Pakistan
in the
Twentieth
Century

A Political History

Pakistan
in the
Twentieth Century
A Political History

Lawrence Ziring

Karachi
Oxford University Press
Oxford   New York   Delhi

Oxford University Press, Walton Street, Oxford OX2 6DP

Oxford   New York
Athens   Auckland   Bangkok   Bombay
Calcutta   Cape Town   Dar es Salaam   Delhi
Florence   Hong Kong   Istanbul   Karachi
Kuala Lumpur   Madras   Madrid   Melbourne
Mexico City   Nairobi   Paris   Singapore
Taipei   Tokyo   Toronto
and associated companies in
Berlin   Ibadan

Oxford is a trade mark of Oxford University Press

© Oxford University Press, 1997

ISBN   0 19 577816 2

Second Impression 1998

Printed in Pakistan at
Mueid Packages, Karachi.
Published by
Ameena Saiyid, Oxford University Press
5-Bangalore Town, Sharae Faisal
P.O. Box 13033, Karachi-75350, Pakistan.

*This history is dedicated to
Manzoor and Amna Hussain,
who live the Pakistan experience with me,
and to the memory of
Hassan Habib and Irving Swerdlow,
much remembered colleagues*

CONTENTS

PREFACE

Compressing the political history of Pakistan into a single volume has been a daunting task. Judging what was to be included and what omitted, how much detail and how much analytic rendering, challenged the author through the two years of its drafting. Needless to emphasize, the research for this volume began several decades ago when, as a young graduate student, I had my first opportunity to experience Pakistan close up. In some of these pages, therefore, the author could not avoid including some of his own recollections. Thus, although I have refrained from injecting myself into the story, I recognize that my account is sometimes influenced by the events I personally witnessed and the many people who shared their insights and performance with me. Arriving in Pakistan for the first time during the administration of H.S. Suhrawardy, I was able to observe the last segment of the initial parliamentary period. During the Ayub era, I was domiciled first in East, and later in West Pakistan. In subsequent years, I was exposed to the Bhutto and Ziaul Haq administrations, and in more recent times, to the Benazir Bhutto and Nawaz Sharif governments. Having devoted so much of my professional life to the study of Pakistan's government and politics, this one-volume history was both a test and an opportunity, that is, a test of my scholarly capacity and an opportunity to raise significant questions.

As a student of the Pakistan condition, I could not ignore the dilemmas of Pakistan's emergence as an independent nation-state, nor have I avoided citing the vainglorious behaviour of so many of its major personalities. This account of Pakistan's role in the twentieth century is, in large measure, a critique of the country's leaders, of men and women who were not only burdened with awesome responsibilities, but who were called to realize a noble, but nevertheless illusive, objective. Unfortunately, these same men and women too readily succumbed to the scramble for power and privilege, and in so doing, they did great damage to the nation, and especially, to its innocent inhabitants. In telling this story I have tried to assure a balanced rendering, but only the reader will judge if my interpretations are true to the objective record.

I cannot cite here the many people who, in one way or another, assisted me in the more than four decades that I have personally been involved in the study of Pakistan. Indeed, many of those individuals are no longer with us and I am mindful of my responsibility to them, given their inability to respond to my work. I can only say in memory of them, as well as to those who will read in these pages events which we have shared, that I have laboured to be fair. Finally, I recognize that this volume will frame a period for Pakistanis today and into the future. I am humbled by that realization, and I also know that despite my arduous efforts, I may have erred. I alone am responsible for what appears in these pages.

I would be remiss in not mentioning two people who assisted me in the preparation of the completed manuscript. I wish to extend my formal appreciation to Chien-Hong Lee, who helped me with the research of the contemporary period as well as with the bibliographic material. I am also indebted to my wife, Raye M. Ziring, whose electronic wizardry was invaluable, but even more so, who took it upon herself to proof and edit the finished manuscript. Finally, I must extend my appreciation to Ameena Saiyid and Yasmin Qureshi of Oxford University Press who asked me to write this history, who honoured me with this rare opportunity to sum up a life of scholarly endeavour, and whose distant presence stiffened my resolve.

Lawrence Ziring
25 March 1997

CHAPTER 1

BEFORE THE BEGINNING

The twentieth century began much as the nineteenth had ended, with Great Britain the acknowledged world leader, ruling a vast realm encompassing one-fifth of the globe, a colossal empire of twelve million square miles of colonies, dependencies, and protectorates, wherein lived a quarter of the earth's inhabitants. And the centrepiece in this expansive imperial system was the Indian subcontinent where, in 1903, King Edward VII, acceding to the British throne following the death of Queen Victoria, was declared Emperor of India in a Grand Durbar presided over by Lord Curzon of Kedleston, the Viceroy of India. Lord Curzon regretted the inability of the King to appear at the ceremony, but he dutifully read the monarch's message to the assembled throng, and especially to the Indian princes who had come to Delhi to swear fealty to the Crown. King Edward's message called for the 'increasing prosperity of my Indian Empire,' and the Viceroy left no doubt that Britain's purpose in India was central to its claim as the world's pre-eminent power.

Largely obscured from the outside world, however, political developments inside the subcontinent already were reshaping the character of the British role in India, and hence in the larger world. Global developments following the Mutiny of 1857 had transformed the administration of India from that of a commercial enterprise to one of geopolitical and strategic importance. Prompted by the European scramble for empire, Britain moved to assure its sustained control over the Indian Ocean region by designing and implementing policies geared to enhancing its Indian administration. Britain had capitalized on existing differences between the major Hindu and Muslim communities, and the Crown's programme of divide and rule aimed at neutralizing the political movements energized in the last half of the nineteenth century. Indeed, Lord Dufferin, who had assumed the station of Viceroy in 1884, successfully manipulated the several, often competing, political forces. It was Dufferin who invited Allan Octavian Hume, a retired civil servant and an Englishman, to organize a body that would work in close association with the government. That charge led to the formation of the Indian National Congress in 1885, an organization which claimed to represent all Indians, but whose initial agenda could not conceal an anti-Muslim bias.

Nevertheless, the Congress drew support from some important Muslim groups, especially the Central Muhammadan Association under the leadership of Amir Ali. And in 1887 a leading Muslim, Badruddin Tyabji, was declared President of the Congress. In 1896, still another Muslim luminary, Rahmatullah M. Sayani, also was elected to that lofty post. A larger number of Muslim leaders, however, hesitated in identifying themselves with an organization that they perceived to be threatening to Muslim causes. Moreover, it was their contention that Congress's anticipated plans for a self-governing India did not include adequate protection for the subcontinent's Muslim population. Fearful of the Hindu community's significantly larger numbers, and the likelihood of a Hindu raj in any scheme pressing majoritarianism, these Muslim leaders insisted on a different constitutional arrangement, one that would guarantee the minority community a special place in any future self-governing experience. Led by Sir Syed Ahmed Khan, the founder of the Aligarh Muslim University, these Muslims joined together in the Jamiat-i-Muhibban-i-Hind (the Joint Committee of the Friends of India) in 1888. Declaring the aim of their party to be direct opposition to the Congress, the association proved to be the forerunner for subsequent Muslim efforts aimed at defining a protected place within a British India that was more responsive to indigenous aspirations.

Hindu revivalist activities had frightened the Muslim leaders, who acknowledged their weaknesses in the decades subsequent to the 1857 uprising. W.W. Hunter (1872) wrote of the plight of the Muslims, who lagged behind their Hindu counterparts in the decades following the events associated with the Mutiny. The Hindus, he noted, were quick to take advantage of the opportunities offered them by the British, and having adapted themselves to the ways and manners of their European overlords, it was they who filled almost all the positions reserved for indigenous peoples in the expanding colonial government. Sir Syed's efforts at closing the gap between Muslims and Hindus were not without success, but they could never overcome the lead enjoyed by the majority community. Moreover, Hindu achievements under British tutelage rekindled the embers of their past glories, of an earlier age before Muslim penetration of the subcontinent. Congress leaders like B.G. Tilak opposed Muslim membership in what they saw as a Hindu organization (Wolpert, 1962). More important, Tilak's fanaticism appealed to the more narrow-minded and militant among his co-religionists, and he enlisted a huge Hindu following by exploiting the glaring cultural differences between the two major communities.

Tilak's use of history, his fashioning of a cult built around the exploits of the Maratha Shivaji, who had strenuously contested Muslim Mughal rule, aimed at transforming a political movement whose original purpose was self-government, to one that was predicated on the intensification of communal hatred and conflict. Moreover, the growth of the Hindu Mahasabha, the Great Assembly of Hindus, alongside this extreme wing of the Congress party, raised serious questions about the course of representative government in British India.

It is doubtful if the British, so committed to their divide and rule policy, fully grasped the depth of Hindu-Muslim antagonism, or how their self-interested programmes had intensified communal bitterness (Mayo, 1927). In fact, the record reveals that the British were little concerned with how their divisive balancing actions contradicted their much heralded law and order programme. But whether or not they were mindful or troubled, it was the manner and character of British rule in India which established the framework of interaction that the indigenous political actors fitted themselves into at the dawn of the twentieth century. Hence it is important to note that it was not the British who constitutionally addressed the reconciliation of rival moral claims between the major communities, nor was this made the purpose of the Hindu-dominated Congress party. That task was left to the Muslims who, anchoring their hopes on the rule of law, sought to bridge the differences between the communities, while at the same time acknowledging a British policy that, in its essence, encouraged the separation of distinct religious orders (Coupland, 1944). Although it is still widely held that the Muslims prevented the creation of a modern unified India, it was the method of British governance in the subcontinent that prompted the political separation of the communities, and that procedure was long in train prior to the climactic events of World War II.

Separate electorates, the institutional device that would safeguard the interests of the minority population, while at the same time granting an appropriate voice to the majority, became the major objective of the Muslim movement. And indeed, it was with the demand for separate electorates in public view that Nawab Viqar-ul-Mulk and the Nawab of Dhaka convened a meeting of leading Muslims in Dhaka on 30 December 1906. As a consequence of their deliberations, the All-India Muslim League was born to promote the cause of the Muslims of the Indian subcontinent. The League pledged itself to the service of all India's Muslims. It also cited its desire to live at peace with the other communities, and hence attempted to allay fears that, because of its all-Muslim character, it had set a course of aggressive militancy. The Muslim League, it was emphasized, was not another extremist organization, but rather a political party committed to constitutionalism and the rule of law in the India of the twentieth century.

Muslim League insistence on separate electorates intertwined with the 1905 partition of Bengal, and the violent reaction registered to that decision by Hindu militants led by the Hindu Mahasabha. The administrative province of Bengal had been the handiwork of the British. Indeed, Britain's early entry into the land of the Bangla speakers had given new significance to the region and, to a large extent, the Bengali cultural experience flourished under British supervision. But Bengal had become an administrative nightmare, and it was with the intention of improving official workways that the scheme to rearrange its administrative character gained the attention of Lord Curzon, then the Viceroy of India. In the course of establishing what they thought would be more manageable conditions, the British separated the districts of Dhaka, Mymensingh, and Rajshahi from united Bengal and linked them with the Chittagong area and the expansive, but sparsely populated, Assam region. But whereas the British purpose was to provide Assam with an outlet to the sea, and the eastern Bengal hinterland with more efficient administration, the colonial rulers did not fully contemplate the human impact of their actions. Almost at once the Bengalis let it be known that they would resist being transformed into Assamese, and Lord Curzon was impelled to assure them that they would be at the heart of the new province. More explosive and less easily controlled, however, the new administrative province had been given a Muslim majority and the adverse reaction of Hindu extremists to the scheme was, at least to the British, surprisingly violent.

While the British argued it was never their intention to pit Hindus against Muslims, or to split the Bengali nation, Hindu militants launched a concerted campaign to force the colonial authority to reverse its decision. The British reaction initially was to resist the extremists and to press ahead with the decision to form a province of eastern Bengal and Assam. Efforts were made to gain the support of the high-caste Hindus of eastern Bengal who dominated the region's economy, but this did not prove successful. The Hindu-dominant elements in Calcutta, notably the Press and members of the legal community, also saw threats to their professional interests in the partition scheme. Their alliance with the militants, coupled with the position taken by the Hindu landlords of eastern Bengal, ultimately forced the .British to reconsider their decision.

The voices of militancy and communalism, best represented by the Hindu Mahasabha, and notably that of Surendra Nath Banerjee, whose fiery speeches centred on opposition to the establishment of a Muslim-majority province, destabilized the region and threatened European commercial enterprise. Weighing the costs, and determined to subdue passions, the British eventually yielded to the extremists. The penned words of Lovat Fraser (1911), whose book on Lord Curzon appeared just months before the decision to reverse course, speaks volumes of the inability of the British, no matter how intimate their association with the people of the subcontinent, to understand the full measure of the communal antagonism they had consciously or subconsciously nurtured. In 1910 Fraser wrote: 'Ten years hence both Bengals will be proud of the new province (East Bengal) which had such a stormy infancy' (p. 386). How wrong he was! The decision to reunite the two Bengals was completed in 1912, following the Royal Durbar in Delhi presided over by King George V and Queen Mary. Bengal was raised to the status of a Governor's Province, equal to the Presidencies of Bombay and Madras, but while Hindu nationalists applauded the decision, the Muslims had suffered still another setback.

It was with this background that the All-India Muslim League was formed and operationalized, albeit in eastern Bengal, and although the League pledged itself to work for communal amity, the partition of Bengal and the ensuing bloodletting, essentially perpetrated by Hindu extremists, proved a harbinger of events yet to unfold. The Muslim League gave voice to Muslim fears in the slogan 'Islam in Danger' and, in short order, it assumed the role of spokesman for a people and a culture which it deemed to be under siege. Indeed, the two-nation theory later pressed by the Muslim League in the formation of Pakistan had its origins in the events that swirled around and through the north-eastern quadrant of the subcontinent in the first decade of the twentieth century (Bahadur, 1954).

The British approached the problem of Hindu-Muslim incompatibilities within the sterile confines of law and order administration, seldom giving expression to the complexities of a human condition they little respected. The British were inclined to benefit those among their colonial subjects who adopted their ways and ensured their mastery of the administrative and legal processes (Tinker, 1954). Seldom were they concerned with the divergent psychological aspects of disparate and complex publics. Colonial policy meant the maintenance of empire, and virtually all the energy of the administrative authority was devoted to controlling and limiting mass expression. Distance and aloofness, indeed condescension and arrogance, shaped the role of India's European guardians. Non-interference in local matters suited the holders of power so long as it assured the enhancement of imperial control. But with one age about to end and another in the early stages of gestation, the colonial mentors of British India were either indifferent to or oblivious of their part in filling the wellsprings of Hindu-Muslim rivalry and hatred.

The Evolution of the Muslim League

The Muslim League's origin in Dhaka was a consequence, not so much of the formation of the Indian National Congress, but rather of the creation of a Muslim-dominant province in eastern Bengal. For the first time since the Mutiny of 1857, and the banishment of the Mughal Emperor to Burma subsequent to that event, Muslims were afforded a pre-eminent political role in a portion of the subcontinent. But by the dawn of the twentieth century, it was the Hindu cause that was better represented in the halls of power. Muslims, who initially rejected British overtures of assistance in return for adopting European codes and manners, came late to the awareness that the Hindus over whom they had once reigned supreme were now a major force in colonial India. At best, some Muslims could try to fill a few of the posts in the prevailing administration, but the Muslim masses needed protection from the more numerous Hindus who, even in a future majoritarian situation, retained the numbers to monopolize official proceedings. Separate electorates were conceived as safeguarding minority interests, especially in the wake of the British decision to reverse themselves on the partition of Bengal. The British had given the Muslims their solemn word that the Bengal partition was a 'settled fact', but in the end, none of their assurances were honoured. Yielding to Hindu agitation, the colonial overlords betrayed and, it can be argued, abandoned their Muslim subjects.

Hindu-Muslim antagonism entered a new stage and, although there was still the lingering belief in some Muslim quarters that the colonial authority would moderate the relationship, there was little evidence to sustain this conclusion.

The early development of the Muslim League was influenced less by its Nawab founders and more by two members of the Muslim literati, i.e., Maulana Muhammad Ali and Abul Kalam Azad. Both men published newspapers in Calcutta that focused attention on the duplicity of the colonial administration, notably its failure to honour commitments made to the Muslim community. Of the two, Muhammad Ali was the more critical, taking issue with British actions not only in India, but in other regions where Muslims were forced to live under European pressure. Abul Kalam proved to be the more restrained of the two, and also the more objectively realistic (Azad, 1960). He cited British self-interested deviousness but also acknowledged their superior power. Irrespective of their different styles, however, Muhammad Ali and Abul Kalam attracted a youthful following that, at least for the period, virtually eclipsed the earlier work of Syed Ahmed Khan at Aligarh. The new Muslim consciousness that was shaped in the controversy over the Bengal partition was driven more by notions of self-determination than colonial mentoring, and the leaders of the Muslim League were forced to come to grips with a new reality: that Muslims in a Hindu-dominant India were at risk and that they had only themselves to fall back upon in times of crisis.

What lay ahead could not be forecast with any degree of accuracy, however, and those leaders of the Muslim community who were compelled to work within a political framework largely determined by their British overseer were given few options. They could either challenge Hindu rule as Muslims had been challenged in eastern Bengal, that is, in the streets—or they could attempt to reconcile their differences in the hope that, with British assistance, the two communities could find the necessary legal formula for accommodation. Moreover, the Congress party, unlike the League, was organized as a secular organ, and many Muslims found it possible to associate with both institutions. This intermingling of Muslims and Hindus made it possible for the two parties to join in common agreement in the 1916 Lucknow Pact. The pact signified the intention of both major parties to combine their efforts toward the achievement of self-government on the basis of dominion status. Most importantly for the League, the Congress accepted the separate electorate arrangements that, in 1909, had been enshrined in the Morley-Minto Reform.

It is important to note that the Muslim League had moved its headquarters from Dhaka to Delhi following the abrogation of the Bengal partition scheme. In Delhi, the League came under the management of members drawn from an array of locations stretching across the subcontinent. All were representatives of either the Muslim intelligentsia or the landholding class. Many had their initial training at Aligarh and later went on to become barristers. Thus, an urbane element ranged alongside the landed gentry, and it was not surprising that the members of the legal fraternity assumed the day-to-day responsibilities in managing the League, or that they should press for legal formulae to protect the rights of the minority community. Mohammad Ali Jinnah, with his base in Bombay, was one of these men (Al-Mujahid, 1981). A successful advocate and a follower of the liberal Hindu thinker, G.K. Gokhale, Jinnah had joined the Congress in 1897, and from the beginning of his political career he was primarily concerned with bridging the gap between Hindus and Muslims. When Jinnah joined the Muslim League in October 1913, he already had established himself as an articulate and effective leader who got on well with Hindus as well as Muslims. In fact, it was Jinnah who defended B.G. Tilak during periods of his incarceration. It was also Jinnah who championed the right of India's politicians to criticize and question the policies of the colonial government. Gokhale's death in 1915 made a deep impression on both Jinnah and Tilak, and the latter's adoption of more moderate ways was, perhaps, linked to his association with Jinnah as well as his respect for Gokhale and his work. Indeed, it was Jinnah and Tilak who led the debate that resulted in the Lucknow Pact, but their success was short-lived.

Even before Jinnah and Tilak could put into operation the

principal features of the Lucknow Pact, especially the demand for self-government, they were upstaged by Mohandas Karamchand Gandhi, who had returned from South Africa in 1915 determined to lead India in another direction. Convinced that the British would only yield to concerted pressure, Gandhi sought to use the technique that had served him so well in South Africa, a technique he referred to as *satyagraha* (truth force), or non-violent passive resistance (Gandhi, 1948). Gandhi's use of *satyagraha* in fighting discriminatory race legislation in South Africa had resulted in the Gandhi-Smuts agreement, and he was confident the colonial authority in India would likewise be compelled to yield to his demands. Indeed, given his early successes in rallying the Indian (notably Hindu) masses, the Mahatma, as he came to be known, soon bypassed Tilak as the major force for change within the Congress Party. Similarly, he neutralized Jinnah, whose tactics were clearly more staid, conventional, and institutional. By contrast with Jinnah, Gandhi made himself a man of the common people, giving up the trappings of his sophisticated development to mix more freely with the masses of the Indian subcontinent. Although a London-trained lawyer, his experience in South Africa had taught him to challenge the legal institutions and, wherever possible, to ignore or reject them. By contrast, both Tilak and Jinnah were, above all, representatives of a westernized middle class; Gandhi removed himself from that class to assume a place among the simple folk who responded to his call with deference and ecstatic adulation. As Percival Spear (1961) has noted:

> While Tilak was to the people a Brahmin calling for respect and a politician immersed in strategy, Gandhi (a Vasiya by caste) was something more than a Brahmin, a holy man, and something more than a realist—a prophet who appealed to moral principles which as Hindus they understood. Gandhi made himself poor like a peasant, and the people made him holy like a saint or guru. (p.359).

For Jinnah, Gandhi was a nemesis he had not factored into his calculations. Convinced that Gandhi's tactics could only deepen the divide between Hindus and Muslims, but also cognizant of his vast popular appeal, Jinnah feared that the British could not long resist his movement. Jinnah clearly was outfoxed by the bespectacled little man in a loincloth, and his frustrations were so great that he believed his only recourse was to leave India for England, where he might better contemplate the future. Jinnah's departure from the subcontinent left the Muslim League without its chief spokesman, and the organization foundered in his absence. Moreover, without significant opposition, Gandhi dominated the Congress Party, which was now wedded to his peculiar style of populist politics.

Genesis of Political Culture

Britain could not successfully fight World War I without major assistance from India, and in spite of the Indian Muslim's affinity for the Ottoman Turks, the Muslim League and its members had sworn allegiance to the Crown. The end of the war seemed to project a new era for the people of the subcontinent and Jinnah's vision was that of a new India, a dominion within the British empire, but nevertheless a fully self-governing and commingled society. Gandhi's seizure of Congress Party leadership, however, and the extralegal tactics he employed, notably influenced by Hindu practices and expressions, destroyed that vision and ended the dream of Hindu-Muslim co-operation. Gandhi may well have transformed a middle-class movement into one of mass emotion embracing all strata, but his appeal to moral idealism played havoc with the ordered rule of law, the only real guarantee in a polyglot society that justice would be rendered equally and equitably to all, irrespective of belief or expression, practice or ceremony.

Thus, the gains that were to be derived from the Great War were not realized. The alliance between the Muslim League and the Congress that was forged during the war did not survive its end. The issue of self-government was raised in the 1917 Montagu-Chelmsford Report, but it was condemned by the Congress as inadequate. The organization split, with the more moderate members organizing a party that better represented their purpose. Gandhi assumed control of the Congress and, while at first he seemed to accept the reforms described in the report, he soon reversed himself and inspired his followers to adopt a resolution of non-co-operation with the colonial government.

Given the unrest spawned by Gandhi's passive resistance movement (and it was often more violent than passive), the colonial government in 1919 adopted a set of coercive measures that were framed in the Rowlatt Acts. The Acts sustained the arbitrary prerogatives of the government, but the use of repressive powers only added legitimacy to Gandhi's now massive displays of popular disobedience. Indeed, the Jalianwala Bagh massacre in Amritsar was a direct outcome of the confrontation between passive resisters and the government. These unfolding events thoroughly demoralized Mohammad Ali Jinnah. Gandhi may have been received as a saint by his followers, but for Jinnah he was merely a contemporary demagogue whose deeds were the antithesis of democratic procedure and promise. Moreover, the rule of law, the only true safeguard for the weakest members of society, was made a shambles by Gandhi's defiance of authority, and by a colonial government that was duty-bound to control him and the excesses of his movement.

External developments also had an impact on the subcontinent and Gandhi was quick to take advantage of them. The Ottoman empire's defeat in World War I threatened the Islamic Caliphate which, since 1517, had been occupied by a Turkish sultan. Maulana Muhammad Ali articulated the fears of subcontinental Muslims when he declared in Paris in 1920 that the Caliphate (*Khilafat*) was the 'most essential institution of the Muslim community throughout the world' (Rajput, 1948, p. 29). The subcontinent's Muslims demonstrated that they were ready to ignore their own circumstances when word filtered into the region that the Caliphate was under threat of being destroyed by Christian forces. And although individuals like Maulana Muhammad Ali had captured the sentiments of their co-religionists, no one among the Muslim leaders was able to organize and direct their passions, and that task was assumed by the Mahatma. Gandhi realized that in furthering the Khilafat Movement he could not only strike a blow against British imperialism, but more important, he could demonstrate the weakness of the Muslim

League. The Khilafat Movement offered Gandhi an opportunity to bridge differences between Hindus and Muslims, and also to wean away the Muslims from their association with the Muslim League. In sum, Gandhi was convinced that his role in taking up the cause of the Caliphate would reveal the dysfunction in the Muslim League and draw its members to the Congress Party.

Gandhi's decision to intrude himself into an essentially Muslim campaign was without parallel. Maulana Muhammad Ali waxed eloquent in singing the Mahatma's praises, calling him a rare visionary and a 'large-hearted man' (Rajput, p.31). At another time Muhammad Ali called him 'Christ-like' and said that, under his leadership, the subcontinent resembled biblical Judea on the eve of the advent of Jesus. The Maulana called upon Muslims to adopt Gandhi's *ahimsa* (non-violence to all living creatures), to practice moral self-discipline, and to follow the Mahatma's call for *swaraj* (freedom). Gandhi's pragmatic approach to the Khilafat issue was similar to that taken in forcing the British to share political power with the indigenous population. On the one side he ordered a total boycott of all British goods, while on the other he urged his followers to shut down the country, to avoid going to work, and to force the government into paralysis. Failing these tactics, Gandhi called upon the subcontinent's Muslim population to consider leaving their homes and migrating en masse from India to Asia Minor, the seat of the Ottoman empire.

Given the emotional circumstances of the time, few Muslims contemplated the threat that Gandhi's leadership posed to their well–being as Indian subjects of the Crown. With the Muslims sworn to eschew violence and directed, if need be, to migrate to an unknown land, the Mahatma's scheme for saving the Caliphate was aimed at pressing the Congress's programme against colonial authority in India; it had little to offer when it came to serving general Muslim causes.

Nevertheless, Congress ranks swelled with the substantial influx of Muslim members. As was to be expected, the Muslim League became a shell of its former self. Moreover, true to Gandhi's urging, Muslims abandoned their professional calling and vacated their businesses, while Muslim students curtailed their studies. Almost twenty thousand Muslims sold off their properties and migrated to Afghanistan. Those engaging in these expressions of defiance paid a high personal price for their behaviour, but the Muslim community also suffered. Only Aligarh University defied the Mahatma's command and continued its usual functions. Moreover, thoughtful Muslims began to wonder why it was that Hindu institutions continued to operate normally during this period of acute crisis and indeed, when Gandhi ordered a suspension of the non-co-operation movement following the Chauri Chaura incident, even the more gullible among the Muslims realized they had been led astray by the Hindu Mahatma.

Given their ultimate disappointment, Gandhi's call to Muslims to pursue *swaraj* as a means to right the Khilafat wrong lost its appeal almost as quickly as it had been aroused, but it was the Turks, not the Europeans or Gandhi's strategy, that finally put an end to the Khilafat Movement (Qureshi, 1965). The seizure of power by Mustafa Kemal Ataturk led to the dissolution of the Ottoman empire and the creation of the modern Turkish republic. It was Ataturk who abolished the Caliphate, believing it to be an antiquated institution. These actions left the Muslims of the subcontinent in a great quandary, given the fact that so many of them had exhausted their savings and squandered their assets on a futile mission. Indeed, India's Muslims had spent much of their psychic as well as physical energy, and had come away from the experience with nothing more than a frustrating emptiness. India's Muslims could reflect on the strength of their faith and derive some satisfaction from their resoluteness, but neither their psychological or material circumstances were enhanced by the Khilafat experience. Moreover, having put such faith in the Mahatma and the Congress Party, and now believing they had been grossly deceived, there was little likelihood that they could again become parties to the actions of the Hindu leaders (Hardy, 1972).

The Hindu Mahasabha, as represented by Madan Mohan Malaviya and Lajpat Rai, used the occasion of the Khilafat misadventure to purge the Muslims from what the extremists conceived to be chaste Hindu orders. The result was more communal riots and more carnage. The Lucknow Pact, which had envisaged a new understanding between Hindus and Muslims, was laid to rest. Its epitaph was written in the hardening of positions between the two major subcontinental communities, as well as in the tempering of exclusive political cultures. In spite of the outward pretences and public declarations about peace and non-violence, even Gandhi could not conceal the fact that he, knowingly or not, had provided succour to the most militant and extreme among his countrymen and co-religionists.

Thus, whereas the Hindu extreme was energized as never before, the Muslims were even more demoralized following the collapse of the Khilafat Movement. Not since the demise of Mughal rule seventy-five years earlier was the community so destabilized. Confused and exhausted, disorganized and ineffectual, the Indian Muslim community was forced to examine its performance and to weigh its future in a fast-changing India. Unlike the nineteenth century, there seemed little likelihood that the British would be a factor in lifting the Muslims out of their despair. Gone were the days when Indian Muslims could not trust anyone but themselves. This awareness was in evidence at the two Round Table Conferences called by the British and convened in London in 1928 and 1930. As a consequence, the Conferences, which were aimed at addressing the deepening rift between Hindus and Muslims, resolved nothing. Maulana Muhammad Ali blamed himself for the plight of his brethren who had left their work, their schools, and some even their homes, to follow the teaching of the Mahatma. Just two days before his death, he wrote a letter to the British Prime Minister in which he beseeched the overlords of the subcontinent to acknowledge the destitution of the Muslim people and to restore a modicum of justice and security to his brethren. Muhammad Ali's last plea, however, proved unnecessary. Knowledgeable Indian Muslims had read the times and they would be forever marked by the events of the immediate post-World War I years. Muslims sensed the need to be less trusting, more suspicious, and at least as clever as their militant neighbours. Cynicism influenced the Muslim mindset and pervaded their political culture, and it would be no simple task to direct the thinking and the energies of a people who had given so much to a cause and had reaped only the whirlwind.

The Jinnah Factor

Jinnah was a son of the Aligarh school of Muslim political leaders who believed that loyalty to the British Raj brought benefits to the entire Muslim community. More than that, colonial authority was to be respected and served, and acceptance of the hierarchical colonial system was a *sine qua non* for moving Indian society away from its traditional autocratic moorings and into a new age of opportunity, mobility, material achievement, and balanced harmony. With the British in indefinite occupation of the subcontinent, and with their power stretched from one end of the earth to the other, it appeared that the European overlords were amply provided with the wherewithal, as well as the wisdom, to not only manage the vast, diverse world of the Indian subcontinent, but to usher it into a new era. Indeed, for a number of educated Muslims, British interposition between Hindus and Muslims seemed to assure an equilibrium, within which the major communities could find common ground for the creation of a future India that would be very different from the one they had known.

Liberal European ideas, philosophy, and workways had already had their impact, especially among those individuals who were exposed to English education and manners. Notions of pluralism and representative government had begun to replace the time-worn experience with oriental absolutism, and a defined secularism had been superimposed over an older order that, heretofore, had been fashioned from spiritual experience and more narrowly conceived identities. The British, therefore, were responsible for creating a new elite, or class, or caste, imbued with a different vision from that of their forebears, and seemingly dedicated to the transformation of the Indian subcontinent from a congeries of disparate tribes, ethnicities, and religions, into a nation of nations, a veritable union of religions and cultures that were capable of addressing a world forced to be modern by the industrial and urban revolutions.

Mohammad Ali Jinnah fitted himself into this rapidly changing and volatile experience. Moved by the possibilities to which his education had exposed him, Jinnah early on set a course for himself that placed him in a select circle of Indian leaders. Inspired and mentored in his developmental years by Hindu leaders, notably Gokhale and Dadabhai Naoroji, he learned to understand the demands and promise as well as the foibles of the parliamentary experience. Jinnah measured himself against a panoply of Indian leaders representing a vast variety of styles and philosophies. Personalities like Tilak, Ranade Pherozeshah Mehta, Lajpat Rai, and Madan Mohan Malaviya challenged his thinking. They also influenced his direction. Jinnah accepted their diversity of thought even as he rejected or modified their actions. Differences for Jinnah were a matter of style and culture, and natural to the human condition, but reconciliation and reasoned judgment, he concluded, were essential to the creation of the India of the twentieth century.

Jinnah's balanced judgment, his objective approach to the monumental changes affecting Indian society, seemed to rule out displays of emotion, and indeed, he believed it to be his task to stand above the crowd, to articulate their sentiments, but at the same time to raise the larger population to heights they had not imagined for themselves. Jinnah's vision of an ordered society required ordered minds, and it was his task to begin a process of human engineering that allowed for the inculcation of those values which he had imbibed from Gokhale, his chief mentor.

Jinnah returned to British India from his self-imposed exile in England in 1934 and immediately took up the cause of the Muslim League, which had wallowed in its own despair in the aftermath of the failed Khilafat Movement. Tempered by the unsuccessful Round Table meetings that he had attended in London, and energized by the British decision to offer more self-government to India than had been given in the 1919 Government of India Act, Jinnah set himself the task of reorganizing, and more important, of revitalizing the Muslim League, which he now acknowledged was the only hope for the Muslims of the Indian subcontinent.

Rebuilding and reinvigorating the Muslim League was no

small undertaking. Moreover, it came at a time when the British government was about to offer India its first taste of genuine self-government. The 1919 Act had been burdened by the dyarchy principle, which meant the Viceroy continued to reign supreme over all legislative and executive functions. Gandhi's passive resistance campaign, especially the Congress's rejection of the 1919 Act, finally convinced the British that they had to be more forthcoming with their Indian subjects. In 1927, therefore, the government appointed a statutory commission headed by Sir John Simon, and charged it with designing a more democratic self-governing scheme for the subcontinent. The Simon Commission Report led to the drafting of the Government of India Act of 1935. Although the Congress rejected the 1935 scheme at its first public hearing, the Muslim League found sections of it acceptable, and Jinnah knew that some version of it would eventually be approved and implemented. Moreover, the new instrument would require all-India elections, and Jinnah did not want to miss the opportunity to range the Muslim League alongside the Congress when the votes were cast.

Reconstructing the League under the pressure of impending elections added to the difficulties Jinnah encountered in breathing new life into the moribund organization. More significantly, however, the League's decline had opened up new opportunities for those who would construct other organizations which, they had argued, were more beneficial to the subcontinent's Muslims. The Muslims of British India in the 1930s were, in fact, divided into a wide range of competing and often hostile camps. Some were localized organizations, while others claimed representation throughout the subcontinent.

Among the more prominent Muslim organizations and movements was the Khudai Khidmatgar, the work of Abdul Ghaffar Khan. An anti-British organization, it was formed in the late 1920s to represent the quest for self-determination by the Pathan population of the North-West Frontier. The Unionists were another, representing a collection of Muslim and Hindu landowning families that were prominent in the Punjab. Fazlul Huq had organized the Krishak Proja Party in Bengal to represent the aspirations of the province's poor peasants and workers; while the Jamaat-i-Islami owed its existence to Maulana Abul Ala Maudoodi who, though something less than a Muslim divine, was nevertheless a disciplinarian espousing Islamic fundamentalist beliefs. The Jamaat drew youthful disciples to its fold and thus cut into Muslim League reserves (Mohammad Ali, 1973). The Khaksars, a reactionary, quasi-fascist group of brown-shirted shock troops, was the conception of Allama Inayatullah Khan Mashriqi, who violently opposed what he asserted were the effeminate teachings of Mohammad Ali Jinnah and the Muslim League (Ansari, 1996). The Ahrars, another religious order with fundamentalist precepts, proclaimed the ideal of the *Hukumat-i-Ilahia*. It opposed all alien borrowing from the European world and proved to be a constant problem for Muslim League organizers. Of lesser importance, but nevertheless a thorn in the side of the Muslim League, were the Momins of the United Provinces and Bihar who followed a curious biological logic that, they argued, made them different from other Muslims of the subcontinent. And finally, there were the Muslim Nationalists, who saw themselves as a Muslim organization that paralleled the Congress. In addition to these not inconsiderable Muslim League competitors, Jinnah had to contend with a variety of Muslim *pirs* (divines) and *mullahs* (theologians), as well as tribal headmen who claimed their own following and who ranked their legitimacy higher than that of more formal groupings like the Muslim League.

Also not to be ignored were the ideas and forces generated in the external world of the 1920s and 1930s that had an impact on the educated Muslims of the subcontinent. Given the tenor of events, a variety of ideologies attracted followers to the communist, fascist, socialist, nationalist, and democratic folds. Even Hitler's Nazism had its admirers within British India, but neither it, nor any of these other creeds, touched more than a minute minority, and their only claim to notoriety was their rigid opposition to either the Muslim League or the Congress Party. Overcoming the appeal of all these organizations, movements, and philosophies was a monumental task that Jinnah did not relish undertaking, but his cause was hopeless if he did not succeed in mastering the situation.

Still another formidable problem facing Jinnah in refashioning the Muslim League was how the organization would relate to the *zamindar,* or landlord, class. The feudals in most respects owed their prominence to the British, who had granted land in return for loyalty and support. The possession of land in agrarian societies was the key to power, influence, and prosperity, and no landlord was prepared to see his holdings diminished, let alone expropriated. Furthermore, landlords not only possessed land, they also controlled and thus ruled over the people who lived upon and cultivated the land. Nowhere was the superior-inferior relationship more obvious than between the landlord and his peasant. The lofty position of the former and the servile character of the latter addressed a relationship antithetical to modern discourse and certainly to the building of contemporary democratic relationships. Prevailing political systems in India, of necessity, were extensions of the rural power structure and Jinnah did not challenge them. Moreover, the Muslim League desperately needed financial backing, and no political organization could survive without drawing upon the largess of the landed aristocracy.

As a political leader with national credentials, and one determined to contest the projected elections alongside the Congress Party, Jinnah was forced to accommodate a variety of interest groups. In like measure, he was forced to come to grips with sectarian rivalry, and notably the on-going conflict between Sunni and Shia Muslims. Nor could he ignore the explosive nature of the Sunni-Ahmedi controversy. Abiding religious differences divided the Islamic community, and Jinnah's call for tolerance was not the message many of his co-religionists wished to hear. None the less, he pursued his single objective of Muslim unity with such vigour that even the most resolute among his detractors were compelled to acknowledge his strength of character and his superior leadership qualities. In the give-and-take of subcontinent politics, Jinnah was not above making deals, but each test gave him that much more experience in developing the negotiating style he needed in his later confrontation with Gandhi, the Congress, and the British colonial authority.

The Two-Nation Theory

Having reclaimed the Muslim League as the chief representative of India's Muslims, Jinnah adopted a separatist formula in guiding the party's destiny. Earlier efforts aimed at constructing Hindu-Muslim unity were cast aside in favour of an exclusive arrangement which highlighted Muslim differences with the majority, but which also sought to rally an otherwise fragmented and disparate community of believers. Jinnah understood that the Indian Muslims could compete with the Congress Party only when they showed they were capable of reconciling their own differences. It was with this latter objective in view that Jinnah declared the Muslims to be a nation with its own

> distinctive culture and civilization, language and literature, art and architecture, names and nomenclature, sense of values and proportion, legal laws and moral codes, customs and calendar, history and tradition, aptitude and ambitions (Rajput, 1948, p. 57).

Jinnah chose the opportune moment afforded by the 1937 election to call upon his brethren to support the Muslim League. And although the community's response was encouraging in that it elevated the role of the party to national status, it did not provide the Muslim League with electoral victory in the provinces. Jinnah was nevertheless acclaimed as the Quaid-i-Azam, the Great Leader of the Muslims, but to the leaders of the Congress Party, he continued to espouse heresy and divisiveness. To many a Muslim, Jinnah was the model of deportment, an articulator of dreams, and the promise of a better future. For members of the Congress, however, and perhaps Hindus in general, Jinnah was arrogant, dictatorial, egoistic, and fanatically ambitious. It would not be an exaggeration to say that the colonial authority agreed with the Congress's appraisal of Jinnah's personality. They also were perplexed as to how they might deal with a revived Muslim League under his command.

British distress can, in part, be attributed to their perception of Muslims as a warrior people. They questioned how Jinnah, having awakened a heretofore somnolent, depressed, and divided people, could exert sufficient control over them now that their more militant instincts had been aroused. Moreover, the British believed that Muslim political culture responded to strong, autocratic, and absolute leaders, and they displayed great misgivings as to how a Bombay lawyer could transform that culture so that it could embrace reasonably sophisticated, representative institutions.

How well Jinnah and his Muslim League did can be measured by the election campaign and the polling results. Although the Congress was the overwhelming winner in the 1937 election, sweeping Madras, the United Provinces, the Central Provinces, Bihar, and Orissa, proving to be the strongest party in Assam and a genuine force in the North-West Frontier, as well as a respectable participant in Bengal, the Muslim League was not without some successes (Sen, 1955). Nevertheless, in none of the provinces was Jinnah's party sufficiently strong to form its own ministries. In Bengal, Fazlul Huq's Krishak Proja Party organized a coalition government. The more regional Muslim organizations demonstrated their strength when the Congress joined with the followers of Ghaffar Khan in the North-West Frontier, the United Party dominated Sindh, and in the Punjab, a Unionist administration presided over the provincial government.

None the less, the elections went more smoothly than had been forecast, indicating that the Indian population had achieved a level of understanding and that they were becoming familiar with the complexities of electoral politics. More significantly, the Muslim League had made a show of it, had played within the rules, and had accepted the results with grace and forbearance. Jinnah was disappointed but not surprised by the results. The Muslim League had demonstrated its competitive capabilities and its spirit was elevated by the experience. But it also was obvious that Jinnah's work in establishing the organization as the premier Muslim entity and the sole national spokesman for the Muslims of the subcontinent was still a distant goal.

CHAPTER 2

THE FORMATION OF PAKISTAN

Great Britain endeavoured to retain its Indian colony, but the early decades of the twentieth century forced its decision-makers to reconsider the state's role in the subcontinent. World War I had been concluded victoriously for John Bull, but the empire emerged from the conflict far weaker than when it had entered it. Moreover, Britain could not have pursued the war without heavy dependence on the colonies, notably for a steady stream of men who were transported thousands of miles to fight, and many to die, in the trenches of France. The enormous human sacrifice that the Great War demanded was translated in the colonies into a commitment and promise that once the war ended, the colonial people would be given a good measure of self-government, if not outright independence. Furthermore, the British were constantly reminded of their promises by a variety of Indian political leaders who, although not necessarily pursuing the same long-term objectives, nevertheless were reasonably unified in their campaign to force the British to honour their commitment.

While the pace of change was never satisfactory to the indigenous politicians, especially those in the Congress Party, the British made significant gestures in the direction of power-sharing. The 1921 Montford reforms altered the principle of dyarchy to conform to democratic initiatives, and the colonial government insisted that 'autocracy' was no longer appropriate for British India. Instability in Britain, however, made it more difficult to execute consistent policy in the colony. Winston Churchill's opposition to Indian self-government and Mahatma Gandhi's street tactics also slowed the process.

Nevertheless, the London Round Table Conferences were evidence of genuine British intention, and even if they could not resolve differences between the parties, they still sustained the drive for popular government. With the 1935 Government of India Act, the colonial government knew what it wanted for India; it also knew what it wanted for itself. Having vigorously repulsed Congress assaults on its authority (thousands were arrested, including Gandhi for what was described as seditious behavior), the Viceroy's administration insisted on an orderly, institutional approach to the question of Indian self-government. Burma was separated from India, the North-West Frontier Province had been given Governor's status as early as 1932, and Orissa and Sindh (which was separated from Bombay) were made separate provinces. The creation of eleven full-fledged provinces illustrated Britain's intention to spread and deepen the experience with representative government.

Federalism, also, was boosted as the structure for framing the political life of the subcontinent. The essential approach emphasized provincial government in indigenous hands with shared responsibility, but overall viceregal control at the centre. The Indian provinces would be accountable for day-to-day governance while, the central government sustained the union and hence continued to oversee questions of security, foreign policy, communications, and finance. The 1935 Act also aimed at establishing coherent relationships between the princely states and the self-governing provinces. In 1930, the princes agreed to accept arrangements wherein their defence, communications, and foreign affairs devolved upon the central government and the monarchs were given the opportunity to nominate one-third of the members of the lower central legislative assembly and two-fifths of the Upper House. But because the scheme was made voluntary, the princes delayed complying with the plan. Rounding out the structure of government, and assuming compliance from the princes, the colonial authority offered to set up a federal reserve bank and a federal court, and the plan was to divide legislative powers into central, provincial, and concurrent lists. The Governor-General of the federation was to reserve residuary powers, which were judged necessary in emergency conditions. Moreover, in fulfilling the purpose of these constitutional changes, the power of the London-based Secretary of State for India and his council were to be significantly reduced.

The reforms and constitutional enactments opened up an array of opportunities for India's political leaders at all levels of government. Ministers were selected from among the local and national politicians, and the governors of the different provinces were authorized not to interfere with the day-to-day work of government. Only in emergency circumstances was executive authority to be utilized. The reforms left the more than 600 princes relatively untouched as to their prerogatives, but their association with the federal structure, even as loosely defined, tended to highlight their weakness vis-à-vis a representative system that largely eclipsed their traditional bona fides. It was ever more clear that it was the British presence in India that reinforced the princes in their conventional roles. In the absence of British authority, it was doubtful that the aristocracy could maintain their hold over their lands and subjects, and this was not lost on the threatened monarchs. Moreover, it was even more doubtful that both citizens and subjects could live side by side in a national or even multinational state, espousing democratic values and purposes, while in their midst, conventional oriental monarchies sustained the traditional aspects of servitude.

But while the British assembled a model of self-government that generally favoured the democratic spirit, they none the less failed to come to grips with the peculiar pluralism found in the subcontinent. True, there was recognition of a need to compensate for the disadvantages suffered by the 'scheduled castes', but little, if any, attention was given to the multicultural character of Indian society. While not uninformed on the differences between Hindus, Muslims, and Sikhs, the British were nevertheless so enamoured of their political structure that they failed to plumb the depths of communal distinctiveness, let alone contemplate how the different communities perceived one another in a self-governing context. In fact, no serious effort was launched to ascertain why the different cultural communities clung to traditions and practices that forever separated them from one another.

On the one side it appears the British proudly, but also blindly, assumed that their political model transcended and encompassed the total communal experience; on the other, they failed to understand that the Indian population, though championed by men with western credentials and conversant with the European idiom, nevertheless expected their leaders to represent their uniqueness and traditional but divergent mindsets. Identity began with a lowest common denominator, with kinship, tribe, religious affiliation, and culturally defined location, and any higher identity, of necessity, had to begin from the bottom up. Leaders who failed to articulate these sentiments were doomed to failure. Nevertheless, those that did understand these conditions and the forces they generated could, and did, use them to elevate horizons and open new vistas.

In their grand design, the British recognized the different communities, cited the plight and the needs of the minorities, but failed to provide them with the requisite power to register their claims in the new political system. The paradox in this observation is how an empire that prided itself on divide and rule, that took full advantage of the differences between tribal groups and social orders, between religious communities and nationalities, all with the single objective of maximizing its own power, could, when the time came to transfer authority, so utterly fail to understand the power factor in relating rival peoples to one another. If the crux of British power and dominance in India lay in the segmentation and exaggeration of differences, how did they imagine that they could eventually depart from India leaving behind a compatible and accommodating population, under a unitary system centred on the rule of Anglo-Saxon law, and dedicated to the cause of liberal, democratic principles? How could the British have genuinely believed that an autocratic experience could be transformed, with almost no preparation, into a free and open, as well as competitive, self-governing political system? How could a multinational state, the majority of whose population remained illiterate, impoverished, and largely uninformed, carry forward an experiment in sophisticated living that even in the European countries of the day was sadly lacking? Britain's failure to follow the logical progression of its rule in India was ultimately the key element in the struggle that followed the implementation of the 1935 Act, a struggle that was writ large in the partition of the subcontinent and the resulting formation of Pakistan.

The Politics of World War II

The Great Depression that seized Europe and the United States divided societies and all but destroyed popular confidence in government. The emergence into prominence of communism and fascism following World War I was a consequence of the instability that overwhelmed virtually all the major world actors. The rise of modern dictators, notably Joseph Stalin in the Soviet Union, Benito Mussolini in Italy, and Adolph Hitler in Germany, signalled the end of the classic empires, as well as the bankruptcy of liberal democratic European experiments, especially the capitalist system. The tremors radiating out from a Europe suffering from anomie and consumed by malaise and despair were not long in registering their impact in the colonies.

India was no exception to these developments. Jawaharlal Nehru, a member of the Congress Party's inner circle, had returned from a European sojourn in the late 1920s impressed with the Soviet experiment in socialist renewal. Still another rising figure in the Congress Party, Subash Chandra Bose, more extreme in his thinking than Nehru, combined both communist and fascist ideas in pressing his views for a modern India free of European interference. Gandhi was compelled by the exigencies of the time to choose between these two young firebrands, and he reached out to Nehru, the son of Motilal, as the more flexible of the two. It was Nehru who sponsored the Indian independence resolution at the Madras Congress meeting in 1927, and it was Bose who cited the growing power of Japan and called upon the Congress to ally itself with that other Asian nation. Gandhi chose Nehru over Bose to lead the Congress Party, in part because Bose was more radical, but also he was more likely to elevate British fears in the broader spectrum of their global interests. The Mahatma was personally uncomfortable with Bose but, for the moment at least, his principal concern was the avoidance of gestures which might distract the British and cause them to reconsider their power-sharing agreements.

Nehru's ascension to the Congress presidency in 1930 signalled the success of the left wing of the party. Elected to a second term in 1936, it became Nehru's task to lead the party into an era that commenced with the formal promulgation of the new constitution in 1937. Nehru's role at the head of the party positioned him to also lead the Indian government, especially given Gandhi's desire to remain above politics and outside the day-to-day administration of state affairs. With the Congress in control of eight of the eleven Indian provinces, this devolution of power to the young Jawaharlal was significant. Nehru headed the Congress high command or Syndicate, and no important decisions could be taken without its approval. Moreover, the period 1937-9 was dominated by the Congress, except for the fact that the Indian princes refused to join the Congress-led federation that had been engineered by the colonial authority. From the time that the new constitution went into force, it was apparent that the princes preferred dealing with the British colonial authority and perceived the Congress governments in the provinces as a threat to their sustained autonomy. It is important to note that the British Viceroy did not try to dispel these fears, let alone pressurize the princes to accede to the federation.

But more importantly, the Congress, sensing its expanding power, did everything it could to undermine the position held by the Muslim League. Claiming to represent Indians of all persuasions, Congress ignored requests made by the Muslim League to share power in those regions where Muslims lived in significant numbers. Moreover, Maulana Abul Kalam Azad had thrown in his lot with the Congress and had assumed responsibility for the Muslim section of the Congress Party. Azad rejected Jinnah's call for co-operation and coalition between the Congress and the Muslim League. Thus Muslims who entertained hopes of occupying ministerial positions in the Congress-dominated governments could realize their expectations only upon joining the Hindu-dominant party. It had become Nehru's strategy, with Congress high command concurrence, to stifle the Muslim League before it could improve its organizational strength and possibly recover from its relatively poor showing at the polls. Confronting the power arrayed against him, Jinnah was left with two options. He could dissolve the League and fold it into the membership of the Congress, or he could increase the pressure on both the Congress and the British to acknowledge the Muslim League as the sole representative of India's one hundred million Muslims.

Nehru's failure to address Jinnah as a national figure, and more so his reluctance to accept the Muslim League as a national party, affected all subsequent developments. The Muslim League's 'Islam in Danger' theme became central to all Muslim League activities. Moreover, Islam was deemed in danger from recalcitrant and demanding Hindu elements. Hinduization was an intolerable thought for Muslims in all walks of life, and only the Muslim League positioned itself to stand between the Muslim believer on the one side and the Hindu devotee of Kali and Vishnu on the other.

When Germany invaded Poland in September 1939, Britain declared it would honour its treaty commitments and World War II officially exploded over the European continent. As a vital extension of the British empire, India was declared a belligerent in the war, even though the Congress had not been consulted and, indeed, had little interest in a struggle which it had judged to be a European affair and of no concern to the people of the subcontinent. The British, however, prevailed, and India was placed on a war footing. Nehru's response to the war declaration was to order all the Congress ministries in the different provinces to resign in protest. Calling the British action arbitrary and unconstitutional, a new campaign of civil disobedience was engineered by the Congress Party and led by Mahatma Gandhi.

Thus the war added several new variables to the Indian political equation. Self-government yielded to wartime colonial administration. No less important, and certainly not lost on Jinnah, the cessation of Congress rule provided the Muslim League with new options it otherwise might not have contemplated. Jinnah threw his party's support behind the British war effort and, with Hindu rule suspended, the Quaid-i-Azam of the Muslims declared a 'Day of Thanksgiving'. The general and widespread Muslim celebrations that followed Jinnah's declaration hinted at the intensification of the struggle between the Muslim League and the Congress as well as between the Congress and British colonial authority.

The war that was to consume the planet for the second time in little more than twenty years affected a myriad of life experiences and, no less so, interrupted what appeared to be a constitutional experiment aimed at providing the Indian population with a modest degree of self-government. While there were some expressions of empathy for fascism in pre-war India, generally speaking the attentive public opposed Hitler and Mussolini and urged London to display more backbone in its relations with the dictators. But once war erupted on a grand scale, Indian opinion was far more reserved and cautious. More significant perhaps, India had begun to think of itself as an independent country, and Britain's decision to commit the country to the war without consideration for Indian concerns was simply unacceptable. Moreover, Bose's speeches and antics were now more popular among the masses, and even Gandhi had difficulty in ranging his own public displays alongside those of the Bengali militant. Disturbances plagued the British colonial administration as allegedly non-violent demonstrations degenerated into riots and sometimes, open rebellion.

In the midst of widespread instability, much of it focused on the Muslim community that largely supported the British war effort, Jinnah called an All-India Muslim League convention in Lahore. Having reiterated just a few months earlier that Hindus and Muslims were separate nations 'who both must share the governance of their common motherland' (Majumdar et al., 1953, 1990), Jinnah now insisted that either a homeland for Muslims be created, namely Pakistan, or at the very least, a federation be formed from the Muslim majority provinces of Punjab, North-West Frontier Province, Sindh, and the territories of Kashmir and Balochistan. Such a scheme had been presented much earlier at the Round Table Conferences and had been dismissed as a 'student scheme'. This time, however, it could not be so cavalierly ignored.

Tracing the origins of the Pakistan idea will never lead the explorer to its fundamental source, but the 1930 presidential address to the Muslim League by Muhammad Iqbal is widely held to be the first serious exposition on the subject. Iqbal's call for a loose Muslim federation highlighted an otherwise uninteresting session. The speech, however, no doubt excited Rehmat Ali, a young Muslim student residing in England, who fashioned and thus coined the name 'Pakistan' in 1933. Rehmat Ali's contribution involved arranging an acronym from the territories mentioned by Iqbal. In addition, the acronym when translated into Urdu meant 'land of the pure', a designation no doubt considered in its drafting. Although somewhat obscure in its origin, the name 'Pakistan' was seized upon by members of the Muslim League, who used it freely in discussing their plans for the future of the subcontinent. At the 1940 session of the Muslim League, however, even though the leaders of the League had discussed the Pakistan idea prior to the convention, no specific reference was given to 'Pakistan' in the resolution that called for the grouping of 'independent states'. Nevertheless, the framers of the Lahore Resolution did not shy away from demanding that the conceived Muslim constituent units be autonomous and sovereign.

The Lahore Resolution, much later renamed the Pakistan Resolution, proved to be the point of no return for those championing the unity of the subcontinent. The French surrender to Germany and Britain's tragic retreat from Dunkirk appeared to signify the eclipse of the once vaunted empires. Seeking to reap advantages from Britain's perceived weakness, an emboldened Congress attempted to force greater concessions from the colonial authority, while more extreme elements within Indian society took to the streets, not only for the purpose of disturbing the peace, but with the intention of reaping havoc on British administrative and military forces as well as their installations. The British were hard put to deal with the insurrectionists, but the knowledge that the Muslim community generally supported the war effort meant that the colonial authority could devote its

energies to neutralizing the Congress threat. It also meant
that the Muslim League call for the establishment of sovereign
Muslim states within the subcontinent could be discounted
as a distant and less threatening dilemma, to be confronted
in quieter and more peaceful moments following the end of
the war.

With Churchill back at the helm of the London government,
the British had every intention of not only defending, but
clinging to, their prize of empire. The Japanese entry into the
war in 1941 and their earlier membership in the German-
Italian Axis, however, complicated the Prime Minister's task.
The Japanese moved swiftly through south-east Asia, forcing
the British to retreat from their stronghold at Singapore and
later from Rangoon. By 1942 the Japanese were on the
frontiers of India, and the British hurriedly assembled a mixed
imperial army to challenge the almost 100,000 Japanese
troops poised in Burma's Imphal region, ready to invade the
subcontinent. The Royal Air Force also operated out of the
Bengal region, primarily composed from volunteers
representing a host of nations as far away as Argentina. The
Spitfires and Hurricanes provided support for the troops and
also offered air defence for Calcutta and the surrounding
area. Among the RAF units, the 136th Fighter Squadron,
otherwise known as the 'Woodpeckers,' operated from the
Maidan in central Calcutta to the sandy beaches at Cox's
Bazaar and, by the war's end, proved to be the most effective
air defence unit in the whole of the Burma-India theatre of
war (Jacobs, 1994). Britain's considerable activity in the
defence of India may be attributed more to the geopolitical
aspects of the war, but it nevertheless demonstrated the
importance that the empire gave to retaining control of the
subcontinent.

India's armed forces swelled from little more than 100,000
troops prior to the outbreak of hostilities, to approximately
two million by the time the war ended. In the course of this
expansion, the once all-English officered force was
transformed into an indigenous army with its own cadre of
officers. Thus the war had not only produced important
political changes, it had also put in place an institutionally
sound armed force overseered by British generals, but with

its own native chain of command. And, unlike the political divisiveness reflected in the rivalry between the Congress Party and the Muslim League, the Indian Air Force and Navy were essentially homogenous. The Army also was raised along integrated lines, and although some units were comprised exclusively of one cultural or ethnic group, notably among the Hindus, in other units Muslims and Sikhs were combined with Hindu troops and in fact, many of the more predominantly Muslim contingents were led by Hindu and Sikh officers. These developments, prompted by the exigencies of World War II, proved of major importance in the post-war political arena.

World War II also brought heightened investment in India's infrastructure as well as its industries. The chief beneficiaries of these inputs were the major port cities of Bombay, Madras, and Calcutta. Thus, in the already more developed areas of the subcontinent, a significant entrepreneurial class emerged with connections to the outside world. Contrasted with these developments were the frontier areas, which remained largely untouched by modernity and which, because of their strategic importance, were little more than military staging areas. The great famine which overtook the hinterland of Bengal in 1942-3 is sometimes traced to the greed of rice farmers who, eager to get maximum prices for their crops, sold all their stores leaving nothing for the society around them, let alone themselves. The local administration also was subjected to major criticism for its failure to effectively manage the distribution of foodstuffs in the province. But what is often overlooked was the disruption of the transportation system, heavily and almost exclusively dependent on small river craft which had been commandeered by the military in order to thwart Japanese infiltration of the Bengal and Assam regions. The development of India's urbanized sophisticated areas and the neglect of the marginal hinterland again can be attributed to the war, but the full impact of these developments would only be registered with the partition of the subcontinent.

Whereas the colonial government led by Lord Victor Linlithgow sought to emphasize the prosecution of the war and, therefore, avoided coming to grips with the political questions, Congress-Muslim League rivalry had intensified and the British were in a poor position to ignore its ramifications. Congress continued to press the theme that the war was an 'imperialist' endeavour, while the Muslim League emphasized its continuing support and eagerly encouraged Muslims to volunteer their services. The contrast was striking, and in the British mind there was little question as to who represented Muslim interests in the colony. Congress's opposition to the war, the resignation of its ministries, almost by default left the field to Mohammad Ali Jinnah, who was accepted as a more trustworthy subject of the Crown than Mahatma Gandhi, whose actions, it was alleged, had incited widespread unrest. A Congress out of office had reduced its role to that of an organization whose principal purpose was agitation at a most inauspicious time. The levelling process between the Congress and the League had thus occurred without the Muslim League or the British having induced it. Congress had done more than just shot itself in the proverbial foot; it had given new significance to the Muslims as a separate nation, represented by a single party and led by a visible and very popular personality. Whereas Gandhi had earlier caused Jinnah to retreat from the fray, the circumstances surrounding the war in the subcontinent had evened the playing field between the Mahatma and the Quaid-i-Azam.

In 1942, Sir Stafford Cripps, a member of the British War Cabinet and a reputed socialist, was sent to India to help gain Congress's support for the war. Cripps was authorized to offer a plan for a self-governing and essentially independent Indian dominion once the war had run its course. The constitution for the new entity was to be drafted by a constituent assembly elected by the existing provincial legislatures. The overall plan was equated with those tying Scotland and Northern Ireland to Great Britain, although India retained the option of seceding from the Commonwealth if the arrangement proved unsatisfactory. An interim government, acting as a cabinet and attached to the Viceroy's office, was to be appointed almost immediately, thus guaranteeing the full implementation of the plan. In spite of the relative acceptance of the Cripps proposal by the Congress high command and the Muslim League, Gandhi interposed himself between his party's leaders and the British and demanded its rejection. Although it is said that Nehru was prepared to break with Gandhi over the issue and indeed, Rajagopalachari quit his position on the Working Committee as a demonstration of disagreement with Gandhi, the Mahatma prevailed. Cripps departed from India exasperated by the experience and moved to press his government to reconsider its approach. Gandhi's motives remained a point of controversy. On the one side he was reluctant to accept an offer from a weakened British empire that addressed an after-the-war scenario, while on the other, he anticipated an imminent Japanese invasion which, he judged, would bring a sudden end to British rule in the subcontinent. It can be argued that Gandhi expected more immediate rewards, not from the British, but as a consequence of a Japanese victory.

A significant aspect of the Gandhi strategy was his perception of the Muslim League threat to India's future unity. The defeat of Britain by Japan opened up the possibility of eliminating that threat. Quite different results were in the wind if Britain succeeded in repulsing the Japanese attack. Indeed, a British victory would appear to guarantee a dominant role for the Muslim League after the war. It is reasonable to argue, therefore, that Gandhi saw less reason to fear Japanese penetration of the subcontinent. What is curious in this discussion is that Gandhi, as a consequence of the war, and particularly the course it had taken in 1942, appears to have shifted his support from Nehru to Subash Chandra Bose, who earlier he had judged to be too radical. Bose had, in fact, left India with the express purpose of linking up with the Japanese, and with the latter's considerable assistance had organized the Indian National Army from captured Indian forces. It was Bose's intention to lead the INA in the campaign designed by the Japanese to 'liberate' the subcontinent from British imperialism. Gandhi appeared not to oppose these actions, and it can be argued that he saw the Bose forces neutralizing the last vestiges of Muslim separatism. Gandhi's call for non-violent resistance to the Japanese and his demand that the British 'Quit India' was followed by a massive civil disobedience campaign which the Mahatma referred to as 'open rebellion' (Spear, 1961, p.405).

The Viceroy was compelled to declare the Congress an illegal organization, and in the ensuing riots more than 1,000 lives were lost and many thousands more were injured. By the end of 1942 the British had arrested more than 50,000 Indians, who were incarcerated in makeshift detention camps, given the lack of prison facilities. Churchill cited the Gandhi-fomented Congress rebellion, calling it a stab in the back from those who otherwise publicized their peaceful intentions and actions. For Britain, the issue was not simply one of preventing the Japanese from penetrating and possibly overrunning the subcontinent; there also was a lesson to learn. London finally acknowledged the depth of animosity between the rival Indian communities. Downing Street would pursue the war because it had no other option, but whether to cling to empire was a matter that needed resolution, and the decidedly ugly character of the social struggle in the subcontinent seemed to argue for withdrawal as quickly and as honourably as possible. Although some of the more conservative members of the British political scene, e.g., Churchill, thought in terms of holding the line in India, opposition to that line of thought was mounting, egged on by the upheavals of 1942-3.

Linlithgow was replaced as Viceroy by General, now Lord, Archibald Wavell in 1943, and the change was very much linked with London's decision to shift the attention in India from military matters to political issues. By the time of Wavell's arrival in India, the Japanese invasion of India had been neutralized and a counter-offensive had forced the enemy to take up defensive positions. India was not again threatened, and Gandhi's forecast of a British defeat turned out to be a gross miscalculation. Even Bose's INA fizzled out, while the Bengali radical did not survive the war. In the general course of events, the Congress Party suffered grievous losses while its counterpart, the Muslim League, succeeded in a number of by-elections and developed into the national party it had always represented itself as being. Britain was now prepared to do serious business with the Muslim League and Jinnah was made a major party to all further deliberations.

As Viceroy, Wavell was charged with bringing as much reconciliation to Congress-League relationships as conditions allowed. He organized a meeting of the parties at Simla in June 1945, hardly weeks after the German surrender, ostensibly for the purpose of pursuing the war against Japan, but with the awareness that it was winding down and that the time to address the future of the subcontinent had arrived. India was swarming with British forces at the time and the atmosphere was one that seemed to favour a confident British initiative. Wavell's intention was to revise the Cripps proposals by calling for a national administration to sustain the war against Japan, and a constituent assembly that would be responsible for drafting a constitution. But at Simla, the Congress continued to insist that it represented all Indians, including Muslims, and argued for the sitting of Muslim representatives of the party. Jinnah voiced his opposition to the manoeuvre, refusing to deliberate in the presence of Muslims that associated with other organizations, and the talks floundered. Congress, unlike the British, still believed the Muslim League could be outfoxed, and continued to act as though nothing had happened in the intervening years to alter the equation between itself and the League. The British attempted to disabuse it of this view, to explain the pledges made to the Muslims in the course of the war, but the stubbornness of the Hindu leaders could not be shaken.

Congress's intransigence appeared to pay off when, in quick succession, Churchill lost control of the government to Clement Attlee and his Labour Party, and Japan surrendered unconditionally to the Allied Forces following the atomic bombing of Hiroshima and Nagasaki. Unlike the Conservatives, the British Labour Party had been long committed to vacating India. An exhausted Britain had all it could do to celebrate the end of World War II, and had little energy remaining to retain an empire that already had come apart. The rapid removal of the Allied Forces from India added to Whitehall's urgency in cutting its losses and retreating with grace and forbearance. India was well along the road to independence in 1945. It had long thought of itself as an independent country; its leaders had achieved international stature; it had received charter membership in the United Nations; and it only remained to consecrate its sovereignty in a formal act of ceremony. At least, that is how it looked to the Congress, and now too, to the new Labour government in London. Lord Wavell attempted to inject reality into the picture, citing the quest of the Muslim League, but the idea of an independent Pakistan had not yet won the attention of the key British policy-makers, and Jinnah's followers realized their work still lay before them.

The Decision to Partition

The Wavell administration decided to hold fresh elections to test the strength of the parties, and thus to determine how and what needed to be done in order to bring the matter of Hindu-Muslim relations to a successful resolution. The election results of 1946 were quite different from those of 1937. The League faced stiff opposition in the Punjab, where a coalition of Muslims and Hindus, led by Khizr Hayat Khan Tiwana, prevented the party from forming the government; and in the North-West Frontier Province, where the Khudai Khidmatgar and the Congress had formed a union under the leadership of Dr Khan Sahib (the brother of Abdul Ghaffar Khan). It was nevertheless obvious that the Muslim League represented the Muslims as much as the Congress spoke for the Hindus. Following this most recent round of elections, and in order to demonstrate its determination, the League openly courted its brethren in both Punjab and NWFP, urging them to reconsider their association with the Congress, as well as the negative impact of their sustained relationship on Muslim causes throughout the subcontinent.

But more than Muslim causes were jeopardized by the intensification of Congress-Muslim League rivalry. In essence, both the Congress and the Muslim League were nationalist and secular parties. Religious ritual was never made the centrepiece of their *modus operandi*. Both parties were more or less modelled after their European counterparts, and both stressed the competitive and universal aspects of their expression. Both claimed to be free of bias and prejudice, and both sought to comfort the minorities in their midst and to assure them that they had every opportunity to engage freely in the political life of the nation. The Muslim League, of course, was organized along communal lines and denied membership to non-Muslims, but it did not win the favour of the more fundamentalist members of the Islamic *umma*. On the contrary, it attracted stiff opposition from the Muslim *ulema*. Jinnah's insistence on balance and fairness to all, irrespective of religious persuasion or cultural identity, projected a secular approach that was now obscured in the Muslim League's struggle to achieve parity with the Congress. In the end, the exclusive natures of Hinduism and Islam were elevated over that of shared experience, and the moderates in each party were forced to assume extreme positions that contradicted their philosophy and caused them to exaggerate their differences. In this way too, a pattern of political engagement emerged which left little room for successful bargaining and compromise.

With Great Britain still reeling from the costs of World War II, London's Labour government had little patience with the culture war raging between Hindus and Muslims. Having decided earlier to leave India at the earliest possible moment, the question was not what kind of India would achieve its independence, but how British interests would fare in the ensuing circumstances. From a strategic and military vantage point, it was clear to Whitehall and Downing Street that British power in the world had been superseded by the Americans, and that with the Japanese surrender, a *Pax Americana* had settled over the planet. Britain could no longer pay the costs of empire. Reconstruction and rehabilitation at home took precedence over matters challenging the colonies. Moreover, the Americans were insistent that the still operating imperial systems must reconsider their purpose in the post-World War II era and yield to the pleas for self-determination from their colonial subjects. Britain, of all the still functioning empires, seemed best to realize the futility of clinging to distant colonies, and, except for generally remote strategic territories, began the process of dismembering its imperial system. High on the agenda addressing the subject of the transfer of power from imperial to indigenous authority was the subcontinent, but still one last attempt would be made to leave behind a whole India, albeit a loosely-arranged confederation that seemed to promise Hindu-Muslim co-operation.

London sent Lord Pethick-Lawrence, Sir Stafford Cripps,

and A.V. Alexander to India to negotiate an understanding between the leaders of the Congress Party and the Muslim League. Known as the Cabinet Mission, or the Second Cripps Mission, the Labour government's representatives laid out a scheme that they believed would do justice to the different political/cultural communities, while at the same time preserving the unity of the Indian subcontinent. The Cabinet Mission proposed offering the Muslim League the opportunity to create a veritable Pakistan that would be autonomous within a larger framework of Indian union. On the one hand, the British proposed the formation of a federal union that also would include the Indian princes and their holdings, and in which all defence matters, foreign affairs, and communications would come under central control. On the other hand, separate clusters of provinces would be formed into individual sub-federations, making it possible for the Muslim-dominant Punjab, the North-West Frontier Province, and Sindh, to form one Muslim entity, while predominantly Muslim Bengal would comprise another. All the Hindu-dominant provinces would likewise be clustered to form yet another relatively self-governing union. In addition, the Cabinet Mission proposed the formation of a constituent assembly which would be given responsibility for drafting a constitution to give meaning and substance to this form of federation/confederation.

The Cabinet Mission cited the need to organize as quickly as possible an interim government that would assume responsibility for governing the country while deliberations on the proposed plan moved forward. The interim government would also be made responsible for the election of the constituent assembly, and would embody all sovereign powers until such time as a new constitution, and hence a permanent government, were put in place.

The federation/confederation plan, somewhat surprisingly, received tacit approval from both the leaders of the Congress and the Muslim League. But the interim government proposal was another matter. Indeed, the larger plan could not be pursued in the absence of agreement on the interim government, and it was here that the two sides once again revealed their inability to collaborate in a scheme that centred on preserving the territorial integrity of the subcontinent. The interim government was projected as consisting of an equal number of Muslims and caste-Hindus. The Congress, however, still insisted that its more secular philosophy permitted it to represent all Indians, and that it could select a Muslim to represent its interests in the interim government. The Muslim League refused to acknowledge that claim, and demanded it be given sole responsibility for choosing the Muslim representatives. Jinnah declared that no compromise was possible on the issue. Meetings between the British representatives and those of India's principal political parties followed one after another, providing opportunity for the Congress officials to gain the confidence of the British mission as well as the Viceroy. By contrast, the League lost ground during these protracted proceedings. Jinnah was perceived as strident and inflexible, and the Muslim League appeared too culture-bound for British tastes. In fact, Jinnah was not in error in perceiving communion between the would-be neutral negotiators and the leaders of the Congress. After considerable haggling between the major antagonists, the Congress Working Committee unilaterally declared that it was prepared to convene the proposed constituent assembly, explaining that it would be a sovereign body and would hence possess the authority to assemble a government. Jinnah's refusal to succumb to this Congress manoeuvre only added to the British perception that it was the Quaid's intransigence which stood in the way of a settlement.

Jinnah's reason for rejecting the constituent assembly aspect of the Cabinet Mission proposal was explained by the Muslim League General Secretary, Liaquat Ali Khan. He cited Congress's decision to back away from its earlier approval of the total plan. Nehru's statement that the Congress was only prepared to accept that portion of the proposal which described the method of election to the constituent assembly, was interpreted as a clever gambit aimed at overcoming League opposition. To Jinnah and his followers, the Congress was seeking a way around the Muslim League that would reduce the party's role in any final arrangements. Acknowledging that the Congress offer, if accepted, would force the Muslim League to agree to a 4 to 1 disadvantage, the League issued a public statement declaring that the organization would be committing 'suicide' if it participated in a Congress-dominated constituent assembly and did not have the safeguards promised in the total Cabinet Mission package. But there was even more to League concerns. From the vantage point of the Muslim League, the Viceroy and his colonial apparatus had retreated from their often stated even-handed role. In British eyes, Jinnah in particular, and the Muslim League in general, had broken all the rules of propriety. Nearing their last hour, the Labour government-directed colonial authority had cast its lot with the Congress, and the Muslim League, deprived of Churchill's wartime support, was left to ponder its much diminished options.

Sensing the loss of a major opportunity, but still obliged to think in terms of some form of a unified subcontinent, Jinnah called upon the Viceroy to honour paragraph 8 of the Cabinet Mission statement of 16 June 1946, which specified that any party which accepted all of the Cabinet Mission's proposals would be permitted to form the government. In so far as the Congress had registered a negative vote on the overall plan, the League said it would accept them in total, and Jinnah called upon the Viceroy to do his duty, that is, to permit the Muslim League to form the government. Lord Wavell feared being outmanoeuvred by Jinnah's action, but the Quaid's demand virtually paralysed his decision-making capacity. Jinnah's next move was to accuse the Viceroy of a breach of faith, and when Wavell called for a postponement of the paragraph 8 understanding, Jinnah was left with no other recourse than to call upon the League and his followers for 'direct action' in the attainment of Pakistan. Citing an Anglo-Congress conspiracy aimed at denying the Muslims their proper place in an Indian union, Jinnah called for countrywide demonstrations, and the mayhem the British so much feared, but had done almost nothing to prevent, spread from one area of the subcontinent to another.

Following Jinnah's call for the achievement of Pakistan, the Muslim League Council passed two resolutions in which the League formally rejected the Cabinet Mission plan and confirmed its support for direct action, making it perfectly clear that the objective was the attainment of an 'absolute

Pakistan'. All Muslim Leaguers who had received titles from the British Crown were called upon to renounce them forthwith. Jinnah was constrained to note that the call for direct action was not to be taken as a declaration of war, but an official League act of self-defence. The party's objective, he said, was the preservation of the League's role as the only national representative of the subcontinent's Muslims. Congress reacted with its own tactics that were designed to further destabilize the League. It now accepted the Cabinet Mission proposals in their entirety, and also received the support of the Sikh Panthic Board, which up to this time had refused to go along with the scheme because it did not give the Sikhs recognition of their claims. Still another blow was levelled against the League when the Viceroy agreed to establish the interim government with Congress in the driver's seat. Following this act, Nehru contacted Jinnah to ask for his co-operation, and the two leaders met on 13 August 1946, but could not resolve their differences, let alone transcend their mutual suspicions. Nehru reported that Jinnah had rejected the interim government proposal, and the British, who now were absolutely convinced they could not work with the Quaid-i-Azam, decided to go ahead and form the government without the League. On 24 August, Jawaharlal Nehru and his colleagues were called upon by the Viceroy to head the new administration.

Jinnah's call for direct action now took on greater meaning. Tensions had been increased, not lessened, by the breakdown in negotiations and the British decision to proceed with a Congress-driven interim government. No one, including the colonial authority, was in a position to control events. Disturbances erupted from one end of the subcontinent to the other, with major riots hitting the cities of Calcutta, Bombay, Delhi, Ahmedabad, and Agra. Bengal and Bihar were scenes of the heaviest carnage, where the intermingled Muslim-Hindu neighbourhoods exploded in orgies of blood. Calcutta, the seat of a Muslim League government, was perhaps the worst case. A Muslim, H.S. Suhrawardy, a lawyer by training, had assumed the office of chief minister of the province of Bengal following the ouster of the Khwaja Nazimuddin administration, which had been tainted by the famine that ravaged the region during the war. Suhrawardy proved to be an effective administrator. He also demonstrated a capacity to transcend communal politics and generally got on well with members of the Hindu community. Nevertheless, given the tensions produced by the Hindu-Muslim controversy, he was prompted to bolster his police establishment, and in so doing, he made the mistake of recruiting Pathans from the North-West Frontier Province. Suhrawardy believed that the martial background of the Pathans suited them for the role. He also was familiar with the British policy that stationed forces of one particular ethnicity in regions inhabited by another. Following in this tradition, and believing the Pathans would be true to their salt, Suhrawardy utilized them in maintaining law and order. What he did not contemplate was Jinnah's call for direct action to achieve Pakistan and the impact this would have on the region; more so, how it would be exploited by a variety of elements concerned with something more than a Congress-Muslim League tug-of-war.

The riots that overwhelmed Calcutta in 1946 were the worst in Britain's colonial history, and because the Suhrawardy government had been compromised by its employment of a Pathan police force, the British were forced to interpose themselves between the warring parties. Only a major military presence was able to restore a modicum of tranquillity to the city, but the magnitude of the killing and the random slaughter had both angered and frightened the colonial authority. Lord Wavell communicated his distress to London, and argued that British troops should not be forced into the quagmire of communal warfare. General Sir Claude Auchinleck, overall British commander in the country, concurred with this appraisal and urged London to move with haste in transferring power to indigenous hands. Both Wavell and Auchinleck were convinced that Great Britain would not be able to reconcile the parties, and that the British troops who were called to put down civil strife would themselves become the target of faceless rioters. With the sacrifices of World War II ever fresh in their memories, the two generals convinced London that it confronted a mission impossible. Their recommendation called for abandoning the subcontinent to the leaders of the Congress and the League, who would have to deal with the situation with their own resources and in any way they considered appropriate.

Amidst the slaughter, the Congress-organized interim government received official sanction on 2 September. Citing British complicity in provoking the killings, Jinnah appealed to the Muslim members of the British Indian Army to reconsider their oath of allegiance. Fearful of an all-out civil war, Wavell invited Jinnah to discuss the conditions under which the League might still agree to join the interim government and after extended talks, assisted by the Nawab of Bhopal, Jinnah agreed to a compromise formula. Neither the impasse nor the rioting, however, was addressed by the agreement. Jinnah continued to reject the formation of a sovereign constituent assembly, and the arbitrary and random killing continued unabated throughout the country. Thus, when the Viceroy called for the creation of the constituent assembly in December 1946, Jinnah prevented his Muslim League from sending its representatives. Leaving open the possibility that the League might yet attend, Jinnah called upon the Congress to agree to the original terms of the Cabinet Mission proposal, as well as the interpretations regarding the grouping scheme which had created a Pakistan state within the projected union.

The Congress, however, had pledged itself not to permit the formation of Pakistan and, in a last desperate act, the British government called a meeting in London that was attended by the Viceroy of India, Lord Wavell; Nehru; Jinnah; his lieutenant, Liaquat Ali Khan; and Baldev Singh, the Sikh representative. Prime Minister Attlee, Lord Pethick-Lawrence, Sir Stafford Cripps, and A.V. Alexander, the Cabinet Mission principals, joined the deliberations in 10 Downing Street, the residence of the Prime Minister. On December 6, the first day of their discussions, the British government called for an end to the impasse on the basis of the original Cabinet Mission proposal. The Congress Party was urged to adopt the grouping scheme and accept the reality of a Pakistan entity. The British insisted that compromise, no matter how painful, was a *sine qua non* for serious agreement. In the British plan, Congress was to agree to a self-governing Pakistan, while the Muslim League was called upon to accept a union government, dominated by the Congress, that controlled defence, foreign policy, and communications. Although total agreement could not be achieved, Jinnah was encouraged by the proceedings and sustained his quest for an independent Pakistan.

The Quaid continued to argue that united India was a historical fiction. Jinnah noted that the only single India in the history of the subcontinent was the one fashioned by the British 'sword', and that India could only be preserved by the sword. Jinnah acknowledged that the geographic division envisaged by the Pakistan quest gave Pakistan the poorest region of the subcontinent, but it would still be a country of approximately 100,000,000 souls, who would then be able to pursue, in peace, their peculiar traditions. Jinnah also alluded to the disparate character of the two major political cultures, expressing the view that Islam was egalitarian whereas Hinduism was caste-ridden and, hence, an intrinsic denial of democratic values and practices. The Muslim demand was not an assault on the rule of the majority, he said, but a plea to permit a distinctive people the right to find their own future in a rapidly changing world.

Long opposed to the independence of India, Winston Churchill appeared to reverse course when he intruded himself into the debate. Echoing Jinnah in some part, he noted the artificial nature of Indian unity and urged the British government to look seriously at the Muslim League demand. Noting that the Muslims 'comprised the majority of the fighting elements of India' (Rajput, 1948, p.141), he questioned how the British Labour government could consciously give advantages to the Congress. Churchill raised the issue of Britain leaving India to its own destiny. He articulated the fears expressed earlier by Wavell and Auchinleck about using British troops to enforce 'caste-Hindu domination upon 90,000,000 Muslims and 60,000,000 untouchables' (Rajput, 1948, p.148). The Labour government's response to Churchill's impassioned address was defensive and chastened. The British government, it was said, must announce its withdrawal from India at a date certain, while it still had essential control over the subcontinent's administrative machinery. If it delayed in doing so, it was said, the empire would face being forced out under a pall of violence and terror. There were now no other options.

Mountbatten and the Final Chapter

Congress obstinacy in matters related to the Muslim League was, no doubt, fed by the Congress-directed Khan Sahib government in the North-West Frontier Province and the Khizr Hayat Khan Unionist government in the Punjab. In the absence of control in these important provinces, the Muslim League could never sustain its claim to represent all the Muslims of India. Muslim League opposition to these governments had crystallized since the 1937 elections, and there was little doubt that in another poll, fairly conducted, the Muslim League would emerge victorious. Thus, the Muslim League leaders in those provinces assumed a more determined stand, and when Abdul Qayyum Khan declared his intention of calling a separate Muslim constituent assembly, and the Khan of Mamdot, along with Mian Mumtaz Daultana, Malik Feroz Khan Noon, Sardar Shaukat Hayat Khan, and Mian Iftikharuddin all courted arrest, the campaign to gain Muslim League control of the NWFP and the Punjab began in earnest.

Sensing the imminent threat to his government, Khizr Hayat lumped the Muslim League with the Hindu extremist organization, the Rashtriya Swayam Sevak Sangh or R.S.S., declared both organizations enemies of the state, and banned them from all public activities. Such tactics did not deflect the Muslim Leaguers, however, and now, supported by rank and file Punjabi Muslims, they increased their pressure on the Unionist government. As these developments were unfolding, the British government declared it would act to determine who assumed power at the centre as well as in the provinces if the parties could not achieve a consensus on the constitution. Khizr Hayat insisted on the call for a meeting of all the political leaders, given the fears expressed by his Sikh and Hindu supporters that the Muslim League had planned a *putsch* in the Punjab. Moreover, the Punjab was already the scene of wide-scale agitation.

The Sikhs, who were especially aroused, demanded the right to carve out their own Sikh-Hindu province, rather than yield to Muslim League domination. The Hindu R.S.S., now noticeably more active in the province, held similar views, and the message went out to their agents to stockpile weapons in anticipation of a violent showdown with Muslim League National Guards. Master Tara Singh, the spokesman for the Punjabi Sikhs, arguing that co-operation with the League was virtually impossible, placed his Akali Fauj, or Sikh Army, on a similar footing. All forecasts projected a test of arms, no matter what the final outcome of the political manoeuvring in New Delhi. Having focused the conflict between Muslim and Hindu/Sikh, and having done nothing to prevent the breakdown of law and order, on 2 March 1947 Khizr Hayat submitted his resignation, after citing the British decision to leave India and his own inability to guarantee the peace of the region. Khizr's abrupt departure forced the main contenders for power in the Punjab to confront the realities of their rivalry.

Khizr Hayat had made reference to the announcement on 20 February 1947 by the Attlee government that Britain had had all it could stomach in the subcontinent and that it was the Crown's intention to transfer power to indigenous hands and depart from India no later than June 1948. Attlee had also revealed that he had replaced Wavell with Lord Louis Mountbatten and, as the last Viceroy, Mountbatten had been instructed to proceed with all deliberate speed in vacating the once prized colony (Raza, 1982). The British decision to quit India was welcomed in most circles, but it was overdue, and the conditions in which the Europeans had decided to make their retreat were not favourable to a smooth transition. Moreover, the choice of Mountbatten as the last Viceroy meant that a pro-Congress personality had been summoned to render the final verdict in the Congress-Muslim League controversy.

Mountbatten was a scion of the royal family and a celebrated hero of World War II, having had overall responsibility for the Allied Forces in the China-Burma-India theatre. Dashing and courageous, Mountbatten had won the affection of the troops under his command. He had also gained the fancy of Jawaharlal Nehru, who greeted his arrival in India with exceptional delight. Mountbatten's reappearance in India on 22 March came just days after the Khizr Hayat government in the Punjab had fallen to the Muslim League. As predicted, the assumption of Muslim power in the Punjab precipitated a violent reaction from the Hindu and Sikh population, and a civil war mentality gripped the province. Quickly concluding that it was either Pakistan or anarchy, Mountbatten opted for the former, but in so doing, decided that there was no reason to postpone the inevitable until June 1948. The new Viceroy set an energetic course for all concerned, believing that time was of the essence, and that only a determined posture would allow Britain to depart with dignity and also allow the people of the subcontinent to find the peace he believed they all wanted.

Mountbatten's first concern was not to tame, because he could not, but how to appease the forces that were tearing the Punjab apart. If that province was not stabilized, he did not see how the slaughter in greater India could be contained. Mountbatten did not seek an end-game course in which the warring parties would reconcile their differences. His major objective was more a hiatus, so that the formal transfer of power could be completed and the British allowed to exit with dignity and safety. Mountbatten was also determined that the British departure from India should be accomplished with pride and a sense of deep accomplishment. Believing in the majesty of his mission, he intended to give it all the pomp and pageantry of a royal coronation.

During the time of the Punjab crisis, Jinnah was residing in Bombay, and it was from that station that he issued a directive to the new Muslim League government there. Jinnah counselled restraint and self-control; above all, he called upon his colleagues to protect the minority population, no matter how extreme the provocations. Mamdot had formed the Muslim League government and had extended peace over-tures to the Sikhs, offering them a share of the government which they promptly turned down. Nevertheless, strenuous efforts were launched by the League that were aimed at quieting fears and lowering the volume of violent rhetoric.

But where the League continued to see possibilities for future reconciliation, Mountbatten saw only more mayhem, and he was not prepared to give the parties the time to see if they could sort out their differences. Indeed, Mountbatten was convinced there had already been far too much foot-dragging. Given his accelerated manoeuvring, he alone would determine the timetable, the character of the transition, and the final outcome. Mountbatten immediately called for Jinnah, Gandhi, and the members of the interim government, including Jawaharlal Nehru, to parley with him. In the crisis of the moment, virtually all the Indian leaders believed that Mountbatten would select the most appropriate device to break the impasse, but the Viceroy cautioned that nothing he could do would ensure a smooth transition if decorum among the major leaders was unattainable.

Mountbatten informed the assembled principals that the subcontinent, that is, British India, was to be partitioned and, however painful the adjustment to that reality, it had become a settled fact and the necessary starting point in the pursuit of a workable solution. The breakdown of the civil administration was a primary problem. The politicians, he asserted, had done great harm to the steel frame of colonial administration and any further display of disaffection would have ruinous consequences for the whole nation. Rebuilding the bureaucracy, notably the police services, required the co-operation of all the parties, especially if they expected to pick up the reins of government once the British had departed from the scene. Finally, Mountbatten cited the misuse of the Press and how the media had been exploited for partisan advantage. He questioned the negative feeding of gullible publics, a practice that only heightened emotions and provoked random and indiscriminate assaults on civil society. Mountbatten appeared to agree with Jinnah when he noted that India was not a nation in the true sense of that term, but rather a nation of nations. It was only when all the major actors acknowledged that reality that the subcontinent could find true peace.

Only weeks after his arrival, it was clear that British India would give birth to two sovereign, independent dominions, India and Pakistan. But that was not the end of the matter. If partition of the subcontinent was indeed inevitable, and if it was to be made along lines that satisfied the Hindu majority areas on the one side and the Muslim majority areas on the other, then it followed that those provinces which were reasonably divided between the two communities should also be partitioned. The Congress leadership demanded that Bengal and Punjab also be divided to reflect the majority residence of the different communities. Jinnah voiced his opposition to the Congress demand, insisting that Pakistan should comprise five established Indian provinces, i.e., Sindh, the NWFP, Punjab, Bengal, and Assam, as well as the territory of Balochistan, which was to achieve provincial status after the transfer of power. Anything less would be more shadow than substance; indeed, H.S. Suhrawardy had drafted a long memorandum to Jinnah, arguing that any partition of Bengal that left Calcutta in India would do serious damage to the Pakistan design.

Mountbatten sent his deputy, General Lord Ismay, to London to lay out the possibilities for the transfer of power. Signalling general acceptance of the partition principle, Ismay indicated that Punjab and Bengal would be divided to represent the majority community in each area, and that a boundary commission would have to be appointed to handle the matter. Barring this, Punjab would most certainly be put to the knife, but Bengal might be preserved intact if a constitutional scheme could be devised granting the province special status in respect to both India·and Pakistan. Ismay was authorized to brief the government on the status of the NWFP as well. Under Muslim League pressure this time, Mountbatten had agreed that fresh elections should determine the character of the Frontier Province prior to the transfer date and, most important, to see whether or not the Congress-led coalition could prevail over the forces of the Muslim League. But having discussed these matters, the question surrounding the future of British India still needed a definitive answer. Jinnah had broached the subject of India's assets and how they would be divided between the two parties, but no understanding had been arrived at. Now, however, the matter could no longer be postponed and all the parties agreed that a complete understanding was critical to the formation of the two new states.

Neither Mountbatten nor Field Marshal Auchinleck wanted to see the division of the Indian Army. Judged to be Asia's finest fighting force at the time, any tampering with its units, chain of command, etc., could only have catastrophic effects, or so at least the British believed. For the first time, the British publicly introduced the subcontinent's strategic needs into the deliberations, especially the British perception of the region's geopolitical position with the onset of the Cold War. The March 1947 Truman Doctrine, establishing the American containment policy, centred on checking the spread of Soviet influence; that policy had suddenly become a factor in the equation of Indian independence. The Indian reaction to this issue was confused, in that although the Congress did not want to see Pakistan provided with a sizeable armed force, it also wanted an independent India that was free of Cold War machinations. The Muslim League, on the other hand, was insistent on a fair distribution of the armed forces as well as the weapons stores, but it had not settled on a Cold War policy. What could not be missed in the debate over the division of the armed forces, however, was that both India and Pakistan would be born into the Cold War and that they could not avoid the impact of the rivalry exhibited by the United States and the Soviet Union.

The issue concerning the future of the Indian armed forces had not been resolved by the time Mountbatten left for London to discuss progress and future actions with the British government. In London, the subject of dominion status for the two new states was finally agreed upon. Whereas the British had always considered Commonwealth status a necessity for the two new states, Nehru had voiced objections, arguing that India would not be really independent if it remained tied to the British Crown. That concern, however, was addressed, and the matter of dominion status within a reconstituted but voluntary Commonwealth was agreed upon and the matter put to rest.

On 2 June, having returned to New Delhi from London, Mountbatten called a meeting of the key Congress, Muslim League, and Sikh leaders to review the decisions taken by the British government. Gandhi met the Viceroy later in a private session. The following day, all the leaders returned to the Viceroy's office to announce their approval of the transfer of power plan. That night the public learned officially over All-India Radio that the British colony would be divided into two states, and that the Punjab as well as Bengal and Assam would be divided, with a part of each going to the respective dominions. In addition, it was reiterated that the plan did not preclude negotiations between the communities for a united India; but in the case of partition, and it was now a certainty, the existing constituent assembly would continue to serve India, and another constituent assembly would be convened for Pakistan. Each constituent assembly could decide to remain in the newly reconstituted Commonwealth or opt out of the arrangement, and if the latter was the chosen course, then dominion status also would be nullified.

Most importantly, a boundary commission was to be organized and given the task of determining the geographic frontiers of the new states, but there was advance agreement that the demarcation would trace contiguous majority areas between Muslims and non-Muslims. Elections, not a boundary commission, were to determine the preference of the people of the NWFP. Dividing and distributing the resources and assets of the colonial government was to be left to the parties following the transfer of power. The same procedure would follow in matters of defence, finance, and communications, as well as the division of the services. Only the position of the Indian princes was left in an ambiguous state and still needed resolution. It was expected that many of the monarchs of India's 600 princely states would opt for one of the dominions, while others would enter into treaties with one or the other dominion government and remain effectively independent. But no one had a clear picture of these developments. In fact, none of these subjects had a simple answer. In the final analysis, it was the ambiance of civil war that weighed heavily on the decision-makers, and in their rush to judgment, British India's political leaders finally understood that they had little, if any, room for further manoeuvring.

CHAPTER 3

THE AGONY OF PARTITION

The 3 June partition plan was heralded as a demonstration of statesmanship: an eleventh-hour agreement had been hammered out which would prevent a tragic civil war and allow the two new states, India and Pakistan, to centre their attention on the immediate needs of their respective peoples. In a radio presentation that addressed all the people of India, Jinnah called upon them to examine the separation plan dispassionately, with calm, and with confidence in their individual as well as combined futures. Citing the magnitude of the undertaking, Jinnah noted that the road ahead would be difficult, but that he had no reason to believe that the transfer of power would be anything but successful. Appealing for discipline and co-operation from the vast population of the subcontinent, his words were especially directed at his Muslim brethren, who, he said, must be gracious and objective in approaching the implementation of the agreement. Jinnah's principal concern lay in keeping the peace, by which he meant the maintenance of law and order in a period of unprecedented change.

Jinnah acknowledged that the partition plan was far from perfect and that there would be those who would, understandably, find fault with it; nevertheless, he felt it offered a workable way out of the long-sustained Congress-Muslim League impasse, and could be said to satisfy the essential demands of both parties. The Quaid cited, in particular, the onerous decision to proceed with the division of both Bengal and Punjab, but said it was done in an act of compromise and with the hope that the riots which had ravaged the provinces would now subside. Jinnah indicated how important it was that the two new countries enter the period of self-government in an ambiance of friendship and accommodation, that much work lay ahead following the grant of independence, notably in dividing and distributing the armed forces, as well as the assets and liabilities of British India. Therefore, the building of trust between the two states was a *sine qua non* for a smooth transition. Jinnah was effusive in his praise of Lord Mountbatten, who had brokered the agreement. The Quaid offered the thought that the Viceroy had been motivated by a 'high sense of fairness and impartiality' (Rajput, 1948, p.201-2), and that his single interest centred on making it possible for the people of the subcontinent to live in peace following the formal British withdrawal.

Given the scheduled referendum in the North-West Frontier Province, Jinnah ordered the Muslim League to terminate its civil disobedience movement. Calling for a free and open election, Jinnah indicated that he would accept the people's verdict, and that there should be no reason to question the results by any of the parties. The Quaid-i-Azam's statement made it clear that the independence of Pakistan was now a certainty, and that Muslims everywhere could take pride in the creation of a new, sovereign Muslim state. It was a particularly proud moment for the Muslims of the subcontinent, whose political expression had been restored after a silence of almost one hundred years.

The Muslim League empowered Jinnah to act on behalf of the party and the Muslim nation in all further negotiations with the Congress and the Viceroy. It was reiterated that the time had passed when the larger Muslim public needed to be directly involved. Given the agreement, all street demonstrations were to cease, and the Quaid and his key lieutenants would speak for and act on behalf of the entire Muslim nation. The League adopted the partition plan as the framework for all further deliberations, and whatever changes might be arrived at were to be made within the limits of legal/political procedure, orchestrated by the highest leadership in the organization. From here on, all the activity

concerned technical issues and data that only the chief
politicians and their expert advisors were familiar with.
Financing the new state was a major responsibility, and the
allocation of resources and the distribution of economic
capacity were matters that only the most knowledgeable
members of the administrative system could assume. In the
controlled euphoria of the moment, Jinnah and the League
stressed two elements: 1) that the Muslim people give their
support to the partition plan and the Muslim League
leadership and remain calm in doing so; and 2) that the
experts be allowed to answer the many questions raised by
the partition scheme. Overall, Jinnah was confident that the
agreement was a settled fact and that it would not be
tampered with by either the Congress or the Viceroy.

Mountbatten appeared to keep to this understanding. Two
days after the formal announcement of the partition plan, he
called a meeting of all the key leaders and formed a Partition
Committee, placing it directly under his office. It was at that
meeting that Mountbatten dropped his first bombshell. He
revealed that it was his intention to complete all the
necessary work in time for the British to formally transfer
power and hence leave India by August, just weeks away.
Originally, the parties believed they had till June 1948 to iron
out all the problems that still lay ahead. Now, however, it
was made clear there would be little time to manage the
details of separation. And in this regard, the Muslims were at
a significant disadvantage. The Congress was far more
organized and would be the direct recipient of the British
legacy. Indeed, India was already a known entity, a charter
member of the United Nations, and a ready-made actor in all
domestic circumstances. The loss of several of its provinces
posed certain problems, but they paled into insignificance
when ranged alongside those facing Pakistan. The Muslim
nation was a totally new endeavour, and its geographic and
demographic aspects were ill-defined. In fact, it had not yet
been decided how Punjab and Bengal were to be divided,
nor was it clear what resources Pakistan would possess when
the transfer of power actually took place. Clearly, the Muslim
League leaders needed more time, and Mountbatten's
decision to stand down within weeks of the issuance of the

partition plan came as a great surprise to Jinnah and his colleagues (Hayat, 1991).

Nine expert committees were organized, ranging from personnel to revenues, from communications to the armed forces, and from trade policy to foreign policy. Moreover, these committees were all expected to submit their reports within four weeks of their charge. The same haste was evident in creating the Boundary Commissions, one for Bengal and another for Punjab. The indigenous members of the committee were announced straight away, with two Congress and two Muslim League members filling the Bengal Boundary Committee slots. The Punjab Boundary Committee comprised two Muslims, one Hindu, and one Sikh member. Only the chairman of the two committees was not announced at that time. That chairman turned out to be Sir Cyril Radcliffe, a leading English barrister, who was appointed on 9 July. Although the Radcliffe appointment was approved by Jinnah and somewhat questioned by Nehru, Radcliffe nevertheless turned out to be Mountbatten's second bombshell. Radcliffe was given responsibility for both committees even though he had never visited India, let alone served there, and did not possess even the most basic understanding of Indian demography or cultures. Moreover, Sir Cyril was given three weeks to complete the work of the two commissions. Mountbatten now set the date for the formal transfer of power at 15 August.

The rush to judgement was unfortunate in view of the complex nature of the assignments given to the many partition committees and especially the Boundary Commissions. There was significant concern on the part of the almost four million Muslims who resided in what was to be India's eastern Punjab. By the same token, there were more than one and a half million Sikhs in western Punjab, which was earmarked to go to Pakistan. The reference point of Muslim majority areas was more than a simple matter of drawing lines. Moreover, although the Sikhs would have preferred their own independent Khalistan, neither Britain nor the Congress wished to see yet a third sovereign state in the subcontinent. The denial of an independent Sikh nation, however, meant that that community had to adjust to a division which placed one group of Sikh believers in India and another in Pakistan.

For a majority of Punjabi Sikhs, this was an intolerable situation.

While the different committees laboured feverishly to meet the deadline set by the Viceroy, the British Cabinet also followed a torrid schedule. The drafting of the India Independence Act was accelerated and the 'Divide and Quit' bill for the first time referred to 'Pakistan' by name. It was decided that a Governor-General, designated by the respective constituent assembly, would be appointed by the King for each new dominion, except where the legislature of either dominion requested the same person to fill both positions. Full powers, however, were vested in the two legislatures, and the Governor-General was relegated to largely ceremonial chores. The Independence Act also affirmed that Acts of the British Parliament would cease to have effect in either India or Pakistan following the transfer of power that formalized the partition of the subcontinent. In the end, it appeared that Britain had chosen to depart from India leaving behind a legal framework that could be managed by its indigenous organizations. According to Prime Minister Attlee, Britain had completed its mission, not abdicated its role in the subcontinent. The parliament agreed to the elimination of the King's title as 'Emperor of India', and during the third week of July, the monarch gave his assent to all of the parliament's actions.

The legislative activity in London was the signal for the formation of two provisional governments, which were set up in New Delhi on 19 July. Until the actual transfer date, the two provisional governments were to act independently of one another but co-operate in areas of mutual concern. Following the official ceremonies granting independence to India and Pakistan, the two governments were to assume all responsibilities in their respective capitals. Indeed, the Muslim League, had a month earlier, selected Karachi as the site for Pakistan's capital.

The Independence of Pakistan

On 20 June 1947 Bengal voted to join Pakistan, and three days later, Punjab followed the same course. Balochistan declared its desire to become part of Pakistan on 29 June. On

13 July the Sylhet region of Assam opted for the Muslim state, and the referendum in the North-West Frontier Province also went overwhelmingly in favour of the Muslim League. In the latter instance, the Congress-dominated Khan Sahib government tried to remain in office even after its defeat at the polls, and when the British governor hesitated in removing the pro-Congress government from office, Jinnah was obliged to take the necessary action that finally placed a Muslim League government at the helm in Peshawar.

A more serious matter, however, developed during the deliberations of the boundary commissions. Radcliffe did not attend the meetings of the two committees, preferring to review their activities in the solemnity of his Delhi office. He was more closely in touch with Mountbatten than were the members of his committees, as his office was just down the hall from that of the Viceroy. Radcliffe's examination of the maps and other records was conducted in the presence of Mountbatten and other individuals not necessarily associated with either of the two bodies. Thus, when the committees failed to agree on the drawing of boundaries between the two dominions, Radcliffe pre-empted their work and made all the decisions for them (Moon, 1962).

Radcliffe assigned Calcutta to India, in spite of the strong claims to the city presented by the Muslim League. Virtually all the wealth of eastern Bengal was concentrated in the port city on the Hooghly. The Muslims who toiled in the jute paddies of the eastern hinterland sent all their harvests to Calcutta for processing, and it was Calcutta that determined the economic life of the region. When the last British governor of undivided Bengal, Sir Frederick Burrows, recommended that Calcutta be made a free port and open to both dominions, Mountbatten overruled him and insisted that the city be given to India. The Viceroy's decision followed the original understanding that only Muslim majority areas would go to Pakistan. Calcutta, Mountbatten noted, was only 25 per cent Muslim. The Viceroy, however, ignored the formula employed in determining Muslim majority areas. Muslim majority areas were only to be drawn in relation to caste-Hindu areas, and in the case of Calcutta, caste-Hindus were not significantly more numerous than Muslims. The issue, therefore, revolved around the scheduled castes, who had aligned with the Muslim League in the expectation that a Muslim government would be more likely to elevate the stature of Hinduism's untouchables.

Given that combination of factors, it was the Muslim League contention that Calcutta was not, strictly speaking, a predominantly Hindu city under the terms of the partition scheme. The Muslim League called for a plebiscite to determine the wishes of the people of Calcutta, but Mountbatten denied the request, having much earlier agreed to award the metropolis to India. In fact, Mountbatten had been closeted with high-ranking Congress leaders and had received their approval to the larger partition plan only after he had acknowledged that an independent India would be a very weak country without Calcutta and that the city must be awarded to India.

The Muslim League's inability to acquire Calcutta meant that the eastern portion of Bengal, where the Muslims were in an overwhelming majority, would be bereft of an economic anchor. Allowed to float free, the eastern hinterland, the poorest region of united Bengal, located more than a thousand miles from the provinces of western Pakistan, would according to H.S. Suhrawardy, be isolated and too enfeebled to assert its bona fides, let alone contribute to the development of Pakistan. Moreover, it would remain dependent on western Bengal, and especially Calcutta, thus bringing into question its future in a single Muslim state whose centre of gravity was located in Karachi. After the Calcutta issue, Mountbatten's secret deals with the Congress slowly began to emerge, and the Muslim League perception that he was a fair and impartial third party was radically altered.

Britain, through its high emissary, the Viceroy, had set a date certain for its withdrawal from India, but the British had also decided it would be foolhardy to leave behind two relatively weak states that could only multiply regional chaos and expose the subcontinent to external manipulation. Mountbatten believed that India's future security, given Pakistan's control of the strategic north-western gateways to South Asia, was dependent on dividing Bengal, so that India remained the overwhelming power from eastern Punjab to the frontiers of Burma. With a view to the martial traditions of the subcontinent's Muslim population, Sardar Patel was to declare later, 'We (the Congress) made a condition that we could only agree to partition if we did not lose Calcutta. If Calcutta is gone, then India is gone' (*Hindu*, Madras, 16 January 1950).

Radcliffe's decision to award the Muslim-majority district of Murshidabad and a portion of Nadia to India was in direct violation of the partition formula; so too was the assigning of the Buddhist Chittagong Hill Tracts to Pakistan. If other considerations were addressed in making those awards, then it must also follow that something different could have been arranged for Calcutta. In the final analysis, it made little difference to Mountbatten and the Congress if eastern Bengal was something less than viable, especially if it meant that India's basic needs had been satisfied. And finally, Mountbatten, Nehru, and Vallabhbhai Patel were all convinced that eastern Bengal, denied Calcutta, would have extreme difficulty in managing its affairs without assistance from India. Eastern Bengal, they surmised, would be more inclined to identify with India than with a distant Pakistan. The entire matter was reduced to a zero-sum game in which India was destined to emerge the stronger party.

On the other side of the subcontinent, the division of Punjab was made much more complicated by the Sikh population, who had long considered the province their homeland. The fact that the British and the Congress had decided against the creation of an independent Sikh state did not mean that Mountbatten could ignore the heavy Sikh presence in the Indian Army, or the community's overall significance in Indian affairs in spite of its relatively small population. The colonial authority, nevertheless, did almost nothing to counter Sikh declarations that they would fight to the death before they agreed to live their lives in a majority Muslim nation. Reluctant to intimidate the Sikhs, Mountbatten agreed to entertain Sikh claims to areas in which the Muslims were in the majority, but in which the Sikhs could argue historic and cultural identity, notably the sites of Sikh shrines. Neither Radcliffe nor Mountbatten used these same tests to demarcate areas considered sacred to Muslims, but the Sikh complaint, especially because there was no intention of granting the Sikhs a self-governing state, meant that the principle of Muslim majority areas would not be followed in Punjab. Thus, as in Bengal, whenever a difficult question demanded resolution, it was answered by requiring the Muslims to yield their claims.

In Punjab it was the Muslim majority districts of Gurdaspur and Batala that were given to eastern Punjab and thus awarded to India. The latter determination, however, had little to do with Sikh demands, but had much more to do with providing India a road link to Jammu and Kashmir. The Muslim majority *tehsil* of Ajnala in Amritsar district also went to India. The same destiny was imposed upon the Muslim *tehsils* of Nakodar and Jullundur, as well as the *tehsils* of Zira and Ferozepore, even though they abutted on western Punjab. It is important to note that, by contrast, not a single Hindu majority area was assigned to Pakistan's western Punjab.

Radcliffe's decisions did great harm to Pakistan in particular they made western Punjab dependent on India's control of the headwaters that fed the region's complex irrigation system. The awarding of the Muslim *tehsils* to India guaranteed that western Punjab's canal systems remained connected to India; it also made Lahore, Pakistan's second largest city, a hostage to Indian machinations. But it was the Gurdaspur award that created the greatest long-term damage. In time, the canal and irrigation systems could be altered by new hydroelectric systems, but the Gurdaspur issue introduced a political dilemma which became the major bone of contention between the two new states.

Gurdaspur district comprised four *tehsils*, only one of which was Hindu-dominant, namely Pathankot. Overall, the district was represented by a Muslim majority population that was contiguous with western Punjab. If Radcliffe had decided to award just Pathankot *tehsil* to India there would have been no opposition from the Muslim League. But the Radcliffe decision to give the entire district to India was another matter. Gurdaspur dominated the only land entry to the state of Jammu and Kashmir from India, and Pathankot *tehsil* did not sit astride this land route. It was obvious, therefore, that

other considerations had convinced Radcliffe to award
Gurdaspur to India, and indeed, there is sufficient reason to
believe that Mountbatten's strategic concerns were some of
them.

But as independence day approached, none of these
decisions had done anything to placate, let alone meet, the
deeper demands of the Sikhs, who were determined to press
their claims in the streets; and the Gurdaspur manoeuvre
merely prepared the ground for a display of arms in which
India and Pakistan were provoked to make war on one another
the very day they became free of imperial rule. Moreover, it
is interesting to note that the Radcliffe partitions were not
made public until 16 August, the day following the formal
ceremonies transferring power to the new dominions.
Mountbatten bears responsibility for the silence. He correctly
anticipated an adverse reaction to the awards, and he did
not want his last day as Viceroy, or the regal ceremony over
which he presided, to be marred by untoward events. It was,
therefore, Mountbatten who urged Radcliffe to wait until after
the grant of independence before making his determinations
public. Jinnah, in fact, had only become aware of the Radcliffe
decisions a few days before the formal transfer of power. By
that time, Sikh militants were already engaged in killing
their Muslim neighbours in eastern Punjab and tribal Pathans
had infiltrated Kashmir from the north-west, bent on
challenging the Hindu Maharajah's rule in that Muslim
majority princely state. Jinnah's dismay over the Radcliffe
awards, therefore, was heightened by the killing fields that
stretched from Amritsar and Lahore to Srinigar. But the
Quaid-i-Azam, true to his beliefs, refused to pour more fuel
on an already raging fire. Alluding to the adverse long-term
impact of the awards, but also citing their irreversible aspects,
Jinnah accepted their binding effect and urged his
countrymen to do likewise. 'As honourable people we must
abide by it (the awards). It may be our misfortune but we
must bear up this one more blow with fortitude, courage and
hope' (Ali, 1973, p.221).

Mountbatten addressed the Pakistan Constituent Assembly,
housed in the old Sindh legislative building, on 14 August
1947. Acknowledging the work of Mohammad Ali Jinnah in
the creation of Pakistan, the last of the British Viceroys

asserted this was not the time to look back, but to consider the future and Pakistan's role in a changing world. The moment was all ceremony and ritual, and as Mountbatten had wished, nothing was done to spoil the day. On 15 August, the last Friday in the month of Ramadan, Mohammad Ali Jinnah became Head of State, the Governor-General of the new state of Pakistan.

Trials and Tribulations

Pakistan was among the first of the new countries to be born after World War II. Of the then independent Muslim states, it was the largest in population and appeared destined to play a significant role in the Islamic world as well as in the changing international order. But the assertion of Pakistan's position was slow in emerging. Conditions within the country and between itself and India were not propitious. Internally challenged by divisive ethnic and provincial forces, denied the essential elements required to govern a contemporary state, destabilized by communal conflict, generally unprepared for the responsibilities of administering to a diverse population, separated spatially and temperamentally, the joy of independence was quickly transformed into the necessity for survival. Externally, Pakistan was forced to contest India in a show of arms over the future dispensation of Kashmir. That conflict introduced a United Nations presence that tested the young nation's diplomatic capacity, just as strife on the domestic front forced the country to come to grips with its *raison d'être* as an integrated state.

All eyes turned toward Mohammad Ali Jinnah, the man who, more than any other, had made Pakistan possible. Already in the seventh decade of his life, limited by illness and exhausted by the long, arduous journey toward independence, Jinnah, unlike Gandhi, who preferred to remain outside the play of day-to-day politics, had assumed the office of Governor-General in the new dominion (Bolitho, 1954). No other Muslim League personality had achieved national prominence in the years prior to the transfer of power, and even Liaquat Ali Khan, who became Pakistan's first Prime Minister, was a refugee from India and hence without a solid constituency in the new country. It is important to recall that the Pakistan movement had been centred in the Gangetic plain, with its tail in the region of Bengal. The territories of the north-western sector of the subcontinent, while overwhelmingly Muslim, had to be induced to join the League and indeed, the opposition to the party came from local Muslims, who questioned the League's protestation that Islam was in danger. Winning their support proved to be a strenuous undertaking and the wounds suffered in the struggle festered long after partition.

There can be no doubt that Jinnah's active presence was needed in guiding Pakistan after the grant of independence. Whether the Quaid-i-Azam could have managed this task outside the formal government structure will forever be a subject of debate. But the fact remains that he chose to become Pakistan's Head of State because he believed that no one else had been groomed for the role, and no less important, no one else had the capacity or the bona fides to realize his vision of a modern state. Jinnah sensed that he alone could manage rival politicians, neutralize dissatisfaction with League policy, and rally both officials and lay citizens in the consolidation of the nation. By contrast, Mountbatten had assumed the role of India's Governor-General, and this had been made possible in part because the higher echelons of the Congress government had more experienced politicians and lawmakers than the Muslim League, but in greater measure, because India had been an established entity long before the transfer of power. But as India's Governor-General, Mountbatten was relegated to essentially ceremonial functions.

Mountbatten had expected to become Pakistan's first Governor-General as well, but the Muslim League feared that the former Viceroy would do more damage than good in that position. Mountbatten had been on the receiving end of a variety of plaudits for his work in directing the transfer of power, but out of the public eye, the Muslim League high command was critical and always suspicious of Mountbatten's performance. India always remained the focal point of Mountbatten's attention, whereas Pakistan was the afterthought that would not go away. As Viceroy, Mountbatten saw no option other than to yield to Muslim League demands for partition, but he was never comfortable with the idea of a divided subcontinent. For Mountbatten, Hindus were more adaptable or more flexible than Muslims, and he philosophically opposed the notion of a state created to serve the interests of a peculiar religious community. The Congress government's emphasis on secularism reflected his own thinking, and his concern that India must assume major power status in southern Asia drove him to overcompensate the country when the time came to divide the subcontinent.

Jinnah's decision to become Pakistan's Governor-General, however, was not driven by any evaluation of Mountbatten's behaviour, or his role in the partition of the subcontinent. Jinnah became Governor-General because Pakistan had been dealt a weak hand at the time of independence, and he had toiled too long and too hard to yield authority to the last of the imperial Viceroys. Independence, to Jinnah, meant the freedom to pursue one's own version of a political state, and because Pakistan was the outcome of a particular religious experience and culture, it was impossible to allow the first head of that new nation to be someone alien to that persuasion. Jinnah discussed the matter with Mountbatten and, although reluctant to accept Mountbatten as Governor-General of both dominions, he nevertheless offered the suggestion that the Crown appoint someone to act as supreme representative during the transition. That representative would be responsible for matters that still required joint control, and would smooth the way for the distribution of those assets that could not be completed by the time of the formal transfer of power. Such a figure could ensure a degree of continuity and sustain a balance between the two new governments, but he would, nevertheless, be a subordinate officer to the Governors-General. Mountbatten, however, refused to consider an office in which he would find himself the lesser of the prevailing powers and the scheme, although never presented formally by Jinnah, was discounted by the Viceroy and the British government and subsequently abandoned.

Jinnah made it clear, however, that he had no intention of playing the role of an Islamic Khalifah. As Pakistan's Governor-General, he intended to see to it that all its citizens, irrespective of religious or cultural orientation, were, politically and before the law, similar and equal. But Pakistan was a fragile experiment at the time of independence and Jinnah's dream of a coherent, secular state, unified in will and spirit, and dedicated to the proposition of democratic development, was still to be realized. It was impossible for him to think that Mountbatten could move Pakistan in that direction; nor did he believe that Liaquat and his cabinet could manage the pressures of governmental responsibility without his assistance.

Jinnah did not deliberately embarrass Mountbatten, but his failure to yield to the former Viceroy's vanity may have been a tactical miscalculation. There is every reason to conclude that Jinnah could have influenced policy, whether in or outside the government. He was too important a figure to be consigned to obscurity should he have chosen not to assume official public office. Moreover, with Mountbatten ceremonially presiding over Pakistan's government, as he did over India's, his opportunity to thwart Pakistan's policy initiatives would have been nil. More important, if free from the day-to-day burdens of government, Jinnah might have found the time to restore his energy; months, perhaps years, might have been added to his life. It could be hypothesized that Pakistan may have had a different beginning had he lived even a year longer. Clearly, as Pakistan's one and only total leader, Jinnah's charisma permeated the nation, and any presiding Governor-General, even a Mountbatten, would have been a lesser figure in the making and implementation of policy. Observing this juxtaposition of personalities from another direction, if Mountbatten had been made Pakistan's first Governor-General it is possible that the Kashmir issue would have been less confrontational, while the communalism which savaged the Punjab might have been addressed more aggressively. But such was not the case. Jinnah and Mountbatten found themselves on different sides of a divide, and both were influenced by their immediate associates and the peculiar circumstances of their very different responsibilities.

On 29 August the two Governors-General met in Lahore with the Joint Defence Council, representing both India and

Pakistan. It was then that the decision was taken to disband the Punjab Boundary Force and to allow both dominions to assume responsibility for policing their respective territories. The disbanding of the 50,000-man force did nothing to restore law and order; in fact, the killing intensified and spread, and on 4 September Delhi too became a bloodbath, as Sikhs and members of the R.S.S. vented their anger on Muslims wherever they could find them. These developments provoked retaliation against Hindus and Sikhs in Pakistan, and the massive movement of people from both sides of the new frontier began in earnest. The Pakistan High Commissioner in Delhi reported to Karachi that the government should be prepared for the influx of millions of Muslim refugees. Percival Spear (1961) laments Mountbatten's reluctance to act decisively before the situation reached a critical stage. 'The key to this problem,' he writes, 'lies in the Boundary Force. If Lord Mountbatten had realized more clearly the do-or-die nature of the Sikhs, its 50,000 men might have been augmented (not disbanded).' According to Spear (1961), the only other alternative

> was the use of British troops. Instead of being withdrawn to the ports for shipment to Britain, they could have been concentrated in the boundary area and withdrawn via Karachi and Bombay after the initial tension had eased...The question remains, should not the British government have insisted on policing the boundary for six months after partition on the strength of its knowledge of conditions and in the name of humanity?

The question raised above remains; that is, had Mountbatten been Governor-General of Pakistan, would he have acted differently, and would he have had Field Marshal Auchinleck fulfil the purpose of his original mission?

Leonard Mosley (1961) also points the finger of responsibility at Lord Mountbatten. Upon visiting Calcutta after partition, and noting that so many people had perished there months before, Mountbatten asked Lieutenant-General Sir Francis Tuker if he would like a boundary force similar to the one he had raised in the Punjab. Tuker's responded negatively, asserting that he could handle the matter with his own forces. Tuker, in fact, had been assisted by Mahatma Gandhi, who spent Independence Day in a Bengali village in Noakhali, the location of an earlier slaughter. Gandhi's view that Independence Day was 'a day of mourning', not celebration, had brought him to Calcutta where, along with the former Muslim Chief Minister, H.S. Suhrawardy, he ministered to the needy and deflected the passions of those bent on spilling more blood. Thus, in a period when violence had stretched all across the Gangetic plain, through Delhi and on to the divided Punjab, Calcutta and most of Bengal remained tranquil. Nevertheless, East Bengal's population had increased by approximately one million refugees, driven to refuge by the slaughter in the neighbouring province of Bihar. To conclude that only Gandhi's presence limited the killing would be a gross error, considering that the Mahatma was not successful in the Punjab. It would be better to argue that different means were required in different regions, and that the appearance of British Armed Forces in Punjab might have produced a different outcome. But even if the questions raised above are never answered, history records that in 1947 the subcontinent was a scene of indescribable human tragedy. It was, in fact, the venue for the largest mass movement of people in all of recorded history. Chaudhri Muhammad Ali (1973) writes: 'Within a matter of weeks over twelve million people had left their homes and gone forth on foot, by bullock-cart, by railway, by car, and by plane to seek shelter and safety in the other Dominion.' Before the orgy of slaughter had run its course, an estimated twenty million people would become refugees, while perhaps as many as three million would perish in the arbitrary butchering of the innocent. Ethnic cleansing, only comparable to the brutalities inflicted on minority communities during World War II, occurred without any effort on the part of third parties to intervene. By the end of 1947, just four months following the grant of independence, Pakistan became a refuge for almost ten million displaced persons. If partition had ruptured the rhythm of the subcontinent, this unforeseen and unplanned-for holocaust fractured Pakistan's already feeble economy, strained its meagre resources, and imposed an impossible burden upon its administrative structure. Just the care, feeding, housing, and basic medical attention required by the millions of homeless, desperate people demanded far more resources than the nation could adequately muster.

Observing the worst carnage in the Punjab, Jinnah ordered Liaquat to operate his government from Lahore, at least temporarily. The Quaid-i-Azam also made numerous trips to the province in order to promote the co-ordination of relief activities between the central and provincial governments, and although there was major co-operation from the civil servants, and the British Governor of West Punjab, Sir Francis Mudie, laboured diligently to address the emergency, rivalries between the different Punjabi ministers were already apparent. Disgusted with the lust for power and advantage at what he judged to be the cost of a desperate humanity, Mian Iftikharuddin resigned his post as West Punjab Refugee Minister, and eventually abandoned the Muslim League for an organization more reflective of his sentiments. Jinnah's concerns were so multidimensional and so awesome in their character that no leader, no matter how eminent of stature, could effectively cope with them. The Quaid-i-Azam on the one side addressed himself to the question of what forces he had available to quell the killing; on the other he was burdened by the spectre of hundreds of thousands of refugees in need of immediate day-to-day assistance. And between both these pressing issues he had to confront and attempt to mediate between political power-seekers who used every opportunity, even the plight of the refugee community, to fashion a more secure place for themselves.

Jinnah was forced to divert too much of his attention away from the immediate needs of the country, to the in-fighting between political personalities within and outside his own party. At the same time, he was confronted by a situation in Kashmir which brought him into direct conflict with New Delhi and the Indian leaders who had masterminded a partition scheme the consequences of which were only now becoming known.

Political Gamesmanship

The idea of an independent and sovereign Muslim homeland in the subcontinent initially attracted a middle-class following, comprised of English- or semi-English-educated professionals and students. It later gained the financial support of some of the members of the Muslim princely community, who were attracted to the notion either for intellectual reasons, or because it seemed to promise greater personal security. The Muslim masses who later responded to Jinnah's call did so with exceptional enthusiasm. He drew strength from their dedication, and was forced to acknowledge that the Muslim League was their party and that Pakistan had become their joint quest. Seldom in the annals of modern history were a people and their supreme leader so intertwined with a common political experience (Wolpert, 1984).

But the Muslim League was far from being the choice of the majority of those who considered themselves politicians in the days of British India. Nevertheless, the meteoric expansion of the Pakistan Movement drew many a personality to join the growing army of Muslim Leaguers. With the passage of time, the Muslim League seemed to promise far more than the British or the Congress had ever offered, and when the Pakistan idea took on a life of its own, the party was expropriated by political characters of varying demeanour and purpose, few of whom demonstrated a political calling founded on selflessness or civic conscious-ness. More likely to be self-aggrandizing, the political world appeared to offer opportunities for wealth, position, and power that no other occupation permitted. Moreover, the name of the game was power, and it was no surprise that only the more egoistic, the most clever, and in too many instances, the cynically ruthless, could effectively compete.

Given their knowledge of the political scene and the resources that they brought to the contest, Jinnah could neither ignore these politicians, nor could he reject them. Socializing them also proved to be an unrealistic goal. Jinnah knew only too well that even their deference to him as the ultimate leader of the Pakistan Movement was hardly genuine and that, once he was out of their presence, they would conduct themselves as they saw fit. Jinnah was no more fooled by the politicians then they were overwhelmed by him. Jinnah's power lay not in the loyalty of the politicians with whom he was compelled to work, but in the Muslim masses who drew strength from his demeanour and envisaged through him a prouder and more brilliant future.

The problem that Jinnah faced in the period immediately following the creation of Pakistan was not just his rapidly deteriorating health. It was the reality that the masses who had carried the Pakistan movement to a successful conclusion, who had sacrificed so much in the process, were now called upon to stand down, to step aside, and leave the matter of Pakistan's future to others, indeed, to those politicians who would populate the institutions of government and, in effect, control the destiny of the nation. The Quaid-i-Azam was forced to labour with those individuals and personalities he had good reason to detest, who he knew would work at cross purposes, and who he also recognized would outlive him. Jinnah believed he had to have formal office in order to balance and, if need be, to check the arbitrary or personal power gambits of ambitious people. This may well have been the key issue in his tussle with Mountbatten over who should become Pakistan's Governor-General. Jinnah understood he was dealing with foxes who were shrewd and determined to have their way, and though a committed constitutionalist, he nevertheless understood the necessity of retaining that power which enabled him to deal with extreme circumstances. Jinnah had hoped to set Pakistan on a course that never deviated from the rule of law, but in reality, because he confronted some of the more unscrupulous of the subcontinent's self-serving politicians, he found it impossible to hold to that discipline.

In assuming the Governor-General's office, Jinnah perpetuated a viceregal tradition that had dominated the Indian scene during the age of the viceroys. Officially a parliamentary state, created along federal not unitary lines, the central and provincial governments were supposed to be the repositories of popular will. As a representative state, Pakistan projected a political character that was to best reflect the diversity of its human condition. But in point of fact, Pakistan was rushed into independence without the necessary opportunity to prepare and instil, in those who would assume representative responsibilities, the popular demands of their calling. As a consequence, those who would represent the national will, who gained control of the political life of the nation, were the same people who dominated the

power relations in traditional society. In the main, the so-
called representatives of the people were the aristocrats and
the landowners, the feudal lords and their sycophants, but
especially the patriarchs who dominated the land as well as
the people who depended upon that land for their sustenance,
and indeed, for their very survival.

The regions from which Pakistan was comprised lacked
the economic sophistication of Calcutta or Bombay. Agrarian-
centred, not urban-based, forces shaped the political life of
the nation. Only in East Bengal, where the estate holders had
been predominantly Hindu, and where the landowners had
abandoned their holdings, did urban power become a
significant factor. But strong urban centres were not part of
Pakistan's inheritance, and East Bengal did not have a
substantial metropolitan vista. Even Dhaka was little more
than an agrarian backwater, servicing the needs of the
surrounding riverain community. *Zamindari* omnipresence,
however, was particularly pronounced in the provinces that
formed the western region of Pakistan. Unlike the deltaic
features of East Bengal, Punjab and Sindh comprised vast
tracts of land, ample space for the evolution of a celebrated
class of landlords. In major part, these landlords were
creatures of a British colonial policy that rewarded favourites
and retired members of the Armed Forces. Moreover, the
development of extensive barrage and irrigation systems
during the nineteenth and early twentieth centuries had made
these lands coveted prizes, and the gifts of land were
instrumental in the consolidation of British power. As a
consequence, the landlords not only developed solid working
relationships with the colonial authority, they also saw to it
that their peasant populations remained obedient and
generally quiescent.

In Balochistan and the North-West Frontier Province a tribal
order had prevailed from time immemorial. The settled areas
eventually came under direct British jurisdiction, but in the
more remote tribal belt that separated the subcontinent from
Afghanistan and Iran, traditional headmen maintained their
pre-eminence. While landlordism as found in Sindh and
Punjab was not a factor, the centrality of individual tribal
authorities in the frontier areas pervaded the social and

political life of the population. It was from such circumstances that Pakistan's politicians emerged into prominence, and although many of them possessed significant education, the learning experience did virtually nothing to alter conventional mindsets or workways.

Even Karachi, which was a relatively small fishing village during the British period, did not develop the character of a city until after Pakistan gained its independence and the site was chosen as the capital of the country. Lahore, the only city of note that was inherited by Pakistan at partition, was historically important as the only genuine reminder of the Pakistani Muslim's Mughal past, but as a city, it lacked the vitality associated with urban living. The other metropolises were hardly more than military staging areas, notably Rawalpindi and Peshawar. Thus when Jinnah, the urbane and sophisticated leader of the Pakistani nation, set about the task of constructing a state and its myriad institutions, he had little to work with save the members of the refugee community whose late domicile had been New Delhi, Bombay, Hyderabad, or Calcutta. The refugee or *mohajir* leaders of the Muslim League, of whom Liaquat Ali Khan was a notable example, with assistance from urbanized members of the bureaucracy, for example Chaudhri Mohammad Ali, were charged with instituting citified reforms in places that knew little of their value, and among people who feared their imposition. The landed interests were hardly prepared to yield their vaunted powers to a system of rules and laws, of procedures and modalities that limited and, in time, were expected to replace their expressions of personalized autocracy. Thus, early efforts at land reform in the provinces of western Pakistan were easily thwarted by powerful politicians who successfully resisted their implementation.

The All-India Muslim League made a fateful decision on 15 December 1947 when it split into two organizations, one representing Pakistan and the other the Muslims of India. In doing so, the party that was to lead Pakistan into a new era cut its ties to its urban lifeline and allowed the organization to be commandeered by persons unfamiliar with its roots, who were more concerned with sustaining their privileges than promoting development and change in a national setting. The creation of the Pakistan Muslim League not only played into the hands of the agrarian-based elites in the western provinces: the latter's hands were strengthened by the ruling, in spite of Jinnah's objection, that denied leadership of the party to a sitting member of the government. Thus, the party began its new life with leaders who were hardly the measure of the entrenched landed gentry, and who could not be expected to follow the organization's policies. The choice of Choudhry Khaliquzzaman as first President of the Pakistan Muslim League proved to be a disaster from which the party never recovered. And the weakness of the League, at the very moment of independence, meant that Jinnah would not have a party to represent his vision or, more immediately, to perform state-building functions. In the circumstances of the time, therefore, it is not surprising that Jinnah looked more to the loyal members of the professional bureaucracy than to his party in assembling the critical state structures, or even in attempting to manage stubborn and/or rival political personalities.

The hopelessness of Jinnah's task was soon all too apparent. The great leader of the Pakistan Movement was too weakened by his debilitating illness to do more than try to reason with difficult foes. But appeals to patriotism and religious principles could not overcome the pursuit of self-interest. *Amour propre* prevailed over social obligations, and the country separated into two camps: that of the masses, whose Islamic motivations remained high but whose political expectations had been reduced to cynicism, and that of the power seekers and power brokers, whose every action was measured by personal gratification and power. Moreover, the federal structure of the League had provincialized politics as never before. With the Quaid-i-Azam no longer President of the League, the party fragmented into its constituent parts, and the political leadership of a particular province determined who was to be rewarded and who denied, what was to be stressed and what was to be neglected. The insularity of patronage reinforced those already in power and whetted the appetites of those aspiring to replace them. Politics became little more than the pursuit of material gain, and only the most cunning manipulators of the process were given any chance of achieving office. The new Muslim League, therefore, ceased being a voice of the masses and more and more assumed postures that reinforced the already powerful. While Jinnah lived, at least the central administration of the Muslim League was able to carry forward its mandate. The raising of the armed forces was a demanding matter, especially with a war raging in Kashmir. The need for a currency and banking system was also most imperative, and such matters were enough to consume the time and energies of the central leadership in those first trying months. Indeed, one of Jinnah's last official acts was to preside over the inauguration of the State Bank, and to laud the work of an exceptional civil servant, Zahid Husain, who had organized the institution in record time. But even as progress was made in these areas, there were divisions and controversies which left many issues in limbo. The Quaid-i-Azam was compelled by the exigencies of the time to travel to all the regions of Pakistan, and the daily work of the government and Muslim League Central Committee was left to Prime Minister Liaquat Ali Khan. Liaquat was a loyal disciple of the Quaid, but unfortunately he did not always command the support of the members of the League's executive committee. Moreover, Jinnah's perpetuation of the viceregal tradition caused him considerable embarrassment, if not pain, in that he seldom enjoyed the power that went with the office. Jinnah's tendency to arrogate powers to himself, his last word on virtually all substantive matters, left the Prime Minister with limited capacity, and his cabinet was less inclined to follow his lead given the long shadow cast by the Quaid-i-Azam. Thus, the serious day-to-day work of the League was more pronounced within the provinces, and rank and file party workers were more likely to take their orders from local bosses than from the central leadership of the party. After Jinnah's death, therefore, it was not surprising that power gravitated to the more parochial extensions of the League. It also came as no surprise when defections from League ranks and the formation of opposition parties challenged the party's heretofore monopoly.

East Bengal

Of Jinnah's many strenuous journeys to heal rifts and mend fences, a few require special attention. They also reveal the difficulties Jinnah and the League faced in consolidating the grant of independence. In March 1948 Jinnah was forced to make an arduous trip to East Bengal. Jinnah knew little about conditions and life in the eastern province, but he put great confidence in the Muslim League government that was led by Khwaja Nazimuddin and Nurul Amin. Jinnah perhaps naively believed that they represented the best interests of the province. In actuality, they represented only the urban aristocracy of Dhaka, and had ignored developing roots in any of the rural constituencies of East Bengal. Moreover, Nazimuddin had been Chief Minister of undivided Bengal during World War II. It was his administration that was heavily criticized for its ineptness during the great famine of 1942-3 which had taken an enormous human toll in the villages of eastern Bengal. Dismissed as generally incompetent, Nazimuddin had yielded his office to Suhrawardy, but he nevertheless remained a powerful force in the Muslim League politics of Dhaka.

When Radcliffe divided Bengal and denied Calcutta to the Muslim League, Dhaka loomed as the only significant urban centre in East Bengal. Nazimuddin, therefore, was still a power to be reckoned with, especially after Suhrawardy offended Jinnah by condemning the division of Bengal. Suhrawardy aroused even more League anger when he was identified as the chief author of the United Bengal Scheme which, it was said, would have produced two separate Pakistans, not one unified one. In effect, Suhrawardy let it appear that he considered himself a Bengali Quaid-i-Azam. Moreover, unlike Nazimuddin, who was ensconced in Dhaka, Suhrawardy was domiciled in Calcutta, and with the 1946 Calcutta riots still a fresh memory, Jinnah believed he had more than sufficient reason to ignore the former Bengali Chief Minister. Finally, although a successful lawyer, Suhrawardy's flamboyance and reputation as something of a profligate did not sit well with Jinnah. By contrast, Nazimuddin was a pious Muslim, reserved and unassuming. Jinnah judged him to be redeemable and, as a very influential figure in Dhaka political and commercial circles, he was his overwhelming choice to lead East Bengal once Dhaka's placement as the capital of East Bengal was announced.

The opposition to the Muslim League in East Bengal, therefore, can be traced to the actions of Radcliffe and Mountbatten. They are also found in the League decision to deny Suhrawardy a place in East Bengal. But perhaps even more important were the philosophical and practical differences that separated Fazlul Huq, the 'Tiger of Bengal' who had been the mover of the 1940 Lahore or Pakistan Resolution, and Maulana Bhashani, a sensitive representative of the Bengali underclass, from the Dhaka nawabs. Like Suhrawardy, both men had been members of the Muslim League in the struggle to achieve Pakistan, but each also represented indigenous political organizations, and they could not reconcile their roles as representatives of the impoverished masses with those played by Nazimuddin and Nurul Amin. Believing they had been sidetracked by the Dhaka-based Muslim League leadership, Fazlul Huq and Bhashani did not approve of the Muslim League's Islamic emphasis which, they concluded, made second-class citizens of the Hindus who comprised approximately twenty-five per cent of East Bengal's population. In effect, although the Hindu aristocracy had fled to India with partition, the poorer masses, in so many ways indistinguishable from their Muslim counterparts, had remained in place. Fazlul Huq and Bhashani endeavoured to represent all Bengalis without distinction; they also sensed the need to establish cordial relations with India, especially with that other segment of the Bengali family in western Bengal. The opposition, therefore, developed significant ideological as well as practical differences with the Muslim League shortly after the transfer of power. Furthermore, when Suhrawardy was denied his seat in the Pakistan constituent assembly, and prevented from making public appearances in East Bengal, he too found the League oppressive and joined this emerging opposition.

But it was not these matters that drew Jinnah to Pakistan's east wing. The Quaid-i-Azam had been provoked to visit East Bengal because a political movement had taken shape within the student community which had as its principal objective the elevation of the Bengali language to a place alongside Urdu. Urdu was the language which the Muslim League promoted as a substitute for English in all official matters. But the use of Urdu seemed to place Bangla-speakers at a disadvantage. Moreover, the Bengali population represented more than half the population of Pakistan, and hardly eight per cent of Pakistanis everywhere were said to be conversant in Urdu. Urdu became a *cause célèbre* when the Muslim League was accused of deliberately undermining Bengali culture. The Bengali language movement had been energized by Shaikh Mujibur Rahman, a young student agitator, but it had already enlisted considerable support in political circles, notably among the expanding ranks of the opposition to the League government. More significantly, however, the movement had elevated Bengali passions to a dangerous level, and many Muslim Leaguers shared the opinion that the whole affair was the work of New Delhi which, it was said, was determined to separate East Bengal from Pakistan. At the heart of Muslim League fears was the belief that the large Hindu minority domiciled in the province was being manipulated from the other side of the border.

In March 1948 Jinnah convened a mass meeting on the Paltan Maidan, the central meeting ground in Dhaka. It was there that he called upon the students not to be misled by alien forces. Acknowledging the importance of the Bengali culture and especially the Bengali language, he emphasized the right of a people to represent their peculiar lifestyle. But he cautioned Bengalis to beware of threats to the young Pakistani nation of which they were an integral and important part. It was only for the purpose of national unity, to ward off threats to Pakistan's security, that the Muslim League had adopted Urdu as its national language. The country, he said, spoke with many tongues, but it was a nation founded on Islamic tradition and with a shared inheritance. It was, therefore, imperative that the nation have a lingua franca that cut across the variety of cultures and, indeed, bridged regional differences. The central purpose of the Muslim League was the formation of one solitary Pakistani nation. Bangla, he noted, would be the provincial language of East Bengal, but he insisted there could be only one national language, and that language, emerging from the Muslim experience within the subcontinent, must and would only be Urdu. Jinnah did not convince the gathered throng that his party had chosen correctly, but he returned to Karachi believing he had reduced the movement to a bargaining chip in the long debate that most assuredly lay ahead.

Jinnah never returned to the eastern province, but that day of his appearance in Dhaka marked the beginning of the end for the Bengal Muslim League. His speech also brought into question another that he delivered in Karachi when he declared that in political and legal matters, there was no distinction between a Muslim or a Hindu; both were Pakistanis, he had said, first, last, and always. But his comments in Dhaka in defence of Urdu as the national language did not reassure those who wanted to believe Pakistan could be a secular as well as a dominant-Muslim state. The defection to India of Jogendra Nath Mandal, the Pakistan Labour Minister and leader of the Pakistani scheduled-caste Hindus, following Jinnah's death, was an early but tell-tale sign that the problem embedded in the Bengal language controversy would not go away.

Sindh and Punjab

Jinnah was detained in Punjab when word reached him that trouble had erupted within the Sindh government. Ayub Khuhro had been named Sindh's first Muslim League Chief Minister, and the phlegmatic politician had long been a thorn in Jinnah's side. A Sindhi of considerable intellectual capabilities, Khuhro had demonstrated a degree of provincial chauvinism that made Quaid-i-Azam uncomfortable. Karachi was the nation's only commercial port at the time of partition; it also was the province's most notable urban community. Jinnah identified with Karachi, the city of his birth, but he was also a sophisticated internationalist, having risen into prominence as a successful English-trained lawyer. Jinnah passed much of his early professional years in Britain and Bombay and seldom visited his ancestral home. Khuhro, a follower of the Pir of Pagaro, on the other hand, was devoted to Sindh. He asserted provincial leadership when Sindh was separated from the Bombay Presidency in 1936, and from his base in Karachi he rose to prominence as a forceful and articulate spokesman of Sindhi causes.

Sindh was a backwater in the period leading up to World War II, possessing little in the way of infrastructure. It had been denied sophisticated educational institutions, and its commercial life was limited to a range of fishing enterprises. Given its relatively tranquil ambience by the sea, Karachi became an attractive retreat for British officers serving in the colonial government, and the beaches at Clifton along the Arabian Sea were lined with cottages for the playful members of the elite class. Karachi, however, stood in vivid contrast with inner Sindh, which was a vast, relatively dry area, made fertile only by the barrage and irrigation systems developed in the 1920s and 1930s. Controlled by a form of landlordism that can only be described as oriental feudal, the landed gentry, the *waderas* as they were known in Sindh, managed their lands with an oppressive firmness that was often ruthless and brutal to their peasant-cultivators. The Sindhi peasant, or *hari*, was a virtual slave in his dependency, and he possessed almost nothing that he could call his own. His labour, his animals, even his wife and his very life belonged to the *wadera,* who housed and fed him and 'protected' him from other *waderas.*

World War II brought dramatic changes to Karachi but did little to alter the lives of those in the Sindh hinterland. The expansion of the port and the development of its harbour placed Karachi on the list of prime seaports on the Indian Ocean. Karachi was also the location for the construction of a modern airfield that, even after the war, gave it a distinctive position in global aviation. The population of the city swelled rapidly from something less than 100,000 inhabitants in the 1930s to approximately 300,000 by the time of partition. Given the city's growing prominence, its likely development as a major outlet to the world, and especially its significant commercial possibilities, Jinnah and the Muslim League opted for Karachi as Pakistan's capital.

Ayub Khuhro had been Mayor of Karachi and a prominent member of the Muslim League, but he had reason to question the selection of the city as the seat of Pakistan's central government. Karachi's prominence made it the destination of

82   PAKISTAN: A POLITICAL HISTORY

hundreds of thousands of refugees fleeing India, and it was not long after the arrival of the first wave of destitute and terrified people that Khuhro expressed the sentiments of a large proportion of Sindhis. Khuhro emphasized the backwardness of Sindh and its limited capacity in caring for such a colossal influx of humanity. Khuhro's concern, however, was not simply with humanitarian questions. He also wondered what the impact on Sindh would be if the Sindhis were overwhelmed by the outsiders. Sensing that the refugee community could dramatically change the politics of Sindh, he urged the central government to seek a capital for Pakistan somewhere else. But the Muslim League response was totally at variance with the province's Chief Minister. The central government had not only decided that it would develop Karachi as the nation's citadel, it also decided to take the administration of the city under its own wing. Karachi was to be severed from Sindh, made into a federal area, and governed separately by an administration created by the centre. Khuhro understood that the loss of Karachi, while perhaps necessary in practical terms, none the less gave even more power to the *wadera* class of landlords. Any effort to improve the self-image of the Sindhi peasantry would be lost, and the *mohajir* community would ultimately come to dominate Karachi politics.

Khuhro, therefore, was incensed by the manoeuvre, and on 2 February 1948 he got the Sindh Assembly to unanimously oppose the action. Appearing to defy his party's leadership, and especially that of Mohammad Ali Jinnah, Khuhro was now slated for removal. Governor Shaykh Ghulam Hussain Hidayatullah had a running quarrel with Khuhro that was not resolved when Pakistan was established. Their relationship after independence was abrasive and often stormy, and Hidayatullah, a major spokesman for the *waderas* had looked for the opportunity to dismiss his Chief Minister. That opportunity came after the 2 February vote of the legislature. But because Khuhro had the confidence of the Sindh Assembly, the Governor could not sack him on procedural grounds. Hidayatullah went around the legislature and notified Jinnah of Khuhro's insubordination. Jinnah authorized the Governor to dismiss Khuhro under special emergency powers noted in Section 51(5) of the Government of India Act 1935 and amended by the Pakistan (Provisional Constitution) Order 1947. Khuhro was accused of maladministration, gross misconduct, and corruption in the discharge of his duty, and removed from office on 26 April 1948. Moreover, a judicial tribunal was assembled to enquire into the charges against Khuhro.

Hidayatullah had reallocated cabinet portfolios prior to the order without seeking the advice or the approval of the Chief Minister. The special order removing Khuhro provided the Governor with the powers to oversee the work of the provincial cabinet, and in·effect the ministers held office 'during his pleasure.' Khuhro was charged on sixty-two counts and the tribunal found him guilty on many of them, but he still commanded the Sindh Muslim League, and shortly after Jinnah's death, he was formally elected its President. The incident was one more indication that Jinnah's stress on the rule of law and due process was contradicted by his actions, which promoted and enlivened Pakistan's viceregal legacy. It also demonstrated the fragile nature of the Muslim League and its general inability to encourage the growth and development of urban leadership. Khuhro's dismissal solved nothing. His successor, Pir Elahi Bakhsh, was removed not long after, when his election to the legislature was disqualified. Sindh politics were muddled and full of controversy, and Jinnah's decision to favour the province's traditional leaders meant that conventional, not constitutional, politics would dominate Sindhi political life.

Jinnah was in Punjab addressing still another thorny issue when Khuhro was surreptitiously dismissed from office. Though tired and ailing, Jinnah had been urged to visit Lahore because of differences between the Khan of Mamdot, the province's first Chief Minister, and his Finance Minister, Mian Mumtaz Daultana, and Revenue Minister Sardar Shaukat Hayat. Punjabi conditions were bad enough in the aftermath of the communal killing, the arrival of thousands of impoverished refugees, and the Indian government's decision to divert the water that fed the province's irrigation canals, but Jinnah was deflected from these problems and, instead, forced to mediate a dispute between political personalities.

The Muslim League, which had replaced the Unionist government of Khizr Hayat, was dominated by *zamindars* and rural power brokers, and rivalries between them made a shambles of Jinnah's vision. Observing what appeared to be unreconcilable differences between Mamdot and Daultana, Jinnah decided that Mamdot would be made a central minister and Daultana left to head the Punjab Cabinet. Daultana, however, was reluctant to accept the arrangement, and Jinnah, despairing of a resolution, left the matter to the British Governor of the province, Sir Francis Mudie. Mudie dismissed both Daultana and Shaukat Hayat and allowed Mamdot to form a new Cabinet.

Jinnah's inability to manage the infighting in the Punjab tended to exaggerate his diplomatic deficiencies. By deferring to Mudie, he not only highlighted his sickness, he also gave more emphasis to the special prerogatives reserved for executive authority in Pakistan. Quaid-i-Azam, it is reported, later called the Punjabi principals to Karachi, but even then there was no resolution to their dispute. In fact, this rivalry in the Punjab continued, and after Jinnah's death, Governor's Rule was established in the province under Section 92-A of the adapted Government of India Act 1935. This time, however, the Governor dissolved the legislative assembly, asserting that the people were demoralized by corrupt politicians, and that even the administrative services had been undermined by their unlimited capacity for intrigue. Nowhere in Pakistan in 1948 did it appear possible to establish the working relationships so necessary to the democratic growth of the nation. But if the country's Bengali, Sindhi, and Punjabi leaders could not accept the responsibility of their offices, what could be expected from the more tribal regions? Certainly the North-West Frontier Province was not the place to find respite from the crass politics that had overtaken Pakistan in its first year.

North-West Frontier Province

In April 1948, Jinnah visited the North-West Frontier Province. His trip was not prompted by a desire to celebrate the area's inclusion within Pakistan or the success of the Muslim League there. On the contrary, Jinnah was troubled by the sustained actions of Abdul Ghaffar Khan's Khudai Khidmatgar and its unconcealed hostility toward Pakistan. Unreconciled to the province's expressed preference for the Muslim League, the Red Shirts, as they were known, had laboured long before the formation of the Pakistan Movement to dislodge the British from the frontier region. And just at the moment of realizing their quest, their goal was snatched from their grasp by a relatively distant Muslim League. Ghaffar Khan, the Frontier Gandhi, was not enamoured of Jinnah, nor did he accept the Quaid-i-Azam as a great leader of the Muslim people. The Red Shirt leader had condemned Jinnah as a lackey of British imperialism, and could not disabuse himself of the view that Jinnah had conspired with the British to set the people of the subcontinent against one another in order to sustain European influence. More inclined to identify with the work of Mahatma Gandhi, whom he considered more a son of the soil, Ghaffar Khan made it clear that he would sustain the struggle against the Muslim League, as well as that party's inclination to make an enemy of India. Among Ghaffar Khan's several purposes was his intention to bridge Indo-Pakistani differences and to promote co-operation between the two states.

Jinnah's face-to-face meeting with Ghaffar Khan followed the January assassination of the Mahatma by a radical member of the Hindu R.S.S. Believing Ghaffar Khan's intimacy with Gandhi would cause him to rethink his position toward Pakistan, especially in the light of this display of Hindu extremism, Jinnah approached his nemesis in a sombre mood, but with the expectation that their conversations would begin a dialogue of understanding. Ghaffar Khan was joined by his brother, Dr Khan Sahib, whom Jinnah had removed as Chief Minister of the NWFP after the plebiscite had revealed that the voters' preference was with the Muslim League. To Jinnah's dismay, but not necessarily to his surprise, both men rejected the Governor-General's overture that they join the Muslim League and work toward the development of the Pakistan nation. Khan Sahib reminded the Quaid-i-Azam that he had refused to swear loyalty to Pakistan, and that the Red Shirts would not be disbanded. Ghaffar Khan noted that his party would continue its programme to provide the Pathans with a higher profile than that envisaged by the Muslim League.

Although Ghaffar Khan did not raise the issue of 'Pakhtunistan', that is, a separate state for the Pathan nation, his reply to Jinnah's queries led the Quaid-i-Azam to conclude that Pakhtunistan was indeed the Khudai Khidmatgar's principal objective. The Khan brothers, he confided to his closest confidants, were determined to destroy Pakistan and hence must be resisted. Jinnah was reluctant to confer more power on the NWFP's Chief Minister, Khan Abdul Qaiyum Khan. Qaiyum Khan certainly was not a Jinnah constitutionalist, nor did he see the utility of using liberal policies in the circumstances obtaining in the frontier province—policies which he fervently believed would only make the situation worse. Jinnah's failure to placate, let alone win over, the Khan brothers, however, released Qaiyum Khan from an earlier promise made to Jinnah that he would avoid the use of arbitrary power in managing the frontier province.

Qaiyum Khan assumed leadership of the frontier Muslim League only a few years after he had denounced the party as opportunistic and comprised of aristocrats and petty power brokers. Shifting his support to the League when it appeared certain that Jinnah would succeed in his attempt to establish a sovereign Pakistan, Qaiyum Khan found it a relatively simple task to gain control of the provincial party. But when he took control of the organization, the League had but fifteen members in the Provincial Assembly to twenty-one for the Congress. Qaiyum Khan's heavy-handed tactics, however, soon influenced seven Congress supporters to drop their affiliation and join the Muslim League, thus turning the balance in favour of the latter. From that point forward there was no stopping Qaiyum Khan. In May 1948, without Jinnah's knowledge, the Chief Minister ordered the arrest of Ghaffar Khan under the Frontier Crimes Regulations, and the Red Shirt leader began the first of many incarcerations in Pakistani prisons. Before his arrest Ghaffar Khan had described Pakistan as a 'house of sand' and Jinnah as a British agent. The government of Pakistan, he argued, was managed by outsiders who had converted 'the native population into refugees in their homeland' (Burke and Ziring, 1990, pp. 68-9).

The unresolved aspects of the Pakistan design at the time of partition had kept alive the ambitions of the Khan brothers

and their secessionist movement. They could well anticipate
outliving Jinnah who, they could see, was a very sick and
aged man. Moreover, they had already concluded that
Jinnah's death would, more than likely, lead to the undoing
of Pakistan. They need only wait, hold to their position, and
maintain the discipline of their followers; events could be
expected to move again in their direction, and without Jinnah
they anticipated little difficulty in forcing the Muslim League
from the NWFP and surrounding region.

Ghaffar Khan's position and behaviour fired the ambitions
of some of the frontier's tribal leaders and several of them
followed a similar course. Principal among them was the
Fakir of Ipi, Haji Mirza Ali Khan, a leader in the Tirah
borderland between Pakistan and Afghanistan. Like Ghaffar
Khan, the Fakir of Ipi was outspoken in his opposition to
Pakistan. The Muslim majority areas, where tribal leaders
reigned supreme, were ill-informed concerning the Pakistan
Movement, and the Muslim League battle cry that 'Islam was
in danger' took considerable time to reach them. Moreover,
from the seclusion of their mountains, surrounded by other
Muslims, it was the British colonial power, not the Indian
National Congress, that appeared a threat to Islam.

Like Gandhi and the Congress, the tribal leaders had
directed all their efforts against British rule, and like the
Hindu leadership, they were eager to force a British
withdrawal from the subcontinent. The tribals had never
yielded their authority to a distant government, and it was
the British, with their 'Forward Policy' in Afghanistan, who
had intruded on their privacy and caused the destabilization
of the region. Britain's three wars with Afghanistan, two in
the nineteenth century and the last occurring immediately
following World War I, had brought major European forces
into the tribal belt. Skirmishes between the mountain people
and English forces were commonplace and sustained. Neither
vanquished or subdued the other, but there were sufficient
victories and defeats on both sides to prolong the conflict.

Britain's contest with Imperial Russia fed these frontier
wars. By the fifth decade of the nineteenth century Russia
had moved its forces into Central Asia, defeating and
liquidating the once-celebrated Muslim kingdoms of Merv,

Bukhara, Khokand, and Samarkand. When the Russians paused at the Oxus river border with Afghanistan, Britain had reason to believe that the Tsar's ultimate goals were in the direction of the Persian Gulf on the one side and India on the other. Britain decided to meet the Russians in Afghanistan, and the 'Great Game', as the contest was known in the nineteenth and early twentieth centuries, plunged Britain into the affairs of the tribal Pathans. Less than a century later, with the British now no longer a presence in the region, Pakistan inherited this history, especially after the settled areas of the North-West Frontier Province opted for the Muslim League. In these circumstances, it was predictable that the tribals, who had sustained the fight against the British, should now turn their attention to Jinnah and his followers. Moreover, many of the tribes inhabiting the region had enjoyed somewhat amicable relations with Afghanistan, and indeed it was Kabul that had demonstrated its friendship for the tribal Pathans by promoting a separate and independent 'Pakhtunistan'.

That Afghanistan harboured ulterior motives was not ignored in Pakistan. Gandhi and the Congress had both promised landlocked Afghanistan an outlet to the sea if Kabul added its voice to those opposing Pakistan. Karachi was considered one possibility if Pakistan did not materialize, Gwadur was another. Thwarted by the success of the Pakistan Movement, but unreconciled to a sovereign Pakistan on its border, Kabul cast the only dissenting vote when Pakistan sought admission to the United Nations. But when Pakistani forces attacked the Fakir of Ipi's redoubt, Kabul failed to come to his assistance. The Fakir of Ipi's defeat sent a signal to the Afghan capital that Pakistan had the necessary means to protect its territorial integrity, and Afghanistan's first ambassador, Shah Wali Khan, tried to placate Pakistani authorities as well as public opinion by declaring that his government had no intention of claiming land belonging to Pakistan. But the ambassador's superiors in Kabul must have seen the matter differently. Shah Wali Khan was criticized for his remarks, his appointment was cancelled, and he was summarily withdrawn. Shortly thereafter the Afghan parliament described the Durand Line that separated Pakistan from Afghanistan as 'imaginary', hence questioning the legitimacy of Pakistan itself.

Jinnah did not live to witness the expansion of the Afghan claim against Pakistan, or the many skirmishes between Pakistani and Afghan forces, but Najibullah Khan, a personal emissary of the Afghan King, did meet with Jinnah in early 1948, and an attempt was made to pressure the Quaid-i-Azam into accepting the tribal border states as a sovereign entity. Najibullah also raised the matter of an Afghan port on the Indian Ocean, and he left no doubt that in case of general hostilities between India and Pakistan, Kabul would remain neutral but that its sympathies would lie with New Delhi. Jinnah characterized Afghan demands and explanations as 'unfriendly' and he rejected all of them. Nevertheless, a hostile Afghanistan made it imperative that Pakistan cultivate neighbouring Iran, and one of Jinnah's last official acts, made from his hill station retreat in Balochistan, was to send Raja Ghazanfar Ali Khan, one of his oldest and most trusted lieutenants, to Tehran as Pakistan's first ambassador.

The Kashmir Issue

The open enmity toward Pakistan exhibited by the Red Shirts and others among the tribal Pathans, as well as by Afghanistan and India, seemed to have its confluence in the Kashmir problem. For individual and collective purposes, the central target of all the actors, both major and minor, was Pakistan. Each party was convinced that Pakistan had denied them the opportunity to reap the benefits of the British withdrawal from the subcontinent. And all of them had common cause in blocking Pakistan's claim to Kashmir. The British role in this matter was not insignificant, however. In fact, it could be argued that the British had set the scene for what was to become one of the more intractable, long-term problems of modern diplomacy.

In the first instance, the British departure from India was completed in such haste that few, if any, of the complex issues were adequately addressed. The princes had some years earlier rejected joining the Indian Federation, and the Viceroy's helter-skelter dissolution of empire failed to answer the question of whither the princes after the independence of

India and Pakistan. The issue of 'paramountcy' went essentially unanswered, that is, whether the technique adopted by the colonial authority in controlling and relating to the almost 600 allegedly autonomous princes of the subcontinent applied after partition and the formal transfer. Given the character of partition, were the princes required to yield to the preferences of their erstwhile subjects, or were they free to determine their futures in accordance with traditional royal prerogatives? Britain's diplomatic silence on these matters, and the more or less official position that the princes would make their own determination, only made a difficult situation much worse. The Kashmir problem was a direct consequence of such indecision.

The dilemma that emerged in Kashmir was made even more complicated by the scramble for advantages by different Muslim actors who made a mockery of appeals to Islamic solidarity. The Khudai Khidmatgar, tribal separatists, and the Afghans, all were capable of meddling in Kashmir, and all had their own reasons for doing so. Kashmir was, from the beginning, far more than a matter of competing religious communities. The Congress had long argued secular credentials, and it had attracted allies in Muslim-dominant regions, notably on the north-west frontier. Although the Muslim League claimed to speak for all the subcontinent's Muslim population, in reality it represented only a portion of them. India's claim to Kashmir centres on the formal accession of the Hindu Maharaja who, it has been argued, legally opted to join the Indian Union. Pakistan's counter-argument questions the legality of the formal accession, but more important, stresses the lapse of paramountcy and the right of the people of Kashmir and Jammu to determine their own political future.

The Indian troops who arrived by air in Srinigar on 27 October 1947 deprived the predominantly Muslim population of Jammu and Kashmir from determining their future. Of the 4,000,000 persons living in the mountain state, 75 per cent were Muslims, and the populated Vale of Kashmir, in which Srinagar is located, was fully 90 per cent Muslim. Moreover, these Muslims did not live in an isolated pocket within the larger subcontinent. The Kashmiris were very much connected to the Muslims of the North-West Frontier Province, as well as to that area of Punjab that was included in Pakistan. Only the reference to paramountcy sanctioned the Hindu Maharaja's right to determine the future of his subjects. In point of fact, however, paramountcy had lapsed, and although the princes were permitted to choose the means that enabled them to come to grips with the transfer of power, Indian actions that forced the princes to vacate their lands would appear to have ended the argument. With the exception of Hyderabad, Junagadh, and Jammu and Kashmir, all the other princely states had acceded to India by 15 August 1947 (Lamb, 1994). All that remained was the consolidation of the Union, the character of the dispensation, and the size and duration of privy purses.

On the basis of 'abrupt termination', the British did nothing; in fact, they encouraged New Delhi to quickly complete the process of inclusion. It need only be mentioned that Mountbatten as India's Governor-General presided over the initial phase in forming a more perfect Indian union. The former Viceroy and the Congress leaders knew that their actions would anger the rulers who were not prepared for the suddenness of the British departure, or the British decision to abandon them to their fate. But not a single major Congress official opposed the procedure, their focus having centred on establishing India as unified, viable, and if at all possible, the most powerful state in the Indian Ocean region.

The British, too, were determined to leave behind a strong Indian state, especially with the onset of the Cold War. But for New Delhi, the Indian princes were ancient history, and an anachronism they could do without. Of the three remaining holdouts, Junagadh was quickly overrun and incorporated into the Indian union, in spite of Pakistani protests. Hyderabad, a large Deccan entity with a Hindu majority and a reasonably progressive Muslim ruler, suffered the same fate in September 1948, on the very day of Jinnah's funeral. But Kashmir was another matter, and although India tried to put the issue quickly to rest, the state's proximity to Pakistan, and the egregious nature of the problem, gave it a life long after its Hindu ruler supposedly opted in favour of the Indian union. Moreover, Pakistan's argument has been consistent, that is, the future of the state should have been left to the determination of its people.

But India remained deaf to such an argument. The Radcliffe Award had given the Punjabi Muslim district of Gurdaspur to India with the full knowledge that New Delhi would thereby have road access to the mountain state. Thus, by air and then by land, Indian troops occupied Jammu and Kashmir soon after the transfer of power, even while the Maharaja's accession to India revealed serious legal flaws that New Delhi refused to clarify. India's claim that it moved into Kashmir only after its Maharaja appealed for assistance against an invasion of tribal Pathans from the north-western region of Pakistan also left a number of questions unanswered. Who were the tribal Pathans who allegedly ignited the Kashmir problem? While a definitive answer may never be found, it is important to cite the continuing rivalries and strife in the region.

Numerous separate but related mixed kingdoms had emerged in the region in the early part of the nineteenth century, many of them *jagirs*, or grants of territory to individuals acknowledging the pre-eminence of more distant rulers. Because of the relationships between them, the different principalities were often in conflict with one another, and the submission of one to the other was cause for constant intrigue and violence. Such was certainly the situation in Poonch, an ancient hill state abutting on and largely subservient to the Maharaja of Jammu and Kashmir. It was just such a conflict that collided with the events leading up to and following the British transfer of power. While the letter *K* in 'Pakistan' supposedly represents Kashmir, there was no immediate claim by Jinnah to Kashmir in the creation of Pakistan. Nor were the Poonch fighters who assaulted the Dogra ruler prompted to action because Muslims were in danger and denied the opportunity to opt for Pakistan. It is now more evident that Muslim Poonchies launched a series of largely sporadic attacks on Kashmiri authority in an attempt to alleviate the strain imposed on them (Sikhs and Hindus were exempted) by the levy of an array of oppressive taxes. Moreover, Poonch had supplied the British with the highest percentage of Kashmiri forces used in both World Wars I and

II, and many of the Poonchie marauders were returned Muslim veterans who were well-schooled in the use of firearms and quick to assert themselves when stressed.

In the climate created by the transfer of power and the Srinagar Muslim displays of support for Pakistan, the Poonch uprising had all the earmarks of a Pakistani *putsch* aimed at seizing Kashmir. In point of fact, Pakistan's Army was only then being formed, and many of its units were scattered throughout the subcontinent and still under alien commanders. Pakistan was hardly in a position to make a grab for Kashmir, but Poonch lay along the border with the new Pakistan state, and the inhabitants of the larger region had always intermingled in one way or another. Also, the Pathans of Poonch were related to tribal groups from Afghanistan, and the creation of new legal frontiers that divided these people from one another was bound to cause repercussions.

There is no doubt that the Poonch rebels had their contacts in Pakistan or that, among the different bands, there were those who envisaged the establishment of a separate and independent state. Sardar Ibrahim Khan, one such would-be liberator, was able to make contact with Prime Minister Liaquat Ali Khan who, without Jinnah's knowledge, registered sympathy for the rebels. In time, the Poonch rebels developed into the force of Azad Kashmiris, who were encouraged to sustain their struggle by Colonel Akbar Khan, an officer in the Pakistani Army. Although acting on his own, some of Akbar Khan's plans fell into Indian hands, and these documents were used to demonstrate Pakistan's official role in the conflict.

Jinnah, however, had no desire to make war over Kashmir. Knowing it would confound his state-building activities, as well as delay the distribution of Pakistan's share of the British Raj's assets, he was too steeped in other matters to embroil the nation in a conflict it might not be able to win. By September-October 1947 Jinnah had agreed to a Standstill Agreement, wherein matters would be left undisturbed pending negotiations on the final disposition of the Kashmiri territory. But this understanding was undermined by irregular forces that had cut the lines of supply between Pakistan and

the mountain state. From the vantage point of the Hindu
Dogra government, Pakistan had authorized the blocking of
road traffic in order to stifle the regime, and when Liaquat
sent Colonel A.S.B. Shah to Srinagar to assess the situation,
the Maharaja's Prime Minister accused the emissary of
pressurizing the ruler to accede to Pakistan. By late October
the Kashmiri government was saying that it would ask India
for assistance and Jinnah, judging the announcement to be
an ultimatum, acknowledged the failure of negotiations. In
actuality, Jinnah was unable to control the tribesmen who
severed the Rawalpindi-Srinagar road and who accelerated
the violence in the region. The Maharaja's government
responded by confiscating weapons and by unleashing
assaults on his Muslim subjects. Armed Sikhs and Hindu
extremists linked with the R.S.S. entered the fray and they,
too, exacted a heavy toll on the Muslim community. It is
estimated in the course of these events some 200,000 Muslims
were slaughtered, and thousands more fled the region for
safe havens in Azad Kashmir or Pakistan.

Although Jinnah hesitated in moving on the Kashmir front,
and as a consequence allowed the tribesmen to prepare the
scene and indeed complicate the conflict, Nehru, but more
notably Vallabhbhai Patel and Baldev Singh, were deeply
committed to intervention. India's massive preparations
involved cutting road links to Kashmir from Pakistan, and by
deploying major Army units in the state, they anticipated
consolidating their hold on Kashmir before Pakistan could
make a concerted response. New Delhi also was engaged on
the political front, and Nehru expected to gain assistance
from Sheikh Abdullah, a nemesis of the Maharaja but a friend
of the Indian Prime Minister. Abdullah led the National
Conference, a formidable political organization in Kashmir
which he once believed would act as the seed for the
flowering of the 'Switzerland of Asia'.

It was now Nehru's task to convince Abdullah that, with
the Maharaja out of the picture, he would lead the new state
of Jammu and Kashmir into the Indian Union. All that was
needed to fulfil this plan, limit the losses, and beat back the
Pakistan threat, was the Maharaja's accession, or at least that
is what New Delhi wanted to believe. The fact remained that

Pakistan was in no position to control the irregulars and tribals, and though Indian strategists could plot their moves, the best they could achieve was to deny the Vale of Kashmir to the Azad Kashmiri fighters. By the close of 1947, tribal Pathans from the Mahsud, Afridi, and Mohmand had entered the struggle. Massacres were perpetrated from one end of Pakistan's north-western frontier all the way to the villages of Kashmir. Army units that were being prepared for separation were set upon by tribal warriors, and along with the killing of rank and file troops that were slated for transfer to India, British officers, sometimes with their families, were also victimized. The Kashmir conflict was hardly a clear-cut encounter between two armies over a fixed combat zone. On the contrary, the Kashmir war was a brutal display of anarchy, from the start of the initial Poonch uprising to the ceasefire arranged by the United Nations Security Council in 1948-9.

Indian forces had entered Kashmir prior to receipt of the Instrument of Accession, and it is doubtful that there ever was such a document. Nevertheless, the Indians justified their action on the basis of saving Kashmiri humanity from wanton destruction. History must be allowed to judge this latter explanation. The record shows that the opposed sides, i.e., India and Pakistan, despite the chaotic aspects of the struggle, finally defined the front lines between them. Neither, however, had managed to effectively neutralize the other. Both India and Pakistan referred to the fighting in 1947-8 as a matter of national honour and possibly even national survival. But it is doubtful whether the belligerents or their victims were aware of these claims or were affected by them. But what is certainly clear is that the war over Kashmir crystallized and deepened the bitterness, the suspicion, and the rivalry between the subcontinent's two most important actors. More immediately, the conflict destroyed what had once been a proud imperial Army. The British had taken great pride in the creation of their Indian Army, and that force had served the empire with distinction in two great twentieth-century encounters. But that army could not survive the partition of the subcontinent, and it is perhaps one of the monumental tragedies of subcontinental history that that army's denouement came from self-inflicted wounds that left it with hardly a memory of its celebrated past.

The Final Agony

Mohammad Ali Jinnah retreated to the cool hills of Balochistan in June 1948, and except for a brief trip to Karachi to inaugurate the opening of the State Bank, he never ventured from there again, that is, until the fateful day of 11 September, when he was flown to Karachi for emergency medical treatment and expired soon after arriving at the Governor-General's house. Jinnah's last months and weeks in Quetta and Ziarat were passed away from the din and clamour of Pakistani politics, and distant from the exacting decision-making process of a new and still inchoate nation. As his illness took its final toll, the Quaid-i-Azam became less and less able to address the affairs of state and, with his sister Fatima in charge, his visitors were few and very select. It is said that the Quaid took on a more critical demeanour in his last days, becoming short of temper and quick to find fault with a world that he had been so responsible in making.

Jinnah's year as Pakistan's first Governor-General was not what he had envisioned when he took the oath of office on that August day in 1947. The year had been spent in not only trying to frame a political structure for the country, but in an all-consuming struggle to keep his abstraction alive. Pakistan was Jinnah's creation, but it was not a healthy baby at birth, and without the nurturing that the Quaid-i-Azam provided in its first year it could, and possibly would, have succumbed to its many contradictions. Certainly there were those who anticipated Pakistan's sudden demise; some among them had even plotted its return to Mother India! But the country did manage that initial, crisis-driven year. In spite of the lack of political cohesion, an empty treasury, a non-existent economy, a jerry-built governing structure, an inundation of millions of desperate people, and a war in Kashmir, there were enough Pakistanis who rose to the challenge and who seemed ready to face future unknowns, strong in the belief that Jinnah had carried the nation to a point where only they could do it mortal harm.

It can be said that Jinnah lived long enough in that he realized his dream of an independent Muslim state within the subcontinent; and yet not long enough to mentor the state in its formative years. After partition, it was his presence alone that prevented the country from imploding on itself. But only his use of extraordinary viceregal powers, combined with the power of his persona, kept the foxes from devouring the fledgling state. Jinnah's spirit, his recorded actions and words, however, could never do for the nation in death what he did for it in his lifetime. Jinnah departed from Pakistan while it was still in its infancy. He lived long enough to recognize that those political personalities who joined with him in realizing a sovereign home for the Muslims of the subcontinent, who laboured with him in the fateful years prior to and following World War II, and who assisted in forcing the British and the Congress to divide the subcontinent, were not necessarily the people best equipped to carry the nation into an independent experience. The essential unity exhibited in Muslim circles during the struggle for Pakistan, and the popular support won by the Muslim League, was a consequence of an uneven contest between essentially two forces, the Muslim League on the one side, and the Congress on the other. The relative solidarity demonstrated by the Muslim community in achieving Pakistan, coming as it did from the Muslim minority areas of India, however, could not be replicated in the lands that became Pakistan after independence was achieved. Except in East Bengal, little thought and even less energy was given to the deeper meaning of Pakistan once the state became a reality. And even in that eastern province, so geographically distant from the other wing of the country, there was far more *amour propre* among its leaders and little display of national responsibility.

This then was the final agony of partition. The real Pakistan experience was moulded and shaped in the period following World War II, and especially in that first year after the transfer of power. The Pakistan of Mohammad Ali Jinnah, his vision and the reality, his promise and the disillusionment, his ecstasy and the desperation, his hope and the frustration, became the story of Pakistan's first fifty years.

Chapter 4

The Pitfalls of Constitution-making

The chaos that overwhelmed Pakistan at independence was a consequence of little planning and virtually no conceptualization. Jinnah devoted all his energy and used all his time in convincing the Viceroy that a sovereign Muslim state within the subcontinent was not only justifiable but also feasible. But neither Jinnah nor any of his immediate circle was moved to lay out on paper the blueprint for the state they intended to create. There is nothing in the archives to even hint that someone was responsible for defining the nature and structure of the state, its purposes and functions, its powers and limitations. Absolutely nothing was done to fit into the larger scheme of an abstract national entity, the very tangible constituent parts from which the country was ultimately formed. Pakistan, in effect, was created without the guidance of an astute, even semi-aloof, savant who might have given thought to the Muslim political experience and how it combined with the conditions of the subcontinent to fabricate a contemporary nation-state. There were no al-Birunis or ibn-Khalduns in the Pakistan Movement! The absence of a Pakistani literary tradition, or a key scribe, meant that there was no pen to record the eloquence of the struggle for independence as it was happening, and no theoretical foundation upon which to rest what was, without question, a unique and singular undertaking.

The movers and shakers of the Pakistan Movement were not only accepting of a British designed 'moth-eaten and truncated state', they also adopted the 1935 Government of India Act as their initial constitution. Even the agreement to function as a dominion within the British Commonwealth was more a display of desperation than an intuitive or learned reaction to the available options and contingencies. Jinnah opted for the more familiar colonial system, in major part because in the final reading of independence, Pakistan was 'a rush to judgment'. But lack of time was no excuse for not having someone, or a group, prepare the necessary study that plotted Pakistan's future. And because no one was given this assignment, or assumed that responsibility, the diverse and disparate peoples that were suddenly made integral components of the new nation were subjected to the vagaries of the period and especially to the machinations of those peculiar personalities who dominated the historical moment.

Pakistan was fitted into a design of parliamentary experience, but the people who suddenly found themselves parliamentarians had neither the training nor the requisite sense of social responsibility, and perhaps no less important, a questionable aptitude. Complicating the situation were the myriad of details that needed addressing, the countless people that demanded emergency services, and the deep-seated fear that the infant state would collapse under the weight of its heavy burden. In the circumstances, it was the members of the former colonial bureaucracy who assumed the major work of stabilization. This pillar of the former colonial 'steel frame' remained relatively intact, and under the guidance of its newly appointed Secretary-General, Chaudhri Mohammad Ali, the career administrators were positioned to provide the essential services expected of a sovereign government. The labours of the bureaucracy, however, were hardly substitutes for a successful political experience. None the less, the strength, the discipline, the dedication, and the expertise of the administrators stood in sharp contrast to the country's politicians, who demonstrated few, if any, of these traits or abilities. In official parlance, Pakistan emerged as a parliamentary entity, but in reality it was a virtual administrative state, less a representative expression and more the recrudescence of a familiar but palatable, if not benign, authoritarianism.

The Liaquat Conundrum

Jinnah was irreplaceable, and his mortality might have been sufficient reason for him to refuse the office of the Governor-General. Perhaps it would have been better had Pakistan's first Governor-General been someone with less credentials and devoid of Jinnah's charisma. It would have made it easier for a successor to follow in that office, and moreover, there may have been some expectation that the successor to a head of state of lesser stature than the Quaid-i-Azam could make a better job of it. Jinnah, however, made his successor's task an impossible one, and in attempting to imitate his style, those who followed him made a shambles of the office and caused great harm to the nation. In spite of all his constitutional instincts, Jinnah had centred attention on executive decision-making, on the centralization of authority, and on crisis management. It could be argued that the times influenced these actions, and had they not been taken, the country's position would have been even more perilous. Arguably, the time was not appropriate for liberal constitutionalism, for the slow, deliberative operation of the democratic process, but it is also questionable if the inaugural period demanded a veritable dictator, and in Jinnah, Pakistan had an authoritative voice that all but silenced the representative institution.

The Quaid's towering personality dominated the Pakistan movement and it, no doubt, lifted the nation after the transfer of power. But his successor did not possess any of his qualities, nor did he command the obedience that had been reserved for Jinnah alone. When it was revealed that Prime Minister Liaquat Ali Khan's choice to succeed the Quaid-i-Azam was the Bengali Chief Minister, Khwaja Nazimuddin, there was the expected disappointment from almost all sectors of the population, including East Bengal. Nazimuddin was the total reverse of Jinnah, in temperament, in bearing, in experience, in oratory, in all the categories whereby personalities, notably leaders, are judged. A pious member of a successful family of Bengali merchants, Nazimuddin was an early member of the All-India Muslim League and had been his party's choice to become Chief Minister of Bengal following the 1937 elections. But he was a failure in that office and was forced to retreat to the familiar confines of his birth city until Jinnah's call for direct action to achieve Pakistan revived his political career. Furthermore, the Radcliffe Award that gave Calcutta and western Bengal to India had revitalized his political life. With the help of an organization assembled by Shahabuddin (Nazimuddin's brother) and Nurul Amin, Nazimuddin took control of a very divided East Bengal Muslim League. And when Suhrawardy, Bhashani, Fazlul Huq, and Abul Hashim were sidetracked on one pretext or another, Nazimuddin was engineered by his very astute brother into the Chief Minister's office.

Only one conclusion explains why Liaquat chose Nazimuddin to succeed Jinnah as Governor-General of Pakistan. Liaquat, long in the shadow of the Quaid-i-Azam, was eager to assert his leadership and he did not want a head of state who could interfere with his style of management. Nazimuddin, from that standpoint, was the perfect choice, but looked at from every other direction, his appointment was an unmitigated disaster. Even when it is argued that Liaquat wished to de-emphasize the viceregal tradition and to elevate the parliamentary experience, as had occurred in India, his decision to go with Nazimuddin focused attention more on himself than on the institution of the parliament.

In being perceived as wanting to arrogate power to his own person, Liaquat challenged the prerogatives of provincial Muslim League leaders whose ambitions were noteworthy during Jinnah's tenure as Governor-General. And there was still another element in the brew. Even if Liaquat's choice was predicated on giving one of Pakistan's two principal political offices to a Bengali, there were those in the western Pakistan provinces who showed discomfort in the presence of East Bengalis. Although slow to surface, hostility between the eastern and western wings of the country had been registered during Jinnah's forced visit to Dhaka. But now the Bengalis demanded recognition of their superior numbers and they clamoured for their proportional share of the representation in the National Assembly. Important Punjabi leaders would have none of it and, asserting that their province was the heart of the nation, they demanded a role far larger than their numbers otherwise permitted.

Jinnah's death caused more than a leadership vacuum in the country. Nazimuddin's appointment as his successor spawned a struggle between the centre and the provinces, and between the provinces of western Pakistan and East Bengal. Politicians, some already vocal, others heretofore dormant, now intensified their actions, and the intrigue and manoeuvring slowed the process of constitution-making and forced many Pakistanis to question what their struggle and sacrifice were supposed to achieve. Moreover, given the indiscipline of the politicians, as well as the fracturing in the ranks of the Muslim League, the way was open to members of the administrative services to play more formidable political roles.

Liaquat was in no position to address the many divisions that threatened his leadership. A loyal follower of the Quaid-i-Azam, it was his urging that convinced Jinnah to leave his self-imposed exile in England, return to the subcontinent, and rebuild the Muslim League. Jinnah was moved by Liaquat's demeanour and he never had reason to question his loyalty or dedication. In Liaquat, Jinnah had the perfect lieutenant. Liaquat's Delhi home became the headquarters for the All-India Muslim League, and Jinnah made him the party's Secretary-General. Assigned responsibilities in the negotiations with the colonial authority, Liaquat proved himself a faithful confidant and an energetic assistant, but he was seldom called upon to display his leadership qualities. Moreover, Liaquat was a Nawabzada and thus a member of the United Provinces aristocracy, but he had little, if any, exposure to conditions in the provinces that ultimately formed Pakistan.

When he arrived in Karachi to take up his responsibility as Prime Minister of Pakistan, he was literally a man without a constituency. Liaquat was a product of the All-India Muslim League, and the decision to split that organization after independence did not redound to his favour. Marked as the Quaid's man, he had minimal opportunity to initiate actions or reconcile differences with the new country's provincial leaders. Much like H.S. Suhrawardy, Liaquat was judged an interloper and, had it not been Jinnah's desire, his situation following partition might have been similar to that experienced by the last Chief Minister of undivided Bengal. Jinnah's support was therefore a mixed blessing. Because the Quaid-i-Azam insisted on handpicking Pakistan's first Prime Minister, Liaquat was welcomed to Pakistan, but the man from central India also found Jinnah's extraordinary powers distressing, and perhaps even suffocating. Jinnah's passing removed both Liaquat's protective shield as well as the limitations that the Quaid's actions imposed on his powers. But if Liaquat believed that now was the time to demonstrate his leadership, he was to be sadly disappointed. Without Jinnah, the Pakistani centre proved to be a weak entity. Liaquat not only had significant problems in managing his federal cabinet, he was also under pressure to yield to the several provincial authorities whose powers in many ways exceeded his own. In an effort aimed at preserving his prerogatives, Liaquat did not flinch from using extraordinary means, but his use of arbitrary measures was not slated to win the affection of his provincial detractors. The Prime Minister justified his use of emergency powers in the name of preserving the central government, but his rivals knew full well that his real purpose was the expansion and consolidation of his personal power.

Liaquat, despite the appellation given him as the Quaid-i-Millat, or Leader of the Nation, realized he could never replace Jinnah, nor command the respect of Pakistan's quarrelsome politicians. Whereas Jinnah could deflect his adversaries with a facial expression or the tone of his voice, Liaquat found it necessary to gamble some, and later all, of his political capital in order to achieve the same results. The exhaustion of that capital was to cost him his life.

Tragedy in Rawalpindi

Liaquat was not cut out for the job as Pakistan's first Prime Minister. Jinnah confided to some of his confidants that he would have preferred finding someone more decisive, and given the circumstances, a person more familiar with the territory. The last stages of Jinnah's illness, however, prevented such action. And following Jinnah's death, Liaquat saw constitution-making as his central task. India had moved rapidly on that front, and by 1950 it would proudly promulgate a detailed document, heralding the country as a genuine democracy. The drafters of the Indian document retained the country's secular ideology, thereby transcending many of the country's inner contradictions. They also elaborated on the 1935 Government of India Act, which speeded the process of constitution-writing and provided a foundation for a more detailed set of laws and fundamental guarantees. Pakistan, however, faced other problems.

Compatibility between political leaders as well as among rank and file politicians was an important consideration in the drafting of a national constitution. Pakistan's Constituent Assembly was charged with that responsibility from the day it was organized. But that body performed a dual purpose: it also acted as the country's central legislature, until such time as the new constitution came into force and a formal National Assembly assumed its proper functions. The Constituent Assembly reflected the different regions of the country, but it was not designed to represent the numerical differences between the provinces, and considerable harmony of interest was needed if the body was to successfully carry out its mandate. That harmony of interest was never achieved, and the work of the Assembly was impeded by sustained conflicts among its members as well as the central leadership of the Muslim League.

Another matter delaying constitution-making was the Assembly's passage in 1949 of the Public and Representative Offices (Disqualification) Act. Better known by its acronym, PRODA, it was ostensibly fashioned to deal with official misconduct and corruption, but it was really meant to instil party discipline, limit defections, and thwart challenges to the central leadership. Unable to control the antics of Sindh's Ayub Khuhro, PRODA was enacted to make it possible to disqualify persons from holding public office for a period up to ten years. PRODA was a power given to the Governor-General, although the central cabinet, especially the Prime Minister, recommended its use. In other words, Liaquat believed that PRODA would facilitate his handling of renegade provincial leaders. He did not contemplate how the act reinforced the authority of the Governor-General, or how another, future Governor-General might ignore the wishes of a Prime Minister and assert his own authority. Conditioned to think short-term, and very much the dominant figure in his relationship with Nazimuddin, Liaquat 'encouraged' the Governor-General to use PRODA against Ayub Khuhro.

Nazimuddin was almost embarrassed to use his special powers, and when the Sindh Governor, Shaykh Din Mohammad, recommended that Khuhro's disqualification stand for seven years, Nazimuddin tempered the punishment and ordered a two-year disqualification. PRODA was to figure prominently in all political contests following this episode, and the act was so sweeping in its arbitrariness that it could only generate displeasure and dissension among the politicians. Clearly, it weakened the League rather than strengthen it. Although the central cabinet was not supposed to be involved in its application, given Nazimuddin's obvious weaknesses, PRODA was really a weapon in the arsenal of the Prime Minister. Moreover, Liaquat had introduced the PRODA bill in the Constituent Assembly and had strongly recommended its adoption. The passage of the bill and its subsequent application did not endear Liaquat to the more ambitious politicians, nor did it draw a clear line between the Prime Minister and the Governor-General. More important, how were the Governor-General's dictatorial powers to be reconciled with constitution-making? If the central objective of constitution-making was the limitation it imposed on government decision-makers, PRODA contradicted the total process.

PRODA also was used against the Khan of Mamdot, with different results and long-term significance. Mamdot had been instrumental in winning the Punjab for the Muslim League, but was engaged in a running battle with Mian Mumtaz Daultana after independence was achieved. The original PRODA charges against Mamdot had been assembled by the Pakistan Central Police, but they were later questioned in a court of law and the disqualification order was not applied. Nevertheless, the episode was cause for widespread disaffection within the League, and although the Punjabi antagonists intensified their fight, the real loser was the central government. A similar problem arose when Hamidul Haq Chowdhury, an East Bengal Minister of Finance, was accused of corruption while in office. His PRODA case raised the issue of 'secret files' being prepared, of charges and evidence being fabricated for the occasion, and of false testimony being offered, all with the purpose of politically destroying him. PRODA did not survive the tenure of the Muslim League, but its practices were perpetuated by successive governments. PRODA ensured that there would be little co-operation among politicians and that the contest between them would have little to do with the governance of Pakistan. Politics in Pakistan, almost from its inception, and at every level, were hardly more than the pursuit of personal power. Whereas Liaquat's introduction of PRODA signalled the decline of the Muslim League, not its evolution, it also sapped the vitality from constitution-making as an idealistic and democratic enterprise.

With PRODA as background, the Constituent Assembly approved the Objectives Resolution moved by Prime Minister Liaquat Ali Khan on 7 March 1949. Drafted in major part by I.H. Qureshi, the resolution established the framework for the drafting of the constitution. It stipulated that the guiding principles of the state were democracy, freedom, equality, tolerance, and social justice. More specifically, it stated that Pakistan was created as a homeland where Muslims would be able to order their lives in accordance with their Islamic tradition, but that minorities would be amply protected and given complete freedom to pursue their different ways of life. Having said this, it is important to note that the resolution begins with a purely Islamic reference, citing that 'sovereignty over the entire Universe belongs to Allah Almighty alone, and the authority which He has delegated to the State of Pakistan through its people for being exercised within the limits prescribed by Him is a sacred trust' (quoted in Callard, 1957). While the resolution was quickly approved, the small minority community remaining within Pakistan found the statement overdrawn, and because it referred specifically to one religious persuasion, they also found it threatening. Noting that the Muslim League remained closed to non-Muslims, and that separate electorates was still a sacred principle of Muslim League doctrine, the Objectives Resolution was another indication that, public statements to the contrary, Pakistan was a country exclusively for Muslims and that non-

Muslims would be advised to accept their lesser place within the country. The resentment registered by the minority communities was expressed in the resignation of the central Labour Minister, J.N. Mandal, the Hindu leader of the scheduled castes and an associate of the Quaid-i-Azam. His subsequent decision to leave Pakistan for India was said to have been motivated by the Objectives Resolution.

The Islamic content of a state comprised overwhelmingly of Muslims came as no surprise to anyone, but at the same time, the fact that Islam predominated left many questions of a political nature unanswered. Islam could never be judged to be under threat in Pakistan. How far then should the state go in emphasizing Islam when Muslims were the vast majority and were free to live their lives as they saw fit? How was secularism to be expressed in a contemporary Muslim nation that was also a modern nation-state? Indeed, should it be expressed? Furthermore, was the state to specify which version of Islam was the preferred version? In point of fact, was it necessary to establish a state religion for Pakistan, or to fashion Pakistan as an Islamic state? How, in fact, could the Pakistan government establish one representation of Islam as the true version and relegate the others to lesser status?

The schism that had divided the Islamic world into Sunnis and Shias centuries earlier had long been a source of turmoil in Muslim lands, but such differences were never a consideration in Jinnah's case. Though born a Shia, Jinnah's secular training, his wide-ranging eclecticism, exposed him to a variety of cultural expressions, and his goal lay in the creation of a solidary national community, not one with narrowly-circumscribed traditions. His championing of Muslim-Hindu amity and political unity is a matter of record. Almost to the moment of the transfer of power, Jinnah was still searching for a way to bridge differences between himself and his Hindu counterparts. And following Pakistan's independence, Jinnah's first concern was the melding of a balanced community of different believers. The only test Jinnah believed necessary was the citizen's loyalty to Pakistan. Nothing else, according to him, mattered, and he urged the majority community to open its arms to the non-Muslims in their midst.

Jinnah, however, was a man of action, hardly a dreamer. He must have anticipated the problem that was to become a major issue following his death. Pakistan had been won on the basis of the two-nation theory, and a separate nation-state had been created in the subcontinent specifically to protect the culture and interests of the Muslim community. But a vast majority of Muslims remained in India, and Pakistan had enough difficulty in absorbing those Muslims who, for one reason or another, left India and opted for the Muslim homeland. Pakistan was never meant to be a state whose principal function was the in-gathering of all of colonial India's Muslim population. This is why it was so important to lay out an outline, in theoretical or practical terms, of the Pakistan that was to be. The failure to do so, the reluctance in coming to grips with this essential matter of ethos, plagued Pakistan in its early years and it continued to do so with the passage of the decades. Jinnah recognized the enormity of the problem when communal bloodletting could not be averted. Always the systematic, methodical practitioner, distressed by passionate, emotional displays, Jinnah had to accept the reality of a condition he could not control. By the time partition was made official it was already too late to address the dilemma. The transfer of power sealed the fate of the millions of the subcontinent, and unleashed sectarian forces in Pakistan that its leaders ignored only at their own peril.

The same day on which the Objectives Resolution was adopted, the Constituent Assembly created a Basic Principles Committee of twenty-five members, representing approximately one-third of the Assembly. The BPC was permitted to appoint an additional ten members who were not supposed to be members of the body. The Bengali Tamizuddin Khan, the President of the Constituent Assembly, was made its President, and Prime Minister Liaquat Ali Khan became Vice-President. The committee later included ten members of Liaquat's cabinet, the Chief Ministers of Sindh, the NWFP, and East Bengal, as well as the Chief Justice of Pakistan, thus making the BPC the most prestigious single committee in the country. The overall responsibility of the BPC was the framing of a constitution for Pakistan. If the problem was in the detail, the BPC was responsible for addressing and reconciling the many constitutional questions before they were overwhelmed by controversy. Working with a subcommittee structure, an Interim Report was completed and publicized by the Constituent Assembly in September 1950.

The Interim Report, though a brief document, elicited immediate criticism because it relied so heavily on the 1935 Act, and made only peripheral reference to the Islamic character of the state. Nevertheless, the report reiterated the Muslim League goal of establishing Urdu as the country's official language, thereby angering the Bengalis, who anticipated a display of flexibility on this unresolved issue. Although not spelled out in the document, it also appeared that the Bengalis were to be denied the representation in the National Assembly that their greater numbers seemed to warrant. Faced with dissension in his own ranks and confronting widespread disapproval, Liaquat was urged to disown the BPC proposals and seek a way out of the dilemma. Constitution-making was delayed once again, but the obvious need lay in finding a workable formula. Sardar Abdur Rab Nishtar, a Punjabi and a disciple of the Quaid-i-Azam, was given that task at the head of a special subcommittee. Nishtar solicited responses from the broader public, but that approach only complicated the work of his committee. The principal replies to committee questions were those emphasizing Pakistan's Muslim character and hence the stress given to the writing of a constitution that laid out in detail the obligations that Islam imposed on its believers. Maulana Abul Ala Maudoodi, leader of the Jamaat-i-Islami, having left India for Pakistan, sent the committee a draft constitution that was based solely on Islamic tradition and practices. Among the *Islam-pasand* contributions were those calling for a head of state who would be officially addressed as a Khalifa or Amir, and all these respondents acknowledged that such a person could only be the most pious Muslim in the land, hence never a practising politician.

The Bengalis, however, centred their attention on more mundane matters, insisting on appropriate representation in the parliament, cabinet, and highest offices of the land. They also gave repeated emphasis to the language issue and demanded that Bengali be given equal status with Urdu. But the prosaic quality of the Bengali requests did not receive the same attention that the BPC gave to those stressing Pakistan's Islamic dimensions. The members of the Islamic *ulema*, a group that had opposed the formation of Pakistan, and clearly an element Jinnah had ignored in the demand for a sovereign Muslim state, was brought into the deliberations in the person of the leader of the Talimaat-i-Islamia, Maulana Syed Sulaiman Nadvi. With Nadvi a principal in committee deliberations, the division between the more secular-minded and the Islamic fundamentalists was firmly established. Thus, in an effort to please everyone, the BPC satisfied no one. Moreover, with indecision, confusion, and essentially weak leadership in the central Muslim League, the pragmatic aspects of constitution-making were either neglected or postponed. In the circumstances, a different form of representation emerged; status was now given to those capable of articulating the sentiments of the marginalized Pakistani masses. By appealing to their overriding consciousness as Muslims, not Pakistanis, the religious clerics, who had so opposed the creation of Pakistan, captured the sentiments of a vast unappealed-to segment of the population. By so doing, an even heavier burden was placed on the shoulders of the rank and file politician.

The key question revolved around the expressed need to produce a constitution whose laws and regulations, as well as its principles and purposes, were in accordance with the Koran and Sunna. Liaquat was careful not to oppose such a theme. In fact, he argued that Islam was the most democratic of the world's religions, and that a country founded on Islamic principles satisfied all the expectations of a democracy. By adopting an Islamic emphasis, Liaquat believed he could move the process of constitution-making to a successful conclusion.

The times seemed to demand a more forceful Muslim League President as well. Chaudhri Khaliquzzaman never won the approval of provincial party leaders, and the weakness of the League was attributed to his utter lack of charisma. In a meeting of the party in October 1950 the League council amended its constitution and removed the restriction imposed on ministers. That very day Liaquat replaced Khaliquzzaman as President of the Muslim League. Given the intertwining of the Prime Minister's office with the presidency of the Muslim League, Liaquat launched a campaign stressing the inherent unity between Pakistan and the organization most responsible for its creation. His reference to Pakistan as 'the child of the Muslim League' would be made over and again as he tackled the hard issue of League disaffection as well as defection (Afzal, p.45).

The one practical problem still before Liaquat, however, was the distribution of seats in the National Assembly and, most important, how the different provinces could be accommodated. East Bengal contained more than a majority of the Pakistani population, and its verbal opposition adamantly demanded the recognition promised them in the 1940 Lahore Resolution. The Bengalis cited their long history with the Muslim League and their steadfast resolve in the formation of Pakistan. On the other hand, East Bengal was historically a deprived region, and although it was Pakistan's one great source of foreign exchange in the years immediately following independence (a factor due solely to the Korean War), its economy was largely in the hands of non-Bengalis. Moreover, the province had a population that was almost 25 per cent Hindu, and the Punjabis, who had experienced the most intense form of communal bloodletting during partition, were averse to any provision that accorded the minority community adequate representation. Some Bengalis, however, read the situation differently, and in October 1950 they formed an ad hoc Committee of Action. Dominated by recently organized opposition parties, the Action Committee warned against reducing East Bengal to the status of a municipality, and they deplored the BPC for its 'undemocratic' proposals. A 'Protest Day' was organized and all Bengali members of the BPC were encouraged to boycott its meetings.

When the Hindu Mahasabha and the Communist Party added their voices to the opposition, Liaquat was constrained to declare that his government 'shall not tolerate these activities any longer and shall put an end to them in the interest of the existence and stability of Pakistan' (*Dawn*, 30

October 1950). Following this declaration, the Prime Minister went to Peshawar where the Muslim League also faced new challenges. Having learned that Mamdot had broken with the Punjab Muslim League and had formed a party called the Jinnah Awami League, he was very disturbed over reports that NWFP Chief Minister Abdul Qaiyum Khan was losing control of his government, and that a clash with the Pir of Manki Sharif had inflicted deep wounds in the ranks of the frontier Muslim League. Moreover, the Pir had also moved to form a new political party. Speaking in Peshawar, Liaquat repeated his now familiar phrase that Pakistan was the 'child of the Muslim League' and that Pakistanis should beware of 'mushroom organizations' (*Morning News*, 5 November 1950). Aware now of the storm the Interim Report had created, the Prime Minister returned to Karachi to call upon the Constituent Assembly to suspend its deliberations on the Interim Report. Additional time was required, he said, and a host of arguments needed to be addressed. But by this time the political opposition had swelled to significant proportions, and halting their momentum was all the Prime Minister could hope for.

H.S. Suhrawardy had quit the Muslim League to assist in the formation of the Awami League, which had its base of operations in the eastern province. In January 1951, free of the 'gag order' that had been imposed on him, he barnstormed East Bengal and, although the Muslim League organized demonstrations aimed at disrupting his meetings, they could not prevent his message from being delivered to enthusiastic audiences. To steal some of the thunder from the opposition, Liaquat offered Fazlul Huq a position in the central government which the old 'tiger' readily accepted. But this move did little to placate the opposition in East Bengal. By December 1950 there were twelve vacancies in the provincial legislature, but the Muslim League government of Nurul Amin was reluctant to hold by-elections. Having lost a contest in Tangail to a dissident Bengali student, the League did not want to test its popularity in other mid-term elections. Liaquat was summoned to Dhaka on 17 December, his first visit in almost one year, to bolster League morale. The Prime Minister laboured to reinvigorate the East Bengal Muslim

League, to boost the credentials of the Nurul Amin government, and to plead for patience as the BPC worked its way through the difficult business of constitution-making. Liaquat argued against the formation of opposition parties, noting that the time demanded solidarity and that the 'Muslim League was the mother of Pakistan,' and he ended with the thought that only a 'real mother' can demonstrate affection for her offspring (*Morning News*, 24 December 1950).

None of the Muslim League's problems were satisfactorily addressed in East Bengal, and Liaquat now turned his attention to Punjab, where provincial elections were scheduled for March 1951. On the day of the balloting Liaquat made a shocking announcement. He revealed that the Army Chief of Staff, Major-General Akbar Khan, and a number of other officers, as well as notable civilians, among them the celebrated leftist poet Faiz Ahmed Faiz, had conspired to overthrow the government, arrest and summarily execute political and army leaders, and establish a communist political system in the country. Akbar Khan had led the tribal irregulars in the stalled Kashmir conflict, but he had risen in the ranks of the army and was angered when Liaquat chose Ayub Khan as the army's first Pakistani Commander-in-Chief. Akbar also had serious differences with Liaquat's foreign policy, and the Prime Minister's 1950 'No-War Pact' with India was especially distasteful. Akbar was alleged to have induced a number of army officers to join with him in refashioning the country's political life, a high priority toward that end being the wresting of Kashmir from India.

Liaquat gave few, if any, details, and many observers were sceptical that there were any, but the Rawalpindi Conspiracy produced an eighteen-month trial in which all the principals were found guilty but later received light sentences which they never fully served. At the time, however, the affair signalled Liaquat's resolve to sustain civilian leadership of the Armed Forces. It also set the scene for the outlawing of the Pakistan Communist Party, and placed the Muslim country firmly on the side of the West in the Cold War. More immediately, it provided the Punjab Muslim League with an enormous boost in the provincial elections of 1951. The party not only won an overwhelming majority of seats in the Punjab legislature, the elections also established Daultana as the most powerful of the Punjabi political personalities. The 'Rawalpindi Conspiracy' more directly bolstered the role of General Ayub Khan, whose consolidation of the army command structure was now assured. While there were rumblings among the officers and some dissension in the ranks, the new Commander-in-Chief began the process of reorganizing the forces along more disciplined lines.

Daultana's stranglehold on the Punjab Muslim League gave him a feel for power he had not enjoyed even as the province's largest landlord. Moreover, there was no avoiding his differences with the Prime Minister, and he began to show strong opposition to any central government scheme which left Punjab in a weak position *vis-à-vis* East Bengal. Daultana did not like the formula that Liaquat had hammered out during his visit to the eastern province. The plan would give East Bengal parity with the combined provinces of western Pakistan, but in so doing, the Bengalis were destined to enjoy far more seats in the National Assembly than those held by Punjab. Daultana never appreciated this approach and he refused to compromise in a matter which he believed relegated his province to second-rate status. Daultana was supported in his opposition to any parity formula by a broad segment of Punjabi leaders, and none was more expressive on this issue than Mushtaq Ahmad Gurmani, a former Prime Minister of Bahawalpur who had been appointed Minister of Kashmir Affairs in 1950, and was made Minister of the Interior in 1951. Like Daultana, Gurmani was an ambitious figure, and also like the Chief Minister, he had reasons to question Liaquat's leadership. Sensing that power had shifted from the centre to the provincial governments, Daultana and Gurmani had visions of the Punjab controlling the flow of Pakistani policy, both domestic and foreign. Indeed, if the Kashmir problem was the key, it was an issue that affected Punjab and through it, the Frontier province as well. East Bengal, it was argued, had only a peripheral interest in the matter, and Liaquat's apparent willingness to find a compromise arrangement with India was more likely to find approval in Dhaka than in Lahore.

On 11 October 1951, with all these issues swirling around

him, Liaquat announced that he would leave Karachi for a five-day tour of Punjab. Among the stops on his agenda was a public speech he planned to deliver in the Company Bagh at Rawalpindi. This speech was scheduled for the afternoon of 16 October but the Prime Minister would never get the opportunity to deliver it. As he was about to address the assembled crowd, he was shot at close range and died soon thereafter. His assassin was reported to be an Afghan by the name of Said Akbar. There were no other identifiable credentials. Akbar was himself killed on the spot by Police Inspector Mohammad Shah, thus sealing the assassin's lips forever. Mohammad Shah lived to face the investigators, but no evidence could be developed indicating that a conspiracy had been hatched to take the life of the Prime Minister. Mysteriously, Mohammad Shah was himself the victim of an assassin in 1960.

Although Scotland Yard was brought into the case at the urging of Begum Liaquat Ali Khan, their sleuths also failed to turn up a single lead that could confirm that high-level plotters were involved in the killing of the Prime Minister. Rumours, however, abound to this day. Some cite the fact that Daultana had lured the Prime Minister to Punjab by stating that he would not force a parity formula on the Punjabis. Liaquat, he declared, would have to sell the programme to the Punjabis himself. Both Daultana and Gurmani, however, bore major responsibility for protecting the Prime Minister during his stay in the province, and the ease with which an assassin took Liaquat's life raised suspicions that they were in some way involved. Others, however, were more convinced that the Rawalpindi Conspiracy Case had so angered a group of army officers that they were prepared to reap their revenge by having Liaquat killed. Still others cited Liaquat's policies toward India, which left New Delhi with a strong hand and appeared to confine the Kashmiris to a condition of permanent servitude. Given the tribal role in the Kashmir conflict, it would not have surprised the authorities if they had found a link that tied disgruntled Kashmiri mujahiddin to Liaquat's death. But none of these suppositions or rumours, and none of the speculations, could be transformed into hard fact. No evidence supporting a conspiracy thesis was ever found. Some years later Mahmud Hussain, then Vice-Chancellor of Karachi University, but a Minister in the central government at the time of the assassination, revealed that there were intelligence reports indicating a plot to take the life of the Prime Minister in Punjab. He personally pleaded with Liaquat not to make this particular journey, but the Prime Minister chose to ignore the reports as well as his Minister's plea.

The loss of Liaquat Ali Khan, a leader who had been honoured with the title Quaid-i-Millat, was a stunning blow to the young nation, but it is interesting to note the passivity of the population at large when his death was made public. There were no disturbances. In fact, there were few indications of public grief at the news. Many observers, in Pakistan and outside, saw this reaction as a sign that the country had come of age, had weathered adversity, and was sufficiently grounded to manage even without its other venerable leader. In fact, Liaquat's passing wrote an end to the beginning. It could be argued that up to this moment, Pakistan was a consequence of the history of the first half of the twentieth century. With Liaquat's passing, the Pakistan Movement ceased to be a factor in people's lives. Moreover, power had shifted from the centre to the provinces, and while something approaching a centrally-guided state had prevailed up to the time of Jinnah's death, during Liaquat's tenure the dyarchical aspects of the Pakistan equation had become more apparent. The test of Pakistan's future would not be found in its capacity to sustain central authority, but rather in how a weak centre could continue to represent its distinctive but quarrelsome parts.

But as it is in history, events are seldom understood when they happen. And the events that overtook Pakistan in October 1951 were not grasped by an unsuspecting public, nor it could also be said, by those who scrambled to fill the power vacuum left by the loss of first the Quaid-i-Azam, and now Liaquat too. Those who stressed sustaining the power of the central government failed to acknowledge what was occurring inside the country, either because their attention was riveted on their personal destinies, or because they were increasingly wary of external matters. By 1951 India had emerged as a formidable actor in world affairs, and even if its Armed Forces were still in a stage of formation, their diplomatic capabilities were acknowledged worldwide. India's role in the United Nations, its decision to challenge the United States in that political forum, and its particular criticism of Washington's policy toward the emerging Third World, had given New Delhi a prominence that could not be overlooked in Pakistan. There were those in Pakistan who insisted on the development of a strong centre to balance this growing power and influence of their near neighbour. Whatever the cost, they believed, the provinces had to accept the pre-eminence of the central government. As a consequence of such strongly held views by determined personalities, a contest was precipitated between the nation's centrists and those representing more parochial ideas. The manoeuvring engaged in by the centrists on the one side, and the peripheralists on the other, guaranteed protracted struggle with unforetold consequences.

The Succession Crisis

There was no special meeting of the central cabinet when news reached Karachi that the Prime Minister had been assassinated. Instead there were a flurry of exchanges between the different principals, all of whom apparently agreed that Liaquat's successor had to be named quickly and before the news had an impact on the nation. The public required reassurance that the country was essentially stable and that the Prime Minister's death, tragic as it was, was not a consequence of something more sinister. Because there had been increasing tensions with India during this period, the government wanted to dispel speculation that Liaquat's murder was carried out by Indian agents and was prelude to an Indian assault on the country. There also was concern as to how the Prime Minister's death would be read in the outside world, and the government was determined to put the tragedy to rest as quickly as possible. More significantly, however, any delay in declaring a successor offered opportunities for the country's more divisive personalities to play their hands. No one appeared to know if the assassin operated alone, was a hired killer, or linked with conspiratorial elements in or outside the government. (If they did know, they were certainly not talking).

Governor-General Nazimuddin was reported to be in shock when he learned that the Prime Minister was dead. As head of state it was his responsibility to find a successors as well as to comfort the nation. Nazimuddin's closest advisor and confidant, also a Cabinet official, was his brother, Khwaja Shahabuddin. Shahabuddin had received the tragic news from his Joint Secretary in the Ministry of Information, S.M. Ikram. He was then contacted by Sardar Bahadur Khan, Fazlur Rahman, Mahmud Hussain, and Chaudhri Mohammad Ali, all urging him to advise his brother to fill the Prime Minister's role. Shahabuddin rejected their entreaties categorically and argued for more time. Begum Liaquat Ali Khan had not yet been informed that her husband was dead and it was decided to send Chaudhri Mohammad Ali to her residence to tell her the sad news. The group agreed to continue their discussions at the home of Fazlur Rahman, where they went after Shahabuddin dropped Mohammad Ali off at the Prime Minister's residence. The discussions at Fazlur Rahman's home were no more conclusive, however, and Shahabuddin returned to his residence.

Soon thereafter, Altaf Hussain, the editor of *Dawn*, arrived to inform Shahabuddin that Chaudhri Mohammad Ali was supporting Nishtar for Prime Minister and that such an appointment would create more problems than it would solve. Fazlur Rahman and Sardar Bahadur Khan were most opposed to Nishtar taking the office. Altaf Hussain informed Shahabuddin that Chaudhri Mohammad Ali was already pressurizing Nazimuddin to appoint Nishtar, and that the only way out of the dilemma was for Nazimuddin to fill the role himself, and allow Ghulam Mohammad to become the ceremonial Governor-General. Moreover, the decision had to be made before Liaquat's body arrived in Karachi from Rawalpindi. Altaf Hussain cited Ghulam Mohammad's poor health, the fact that he had recently suffered a stroke, and that he would be too feeble to interfere with the work of the Prime Minister and his cabinet. The removal of Ghulam Mohammad from the Cabinet would also strengthen Nazimuddin's hand as Prime Minister. Altaf's assurances and reasoning convinced Shahabuddin that this was the best course of action and he agreed to urge his brother to take up the new assignment.

Nazimuddin, however, had already been approached by Chaudhri Mohammad Ali and, in the excitement of the moment, had agreed to the change. Believing that he was needed to save the nation at a difficult time, Nazimuddin naively accepted the arrangement wherein he would become Pakistan's second Prime Minister. Flattered that it was he who had been selected to follow Jinnah, and now Liaquat, Nazimuddin resigned the office of Governor-General and was officially sworn in as Pakistan's new Prime Minister.

It should be noted that Liaquat's cabinet had been deeply divided, with Fazlur Rahman, the Commerce Minister, on the one side, and Ghulam Mohammad, the Finance Minister, on the other. Liaquat had managed to keep the major antagonists in relative balance, but in matters judged to be of vital importance, he was more likely to favour the Fazlur Rahman group. The devaluation of the Pakistani rupee was one such occasion. Ghulam Mohammad was in favour of devaluation in so far as India had already done so. Fazlur Rahman, however, opposed the devaluation scheme and Liaquat had sided with him. Zahid Hussain, Governor of the State Bank, also supported Ghulam Mohammad's position; however, the country's leading financial experts could not move the Prime Minister. One reason for Liaquat's obstinacy in this matter was the Punjabi-Bengali controversy that surrounded devaluation. As a consequence of the then raging Korean War, the Bengalis had reaped heavy profits from the sale of jute, and hence were the beneficiaries of an unchanged rupee. The Punjabis, on the other hand, conducted much of their trade with India, and they stood to lose if the rupee was not devalued parallel with Indian currency. Liaquat's tilt toward East Bengal, therefore, antagonized many of those power-brokers who identified with Punjab.

Nevertheless, with the exception of Ghulam Mohammad, who was consistently supported by Gurmani, the other cabinet members largely deferred to Liaquat. The Prime Minister, however, was visibly distressed over his inability to control his Finance Minister. Liaquat confided in Mahmud Hussain, a Minister of State at the time, that he was planning to change the composition of the central cabinet, and that his highest priority was removing Ghulam Mohammad. In fact, efforts had already been launched to make him the new ambassador to the United States. On learning of Liaquat's plan, Ghulam Mohammad is said to have remarked that he would rather 'commit suicide' than assume a post in Washington.

Liaquat, however, was not given to sharing too many confidences with Mahmud Hussain. He was heavily dependent on Chaudhri Mohammad Ali, Pakistan's leading public administrator, and it was he who best knew Liaquat's inner thoughts and concerns. There were no secrets between the Prime Minister and Chaudhri Mohammad Ali, and only on two occasions did Liaquat go against his advice. The first was when Liaquat insisted on Ayub Khan being named Commander-in-Chief of the Pakistan Army. Ayub was not the choice of those planning a major role for the army, and especially those from Punjab. But he was Liaquat's choice, and he was also rumoured to be Begum Liaquat's choice, and the Prime Minister held to his decision. The Rawalpindi Conspiracy was in major part believed to be linked to this appointment. The second was Chaudhri Mohammad Ali's support for Ghulam Mohammad on the devaluation matter, and Liaquat's determination to reject the advice of all his experts. Despite their differences on these issues, Liaquat met with Mohammad Ali before all cabinet meetings, and made a place for him above the cabinet, a post that was equivalent to that of a Deputy Prime Minister. Chaudhri Mohammad Ali therefore played an instrumental role in the selection of Liaquat's successor, and in doing so he had to outfox the Bengali group led by Fazlur Rahman and Khwaja Shahabuddin.

Citing the many problems confronting the central government, the Bengali contingent noted the importance of placating the people of the eastern province. The Bengalis in the Cabinet also believed that a conspiracy had taken the life of the Prime Minister. They could not dispel a fear that Liaquat had been killed because he leaned toward the east, and that in the silencing of the Prime Minister, their voices too had been muted. Moreover, given the negative Punjabi reaction to all the issues that conferred status on East Bengal, the Bengalis were convinced that high members of the central and Punjab governments were implicated in Liaquat's death. Ghulam Mohammad and Gurmani were both in Rawalpindi on the day of the assassination, thus feeding the rumour mill about their likely complicity. It was during this period of uncertainty and rumour-mongering that Sardar Abd'ur Rab Nishtar's name emerged as the candidate best suited to become Pakistan's next Prime Minister.

Nishtar identified himself as a Pathan although his residence was in Punjab, and indeed he was Governor of Punjab at the time of the assassination. Nishtar, however, was perceived as too friendly with Abdul Qaiyum Khan, and the latter's chief nemesis in the cabinet was Sardar Bahadur Khan, who had opposed Qaiyum Khan and now forcefully objected to the selection of Nishtar as well. Chaudhri Mohammad Ali also revealed that the army, and notably Ayub Khan, opposed the selection of Nishtar. Given the degeneration of the deliberations into what were described as 'Pathan politics', Fazlur Rahman recommended that Nazimuddin step down as Governor-General and assume the Prime Minister's role. Nazimuddin was an acknowledged lightweight, but Liaquat had strengthened the office of the Prime Minister, and if Nazimuddin received the approval of the army high command and gained the loyalty of the senior members of the bureaucracy, he could be the best choice. Moreover, Punjab could also be served by making Nishtar the Deputy Prime Minister. And if Nazimuddin and Nishtar could be made to work as a team, many of the differences straining East Bengal-Punjab relations may well dissipate.

Once Nazimuddin agreed to the shift from the office of the Governor-General to that of the Prime Minister, and he appeared eager to make the change, it only remained to determine who would fill the office of Governor-General. In the critical hours following Liaquat's murder, no time was given to Jinnah's role as Governor-General. More consumed with filling Liaquat's office, most of the key decision-makers gave little thought to a proactive Governor-General. Others, however, did not overlook the opportunity to install a potent officer. And because they were convinced that Nazimuddin would be a weak Prime Minister, they saw the necessity for a Governor-General who could act decisively at home and abroad. Mushtaque Ahmad Gurmani belonged to this latter group. Gurmani, it is said, was the first member of the cabinet to propose that Ghulam Mohammad be allowed to fill the post left vacant by Nazimuddin, but instead of addressing the Finance Minister's strengths, the Interior Minister cited his poor health and the fact that he would be little more than a ceremonial head of state. Gurmani noted Ghulam Mohammad's long and distinguished service to the nation, and his having been honoured by the Quaid-i-Azam, who had once called him his 'financial wizard'. Ghulam Mohammad's appointment as Governor-General, therefore, would not only honour an old and ailing civil servant, it was said, but would also assure the Prime Minister that the head of state would not threaten his prerogatives. When Chaudhri Mohammad Ali declared his support for the Gurmani proposal, opposition to the appointment failed to materialize. East Bengal could take pride in one of its own becoming the nation's second Prime Minister, but a Punjabi-bureaucratic manoeuvre had secured the Governor-General's office for one of its own.

As Liaquat's body was taken from the plane at Karachi airport, Nazimuddin had already assumed his responsibilities as head of the Pakistan government and Ghulam Mohammad had been declared the country's third Governor-General. But it did not take very long to realize that the two men, so different in outlook, in experience, in temperament, in attitude, and in behaviour, would make a very odd couple, and that their relationship would be as dramatic as it was short.

The Nazimuddin Interregnum

Nazimuddin's appointment was a stop-gap measure, made necessary by the circumstances surrounding Liaquat's death and the desperate need for a quick and decisive transition from the one government to the other. Nazimuddin assumed an office that was immersed in crisis. Constitution-making had been Liaquat's first priority, but the obstacles thrown in his path, notably by different provincial leaders, had proved to be more than he could manage. It is still believed that he died because he could not reconcile opposed forces articulating different constitutional objectives. Nazimuddin inherited an impossible legacy. Moreover, he was a far weaker personality than Liaquat, and totally devoid of those qualities that leaders are supposed to be made of. Reserved, shy, indecisive, introverted, and generally slow-witted, Nazimuddin could not have been expected to move a programme that Liaquat had died promoting. All the problems that challenged Liaquat had become Nazimuddin's responsibility, and no one expected the new Prime Minister to succeed where the Quaid-i-Millat had not.

Nazimuddin's task was to relate the centre to the provinces and to emphasize the pre-eminence of the former, but to do so in a way that did not add more fuel to the fire of provincial passions. As a Bengali, he might have been expected to lean toward his native surroundings in constitutional matters, but Nazimuddin was hardly the type to use his office to satisfy the parochial demands of his brethren in the east wing. Nazimuddin envisaged a role that inspired bridge-building between and among the several Pakistani cultures. A cosmopolitan in his heart of hearts, Nazimuddin did not speak the native language of his home province and his speeches, generally in Urdu or English, had to be translated into the Bangla of his rural constituents. Committed to Jinnah's dream of a single, unified Pakistan, he had been a tireless worker for Muslim League causes, and he could not back away from that quest as head of the Pakistan government. But while he stoically accepted his noble mission, the new Prime Minister did not possess the essential power to realize his goals. With his frailties well known, Nazimuddin was exploitable by those who did not share his belief in a fully integrated and united Pakistan. As a compromiser, Nazimuddin was eager to blend his ideas with others', but his yielding nature was judged weakness, and rather than follow his lead, his detractors sought advantages whenever he equivocated. Instead of sensing the eloquence in Nazimuddin's appeal for unity, the power-brokers considered him a pathetic figure who could be freely manipulated to satisfy their peculiar purposes.

Nazimuddin's problems were all around him, in the central government as well as in the provinces. Ghulam Mohammad may have suffered a stroke, and may have lost some of his mobility, but he remained a determined, strong-willed figure, and he had no intention of yielding to the Prime Minister in matters of policy. Aggressive and self-confident, Ghulam Mohammad was uncomfortable in ceremonial roles and he refused to leave the management of the country to Nazimuddin. The Governor-General had little confidence in the Prime Minister's abilities, and he also questioned the vitality and the expertise of his cabinet. Moreover, that cabinet closely resembled Liaquat's, and there were several of its members he wanted removed. Overall, Ghulam Mohammad was the consummate administrator; he detested politicians and believed the country would be better served by men with professional callings. The country, in his opinion, needed the skills and talents of trained and experienced practitioners, men of integrity and bearing, who knew their tasks and were efficient in fulfilling them. He also knew what the country did not need, that is, the bickering and the petty intriguing that is the stuff of everyday political life. Politicians, in the eyes of the Governor-General, were not only untrustworthy, they were crass opportunists who were too eager to feather their individual nests at the expense of national needs. Nazimuddin might well seek to reconcile contesting political factions, but for Ghulam Mohammad, that was a wasteful enterprise. Nazimuddin consumed precious time and resources and, in the ambience of Pakistani politics, he could not succeed.

From the outset, Ghulam Mohammad intended to play Jinnah to Nazimuddin's Liaquat. And just as Liaquat subordinated himself to the Quaid-i-Azam, so too Nazimuddin had to learn to live in the long shadow cast by the Governor-General. Ghulam Mohammad did not deliberately seek to demean the office of the Prime Minister, merely to re-establish that governmental framework erected during Pakistan's first year. As a member of the team that laboured to keep Pakistan alive in those initial weeks and months, the Governor-General knew the mindset and the style of the Quaid-i-Azam, and he was convinced that the country needed a leader who demonstrated the forcefulness of character associated with the country's founder. Although only a marginal Muslim Leaguer, and never really a politician, Ghulam Mohammad was enamoured of Jinnah's persistence, his intuitive gifts, and especially his single-minded dedication. The two men functioned well together and neither ever displayed discomfort with the other's performance. Moreover, Jinnah leaned heavily on the civil bureaucracy, and he knew from the very moment of the transfer of power that Pakistan would remain dependent on the steel frame of colonial administration while its leaders went about the business of fashioning a new state apparatus.

In spite of his infirmity, therefore, Ghulam Mohammad remained a man of action, a secular pragmatist, a man with a short temper and an aggressive turn of mind. A graduate of Aligarh University, before partition he served in the Indian Audits and Accounts Service, was Hyderabad's Finance Minister, and became a director in one of India's foremost commercial operations, the Tata industrial complex. Opting for Pakistan at Jinnah's urging, Ghulam Mohammad assumed the finance portfolio in the central government and was a major figure in creating and stabilizing the nascent state's financial institutions. As Governor-General, Ghulam Mohammad knew what he wanted for the nation, and with the assistance and abiding loyalty of a civil bureaucracy that was shaped and influenced by its Secretary-General, Chaudhri Mohammad Ali, he was ever confident that his objectives could be realized.

The Governor-General also counted on support from within the political community of western Pakistan, especially those politicians in the Punjab whom he most closely resembled in temperament and ambition. Like his Punjabi counterparts, Ghulam Mohammad saw little future in an East Bengal shorn of its Calcutta metropolis and forced to fall back on the denizens of the Dhaka hinterland. Moreover, his having been paired with Nazimuddin, the major personality of the east wing, only reinforced his determination to dominate the central government. Ghulam Mohammad knew all the details that led to the decision wherein Nazimuddin assumed the Prime Minister's office. More than that, he was an active behind-the-scenes participant in the discussions that won over the hesitant members of the Cabinet to his own appointment, especially Khwaja Shahabuddin. Granted Ghulam Mohammad's health was poor, but so too was Jinnah's when he assumed the responsibilities of the office. Indeed, Ghulam Mohammad, despite his affliction, believed he possessed far more endurance than the Quaid-i-Azam at the time of the country's independence. Thus, Ghulam Mohammad's promotion to the high position of Governor-General was a strategic manoeuvre, developed in major part by Chaudhri Mohammad Ali and Mushtaque Ahmad Gurmani, but encouraged by a wide array of civil and military officials as well as some very prominent Punjabi politicians.

Nazimuddin was unaware of the strategy that was developed to bypass, and in time, to discredit and finally drive him from office. Nor was he privy to the machinations of clever politicians, both east and west, who were intent on destroying his provincial power base. There is little in the historic record to suggest that events took their own course, that they were surprise occurrences, or that no one could have contemplated their evolution. In fact, the ground had already been prepared, the objectives had been clearly stated, and the actors needed only their cues to play out their roles. Nazimuddin had become a target of the power-brokers, and the best place to begin the campaign to dispose of him would be in his own province, and indeed, in the very city that formed his power base.

East Bengal

Several months after assuming their respective offices, Ghulam Mohammad and Khwaja Nazimuddin agreed that a visit to East Bengal was imperative, not only to demonstrate that the centre controlled events, but that the government was moving ahead with its many programmes, most importantly, the drafting of the constitution. The Governor-General decided that he would precede the Prime Minister, thus both upstaging Nazimuddin as well as setting the scene for the Prime Minister's later visit. When Nazimuddin arrived in his home province, he found that Ghulam Mohammad had stirred up considerable opposition to the Muslim League government in the province and at the centre. The Governor-General's demeanour as well as his public statements had belittled the East Bengali contribution in the formation and consolidation of Pakistan, and had aroused the unpleasantness that confronted Nazimuddin as he stepped from his aircraft. Instead of a welcome ceremony praising the successor to both the Quaid-i-Azam and the Quaid-i-Millat, Nazimuddin found himself in a hostile atmosphere that intensified with his every utterance.

On 27 January 1952, Prime Minister Nazimuddin read a lengthy speech before a multitude assembled on the same Paltan Maidan that Jinnah had used for a mass public meeting years earlier. Nazimuddin appealed for unity, and in the course of a long presentation, cited the need for a national language that could bridge the many cultural divisions that separated one group from another, and one province from another. Nazimuddin referred to Jinnah's call for a lingua franca, and he cited the Quaid-i-Azam's visit to East Bengal in 1948 and his insistence that only Urdu met all the requirements of the young nation. Nazimuddin repeated Jinnah's words and said that his thoughts on the subject were no different from those of the country's founder. Only Urdu tied the different segments of the nation to one another, and even though a larger percentage of Pakistanis spoke Bangla, Urdu was the bridging mechanism to bring the Muslims of the subcontinent together. On the one side, it is said that Nazimuddin simply read the contents of a speech that had been prepared for him by his staff, and that he did not have the time to screen the speech before it was delivered. On the other hand, Shahabuddin later questioned his brother about the Urdu item in his presentation, and why in fact he had decided to mention the language issue, given the known sensitivities of so many of his Bengali constituents. Nazimuddin's response was simple and straightforward. He said that he believed in the case for Urdu, that he was a Bengali who was comfortable with the Urdu language, and that he believed as Jinnah did (who did not speak chaste Urdu) that it was the only Muslim language that could unify an otherwise diverse and geographically separated Muslim nation.

But whatever Nazimuddin's convictions, the Prime Minister did not contemplate the extent to which his Urdu statement would precipitate an explosive response. True, he was not oblivious to the demonstrations denouncing Urdu that had rocked Dhaka following the transfer of power; indeed, he was the province's Chief Minister during those disturbances. But like his colleagues in western Pakistan, Nazimuddin saw the protestors as Hindu agitators and Indian sympathizers who were bent on undermining the new Muslim state. Although the Bengali language movement was led by a Muslim student, Nazimuddin believed that Shaikh Mujibur Rahman was either duped by, or in the pay of, Indian agents. As a non-speaker of Bangla and as a member of the most successful Muslim family in East Bengal, Nazimuddin had little association with the Bengali milieu. He had long shown indifference to the development of the Bengali literary tradition, and even Rabindranath Tagore's achievement in winning the Nobel prize for literature had not impressed him. By the same token, the work of Muslim Bengali poets failed to stir him—in major part, because he did not read their renderings. If he had been more sensitive to the Bengali oral tradition and the later development of Bengali literature, especially Bengali poetry, he would have been more aware of the yearnings of his provincial countrymen, but that was not his intention and it was not to be.

As Chief Minister in 1948, Nazimuddin had met with the leaders of the Bengali language movement, and he had agreed to a seven-point formula in which he assured the students that his government would do everything in its power to impress the federal authorities with the need to make Bengali coequal with Urdu. On that occasion, he spoke of the spontaneous nature of the language movement, noting that it emerged from the hearts of his countrymen and that 'the movement was not inspired by the enemies of the state' (*The Statesman*, 16 March 1948). But when Nazimuddin presented the compromise formula to the provincial legislature, the legislators ignored it and some even denounced it as unworthy of consideration. When the students learned that their work on behalf of the Bengali language had been ridiculed and cast aside they again took to the streets, and this time Nazimuddin condemned the demonstrators, arguing that they were using the language issue to destroy the country (*The Statesman*, 18 March 1948). These were the events that prompted Nazimuddin to make an emergency call to Karachi in which he pleaded with Jinnah to come to the province.

Jinnah answered Nazimuddin's call, and during a presentation at Dhaka University, the Quaid-i-Azam warned the students to beware of 'Fifth Columnists' who were injecting the 'poison of provincialism' into the public debate. It was then that he justified the adoption of Urdu as the national language, declaring that it was understood from one end of the country to the other, and that it best reflected Pakistan's Islamic culture (*The Statesman*, 25 March 1948). 'Make no mistake about it,' he concluded, 'there can be only one State language if the component parts of the State are to march forward in unison, and that, in my opinion, can only be Urdu' (*The Statesman*, 25 March 1948).

Following Jinnah's Dhaka visit, the language movement was largely neutralized by the arrest and incarceration or the bribing of its leaders. But in 1950, the Interim Report of the Basic Principles Committee contained a passage that again highlighted Urdu as the national language of Pakistan, and once again the Bengalis were sufficiently aroused to revive their cause. The subsequent withdrawing of the Interim Report again put the language movement on hold, that is, until Nazimuddin's return to East Bengal in 1952. Nazimuddin's speech on the Paltan Maidan had unleashed a fury of criticism, but his defence was weak and ineffectual. Arguing that he was merely presenting government policy, not his personal opinion, Nazimuddin's explanation only intensified the attack on himself and his administration.

Declaring they had lost all confidence in the Prime Minister, and determined to register their displeasure with central government policy, the Bengali language movement was reconstituted, and on 21 February 1952 a group calling itself the All-Party State Language Committee of Action took to the streets. Led by the recently formed Awami League party of Shaikh Mujibur Rahman, the demonstrators called a general strike that was aimed at paralysing the province and embarrassing the Nurul Amin government. The government retaliated by banning the publication of *The Pakistan*

Observer, an English daily that had championed the Bengali language issue. Section 144 of the Code of Criminal Procedure was also imposed, making it illegal to organize processions, demonstrations, and assemblies of more than five persons. The Language Committee, however, ignored the provincial government's order, and it called upon its followers to take the issue into the streets. Shopkeepers were induced to shutter their establishments, and vehicular traffic was curtailed. Because the Dhaka University students were at the centre of the demonstration, the police were ordered to take up stations around the campus while the Superintendent of Police, the District Magistrate, and the Vice-Chancellor of the University tried to address the angry students. The officials noted the unlawful character of the activity and they pleaded with the students to cease their actions and disperse. The students, however, were too aroused to listen to their appeal and, according to a pre-arranged plan, they proceeded to leave the university compound in order to carry their message to the city's inhabitants.

Once outside the university gates, a general free-for-all provoked brickbatting by the students and lathi charges by the police. What had been a swarm of students now escalated into a multitude, and the police were unable to prevent the young people from moving through the streets, attacking targets of opportunity as they rampaged their way through Dhaka's busier neighbourhoods. The police were forced to use tear gas and the crowd broke into segments, thus spreading the area of confrontation and conflict. By afternoon, numerous injuries were reported, including those to the District Magistrate, the Deputy Inspector-General of Police, the Superintendent of Police, and the Additional Superintendent of Police. With the demonstration now having degenerated into a riot, with thousands involved in the mêlée, and with the police numerically overwhelmed, the District Magistrate gave the order to the Superintendent of Police to open fire on the demonstrators. One student died immediately and three others succumbed to their wounds later in the hospital, but the rioting continued. The language movement had claimed its first martyrs, and with their bloodstained clothing held aloft, the crowd was urged to take their revenge. Only darkness ended the disturbances that day, but with the dawn the hostilities flared again. The pro-Muslim League English newspaper the *Morning News* was assaulted, its equipment was destroyed, and the building was set ablaze. When the fire brigade arrived, they were prevented from putting out the flames when their hose, drawing water from the nearby river, was cut in several places. Other installations were similarly attacked, and although the damage was minimized, the work of the city was paralysed.

That evening the provincial legislature unanimously adopted a resolution asking the central government to adopt Bengali as one of two national languages. But it was a gesture too little and too late and it did not end the mayhem. By this time a base element of society had seized the opportunity to loot and pillage, and now there was talk in the streets that the army would be called in to put an end to the turbulence. In fact, Nurul Amin was left with no other alternative. Having exhausted his own remedies, he deferred to the military and the army responded, restoring order soon after arriving on the scene.

Nurul Amin's government spread a broad net in identifying those it claimed had provoked the disturbances. The government arrested a number of high-placed individuals, including four members of the provincial legislature, as well as Abul Hashim, the former secretary of the Bengal Muslim League, and Hamidul Huq Choudhury, publisher of *The Observer*. They also moved into Dhaka University and arrested Dr P.C. Chakraverty, Head of the Department of International Relations. A number of other university lecturers were also incarcerated for alleged communist activities. Twenty-eight students were arrested in Salimullah Hall, a university hostel, while the entire university was ordered closed indefinitely.

The closing of the university and the scattering of the students to their homes all over the province meant that their narration of the riots would be repeated over and again, often with exaggerated embellishment. Where, in fact, four students had died in the rioting, the students would report that more than 200 had been slaughtered by the Muslim League government. The Nurul Amin administration was described as a despotism, and the energies of its opposition were directed at its elimination. The Bengali language movement had not only matured into a full-blown political issue; 21 February 1952 from then on would be known as 'Shaheed Day', the day of the Bengali martyrs. In time it would also become a focal point for Bengali nationalism and, ultimately, secession. More immediately, however, the mishandling of the language issue by the Muslim League government in East Bengal destroyed the party's provincial base and, not to be overlooked, Nazimuddin had been repudiated by his own people.

The Basic Principles Report Revisited

The Basic Principles Committee Interim Report was rejected by East Bengal because it did not give the province the representation its numbers demanded. On 4-5 November 1950 East Bengal convened its own constitutional convention which drafted still another document. Its guiding principles described a republican form of government with two autonomous regional administrations, one for East Bengal, the other for the combined provinces of western Pakistan. The Bengali version of a central parliament called for a body reflecting the country-wide distribution of the population, but its functions were relegated to foreign affairs, the printing of money, and national defence. The Karachi-based government, however, decided to ignore the Bengali initiative and, in so doing, provoked still more disturbances in the eastern province. Liaquat Ali Khan was compelled to visit the region, and it was after these meetings with Bengali leaders that he apparently had a change of heart. For the first time, Liaquat saw the sincerity in the Bengali argument, and decided that the original report was irreparably flawed. Liaquat focused his attention on the parity question, but by the time the second draft was published, Liaquat was dead and Nazimuddin had become Prime Minister. It thus fell to Nazimuddin to present the second BPC report to the Constituent Assembly.

This second report, made public on 22 December 1952, described a federal structure comprised of two parliamentary bodies, one a House of the Units and another a House of the

People. Both Houses were to function on the basis of parity, with East Bengal being granted half the seats in each Assembly, while the combined provinces of western Pakistan made up the other half. The House of the People was projected as another House of Commons, and hence, given greater notoriety and importance. The House of the Units, representing the different provinces, was considered a lesser body, and along with a Council of Ministers, it was made to answer to the House of the People. In the likelihood of a conflict between the two Houses, the report envisaged joint sittings and decisions based upon majority principles. All money bills, however, originated in the House of the People, and the House of the Units was envisaged more as a court of last resort, or deliberative institution, that could counter hasty or arbitrary legislative manoeuvres in the other body. The central feature of the second report, however, was the issue of East-West parity, and while the Bengalis were apparently ready to go along with the formula, now it was the Punjabis who demonstrated displeasure.

The second BPC report, therefore, was no more successful than the previous one, but this time it was the Punjabis who decided to convene a meeting and air their grievances. On 11 January 1953 a conference was held in Lahore that included high Punjabi government officials. The conferees wasted no time in condemning the parity formula, arguing that it overcompensated the Bengalis at the expense of Punjab. The Punjabis were agreeable to representation in the House of the People on the basis of population, but in the House of the Units, they argued, the institutions should be equally represented, i.e., one unit one vote. Moreover, they demanded the giving of equal powers to both Houses, neither having supremacy over the other.

Punjabi opposition to the second BPC report was sufficient to force Nazimuddin to again postpone the process of constitution-making. It is interesting to note that, despite Punjab's apparent defence of the provinces of western Pakistan, the North-West Frontier Province found no fault with the parity formula and appeared to fear its near rather than its distant neighbour. In effect, the NWFP did not want to confer inordinate powers on the Punjab, notably those that would allow it to enhance its role as the country's dominant province. Nazimuddin, however, was in no position to thwart Punjabi ambition, and rather than proceed with the implementation of the BPC recommendations, he decided to freeze the proceedings. Thus the country faced still more delays in drafting a constitution and, as the process was allowed to drag on without a resolution, constitution-making became the plaything of the provincialists, and the national ethos remained unreconciled. Moreover, not a single provincial leader showed the courage or the wisdom to break the impasse. The wrangle over the BPC findings merely intensified the rivalry between the provinces and left the nation deeply divided and uncertain as to its future.

Nazimuddin demonstrated by his inaction that he was unequal to the test of national leadership and, instead of bridging differences between the units, his behaviour imposed even heavier strains on the fragile nation. Pakistan may have been created as a homeland for the Muslims of the subcontinent, but it was already too clear that the theory of the nation-state and the reality of nationhood were seriously out of balance. Islam may have fuelled the Pakistan Movement, but Islam proved not to be the ingredient needed to unify disparate cultures, let alone assure the formation of a modern nation-state.

The Ahmedi Controversy

Islam requires total conformity to the tenets of faith, and ritual is a manifestation of that faith. Abiding conviction in the absoluteness of Islamic tradition is fundamental, and deviation from established doctrine cannot be casually tolerated. Islam requires of believers complete submission to an eternal and omnipresent God who influences the Muslim's every mannerism, expression, and deed. Islam, in the Indian setting, could not be more defined. Alongside the pantheistic complexities of Hinduism, Islam projected a revealed simplicity, a steadfastness of belief, a devotion to principle, and a resoluteness of will that ensured the purity of the religious experience into and through the twentieth century No two religious representations could be more distant from one another than Islam and Hinduism, and the history of the subcontinent bears testimony to the distance that separated the communities from one another. While political and strategic matters intruded on the relationship and, to some extent, encouraged a modicum of interaction between the communities prior to the arrival of the Europeans, it was not until the British imperial intrusion that some gains were made in modifying conventional mindsets. The importation to India of national and political secularism, the imposition of an Anglo-Saxon legal system, and the considerable effort that went into the fashioning of the colonial administrative structure, enlisted members from all the religious communities. Common responsibilities in many ways offset their otherwise acknowledged, but very personal, differences (Jennings, 1957).

But the British presence in India also highlighted the distinctiveness of Muslims and Hindus, and the British were not eager to disturb familiar lifestyles or tamper with avowed obligations. Thus, while the colonial authority was inclined to promote change, and it had been stated policy early in the nineteenth century to transform the native population into 'brown Englishmen', they were equally mindful of the need to respect time-worn practices. Christian missionaries mingled with the different communities, and some converts to Christianity were drawn from among the poorer Hindus, but programmes of serious proselytization were not government policy, and the British were genuinely tolerant of the beliefs of the vast majority. It is important to note that the British did not go to the subcontinent for the purpose of spreading their faith. Motivated to compete with rival imperial systems, their objective was initially commercial. But as time passed and more secure arrangements were deemed necessary, the British involved themselves in political and bureaucratic engineering, ultimately coming to believe that they had a divine mission to spread the genius, but not the substance, of western civilization.

The British presence and its role somewhere between the two major cultures of the subcontinent, however, acted as a catalyst in the fusing of European ideas with those long prevalent in the region. Where the Muslims were concerned, a major transformation occurred through the labours of Syed

Ahmad Khan and the Aligarh School he founded. Mohammad
Ali Jinnah, Liaquat Ali Khan, Ghulam Mohammad, Mushtaque
Ahmad Gurmani, Sardar Bahadur Khan, and Ayub Khan were
some of the graduates of that Anglo-Muslim university, and it
was there that each of them imbibed the training that
augmented their lives as Muslims of the Indian subcontinent.
The British-created schools and colleges also aided and
abetted this transformation, and the men who rose to
challenge colonial authority were the same ones who drew
so heavily from a reservoir of European-prompted learning.
The broadening of experience, the fashioning of cosmopolitan
views, the conceptualization of liberal constitutionalism and
democratic government, were largely the endproduct of a
British-nurtured experience (Faruki, 1974). Although the
Crown and its representatives in the subcontinent acted as
though the empire would endure through the ages, any
historic perspective would have forced the conclusion that
with the passage of time, the very introduction of alien
notions of self-government must perforce mean the
abandonment of empire.

But if the British concluded that the people of the
subcontinent had yielded their essential traditions for some
new hybrid order, they were tragically deceived. None of the
outward signs of co-operation and accommodation measured
up to intrinsic changes in the life-world of the region's
inhabitants. In fact, little change had actually occurred where
the different religious communities were involved. Gandhi's
appeal to Hindu experience, and Jinnah's oratory defining a
threat to Islam, captured the attention of their co-religionists,
and they became compelling features of their respective
campaigns. Moreover, the very character of those campaigns
denied the building of bridges, which both Gandhi and Jinnah
had said was their real objective. India's pre-independence
leaders, paradoxically, were compelled to follow, as well as
lead. In point of fact, the unchanging aspects of the human
condition in the subcontinent proved more durable than
anything that either the British could impose, or Gandhi and
Jinnah might innovate.

Words were important in the creation of Pakistan, but they
were wholly inadequate in building a nation from the

remnants of the British Indian Empire. Jinnah's appeal to faith, unity, and discipline, like his plea for inter-communal harmony and ethnic and tribal integration, did not even begin to modify the long pre-established attitudes, associations, or thinking of the millions that populated the Pakistan landscape. Jinnah implored his countrymen to follow his example, and although they appeared moved by his expression, they none the less preferred their familiar circumstances, and their actions were remarkably at variance with virtually everything he tried to teach. And if Jinnah was unsuccessful in changing conventional behaviour, his disciples were doomed to even greater failure. Nazimuddin's denouement came in just this form. A man of acknowledged piety, Nazimuddin consorted with the Muslim *ulema*, confided in them, and catered to their whims. Nazimuddin was not the man to reconcile the needs and aspirations of the multicultural state he led with the demands of the more orthodox members of his religious community.

Differences between Muslim Sunnis and Shias have been cited, but as deep as those differences are in Pakistan, they pale into relative insignificance in the juxtaposition of Sunni Muslims and the Ahmedis, who also consider themselves Muslims. The Ahmedis are the contemporary followers of the nineteenth-century personality, Mirza Ghulam Ahmad, and they accept Ghulam Ahmad as a prophet because they believe God revealed His eternal message through him. A Punjabi phenomenon, the Ahmedis, also known as Qadianis because Ghulam Mohammad's revelation came while he lived in Qadian, assails the fundamental Islamic belief that the Prophet Mohammad (PBUH) is the last or seal of the prophets and that after him there can be no other prophets.

Nazimuddin inherited a long-festering Ahmadi problem, made more critical with the declaration of the Objectives Resolution and the inclusion of members of the *ulema* in the committee responsible for drafting the nation's constitution. The provision that would bring all laws into conformity with Islamic principles was a key demand of the leaders of the different orthodox religious orders, especially *ulema* insistence that they be granted veto power in scrutinizing legislation believed to be repugnant to the teachings of Islam.

Reserved seats for women in the National Assembly and provincial legislatures were judged to be un-Islamic. The *ulema* also argued that Muslim ministers and legislators must be sworn into office by special Islamic oaths. Given such pressures, it was already assured that the Pakistani head of state would take such an oath. All political figures were obliged to live exemplary lives, and piety was judged a principal consideration in their right to wield power. Moreover, all government officials were to acknowledge that they enjoyed power only as a trust from God.

But perhaps the most controversial aspect of the *ulema* role in constitution-making was the demand made by the Board of Taalimat-i-Islamia that the Ahmadis be declared a non-Muslim minority and given separate representation and hence, separate constituencies. The issue had been debated among the Muslims of the subcontinent from the inception of the new sect. Prior to Pakistan's independence, the Ahmadi matter engaged theological questions, with the larger community generally concluding that the Ahmadis had attacked the basic principles of Islam, namely the finality of prophethood. Viewed as a rebellious and divisive element within the body of Islam, both clerical and lay figures raised their voices against it, none more vehemently than the poet Iqbal, who wrote: 'it is in the interest of this (Islamic) solidarity that Islam cannot tolerate any rebellious group within its fold' (quoted in Binder, 1961, p.273). But in spite of this struggle between the Ahmadi sect and the orthodox representatives of the faith, the British colonial authority had assured the Ahmadis that they would be free to express their religious beliefs, and nothing was done to discourage active Ahmadi proselytization.

Thus, under the protection of a British policy that denied interference in matters of faith, the Ahmadis thrived, and although their numbers were never great, their close-knit community stressed collective endeavour and encouraged self-discipline and, above all, education for its children along lines that allowed them to enter the mainstream of subcontinental life. Moreover, Ahmadi missionaries were active abroad, notably in sub-Saharan Africa. But the principal Ahmadi activity was associated with the subcontinent and, following Pakistan's independence, a good portion of the community, considering themselves Muslims, opted for the Muslim nation. Among this group was Chaudhri Zafrulla Khan, a Lahori graduate of Government College and, later, King's College in London. He was called to the bar at Lincoln's Inn, and returned to Pakistan to practise law in Sialkot and Lahore. In 1926 Zafrulla had been a member of the Punjab Legislative Council, was a delegate at the Round Table Conferences in London in 1930-2, and a member of the Joint Select Committee on Indian Constitutional Reforms. He was elected President of the All-India Muslim League in 1931, served as a member of the Viceroy's Executive Council, and as India's Agent-General in China in the early years of World War II. In 1942 he was named a judge of the Indian Federal Court and, just prior to the transfer of power, he acted as constitutional adviser to the Nawab of Bhopal.

When Pakistan gained independence, Zafrulla Khan opted for the new Muslim state, and Mohammad Ali Jinnah asked him to join the central cabinet as Pakistan's first Foreign Minister. It would be very difficult to find a personage of greater accomplishment· than Chaudhri Zafrulla Khan, but the fact that he was also an Ahmadi made him a lightning rod for criticism from the orthodox religious organizations, notably in Punjab. Jinnah was urged to drop him from the cabinet, but the Quaid-i-Azam was not one to yield to the complaints of the orthodox leaders, and he sustained his support for a friend and associate, always noting that he was the best person to serve Pakistan's foreign policy needs. Jinnah had suffered numerous personal attacks from the same quarters, especially during the struggle to achieve Pakistan. Each time he had deflected assaults on his behaviour, and now he defiantly defended his Foreign Minister. Jinnah's death, therefore, exposed the Ahmadis to new and even more intense criticism from the clerics, and again Zafrulla was made the principal, but not the only, target of their abuse.

A number of Ahmadis had risen to high rank in the Pakistan Army, but in 1948 an Ahmadi army officer was murdered when he innocently approached a meeting near his station in Quetta where speeches were being delivered on the subject of the seal of the Prophet (PBUH) (*khatm-i-*

nabuwat). With the blood of the officer a constant reminder of the perilous condition of the community, the Ahmadis demanded protection from the government, but these demands only added more fuel for those building the fire against the minority community. Moreover, police intelligence, particularly in Punjab, reported the intensification of the campaign against the Ahmadis and warned the government that, if allowed to go unchecked, it would bring 'disaster' to the country because law enforcement would collapse under the impact (Feldman, *A Constitution for Pakistan*, n.d.). The Daultana government ignored all such intelligence reports, however, and since the central government always deferred to the provincial leaders, they too did nothing. Even the British Deputy High Commissioner in Lahore worried about the calumny directed against the Ahmadis, and cited the blind eye of the government which had provided the purveyors of hatred and violence with seeming *carte blanche* to perpetrate their barbaric acts. Just slightly more than five years after the terrible bloodletting between Muslims and non-Muslims in Punjab, Muslims now enthusiastically targeted their own brethren. A principal nemesis of the Ahmadis was the Majlis-i-Ahrar-i-Islam, founded in 1931 by Muslim Punjabis as a political party opposed to the Muslim League. The Ahrars had a chequered background as supporters of the Congress and later, as agitators opposed to the Maharaja of Kashmir. The Ahrars opposed the Ahmadis not only for their unorthodox beliefs, but because the latter had joined the All-India Kashmir Committee which sought to restore peace to the valley following an Ahrar-inspired Srinagar riot in the 1930s. The Ahrars remained somewhat aligned with the Congress right until the independence of Pakistan, and in a public paper issued from New Delhi they had described Pakistan as '*palidistan*,' the 'land of the filthy'. Once Pakistan had been won, however, the Ahrars claimed support for Pakistan, but given their political weakness, organized themselves as a solely religious organization holding periodic *tabligh*, or preaching conferences.

It was in the course of this incarnation as a religious order that the always militant Ahrars began their vituperative campaign against the Ahmadis, centring their venomous attacks on Zafrulla Khan and Mian Iftikharuddin who, they argued, pursued un-Islamic beliefs. The Punjab Muslim League not only did not challenge the Ahrars where the Ahmadis were concerned, they readily formed an alliance with the violence-prone fundamentalists. Thus the Ahrars became active supporters of the Punjab Muslim League, and assisted the party in winning the 1951 provincial election by an overwhelming margin. But in spite of League victories at the polls, it was the Ahrars that made the notable gains. The Ahrars had demonstrated that they could harvest advantages in circumstances where the League needed its support. Moreover, League dependence on the Ahrars translated into duplicity when the Ahrar leadership ordered a bloody vendetta against the Ahmadis and the Daultana government did nothing to prevent it.

The riots that tore the Punjab apart began with the assault on the Ahmadi community, but because the authorities were not inclined to take the necessary counter-action, the disturbance intensified and spread until much of the province was engulfed in mindless destruction and killing.

Nazimuddin had inherited a situation that now deteriorated along a broad plane and in all regions of the country. His travels were arranged to address the nation's many problems, but their complexity and the interplay of the different actors and groups prevented him from achieving even token success. Black flags, symbols of extreme dissatisfaction, confronted him wherever he went, and in Lahore the fury of the malcontents was perhaps most evident. Both the secular authority of Mian Mumtaz Daultana and the many religious orders, including that of the Jamaat-i-Islami and the anarchy-prone Ahrars, had joined their legions to those of the orthodox *ulema*, and they all centred their attention, and notably their hatred, on the Ahmadis community. On returning to Karachi, Nazimuddin was confronted by a Muslim Parties Convention that demanded the immediate excommunication of the Ahmadis.

Nazimuddin acknowledged the need for governmental firmness, and he ordered the arrest of some of the more radical and violent members of the Karachi religious community. Daultana, however, was reluctant to imitate the Prime Minister's actions. Determined to deflect mounting opposition to his provincial government, Daultana avoided taking the timely action required to prevent a full assault on the Ahmadis community. In defence of his passivity in the face of provocation, the Chief Minister cited the popular character of the criticism against the Ahmadis, and, never one enamoured of the liberal notions of pluralism or free expression, he knowingly aided and abetted those bent on punishing the minority sect..

The Punjab riots targeting the Ahmadis began on 27 February 1953, sparked by the Ahrars and fully supported by Maulana Maudoodi and his Jamaat-i-Islami. With the most visible religious movements in the province forming the nucleus, a broad cross-section of Punjab society that ranged from distinguished members of the *ulema* to respected journalists, and from established politicians to rank demagogues with their retinues of squalor-based miscreants, joined in the assault on the Ahmadis community. When the agitators demonstrated their considerable strength, the Punjab government quickly yielded its authority and thereby emboldened the hatemongers, who now issued a set of public demands that would declare the Ahmadis to be a non-Muslim community, that would gain the immediate removal of Zafrulla Khan from his post as Foreign Minister, and that called upon the central and provincial governments to dismiss all high-ranking Ahmadis who were members of the civil-military apparatus. Forming themselves into a Committee of Action, they urged the Daultana and Nazimuddin governments to act with due haste or face the consequences of their hesitation.

Nazimuddin ordered the Karachi police to take the necessary steps to prevent disorder in the city. He expected the same from Daultana in Punjab. But whereas the Karachi disturbances were nipped in the bud, Daultana took virtually no preventive measures in Punjab. The protestors proceeded to intimidate shopkeepers, disrupt transport, and generally paralyse activity in Lahore and the surrounding towns and villages. Deaths at first were scattered, but as the mayhem spread and intensified, the killing and destruction of property quickly mounted. By the time the Daultana government realized what it had unleashed, it was too late to prevent the widespread anarchy that spread over the region.

On 6 March Daultana called for negotiations with the perpetrators of the disturbances, offering to bargain on the basis of their original demands. Daultana's words and behaviour betrayed his position alongside the protestors, and the later court of inquiry would single him out for condemnation, citing his duplicity, his perfidy, as well as his dishonesty (*Report of the Court of Inquiry into the Punjab Disturbances of 1953*, 1954). The central government could no longer wait for the Chief Minister to take the necessary action, and Nazimuddin ordered martial law throughout, Punjab, but only after conditions in the province had reached a critical stage.

Daultana's desultory behaviour forced Nazimuddin to return to Lahore, where he obtained the resignation of the Chief Minister, and with the adoption of stern measures, the arrest of many of the perpetrators of the disorder, and the banning of a number of religious-cum-political orders, including the Ahrars, calm was finally restored to the province, but Punjab and the Pakistani nation had suffered a grievous wound.

The Consequences of Inaction

Nazimuddin could not escape his personal responsibility in the disaster that overwhelmed Punjab. His hesitation in responding to police and intelligence reports, even when he knew Daultana was sympathetically disposed toward the anarchists, was attributed to his piety, his affinity for the *ulema*, and his personal opinion that the Ahmadis had deviated from the true teaching of Islam. Moreover, Nazimuddin, more than Liaquat, had insisted on the inclusion of the *ulema* in constitution-making, and hence he bore responsibility for their largely obstructionist role on the Basic Principles Committee. As head of government, Nazimuddin was associated with all the disadvantages stemming from the Punjab riots. The disturbance fractured the Punjabi economy at a time when the Korean War ground to a halt and the conditions that had driven East Bengal's economic boom evaporated. Taken together, the country's economy faced total collapse; foreign exchange was virtually impossible to generate, and productivity had stagnated. Repairing the damage to Punjab's infrastructure alone proved a costly venture that took years to complete. Restoring investor confidence, let alone stimulating it, was never successfully achieved. Faced with sustained political unrest, and with socio-religious issues unresolved, with constitution-making at a virtual standstill, and with the Muslim League a lifeless national entity, the central government never appeared more helpless. Moreover, the declaration of martial law in Punjab had energized the army, notably its high command led by General Ayub Khan, and together with the powerful members of the bureaucratic *nomanklatura*, they began to question the country's future if left in the hands of its overly ambitious, divisive, and indecisive Muslim League leaders.

Governor-General Ghulam Mohammad, in spite of his infirmities, could not be expected to ignore the circumstances which seemed to threaten the very existence of the state. Falling back on his own experience as a member of the colonial steel frame, he called upon Nazimuddin to strengthen his government by sacking Abdus Sattar Pirzada, his Food Minister, and Fazlur Rahman, his Commerce Minister. But this order to the Prime Minister was more a ploy than an effort to assist Nazimuddin in improving his hand. The Governor-General knew Nazimuddin would not fire his Bengali Commerce Minister. Already judged a pariah in East Bengal, Nazimuddin was a significant liability, and his failure to act more aggressively in Punjab only provided additional justification for his removal. Thus on 17 April 1953, when Nazimuddin hesitated in complying with the order to terminate his key ministers, Ghulam Mohammad, with encouragement from the army high command, and even though the Prime Minister appeared to retain the confidence of the Constituent Assembly, dismissed Nazimuddin and his entire cabinet.

An official announcement issued through the Chief Executive's office declared that the action had been necessitated by the breakdown of law and order and the resulting economic dislocation that had forced the country to the abyss. Approval for the Governor-General's decision was observed in the generally quiet public response to the news of the sacking. The delay in constitution-making, the orgy of blood and destruction that had coursed through Punjab, and the economic misery visited upon the nation appeared to call for a strong hand and stern measures; indeed, for a return to the benign authoritarianism of the colonial period.

Chapter 5

The Failure of Conventional Politics

The inability of the Muslim League to transform itself from a movement to a vibrant, unified, and coherent political party, as well as Jinnah's death so early in the formation of Pakistan, unleashed the divisive forces that, more than India, threatened the survival of the young nation (Suleri, 1962). The traumatic events experienced immediately following partition caused deep wounds in the country's delicate social fabric which the League could not heal. With the murder of Liaquat Ali Khan and the Punjab disturbances to remind the nation of its violent tendencies, there was little concern registered for Nazimuddin, or the sacking of his government. Moreover, up to this moment, Pakistan governments had performed their tasks under a temporary arrangement whose constitutional underpinnings were rooted in a colonial experience. The Muslim League not only ignored the normal processes of post-independence political life, it allowed those heretofore opposed to the Pakistan idea, namely the Muslim clerics, to intrude themselves into the nation's constitution-making activities. Ironically, it was these self-appointed protectors of the faith, and Maulana Maudoodi was a notable example, who, following the death of Quaid-i-Azam, tried to dictate the character, structure, and dimensions of the Pakistan political system.

Confronted by its own crisis of legitimacy, unable to discipline its chief representatives, deprived of national leaders who were prepared to make the tough choices, by 1953 the Muslim League found itself trapped between a colonial legacy and an ill-defined spiritual inheritance. Gone was the dream of Mohammad Ali Jinnah to construct a Muslim-dominant state guided by European expressions of liberal constitutionalism and motivated by eclectic and essentially secular appeals. Jinnah's vision of a modern state could not be imparted to a grossly illiterate population, nor could the Pakistani masses imagine a life different from the one they had always known. After independence, Jinnah found it almost impossible to represent the faceless millions, and even those relatively few sectors of the body politic that recognized his idiom were too consumed in defending privileged lifestyles to seriously contemplate adopting a message that they themselves had difficulty digesting.

People are products of their environment, and their life experience is a kaleidoscope of elements, all of which shape and mould their character and outlook. Differences abound in any given society, and the wonder of it all is that equilibrium is achieved between and among representations of humanity that are so much at variance. Harmonies of interest, however, are never automatically arrived at. There is nothing predetermined, nothing inevitable, in any configuration that draws together multitudes of expression for the purpose of forming a solidary community. Time, patience, a willingness to experiment, but above all, human ingenuity, a sense of collective purpose, the building of a civil society, and great expenditures of energy, are what give substance to the contemporary nation-state. The absence of any of these elements brings into question the viability and the *raison d'être* of the national entity.

Pakistan confronted this reality at the moment of its independence, but it was grasped by only a few of its principals. Thus, after the passing of the Quaid-i-Azam, the responsibility for guiding Pakistan fell largely to those with an awareness of cosmopolitanism, but who were, nevertheless, profoundly influenced by the colonial experience. Thus, too, the Muslim League was forced to yield its mandate and to allow a reconstituted steel frame of civil-military administrators to assume power. The nation's guardians paid homage to the memory of the Quaid-i-Azam, but they did not hesitate in deviating from his policies.

Ghulam Mohammad's intrusive manoeuvre in dissolving the Nazimuddin government changed more than the character of the debate; it also changed forever the Pakistan phenomenon. Ghulam Mohammad's action diverted the nation from its Jinnah-inspired course as a somewhat modified, quasi-European expression toward a more realistic representation of its political culture and history.

Pakistan was the indirect consequence of forces nurtured and accelerated by two world wars. American-conceived ideas of self-determination, consciously or subconsciously, provided the justification for that pursuit to which Jinnah committed his Muslim League. But the foibles inherent in the Pakistan phenomenon were better understood by the civil-military complex than by the political organization that Jinnah led. The League had been organized for one essential purpose, to force the Congress, and especially the British, to partition the subcontinent and in so doing, to establish Pakistan as an independent, sovereign state. The Muslim League accomplished that task but it was unprepared for the ensuing responsibility, that is, giving form and substance to what had been created. The years immediately following partition and up to the dissolution of the Nazimuddin government prove the validity of this argument. And Ghulam Mohammad's arbitrary seizure of power not only wrote an end to the Muslim League, it also pointed to a new beginning, based not on imported ideas but on experiences that were all too familiar to Pakistan's diverse population.

The Politics of Bureaucratics

Ghulam Mohammad's principal objective, and likewise the objective of his most important supporters, i.e., General Ayub Khan, Commander-in-Chief of the Pakistan Army, the Defence Secretary, Iskandar Mirza, and Chaudhri Mohammad Ali, Secretary-General of the administrative services, was the tempering of religious experience. Nazimuddin's piety was respected, but Pakistan's apolitical leaders believed that religion should not be confused with politics. Moreover, Islam was hardly under threat in a country where the vast majority of its inhabitants followed the Islamic *shari'a* in their daily lives. Religious conflict between Muslims was a dagger pointed at the heart of the nation, and the higher bureaucrats could not understand how a people who had sacrificed so much to establish a homeland could harm one another because they had disagreements on the interpretation of scripture. Pakistan's new leaders attributed sectarian conflict to the machinations of demagogues, pervasive ignorance, and the gullibility of the masses. Arguing that little had changed from the colonial period save that the British were no longer the watchmen, Ghulam Mohammad set a course which he said would accelerate constitution-making while minimizing the strains of the bargaining process. Ghulam Mohammad deferred to the experts, minimized the role of the politicians, and tried to isolate the clerics. Asserting that the country had had enough of demagogic displays, he stripped from the Cabinet the more controversial personalities.

Thus, along with Nazimuddin, Sardar Abdur Rab Nishtar, the Deputy Prime Minister and an ardent advocate of the Islamic state, was 'retired'. Fazlur Rahman, Abdus Sattar Pirzada, Mahmud Hussain, Azizuddin Ahmad, and Syed Khalilur Rahman were all terminated. Chaudhri Zafrulla Khan, it is important to note, retained his portfolio as Foreign Minister; he eventually became President of the United Nations General Assembly and later, Pakistan's Justice at the International Court. True to their commitment on the subject of experts, the new leaders brought A.K.Brohi, a most successful Karachi barrister, into the new Cabinet as Minister of Law, and Shoaib Qureshi, a long-time colleague of the Governor-General, was appointed Minister of Finance. Abdul Qaiyum Khan was shifted to Karachi from his post in Peshawar, and a less controversial and more pliable Sardar Abdur Rashid assumed the role of Chief Minister in the NWFP. A number of Nazimuddin's other cabinet fellows, with proven records of performance, retained their positions. Among this group were I.H. Qureshi, Mushtaque Ahmad Gurmani, Sardar Bahadur Khan, and most notably, Chaudhri Mohammad Ali. Qureshi, like Bahadur Khan and Gurmani, was an Aligarh graduate, and prior to partition had been the Dean at St. Stephens College in New Delhi. As Minister of Education, his interest lay outside the realm of politics, and hence his reappointment met the requirements laid down by the new leadership.

But more than rearranging the central government, Ghulam Mohammad's gambits altered the role of the Governor-General. No longer the impartial arbitrator, the office of the Governor-General towered over the role played by the Constituent Assembly. It also circumvented cabinet government, but only in theory. In actual fact, the Governor-General had always retained prerogatives that pre-empted the power of the legislature, and the Muslim League never seriously challenged the institution or its occupants. Nor had Nazimuddin's brief tenure as Governor-General weakened the character or limited the power of the office. Nazimuddin's personality and manner in no way diminished the majesty of Pakistan's viceregal tradition, which remained intact when he became Prime Minister. Moreover, the essentially uncontested action of Nazimuddin's successor in dismissing the government was vivid testimony to the Governor-General's awesome but self-perpetuating inherent powers.

But after assembling the reconstituted cabinet, the question that still required an answer was who would succeed Nazimuddin as Prime Minister and head the new government? That answer was not long in coming. Pakistan's ambassador to Washington, Mohammad Ali Bogra, was summoned home and sworn in as Pakistan's new Prime Minister. Bogra, a Bengali, appeared to satisfy the unstated requirement that the heads of state and government must come from different wings of the country. But Bogra was also an ambitious politician and administrator. He had served in the pre-partition Bengal Legislative Assembly, becoming Parliamentary Secretary to the Chief Minister of undivided Bengal. He was appointed ambassador to Burma after the transfer of power, became ambassador to Canada in 1949, and was finally made ambassador to the United States in 1951. His out-country experience, his administrative acumen, and his generally apolitical behaviour influenced Ghulam Mohammad to select him for the Prime Minister's post. Nor was it public knowledge at the time that Bogra had worked with General Ayub Khan and Defence Secretary Iskandar Mirza in approaching the United States government for military assistance. The Americans had only then inaugurated a new President, Dwight Eisenhower, and a new Vice-

President, Richard Nixon, both of whom were interested in pursuing a United States-Pakistan mutual security agreement. With one eye focused on the domestic condition and the other on the country's external needs, Pakistan's new leaders believed they had the perfect choice in Mohammad Ali Bogra.

The decision to draw closer to the United States was taken by Ghulam Mohammad, with support from Ayub and Mirza. Ghazanfar Ali Khan, from his post in Tehran, had arranged for Pakistan's leaders to visit the Soviet Union, and he urged a linkage with Moscow as a counter to the Indian threat. Ghulam Mohammad rejected that approach, however, arguing that Pakistan was not like India, and could not play one superpower off against the other (interview with Mahmud Hussain, 29 January 1975). The Governor-General insisted that Pakistan's lot lay in Washington's camp, and that a firm commitment to stand against international communism would not be lost on the Americans. Compared to the Soviets, whom he did not trust, he believed that the Americans offered more leverage in the country's tussle with India. Moreover, India had angered the United States by its repeated attacks on American foreign policy, and especially by New Delhi's condemnation of the United States' action in Korea.

Given Pakistani initiatives, but also aware of the Eisenhower administration's desire to construct a Middle East Defence Organization, Pakistani officials had met with Secretary of State John Foster Dulles and Joint Chiefs Chairman Admiral Arthur Radford, who long held the view that 'two men can sometimes learn more of each other's minds in two hours, face to face, than in years of correct correspondence' (McCullough, 1992, p. 801). Vice-President Nixon shared these sentiments. He had also developed a distaste for the Indians, whom he found far too sanctimonious and generally unapproachable. His private discussions with members of the Pakistani diplomatic corps and defence establishment, however, were another matter, and he strongly recommended a United States-Pakistan connection to President Eisenhower, not long after Bogra became Pakistan's new Prime Minister.

Bogra was expected to work with Ayub and Mirza in forging the security arrangements with the United States, while

Ghulam Mohammad, Chaudhri Mohammad Ali, and their bureaucratic colleagues were supposed to centre their attention on restoring popular confidence in government by tackling the difficult economic questions. A wheat deal was arranged with the United States, and the new leaders anticipated substantial American technical and economic assistance in an expanding relationship with Washington. And while the country's essential law and order needs were managed by the administrative services, the politicians were encouraged to accelerate the process of constitution-making.

Ghulam Mohammad, like the Quaid-i-Azam earlier, was the stage-master of all these activities. As such, he anticipated more than the usual co-operation from his colleagues. But in spite of the heightened expectations, it was obvious that the Governor-General was a very sick man, and that his mental state had been affected by his physical disability. Ghulam Mohammad had been a much respected public official but his health had continued to deteriorate, and coupled with the pressures of his office, his personality had undergone a significant metamorphosis. Always a hard taskmaster, Ghulam Mohammad became more demanding, far more impatient, and abusive with everyone around him. Moreover, he began to insist on blind obedience from his subordinates, found fault in their workways, and never hesitated in pre-empting the Prime Minister's prerogatives.

Ghulam Mohammad, however, was carefully monitored by Iskandar Mirza and Chaudhri Mohammad Ali, as well as Ayub Khan, and few of his actions were possible without their concurrence. And, in so far as all were in agreement on the course to be followed and each had his individual responsibilities, they seemed prepared to tolerate the mannerisms, antics, and vituperative remarks of the Governor-General. Moreover, Nazimuddin's removal had received positive notices, especially in East Bengal, where H.S. Suhrawardy had characterized the sacking of the government as 'forthright'. Now a leader of the Awami League opposition party, Suhrawardy urged the Governor-General to do the next best thing, that is, to dissolve the Constituent Assembly and organize a new body that he said would be better suited to constitution-making (*Morning News*, 15 June 1953). Suhrawardy repeated this thought several weeks later, intimating that the Assembly was comprised of Muslim Leaguers who no longer represented their constituents. Nazimuddin's attempt to continue as President of the Muslim League, and his refusal to include Bogra as a member of the party's Working Committee, illustrated Suhrawardy's point. Muslim League failures were mounting, and even though the party supposedly remained the organizing force in the central and provincial governments, it was all too obvious that its fortunes had waned and were about to disappear.

The East Bengal Elections

Of Pakistan's five provinces, only East Bengal had not held provincial elections by the end of 1953. In major part, the delay was the result of Muslim League weakness and the fear expressed by its provincial leaders that the party could suffer grievous losses if the polling were conducted. Opposition to Chief Minister Nurul Amin had mounted after Nazimuddin became Prime Minister, and the sustained rioting that followed his visit to the province had greatly undermined party discipline. Yusuf Ali Choudhury, a vital actor in the Pakistan Movement, developed irreconcilable differences with Nurul Amin and he publicly demanded the Chief Minister's resignation, lest 'the (Bengali) people perish and the Muslim League go to the dogs' (*Morning News*, 14 May 1953). Nurul Amin responded to Choudhury's demand by expelling him and other dissident members from the party, but this desperate action merely complicated the Chief Minister's administrative tasks. Moreover, the East Bengal legislature which had been elected in 1947, before the transfer of power, saw its term expire in 1951, but still the Chief Minister resisted calling elections. Furthermore, in 1952 the East Bengal legislature followed the Chief Minister's lead and extended the life of the body. It did so again in 1953, but this time it aroused such public indignation that the opposition was forced to raise its voice. Suhrawardy was among those to note that thirty of the 170 seats in the legislature were vacant, and that any further delay in holding elections would be cause for open rebellion.

Nurul Amin was finally persuaded to accept the inevitable, and, in the last weeks of 1953, the date for the East Bengal elections was set for 16 February 1954. Although there was little time to marshal their forces, the principal challenge to Muslim League power came from Maulana Bhashani and Surhawardy's Awami League and Fazlul Huq's Krishak Sramik Party. Fazlul Huq had resigned his central government post as Advocate-General in order to contest the elections in his native province, and his principal theme was that the Muslim League had 'sold out the interest of the Bengalis' (*Morning News*, 14 November 1953). Bhashani and Suhrawardy echoed a similar theme, and after evaluating their chances of defeating the Muslim League, the main opposition parties agreed to form a United Front. The sole purpose of the Front was to 'smash the oppressive Muslim League regime' (*Morning News*, 14 November 1953).

The United Front was formally announced by Maulana Bhashani and included the Awami League, the Krishak Sramik Party (a successor to the Krishak Proja Party), the Ganatantri Dal, the Nizam-i-Islam, and the Youth League. A marriage of convenience, the only issue unifying the diverse grouping of political organizations was their hatred for the Muslim League and their determination to destroy its role in the province. Moreover, no effort was made to paper over differences between the parties, or even the intra-party feuds that developed between personalities like Suhrawardy and Bhashani. Noticeably worried by the strength of the now unified opposition, the provincial government moved the election date from February to March, ostensibly to allow time for central government officials to visit the province. Prime Minister Bogra's appearance, however, did nothing for the Nurul Amin government, and his speeches warning the public that Pakistan would die if the Muslim League died fell on deaf ears. While Bogra sought to win Bengali favour by championing the language issue, Abdul Qaiyum Khan, who also visited the province, raised the communal issue, warning Muslim Bengalis that the Hindus in the opposition parties were out to subvert Pakistan. But it was too late for such tactics. The United Front opposition organized a 'Martyr's Day' to commemorate the anniversary of the language riots of 21 February 1952, and Bhashani led a procession of barefooted, bareheaded youth to the burial ground of the students killed on that day. A public meeting on the Paltan Maidan followed that solemn event, and with tens of thousands in attendance, the leaders of the United Front took turns in pillorying the Muslim League government of Nurul Amin.

Facing imminent defeat, the Muslim League leadership desperately despatched Fatima Jinnah, the sister of the Quaid-i-Azam, to Dhaka. Addressing some fifty thousand people on the Paltan Maidan, Miss Jinnah spoke of the 'poison' spreading through the body politic and warned that 'our hard-won independence' was at stake. 'Our future as Pakistanis,' she declared, was 'on the brink of disaster and our sacrifices on the verge of going in vain' (*Morning News*, 1 March 1954). In spite of a number of electrifying speeches, there was no saving the provincial Muslim League from a humiliating defeat. The performance of the East Bengal Muslim League had been something worse than miserable, and the numerous abuses of privilege and rampant corruption could not be erased by the impressive oratory, no matter how eloquent.

The people of East Bengal went to the polls for the first time on 8 March 1954; and by 12 March the last ballot had been cast. Governor's Rule was imposed in anticipation of a strong popular reaction to the results, but there were no cliffhangers in the election. When the tally was made official, the United Front was declared the winner. In fact, it had won so decisively that the Muslim League could barely retain ten of the 309 seats contested. The demolition of the East Bengal Muslim League all but eliminated its role in the province. No less important, it sent a signal to central Muslim League headquarters in Karachi that the party had not only lost its monopoly, it faced the stark reality of being defeated in the provinces of western Pakistan as well.

Crisis and Reaction in East Bengal

The Bengali members of the Constituent Assembly were pressurized to resign so that a new provincial government could appoint its own members to the constitution-making body. Prime Minister Bogra, however, argued that the East Bengal elections could not directly or by implication affect the character of the central government or central legislature.

The United Front response to Mohammad Ali was equally pointed. It was noted that every Muslim League member of the Constituent Assembly had been defeated, and that the Bengali voting public had demonstrated that they wanted nothing to do with a constitution conceived and drafted by Muslim Leaguers. But while this tug-of-war continued, East Bengal looked to the creation of a new government, and all indications pointed to Fazlul Huq being acknowledged as the new Chief Minister. Before he could assume his new responsibilities, however, labour unrest in the jute mills and paper-making factories south of Dhaka, suddenly degenerated into uncontrollable rioting.

The factories most affected were largely owned and managed by non-Bengalis, and it was widely believed that the riots were sparked by Bengali nationalists and radicals who were anxious to reap advantages from the recent elections. But although the actions of the more violent elements revealed considerable planning, no particular agent or group could be clearly identified as fomenting the disorder. The fact that factory machinery was spared, and that only the non-Bengali managerial class was targetted, raised a host of unanswered questions. Moreover, when the unrest spread to other manufacturing enterprises, and especially to the Adamjee Jute Mills and the Khulna Match Factory, the central authority in Karachi could not fail to notice the damage done to the nation's economy. East Pakistan had become the country's chief foreign exchange earner, and the labour disorder threatened to derail economic growth. If not resolved, festering labour problems would discourage foreign investment, and Pakistan had never been very high on the list of attractive locations for international entrepreneurial activity.

The violence in the province's industrial units coincided with the election results and happened well before Fazlul Huq's new government had been sworn in. When the new Chief Minister finally took charge of the administration on 4 April, he not only confronted widespread labour unrest and economic paralysis, he also had to contend with a United Front organization that had won the election but did not know how to manage the successful consequences. Fazlul

Huq could only enlist the services of members of his own
party in forming the cabinet, and in negotiations with
Suhrawardy, he baulked at the Awami Leaguer's demand for
a disproportionate number of ministerial positions in his new
government. Fazlul Huq also displayed his more conservative
temperament when he took issue with Maulana Bhashani's
radicalism and condemned the 'satanic and Godless'
behaviour within the Bengali student community. Indeed,
having achieved his coveted prize, Fazlul Huq seemed to
forget who it was that gave him the opportunity to govern the
province.

Appearing to ignore the divisions within his United Front,
and seemingly oblivious to the continuing labour unrest in
the province's key industries, the East Bengal Chief Minister
flew to Calcutta to be entertained by his Indian hosts. Already
an octogenarian, the old man returned to the scenes of his
earlier life and was overwhelmed by the experience and the
affectionate welcome. Speaking in Calcutta, in an unguarded
moment Fazlul Huq declared he did not believe in the
'political division of the country (India)'. Stating he was not
familiar with two new words—'Pakistan and Hindustan'—he
said the term 'India' was sufficient to describe both countries.
'No power in the world will be able to divide them' (the
people of the subcontinent) he was reported saying to his
Indian hosts.

Fazlul Huq's expressed sentiments may have been
appreciated in Calcutta, but they raised a storm of controversy
throughout Pakistan, and this was one problem the new Chief
Minister could not ignore. When challenged on his return to
Pakistan, Fazlul Huq defended his statements as being
general in nature and sentimental in content. He reminded
his critics that it was he who had moved the Lahore
Resolution in March 1940, that he remained loyal to Pakistan
and was dedicated to serving its people. But when his
explanation and plea failed to extinguish the fires that now
enveloped him, Huq became defiant and accused his enemies
of perverting his words. 'Pakistan has come to stay, and the
sovereignty and integrity of Pakistan will be defended by
myself and every true Pakistani,' he said (*Morning News*, 10
May 1954). These words would be repeated over and over,

but those who would find fault with the old man would not
relent in their attacks. Needing deeds as well as support to
back up his words, Fazlul Huq was forced to accept Awami
League demands for substantial power within the coalition
government. A number of cabinet seats were given to
Bhashani's party, but just as the cabinet controversy and the
many labour disorders seemed to be subsiding, and just when
the new government was being sworn into office, riots again
struck the Adamjee Jute Mills. Far more vicious than earlier,
upwards of six hundred people were reported to have died
in what was described as an inter-ethnic bloodletting. Unable
to restore calm to the region with the police constabulary, the
Pakistan Army was pressed into duty. Moreover, reports
reached Karachi indicating that provincial communists were
behind, and ultimately responsible for, the carnage.

Just a few days earlier, Pakistan and the United States had
entered into a Mutual Defence and Assistance Pact. The
April 19 agreement had been opposed by the Awami League,
the Ganatantri Dal, the Youth League, and the Communist
Party, and these new riots were believed to be the work of
Bengali subversives out to discredit the central government,
not the new Huq administration. The Dhaka-based *Mail*, a
small but nevertheless influential newspaper, in fact accused
the Awami League, and in particular Maulana Bhashani,
who was President of the Adamjee Jute Mills Mazdoor
(Workers) Union, of fomenting the disorder (23 May 1954).
Few believed that Fazlul Huq had instigated the rioting, but
the octogenarian also denounced those who would blame the
communists for the trouble. The Chief Minister claimed that
other elements were responsible for the province's trouble,
but he chose not to identify them.

Fazlul Huq's quixotic behaviour was well known in
Karachi, but Ghulam Mohammad none the less ordered him
to appear before the key officials of the central government.
Huq complied with the order, but his appearance and
answers to questions only heightened tensions between the
Bengali Chief Minister and his superiors. While in Karachi,
Fazlul Huq agreed to an interview by John Callahan, a
reporter for *The New York Times*. In that interview, Fazlul
Huq was quoted as desiring the independence of East Bengal.

He criticized the exclusion from high governmental positions of qualified Bengalis, and he ended by declaring that Bengalis would not be denied their freedom (23 May 1954).

The *Times* article appeared on 23 May and by 25 May the repercussions were felt from Pakistan to the United States and back. In Pakistan, Fazlul Huq's comments were described as a 'horror,' 'irresponsible,' and 'treasonous'. When the Chief Minister again tried to defend himself, only a few were willing to listen. Fazlul Huq said his words were simply part of the protracted autonomy debate and were not meant to question the integrity of Pakistan. This time, however, he would not be given a chance to make amends. Chaudhri Khaliquzzaman, the sitting Governor of East Bengal during this calamitous period, had his well-publicized weaknesses, and the central government decided that his kindly, gentle nature made him the wrong man to do a lion's job. The old Muslim Leaguer was recalled and Iskandar Mirza, the Defence Secretary, who was on holiday in Europe at the time of the central government deliberations, was ordered to return to Pakistan with all haste. Stopping briefly in Karachi for his orders, which were handed to him personally by Ghulam Mohammad, Mirza boarded his plane that very day, flew non-stop to Dhaka, and assumed his new duties as East Bengal's Governor and chief administrator.

Mirza had been educated at Elphinstone College in Bombay and upon joining the British Indian Army, he had been singled out for study at the Royal Military Academy, Sandhurst. He entered the Indian Political Department in 1926 after a brief stint in the forces, where he received recognition for his firmness and discipline in working with the tribes of the NWFP. Opting for Pakistan, he was named the country's first Defence Secretary and was made an honorary Major-General in the Pakistan Army. A favourite of Liaquat and Begum Liaquat Ali Khan, it was Mirza who recommended that Ayub Khan be made Pakistan's first Army Commander-in-Chief. Concerned with security matters throughout his professional life, Mirza straddled the civilian and uniformed members of the higher bureaucracy, and his assignment as Governor of East Bengal was a calculated action, aimed at depoliticizing what was perceived from Karachi to be a volatile situation.

Fears had mounted over the possibility of a Bengali secession, and Mirza's orders were to ensure the effectiveness of the police and civil-military bureaucracy in the province. The fact that the province had experienced its first election and had displayed a preference for leftist programmes and leaders was distracting to a central government which had just entered into a pact with the United States on the basis of its anti-communist credentials.

Mirza's initial action, therefore, was to impose Governor's Rule throughout the province, thereby suspending all political activity. The Governor-General's office in Karachi justified the action, declaring, 'the administration of East Pakistan had virtually broken down and the Fazlul Huq ministry was not able to secure the lives and properties of the people of the province' (*Morning News*, 31 May 1954). The imposition of Governor's Rule nullified East Bengal's election and suspended the work of its government. During Mirza's administration, the province would be governed with an iron hand, and draconian measures were used to isolate those who were perceived as harbouring separatist tendencies. Only the most loyal Muslim Leaguers in the province drew satisfaction from the actions of the central government. The vast majority of Bengalis was appalled and angry that the Ghulam Mohammad government had used the pretext of labour unrest and the behaviour of an errant old politician to scuttle their collective expression. Pakistan had passed from crisis to crisis, East Bengal had become the main theatre testing Pakistan's territorial integrity, but with each dramatic event, the fissures dividing the body politic grew deeper and more menacing. Politically speaking, the country was allowed to drift in a realm of uncertainty as the attentive public waited for the civil-military leaders to make their next move.

The Constituent Assembly Crisis

In spite of the disorder and resulting conflict between rival groups, the use of extraordinary powers by the Governor-General had elevated concerns in the country, and especially among those politicians who had so much to lose if the vice-regal tradition prevailed over their purported democratic projections. However, to see this clash between the politicians and that higher bureaucracy as one between the advocates of democracy on the one side and authoritarianism on the other, only confuses the issues. The politicians were less than gifted democrats, and the bureaucrats were something more than traditional autocrats. Viceregalism was written into every programme granting self-government to the people of the subcontinent. Never was the grant of authority so circumscribed as to rule out the intrusion of the Viceroy and his subordinate Governors in the everyday political life of the colony.

When Pakistan became independent, the power of the Viceroy was not lost on his successor, and the relationship between the head of state and the head of government remained much as it was before the transfer of power. The head of state reserved the right, under Section 92A of the Government of India Act 1935, to impose Governor's Rule, i.e., to interfere in the provinces, if, in his judgment, the security and general well-being of the nation were threatened. Moreover, the India Independence Act had hardly altered the Government of India Act of 1935, and it was that 'constitution' under which Pakistan organized its governmental life during the long period of constitution-making. Pakistan's dominion status within the Commonwealth also sustained ties to the British monarch, and after Nazimuddin's dismissal, the erstwhile Prime Minister appealed to the Commonwealth Relations Office for a judgment on the Governor-General's action. Section 10 of the Government of India Act of 1935 permitted the Governor-General, in acknowledged circumstances, to dismiss a sitting Prime Minister without the advice or consent of the Council of Ministers. In the Nazimuddin case, that emergency power was sustained when the Queen preferred not to answer Nazimuddin's call.

Noting their inability to reverse Ghulam Mohammad's decision, the members of the Constituent Assembly, who considered their body sovereign, searched for answers to very perplexing questions and, most importantly, they looked for ways to ensure their own survival. How could sovereign powers be lodged in two such different institutions as the Constituent Assembly and the Governor-General? Indeed, how could sovereignty be divided without denying it altogether? Crucially, if the Governor-General could use his special prerogatives to pre-empt and supersede the powers conferred on the central and provincial governments, how could the Constituent Assembly protect itself against the arbitrary use of those powers? Moreover, if the Constituent Assembly was a law-making institution and sovereign, did it not possess the necessary power to augment, and possibly eliminate, the powers conferred upon the Governor-General?

The Constituent Assembly confronted this singular dilemma at a late hour. The Governor-General's extraordinary powers had been used and not found illegal. Had the Constituent Assembly acted immediately following the transfer of power, when Jinnah presided as Governor-General, their task might have been different. Coming as it did after Jinnah's approved and enhanced authoritative actions, and now in the wake of the Nazimuddin ouster, as well as the imposition of Governor's Rule in East Bengal, whatever the Constituent Assembly expected to accomplish, it was destined to be a very feeble effort. In fact, it was made more feeble by the elections in the eastern province that had raised important questions concerning the bona fides of the Muslim League members who lost their seats in the East Bengal provincial legislature. The virtual cancellation of East Bengal's election results would appear to have given the East Bengal Muslim League members a new lease on their offices in the Constituent Assembly; but the paradox in this equation was that the power that had extended their individual tenure in the Assembly was the same power they opposed when it threatened to overwhelm the parliamentary institution.

In what was assumed to be a race against time, the Constituent Assembly amended the Government of India Act 1935 by inserting a new Section, 223A, that conferred upon the High Court the power to issue prerogative writs. The Constituent Assembly took a more significant step some weeks later, when it repealed the Public and Representative Offices (Disqualification) Act (PRODA). PRODA had given the Governor-General exceptional powers to investigate the activities of members of the government and, if deemed necessary, to prevent persons from holding public office who were accused of maladministration or corruption. These special powers were performed outside the law courts, and could be initiated by anyone lodging a complaint with the Governor-General, or as the case may be, with a provincial Governor, who could order an inquiry by the High Court judges. If the juridical inquiry found grounds for the complaint, the Governor-General or Governor could prevent the charged politician from holding public office for up to nine years. M.A.Khuhro, Kazi Fazlullah, Ghulam Nabi Pathan, and Hamidul Huq Choudhury had already suffered disqualifications under the PRODA rules.

Moreover, following the imposition of Governor's Rule in East Bengal, Chaudhri Mohammad Ali had introduced a bill in the Constituent Assembly that would have dissolved the existing provinces in western Pakistan, and in fact, would have merged them into a single province. Clearly a manoeuvre aimed at giving the Punjab relative balance *vis-a-vis* East Bengal, the 'One Unit' scheme was the work of Pakistan's higher bureaucrats, who argued that the move would not only make constitution-making easier, it would also reduce ethnic tensions in the country. It was with this structural adjustment in view that Chaudhri Mohammad Ali called for significant changes in the Basic Principles Report. The One Unit scheme had the enthusiastic support of the Governor-General, and it was his task to pressurize endorsements from Sindh's Pirzada and the Frontier's Qaiyum Khan. When the two provincial leaders hesitated in lending their support to a policy that would eliminate their provinces and political identities, and bestow greater powers on the Punjab, Ghulam Mohammad threatened to PRODA them out of the political game. Their eventual public support of the One Unit scheme was ample proof that, in the hands of Ghulam Mohammad, PRODA was an effective weapon.

PRODA was also a ready device for Muslim League leaders who wished to punish renegades in their ranks. And although the Constituent Assembly repealed the Act on 20 September 1954, the deliberative body had attached a proviso to their bill stating that its cancellation did not interrupt tribunal proceedings which had commenced before September 1. The sitting members of the Assembly demonstrated that they were not opposed to PRODA, only to Ghulam Mohammad's capacity to use it. Indeed, on 20 October Ghulam Mohammad used the Muslim League's repeal of PRODA to reduce the sentences meted out to some of the party's chief detractors.

As the cat and mouse game continued, the Constituent Assembly moved to curtail the Governor-General's special powers. Having amended the 1935 Act in order to guarantee that an arbitrary dismissal could be challenged by a writ petition in the courts, and no less important, that no inquiry questioning the actions of those holding public office could be made, the Assembly members seemed assured of their sovereign status. Thus, on the day following the repeal of PRODA, a bill was introduced in the Assembly to amend Section 10 of the Government of India Act 1935. This time the Constituent Assembly took direct aim at the emergency powers of the Governor-General, notably his right to dismiss a sitting Prime Minister. Prime Minister Mohammad Ali had been appealed to by a variety of influential politicians, all of whom wanted to see the Governor-General's power circumscribed. Led by Fazlur Rahman, who had scores to settle with Ghulam Mohammad, the Assembly passed the measure within a few hours, and without revealing its intentions to the ailing Governor-General, who was resting in the Abbotabad hill station north of Rawalpindi, more than 800 miles from Karachi. In fact, the Act was published in the Gazette on the very day it passed the legislature, thereby giving it the firmness of law at the moment of passage.

Like the Governor-General, the public had not been informed prior to this parliamentary manoeuvre, and the intelligentsia seemed more disturbed by the antics of the Constituent Assembly than the actions of the Governor-General. The constitution-making body had committed too many mistakes, had dashed too many hopes, had threatened too many sectors of society, to anticipate a positive response from the people. Not unfamiliar with the viceregal tradition, the attentive public was not totally opposed to the authoritative actions of the Governor-General. Indeed, there was considerable respect for the office of the Governor-General in the autumn of 1954, and Nazimuddin's dismissal had not caused significant public reaction. The imposition of

Governor's Rule in East Bengal also received more than the anticipated popular support, and many of the country's newspapers had editorialized in favour of dissolving a no longer representative Constituent Assembly. The assault on the powers of the Governor-General, therefore, left popular sentiments confused and muddled, but there was none the less little, if any, confidence in the Constituent Assembly. Moreover, the politicians had promoted their personal needs to excess, and in the absence of the Governor-General's extraordinary powers, the attentive public doubted they could be trusted with the country's future.

Ghulam Mohammad, however, was not one to weigh Pakistani public opinion. More concerned with managing the country, the Governor-General had nothing but contempt for most of the members of the Constituent Assembly, and especially for Bengali provincialists and Punjabi fundamentalists. Less than impressed with Bengali politicians, whom he had come to loathe, he was even more contemptuous of Muslim clerics dabbling in politics. Convinced that both groups were divisive, uninformed, and ill-prepared for the challenges of statehood, he was determined to neutralize their political activities. Moreover, the conflict between and within the two groups had divided the Constituent Assembly, had caused repeated delays in constitution-making, and had brought the nation to the brink of disaster. Pakistan had been deeply wounded by the Punjab riots and the East Bengal labour disorder of 1953-4, and Ghulam Mohammad was convinced that only the country's steel frame of civil-military administrators could save the nation. Thus, with Gurmani acting as his chief confidant, Ghulam Mohammad decided that the Constituent Assembly was not just a threat to his powers, but to the nation at large. Pakistan's survival as a modern community, once threatened by external forces, he now believed was confronted by domestic forces that were far more dangerous.

Normally, the Rules of Procedure of the Constituent Assembly required fifteen days notice for the introduction of a bill, and it was standard procedure to circulate copies of the legislation among the members at least three days prior to its presentation. Acting in haste, the Constituent Assembly had ignored all procedures, and hence had failed to give proper notice. Learning that Ghulam Mohammad was aware of the cabal and was returning to Karachi from Abbotabad, the bill was hastily proposed at 9 a.m. and approved fifteen minutes later, without any indication of a debate. The Karachi-based Muslim Leaguer, Mohammad Hashim Gazder, led the abbreviated floor fight, arguing that the bill was necessary for the 'advancement of democratic conditions' (*Morning News*, 22 September 1954). The amendment divested the Governor-General of his powers to dismiss the Council of Ministers, and to claim that they held office at his pleasure. It also meant that the government was solely responsible to the Constituent Assembly. Moreover, if this 'constitutional *coup*' were allowed to stand, the country's most powerful institutions, including the Armed Forces and the civil services, would come under the control of a constitution-making body dominated by Muslim Leaguers whose legal bona fides, in light of the Bengal elections, were questionable at best.

Nevertheless, on the day following the extraordinary action 'eliminating' the power of the Governor-General, Prime Minister Mohammad Ali declared that he was in full agreement with the Constituent Assembly action, and that the limitations on the powers of the head of state would be written into the new constitution which, he said, was being rushed to completion. Declaring that Pakistan would become a republic on 25 December 1954, when the constitution would be formally presented to the nation, Bogra called upon the people to celebrate the moment. On that very day he left the country for the United States, firm in the belief that he was secure in his post and that the country had, at long last, broken free of its colonial legacy.

It is said that Ghulam Mohammad encouraged the Prime Minister to make the transatlantic journey. Bogra was intent on placing his children in school in England, a stopover both going and returning to Pakistan. The Prime Minister required little coaxing to make this trip. Bogra's advisors, however, notably Fazlur Rahman, struggled to get him to postpone his journey, citing the delicate situation in the country and the anger of the Governor-General who, they anticipated, would not yield his powers quietly. In addition, they cited Suhrawardy's championing of the dissolution argument, and the forces in East Pakistan that were merging with those in West Pakistan, notably with Dr Khan Sahib, whose long association with Iskandar Mirza was rooted in the pre-colonial era, when the latter was a political agent on the north-west frontier. Bogra was also informed that General Ayub Khan, Iskandar Mirza, and Chaudhri Mohammad Ali, all very powerful actors on the Pakistan scene, would side with Ghulam Mohammad in any determined showdown. Bogra, however, was emboldened by the ease with which the Constituent Assembly had moved and passed the restrictive amendments, and now, confident that he could deliver a constitution to the country on a date certain, he refused to believe that a cabal, no matter how constructed, could succeed.

Meanwhile, Iskandar Mirza had gone to London to meet with M.A.H. Ispahani, who had been transferred from his post in Washington and now served as Pakistan's High Commissioner in the United Kingdom. Ispahani met Mirza in his hotel room, and after discussing prevailing conditions in Pakistan, they left for the airport to receive Prime Minister Mohammad Ali Bogra, who was returning from his sojourn in the United States. Joined by Chaudhri Mohammad Ali, the two men met Bogra as he deplaned. The Prime Minister was in an agitated state on approaching his welcoming party, having received messages *en route* that the Karachi scene was unsettled and that a crisis of major proportions threatened the stability of his government. Bogra asked Mirza if he had heard that Ghulam Mohammad was about to declare martial law. Mirza's response was negative. But soon thereafter, General Mohammad Ayub Khan, somewhat to Bogra's surprise, also arrived in London after his meetings in the United States.

Ayub joined the impromptu conference, and the Prime Minister realized that the assembly of Pakistan's dominant personalities was hardly an unplanned event. It was Ayub who informed the others that the Governor-General had summoned him back to Pakistan and that Ghulam Mohammad had demanded an army takeover. On learning this, Mirza pleaded with Ayub not to follow Ghulam Mohammad's orders, arguing that he was a very sick man and no longer in control of his faculties. Mirza warned Ayub that any action on his part would be detrimental to himself as well as to the nation. Instead, he insisted that they should all return to Karachi to see what could be done to reconcile the principal rivals and set a proper course for the country. All seemed to agree that only their concerted and collective action could prevent a worsening of the situation. Moving with great haste, Mirza tried to secure a Royal Air Force Canberra that could take the party directly to Karachi. Failing in that effort, another plane was made available by British authorities and the entire entourage, including Ispahani, who had not even informed his wife of his departure, flew to Karachi, where they found themselves in a tense environment.

Bogra asked General Ayub and Mirza for special police protection, sensing an assault on his person. The Prime Minister understood that he had become the principal target of a host of enemies. General Musa, Ayub's chief of staff, was instructed to assist Bogra. According to Mirza, all law and order had broken down in Karachi. 'The whole place was like a madhouse' (interview with Iskandar Mirza by M.A.H. Ispahani, 23 September 1967 in London). Ispahani then escorted Bogra to the Governor-General's residence, while Mirza and Ayub took another vehicle that followed a different route and brought them to the house earlier. Finding Chaudhri Mohammad Ali already in the residence, the three men approached the Governor-General, who was wrapped in a white sheet and gesticulating wildly to the visitors as he lay rolling on the floor of his bedroom. The entourage concluded that Ghulam Mohammad was not in control of his full senses, and they sought to placate him by appealing to his cries of injury. Ghulam Mohammad's response was a tirade against the Prime Minister, in which he claimed that Bogra had betrayed him and that he wanted him out of office and out of the country. Iskandar Mirza, in time, convinced the Governor-General that it would be tactically wrong to sack the Prime Minister, but that it was appropriate to dissolve the cabinet and form another of his choosing.

After protracted but highly animated talks, decisions were taken to dissolve the Constituent Assembly and terminate the Bogra government. Chaudhri Mohammad Ali was given the responsibility of drafting the edict that explained and justified the manoeuvre. Ghulam Mohammad listed the people he wanted in the new cabinet, i.e., Ayub Khan, Mirza, Ispahani, Gurmani, and Chaudhri Mohammad Ali. Mirza and the others were told to add to this list any persons whom they judged suitable for the new cabinet, and given that responsibility, they argued for retaining Bogra until the crisis had passed. Despite Ghulam Mohammad's vehement objections, Mirza prevailed, and it was obvious to all the major actors in this scenario that Iskandar Mirza would soon become Governor-General.

Thus, on 24 October 1954, the Constituent Assembly was dissolved and the Bogra cabinet gave way to one now dominated by a non-Muslim League, civil-military complex. Justification for the drastic action was found in the argument that the Assembly had 'lost the confidence of the Pakistani nation'. The record, however, reveals that the Constituent Assembly had finally resolved most of its constitution-making problems and that the Prime Minister anticipated presenting the constitution to the nation in December. Ignoring these developments, Ghulam Mohammad, but in essence Iskandar Mirza, supported by his like-minded colleagues in the army and civil bureaucracy, opted for what Dr Khan Sahib had described as 'controlled democracy'. Indeed, that term had also been used by Iskandar Mirza, and which of the two men originated the phrase proved impossible to trace.

Nevertheless, Pakistan's dominant personalities had concluded that the Pakistani nation wanted strong rulers, not weak democracy, but they also realized that they needed to give legitimacy to their policies, and that their plans could not be executed without the legal sanctions that could only be provided by a constitutional structure. They therefore avoided declaring martial law and gave both the country and the world the impression that a political crisis was being resolved with proper legal and political remedies. Calling for the convening of a second Constituent Assembly, their intentions were to give Pakistan a constitution, but it had to be one that allowed the guardians of the Pakistani experience to preserve their protective role.

It was Ghulam Mohammad who announced that the country's constitutional machinery had broken down, that the people no longer had confidence in the Constituent Assembly or the Bogra government, and that a temporary state of emergency was required to stabilize conditions before more serious fissures opened in the body politic. Bogra, however, remained on as Prime Minister, and during the transition period that followed, elections would be held for a second Constituent Assembly. Bogra was surrounded by powerful figures and, fully intimidated, he was stripped of his powers. Mirza assumed the Interior portfolio and relinquished his duties in East Bengal. General Ayub took control of the Defence Ministry, and Dr Khan Sahib became the first individual from a non-Muslim League party to hold a cabinet position. Moreover, in the absence of a formal legislature, the new cabinet became an extension of the executive office of the Governor-General, a precursor of events that would lead to the scrapping of the parliamentary system and its replacement by a centralized, presidential power structure. Although hardly a month had passed since the Muslim Leaguers in the Constituent Assembly believed they had terminated Pakistan's viceregal tradition, the events of late October revealed that it was they who had outlived their importance.

The 'Cabinet of Talents' swelled to include Chaudhri Mohammad Ali and the Awami League leader, H.S. Suhrawardy. The latter assumed the responsibilities of Law Minister, a post he retained for a relatively brief period. But nothing could conceal the take-over of the government by men with strong convictions, men who were as wedded to the notion of authoritative government as they were to the survival of Pakistan. In fact, the two issues were so intertwined that they believed the one was impossible without the other. The many divisions within the country, the lack of civility in the resolution of secular-religious issues, the increasing demand but repeated failure to achieve economic gains, seemed to rule out the kind of competitive politics that had sapped the energy of the nation and now threatened its dissolution. Moreover, Pakistan had become a party in the Cold War, had chosen the United States as its most important ally, and had openly challenged the Soviet Union. Even Suhrawardy urged his party to accept the United States-Pakistan security pact, which he now proclaimed was a necessary instrument in the worldwide struggle against international communism.

The Muslim League would continue to speak for the nation in the period ahead, but it was a Muslim League only in name, and far different from the one receiving the transfer of power. The Muslim League had failed to satisfy the basic needs of a political party. A movement, it never developed the coherency of a political organization. Its demise was foreseen in the elections in East Bengal, but it was its contest with the country's viceregal tradition that ended its claim to represent Pakistan. Focusing its struggle on the personality of Ghulam Mohammad, the Muslim League tampered with an institution far more important than the then holder of that office, and certainly more significant than itself. The Muslim League demise wrote an end to a singular chapter in Pakistan's political history, but more than that, its failure to realize the promise of independence influenced the course Pakistan would follow through all the decades of the twentieth century.

Crisis Government and Constitution-Making

The Muslim League took their dispute with the Governor-General into the Chief Court of Sindh, where Maulvi Tamizuddin Khan, Speaker of the Constituent Assembly and a quietly-spoken, erudite Bengali, argued that the Governor-General's action was 'unconstitutional, illegal, *ultra vires*, without jurisdiction, inoperative and void' (cited in Choudhury, 1959, p. 148). Tamizuddin called upon the court to issue a writ of mandamus that would restrain the government from interfering with the functions of the Assembly, and for a writ of *suo warranto* that would enable the court to determine if the Governor-General had acted under the law in assembling a new cabinet. The Sindh Court ruled quickly on the two petitions, arguing in favour of the plaintiff and asserting that the Governor-General had no power to dissolve the Constituent Assembly because it was sovereign and beyond the scope of his jurisdiction. Only a two-thirds majority of the Constituent Assembly could call for its dissolution, in the reasoning of the court. Furthermore, the Crown was no longer empowered to terminate the Constituent Assembly, and the Governor-General, whose power stemmed from the Crown, could not be deemed to possess power not granted to the monarch.

Given this ruling, the government appealed to the Federal Court, which also acted with haste in rendering its decision. In a four to one vote, the Federal Court reversed the rulings of the Sindh Court, citing modified Section 223A of the 1935 Government of India Act, which had not yet received the necessary assent of the Governor-General and hence was not law. The substance of the ruling meant that the Sindh court could not issue the writs requested by the Constituent Assembly through its Speaker. The Federal Court stated it would not examine the legality of the dissolution order, and allowed its decision to rest on the question of the Governor-General's assent to an act of the legislature.

While the Federal Court had demonstrated a lack of will in challenging the viceregal tradition, its action also brought into question most of the bills passed by the Constituent Assembly, which had also acted as the national legislature since the country's independence. No one in the judiciary, however, was prepared to deny the legality of the approximately forty-six Acts which were now an intrinsic segment of the country's statutory system. With the courts paralysed by the constitutional struggle, Ghulam Mohammad promulgated the Emergency Powers Ordinance IX of 1955, in which the Governor-General assumed responsibility for the framing of the constitution, for the creation of the One Unit of West Pakistan, for the validation of all laws currently in force, for the authentication of the national budget, and for the renaming of East Bengal as East Pakistan.

The declared state of emergency provided the cover for these extraordinary executive measures but the Federal Court, chastened by its earlier non-ruling, on 13 April 1955 acted more forcefully in Usif Patel v. the Crown, when it declared that the Governor-General had neither the right nor the power to rule the country by ordinance and executive decree. Constitutional questions, they argued, could only be answered in the Constituent Assembly. Speaking for the Law Ministry, Suhrawardy acknowledged that the country faced its gravest constitutional crisis, because the Usif Patel decision implied that none of the country's institutions possessed legal status, and that included the courts, the provincial legislatures, and indeed, even the administrative system. Confronting a country-wide breakdown of government, the Governor-General was advised by his colleagues to act decisively. His response was the summoning of a 'Constituent Convention', and the Governor-General called on the Federal Court to sanction the action and to establish the interim steps needed to validate the laws in force which, it claimed, the Governor-General could not do. The ball was now in the Federal Court's hands and the justices could no longer escape their responsibility in reconciling the dissolution of one Constituent Assembly with the formation of still another.

The Federal Court acknowledged the chaos into which the nation had been plunged and, carefully weighing the possibilities, it concluded that going back to the status quo ante would further complicate matters and undoubtedly force the army to intervene in the country's political life. On 10 May 1955 the Court finally made its definitive statement on the dissolution, arguing that the Governor-General possessed the power to dissolve the Constituent Assembly, and that he was within the prerogatives of the office when he called for a Constituent Convention. It followed from these rulings that the Governor-General had the power to retrospectively validate the laws in force and that this task was accomplished under the terms of the Emergency Powers Ordinance. The Federal Court's ruling put an end to the immediate constitutional crisis, but it also set the scene for others to follow.

The 'Cabinet of Talents' assembled by Ghulam Mohammad and Iskandar Mirza was denied the opportunity to give Pakistan a constitution, but it nevertheless had the power to establish the Constituent Convention, which convened in Karachi on 10 May 1955. Operating on the basis of parity, East Bengal received thirty of the sixty seats, with the West Pakistan units dividing the remaining thirty among them.

The Punjab was awarded sixteen, the NWFP three, the tribal areas two, Sindh four, and Balochistan, the Frontier states, the Khairpur states, Bahawalpur state, and Karachi one each. Election to the second Constituent Assembly followed the same procedures adopted in creating the first one, i.e., by proportional representation with a single transferable vote. Later, the Governor-General expanded the Assembly to eighty members and declared it would function as a federal legislature and be guided by the same provisions of the India Independence Act that had instructed its predecessor. All the provinces received added representation, but the parity principle remained; in effect, East Bengal now had forty members in the body and the Punjab count rose to twenty-one. East Bengal also regained control of its parliamentary process during this period, and that act gained the support of the non-Muslim League Bengali politicians, who now hailed the second Constituent Assembly as a welcome successor to the first one.

The first Constituent Assembly had been transformed into a relic of history and the new constitution-making body, comprised of a variety of political orders, reflected the changes wrought in Pakistan's political life since the grant of independence. After the Federal Court ordered that the Constituent Convention be renamed the Constituent Assembly; that the Governor-General's power to dissolve the Assembly could only stem from the India Independence Act; that the representation granted the tribal areas and states must be determined by the Constituent Assembly, not the Governor-General; and that the Governor-General could not appoint members to the Assembly, it was only a matter of finding the legal ground for its summoning. On this score, the court determined that paragraph 18 of the Cabinet Mission Plan of 1946 would apply. Thus the earlier declarations of the Governor-General were superseded by the Federal Court's rulings, and the members of the Constituent Assembly were elected indirectly by members of the provincial legislatures. Where no provincial legislature existed, as in Karachi and Balochistan, special provisions were arranged. The one glaring procedural difference between the constitution of the first and second Assemblies was the parity formula that acknowledged East Bengal's larger population while continuing to deny representation in accordance with its size.

In political performance, however, the second Constituent Assembly was decidedly different. Rather than a single political party dominating proceedings, the new body was comprised of a wide array of parties that had been organized since the formation of Pakistan. The United Front of Fazlul Huq and the Awami League of H.S. Suhrawardy were active and important actors from East Bengal. And although the West Pakistan Muslim League parties continued to function in the new Assembly, deep divisions within Muslim League ranks, notably in the Punjab, further enfeebled it. Moreover, the League had been taken over by apolitical bureaucrats, whose association with the party was at best token, and at worst, a Trojan horse. Chaudhri Mohammad Ali was hardly a Muslim League politician, nor was Iskandar Mirza; and Dr Khan Sahib, Mian Iftikharuddin, Malik Feroz Khan Noon, Ghulam Ali Talpur, and Mian Mumtaz Daultana were more inclined to destroy the League than save it. So while the Muslim League had the largest number of representatives in the second Constituent Assembly, some twenty-five of the eighty members, it had neither the power nor the influence to fashion a coalition that could work toward its preconceived goals. Moreover, some of the most prominent leaders of the Muslim League, e.g., Nishtar, Qaiyum Khan, and Nazimuddin, were not elected to the second Constituent Assembly.

The election of the second Constituent Assembly also shattered the Cabinet of Talents, after several cabinet officials failed to win their elections or declined to become candidates. The formation of a new government also necessitated a change in Prime Ministers, and Mohammad Ali Bogra was relieved of his duties and again made Pakistan's ambassador to the United States. Ghulam Mohammad and Iskandar Mirza, with support from Mushtaque Ahmad Gurmani, at first considered offering Suhrawardy the Prime Minister's role, but opposition developed in political circles, notably from Fazlul Huq and Dr Khan Sahib. Suhrawardy had also demanded a number of concessions, i.e., the substitution of joint for separate electorates, that regional autonomy be recognized, and that Bengali be made a national language along with Urdu. Suhrawardy's demands, as well as the posturing of key actors, forced Mirza to look elsewhere, and attention shifted to Chaudhri Mohammad Ali who, admittedly, was most reluctant to assume the post.

It was during the negotiations with Chaudhri Mohammad Ali that Ghulam Mohammad's health totally collapsed, and as he was no longer able to perform his duties, they passed to Iskandar Mirza, who became the acting Governor-General. Chaudhri Mohammad Ali was summoned before Mirza and offered the Prime Minister's office, but Pakistan's chief bureaucrat argued against his selection. He told Mirza of his great discomfort and that he did not believe he could manage the vast array of ambitious political personalities. Moreover, the Muslim League had been hollowed out by years of controversy, and party leaders no longer commanded the obedience of their members. He also cited his concern that the head of state and head of government would both be lodged in West Pakistan. Mirza rejected all his arguments, however, and by appealing to his patriotism, he literally forced Mohammad Ali to accept the appointment. Moreover, Pakistan had taken bold action by developing intimate contacts with the United States, and Mirza needed the unqualified support of all his close associates. Thus a most hesitant Chaudhri Mohammad Ali became Pakistan's new Prime Minister, and along with I.I. Chundrigar, who replaced Suhrawardy as Law Minister, he assumed primary responsibility for guiding the second Constituent Assembly through its constitution-making tasks.

At the same time, Iskandar Mirza and Mohammad Ali had teamed with Fazlul Huq to assure the success of the One Unit scheme. Major opposition to the scheme, had however, emerged from within the United Front which even Fazlul Huq could not blunt. The Awami League severed its ties to the coalition and rejected One Unit as detrimental to the interests of the east wing. Indigenous, somewhat younger leaders had begun to replace the old line politicians in East Bengal, and their more radical views challenged the old guard. Moreover, the newcomers accused Fazlul Huq of betraying Bengal when he answered Mirza's call for assistance. Indeed, the 'Sher-i-Bengal' was now seen running with West Pakistani foxes. This metamorphosis not only confused the politics of the eastern province, it also exaggerated the extremism of a new generation of Bengali politicians. But Suhrawardy was still a figure to be reckoned with and, although relieved of his duties in the Law Ministry, he was nevertheless chosen to lead the political opposition in the second Constituent Assembly. Suhrawardy found sufficient fault with the drafting of the new constitution to deny it his support, but his overall performance was statesmanlike and generally free of obstructionism.

Although it was difficult to say that one Constituent Assembly was more democratically representative than the other, the second resembled more the structure and character of contemporary Pakistani politics than the first. Gurmani was chosen by the Governor-General to call the second Constituent Assembly into session and it was convened on 7 July 1955. The inaugural session in Murree lasted a few days before adjourning and reassembling in Karachi. Its first serious business, however, was not constitution-making, but the revalidation of laws in force in the country. With this matter quickly accomplished, the Constituent Assembly moved to the next important prerequisite, i.e., the restructuring of the federation.

The Governor-General had already publicized his desire to amalgamate the provinces of West Pakistan and, indeed, to form a single administrative province in the west wing of the country. Prime Minister Mohammad Ali Bogra had, in fact, declared the government's intention to form One Unit as far back as 22 November 1954, arguing that it would eliminate all provincial designations and that thereafter there would be 'no Bengalis, no Punjabis, no Sindhis, no Pathans, no Baluchis, no Bahawalpuris, no Khairpuris', and that their 'disappearance' would 'strengthen the integrity of Pakistan' (*West Pakistan As One Unit*, Government of Pakistan, Karachi 1954). This was a spurious argument. It can only be conjectured whether the Prime Minister really believed that a change in official terminology, or the creation of a single administrative province, could cancel out centuries of locational, cultural, and tribal identity.

But whether Bogra believed his words or not was irrelevant after the second Constituent Assembly convened to deliberate the matter. In point of fact, there was precious little debate on the One Unit scheme, because the West Pakistani provincial assemblies had been pressurized to declare their support for the plan months earlier (Callard, 1957). On 30 September 1955, therefore, the vast expanse of West Pakistan, i.e., the several provinces and princely states, were merged into the single province of West Pakistan. Unlike when Lord Curzon sought to improve and rationalize the administration of Bengal and authorized splitting the province into two parts, in this instance Pakistan's chief mentors believed they were simplifying complicated issues, calming provincial passions, and generally ensuring the unity of the country by fusing the many disparate territories into One Unit.

The fusing of the provinces of West Pakistan, however, was hardly a peaceful process, nor was it celebrated in the several regions that comprised the new administrative province. Done mainly to balance the power of East Pakistan, to deny it representation commensurate with its population, it was a divisive action, hardly one geared to promote national unity. On paper the scheme appeared rational, but the issues that separated the provinces and nationalities were sentimental and emotional, psychological and historic, and no paper reorganization could change, let alone replace, the underlying realities.

Mushtaq Ahmad Gurmani became West Pakistan's first Governor and Dr Khan Sahib was named its first Chief Minister. Each man had a reputation for sternness, and the secular mindsets as well as forceful natures of both ensured strong ties with the Mirza government. Clearly, both men were more comfortable with the administrative rather than the political process, and their principal task lay not so much in giving meaning to a new constitution as in neutralizing the political opposition. Pakistan stood on the eve of launching a new constitutional order, but One Unit foretold a diminution in political activity and a heightened role for the country's civil-military bureaucrats.

Unlike its predecessor, the second Constituent Assembly made short work of constitution-making, in part because the laborious tasks had been done by the first Assembly. But perhaps more important, constitution-making was engineered by a combination of professional administrators and secular-minded politicians who better understood the need to keep pace with the country's expanding and modernizing military establishment. Pakistan's immediate past also shaped the behaviour of the second Assembly and, although it embraced diverse callings and interests, it had little difficulty and sufficient reasons to find the necessary consensus. Thus, deliberations from start to finish were completed in less than six months. On 8 January 1956 a draft constitution was laid before the public, and on 29 February it was formally adopted. On 23 March 1956, the sixteenth anniversary of the Lahore Resolution, the Constitution of the Islamic Republic of Pakistan was officially promulgated. Pakistan was given a parliamentary system, and Iskandar Mirza, the presiding Governor-General, was inaugurated as the nation's first President.

In the end, the realists appeared to have prevailed. The ideologues, who had made a shambles of the constitution-making process during the tenure of the original Constituent Assembly, had been ·isolated and at least temporarily neutralized. Pakistan's apolitical leaders were generally more disciplined, more specialized, and more cosmopolitan than those who had preceded them. Relatively familiar with the post-World War II setting, largely schooled in foreign institutions or by foreign teachers, their attitudes more accurately reflected international conditions. Their speed in producing a constitution was, on the one side, induced by increasing societal impatience, but on the other, it was deemed essential to block manoeuvring by traditional elites who were prone to exploit the more limited life experience of the country's uneducated and largely illiterate masses. In a race against time, the agents of change saw their principal task as shifting public attention from its conventional moorings to a more eclectic awareness of unfolding events. They proved successful in delivering the much-promised constitution; but when weighed against all the arguments that had gone unanswered, their victory was hardly complete.

The framers of the constitution did not resolve the separate versus joint electorate question, nor did they effectively settle the issue of the separation of state and religion. Federalism was also a major conundrum in a country with only two politico/administrative units. Moreover, their separation by a thousand miles of hostile Indian territory was an added complication. Nothing had been done to satisfy the proponents of centralism on the one side and provincial autonomy on the other, and only the determined actions and pleadings of Prime Minister Chaudhri Mohammad Ali and his Bengali ally, Fazlul Huq, prevented a breakdown in the deliberations. The Prime Minister stressed the counterproductivity of delaying tactics and, recalling that martial law had been in the air during the 1954 crisis, he urged his compatriots to cast aside their differences, to give the country its long awaited constitution, and to leave for another time and another forum the questions that divided them. While this was a successful tactic, and indeed it broke the impasse, Chaudhri Mohammad Ali had merely postponed a struggle which resumed shortly after the promulgation of the much-heralded political charter.

Pakistan was declared a federal republic, but its parliamentary system had allowed roles for a President and Vice-President. Although the power of decision was vested in the parliament and the Prime Minister and his cabinet, the President was provided expanded powers and the central government was strengthened to meet anticipated emergencies. Provincial autonomy was included in the document, but a strong centre was fashioned to assure solidarity of purpose, and especially to safeguard the state's territorial integrity. The constitution also appealed to the social conservatives, that is, the proponents of the Islamic state. While the country was declared an Islamic republic and not an Islamic state, the constitution's blend of spiritual and secular ideas and expression was sufficient to win the favour of the more orthodox members of the Muslim League, and no less significant, the chief religious parties, i.e., the Nizam-i-Islam and the Jamaat-i-Islami. In fact, the loudest voices of opposition came from the more secular Awami League of East Pakistan and the smaller Hindu and leftist organizations in both provinces. The banning of the Pakistan Communist Party in 1955 had somewhat silenced its voice, but its position was none the less registered through some of the latter groups.

The Awami League, however, posed the most significant challenge, insisting on the incorporation of a 21-point programme that would limit the centre's power to defence, currency, and foreign affairs. Maulana Bhashani led the more extreme faction of Awami League dissidents and, along with Shaikh Mujibur Rahman, he called the constitution a sell-out to the Americans and a black day for Bengalis. Bhashani had vehemently opposed the military agreement with Washington, and the constitution, in his judgment, was rammed through the second Constituent Assembly only to satisfy the United States' demands. Moreover, a strong centre did not sit well with those pressing for a different version of Pakistan than that engineered by (what was perceived to be) Pakistan's civil-military elite. Provoked by the vituperative comments of Bhashani and Mujib, a majority of the Awami League membership condemned the constitution's supporters and demanded immediate recognition of East Pakistan's distinctive character. Their general argument supported the idea of two separate countries that were bound together only by a common religion. Although Suhrawardy tried to play down this argument, Iskandar Mirza threatened a sharp response if such statements were repeated.

The nation had received its long awaited constitution, but the road had been twisted and difficult, leaving many of the principal actors exhausted and the general citizenry sceptical. Moreover, too many battle lines had been drawn through the course of these events, and once established, they could not be erased.

Antecedents to Martial Law

The most outspoken proponent of the separation of state and religion was Iskandar Mirza. Disposed to secular ideas and manners, the President believed religion was a personal matter and should not be imposed from above, whether by government or groups whose central concern was religious performance. Mirza accepted the multiplicity of beliefs expressed within the subcontinent and, somewhat true to

Jinnah's vision, he projected a nation wherein people representing a variety of persuasions could find the necessary security to practise their traditions, while at the same time offering the nation their supreme loyalty. Mirza refused to see conflict in the projection of a particular faith, between making commitment to a spiritual Superior and showing solidarity with a national entity. On the other hand, he was concerned that, because religious experience had its variations, because different religious expressions too often separated peoples from one another, an undue emphasis on religious exclusivity would divide the state more than it unified it. The Ahmedi riots in the Punjab had added special significance to this concern. Moreover, although Pakistan was a predominantly Muslim country, a sizeable Hindu minority lived in East Pakistan, and West Pakistan was ritualistically divided between Sunni and Shia Muslims who were not always compatible. Religion, therefore, in Mirza's opinion, would be best left to personal tests of commitment, and never made a measure for Pakistani citizenship.

Mirza had been quoted in *The New York Times* as saying, 'We can't run wild on Islam; it is Pakistan first and last' (7 February 1955). The President had no intention of minimizing Islam, nor did he believe that a likely prospect in a country more than 90 per cent Muslim, but he was charged with presiding over a new nation-state, and it was the state's stability and progress that challenged his abilities. Pakistan had been created to provide the Muslims of the subcontinent with a homeland in which they could nurture their cultural experience, but it was never specified what, if any, particular Islamic experience best represented the Pakistan ethos. Pakistan may have been propelled along the road to independence by people who saw danger in an India ruled by Hindus, but its emergence as a national entity addressed a kaleidoscope of issues that went beyond the spiritual quest. Once Pakistan achieved independence, it was assumed by those most responsible for articulating its presence that Islam was no longer in jeopardy, and that other matters demanded attention. Moreover, the *ulema*, in all their numerous representations, had chosen not to associate with the Pakistan Movement. Their absence from the struggle confirmed in the minds of those who had been immersed in it that Pakistan was destined to become a nation-state, and it would not be so different from the many others then emerging from the colonial experience.

During that earlier period, the thinking of those in the professional services was not very different from that of the intelligentsia, the students, or even the landed Muslim aristocracy. But it diverged markedly from that portrayed by the religious clerics. By every measure, members of the higher civil-military establishment had been exposed to a wider and deeper life experience than the majority of their countrymen, and their range of interests encompassed a variety of expressions that influenced their development and outlook. Called to do public service, their appreciation for order and decorum, for co-operation and efficiency, transcended the immediate circumstances of their personal .lives. While they may, by choice, have retained and continued to practise the fundamentals of their faith, they were less likely to find their personal experience an obstacle in the performance of their secular and professional duties. Serving a nation of multiple expressions was central to the purposes of a professional calling, and vital to the survivability of the national design.

Pakistan's constitution was engineered by men who, in the main, represented secular vision, but they were nevertheless uncomfortable when conceptualizing the subordination of religious experience to that of the state. Pakistan had been the outcome of a religious movement made political; it could not therefore be true to itself if it did not sustain the religious circumstances of its origin. The Objectives Resolution was their response to this awareness. The legitimacy of what they had achieved could be shown only in their continuing devotion to a higher power than that represented by the nation-state. Defining sovereignty proved to be a challenging experience, and it was only after notions of electoral and popular sovereignty were discarded that the constitution's framers opted for the expression that made God synonymous with ultimate political authority. The sovereignty of the state was considered meaningless in the absence of God's Will, nor did God delegate authority to mortal humans. The essential connection between God and man was trust, and hence Pakistan's Governors ruled not by dint of human contrivance, but as an act of religious responsibility.

Thus, although the framers had avoided constructing an Islamic state, they did form an Islamic republic, and the republic would not be considered legitimate if it could not demonstrate that the state's procedures and operations were in accordance with Islamic principles. Moreover, if an act of state was considered repugnant to the teachings of the Koran, that act could not be allowed to stand. And because Pakistan's more secular officials were not judged the appropriate source to reconcile Koranic teachings with governmental practices, a way was made for the country's spiritual leaders to manage that process. If it was the intention of Pakistan's mundane Governors to maintain a strict separation between state and religion, the intrusion of the *ulema* as ultimate arbiters in constitutional matters made that goal impossible.

Even the most secular of Pakistan's leaders could not avoid their commitment to holy doctrine, nor could they avoid becoming targets of those members of society who claimed a more learned, and perhaps more puristic, religious experience. In point of fact, it would prove difficult to reconcile those espousing the virtues of the Islamic republic with others demanding an Islamic state. Both the first and second Constituent Assemblies struggled with these different approaches, and both found a synthesis between modernity and tradition the preferable course of action. Reference was made to the expression of the Quaid-i-Azam that Pakistan was to be a democratic state, guided by Islamic principles of social justice. But by the time the drafters of Pakistan's constitution had completed their work, they were forced to acknowledge that that vision was too limited for the circumstances prevailing within the nation. In the end, Pakistan's sudden appearance as an independent state did not leave time to secure the meaning of nationhood among a far-flung, disparate, and largely uneducated population. The survival of the state rested on the belief that the central purpose of the nation was a common religious experience; moreover, deviations from commonality were not contemplated at that moment of creation. Thus the Directive

Principles that were written into the constitution were necessary, but at the same time, they were to be employed only as a guide in the formulation of laws and policies.

Chaudhri Mohammad Ali articulated the thoughts of the framers when they delicately balanced secular needs with religious commitment. Addressing the issue he declared: 'We may have differences as to the interpretation of the injunctions of Islam, or the legal system of Islam...but Islam enjoins upon us not compulsion but discussion and consultation together' (Debates, Second Constituent Assembly, January-February 1956, cited in Choudhury, 1959, p.180). The men who ruled Pakistan anticipated a rational and balanced response to their notions of a nation-state, but they also prepared themselves for the assault that would not be long in coming from those whose life experiences were at variance with their own, and whose different objectives ensured a collision of epic proportions.

I.H. Qureshi, the central author of the Objectives Resolution, revealed that the description of Pakistan as an Islamic republic

> had no thought or religious pressure behind it...It was first proposed and carried by a snap vote in a meeting of the Muslim League Party...and it was passed because of the discipline of the majority party in the house. However, there was no thinking behind it (Qureshi, Islamic Elements in the Political Thought of Pakistan, manuscript, 1957, p.24).

Although it is difficult to believe there was 'no thinking' behind the terminology, what Qureshi no doubt wished to express was the instinctive perception of the Muslim League that contemporary Pakistan was first and foremost a religious expression.

That 'thinking' was certainly in evidence during and following the promulgation of the constitution, when the debate continued over the retention of separate electorates. The East Pakistan Muslim League had led the fight to eliminate the separate electorates. The Bengali party had concluded that it was time to adopt a joint electorate scheme, which meant there would be no distinction at the polls between the different religious communities. Although a central demand of the Muslim League during the colonial period, its continuation after the establishment of Pakistan was deemed to be unnecessary and demeaning. In a country predominantly Muslim, and in a modern state that claimed to practise equality of citizenship, the need for separate electorates appeared anachronistic at best. The Awami League was Pakistan's first true experiment with a secular political party. The Muslim League continued to restrict its membership to Muslims, and in spite of its protestations of democracy, the country's minorities were forced to find expression in those parties that sustained their exclusivity, or the few fringe organizations that ignored religion as a requirement for membership. But when the Awami League decided to open its rolls to non-Muslims, it followed that they would seek to rescind the separate electorates that underpinned the Muslim League ethos. In fact, the Muslim League, which had long considered itself synonymous with Pakistan, had adopted separate electorates as its ideology, and any attempt to strike it down was considered an assault not only on the party, but also on the country. The intensity of this struggle came at a time when the more secular-minded members of the Pakistan experience questioned the deepening intrusion of religious elements in the political life of the nation. Thus, with the Awami League already the pre-eminent party in East Pakistan, the stage was set for a contest that would determine the Muslim League's future in West Pakistan, and hence in the nation.

The principal opposition to the Muslim League in West Pakistan emerged in September 1956, with the inaugural convention in Lahore of the Republican Party. The Republican Party was considered the brainchild of Iskandar Mirza, but it was more than likely the joint enterprise of Ahmad Mushtaq Gurmani and Dr Khan Sahib. Mirza insisted that he was in his residence in Karachi when a call came to him from Dr Khan Sahib informing him that a Republican Party had been organized in Lahore. When Mirza questioned Khan Sahib about the origins of the organization, the former Red Shirt and Congress leader disclosed that Gurmani had generated the idea, but that both had agreed an alternative had to be found for the Muslim League. It was their opinion, as well as that of a goodly number of Punjabis, he said, that the Muslim

League had become bogged down in ideological and religious issues, was too heavily influenced by elements among the *ulema*, and was unable to adapt itself to the changing political scene in both East and West Pakistan.

Dr Khan Sahib cited the vast changes in East Pakistan and the sharp division in outlook and behaviour between the Awami League and the Muslim League. Coalition government was unavoidable in both the National Assembly and West Pakistan legislature, but the Muslim League could not coalesce with the Awami League and the National Assembly had suffered from paralysis; in similar fashion, the Muslim League could not escape the influence of the mullahs who threatened the labours of the West Pakistan legislature. By contrast, the Republican Party was comprised of pragmatists, most of whom were Muslim League defectors, and they believed that a clean start was not only possible, it was imperative. Furthermore, the Republican Party sympathized with the Awami League in moving toward joint electorates, and even if they were not accepted for West Pakistan, the Republicans called for their establishment in the east wing.

Mirza told Khan Sahib that he did not want to see the further fragmentation of the Muslim League but, in so far as he and Gurmani had already formed their new party, he would not oppose it. According to Mirza, it was shortly after this telephone conversation that a distraught Chaudhri Mohammad Ali came to him saying that he had been betrayed by both the Governor and Chief Minister of West Pakistan and that he had heard rumours that the President had, in fact, prompted his colleagues to form the Republican Party. Mirza said he had only then heard about the new organization from Dr Khan Sahib and that his (the Prime Minister's) 'close friend Gurmani' was the central figure in its formation. Mirza revealed that he had discussed the threat the Republican Party posed to the Muslim League, but that he had decided not to interfere. Mirza's statement was not meant to satisfy the Prime Minister. If the President intended to countenance the formation of the Republican Party, Mohammad Ali said, he would resign as President of the Muslim League and allow Sardar Abdur Rab Nishtar to assume that post.

According to Mirza, their conversation ended on that note,

but the President pondered the Prime Minister's statement, and before leaving for a tour of the Chittagong Hill Tracts, he called Chaudhri Mohammad Ali to his residence and instructed him not to appoint Nishtar as President of the Muslim League. Noting that Chaudhri Mohammad Ali had known Nishtar no more than ten years, Mirza said his own association spread over a thirty-five year period. 'Please listen to me,' Mirza pleaded, 'don't make him President of the Muslim League or you will be in trouble. He (Nishtar) is a religious fanatic and he will work against you behind your back. He will try and control the whole government as President of the Muslim League because he seems to think he is no less a man than the Quaid-i-Azam' (interview, September 1967, M.A.H Ispahani and Iskandar Mirza). The Prime Minister did not reply to the President's admonition, and not knowing who or what to believe, but having lost all trust in those he had worked with so closely in years past, a dejected Chaudhri Mohammad Ali silently left the President's residence.

In the end, the Prime Minister did as he had originally planned. He decided not to take the advice of the President, he resigned his position in the Muslim League, and he permitted Nishtar to take control of the party.

While still on his tour of East Pakistan, Mirza received a distress message from the Prime Minister who urged his return. Mirza cancelled a planned hunt in the Sunderbans and immediately returned to Karachi. Chaudhri Mohammad Ali met him at the airport and was forced to admit that Mirza was correct in his assessment of Nishtar, and that the Muslim League President, in a relatively short period of time, had made it impossible for him to preside over the government. Mirza told the Prime Minister that his problems would increase. He then asked him a pointed question. 'Why did Liaquat Ali Khan take the Presidency of the Muslim League after the death of the Quaid-i-Azam?' Rhetorically responding to his own question, Mirza said it was necessary to keep Nishtar out of the role because he had a different vision for Pakistan, was too involved with the mullahs and reactionary forces in the country, and would do everything in his power to convert Pakistan into a quasi-theocratic state. Moreover, Mirza believed that Nishtar had been involved in fomenting the disorder in the Punjab and that he could be expected to continue to exploit secular-religious differences.

Chaudhri Mohammad Ali met with Mirza on one final occasion, this time to tender his resignation from the government. Stating he had made 'too many mistakes,' Chaudhri Mohammad Ali told the President he was exhausted, frightened, and simply unable to continue as Prime Minister. With a weeping Chaudhri Mohammad Ali before him, Mirza concluded that 'the man had lost his nerve' and, indeed, should not remain in office. In a later meeting with Gurmani, Mirza discussed Mohammad Ali's state of mind and both agreed they should accept his resignation. But before doing so, and in order to ease the transition, the Prime Minister should be sent to London for medical treatment and Mirza would administer the country from the President's office. It was at this time, with the constitution in force only a few months, that Mirza concluded it could not work. Parliamentary politics required a willingness on the part of those involved in the political process to amicably work through their differences and most of all, not only to accept the will of the majority, but to appreciate the pluralistic character of the nation (Afzal, 1976). Respect for views and positions, for ideas and expressions, was fundamental to the success of any deliberative body, and at some point, consensus was required in doing the people's business. These elements may have been evident in the British system, but according to Mirza, they were absent in Pakistan, and hence its leaders were charged with finding another formula if the country's problems were to be made treatable.

Firm in the belief that an 'unworkable constitution' had destroyed Chaudhri Mohammad Ali's mental capacity, Mirza met with Gurmani and Khan Sahib and told them it would be best to return to the 'old Muslim League idea' but not to the Muslim League itself. By this he meant that there had to be an overwhelming political force in both the National Assembly as well as in the West Pakistan legislature. He therefore wanted to call upon H.S. Suhrawardy to form a new government. Moreover, Suhrawardy's party would prove compatible with the Republican Party, and the coalition would not only blunt Nishtar's aspirations, it would also stymie the reactionary forces that had taken control of the Muslim League. Mirza noted that Suhrawardy was strong-willed, an experienced politician and administrator, an artful lawyer, a modernist, and a 'brilliant parliamentarian'. Not one to retreat from a good fight, he could be counted upon to maintain his calm whatever the provocation. The three men agreed that the Awami Leaguer was the best choice in the circumstances, and Mirza summoned him to a private meeting. Acknowledging that he had refused to yield to Suhrawardy's earlier demands, Mirza cited his error in selecting Chaudhri Mohammad Ali and asked him if he would assume the office of Prime Minister in concert with the Republican Party and 'the Hindu members of the Assembly'. This time Suhrawardy did not insist on a prior agreement. Having weighed the alternatives, he knew he had an opportunity to press a programme close to his interests and he did not hesitate in supplying an affirmative answer. Mirza then asked him to meet with Dr Khan Sahib in order to work out the details of their coalition. Suhrawardy said he would do so and return the following day with a list of names that he would recommend for his cabinet.

Dr Khan Sahib and Suhrawardy had no difficulty in reaching an agreement, given the former's willingness to promote the establishment of joint electorates in East Pakistan. Moreover, he assured Suhrawardy that West Pakistan would adopt joint electorates at a later date. Like the Awami League before it, Khan Sahib also intended to open the Republican Party to non-Muslim members. The two men acknowledged the need to forge co-operative ventures between the wings and to manage the distribution of development resources on a more equitable basis. Believing he had adequate assurances, Suhrawardy met with Mirza to run down his list of cabinet choices. Only one person was held over from the previous government, namely Amjad Ali. All the others would be first-time appointments, but some of them, like Firoz Khan Noon and Ghulam Ali Talpur, were hardly newcomers.

Suhrawardy's tenure as Prime Minister began on 12 September 1956, and it dramatically altered what appeared to be a hopeless condition. Under his leadership the government displayed a new resiliency, and the relative stability that Pakistan enjoyed drew increasing interest from the United States. But perhaps that which really drew American attention to Pakistan was its membership in the Southeast Asia Treaty Organization in 1954, and more notably, the Baghdad Pact, which it joined in February 1955. Although both arrangements were made during the administration of Mohammad Ali Bogra, it was Suhrawardy who made them credible. Only weeks into his new responsibility, the French and British assault on Egypt's Suez Canal, followed by Israel's strike across the Sinai, aroused popular passions throughout Pakistan. The Suez crisis was exploited by forces on both the right and left, but in spite of the attendant pressures, the Prime Minister refused to sever Pakistan's ties to the western alliances. Undaunted by criticism that his obstinacy could kill his government, Suhrawardy remained true to his convictions. Some years later, Mirza would be compelled to acknowledge that it was Suhrawardy's defiant stand against both his friends and foes that had saved Pakistan's association with the United States.

In the course of those critical events, Suhrawardy found himself dependent on the Republican Party. Moreover, the alliance issue had split the Awami League, and the Bhashani faction weighed the possibilities of forming still another opposition party. Though pretending to be unmoved by these developments, Suhrawardy none the less defended his decision to defy the popular complaint. Claiming that Pakistan had developed an 'independent' foreign policy and was not a camp follower of the Americans, the Prime Minister cited his role in solidifying Pakistan's relations with the People's Republic of China. The Prime Minister wanted everyone to know that his country's ties to the United States had more to do with the threat posed by India than with Cold War strategy. Pakistan's concern, he intimated, was with New Delhi, not Beijing, let alone Moscow.

The Suez crisis, in fact, had developed while Suhrawardy was on a state visit to China, and he returned home to find Pakistan seething with discontent. Pakistani crowds had already burned and looted British, French, and American installations in the country, and there was hardly a politician who had not seized the opportunity to denounce the West, or to express their solidarity with a brother Muslim nation. Demands that Pakistan quit its western alliances came from every sector of society, but Suhrawardy brushed them all aside. Instead of yielding to popular sentiment, he declared, 'far from being scrapped, the alliances are to be supported' (*Morning News*, 11 November 1956). Dr Khan Sahib, at least in public, decided against giving his support to the Prime Minister. But his attack on Suhrawardy was mild when compared with those launched by Mian Iftikharuddin and Maulana Maudoodi, who combined forces to condemn the Prime Minister as both a traitor to Pakistan and a threat to the Islamic world. The verbal fulminations of the extreme left and right in Pakistan provoked their followers to more deliberate acts of violence, but Suhrawardy stood his ground and, finding support in President Mirza and General Ayub Khan, he prevailed, at least for the time being. Moreover, the permanent services, namely the higher officials in the bureaucracy and army, were only too pleased to have the Prime Minister take the heat.

Speaking forcefully in the National Assembly, Suhrawardy acknowledged he was flying in the face of popular opinion, but he warned his countrymen that

> our enemies are most anxious to isolate us...I refuse to be isolated. So long as I am Prime Minister, I will not do anything which will weaken Pakistan. We are living in dangerous and difficult times and we must have friends upon whom we can rely (*Morning News*, 15 November 1956).

Suhrawardy's problems eased somewhat when the British and French withdrew their forces from Egypt. But serious damage had been done to Suhrawardy's support base, especially in East Pakistan. Now he was even more dependent on the Republican Party, and Iskandar Mirza held the key to his future. And Mirza had already concluded that Suhrawardy was a declining asset, that he had largely served his purpose, and that his successor would have to be found from among the growing opponents to the regime.

But if plans were underway to replace the sitting Prime Minister, the events of January 1957 postponed their execution. New Delhi saw advantages in Pakistan's political instability and Jawaharlal Nehru moved forcefully, and in violation of all United Nations directives, to annex the disputed mountain state of Kashmir. This blatant display of Indian imperialism reignited the street demonstrations, but it also extended the life of the Suhrawardy administration. Suhrawardy used the occasion to repair some of the damage done to his reputation by citing the capacity of some nations to operate on the basis of 'force and fraud'. Finding renewed justification for Pakistan's membership in the western alliances, he noted that France and England 'had walked out of Egypt' but that India and the communist countries 'did not walk out of the lands they forcibly occupied' (*Pakistan Times*, 7 February 1957).

With a new air of confidence, and with his credibility enhanced, Suhrawardy met with his Awami League associates at Kagmari, not far from the home of Maulana Bhashani. Suhrawardy had come from a meeting with the students of Dhaka University who had listened patiently to his remarks, and he was not about to compromise his position with his party's critics. Bhashani had little interest in compromise in any case, and he defiantly ordered Awami League officials to resign their posts. Many party members responded affirmatively to this demand but others, including Shaikh Mujibur Rahman, who saw his opportunity to gain absolute control of the party, agreed to stand with the Prime Minister. The Awami League was hopelessly divided. Maulana Bhashani declared virtual war on both the federal government and the West Pakistani power-brokers, insisting that East Pakistan was an exploited province and hardly more than a colony of the western region. In still another of his emotional moments, he declared that East Bengal had the right to establish itself as an independent and sovereign state (*Pakistan Times*, 8 February 1957).

Bhashani's secessionist threat did nothing to strengthen the Suhrawardy administration, and the Prime Minister did what he could to minimize its impact. Seeking to downplay the statements at Kagmari, Suhrawardy endeavoured to shore up his shaky coalition by defending his foreign policy. A political realist himself, he searched for a way to temper the nation's subjective character. Opening a debate in the National Assembly, the Prime Minister made it abundantly clear that Pakistan was in no position to take on India in an all-out war. Citing India's greater ability to purchase a vast array of weapons, the Prime Minister said Pakistan could only compensate for its weaknesses by allying with the United States. Suhrawardy insisted that the pacts had already thwarted New Delhi's aggressive tendencies and, moreover, had begun to 'advance the political and economic strength of the nation. Pakistan's modernization programme must not be made hostage to the Indian threat,' he declared, and the country's capacity to attract foreign investment was a *sine qua non* of its economic health. 'Neutrality,' he said, is not possible for Pakistan because 'we are not big enough, we are not strong enough to defend ourselves' (Government of Pakistan, *Statements on Foreign Relations and Defence* by H.S. Suhrawardy, Prime Minister of Pakistan, 1957, pp.10-14).

In spite of a courageous performance, the Prime Minister still had his many detractors. Opponents like Daultana, Ayub Khuhro, and Iftikharuddin found sufficient fault with his arguments to raise a demand that he step aside. Mirza and Gurmani, however, had not yet decided to rid themselves of their frontman. They rallied sufficient votes in the National Assembly to give the Prime Minister a vote of confidence, albeit with the Muslim League and Fazlul Huq's Krishak Sramik abstaining. But Suhrawardy's success was hardly more than a Pyrrhic victory. New political combinations were forming in both East and West Pakistan. Defections from the Awami League had given new vigour to the Krishak Sramik, and the latter was eager to make alliances with the Muslim League or, if the opportunity arose, with the Republican Party.

Suhrawardy had become a Prime Minister without a political party. He had been discredited in East Pakistan by his intimate association with the Republicans, and Shaikh Mujibur Rahman, in the absence of Bhashani, had assumed total control of the Awami League. Moreover, Bhashani had begun to branch out and had found willing associates in the west wing. Finding Iftikharuddin's regional autonomy argument similar to his own, he linked forces with the Punjabi dissident, and through him, with G.M. Syed in Sindh, A.S. Achakzai in Balochistan, and Abdul Ghaffar Khan in the NWFP. Claiming to work within the system afforded by the new constitution, Pakistan's most publicized provincialists agreed to pool their efforts and their organizations, and in the summer of 1957 they inaugurated the National Awami Party on Dhaka's Paltan Maidan.

Operating on a programme that had as its main objectives the dissolution of One Unit and the termination of the western alliances, the NAP became an important actor from the moment of its formation. Emerging at a time when the Muslim League had little likelihood of ever again securing a majority role, with the Republican Party in disarray and more and more dependent for its survival on President Mirza, and with the Awami League undergoing significant reorganization, the merging of the heretofore marginal groupings opened the NAP to mainstream political activity. Moreover, with none of the national parties in a position to discipline their members, the ideological commitment and solidarity represented by the NAP gave it an advantage that frightened the very centres of state power.

Dr Khan Sahib declared his inability to manage the West Pakistan government, and he called on President Mirza to impose President's Rule. East Pakistan, however, also confronted anarchical conditions. The East Pakistan legislature had approved a motion calling for immediate provincial autonomy, and Mujibur Rahman had stirred popular passions when he accused the central government of transforming East Pakistan into a colony. Echoing Bhashani's earlier talk about secession, Mujib demanded more equitable treatment if a monumental crisis was to be avoided.

With little time to save his party and government, Dr Khan Sahib was ready to ally himself with any combination that would guarantee his survival. Constrained by the constitution, his call for a 'revolutionary council' had little chance of success, but, on 12 August 1957, he met with Maulana Bhashani, and the two leaders agreed to form a coalition government that included the Republican and National Awami parties. Mirza was obliged to withdraw President's Rule, but he was most apprehensive when a Republican-NAP motion was approved in the West Pakistan legislature calling for the dissolution of the One Unit. Following its easy passage in Lahore, the matter was placed before the National Assembly in Karachi, where it became Suhrawardy's task to save the scheme. Suhrawardy had been reserved for one more floor fight. Mirza broke ranks with Khan Sahib and General Ayub Khan, who was attending a Commonwealth Commanders-in-Chief' Conference in the United Kingdom, was told to break off his conversations and return immediately to Pakistan.

Mirza joined with Suhrawardy in issuing a statement that cited a threat to the integrity of Pakistan. They condemned the tampering with the constitution, and argued that it dangerously weakened the nation's already frail political fabric. Suhrawardy also noted how the One Unit matter would affect the holding of national elections, which were slated for 1958. Even ten years after the transfer of power, Pakistan had not yet experienced a national election, and the dissolution of the One Unit would postpone that experience for at least another year and possibly longer (Aziz, 1976). The full implementation of the 1956 Constitution was intertwined with the anticipated elections and, according to the Prime Minister, all efforts at institutionalizing the country's political experience were jeopardized by the Republican-NAP alliance.

But while Suhrawardy pressed a constitutional argument, Mirza, and notably Ayub Khan, were concerned with the manageability of the country if the old provinces of West Pakistan were reconstituted. Ayub may well have been the original source of the One Unit scheme, as his private secretary, Colonel Mohammad Ahmad, had indicated (Ahmad, 1960). Something of a socio-political engineer, the Army Commander had his own vision of a restructured Pakistan, but that vision required the maintenance of One Unit. Furthermore, Ayub feared that the reinstatement of the older provinces would legitimize the work of the NAP and radicalize large segments of the population. And he did not need convincing that NAP leaders were essentially anti-Pakistan and in league with external forces who were inimical to Pakistan's fundamental interests. Any threat to Pakistan's membership in the western alliances also threatened the Pakistan Army's modernization programme. Concerned that NAP activities might infiltrate the Armed

Forces, and ever mindful of the Rawalpindi Conspiracy, Ayub could not risk another breakdown in army discipline.

Suhrawardy, however, had the major responsibility for defending One Unit. Despite his opposition to the scheme when it was first publicized in 1955, the Prime Minister cited his love for Pakistan, and he condemned those who would 'spread the poisonous hymn of provincial hatred' (*Morning News*, 5 October 1957). Rising to his oratorical best, Suhrawardy's eloquence and the sincerity of his delivery captivated his audiences as he toured the country. Can it be, he conjectured, that there is so much sentiment for Pathans, Punjabis, Sindhis, Bengalis, and Balochis but no room 'in your hearts for Pakistanis?' But not everyone found Suhrawardy's speeches stirring, patriotic, or, indeed, beneficial.

Increasingly uncomfortable with Suhrawardy's campaign, Khan Sahib pleaded with Mirza to dismiss him. The West Pakistani Chief Minister said he was prepared to break his pact with the NAP if the President would heed his plea. Mirza indicated his interest in a new understanding but urged Khan Sahib to 'go slow,' to ponder the role played by Ayub Khan, and to lower his rhetoric while he met with the Army Commander-in-Chief. The President and Army Commander met shortly thereafter, and although their deliberations were never recorded, it appears Mirza convinced Ayub that it was the Republican Party, not Khan Sahib, and certainly not Suhrawardy, that needed saving. Mirza argued that both men were expendable, but the Republican Party was the only organization that the President believed capable of warding off a possibly resurgent Muslim League and, more important, an increasingly more popular National Awami Party. But in order to bolster Mirza's Republicans, it was necessary to choose between Khan Sahib and Suhrawardy, and the decision was taken to sacrifice the Prime Minister.

Suhrawardy had saved One Unit. And by exposing the ephemeral nature of the Republican-NAP alliance, he had also added to the strength of the Army Commander-in-Chief. Mirza, however, like Khan Sahib, had lost stature, and it was doubtful that their reputations could be saved by Suhrawardy's removal. Nevertheless, on 10 October 1957,

Khan Sahib announced that his party and the West Pakistan government would no longer support the Prime Minister. Mirza, true to form, took his cue from his Chief Minister and immediately called for Suhrawardy to submit his resignation. The old politician, however, was never one to run from a political fight, and knowing this would be his last good struggle in a long political career, he refused to comply with Mirza's request. Suhrawardy demanded a special session of the National Assembly that would determine his fate. This time it was Mirza who refused to budge. With no alternative in sight Suhrawardy, unable to perform the duties of his office, presented his resignation. Mirza displayed no remorse in accepting it. But C.B. Marshall, whom Mirza had brought from the United States to assist the federal government in setting up its new constitutional structure, and who had worked closely with Suhrawardy during the period of his Prime Ministership, condemned the President's action and lamented the elimination of a unique visionary.

> This last piece of folly was of determining importance. It violated the canons of parliamentary order...the action was taken on the basis of issues with respect to which the Prime Minister was clearly acting in the interest of national unity and responsibility in policy. It sent out of office the only available man with aptitude as a politician and giving reasonable promise of national leadership (Marshall, 1959).

Suhrawardy's ouster marked the end of Pakistan's parliamentary experiment. It was also the end of an era. Only Pakistan's viceregal tradition had survived the political bloodletting of the nation's first decade, and even Mirza's ill-conceived attempt to preserve the Republican Party was doomed to fail. If the President had seriously contemplated Pakistan's future, had faced the realities of the political monstrosity he had foolishly nurtured, had taken the true measure of the men who ruled the nation, he would have acknowledged the special qualities of H.S. Suhrawardy. Of all the politicians, Suhrawardy was the only one of national stature whose power lay neither in feudal connections nor ideological expression. Suhrawardy was the consummate politician. His calling highlighted the role of the political servant, but it was a calling little appreciated in a land of angry people, of suspicious and self-serving officials, a land in which the many were so dependent on the few, and where the few seldom honoured their public trust. Pakistan began its political life in chaos, and it was chaos that tracked its destiny. Suhrawardy was mustered into service at the eleventh hour to preserve a political order that was more myth than reality. His passing dramatized the fiction of Pakistani constitutionalism, as well as the nation's inability to transcend parochial loyalties or suppress personal ambition. Others would follow in Suhrawardy's wake, but never again would the country innocently pay homage to its political leaders.

CHAPTER 6

THE COMING OF MARTIAL LAW

Ten years after the transfer of power, Pakistan was still in search of its destiny, let alone an identity. The integration of the nation, split at its birth into two segments separated from one another by a thousand miles of Indian territory, was a daunting exercise. But no less than that, the amalgamation of the different ethnicities, especially in West Pakistan, was particularly challenging. One Unit was supposed to answer the representational question that plagued constitution-making. It also aimed at creating a Pakistani identity among peoples long accustomed to thinking and behaving in more limited surroundings and circumstances. For the people of West Pakistan, however, it was the reality of their more intimate, daily lives that influenced popular attitudes and shaped outlooks. Moreover, One Unit was not a balanced programme. Whereas Punjabis, Sindhis, Pathans, and Balochis were urged to shed their historic identities for an all-encompassing, but nevertheless more abstract, role as Pakistanis, the Bengalis of East Pakistan were given new credence as a distinct nationality. East Bengal may have been renamed East Pakistan, but the Bengali character of the province had not been altered, nor could it be. Bengalis would ever remain Bengalis. By contrast, the different ethnicities of West Pakistan were to be measured by their Pakistani qualities, and any replay of Sindh for the Sindhis, or Pakhtunistan for the Pathans, was judged divisive, parochial, and a threat to the integrity of the state.

The 1956 Constitution complicated conditions because it did not adequately address the prevailing circumstances in the different regions that comprised Pakistan. East Pakistan was an artificial state, carved out of greater Bengal in sudden and confusing circumstances. Its economic and social history was intertwined with that other region that was included in the Indian Union. Its leaders straddled two epochs, the colonial and the post-colonial, and their disorientation was compounded by the Radcliffe Award that also divided them into beneficiaries on the one side and outcasts on the other. Thus the former were lauded and offered high office, whereas the latter were demonized and made to feel tainted and unwanted. Similar, yet different, dilemmas burdened the people in the western portion of the country. Historically and instinctively more independent and combative than their eastern brethren, the north-western provinces of the subcontinent had a long tradition of local rule. Tribalism remained the defining feature of life in the Pathan and Baloch areas, and even the people of the settled regions were inclined to follow known personalities with habits and virtues much like their own. Patriarchy and feudalism also pervaded the Punjab and Sindh, where the *baradri*, *patti*, caste, *zamindar*, and *wadera* dominated the lives of the population.

The constitution also fell short in explaining the role of religion and its place in what was projected to be a pluralistic, secular state. Although no state religion was contemplated by the framers, they nevertheless felt compelled to exaggerate the Islamic nature of the country. Islamic experience generated the psychic forces that created independent Pakistan, but there also was a practical and a pragmatic dimension in the Pakistan design, and that latter element centred attention on the formation of a nation-state fashioned from the British colonial experience. While the former provided the instinctive justification for the state, it was the latter which framed its structure, influenced its processes, and placed Pakistan in the firmament of the world's independent nations. The delay in producing a constitutional framework made the reconciliation of these two dialectically different inheritances a far more difficult and almost hopeless task. At first blush, the euphoria of independence was supposed to solve all issues and, most notably, fuse peoples of disparate cultures and aspirations, with different perspectives and expectations, into a single national entity. The first ten years of Pakistan's independent life were passed in that endeavour, and the lack of progress, the repeated failures, and the deepening crisis, pointed to the need for a course correction of significant magnitude.

Reviewing the sequence of events, and given the circumstances of Pakistan's emergence as an independent state, it is clear that Pakistan needed a leader who, on the one side, could pick up where Jinnah left off, and on the other, offset the viceregal tradition inherited from the colonial period. Pakistan did not require a substitute Quaid-i-Azam, but it did need someone who stood above petty feudal and tribal rivalries and who, while acknowledging the country's dominant religious tradition, nevertheless transcended scriptural interpretations of constitutional procedure. Some countries are fortunate in that they possess an abundance of gifted statesmen at independence, but Pakistan was not one of them. Liaquat lacked the necessary political perspective, Nazimuddin was a perennial neophyte, Ghulam Mohammad possessed a hopelessly flawed ego, and Iskandar Mirza was too blinded by power to use it effectively. In the larger scheme of things, Chaudhri Mohammad Ali, Mushtaq Ahmad Gurmani, Mian Mumtaz Daultana, Abdul Qaiyum Khan, Ayub Khuhro, Shaikh Mujibur Rahman, Maulana Bhashani, Fazlul Huq, and Sardar Abdur Rab Nishtar were all minor figures in a major scenario. None measured up to the demands of national leadership, and none were comfortable with the configuration that represented contemporary Pakistan.

Moreover, the events leading up to the transfer of power caused Jinnah to find dissatisfaction with and hence to reject the only Muslim League politician who had governed a Muslim-dominant province prior to partition. H.S. Suhrawardy had been the last Chief Minister of undivided Bengal, but he was forced to leave his party and find an alternative route into the Pakistani political mainstream. Suhrawardy was hardly Pakistan's saviour, but the record reveals that among all the other Pakistani politicians, he was the only one with an appreciation of the historical moment, with the political acumen and the rational mindset needed to reconcile rival moral claims; furthermore, his detached status afforded a flexibility of judgment not available to others more dependent on filial, tribal, or landed associations. Suhrawardy's second coming, however, was no more successful than his initial effort at finding a place in the Pakistan design. His rejection at the beginning, and again after ten years of independence, signalled the end of Pakistan's political experiment with representational politics.

The Politics of Confusion

Following Suhrawardy's ouster, Mirza found himself in a race to outdistance General Ayub Khan. Having worked with Ayub as Defence Secretary, as Governor of Bengal, Interior Minister, and as Governor-General and President, Mirza knew the General's thought process and concerns. Ayub had been Mirza's choice to head the Pakistan Army, and he had recommended him to Liaquat largely because he believed he had the determination, the character, and above all, the balanced personality needed to modernize and expand the forces, while at the same time holding in check the more gregarious and aggressive of the uniformed risk-takers. But Ayub's dedication to the restructuring of the army was not less than his concern for the future of Pakistan. Caught up in the disturbing events that followed his becoming Commander-in-Chief, Ayub's perceptions were sharpened by the sustained political instability.

Less a combat officer and more an administrator, Ayub had examined the Pakistan ethos and had concluded long before Suhrawardy's removal that the nation was ill-suited for the political experience that emerged from the colonial setting. Pakistan's politicians were judged wanting in all categories. Self-serving, narrow-minded, suspicious, and divisive, politicians in Ayub's estimation were a detriment, not an asset to the nation. But, although holding them in contempt, he acknowledged the country's aspiration for democratic expression, and he wondered how the politicians could be directed to that objective. Failing that, he also accepted responsibility for guiding the country along another path.

Mirza and Ayub had interacted in personal ways, socializing with one another and often sharing experiences and ideas. Of the two men, Mirza was more the doer while

Ayub was, by contrast, contemplative, calculating, and deliberate. Mirza operated largely from instinct influenced by a quasi-imperial attitude. His relatively brief military experience had done more to bolster his aristocratic nature than hone his tactical thinking. Ayub was more systematic, better organized, more given to routine, and highly disciplined. More familiar with the Pakistan scene in West Pakistan, his roots intertwined with the lives of the rural folk who settled the Frontier and Punjab areas. Mirza could never escape his Murshidabad birthplace and he always appeared more at home in distant places, far from Pakistan.

With the parliamentary institution in a shambles, Mirza had only his Republican Party to fall back upon. A jerry-built organization, it had no philosophical underpinnings and functioned only as an extension of autocratic forces with essentially landed interests. Although Dr Khan Sahib had claimed leadership of the party, Mirza had no compunctions in abandoning him, given his tryst with the NAP and that party's secessionist rhetoric. Determined to preserve the One Unit, and pressurized by Ayub to act decisively in neutralizing the NAP, Mirza attempted to assume direct control of the Republican Party and immediately entered into negotiations with members of the Muslim League. Bypassing Nishtar, he called on I.I.Chundrigar, a former Law Minister and a primary actor in the constitution-making process, to form a new ministry in combination with the Republican Party. Chundrigar responded quickly to the President's call, fearing a total collapse of the constitutional system if he delayed his decision. But Chundrigar none the less struck a hard bargain. In return for Muslim League support for One Unit, he expected Mirza to force the Republicans to retreat from their acceptance of East Pakistan's joint electorate. Knowing this would inflame passions in the east wing, Mirza nevertheless concluded that risking the enmity of the Bengalis was a lesser price in his struggle to save the Republican Party. It did not follow, however, that the Republicans saw the problem in quite the same way, or that they were prepared to substitute Mirza for Khan Sahib.

Chundrigar's government was a curious combination of old, somewhat tired, often conflicting personalities. Firoz

Khan Noon, Ghulam Ali Talpur, Mian Jafar Shah, and Amjad Ali were holdovers from the Suhrawardy Cabinet, but Fazlur Rahman, Mumtaz Daultana, and Yusuf Haroon were also added to highlight representation from the different provinces. In party make-up, the cabinet included the Muslim League, the Republican Party, the Krishak Sramik, and the Nizam-i-Islam, with the Muslim League a minority in its own government. Thus, the Chundrigar administration had built-in difficulties that the Prime Minister could not manage, no matter how sincere his efforts at reconciling the many disparate programmes. In fact, the Prime Minister was betrayed even before he could describe his intentions. Dr Khan Sahib challenged Mirza's right to speak for the Republicans and he manoeuvred behind the scenes, canvassing the members on the electorate issue. As a consequence, the Republicans refused to go along with Mirza's scheme, and Chundrigar was prevented from moving the matter in the National Assembly. Chundrigar was immediately pressurized by his party, as well as the Nizam-i-Islam, to bring the issue to a vote and, if unsuccessful, to tender his resignation.

Mirza sensed still another crisis, and called for time to work out the difficulties between the competing politicians. A Republican Fact-Finding Committee was assembled which was slated to leave for East Pakistan to ascertain popular sentiment, but before it could depart, Nishtar organized a Muslim League demonstration outside the National Assembly building in Karachi. I.I. Chundrigar was called to address the assembled crowd, which had paralysed commercial activity in the city and which threatened violence if its wishes went unanswered. When Chundrigar appeared, his words were measured and carefully modulated. Informing the throng that he had received their message, he assured them that their demands had been accepted. Separate electorates were an article of faith, and he would not allow politics to compromise that position. Urging the crowd to disperse, the Prime Minister thought he had achieved the desired result when Suhrawardy's vehicle approached the Assembly grounds. Recognizing the former Prime Minister, the crowd surged toward the car shouting obscenities, while some of the more violent-prone unleashed an assault of rocks and brickbats. Although Suhrawardy was not injured in the mêlée, his car was badly damaged, and the episode illustrated the brittle and volatile nature of the Pakistan scene.

Chundrigar apologized to Suhrawardy for the misbehaviour of the demonstrators and called for a higher degree of security around the National Assembly building. The Awami League opposition, however, saw the opportunity to harangue the Prime Minister, to question his authority, and to belittle his efforts at reconciliation. Suhrawardy, clearly shaken by the experience, charged the government with a failure to maintain law and order, and he characterized the incident in front of the Assembly as a premeditated conspiracy. Shaikh Mujibur Rahman followed with a motion calling for the adjournment of the House so that the entire affair could be thoroughly investigated. Moreover, Dr Khan Sahib, in a blatant attempt to embarrass Mirza, agreed to support Mujib's complaint. Khan Sahib called for an end to the charade of parliamentary government. 'We are unfit for democracy,' he exclaimed (*Morning News*, 1 December 1957). The old Pathan warrior revived his call for a 'revolutionary council' and for the 'ten best men' to be chosen to run the country. But the most venomous speeches were reserved for Shaikh Mujibur Rahman and Ataur Rahman Khan, leaders of the East Bengal Awami League. They declared that the preservation of law and order in the east wing could no longer be guaranteed. Bengalis, too, were capable of organizing demonstrations, and, added Mujib, 'if the Muslim League could bring a few thousand people to show that it had the people's backing in its demands for separate electorates, I can bring one lakh (100,000) people to show that the people were for joint electorates' (*Morning News*, 1 December 1957).

Following the stormy debate in the National Assembly, the Republican-Fact Finding Committee left for East Pakistan, where in one week they visited eight different districts and received sixty deputations from representatives of various communities. In the end, the committee was even more confused than earlier, except that they had occasion to note the work of the caucuses behind the political parties 'and their power of mobilization that regiments and parades the unwary common man into various gatherings and makes (him) shout slogans, and raise hands in favour of or against an issue which he hardly grasps' (Mahmud, 1958, p.10). The Republicans, nevertheless, decided they could not support the rescinding of the joint electorates in East Pakistan, and on 11 December 1957, hardly two months after taking office, I.I. Chundrigar announced the resignation of his government.

Mirza had plotted the whole sorry mess, and sensing a considerable loss of personal prestige, he urged Chundrigar to reconsider his decision. He also moved to block the actions of Dr Khan Sahib, who he held chiefly responsible for the unrest that had spread to all regions of the country. Khan Sahib, however, had become more intimate with the NAP, and his courting of the Awami League gave him substantial leverage in his contest with the President. Chundrigar, prodded by Mirza, made one last desperate attempt to rally his dispirited forces, but it was a futile gambit. On 13 December Mirza had to admit defeat, and he called upon Malik Firoz Khan Noon, a former Governor of East Pakistan and more recently the Chief Minister of Punjab, to form yet another government. Firoz Khan Noon had been the Foreign Minister in both the Suhrawardy and Chundrigar administrations. He also was a charter-member Republican, having joined the party at its inception. More significantly, Noon was Pakistan's seventh Prime Minister in little more than ten years.

The strength of the Firoz Khan Noon government was also its weakness. It was a coalition like none before it. The cabinet was comprised of seventeen members, drawn from the Republican Party, the Awami League, the National Awami Party, the Pakistan National Congress (a Hindu organization), the Scheduled Caste Federation, and the Krishak Sramik Party. Only the communal parties, i.e., the Muslim League, the Nizam-i-Islam, and the Jamaat-i-Islami, were left in the opposition. Furthermore, Dr Khan Sahib and H.S. Suhrawardy entered into an agreement that, on the surface at least, suspended their running feud. Khan Sahib explained the manoeuvre by stating that, 'I and Mr Suhrawardy are determined to sit together and make the new Cabinet work smoothly' (*Pakistan Times*, 16 December 1957). Khan Sahib's actions behind the scenes led Chundrigar to note that Noon was little more than the spokesman for a small elite that acted as 'a sort of presidium outside the cabinet' (*Morning News*, 19 December 1957). Mirza drew the same conclusion. Moreover, he was convinced that the combined Opposition, led by Dr Khan Sahib and the members of the President's erstwhile party, were determined to neutralize his authority. Recalling the efforts made to reduce the power of Ghulam Mohammad, it was Mirza who now contemplated taking the drastic action that his successor had used to defend his position.

Mirza publicly warned the politicians that their actions would be weighed carefully and, if the people of Pakistan did not reject the political manoeuvring, he might have to do so in their behalf. Mirza dilated on Pakistan's utter lack of mass education, and how important such experience was to a mass population confronted by political chicanery. In a moment of considerable exasperation he noted that, 'our political headaches will continue in a greater or lesser measure till we are able to increase our percentage of literacy' (*Pakistan Times*, 23 December 1957). Later Mirza attacked the politicians as callow opportunists whose loyalties shifted 'with each passing wind'. No government could be expected to 'tackle the serious problems facing the country if it is made to feel that it is sitting on the apex of a shaky pyramid'. Perhaps conscious of his own indiscretions, President Mirza admitted that the 'challenge of freedom' demanded more sustained and dedicated efforts than the strength required to attain it (*Pakistan Times*, 26 December 1957).

Mirza's lament centred on the politicians he could not control, but his principal target was a constitutional system that protected diverse expression but did not guarantee political stability (Von Vorys, 1965). Moreover, the proliferation of political organizations had complicated the work of doing the country's business. Those parties not in power were obliged to use every opportunity, every tactic, to prevent those in power from managing the public's affairs. Thus, if satisfaction could not be achieved inside the parliamentary institution, it was not unusual to take the struggle into the streets, where the emotional and easily mobilized masses were all too eager to demonstrate their disfavour with the prevailing order.

Crisis Politics in East Pakistan

In March 1958 the Awami League provincial government in East Pakistan issued a series of ordinances designed to limit the power of the Speaker of the Legislative Assembly. Under the terms of the Secretariat Act of 1956, the Speaker presided over the Assembly secretariat and possessed exceptional powers in the legislature. The purpose of the Act was to place the Speaker above politics, but in the ambience of East Pakistani politics, the Speaker, Abul Hakim, was easily compromised. Won over by the opposition, he was deemed a threat to the Awami League government; hence its decision to use extraordinary measures against him. The ordinances forbade the Speaker from adjourning the proceedings of the House until he had the concurrence of the majority leader. They also eliminated the autonomy of the secretariat, and passed control in the Assembly to the members of the ruling party. Not unexpectedly, the opposition reacted negatively to the government orders, saying they had no legal foundation and would not be allowed to stand. The Krishak Sramik spokesman argued that the Awami League had reduced the secretariat to ashes, while the NAP accused the provincial government of 'murdering democracy' (*Morning News*, 13 March 1958).

When the Awami League Chief Minister, Ataur Rahman Khan, placed his government's budget before the legislature, an NAP legislator argued that the bill should be circulated among the population before being brought to a vote. In the ensuing debate, and failing to get the House to pass the measure, Ataur Rahman called upon the Governor, who just happened to be Fazlul Huq, the sworn enemy of the Awami League, to prorogue the Assembly. Fazlul Huq refused that order and instead, issued one of his own demanding the resignation of the Awami League government because, in his view, it no longer controlled a majority in the legislature (*Morning News*, 1 April 1958). Ataur Rahman ignored the Governor's order and argued that he was prepared to call for a vote of confidence. Moreover, the Chief Minister publicized that his cabinet had earlier recommended the removal of the Governor, and that Fazlul Huq had acted from personal pique and in a rash attempt to save his office. With passions rising on both sides, Fazlul Huq declared the Awami League government defunct and, that evening, swore in a member of his Krishak Sramik Party, Abu Hussain Sarkar, as the new Chief Minister of East Pakistan. The Governor's action was made in the middle of the night and without prior notice, thus bringing into question its constitutionality. Only Pakistan's arbitrary, viceregal tradition underpinned the action, but this time that tradition would not go unchallenged.

Fazlul Huq prorogued the provincial legislature, something he had refused to do for Ataur Rahman, but which now had to be done to give Abu Hussain Sarkar the time necessary to form a parliamentary majority. The Awami League leaders, however, made an immediate appeal to the central government for assistance, arguing that the Governor's actions were illegal and undemocratic and warning that if they were not reversed, East Pakistan would be plunged into violence. Energized by the call, the central coalition, of which the Awami League was a major component, was called into midnight session and it was their judgment, crystallized by Dr Khan Sahib, that Fazlul Huq must go. A telephonic message was then relayed from Karachi to the Chief Secretary in East Pakistan, the highest ranking administrative officer in the province. The call specified that Fazlul Huq had been dismissed by the central government and that he, the Chief Secretary, was to assume the duties of the Governor. The Secretary, and now Interim Governor, was told to dismiss the Krishak Sramik Chief Minister, who had been sworn in just hours earlier, and to swear in Ataur Rahman Khan who would reassemble his government. Following these events, the reinstated Awami League leader declared the 'victory of democracy', but his statement appeared overdrawn and hinted that the struggle had yet to reach its climax (*Morning News*, 2 April 1958).

Only the communal parties protested against the actions of the central government. Chundrigar spoke for the Muslim League, condemning a decision that did not allow Fazlul Huq's Krishak Sramik to face the East Pakistan Assembly.

Although nothing came of the complaint, Fazlul Huq was yet to respond. Reassuming control of his party, he cited the anticipated national elections that were forecast for a date in 1959, and although an octogenarian, he expected to contest those elections in the most vigorous fashion. Moreover, his call for still another United Front drew the attention of Maulana Bhashani, who had been active in the formation of the Krishak Samity, a peasant organization which he hoped to integrate with the NAP. An alliance with the Krishak Sramik not only would blend the two peasant organizations, but also held out the prospect of a more radicalized Bengali population. It was Bhashani's strategy to focus on rural issues and 'ultimately' to mobilize a peasantry that could challenge the urban elite which had controlled the province since independence. Bhashani's public statement on 4 May 1958 cited 'a tremendous awakening among the East Pakistan masses for whom the solution of the present-day ills lay in class struggle'. And although he denied previously calling for East Bengal's secession, he was unambiguous in noting that the time was approaching when the only alternative was to say 'goodbye to Pakistan' (*Morning News*, 5 May 1958). The Maoist character of Bhashani's performance, his repeated call for the termination of the western alliances and for the breakup of One Unit, and his championing of joint electorates, did not escape the notice of President Mirza.

The sudden death of Sardar Abdur Rab Nishtar altered the role of the Muslim League, and the emergence of a new power structure hinted at a more co-operative arrangement between the party and the central government. Mirza welcomed Abdul Qaiyum Khan when he was named to succeed Nishtar; as President of the Muslim League, Qaiyum was expected to work more closely with the Republicans. Mirza also entered into an alliance with Ayub Khuhro, and his relatively new and independent Sindh Muslim League was added to the growing Republican coalition. Mirza's attempt to gain control of the Republican Party received an unanticipated boost when word reached Karachi on 9 May 1958 that Dr Khan Sahib had been assassinated by someone described as an unbalanced malcontent. A number of persons were initially implicated in a plot to kill the Republican leader, but no evidence was ever found to demonstrate that the incident was anything but the act of a deranged individual who had acted alone. Nevertheless, Khan Sahib's sudden demise had opened the way for Mirza to re-establish his claim to leadership of the Republican Party.

The Awami League now joined with the Muslim League in accusing the President of compromising his office by assuming control of the Republican Party. Shaikh Mujibur Rahman travelled to Karachi to personally attack Mirza as unworthy of the high office he held. The President, he said, more than 'dabbled' in politics, he was the 'band-master' of the most elitist and privileged organization in the country (*Morning News*, 6 June 1958). Mujib declared he was ready to rally the masses in both wings of the country to counter Mirza's moves. Qaiyum Khan echoed Mujib's sentiments, believing the time was right to force Mirza from office and, in so doing, to destroy the Republican Party. The new Muslim League President rejected all Mirza's overtures for co-operation and instead vilified him, insisting that the President was 'plotting the annihilation of both the Muslim League and the Awami League'. Qaiyum wanted the Pakistani public to believe that Nishtar's passing had turned the Muslim League back to its Jinnah orientation. He also reflected on Dr Khan's Sahib's sudden and violent death and lamented the loss of a brother Pathan. Later, Qaiyum would declare that he had no serious quarrels with H.S. Suhrawardy or the Awami League, and that only a resolution of the electorate question prevented the merging of their organizations.

Qaiyum's attempt to win over the Awami League drove Fazlul Huq to accept Bhashani's earlier offer of an alliance. After secret talks between Huq and Bhashani, the NAP announced it would transfer its support from the East Pakistan Awami League to the Krishak Sramik. The decision was sufficient to bring down the Ataur Rahman government and to replace it with another led by Fazlul Huq's successor, Abu Hussain Sarkar, who formed a coalition of the Krishak Sramik, the NAP, Nizam-i-Islam, the Muslim League, the Scheduled Caste Federation, the Congress Party, and the United Progressive Party. Not quite a United Front, the situation allowed Shaikh Mujibur Rahman to approach high members of the NAP and, in confidential talks with Mahmud Ali, to promise support for the NAP manifesto, i.e., for the break-up of One Unit and the termination of the western alliances, if the organization withdrew its support from the Krishak Sramik. Seeing an opportunity to extend its influence, the NAP agreed to do so.

Therefore, only three days after the Sarkar government had assumed its responsibilities, Mujib moved a motion of no-confidence in the provincial legislature. True to their secret arrangements, the NAP voted with the Awami League, and the almost-to-be United Front government collapsed. Sarkar emotionally asked, 'while in this House we are making and unmaking ministries...how many of you can give thought to the suffering and hardship of our common men and women?' (*Pakistan Times*, 24 June 1958). Mujib's action had not only crippled the province's parliamentary process, it had also destroyed Suhrawardy's credibility in the central government. More important, it forced Mirza to impose President's Rule in East Pakistan, and rumours spread that he and Ayub had reason to suspect a communist plot. Provoked by President's Rule, Mujib condemned the President and the Republican Party, but his criticism was also directed at Pakistani industrialists who, he said, had turned East Pakistan into a 'colony'. Either the central government would restore self-government to the province, or the Bengali people would find another way to regain their independence, he said (*Morning News*, 7 July 1958).

Suhrawardy hurriedly met with Mirza in order to head off a showdown that appeared to threaten the very character of the state. Convincing Mirza that President's Rule should be revoked, on 24 August, Ataur Rahman Khan once again was called to assemble a government. Mujib, however, was hardly satiated, let alone satisfied. Sensing the weakness of the central government and ignoring threats of a military takeover, he demanded reparations, citing the '710 million dollars received by the Pakistan Government from the United States' and the mere '115 million dollars sanctioned for East Pakistan' (*Morning News*, 7 September 1958). Arguing that the imbalance had played havoc with East Bengal's economy, Mujib went to Karachi to demand immediate compliance with his demand. Finding Mirza in no mood to yield to his pressure, Mujib returned to East Pakistan to inform his followers that the central government was eager to destroy the indigenous leadership in the province and impose a dictatorship. Suhrawardy's call for decorum and calm, for rational discussion and compromise, was no longer appreciated by either side. The lines had hardened between the more conservative and the radical forces, and any attempt at reconciling their positions appeared doomed to failure.

Bhashani added his voice to that of Mujib's and his rhetoric was more bombastic than previously. Speaking about breaking the 'shackles of imperialism', he cited the shattered provincial economy, and insisted that the food crisis was directly linked to Pakistan having become a 'slave of Anglo-American imperialism'. He added that it was time to punish the Pakistani 'agents' of the alien powers, and he identified Suhrawardy as one of them. 'In no time his name would be obliterated,' he prophesied (*Morning News*, 15 September 1958). On 17 September a confident Maulana Bhashani announced that Suhrawardy no longer represented the Awami League and that there were no longer any differences between the NAP and that party.

The Loss of Innocence

The solidification of the Awami League-NAP coalition energized separatist forces as never before. On 20 September the Awami League government issued additional ordinances reshaping the role of the Speaker so that he could not act without the approval of the Awami League government. Moreover, the Speaker was deprived of his neutrality when the government claimed the right to dismiss him without the customary debate in the Assembly. The Speaker, Abul Hakim, had infuriated the Awami League leaders by his parliamentary manoeuvres, and notably by his disallowance of a motion that would have called for an end to One Unit. He also angered the radicals when several of their number were disqualified from membership in the Legislative Assembly due to conflicts of interest. Appealing to Prime Minister Firoz Khan Noon, the Awami League made its case against the Speaker, and Noon responded by calling Hakim's

actions illegal and hence null and void. Not yet ready to
yield to the Awami League pressure, Hakim sent an urgent
cable to President Mirza in which he outlined a terrible
situation that continued to deteriorate. He cited threats to his
life by Mujib and the fact that a member of his family had
already been assaulted by Awami League toughs, while others
had been arrested or thoroughly intimidated. The work of the
provincial Assembly, he concluded, was at an impasse
(*Report of the Enquiry, 1958*).

Mirza did not respond to the telegram, and the Speaker
made an appearance in the Assembly in spite of his fears.
The Awami League legislators whose seats were questioned
also appeared, thus increasing the tension in the House.
When the latter were challenged and the Prime Minister's
directive allowing them to assume their roles was read, little
could be done to calm the opposition. Moreover, a government
action seeking a no-confidence vote against the Speaker added
to the frenzy. Hakim called the motion curtailing his powers
out of order. Mujib, however, gestured his supporters in the
Assembly to rise and be counted as approving the motion.
The Opposition saw itself trapped on all sides and, with their
combined temper no longer controllable, pandemonium
overwhelmed the House. Representatives from both sides of
the aisle clashed near the Speaker's rostrum, chairs sailed
through the air, and any loose object became an improvised
weapon. The Speaker's microphone became a bludgeon; even
the National Flag was transformed into a potentially lethal,
freewheeling lathi. Outsiders who were in the House also
joined in the mêlée. The Speaker, fearing for his life,
adjourned the session and fled from the building. When the
near riot subsided, the government benches refused to vacate
the premises. Instead, they moved and passed a motion
declaring the Speaker not to be of sound mind and calling for
a competent board of doctors to be assembled to confirm his
condition. The government did not permit a debate on the
matter and the Deputy Speaker, Shahid Ali, ruled that the
motion had carried.

The scene in the Provincial Assembly was subsequently
described as among 'the ugliest incidents ever witnessed
inside a legislature in the parliamentary history of the

subcontinent' (*Morning News*, 21 September 1958). Nevertheless, the Assembly convened the next two days without incident, although neither the Speaker nor the Deputy Speaker entered the hall. The debates on those two days were essentially procedural and centred on the motions voted upon during the earlier fracas. In the end, the exchanges proved nothing, and all the issues remained unresolved. When the legislature convened again on 23 September, no spectators were permitted entry. The Deputy Speaker had been pressured to appear and, in spite of his poor health, he moved fitfully to his seat.

The Opposition was taken by surprise, however, and following some sharp and acrimonious speeches, the legislators again scuffled with one another. It was in the midst of a general free-for-all that an object, said to be the top of a writing desk, was hurled at the Deputy Speaker. Shahid Ali was struck on the bridge of his nose and fell to the floor. Suddenly the District Magistrate, the Inspector-General of Police, and a contingent of steel-helmeted police burst into the Assembly. In the ensuing confusion, the Opposition found themselves in hand to hand combat with the police while the government benches looked on in amusement. The Inspector-General of Police ordered his forces to clear the Opposition from the House, and as they ushered the legislators out of the building, several of the latter were beaten in the entrance to the Assembly, their wounds requiring hospitalization. Shahid Ali, however, had suffered a mortal blow. He died on 25 September, before a specialist who had been summoned from Calcutta could reach his bedside.

The official government announcement stated that the Deputy Speaker had died from a blow received in the mêlée. Several officials of the Krishak Sramik hierarchy were arrested and charged with an attempt to murder (*The Mail*, 27 September 1958), and with several members of the opposition in prison, the Awami League gained complete control of the East Pakistan Government, the Legislature, and the secretariat. But the Awami League was not the only actor in the unfolding scenario. In East Pakistan Army Headquarters, General Umrao Khan sent a highly confidential report to his Commander-in-Chief, General Ayub in

Rawalpindi. Umrao Khan detailed the events of the preceding days and concluded that only army intervention could prevent a radical takeover of the province. Ayub read the message with considerable interest, more so because conditions in West Pakistan also appeared to have taken a desperate turn.

Although less dramatic than the events in the East Pakistan Legislature, West Pakistan had been destabilized by the assassination of Dr Khan Sahib and the death of Sardar Abdur Rab Nishtar, and Qaiyum had added his voice to the chorus of those demanding an end to the western alliances. Moreover, Qaiyum and Chaudhri Mohammad Ali cited the perfidy of India in Kashmir and had urged a military response. The Muslim League had organized its own para-military force, and after a number of threatening Muslim League gestures toward Kashmir, the government felt compelled to ban the wearing of uniforms by all political organizations. Qaiyum, however, defied the government order and forced the Republicans to either act against him, or expose their weaknesses. Meanwhile, Abdul Ghaffar Khan was inciting his followers to engage in a *jung* (war) against the central government. Renewing earlier, non-negotiable demands for self-determination, he declared, 'Bengalis, Punjabis, Sindhis, and Pathans, each group has a homeland of their own and had better be the masters of their own destinies.' Ghaffar Khan's call for the virtual breakup of Pakistan was echoed in East Pakistan by Maulana Bhashani, who inaugurated his personalized Krishak Samity, or peasants' association. Speaking to the assembled crowd, the Maulana said the time was approaching when it would be necessary 'to launch a country-wide vigorous movement to end the tyranny in the present social order'. The Maulana's statements were judged a call to make class war, and Umrao Khan's urgent message to Ayub dramatically took on new meaning.

Firoz Khan Noon was not oblivious to developments in the different sections of the country but his government was burdened by contradictory elements, and when the Prime Minister was forced to add seven more cabinet members, his government's ineffectiveness was apparent to all. The unprecedented number of central government officials in the cabinet guaranteed paralysis in the decision-making process, and the government's inability to act in decisive arenas only energized the opposition to demand additional advantages. By early October 1958, approximately one-third of National Assembly members held cabinet positions. All the parties were represented, save the Muslim League and the Nizam-i-Islam. The NAP was on record as supporting the government but it, too, did not hold any cabinet positions. Given the chaotic use of the inclusionary principle, the Noon government could hardly maintain discipline, and it was impossible to check rampant corruption and inefficiency. The civil service, too, was affected, as career administrators consorted with politicians, or took advantage of the anarchical situation to maximize personal interests.

As the troubled days of September turned into a new October, it was all too obvious that the political process had broken down and that the prevailing disaffection and alienation threatened the survival of the Pakistan nation. Threats of rebellion and acts of civil disobedience had become commonplace, and the central government had lost all popular respect. It was at this juncture that word reached Karachi that the Khan of Kalat, Mir Ahmad Yar Khan, had seized the Miri Fort in Balochistan, removed the Pakistan flag, and raised his own ancestral standard in its place. In what was judged to be an open break with the central government, the Khan of Kalat signalled the independence of his realm. This incident, in combination with untoward and uncontrollable events in almost all the provinces of Pakistan, weighed heavily on and eventually broke the back of the Noon government. Unable to respond effectively, ignored and humiliated by every sector and region of the country, Pakistan's political leaders were not asked to step aside, they were about to be cast away.

On 6 October 1958 the Pakistan Army moved against the Khan of Kalat, deposed him, stripped him of his titles, and subsequently arrested him. Although in the larger scheme of things a minor encounter, the Kalat incident was the signal for a major course correction. The very next day, the army, under General Mohammad Ayub Khan's command, seized control of the radio and telegraph stations in Karachi, Lahore,

Peshawar, and Dhaka. Troops invaded and occupied the major railway and air terminals. The ports of Karachi and Chittagong were locked in a steel vice of flashing bayonets. The National Assembly and provincial legislatures were surrounded and sealed. The sanctity of the newspapers was violated, and strict controls were imposed on their operations. The Constitution, nine years in the making, although only promulgated in March 1956 and never completely implemented, was formally abrogated. With the legislatures closed, the political parties were hardly needed; all were banned and their assets seized or frozen. The politicians had played at representative government for a little more than a decade, and the Pakistan Army, its patience exhausted, ended the charade.

The magnitude of the military intervention pointed to a carefully planned country-wide operation that was months in preparation. Martial law was imposed throughout the country under the authority of President Iskandar Mirza, who declared that General Mohammad Ayub Khan had been made Chief Martial Law Administrator. While the attentive public had reason to expect this military intrusion, the wholesale repudiation of the political process pointed Pakistan in a different direction from that envisaged by Mohammad Ali Jinnah. President Mirza issued the proclamation that abrogated the constitution, dissolved the National and Provincial Assemblies, and banned the parties and all political activity. But it was General Ayub Khan who controlled the armed services, as well as the civil bureaucracy.

The *coup* had been engineered by both Mirza and Ayub but it was obvious that the General, not the President, was the key figure (Wheeler, 1970). Moreover, the two men represented views at variance with one another. Whereas Mirza intended to use martial law to stabilize the political process, and essentially to eliminate those members of the opposition who were undermining his authority, Ayub was determined to chart an entirely different course for the nation. Mirza was a decision-maker whose goals were all short-term and largely self-serving. By contrast, Ayub was given to measured thought, and because he had been distant from day-to-day political activity, he enjoyed a perspective not available to the President. Ayub's tenure as Army Commander-in-Chief reflected stability in a country otherwise in great disarray. When compared with political developments, Ayub's success in building a sophisticated military apparatus gave him the confidence necessary to reconstruct the national ethos. Mirza, of course, perceived a personal threat in Ayub's visionary expressions, and, believing he would be written out of the General's projected programme of national renewal, he was confronted with two options: he could try to neutralize him, or he could make a graceful retreat. The latter had never been a feature of Mirza's character, however, and a final showdown was not long in coming.

Mirza believed he could woo some of the high-ranking officers around Ayub, win their favour with promises of advancement, and thereby protect an important role for himself. On 10 October Ayub gave a press conference which suggested he knew nothing of Mirza's plans to unseat him, nor did he indicate that he had plans to remove the President. Ayub said that, 'martial law was still subservient to the President of Pakistan', who remained in his office even after the abrogation of the constitution (*Pakistan Times*, 11 October 1958). Ayub acknowledged that questions surrounding the governance of the country still required answers and that Supreme Court Chief, Justice Mohammad Munir, had been requested to render a legal opinion on the legitimacy of the revolution. He cited the Continuance in Force Order, 1958, that declared the courts to be fully functional and hence open to serve the public's juristic and administrative needs. Ayub left little doubt that it was only the prior political system that had been scrapped and that plans were in motion to replace it with one more suited to Pakistan's political culture and circumstances.

Mirza, however, had reason to fear a substitute political system. He had had long discussions with Ayub and he knew that the General preferred a presidential to a parliamentary arrangement. Ayub had privately expressed the opinion that Pakistan was not ready for European-style representative government, and that the parliamentary experience weakened rather than strengthened national unity. Mirza had expressed similar views on numerous occasions; for example, he had recently publicly aired his frustrations over the country's massive illiteracy problem. Mirza did not have to be told that responsible self-government required an informed, alert, and collectively intelligent public, or that Pakistan did not measure up in any of these categories. Moreover, Mirza's stated preference for a ruling council to govern Pakistan was ill-defined and hardly pointed to a revolutionary course correction.

Compared to Mirza, Ayub was more decisive and less given to deal-making. Unlike the President, who was always prepared to equivocate, to reverse himself, Ayub had no intention of returning to a *status quo ante*. He saw his task as something considerably more than the mere isolation of troublesome politicians. The abrogation of the 1956 Constitution was a seminal event in the history of the nation, and Ayub understood that it had to be followed by major changes. Ayub was convinced that Pakistan needed more, not less, centralized government, that the decision-making process had to be narrowly focused and made the responsibility of experts and specialists. Precious time had been lost in petty political manoeuvring, the country's development had suffered from a decade of neglect, and a diverse and impatient population had become restive and more difficult to control. Ayub rejected modifications in the prevailing system, nor did he envisage another that could accommodate two headstrong chief executives.

On 15 October Mirza addressed a group of foreign correspondents who were eager to learn how long the country would experience martial law. Mirza's comments were recorded verbatim, and it was obvious that he expected to organize a new government and return the army to the barracks. 'I shall run martial law for the shortest duration possible. Then we shall have a National Council of not more than twelve or fifteen persons' who would be responsible for cleaning up the country. According to Mirza, a new constitution would be crafted by 'thirty or forty good men' and 'examined by people of international repute' who would check every article and every clause to be certain it was 'workable'. A referendum would then be conducted to affirm the product before putting it into force (*Morning News*, 16 October 1958). There was nothing specific in Mirza's thinking, no indication of the form of political experience that he believed best suited the Pakistani nation. What was clear, however, was the President's discomfort with any protraction of martial law. The longer martial law remained in force, the more his personal prerogatives diminished, and indeed, the more his powers shifted to the office of the Chief Martial Law Administrator.

Shortly thereafter, Ayub exposed the differences that separated Mirza from himself. Ayub was emphatic that martial law was a long-term proposition because it would take time and considerable energy to realize the purposes of the *coup*. He reminded all those who would listen, including Mirza, that drastic measures had been introduced. A constitution had been abrogated and it could not be resurrected. An entire political system had been dismantled and it could not be reassembled. The country was passing through a major, irreversible transition, and simple remedies, let alone ambiguous thinking, would not suffice. 'The country has to be brought back to a state of convalescence, if not complete health,' declared Ayub. 'In addition certain major reforms have to be introduced. All these things will need the cover of Martial Law...there is no intention to allow things to revert to the old ways'. And pointing in Mirza's direction, he said: 'Don't let anyone have doubts or fears on this score' (*Dawn*, 18 October 1958).

In need of political leverage, Mirza fell back on the landed aristocracy who had flocked to the Republican Party. Ayub had appointed a Land Reform Commission, and the feudals at first feared the loss of their vast holdings and hence a diminution in their influence and power. Ayub laboured to offset that alliance and to overcome such fears. He appealed directly to the agrarian elite, and he assured them that his plans did not entail a reduction in their stature, or the loss of their property. On the contrary, Ayub was not about to turn the life of the country over to untried, inexperienced, uneducated peasants. The country's principal need was law and order, and national unity was a consequence, as well as a requirement, of that objective. The landlords were a stabilizing influence in the country and, in concert with the civil administration, they were the ones likely to restore the country's equilibrium. Land reform, he affirmed, was neither ideologically driven, nor was it aimed at taking holdings from the few and distributing them among the many. Ayub sought stability and a predictable order in which national growth could be energized. He also envisaged a new, more constructive alliance with the country's landlords. Stabilizing the political scene meant more resources could be devoted to development, and the successful execution of economic and social programmes implied a more satisfied and less exploitable population. Ayub envisaged a long learning experience and a major role for the landed aristocracy.

Ayub's capacity to attract support from Mirza's constituency exposed the weakness of his presidency. It also forced Mirza to take direct aim at the General. It was now apparent that only one of them could emerge the victor. Ayub was clearly the more advantaged in this context. Not only did the General control the forces of violence, he also had the only systematic plan for Pakistan's future. Mirza's *ad hoc* methods, and almost absence of forethought, made him a poor match for a determined Ayub Khan. Ayub was on tour in East Pakistan when word reached him that Mirza had constituted a new government and had appointed him the Prime Minister. Three other generals were also appointed to the cabinet, and civil administrators filled the remaining positions. The formation of such a government revealed that Mirza was inclined to recreate the parliamentary process; if allowed to stand, it would elevate the role of the President and, of course, place the Prime Minister under his charge.

But to prevent Ayub from challenging his scheme, Mirza had to penetrate the army and win its confidence, much as Ayub had begun to win over key members of the landlord caste. Moreover, having given Ayub the post of Prime Minister, Mirza was then in a position to replace him as Commander-in-Chief of the Army. Mirza had, in fact, announced that he had promoted Lieutenant-General Mohammad Musa to the most senior rank, and that Musa would assume command of the Pakistan Army. Mirza also issued numerous promotions and raised the salaries of serving officers and troops. In the same stroke, Mirza made Ayub Supreme Commander of the Armed Forces, but this was hardly a promotion; it was quickly seen as little more than an empty title. The contest of wills between the President and the General had reached a climax.

Ayub could not reverse Mirza's decisions without causing significant disruptions within the army. He could not reduce men in rank who had been promoted, nor could he deny increases in pay once they had been publicized. Ayub had not yet been retired from the army, but his hold on the troops was in the process of being undermined and he had little time to find a solution to what had become his personal problem.

Mirza had not only hastily moved to establish a new government, he had also drafted a new oath of office especially for the Prime Minister. It read:

> I solemnly affirm that in the office of Prime Minister I will faithfully discharge such duties as the President may assign me, that I will bear true faith and allegiance to Pakistan, and that I will do right to all manner of people according to law without fear or favour, affection or ill-will.

For Ayub, to submit to such an oath was tantamount to an abdication of his goals and purposes. The revolution would have meant nothing more than safeguarding the prerogatives of the President. Moreover, the army, which had been popularly acclaimed as a saviour, would have sullied its reputation by appearing to throw in its lot with the nation's most discredited politician. Ayub therefore refused to accept Mirza's offer. Moreover, on the day set aside for the swearing in of the new cabinet, Chief Justice Munir rendered his judgment on the revolution. Munir wrote that a 'victorious revolution or a successful *coup d'etat* is an internationally recognized method of changing a constitution' (Callard, 1959, p.35). The revolution was declared an appropriate act and Ayub in effect had the ruling he needed to legitimize the next stage in the transformation process. Tactically, Ayub accepted the new government, but strategically he moved to rid himself of Iskandar Mirza. He ordered three of his closest associates, Lieutenant-General K.M. Sheikh, Lieutenant-

General W.A. Burki, and Lieutenant-General Azam Khan, to advise the President that it would be in his interest to step down, in fact to leave the country as soon as possible. Unable to gain the necessary support, and not wanting to divide the military, but also assured of a substantial pension in his London retreat, Mirza announced his retirement from the presidency on 27 September 1958. Iskandar Mirza noted in his final public statement that any semblance of dual control was likely to hamper the effective performance of the martial law government; and he did not want to leave the impression at home or abroad that:

> General Ayub and I may not always act in unison. Such an impression...if allowed to continue, would be most damaging to our cause...I wish General Ayub Khan and his colleagues the best of luck (*Pakistan Times*, 28 October 1958).

The office of Prime Minister was eliminated immediately following Mirza's resignation, and Ayub Khan overnight became President Mohammad Ayub Khan. Later, he would confer upon himself still another title, that of Field-Marshal of the Pakistan Army. In the latter instance, he found the opportunity to honour the recent Army promotions while assuring his continuing pre-eminence in all military matters. In the former, he made it absolutely clear who would be the legatee of the country's viceregal tradition and its maximum authority in all political matters.

On learning the news of Mirza's resignation and departure, spontaneous celebrations spread throughout the country. The sister of the Quaid-i-Azam, Miss Fatima Jinnah, summed up prevailing sentiments in the following words:

> A new era has begun under General Ayub Khan and the Armed Forces have undertaken to root out the administrative malaise and the anti-social practices, to create a sense of confidence, security and stability and eventually to bring the country back to normalcy. I hope and pray that God may give them wisdom and strength to achieve their objective (*Morning News*, 29 October 1958).

Not everyone echoed the thoughts of Fatima Jinnah or was pleased with the Army's intervention (Gardezi and Rashid, 1983). Nor were the obvious losers in the scenario about to shed their graces on the Chief Martial Law Administrator and his cohorts. The more jingoistic, if now less vocal, among the opposition were convinced the *coup* had been initiated by the United States which, they argued, had won over the higher members of the Pakistan Armed Forces. The Americans, it was said, wanted to prevent Pakistanis from going to the polls. Elections that were forecast no later than 15 February 1959, hardly four months away, threatened to end the rule of the western-influenced elite, and a newly constituted Pakistani government was perceived as likely to steer a course away from Pakistan's Cold War involvement. Washington, they asserted, anticipated repudiation at the polls, and the Pakistan Army was the only available instrument to deflect that outcome.

Less radical, but nevertheless unhappy, members of the failed political system refused to acknowledge that it had taken ten years of political turmoil to expose the ruling elite, and to demonstrate their self-aggrandizing and patronizing ways. In the view of these critics, the constitution was not at fault, nor were the politicians unfamiliar with its operations. A modified parliamentary system was in use prior to, and immediately following, the transfer of power. President Mirza's assertion that the constitution was hopelessly flawed, and hence needed to be cast aside, did not stand scrutiny. Moreover, in the absence of general elections the constitution's suitability could not be measured. If there was a problem in working the constitution, it was not found in its republic state structure or its parliamentary procedures. Thus it seemed logical to suggest that the violation of constitutional order was a consequence of foreign machinations working hand in glove with members of the Pakistan Armed Forces, who had much to gain from the situation.

But for the vast majority of Pakistanis, martial law was the inevitable outcome of a political experience gone wrong (Rizvi, 1986). At the core of the problem were the people who had been charged with giving significance to representative government and democratic experience. The persons most responsible for the execution of constitutional rules and principles had failed to resolve their inter-personal relationships, and their persistent feuding affected the larger society in the most negative fashion. The Pakistani nation required a particular form of selflessness from its leaders, a transcendent awareness of national need and public accountability. The politicians had revealed little of that, and instead had allowed their personal insecurities to infect the different communities that comprised the nation.

Notwithstanding all the arguments against the abrogation of the constitution, the populace at large received word of its demise with resignation and considerable expectation. As with Fatima Jinnah, and outside the circle of politicians whose way of life was severely interrupted by the military action, the general public appeared to welcome the army's intrusion. The Pakistan Army did not need the United States to prod it to take action against the politicians; indeed, the military *coup* was an internal affair, provoked by indigenous forces for a multitude of domestic reasons. Some would continue to see the hand of some sinister foreign intriguer in the events of 1958, but the destiny of Pakistan was, and remained, in the hands of its own people.

The Ambience of Martial Law

The period prior to World War II and after, in fact, up to the moment of partition and beyond, had witnessed phenomenal physical development in the subcontinent. The construction of elaborate infrastructure, i.e., airfields, roads, telephone and telegraph lines, port facilities, etc., during the great conflict, as well as the logistic needs of substantial armed forces, brought with it wealth and status for particular individuals and groups who were in any way connected with these developments. But while some were engaged in servicing the war effort, others engaged in corruption, nepotism, brigandage, and jobbery. The latter padded their pockets, spread and deepened their power base, and assumed a future of sustained well-being. Public morals suffered during this period of transition, and the men who came to govern Pakistan after independence were some of the very people who had aggrandized themselves during the war. Moreover, those who contested their power were no less corrupted. While not the immediate beneficiaries of wartime developments, they none the less demonstrated in their struggles with those who were, a peculiar indifference to matters of decorum. Coupled with the failure to adapt the conventional roles of the feudal landlords, the indomitable tribal leaders, or the religious fundamentalists, these otherwise more sophisticated leaders failed to give their attention to the creation of a civil society.

In spite of the many declarations of principle and high purpose, it was power that generated the political actions of Pakistan's politicians, but in the end they were no match for the members of the permanent services or military establishment. The steel frame of colonial administration remained intact long after partition and, given the obvious weaknesses in the political process, the country's higher civil-military leaders took what they believed was the necessary initiative. The transfer of power had been made the responsibility of a Muslim League party that, by 1958, no longer resembled the organization that had powered the Pakistan Movement to victory. Power at the time of independence was conferred upon the Muslim League, and the permanent services had pledged their support to the party which took responsibility for the management of the Pakistan government. But the passage of time and the problems encountered along the way took their toll of the Muslim League, and with the loss of its most important leaders, its power gravitated to others less informed about its national purpose.

Provincialism, not nationalism, galvanized these political successors, and the more they narrowed the range of their opportunities, the more they exposed themselves to competitive expressions that were even more limiting and hence more divisive. The supporting cast of civil-military administrators, believing that their professional calling imposed on them emergency responsibilities, and observing the changed and threatening character of the political experience, concluded that their only option was the seizure of the government. In their opinion, the political facade had fallen away, exposing the steel frame, and instead of the politicians being given the opportunity to repair the damage, that task had become the responsibility of the career bureaucrats. The country's civil and military officials sensed that only they could bridge the nation's different regions and expressions and only they were truly representative of national interests and purposes. They, therefore, not the politicians, best understood Pakistan's role in the modern world, and they more or less, but somewhat reluctantly, concluded that the future of the republic was bound up in their capacity to reconcile, if not satisfy, the demands of the different publics.

General Ayub believed that necessity had forced him to retreat from a 1951 admonition to his troops that they should stay out of politics. Ayub knew then, and he acknowledged again following the October 1958 *coup,* that the Army would be better subordinated to civil institutions, but otherwise free to improve on its performance and capability. Modernization of the armed forces was Ayub's principal objective, but his position at the highest level of political authority, and especially his interaction with administrators who had assumed political roles, had augmented his thinking.

Influenced and nurtured in a disciplined environment, infused with dedication and devotion to country, the military mind and lifestyle stood in sharp contrast to the stable of Pakistani politicians who assumed the sole right to govern the country. The latter, accustomed to more lavish living, to freewheeling expression and behaviour, however, could not be compared with the austere professionalism of the trained army officer. Nor could Ayub and his comrades in arms ignore the numerous occasions in which the army had been pressed into service to correct problems which they knew instinctively were precipitated by both ruling and contesting politicians. The Pakistan Army could not take satisfaction from the many times its firepower was used against its own people. It did not relish its role in riot suppression or putting down social unrest. Such deployments weighed heavily on the army high command, which saw its mission in terms of external defence, not domestic policing. Moreover, anything less than a harmonious relationship between the armed forces and Pakistani society compromised the former. It also raised unnecessarily the spectre of an oppressive military institution whose singular purpose was the maximization of its own power.

Martial Law Reforms

The moral decay experienced during the war years was perpetuated after Pakistan's independence. It was most pronounced in the economic sphere, where people of whatever station or calling endeavoured to aggrandize themselves. Complicated by the perils of independence that forced millions of refugees to pass from India to Pakistan, the prevailing insecurities were first personal and only later social. Muslims fleeing their homes and treasures in India sought compensation in Pakistan from properties abandoned by Hindus fleeing in the opposite direction. Evacuee property problems raised volumes of questions concerning its distribution and ultimate beneficiaries. It also burdened the work of the administrators, as well as members of the judiciary and legal system, who were called upon to produce fair and equitable settlements. Clearly the situation lent itself to corrupt practices, and chicanery on both sides of the question became a fact of life. The benefits derived and those denied were too often influenced by political matters, and the overall problem frustrated efforts at instilling discipline and professionalism in the persons charged with handling the matter. The same was true in other economic spheres, where government was made responsible for promoting growth and development. Industries were few in the areas that became Pakistan, and the creation of an industrial sector was a consequence of joint government and private sector co-operation. Here too, the matter of offering licenses, of setting standards, or determining ownership, was not always conducted in an atmosphere of calculated neutrality.

Prices for essential commodities were often arbitrarily established, and seldom in the collective interest. Collecting taxes was a virtual impossibility, and indeed, few if any efforts were made in the agrarian sector. Prosperous landlords and entrepreneurs became exceptionally wealthy as well as powerful, while the general public suffered shortages, high prices, and massive unemployment. Black marketeering, hoarding, smuggling, the trafficking in permits, the adulteration of food and medicines, nepotism, and a host of assorted other anti-social activities pervaded the entire country and burdened an already destitute society.

It was not unexpected that the Martial Law government should try to correct many of these problems. Whereas some of the difficulties required time and restructuring, others could be addressed immediately and without the necessary deliberation. Prices were lowered and regulated for basic foodstuffs; similar policies had an impact on the sale of certain manufactured products, such as textiles. It became declared policy to restrict the importation of foreign-made goods, as well as to save foreign exchange by limiting consumption of externally-produced products. Public corporations multiplied, and military personnel assumed responsibility for managing extensive enterprises. Arrests for economic crimes skyrocketed, and although the government said it would not apply directives retroactively, fear of punishment and sheer intimidation gave the country respite from the price gougers, the black market operators, and the petty criminals.

An Export Bonus Scheme was introduced in January 1959, which enabled a Pakistani exporter to import a percentage of the value of his sales in foreign-made goods. Aimed at expanding exports, the plan benefited the exporter twofold: first, because he was encouraged to export his products, and second, because his increased sales allowed him to earn import vouchers that could be traded for a higher value on the open market. The Bonus plan proved useful in that it not only acted as a stimulant to the economy, it also gave government a modicum of control over imports and, in some ways, made it easier to cope with the black market. The fact that the programme also had its drawbacks, that it could not be totally policed, that it prompted corrupt practices within the administrative system, was one of the prices paid in trying to promote a more successful economy. Suffice it to say that corruption could not be eliminated in any sector, but that the overall results were sufficiently positive to attract foreign assistance and stimulate investment.

The Martial Law Government's crackdown on illicit business practices, its seizure of several prominent firms, the sealing of offices, and the examination of accounts books were received with considerable enthusiasm by the consuming public. So too was the reported recovery of large stores of gold, much of it retrieved from the seabed in the port of Karachi.

But the satisfaction registered by the public was not echoed in the business community, which bore the brunt of the attack. Business leaders found themselves under pressure to conform to ordinances and rules that appeared arbitrary and capricious. The arrest of prominent business leaders singled out for punishment not only frightened the commercial community, the draconian measures drove many from the country. Moreover, so many businessmen had secreted their wealth in foreign banks that their flight from the country also meant that their capital went with them. Efforts to recover monies held outside the country were not very successful. Nevertheless, the martial law authority forcefully collected huge sums of unpaid revenue. Hidden wealth was uncovered in a number of high-profile cases, and for the first time the country began to understand the extent to which the country's wealth had become concentrated in relatively few families.

Concentrations of wealth within the subcontinent were not an unusual occurrence. Even before partition, the industrial, insurance, commercial, and banking sectors were dominated by a few very successful kinship groups. Like India, Pakistan inherited this condition, and the concentrations could only grow larger as the country struggled to find its place in the world economic arena. Thus, all the efforts of the Martial Law authority to limit opportunism and to provide greater benefits for the consuming public did little to change the sources of economic and financial power. Moreover, the martial law authority was wedded to a free-enterprise philosophy and, although it promoted government intervention in several sectors, the mixed nature of the economy at no time suggested a shift toward socialist norms.

An open market philosophy produced associated policies, as was demonstrated by the government's formation of the National Investment Trust. The NIT encouraged small entrepreneurial activities, but in order to make such institutions viable, it was necessary to enlist the services of the larger economic units. The result was a working relationship between the Martial Law Administration and those major business families that it otherwise sought to regulate. Later in his administration, Ayub would be accused of encouraging the development of Pakistan's 'twenty-two' leading entrepreneurial families. In point of fact, the families had existed some time before Ayub's ascendence, and perhaps the more telling accusations were those centring on the assistance Ayub was said to have provided to members of his family who entered the business sector and subsequently assembled sizeable personal fortunes.

The martial law regime also introduced land reforms. A Land Reform Commission hurriedly framed a series of reforms that were approved with little discussion. The reforms ignored East Pakistan, where land ownership was limited to relatively small holdings. West Pakistan was another matter, however, and the alleviation of social distress was given high priority. Land reform ordinances were supposedly aimed at breaking up the feudal estates; thus regulations were authorized limiting holdings of irrigated lands to 500 acres per individual and 1000 acres for non-irrigated property. 150 acres of orchard land were also sanctioned, as well as the transfer of lands to family members, including female dependents. All lands in excess of the maximum allotted were to be transferred to the government, and compensation was to be made for such property in the form of redeemable interest-bearing bonds. Other lands recovered included *jagirs* (income drawn from land that had been granted to a beneficiary by the state) that were a throwback to the colonial period. Exceptions to land seizure were made for holdings used for religious, educational, or charitable purposes. Fragmented holdings, a consequence of Islamic inheritance laws, were ordered consolidated if they were shown to be unproductive. Reforms were also developed to protect occupancy tenants from the more rapacious landlords. But a recommendation that occupancy tenants be given options to purchase the lands they cultivated was not implemented.

A West Pakistan Land Commission, comprised of the province's Governor and five officers selected by him, was established to implement the reforms. In time, the Commission took control of more than two and a half million acres of farmland and paid approximately 75 million rupees in compensation to some 900 landowners. Despite all the fanfare that accompanied the reforms, the total recovered was considerably less, roughly five per cent of the cultivated land, and much less than anticipated. Moreover, the distribution of these lands to tenant farmers did not dent the armour of the feudal lords. While tenants then cultivating the surrendered lands were supposed to have first option to purchase the property, many did not or could not buy it, and hence others were allowed to declare their intentions. The landless peasants did not improve their status, and with the Khan of Kalabagh, one of the province's principal *zamindars*, as West Pakistan Governor, the rural scene remained firmly in the grip of the landed gentry (Feldman, 1967).

The power of the big landlords was altered, but hardly affected, by the reforms. Agriculture was Pakistan's principal economic sector, and the large holdings were also the more productive enterprises in the country. Although political competition might be expected from the growing industrial and financial centres, the landlords sustained their edge in the political debate and they continued to demonstrate their superiority in political organization. In part, this condition was influenced by the larger portion of the country's population, residing in rural areas, and their historic dependency on the landed elites. A landlord's voice is multiplied many times, whereas members of the commercial and financial world, like those of the intelligentsia, generally speak for themselves. Simply put, the industrialists and bankers were denied constituents and their politicking was a more difficult and often less rewarding task. Only urban-rural linkages enabled the former to assume higher stations in the political arena; this was not the fashion during the rule of Ayub Khan, and it changed little after him.

Nor was the Ayub administration meant to be simply punitive. West Pakistan agricultural land had been abused since the British constructed the barrage and irrigation systems of the Punjab and upper Sindh. Built to return the land to fertility, the system was overused and misused, and by the time Pakistan had become a nation, more land was lost each year as a consequence of salinity and water-logging than went into cultivation. No serious response was made to the problem until the martial law regime launched a salinity control project and a master plan was drawn up with the assistance of foreign consultants. Dr Roger Revelle was sent to Pakistan by the United States government to investigate the problem and make recommendations. His report became the hallmark for an extensive programme of land reclamation that, at one time, anticipated restoring a million acres of lost land each year. In addition to the engineering schemes developed for that purpose, the cultivators were to be instructed on the proper use of irrigation systems as well as the more approved methods of cultivation. The task was monumental in all its aspects, and although some progress was demonstrated in replenishing land resources, the programme did not achieve that level of success envisaged by the agronomists, engineers, and scientists who were contracted to execute the programme.

But the martial law authority had to be given credit for exposing the problem, and for seriously trying to remedy it. The same could be said for Ayub's work in enlisting United States' financial and technical support in building a vast hydroelectric and water storage system in the northern areas of Pakistan. India's control and diversion of the headwaters that fed Pakistan's agricultural heartland caused an increase in tensions that brought the two countries dangerously close to war. The intercession and pledge of financial and technical support by the United States, and the resulting Indus Basin agreement between Ayub and Jawaharlal Nehru in September 1960, which called for the construction of several new dams on the Indus River system, dispelled that possibility. The treaty not only guaranteed the continued flow of precious water to Pakistani farmlands, it also meant regions heretofore without electricity would be assured an adequate supply of power. While such projects were of the utmost importance to national development, and in spite of the jobs they created or the benefits derived from their operation, there was little positive public response to the programme. The same was true when the Ayub administration exposed Pakistan to the 'Green Revolution' and thereby endeavoured to raise the level of agricultural productivity. Again, the foreign component in the programme tended to obscure indigenous inputs, and although the introduction of new hybrid wheat strains proved to be a delicate and risky affair requiring careful and knowledgeable use of water, seed, and fertilizer, the advantages outweighed the disadvantages.

Ayub Khan revealed soon after assuming control of the country, that his ideas were meant to have application. Operating on a broad front, he enlisted the services and expertise of persons at home and abroad. In the latter category, the United States played the primary role, but it was not the only country to send its experts to Pakistan. The foreign community swelled during the Ayub years, and by 1965, approximately 8,000 Americans were said to be living and working in the Muslim nation. Scandinavia and the United Kingdom were also well-represented, but it was the Americans who cut the most noticeable profile. Thus, when Ayub called for reforms within the administrative services, he turned to the Americans and, to a lesser extent, to the British for assistance.

Administration during the colonial period centred on the professionalism and unquestioned integrity of the serving officer (Kennedy, 1987). Observing a decline in administrative probity and a lack of contemporary skills, Ayub was determined to return to a time when the public servants assumed their responsibilities with purpose and dedication, and with the necessary wisdom and enthusiasm. In the immediate aftermath of partition, it became necessary to assemble an administrative structure from the remains of a European empire and, given the press of events, there was little time to plan for the future. Moreover, independence opened up possibilities for those in administrative posts, not all of whom were concerned with the well-being of the nation. On the contrary, opportunities for self-aggrandizement were plentiful and the temptation to advantage one self was a common occurrence. The services suffered a significant loss in professionalism during the parliamentary period, and official corruption, no stranger to any society, became rampant and all-pervasive (Goodnow, 1964). Ayub's efforts to reform the civil bureaucracy, therefore, were a major aspect of a countrywide transformation process.

Among the first of the martial law regulations was one in January 1959 that punished civil servants with up to fourteen years rigorous confinement if found guilty of taking bribes or in other ways abusing their powers. Moreover, such cases were turned over to military tribunals where the punishment could be expected to be swift and harsh. Still another ordinance established the machinery to investigate officers accused of misconduct and inefficiencies. More generally civilian bodies, these committees were armed with quasi-judicial powers, thereby allowing them to administer oaths, take evidence, and render judgments. Meeting out of the public eye, the results of these sessions were not subject to question in other courts. Officials brought before such tribunals were called upon to respond in writing or verbally to the charges brought against them. Appeals on judgments were permitted, but if found guilty of the offences described in the complaint, the accused officer was subject to dismissal, retirement, or reduction in rank. When the initial directives failed to cover all eventualities, more thorough rules were published which further examined the conduct, character, loyalty, and the capability of the serving officer.

Approximately fifty-seven committees were assembled for the purpose and, by the end of June 1959, some 1,662 central government officials, and more than 4,000 provincial officers, were caught in the martial law net. A number of these were punished, more were retired, but the large majority suffered reprimands and lesser penalties. This is not to say that all the guilty, let alone the accused, represented the totality of those who had committed infractions or crimes, or simply did not perform their jobs adequately. Many slipped through the net, but on the whole, the programme was conducted with considerable precision, and it did not fail to register an impact on the serving agents. On the other hand, the closed-door nature of the proceedings left reputations reasonably intact, and many retired officers were free to seek other employment, generally in the private sector, where their relative experience could be utilized in financial, industrial, or commercial circles.

Fear of condemnation, however, did have its positive effect. Officers who otherwise might have dallied in less than proper behaviour tightened their methods and carefully avoided compromising situations. Self-correction was perhaps one of the intended objectives of the martial law authority, and in the end, hardly five per cent of Class I officers, including the elite Civil Service of Pakistan (CSP), were found guilty, and less than half of that number were punished in any way. Class II and III categories showed similar results, and in fact, the percentages of the punished in the lower categories were even smaller than those in Class I. In point of fact, the services examined and penalized their own, and the senior officers who comprised the different scrutinizing committees were more interested in preserving the morale of the services than in sorting out the most offensive officials. Generally speaking, the anti-corruption measures were never very successful, and in 1961 a Governor's Conference set up yet another committee to review developments. Additional machinery was created for the purpose of ferreting out undesirable elements in the services, but the goal was always beyond the reach of those engaged in the pursuit of offenders.

The creation, at Ayub's order, of a number of civil in-service training schools was another outcome of these endeavours. Ayub's plan for national development included an important role for the public administrator. The probity of the career official was one concern, but so too was the expertise and the mindset of the civil servant. Colonial administration had catered to the generalist administrator, the virtual ruler in the colonial system. His concern with law and order and the collection of revenue described his duties, and these also were the persons who assumed the responsible government posts following the transfer of power. The new nation, however, required more than policing, and with the aid-giving countries in the wings, Ayub's vision was that of administrators who not only kept the peace, but who also addressed questions of poverty, population control, and modern agriculture. Specialists ranged alongside generalists, each with a particular mission, but all with a common responsibility. The training institutions envisaged by the martial law authority would provide educational experiences wherein the generalist and specialist administrators would interact, learn to co-operate with one another, and pool their talents. The courses of instruction also aimed at changing attitudes and behaviour, and hence the administrator's role in a developing country. Promoting self-reliance, energizing as well as educating a largely illiterate public to adopt methods and techniques otherwise alien to them, was no small undertaking.

Ayub ordered the seizure of the elitist, pre-independence Punjab Club, and after a report was given to him by representatives of the British Staff College at Henley-on-Thames and the Maxwell School at Syracuse University in the United States, he had the building and grounds converted into a school for senior public administrators. The first session of the Administrative Staff College commenced in 1961. This apex institution was supported by in-service training institutions at the middle manager level, hence the development of the National Institutes of Public Administration, as well as the rural institutes that centred their work on serving agricultural needs. Promotion to higher rank was made dependent on in-service training. The availability of indigenous courses of instruction also avoided the need to send administrators abroad; the instruction was made more relevant, it saved foreign exchange, and it also saved time. Although most officials attending the courses were known to grumble over their student status or, when they returned to their assignments, ignored their training, the experience was not without merit. If nothing more, it sustained the idea that the civil service was a profound calling and a major responsibility, and that the probationary training on entering the service was only a beginning in a career that required periodic and continuous learning.

Ayub was also responsible for, and presided over, the Bureau of National Reconstruction. Picking up on the idea that the administrators needed redirection, the Bureau focused on the re-creation and reformulation of ethical and civic values throughout Pakistani society. The people of Pakistan had yet to demonstrate their co-operative and integrative capacity. The first ten years after independence had witnessed fratricidal conflict that appeals to Islamic unity could not control. Ayub acknowledged the necessity for modifying behaviour among the country's rulers, but the matter did not end there. The society was prone to divisiveness, to representations of regional exclusivity, and was too likely to follow demagogic appeals to its vanity and base instincts.

Ayub toyed with the thought of socio-psychological engineering, and, with the leverage afforded by martial law, he pursued avenues for the bridging of sectarianism and provincialism, of tribalism and clanism. He also emphasized giving public roles to women, and encouraged female education and self-assertion. But public toleration for such policies remained an obstacle, and even the heightened intellectual activity did little to modify the prevailing political culture. The same was true for Ayub's austerity programme. His call for simple living meant rejecting all aspects of ostentatious expression, but the more fortunate in Pakistani society had already built, or were in the process of constructing, luxurious family structures. Lavish living ranged alongside abject poverty, and no authority could seriously anticipate closing the gap. The austerity programme never moved beyond the propaganda stage.

Nevertheless, a Woman's Voluntary Group, led by the President's wife, was formed in March 1959 to publicize the renunciation of all non-essential items. Foreign-made clothing was frowned upon home-spun cloth, and efforts were launched to reinvigorate home and cottage industries. The Woman's project fizzled out quickly, however, exposing some of the more shallow aspects of the Ayub reforms. Well-to-do Pakistanis were not eager to adopt belt-tightening measures, especially when the flouting of wealth signalled power and influence and generated respect from others at different stations in Pakistani life. Nor could acquired tastes for foreign goods be controlled by appeals to patriotism and national honour. Moreover, the fact that the Bureau of National Reconstruction, the organ responsible for the social engineering projects, became associated with the Ministry of Information and Broadcasting, pointed to the propaganda, not the material, value of the various projects.

The lacklustre record of the Bureau of National Reconstruction could not however, conceal the serious work done to rehabilitate and find accommodation for the almost ten million refugees who had flooded into Pakistan from India. When martial law was declared, there remained almost a million refugees subsisting in filth and squalor in make-shift shelters in Karachi alone. Previous governments had ignored the plight of the most impoverished among the refugee influx. More privileged members of the community, given connections and wealth, found Pakistan a welcome place to begin their lives anew. But this was in sharp contrast to the mass of rural-based refugees, who received almost no attention at all. It has been argued that the sustained agony of the refugees served some government purpose in that it fed the continuing rivalry with India (Feldman, 1967). Ayub, however, declined to use the refugees for political purposes. He made Lieutenant-General Azam Khan his Minister for Rehabilitation, and urged him to find a solution for the refugee dilemma. Azam responded to the challenge with alacrity, and by January 1959 rural land was made available in the Punjab region, while housing was erected in and around Dhaka and Karachi. Slum dwellings were bulldozed and the recovered land was put to productive uses. The refugee problem was far from solved, but a serious beginning had been inaugurated.

The martial law government gave attention to the employment issue, notably the relationship between workers, managers, and owners (Jalal, 1990). With strikes and agitations outlawed, the authorities pressed for improved relations between management and labour. Labour unions were not discouraged, but the government pre-empted their demands for higher salaries and better working conditions. Under the pressure of martial law, and with their operations under close scrutiny, management was induced to consider higher pay scales, as well as safety in the workplace and tolerable hours of employment. A profitable enterprise, it was stressed, required a reasonably satisfied workforce. An Industrial Disputes Ordinance aimed at improving the dialogue between labour and management, and an Industrial Court that was established to handle intractable problems underlined the importance given to this economic sector. These reforms were to score few successes, but they nevertheless elevated the role of labour, reduced the possibility of strikes and lock-outs, and generally contributed to higher productivity levels. The government, for the first time, also addressed the needs of semi-educated and illiterate workers, and abuses associated with their exploitation by a venal management were targeted, even if they could not be eliminated.

Numerous additional commissions were created to examine law, education, medical practices, and the role of the Press in Pakistani society. The Law Commission examined the court system, its powers, and performance. Special attention was given to legal procedure and the rules of evidence. In all, the commission made 368 recommendations that aimed at providing the nation with a more efficient legal system. Most significant was the call for special family courts where problems related to marriage and divorce, as well as the care of children, could be resolved. Family laws, however, were a separate category, involving issues that transcended legal approaches. In the summer of 1959 President Ayub announced his plan to tackle the problem of over-population. Calling attention to the relationship between food supply and population growth, he argued in favour of limiting the size of families, and thus called for the establishment of hundreds of clinics nationwide to dispense birth control information and devices. Not unaware of Muslim sensitivity in this area of personal responsibility, Ayub tried to assure his countrymen that family planning was neither anti-Islamic nor a threat to religious precepts.

Resistance to family planning was almost instantaneous in spite of Ayub's preachings. He none the less pressed the implementation of his programme, while at the same time counselling parents to acknowledge their responsibilities and be aware of how family size affected the national condition. Concern for the family also led Ayub to introduce the Muslim Family Laws Ordinance. For the first time, Pakistani marriages and divorces were required to be registered. Ayub here again insisted that the Family Laws were not in conflict with Koranic injunctions, and that their purpose was the preservation of the family and the protection of its weakest members. Thus the reform brought into public view the institution of polygamy and, while not outlawing it, aimed at protecting the weaker female. To that extent, a limitation was placed upon the age of the marrying male and female, and some restrictions were imposed on the husband's right to divorce his spouse. The wife's contracted and agreed-upon dowry was also safeguarded, as were her rights and those of her children to specified property. But because the Family Laws were tied to religious practices, the fact that practices varied between orders and were different between Sunni and Shia Muslims complicated their execution. Moreover, the several interpretations used by a variety of schools of Islamic jurisprudence made impossible the uniform enforcement of the laws.

Although the Muslim Family Laws Ordinance was generally well received by the attentive public, the problems that it confronted and the inability to reach consensus on the issues dashed the many hopes that it had raised. Arbitration councils were created to assist in resolving some of the more difficult questions but they too proved ineffective.

Confronted by the Muslim *ulema* who denounced the Family Laws and thus refused to sanction them, Ayub was constrained to limit his invasion of the scriptural argument. Whereas the Field Marshal was convinced of the correctness of his efforts, that what needed changing was not religious precept but social evils, the voices of the religious opposition would not be silenced. Ayub, for example, opposed the use of the Muslim *burqa*, or veil, as not having anything to do with religious practice. His concern that women were an integral and massive segment of national development, and that the country could not progress with half its population denied opportunities that were open to the other half, failed to resonate in the more traditional circles of Pakistani life. The *burqa* became a symbol of resistance in more puritanical vistas and, like family planning, so too the Muslim Family Laws were ultimately defeated by an aroused populace which had been led to believe that its sacred traditions were threatened.

The establishment of the Central Institute of Islamic Research was Ayub's answer to his Islamic critics. Set up as the premier institution concerned with defining the role of Islam in the modern state, its bona fides were the intellectual virtuosity of its directors and their staff. Called to expand upon themes of Islamic brotherhood, tolerance, and social justice, its responsibility lay in scholarly analysis of Islamic tradition and contemporary practices. The Institute was charged with the academic study of Islamic thought, and a corollary concern was the influence of science on religious experience. Funded to produce literary works on Islamic history, law, jurisprudence, philosophy, and culture, the institution laboured to meet its charge, but in so doing it also exposed itself to attacks from leaders of several Muslim sects. I.H. Qureshi and Fazlur Rahman, acknowledged scholars with international reputations, assumed responsibility for guiding the institute during those formative years. But, like Ayub, they too found themselves open to public scrutiny. Fazlur Rahman's defence of the use of contraception during the intensification of the family planning controversy eventually forced him to leave his post, and indeed to flee the country when threats were posed against his life.

Ayub had been influenced by another army leader of a Muslim country, but in attempting to emulate the work of modern Turkey's Mustafa Kemal Ataturk, he found the circumstances and the conditions prevailing in Pakistan almost twenty years after World War II far different from those in Asia Minor after World War I.

Nevertheless, Ayub was a bold innovator, an initiator of events, and a builder of modern society, much in the Ataturk tradition. Nowhere was the comparison better observed than in Ayub's desire to see a new Pakistani capital constructed on the Potwar plateau outside Rawalpindi. As with Ataturk's Ankara, a citadel on the Anatolian plateau, Ayub envisaged a Pakistani capital city built from the ground up, far removed from the impact of competing ideas, and safely ensconced in the remote foothills of the Hindu Kush.

Karachi had been chosen the federal capital at independence primarily because of its location on the sea, its accessibility to the outside world, and because it was the birthplace of Mohammad Ali Jinnah. Never considered a permanent site, the capital's placement at Karachi had raised considerable controversy when it was separated from Sindh province. Lacking in installations to house the federal government, the city received major attention in the early years. In close proximity to western India, it also drew the bulk of the Muslim refugees fleeing India after partition. As a crossroads of inter-Asian activity, with a major airfield located there during World War II, Karachi quickly grew into a major metropolis for commerce, trade, and industry, as well as for central government operations. Indeed, the rapid growth of the city into a bustling commercial community of several million people made it quite evident that the nation's capital would be better placed elsewhere. But while attention was given to constructing a new capital somewhere near Karachi, it was Ayub Khan who chose the permanent home of the federal government.

As early as June 1959, while presiding over a Governors' Conference, Ayub revealed that he would make Dhaka the second or administrative capital of Pakistan. Arguing the need to satisfy the aspirations of the Bengali people, Ayub said that similar concern should be given to the West Pakistani population, and that in his view the nation's first, or executive, capital would be better placed in the northern areas of West Pakistan, away from the hubbub of commercial transactions that characterized the southern portion of the country. He called the new city Islamabad to represent the binding of Muslim peoples, east and west, and he identified the region near Rawalpindi as providing the required space, an acceptable year-round climate, and a generally secure location in the shadow of the major staging areas for the Pakistan Army. Moreover, whereas Karachi allowed for very little if any planning, the Potwar plateau permitted the nation's creativity and ingenuity to express itself like never before. A *tabula rasa*, the people of Pakistan could build the kind of capital that best reflected their genius and, at the same time, they could look forward to a new beginning.

National renewal was inherent in all of Ayub's reform programmes and his crowning achievement, that is, Islamabad, became his permanent monument. But here too there was criticism. It came from East Pakistan, where the idea of being 'second' was not immediately appreciated. It came from the suppressed politicians, who argued that the building of a new city would bankrupt the country for decades to come, and even more critical, that Ayub's decision was based on personal ambition, that Islamabad would be little more than an over-blown and terribly expensive army cantonment. It came from the civil administrators who had built their costly residences in Karachi near the established ministries. It came from foreign governments who had purchased land in Karachi and who had built, or were in the process of constructing, their permanent facilities. Ayub brushed all these arguments aside, noting that he was called to serve Pakistan to the utmost of his ability and nowhere did he see a greater need to act firmly and decisively. Ayub ordered his subordinates to prepare their plans. He expected that ground-breaking ceremonies should begin almost immediately, and that by 1965 the foreign embassies would commence their move from Karachi. Given the freedom that comes from being able to answer your own questions, the decision was never debated.

Ayub and Political Culture

Ayub Khan was a dictator, but his method was neither vindictive nor bitter. Unlike other Army officers in so many other countries, he was neither vengeful nor mean-spirited. His martial law regime demanded obedience, but by its acts, it also displayed compassion and a genuine concern for the national condition. Ayub emerged from a tradition that called for discipline and demanded loyalty and solidarity, but he was also a staff person, given to delegation of responsibilities and dependent on his comrades and all those who worked with and for him. Ayub was guided by his own inner light, but he was open to counter-argument and he did not surround himself with 'yes-men'. His working cabinet comprised of army officers and civilians and, as an admirer of youth, he was prepared to let the younger members of his inner cabinet vent their views.

Ayub assumed the power to guide Pakistan after an extended period of trial and failure by the country's political elite (Ayub Khan, 1967). It cannot be argued that he acted hastily, although it is clear from the timing of the takeover that the 1956 Constitution was not what he envisaged for the new country. Drafted by people few of whom he respected, the new constitution was seen perpetuating the difficulties encountered with the transfer of power. Although the constitution was publicized as Islamic in character, Ayub questioned that assertion, and saw even greater problems when the political system it legitimized failed to live up to the expectations of the more fundamentalist among the Muslims. The new political system, in his judgement, was a shadow-image of the one that preceded it. The parent system had failed repeatedly, and nothing had changed to even hint that a constitutionally endowed parliamentary order would be any more successful than the one put into operation with independence.

The issue of ethos and political culture burdened Ayub, and he struggled to come to grips with a country whose human condition was demonstrably Muslim, but whose lifeforce reflected so many diverse representations of the human psyche. Ayub was charged with creating a nation from peoples whose identities were rooted in regional and ethnic circumstances, a people who, until Pakistán, were never asked to give expression to an expanded community. Having experienced little, if any, physical mobility, the vast majority of Pakistanis lived out their lives in relatively secluded environments, and seldom were any of their number energized to consider the circumstances of those far from their kith and kin. The colonial imposition did not disturb the isolation of the different tribes and nationalities. On the contrary, colonial policy gave specificity to each human order, and sustained separation was the centrepiece of imperial control and administration. The British entered into agreements and treaties with local rulers and tribal leaders, and only when the defence of the realm was an issue was the private nature of the experience intruded upon. The hundreds of formal potentates that dotted British India did not even begin to describe the thousands of relationships between local headmen and those Englishmen serving in the Indian administrative services.

The rules of the game were long in place when Pakistan became a free nation. The political movement that engineered the independence of the state only marginally absorbed the different nationalities, and even that was done through appeals to entrenched authorities who themselves had to outfox others of their ilk in order to register their preference for Pakistan. There was nothing in these arrangements between major political actors to suggest that they had done more than commit themselves to a temporary understanding. This relationship, largely based on personal rather than collective aspirations, would be sustained only so long as the perceived advantages were realized. Failing this, there was no commitment to endure one relationship when yet another was deemed more beneficial.

The opportunism that was so embedded in Pakistani political culture was a feature of a history that predated the state (Symonds, 1950). 'Appeals to a higher loyalty, to patriotism and love of country, were not unanswered, but the response could only be measured by conditions prevailing at the local level. Pakistani identity would take time to develop, and its cultivation involved a delicate balance of otherwise narrow-minded political leadership and positive societal payoffs. The legitimacy of the Pakistan experience was made dependent on the day-to-day manipulation of political forces. Ayub knew instinctively that the millions of subcontinental inhabitants who had overnight become Pakistanis would not fully grasp the logic of the exercise. Only their leaders could interpret its meaning, and hence it was they who were called upon to articulate the significance of belonging to a place called Pakistan. The demonstrated reluctance of those endowed with that responsibility to accept this supreme test of nationhood explains Ayub's distress with the 1956 Constitution. It was neither the constitution nor the politicians separately, but their collective chemistry, that proved troubling. The politicians were not honest with the people, and the constitution was beyond the capacity of the nation to successfully manage. But whereas the constitution could be replaced, the country was saddled with the political leaders it had produced. Thus the one could be rejected but the other had to be included in any substitute arrangement.

To have allowed the constitution to become fully operational, in the eyes of this soldier, would have posed an even greater threat to a nation whose survival was already in question. Ayub did not want to chance such a prospect. He did not believe Pakistan was ripe for a full-blown experiment in parliamentary politics, he did not have faith in its political leaders, and he was convinced that sustained public disorder would destroy the state. His answer to the central question, the issue of national survival, was protracted martial law. Showing confidence only in the Pakistan Armed Forces, Ayub firmly believed that only the men in uniform could save the national design. But he also understood that involving the Army in politics was a temporary affair. In time, governance would have to be transferred to political figures. How that transition was to be accomplished became the acid test.

Ayub conceived of a political order without political parties, one in which politicians reflected loyalties that were not compromised by special and particularly personal interests. He envisaged a modern nation-state that was true to its diverse experience and hence secular in function and process. He nurtured the idea that Islam could be expressed in non-political terms, and that the religious preferences of a polyglot society could be registered without state interference, and above all, without the injection of the spiritual middle, man or guide, whose more inherent tendencies denied the importance, if not the very existence, of the modern nation-state. And most importantly, Ayub considered it essential that government reach out to the masses of faceless Pakistanis, that they be included in the larger political framework, that they too should have opportunity to give voice to their thoughts, and that they were the ones who needed to be infused with the idea of citizenship and educated to think of themselves as Pakistanis and members of a formidable nation.

Ayub held out the prospect of encouraging national pride among the nation's sizeable but politically unconscious population. He also endeavoured to point them in a direction that circumvented, and thus undermined, their traditional leaders. This was not a programme geared to promote associates among the political elite. Nor was it one that endeared him to the self-appointed protectors of Islamic tradition. Ayub deliberately alienated both the politicians and the religious divines, but this was the inevitable outcome of a plan to incorporate the masses into the political process. It also aimed at sheltering them from those individuals and groups who, Ayub believed, had led them astray. When the old line leaders learned of Ayub's intention to substitute their conventional rule for a form of grassroots government, their anger could not be contained. Ayub introduced the Basic Democracies system on the first anniversary of his assumption of power. The order declaring it in force framed Ayub's thinking on the course of Pakistani politics. It also heralded the beginning of a new domestic order that was to dominate Pakistan's national life during the next ten years.

CHAPTER 7

THE AYUB KHAN ERA

Mohammad Ayub Khan was born in 1907 in the village of Rehana, some fifty miles north of the major military cantonment at Rawalpindi. He was the eldest son of his father's second wife. His father was a Risaldar-Major in Hodson's Horse, a celebrated cavalry unit in the British Indian Army. Ayub speaks of his father as a tall, powerful man who commanded the respect of his children as he did of the men in his military unit, but who was also a sensitive and pious Muslim who inspired his children to honour their traditions and to excel in their life's work. Ayub was a Pathan of the Tarin tribe that had ranged over the Hazara and Campbellpur districts, and the history of the clan traces to a period of Afghan glory and accomplishment, notably in contesting the power of the then invading Sikh nation. Beginning his schooling in a local *madrassah*, Ayub was soon shifted to an English language school where his talents began to flower. But it was his study at Aligarh Muslim University that opened the young man to a world beyond his village, and it was from there that he was selected to continue his academic preparation at the Royal Military College, Sandhurst. Deciding to follow in the footsteps of his father, Ayub Khan was commissioned in the British Indian Army in 1928. He was to command an infantry battalion in World War II, and opted for Pakistan following the transfer of power. Made a member of the Services Selection Board by Prime Minister Liaquat Ali Khan, he served in the Punjab Boundary Force that oversaw the division of the province. He was a colonel on the day Pakistan became independent, but Jinnah promoted him to

Brigadier. Serving in tribal Waziristan on the north-west frontier, he was given responsibility for moving the regular forces to more settled installations. He was soon promoted to Major-General and made General Officer Commanding in East Bengal in 1948. The retirement of British General Sir Douglas Gracey opened the way for Ayub to become the first Pakistani to command the Pakistan Army, a position he assumed on 6 September 1950.

Ayub Khan will be forever tied to the history of Pakistan. Pakistan is the context and the framework whereby a young boy from the rural hinterland of a region somewhere between Central and South Asia grew into manhood, expanded his horizon at Aligarh and Sandhurst, became a professional soldier, served an alien imperial system, and came to command a national army (Ayub Khan, 1967, pp.1-8). The totality of that experience shaped Ayub Khan's character and forged his outlook. It was his destiny to be a mature actor when Pakistan burst upon the scene as an independent country. Motivated by aspirations that were essentially nationalistic but inherently Islamic, Pakistan resulted from complex historic phenomena, but it also was the immediate consequence of a changing world order, prompted by two twentieth-century global conflicts. Ayub was positioned to play a major role in the era unfolding after World War II, but he was very much a product of the first Great War. He had been true to his salt, true to his mentors and superiors, and true to himself. While not the most distinguished combat officer, he was a tried and tested veteran who laboured to fulfil the commitment made to his calling when he first entered the service. Ayub was gifted with a rational mind and used his endowment to come to grips with the world immediately around him, a world of limited human opportunity but strong in popular sentiment, a world chastened by subordination and hardship, but ever proud and determined to project its peculiar life experience.

When Ayub Khan the General became Ayub Khan the Field Marshal and President of Pakistan, not everyone was pleased with his self-proclaimed promotions. In an age when civilian politicians are supposed to control and direct the men in uniform, Ayub's power grab, his liquidation of the political system, and the banishment of his civilian superiors, were a breach of faith and discipline. More than that, his actions were judged personal, not societal. Ayub, his critics have argued, illustrated how power and personal ambition are intertwined, and how an essentially minor actor, given command of the principal sources of violence, could seize the centre stage. Moreover, those same critics were convinced that Ayub did not act alone, that his primary support came from outside Pakistan, that is, from the United States which, in manipulating Ayub, also sought to manipulate the Muslim nation. Such argument ignores the realities of the interwar period and the maturation of a subcontinental Muslim soldier whose original domicile lay between a tribal Afghan frontier and the settlements along the Indus river system. Nevertheless, they persist.

Thus Tariq Ali, in his self-acknowledged polemic, can write about Ayub's ultimate fall from power with caustic certainty:

> Unfortunately for the ruling clique, their leader was a mediocrity in every way (as a casual glance at his ghosted autobiography would confirm). He was completely lacking in political imagination, and even in the barrack-room horse sense which he was supposed to possess and which endeared him to the readers of the *Daily Telegraph*. Any sense he may have possessed had been sucked out of him over the years by the abject sycophancy of his courtiers, who had succeeded in isolating him from the political realities of Pakistan. In the end the Army had no option but to dump him (Tariq Ali, 1970, p.20).

Tariq Ali's 'history' reveals more about himself than about Ayub Khan. Nevertheless, his expression must be taken seriously. Ayub had been President of Pakistan for more than a decade when his end came. He had performed long enough at the highest level of Pakistan government to attract an army of enemies—enemies who represented different ideologies, different regions, different constituents, and different purposes. Never reconciled to the General's claim to speak for Pakistan, they would bear their grudges throughout their lives. In so far as Ayub's detractors were concerned, the General, now Field Marshal, could do no right. His dismantling of constitutional order, and his audacity in replacing it with another, were actions they never could countenance (Sayeed, 1980). Nor were they prepared to forgive what they considered his contemptuous attitude, his imperious demeanour, or his blatant self-confidence.

Ayub was not only a staunch and dedicated adversary, he frustrated the ambitions of a generation of expectant leaders. For the latter, Pakistan was a vast playground offering a variety of possibilities. Only Ayub blocked their path, and because their objectives were essentially self-serving, they naturally assumed that his were hardly different. It is left to history and future historians to judge if Mohammad Ayub Khan should be more remembered for his constructive or destructive works. But howsoever the record reads, it will be noted that the Ayub era marks the end of Pakistan's age of innocence. After Ayub, the Pakistan envisaged by its founding fathers would be barely a memory, recreated only on ceremonial occasions by elites whose motivations reflect the insecurities of half a century of political instability.

Basic Democracies

The Basic Democracies Order of 27 October 1959 coincided with Ayub Khan's promotion to the rank of Field-Marshal. No other army officer would attain such status during the first fifty years of Pakistan's existence as an independent state, and no doubt there was a symbiotic relationship between the one event and the other. Basic Democracies was pure Ayub Khan. So too was the Field Marshal rank which, more than a display of ego, was meant to impress upon everyone in the operative system, both civilians and army officers, that the man at the helm was pre-eminent, occupying a singular position over all the country's self-proclaimed leaders and institutions. Basic Democracies was intended to merge all aspects of Pakistani life. It was the device slated to bring together the different sectors of society and its many structural arrangements; it was meant to pool and blend the talents and skills of the more sophisticated with the most common in the nation's teeming population. Basic Democracies envisaged an integrative system of operative representative bodies that functioned without resort to political parties. More apolitical in form and content, Basic

Democracies was designed as an inclusive system whereby ordinary people could assume responsibility for their own development.

Basic Democracies was a political and administrative experiment, but it also was a foray into grassroots economic reform and social change. In introducing the programme Ayub declared:

> We have given the name Basic Democracies for the obvious reason that we want it to grow and evolve from the very first rung of the political ladder so that it finds roots deep among the people starting at the village level in rural areas and at the *mohalla* level in towns (President's Broadcast from Dhaka, 2 September 1959).

Basic Democracies, Ayub noted, recognized the need to move the larger population from a traditional to a contemporary setting. As a learning experience, it aimed to provide simple folk with opportunities for self-growth and heightened awareness. It built upon experiences long in vogue in the subcontinent wherein village people communicated their needs and resolved their differences through local councils comprised of elders. But Basic Democracies also advanced national identity by linking villages and towns in a network of tiered groupings and to the highest levels of government. As such, Basic Democracies utilized an administrative structure long in place, and indeed, in some ways it represented a throwback to the colonial period.

Although it was said that the villagers would determine their individual needs from among their own immediate constituents, the system was made dependent on the services and expertise rendered by the civil administration which controlled the resources that were distributed among the units, and whose experience was required in all matters beyond that of the simplest daily chores.

The unveiling of Basic Democracies was not well received in the nation's cities where the more enlightened and educated members of Pakistani society were likely to reside. The very use of the term raised the hackles of many an urban dweller who sensed being isolated—along with the politicians. The semantic question that emerges from the use of the term to describe a reform concerned with raising the level of mass awareness is not at issue. No bona fide

contemporary would find solace in a description of
democracy as basic. Moreover, the creation of a basic form of
democracy ruled out the return to more sophisticated
expression. Hence, the urban elites were generally distressed
with the order, believing it gave the martial law government
direct control over the rural population while stunting their
own development. The system was simply too colonial in
format and content for the tastes of those who acknowledged
the need to correct an ailing political system, but who were
reluctant to lend their support to an arrangement that denied
them a prominent place in the overall process.

Basic Democracies, in fact, was a simple structure
involving five tiers of administration, at the base of which
were the union and town councils. Each local unit was to
represent between ten and fifteen thousand people and each
population group was to elect its own representatives, or
roughly one elector for every fifteen hundred persons. A
village council of ten to fifteen members would serve a five-
year term, and additional members could be appointed by
government order to represent groups otherwise under-
represented or not represented at all. But the number of
appointed members could not exceed one half of the total
number of elected members. Each union council was given
responsibility for electing a chairman from among the elected
members. Union councils were made responsible for public
needs such as sanitation, open thoroughfares, and the general
safety of the community. Union council chairmen also were
given representation at the next tier, which was described as
the *tehsil* in West Pakistan and the *thana* in East Pakistan. At
this level, the formal administrative system kicked in and the
subdivisional or circle officer became the *ex officio* member
of the council. This higher tier of administration was made
responsible for co-ordinating union council activity, and it
was usually the conduit for the distribution of resources and
technical services to the lower units.

The still higher tiers of administration were located in the
district, and above it, in the division. These tiers were
radically different in composition. All the councils in these
categories were comprised of officials, meaning civil servants,
and appointed members, possibly more civil servants or

attendant experts, but a quota system also guaranteed that some union council chairmen would sit on these higher councils. Nevertheless, both the district and the divisional councils were managed by government officials, with the District Magistrate or Deputy Commissioner presiding over the district council and the Divisional Commissioner conducting the affairs of the division council. The district tier was the key to the success of the Basic Democracies system. Made responsible for matters relating to education, medical care, roads, and agricultural and industrial development, all the major resources allocated for the operation of the Basic Democracies were funnelled through this tier of administration.

The fifth or highest tier in the system were the two Provincial Development Advisory Councils that were set up for East and West Pakistan. Members of these Councils were appointed by the President on the recommendation of the Provincial Governors, and at least one-third were to be chairmen of union councils. Composed of forty-eight members each, these highest councils were presided over by the Governors of the provinces, who answered to the President in all matters pertaining to the operation of the extended system.

The character and disposition of the Basic Democracies ruled out any kind of political activity other than that related to the work of the union councils. Moreover, in so far as the system applied more or less equally to both the cities and the rural regions, traditional politicians who sustained an interest in participating in the political process were called to make their interests known through the apparatus of the union councils in the villages, and the union committees in the metropolitan centres. Those politicians who decided not to contest elections at that level, by default opted out of the political game. The larger objective of Basic Democracies, in fact, aimed at discouraging traditional politicians from becoming involved. The purposes of Basic Democracies were better served if they involved new entrants into the political arena, and in so doing, success would be determined by the elevation of political consciousness among an otherwise distant, unknowing, or apathetic public.

The original number of Basic Democrats was pegged at 40,000 for each of the two provinces, but the total of 80,000 was eventually raised to 120,000. Thus, the first Basic Democrats were primarily persons who had never before engaged in formal political activity, and it was only after the system had become a significant feature of Pakistani life that some of the more professional politicians found it in their interest to gain a seat on one of the elective bodies. But that was to come later.

Shortly after the announcement establishing Basic Democracies, Ayub dramatized the innovation in a week-long train excursion throughout West Pakistan. Calling his train the Pak Jumhuriyat Special, the President mingled with the very people his programme was aimed to reach. His speeches and answers to questions also revealed Ayub's thinking with reference to the country's constitution. It was clear from these proceedings that he had no intention of restoring the 1956 Constitution, and that any new constitutional order would be one that avoided decentralizing power. Ayub said he had come to realize that the Pakistani genius and political culture were not suited to the parliamentary model, that political representation in Pakistan was more than a theoretical question, and was certainly at variance with western political thought. Ayub argued that parliamentary politics demanded an educated and relatively secure population, but Pakistan's widespread illiteracy, coupled with an impoverished people, called for a different approach to political democracy (Ziring, 1966).

Citing the abuses of democratic experience in Pakistan as well as the arrogance of those in leadership roles, Ayub called for a new order that allowed the average Pakistani citizen to enter the political arena. Essentially an educating experience in Ayub's view, Basic Democracies were to evolve as the people matured, grew in confidence, learned to discriminate, and overall, assumed responsibility for their own communities. Ayub brought his message to East Pakistan in January 1960. It was during this tour that the elections to the union councils and committees were conducted, and as Ayub had insisted, the elections were personal pursuits, managed without a single reference to party affiliation.

Ayub implored his countrymen to vote for the best representatives, and by 23 January 1960 the 80,000 Basic Democrats had been chosen and given their first major task. Ayub asked the people's new representatives to indicate whether or not they had confidence in his leadership. Given secret ballots, the elected Basic Democrats were asked to mark them with a simple 'yes' or 'no'. The future of Basic Democracies was said to hinge on the results of the balloting. But the outcome was never in doubt. Having just been elected to the union councils and committees, there was little likelihood that the electors would choose to dissolve the very bodies they had been elected to serve. When the ballots were counted, less than 3,000 voted to reject the system. Thus Ayub had his vote of confidence and Basic Democracies was ensured a prominent place in any future political scheme, at least so long as the Field Marshal sustained an unassailable position.

Ayub took advantage of the 'vote of confidence' to ceremonialize the occasion by having the Chief Justice swear him in as the country's 'first elected President', but his detractors found the whole affair distasteful and condemned the procedure as an affront to democratic practices. Ayub, however, had anticipated the reaction, and was somewhat amused that the same politicians who had intrigued and aggrandized themselves during the parliamentary period now chose the high ground from which to criticize his behaviour. Basic Democracies changed the rules of the political contest; moreover, the scheme guaranteed sustained confrontation between the President and the ostracized politicians. The politicians never accepted Ayub's intrusion into and domination of the political arena, and they refused to confer legitimacy on his policies. Furthermore, they never committed themselves to a change in political direction. Believing they would endure long after Ayub had left the scene, the country's career politicians ignored Ayub's inclusionary ideas and never adjusted their positions to conform with the country's peculiar political culture. Seeing only the usurpation of power, the imposition of a dictatorial regime, and the personalization of political authority, the politicians refused to work with Ayub Khan, but in so doing, they failed to recognize the underlying forces that were reshaping the national design.

Therefore, when Ayub created a Constitution Commission and authorized its members to listen to and ponder on the views of the public, the professional politicians scoffed at the seriousness of the directive. Asserting that Ayub had already determined the character of the constitution, and arguing that the new document would only reflect the desires and aspirations of the country's maximum ruler, the politicians decided to oppose the Commission and its final product. Indeed, Ayub had laid out the design and the procedures in his many public appearances, and the Constitution Commission was given the task of bringing the President's ideas to life. Ayub, for his part, had seriously questioned the moral character of the country's political leaders and, having argued that their purposes were venal and unscrupulous, he called for a constitutional order that safeguarded the interests of the more gullible and easily manipulated masses. Ayub's declaration that only a presidential form of government would suffice in the Pakistani milieu, that only a strong centre could deliver the necessary services to the nation, promote self-help, and accelerate national development, impressed members of the higher bureaucracy and attracted support from among some members of the country's intelligentsia, but it never won the favour of the conventional and fundamental political elites.

The gap between Ayub and the politicians was unbridgeable. Indeed, Ayub's ideal was a nation without politicians. Ayub formally rejected the reinstatement of political parties, which he continued to vilify as more destructive than competitive. He even discounted the creation of a one-party system, and offered the view that a form of Islamic Assembly would be more suitable because each Assemblyman would be free to express himself, unbeholden to any organization, region, or nationality. Elections of such individuals could also be done, according to Ayub, along what he judged to be Islamic lines, that is, by community consensus or expressions of public need. But whatever the outcome, nothing would be allowed to interfere with the Basic Democracies system. More than any other development,

Basic Democracies had become the bedrock upon which any constitutional order would be constructed (Mahmood, 1964).

Ayub had come to believe that Basic Democracies was a manifestation of Islamic democracy and hence was the 'foundation-stone' of a durable and appropriate constitutional order. For him, there was nothing in the system that could not be judged Islamic in spirit as well as content. Ayub questioned the attacks on Basic Democracies but he also encouraged criticism, declaring that it was the Muslim manner to contest views, to challenge ideas, as long as the purpose of argument was the realization of a majority viewpoint. Controversy, according to Ayub, so long as it remained constructive, was welcome. Moreover, it gave the people the opportunity to examine an issue from different vantage points, and in so doing, it assisted them in reaching a higher level of understanding. Ayub acknowledged that the maturation process would be slow and deliberate, but given an ambience of relative good will and co-operation, he anticipated marked improvement in mass political awareness.

Ayub, however, received far more criticism than he anticipated. Ridiculing his association of Islam with Basic Democracies, his antagonists insisted that the system was a contemporary form of the Hindu *panchayat*. They also criticized the subordination of the elected council members to the nation's bureaucrats, and the likelihood that the administrator's power of decision would run roughshod over the opinions of the people's representatives. Moreover, the use of the elected officials as an electoral college denied the larger population their right to directly elect the President. Lacking any trust in Ayub Khan, they argued that the electors could be bribed, bought, and paid for, and their roles easily compromised. The indirect method of elections left few serious opportunities for an opposition, and Ayub was assured overwhelming advantages in any future contest. The politicians were appalled that Ayub would raise the issue of their self-serving behaviour when his own was so blatantly opportunistic.

Ayub, however, was not deterred. Dilating on the need for citizenship training, and believing he had found the necessary technique, he claimed to find justification for his ideas, and especially for the Basic Democracies, in 'the book of Pakistan' (Feldman, 1967, p.112). A firm believer in human progress, Ayub acknowledged the dependence of the Basic Democrats on the administrators, but he also cited the temporary aspects of those relationships. The Basic Democrats, he explained, would in time cease being basic, and by their own actions they would eliminate the need for bureaucratic supervision. Ayub cited the divisiveness of majority decision-making, and rather than suffer the consequences of a win-lose situation, he called for an enduring harmony that could only come from consensus decision-making. Ayub had convinced himself that his elected village and town councillors would learn co-operation by simply working together toward common community goals.

The President's optimism, however, was not shared by the more activist members of the public. Self-government had been assured with the transfer of power. Great Britain had deemed Pakistan ready for independence, and the country had been launched with a sophisticated, functioning political model. The politicians seemed prepared to acknowledge their early aggressiveness, but they passed it off as natural and hardly an extraordinary occurrence in a new nation. Time and experience would bring the necessary improvements, and the politicians anticipated finding that level of discourse which promised a stable national future.

If Ayub believed the simple folk would in time rise to the level of sophisticated citizenship, then how could he conclude that the more professional politicians were not capable of overcoming the political and cultural obstacles made manifest by the colonial legacy? In other words, Ayub's argument justifying Basic Democracies virtually negated the progress already achieved in promoting national democratic behaviour. Ayub failed to seize the opportunity to link Pakistan's higher and lower political experiences, and he leaned too heavily on the steel frame of colonial administration. He could, therefore, not escape the abrasive features of his own dictatorship, and he was forced to struggle against a political opposition which could only grow stronger as the soldier President gradually distanced himself from the barracks and was metamorphosed into the very politician he had taken such pains to neutralize.

Constitution-making was an entirely different experience under the restrictions of martial law. Ayub Khan provided the outline and Manzur Qadir filled in the details. Manzur Qadir was a most able member of the legal Lahore fraternity, an articulate spokesman for the revolution, and Ayub's most adept partner at transforming abstract ideas into legal language. Qadir had studied at Cambridge and was called to the bar from Lincoln's Inn in 1935. He became a senior advocate of the Federal Court of Pakistan, where he had pleaded cases in constitutional law. It was Manzur Qadir who buttressed Ayub's determination to replace the 1956 Constitution with one more geared to presidential politics. An intellectual with impressive international credentials, Qadir transcended the mundane and more limited vistas of the Pakistani experience, and it was he who also encouraged Ayub to pursue secular themes.

Thus, when completed, the 1962 Constitution avoided referring to Pakistan as an Islamic republic, and in effect sustained the order signed by Iskandar Mirza on 11 October 1958 that dropped the religious appellation from the country's official designation. Both Ayub and Qadir saw little to gain in restating what was so obvious, that Pakistan was an overwhelmingly Muslim nation. Moreover, both men were determined to put sufficient distance between the country's theologians and its political future. Political education, they asserted, was not a responsibility of the country's spiritual leaders.

Nevertheless, the failure to include the Islamic state in the final draft of the 1962 Constitution prompted serious objections from a body politic that was determined to find fault with the new document (Burki, 1986). The issue refused to go away, nor was Ayub in a position to ignore the rising tide of negative public opinion. Realizing his claim to legitimacy had been further undermined, Ayub yielded to his detractors and, following the constitution's promulgation, the term 'Islamic Republic' was reinserted. Ayub had been prepared to resist the pressure, but another member of his cabinet, namely Zulfikar Ali Bhutto, had gained his confidence and, over Manzur Qadir's objections, Ayub was convinced by his young Minister of National Reconstruction, Broadcasting, and Minorities that it would be in his government's interest not to sustain the controversy. Although perhaps not fully grasped at the time, Ayub's capitulation represented a weakening of his authority and a diminution in his powers. Also not observed at the time, Ayub came to rely increasingly on Bhutto's counsel, especially after the lifting of martial law.

The 1962 Constitution

Ayub and Manzur Qadir had been assisted by a Constitution Commission that was assembled on 17 February 1960. The charge to the Commission called for a report indicating how a modern democracy could be developed from the Islamic principles of justice, equality, and tolerance. Ayub had established the framework for the Commission's deliberations, and it was not permitted to deviate from the presidential model envisaged by him. The Commission began its work by circulating a questionnaire in English, Urdu, and Bengali, and anyone could obtain a copy, respond to the questions, and send it on to the Commission. Of the 28,000 circulated copies of the questionnaire, a little more than 6,000 were completed and deposited for scrutiny. When some of the questionnaires were leaked to the Press, the martial law authority was compelled to warn the perpetrators that they were in violation of the order denying political activity, and that if the practice persisted, stern action would be taken against the newspapers and the persons disclosing the information.

But in spite of this effort to stifle public debate, the circulation of the questionnaire renewed interest in politics, and when the union councillors in the Basic Democracies system became involved, the authorities reminded all the politicians that they were violating the autonomous character of the Constitution Commission and thus preventing it from doing its work. Although the labours of the Commission were sometimes interrupted by external controversy, Ayub's prodding and Manzur Qadir's acumen moved the process along so that in May 1961 its report was placed before the President. After examining the report's contents, Ayub passed it to a five-person subcommittee under the chairmanship of Manzur Qadir, which five months later deposited a draft constitution on Ayub's desk. The new constitution was announced on 1 March 1962, when copies were made available to the public.

Given the circumstances of its gestation, the constitution was never popular and there was no celebration to herald its launching. When the voices of dissent hinted at the eventual return to the parliamentary system, it was Ayub who talked publicly of 'bloody revolution' (*Dawn*, 8 April 1962). Ayub acknowledged that the constitution was not even roughly equivalent to the presidential form adopted in the United States, but he countered such comparisons by citing the long period of trial and error in that country and that Pakistan was engaged in a totally new experiment. What Ayub could not argue away, however, was the awareness that the constitution had been produced during a forty-four month period of martial law; that even after its promulgation and its coming into force, i.e., the indirect elections to the national and provincial legislatures, it was the handiwork of the military. Moreover, the head of state did not have to stand for re-election because Article 226 of the new constitution stated that the referendum of February 1960 confirming Field Marshal Ayub Khan as the country's first President *ipso facto* made him the first President under the new constitution.

Ayub's continuance as President, the fact that he was not called to compete in an open election, even in an indirect one, could be viewed as a further usurpation of power, or it could be interpreted as security for the new constitution. On the one side, it is known that as early as January 1960, Ayub had voiced the thought of retiring in 1963 or 1964 (*Dawn*, 16 January 1960); on the other, he recognized that the constitution was his handiwork and that he would have to prove its effectiveness before he allowed his successor to assume the Presidency. But whichever argument was more accurate, there was no gainsaying the fact that Ayub had foisted a constitution on the nation and that he remained in power to see that it was brought into force. Although martial law was officially terminated, the Field Marshal's adversaries could still argue that Ayub's dictatorial powers remained intact, and that they still had to risk losing their freedom and their property by appearing to challenge him. In the final analysis, the new constitution did not have an auspicious beginning.

The principal features of the 1962 Constitution called for a President, who must be a Muslim, and a National Assembly comprised of 156 members who were divided equally between East and West Pakistan (Gankovsky and Moskalenko, 1978). Both the President and the National Assembly members served five-year terms, but the latter was subject to dissolution for extraordinary reasons. Both the President and the national legislature were elected indirectly by the electoral college of Basic Democrats. The constitution also made provision for a Supreme Court as well as High Courts in the respective provinces.

The President was the key figure in the constitutional structure. All legislation passed by the National Assembly required his assent. In the case of an impasse between the legislature and the President, the latter could refer the matter to the electoral college of Basic Democrats for an up or down verdict. While the President held the pre-eminent position in the political system, the National Assembly was given the power of impeachment, but only if one-third of its members signed a written notice, addressed to the Speaker, stating their intention to move a resolution calling for the Chief Executive's removal. Such a petition had to prove a wilful violation of the constitution or extraordinary misconduct on the part of the President. But the President also retained the power to dissolve the National Assembly, with the proviso that 120 days after the dissolution order, the President too must step down. The President also reserved the right to promulgate legislation, to issue ordinances when the Assembly was not in session or had been terminated. Finally, the President was given the power to declare an emergency if the country's security was threatened from without, or if a deteriorating domestic economy endangered the life of the nation. During a state of emergency the Chief Executive had absolute powers, with which the Assembly could not interfere. The President's power was virtually total and his decisions passed directly to a Council of Ministers for execution.

It was never a question of whether this constitution or the previous one was better for Pakistan. It was not even a question of whether a parliamentary or presidential system was more appropriate. Either constitution would have sufficed. In the end, it was not the wording of the documents, the structures they described, or the promises they made to the citizenry. Constitutions are words, and only words. It is in their operation, in the intent and purpose of their implementors, that success or failure is judged. In other words, it is how constitutions play out in the everyday circumstances of a nation that determine their utility or inutility. But do constitutions really succeed or fail? The very question supposes an animate quality to constitutions which they do not possess. Constitutions are made by men and they are orchestrated by men. They do not succeed or fail until the men responsible for their execution are judged. The most perfectly drafted constitution is no guarantee of its success. And the poorest drawn document might well prove sufficient if the people responsible for its implementation are true to their purposes. Constitutions are limitations on the power of government; they are contracts between the rulers and the ruled, the governors and the governed; it is in their performance, not in the written word, that answers are found and constitutions judged.

With such observations, it is noteworthy that the 1956 Constitution was never adequately tested, and that the 1962 constitution was negatively judged before its promulgation. At best, the 1956 Constitution centred on the urban scene, but was made the responsibility of rural power-brokers. The feudal elements that dominated Pakistan's political life were hardly the ones to be entrusted with a political structure that limited their expression or reduced their power.

The 1956 Constitution catered more to an intelligentsia who resettled Pakistan after the agony of partition, that is, to a *mohajir* community fervent in its support of Pakistan, but which lacked the power constituencies that moved and shaped the political process. The 1956 Constitution was doomed, not by the intrigue of the army or higher bureaucracy, but by the politicians whose domicile was rooted in agrarian Pakistan and who represented traditional power structures (Maluka, 1995). The 1919 Government of India Act, that called for a dyarchic form of rule, had delegated responsibilities to the provinces, to local authorities in the respective constituencies. This delegation came at a time when the rural power structure was already pre-eminent. It was the *zamindars* and their cohorts who reaped the benefits of the self-governing experience, and it was they that occupied the key political positions. Partition and independence eliminated the colonial centre, but it left the extended units virtually intact. The 1956 Constitution failed to appreciate this order of power, and the creation of a new national centre did not meet with the same deference previously shown the colonial power (Yunas, 1995).

The Ayubian Constitution of 1962 attempted to bring political theory abreast of political reality. It acknowledged the dominance of rural expression, but it also aimed at neutralizing the feudalists and their parochial interests. But while the 1962 Constitution attempted to constrain the landlords, it did not prevent Ayub from enlisting their services. Ayub's dependence on the Khan of Kalabagh, who he made Governor of West Pakistan, was a notable case in point. The landlords would be recognized as the source of traditional power, but their illiterate and dependent workers were to be instilled with ideas of self-worth. Ayub interposed the bureaucracy between the landlords and the cultivators, and it was the former who were expected to elevate peasant awareness and direct their energies. But the process was a long and tedious one, and while it was in train, it would be necessary to hold the more articulate urban elements in a form of limbo. Ayub's principal detractors, therefore, would stem from among the urban elites, especially those whose objectives appeared to be frustrated by the Field Marshal (Hussain, 1979). The clash of interests was inevitable, but the path chosen by Ayub appeared better suited to the cultural conditions prevailing within the country. Most important, the Ayubian Constitution aimed at neutralizing the major political centres, i.e., the landlords, the *ulema*, and the urban intelligentsia.

Ayub was the first Pakistani leader to take a full reading of the Pakistan scene, the first to experiment with holistic change, and the first to fashion a programme that united the needs of the state with those of its humanity. The most significant limitation in Ayub's plan, however, was its inability to measure the Bengali factor. Ayub's political system had considerable merit for the regions of West Pakistan, but it had little meaning in the east wing. The modalities were different in the eastern province, and the combination of power-brokers that framed the West Pakistan political scene were not replicated in East Pakistan. Ayub's shortcomings in East Pakistan are surprising, because he had served there as General Officer Commanding in 1948. It was during his duty there that he gained the attention of Liaquat Ali Khan, who in September 1950 selected him over more senior generals to become Commander-in-Chief of the Pakistan Army. Ayub had received high marks for his work in the eastern province, and it is therefore even more surprising that Altaf Gauhar, one of his closest associates, could later write that

> Ayub did not have much direct information about the views and reactions of the intelligentsia in East Pakistan...His personal contact with East Pakistan was limited to official contacts and meetings with pro-government East Pakistani politicians and academics. Ayub did not receive a single letter from any Bengali who was not a government official about the future constitution, which showed how distant and alien he must have appeared to the people of East Pakistan (Gauhar, 1993, p.186).

The 1962 Constitution did not reflect the political culture of the Bengali nation that had emerged from the colonial-imposed Permanent Settlement. Ayub's deference to and dependence on the bureaucracy reminded Bengalis of an earlier period of colonial servitude. Moreover, Ayub's determination to build a strong centre, one even more remote from the eastern province, was judged a dire threat to the life and future of the Bengali people. The new political system reinforced the thinking of those who had earlier determined that the province was being transformed into a 'colony' of West Pakistan. Nor could Ayub alleviate such concerns by offering to build a 'second capital' in Dhaka, or by promising to provincialize the services. The Bengalis demanded a larger voice in the halls of power, and the passing of their older and venerated leaders had opened a political vacuum that could only be filled by the most radical members of the Bengal political fraternity.

Ayub made an effort to win over the more moderate Bengalis, but his talks with Maulvi Tamizuddin Khan failed when the latter insisted on the reinstatement of the parliamentary system. Tamizuddin even raised the issue of separate provincial constitutions for each of the two wings, but Ayub refused to consider such thinking. More inclined toward the unitary rather than a federal model, Ayub's presidency was Gaullist or Nasserist, and East Pakistan judged it too remote for its tastes. Moreover, the three Bengali members of Ayub's cabinet, A.K. Khan, Minister of Industries, Hafiz-ur-Rahman, Commerce Minister, and Mohammad Ibrahim, the Law Minister, were all dismissed after the promulgation of the Ayubian Constitution. Thus, not only was Ayub cut off from mainstream Bengali politics and thinking, he also appeared indifferent to the province's needs and aspirations. Failing to develop the necessary sensitivity, Ayub's Constitution was to face its acid test in the eastern province.

Constitutional Politics

The 1962 Constitution brought an end to martial law and ushered in a period of revitalized political activity. The politicians, who had been silenced by martial law, were now again in the forefront of the political debate, and they seized every opportunity to ridicule the President for what they described as his dictatorial, self-serving behaviour. Ayub remained steadfast in his resolve, in spite of all the personal criticism levelled against him. Moreover, he was steeled in his view that democracy was his ultimate objective and that his purpose during those forty-four months of military rule was not retribution, but education and development. The country, Ayub believed, needed a respite from the political struggles that followed independence. Time was needed to reflect on the meaning of Pakistan and the course the nation might follow in realizing its destiny. Thus there was no reason to act harshly, and indeed, it was only the rhetoric that seemed to hint at a punishing style of government. In the end, however, the martial law regime abstained from the use of cruel methods, and even the numerous prison sentences were cancelled soon after their issue. Convicted miscreants were released, and the heavy fines imposed on those found guilty of crimes against society were never recovered. Ayub was convinced that a mixture of intimidation and public embarrassment was a better form of punishment than physical distress, and his regime was generally benign and largely forgiving.

Herbert Feldman (1967) questioned a martial law administration that claimed to be democratic, even apologetic. But he was on the mark in noting Ayub's training as a soldier and officer in the British Indian Army. The British, too, were more paternalistic than vindictive, and their style of administration influenced Ayub's behaviour and mannerisms. Ayub had every intention of restoring civilian government. Also he was aware that the longer the men in uniform remained in political roles, the more difficult it would be both to counter public disdain and, no less important, to construct a formidable, disciplined, and professional army. The military's time in the public arena would best be brief, but Ayub did not quickly return responsibility to civilian hands. Moreover, Ayub had to, all intents and purposes, become a civilian. Mirza had replaced Ayub as head of the army when he named him Prime Minister. General Mohammad Musa had become Commander-in-Chief of the Pakistan Army in 1958, and with the lifting of martial law in 1962, he could not be expected to yield that position to Ayub. Furthermore, Ayub was not yet ready to retire from public life, and his decision to remain in place as the country's first President under the new constitution was a calculated move aimed at preserving the reforms he had set in train.

Ayub's civilian status was more apparent following the promulgation of the constitution and the lifting of martial law. If, as Chief Martial Law Administrator, he had proved to be a less than severe taskmaster, as the constitutional President of Pakistan he was subjected to restraints for which he himself was responsible. Ayub's rule was governed more by persuasion than coercive methods, but the system he had put in place answered to him, not to the government, and certainly not to the public. Dominating the political institutions, Ayub did not have to satisfy the National Assembly, and the Basic Democracies were better left to the responsibility of the civil administration. Ayub's ministers served at his pleasure and answered only to him, but this too only burdened his office and absolved his colleagues of any wrongdoing. Ayub took all the credit and all the blame for what he had produced, and while he drew from what he understood to be the history of the subcontinent, his thinking was more a matter of discretionary reasoning than deep political thought. Ayub was hardly the philosophical type. Given to quick, almost simple, solutions, even his more astute and most intimate cabinet colleagues did little to add to his knowledge. Nevertheless, his rule focused on conciliation, and he was often prepared to retreat from a position if sufficient resistance was encountered. After martial law, Ayub managed Pakistan with considerable flexibility, but he could never overcome his popular image as an oppressive ruler.

This explains why Ayub backed away from educational reforms when resistance was encountered from the student community. For the same reasons, his land reforms were not implemented when the landlords showed their displeasure (Hasan Khan, 1981). So, too, there was little success to show for all the effort demanding greater credibility and honesty from the business community. Family planning programmes were stymied by the mullahs who argued against their validity in a Muslim nation. Both public and private corruption, and a variety of malpractices, were little changed by martial law. Nevertheless, the economy did show improvement during Ayub's tenure. The building of state infrastructure, improved agricultural performance, and an expanding industrial base were no small achievements.

Ayub enlisted the support of the United States government in many of his enterprises. A Washington-supported Rural Works Programme replaced the older Village-AID exercises, and public monies were pumped into the rural scene, to be managed by the Basic Democrats in concert with their omnipresent civil administrators. Funds were made available for projects in education and family planning, for road construction, communications, and rural electrification. The martial law period was not without its accomplishments, but the real test of Ayub's rule came after the constitution went into effect in June 1962.

Ayub ruled out the formation and interplay of political parties. Candidates for public office had to prove themselves

to the electors on the basis of merit alone, and he
emphatically rejected any intention to form his own political
organization. Thus, when the elections to the National
Assembly and provincial legislatures were conducted, there
was little excitement and very little balloting. With the Basic
Democrats serving as electors, and with the latter divided
into constituencies, very few votes were tallied to register a
victory or defeat. But the seating of the National Assembly
was a different matter. It was one thing to 'elect' members
without designation of party it was yet another matter to
conduct the business of the House on an individualized basis.
Almost immediately, the Assemblymen divided into factions
and groups that represented different programmes and
interests.

Ayub soon realized the futility of pressing his prohibition,
and only weeks after the convening of the National Assembly,
the President gave his consent to a Political Parties Act. But
the reinstatement of the political parties was made dependent
on the maintenance of party discipline, and no member of
the Assembly from one party was allowed to transfer his
allegiance to another. Nevertheless, party politics were again
in vogue, and even Ayub could not avoid being caught up in
their many practices.

The Muslim League was reactivated almost immediately,
but differences among the politicians could not be resolved
and the organization split, with one group joining the Council
Muslim League, while a renegade movement called for the
establishment of a Convention Muslim League. Some
observers believed the Muslim League was Ayub's for the
taking, but his reticence seemed to leave the party in
disarray. It was soon apparent, however, that the
Conventionists represented the policies of Ayub Khan, and it
was they who eventually formed the government.

The political scene was more complex than seen at first
glance. Efforts to revive the Nizam-i-Islam, the National
Awami Party, and the Awami League met with stiff
opposition from both Muslim League parties. After
considerable debate, the National Assembly divided between
those favouring the government and those opposing it. Older
rivalries surfaced which Ayub's supporters successfully

exploited, thus swelling his government's support base. Under the 1962 Constitution, the President did not require a majority in the National Assembly, but Ayub's preponderance of support was none the less welcome and he wasted no time in using it.

The restoration of the politicians was not without cost, however. Ayub was required to sanction or promote amendments to a constitution not yet fully in force. The Islamic features of the 1956 Constitution were thus incorporated in the new document as Ayub sought a truce with the orthodox members of the religious community. He also authorized modification of election procedures for the presidency which more or less guaranteed his serving another term in 1965. Another amendment lifted disqualification orders from specific categories of individuals, and made it possible for those favouring Ayub to stand for public office. Still another gave the President control over the civil service in that it permitted him to retire members who completed twenty-five years of service, while others were permitted to extend their tenure five additional years beyond the fifty-five year age limit.

On 15 December 1962 Ayub crossed his personal Rubicon when he allowed himself to become a candidate for the presidency of the Convention Muslim League. Subsequent to that action, and in an effort to legitimize his all-Pakistan credentials, Ayub announced publicly that he was 'a two-anna member from both East and West Pakistan' (Dawn, 23 May 1963). Ayub had cast himself in the role of a politician, obviously believing he could bridge the divide between the east and west wings of the country. Moreover, he seriously entertained plans of reviving the Muslim League, especially in East Pakistan, where it had almost disappeared. It was therefore in Dhaka, on 24 December 1963, that Ayub accepted the unanimous vote of the Pakistan Muslim League Conventionists and became their President.

As politician, Ayub had an impact on his cabinet colleagues in a variety of ways. Manzur Qadir, who had shaped Pakistan's domestic and foreign policy, and whom Ayub had come to depend upon for intellectualizing his ideas, left the cabinet after the promulgation of the 1962

Constitution. Justice Munir also returned to his law practice following the report of the Franchise Commission, which Ayub cast aside when it did not approve his indirect election programme. Causing distress among his erstwhile supporters, Ayub appointed a Special Committee which overruled the Franchise Commission. The Special Committee rejected direct national elections, calling them an unreliable index of public opinion in a country that was almost eighty per cent illiterate. Thus Ayub got his way, but it cost him some very important friends and colleagues. Without Manzur Qadir and Mohammad Munir to advise him, the critical role of articulating the President's sentiments fell to the youngest member of the cabinet, namely, Zulfikar Ali Bhutto. Also a lawyer, the erudite Bhutto assured Ayub that he had taken the necessary action and should hold to his convictions.

The reinstatement of the political parties, and Ayub's decision to become yet another politician, had placed him on the defensive. Ayub called for unity and requested both Suhrawardy and Nazimuddin to join the Conventionist Muslim League. Both men, however, declined the invitation rather than add legitimacy to Ayub's actions. In fact, they found common cause in their struggle against the Ayub government, that is, until Suhrawardy's death in December 1963, and Nazimuddin's passing in October 1964. Rejected by or denied the support of Pakistan's elder statesmen, it came as no surprise when Ayub turned to the younger members of his entourage, and especially to Zulfikar Ali Bhutto.

Bhutto was moved by the opportunity to assist Ayub in the restructuring of the Pakistan experience. Sensing that the Field Marshal was not forever, Bhutto's personal ambitions were energized by his high station. Moreover, after Manzur Qadir passed his foreign affairs responsibilities to Mohammad Ali Bogra, and the latter suddenly died, it was Bhutto who assumed that important portfolio. Bhutto's meteoric rise was a direct consequence of Ayub's limited political credentials, and the young man wasted no time in making himself a major figure in the Ayub administration.

Bhutto, a scion of the Shah Nawaz Khan Bhuttos of Larkana, was born into the most notable circle of Sindhi aristocracy. The Bhutto tribal following included affiliations in Balochistan, Punjab, and Rajputana in India. An honour graduate in Political Science from the University of California at Berkeley in 1950, he went on to Oxford where he studied in Christ Church College, receiving a graduate degree in jurisprudence in 1952. He also completed the bar at Lincoln's Inn that same year. Recognized as an orator and debater, he began a teaching career at the University of Southampton and, finally, at the Muslim Law College in Karachi, where he taught both constitutional and international law. In 1958 he served with the Pakistan delegation at the United Nations, and later led his country's representatives at the Law of the Sea Conference. Originally appointed to Ayub's cabinet by Iskandar Mirza, who acknowledged the prowess and influence of the Bhutto clan, Ayub retained the young man and, in time, came to dote upon him. The Field Marshal saw Zulfikar as a superb example of a second-generation Pakistani, a civilian leader who seemed to embody all the attributes Ayub considered necessary in moving Pakistan beyond its colonial heritage. He therefore nurtured the young man, brought him into his inner circle, and after several years of near intimacy, began to confide in him, as well as seek his advice.

Bhutto responded to Ayub's display of patriarchal affection by reinforcing Ayub's ego. More than that, Bhutto played Machiavelli to Ayub's need for counsel. Manzur Qadir was ill-suited for such a role, but Bhutto was also a Sindhi feudal lord, and his aristocratic demeanour focused attention more on statecraft than state-building. For Bhutto it was not so much a matter of educating the masses as it was imperative for the ruler to manipulate them (Gauhar, 1994). The end-game was not the enlightenment of the nation but the symbolic uses of power, and indeed the development of techniques needed to sustain political advantage. Moreover, the more Ayub found himself engaged in the day-to-day politics of the country, the more he became dependent on the assurances provided by his most perspicacious and erudite political counsel.

Bhutto avoided outward displays of bravado in cabinet meetings, preferring to meet with Ayub in the solitude of his

study or remote retreats. Allowing other ministers to speak
their minds or to quarrel with one another over the choice of
policy may have been interpreted as respect for the more
senior members of the ruling council, but for Bhutto it was
strategically necessary to place himself outside the entourage
and hence, in a more formidable position to gain the
President's ear. Thus, whereas the other ministers came and
went, Bhutto grew in stature and responsibility, and apart
from the President, he became the most noteworthy of
Pakistani officials. He was also the most quoted, both at home
and abroad. Bhutto's youth and magnetic personality also
drew the younger generation to his side. Symbolic of a
generational transition, Bhutto's passionate oratory was tailor-
made for the politicized student body, especially in Punjab
and Sindh. The students flocked to his call, and responded
enthusiastically to his emotional speeches that called for the
liberation of Kashmir and the termination of Pakistan's
dependence on the United States. Clearly Ayub saw in Bhutto
an indispensable asset, because the articulate young man,
unlike the aging soldier that he was, could bridge the
generation gap. Ayub was so enthralled with his Sindhi
minister that he even called upon him to orchestrate his 1964
electoral campaign.

Kashmir and the Elections of 1965

Ayub's state visit to Washington in 1961 marked the high
point in United States-Pakistan relations. In 1962, however,
China's attack on India provoked a US reaction that disturbed
the Pakistanis and brought Ayub's dependence on the
Americans into question (Rahman, 1982). Washington ignored
Nehru's provocative statements in the Indian parliament
which triggered the Chinese action. Washington also leaned
heavily on Ayub not to take advantage of a retreating Indian
Army, and in spite of pressure at home, he did not move his
forces into disputed Kashmir. Ayub's dependency on the
Americans provided more fuel for his political opposition,
and an already unpopular ruler was hard put to it to reconcile
his actions with his public statements of national
reconstruction. The modernization of the Pakistan Army was
well in train in 1962-3, but hardly beyond an early

developmental stage. Moreover, that modernization was almost totally dependent on American assistance, and Ayub was in no position to anger Washington if the needed assistance was to continue. Ayub was, therefore, caught between placating the United States and responding affirmatively to those who might ensure the success of his domestic programme. Bhutto's elevation to Minister of Foreign Affairs in January 1963, therefore, could not have come at a more difficult or fortuitous moment. Bhutto was needed to tranquillize the opposition, to assure the public that the country had an independent foreign policy, but above all, to help Ayub prepare for the presidential election slated for 2 January 1965.

If Bhutto's ego was inflated by his high profile station in the Ayub administration, it was immeasurably expanded by his singular role at Ayub's side. Bhutto came to believe that he alone could make or break the Field Marshal. Indeed, Ayub's reform programme appeared to rest on Bhutto's performance. Nor was the Ayub-Bhutto relationship lost on the military establishment. The army high command had given considerable thought to Ayub's civilian successor, and more and more Zulfikar Ali Bhutto seemed the person most likely to follow Ayub. In fact, by his own actions, Ayub was letting it be known that the young man would make a suitable successor. One observer put it this way: 'The most probable heir for the mantle of Saviour is Zulfikar Ali Bhutto. Mr Bhutto seems to be idolized by practically everyone' (Askari, 1964).

Bhutto's rise to prominence coincided with Ayub's overall decline. By 1964, many of the President's earlier associates had deserted him. But Bhutto's advice to Ayub was for firmness on both the domestic and external fronts. Urging a more aggressive posture on Kashmir, Bhutto convinced Ayub that his domestic reforms would be more manageable if he stopped dwelling upon them and, instead, exploited the emotional dimensions of the Kashmir question. Bhutto also counselled Ayub to ignore the country's Cold War commitments which the Pakistani elector knew little about, and to focus his sights on regional matters, especially the Hindu-Muslim issue, which everyone had an interest in. Moreover, with the presidential elections only weeks away, Bhutto cautioned that the indirect polls did not guarantee an Ayub victory. Indeed, Ayub had been forced to do battle with the sister of the Quaid-i-Azam, Fatima Jinnah, who had long since withdrawn her support from the uniformed officer. Representing the Combined Opposition Parties (COP), Fatima enjoyed the name recognition that Ayub could have significant difficulty in overcoming, even in the context of indirect elections.

Bhutto not only believed that exploiting the Kashmir question was solid election strategy, he also linked Kashmir with Pakistan's *raison d'être*. 'Kashmir,' Bhutto wrote, 'must be liberated if Pakistan is to have its full meaning' (Bhutto, 1964, p.13). The Foreign Minister stoked the fires of the Kashmir dispute, and seemed to enjoy antagonizing Washington with his overtures to China. Bhutto also completed the work begun by Manzur Qadir and Mohammad Ali Bogra when Pakistan and China entered into a border agreement in March 1963. The settlement was condemned by New Delhi but played well in Pakistan, and Bhutto was the immediate beneficiary of a very positive Press. Altaf Gauhar, Ayub Khan's Information Secretary, counselled the President on the need to regain the foreign policy spotlight lest Bhutto receive all the accolades. Taking a page from his Foreign Minister, Ayub used the occasion of a visit by W.W. Rostow, President Kennedy's National Security Advisor, to publicly criticize the American transfer of military hardware to India. Ayub warned Rostow that India would be more inclined to use the weapons against Pakistan, and that American assurances to the contrary were not sufficient. Ayub was reluctant to take the matter further. Nor was he given to emotional displays, and his admonition to the Americans was hardly meant to be a repudiation of support.

Bhutto, therefore, continued to enjoy a higher profile in foreign affairs, and he used the spotlight afforded by meetings of the Southeast Asian Treaty Organization (SEATO), the Central Treaty Organization (CENTO), and the Pakistan National Assembly, to shout defiance at India. Convinced of the merit of his cause, Bhutto did not always consult with the President before launching an attack on New Delhi, nor had Ayub been informed when he publicly announced that the administration was on the verge of making a 'fundamental decision' that led his listeners to believe a rupture in US-Pakistan relations was imminent (Ziring, 1971, p.53). Bhutto's rhetoric, however, received popular acclaim in Pakistan, and because it appeared to deflect some of the domestic criticism away from the President, he was allowed to sustain his initiatives on a variety of foreign policy questions.

In December 1963 Pakistan lodged a protest with India against the latter's aggressive moves in Kashmir. A sacred relic, alleged to be a hair from the beard of the Prophet (PBUH) was reported stolen from the Hazratbal Shrine in Srinagar during this same period. The incident provoked riots in the mountain state which sparked similar disturbances in both India and Pakistan, and especially in East Pakistan, where a significant Hindu minority continued to reside. Both the Indian and Pakistani governments voiced concern about the plight of their brethren in the respective countries, and with tensions building between them, the United Nations Security Council became seized of the question. Bhutto presented the Pakistan case at a special meeting of the UN Security Council, where he used his oratorical gifts to excoriate the world body for its inaction. Revealing frustration with the deliberations, instead of sustaining the debate he broke off contact, demanded a suspension, and returned to Karachi just in time to welcome Zhou Enlai. Unlike the United Nations, which was characterized as indifferent to the plight of the Kashmiri people, the Chinese leader's declaration of support was considered a plus for Pakistan, and especially for Zulfikar Ali Bhutto, whose popularity continued to soar.

Again it was Bhutto, not Ayub, who identified with the Chinese leaders and extolled Pakistan's relationship with Beijing. Moreover, Bhutto's energetic activities were not lost on New Delhi, nor was Pakistan's China card taken lightly in the Congress Syndicate. In a gesture aimed at relieving some of the tension over Kashmir, Prime Minister Nehru ordered the release of Sheikh Mohammad Abdullah. He also signalled Karachi that it might be time for direct talks between key officials of their two governments. It was Bhutto, however, who stole a lead on the Indian leaders by inviting the 'Lion of

Kashmir' to visit Pakistan. Like Ayub, Nehru was caught off guard by Bhutto's aggressive diplomacy, but the Indian leader was quick to acknowledge the invitation and to sanction Sheikh Abdullah's trip to Pakistan.

New Delhi believed it had gestured its good will by allowing the Kashmiri leader to visit Pakistan in May 1964. Moreover, Abdullah went to Pakistan as a peacemaker, not an angry belligerent. The celebrated leader of the Kashmiri people called for moderation from all the parties, and noted that a settlement was possible which satisfied the different claims. Nehru buttressed that theme when he called for a meeting with President Ayub and hinted at a willingness to resolve the Kashmir dilemma. A June meeting between the two leaders appeared to be in the offing when suddenly, weakened by a stroke earlier in the year, Nehru suffered still another that hastened his death. Instead of the long awaited summit on Kashmir, Sheikh Abdullah and Zulfikar Ali Bhutto travelled to New Delhi to attend the funeral of the Indian Prime Minister.

Lal Bahadur Shastri, Nehru's successor, lacked Nehru's political leverage, and whatever peace-offering Nehru had planned to bring to the negotiating table was burned with him on his funeral pyre. Relations between India and Pakistan did not improve, anti-Americanism in Pakistan continued to spread and deepen, and the Ayub government turned its attention to the election campaign which was now under way in earnest. Indeed, Bhutto and other government ministers exploited the American factor, citing the US C.I.A. as being in league with the COP and its presidential candidate, Fatima Jinnah. By contrast, the same ministers stressed what they now referred to as Ayub's independent foreign policy. It was Zulfikar Ali Bhutto, however, who received the most attention. On 28 December 1964, just days away from the balloting, Bhutto declared that the Pakistan government would 'take retaliatory steps to counter the Indian attempt to merge the occupied parts of Kashmir with India.' He followed this warning with renewed emphasis on Pakistan's capacity to respond to the Indian initiative. 'You will see better results in the very near future', he counselled (*Morning News*, 28 December 1964).

Bhutto's role in managing the presidential elections via the Kashmir dispute offset Fatima Jinnah's initial success in winning the favour of the electors. Miss Jinnah had accused Ayub of bartering away Pakistan's Indus waters to India. She also reminded the Basic Democrats of Ayub's offer to Prime Minister Nehru in 1959 for joint defence of the subcontinent. At the same time, she appeared to damage her candidacy when she described the United States as Pakistan's 'only friend' and gave Bhutto still another opportunity to boost his government's independent foreign policy. Miss Jinnah's ineffective defence of her position caused rifts to develop within COP ranks, with the more leftist organizations questioning the lady's capacity to govern Pakistan. COP defections also made it possible for Ayub to gain the advantage in their 'Confrontation Meetings', and the strategy of mixing domestic and foreign policy questions began to pay off in Ayub's favour.

The Confrontation Meetings were little more than charades, given the absence of the public and the separate questioning of the candidates. Moreover, the questions posed to the candidates were stacked against Miss Jinnah, and her lack of public experience, as well as her imperious personality, did not inspire the Basic Democrats. Miss Jinnah accused the government of rigging the meetings, but even when her party tried to pack the Rawalpindi programme with her supporters, her ineffectiveness as a debater demonstrated her weaknesses more than her strengths. Moreover, the government-controlled broadcasts aired only those portions of the questions and responses that demonstrated Ayub's superior command. But even without the government editing the 'exchange', Miss Jinnah's lack of understanding, and her inability to frame coherent replies, magnified Ayub's more substantial leadership qualities.

The behind-the-scenes activity of the government in doctoring the statements of the candidates was replicated by the COP's campaign of intimidation and threat, as well as its extensive propaganda programme. Wild and unfounded charges were thrown at Ayub, and one that registered considerable impact was the rumour that Ayub anticipated losing the election and had drawn up plans to leave the country even before the results were tallied. Ayub parried the attacks on his character and demeanour, but the personal assaults redounded to the favour of Miss Jinnah; in spite of her poor showing in the debates, she was still the sister of the Quaid-i-Azam. The juxtaposition of the two candidates indicated that the election would be a close one.

Army, police, and other security agencies protected the polls as the electors cast their ballots. Generally speaking, the election was conducted in an atmosphere of calm and contemplation, despite indications of COP harassment. Ayub also prevented the execution of an order that would have imposed pre-censorship on newspapers reporting the results. Believing that everything had been done to assure his victory, Ayub ordered full disclosure as soon as the ballots had been counted.

The initial returns from Dhaka and Karachi went against the President. Lahore, however, did go Ayub's way, and when the votes were counted in the towns and rural areas, there was an overwhelming outpouring of support for Ayub. Miss Fatima Jinnah and the COP suffered defeat, but the margin of Ayub's victory was far from a mandate. The Chief Election Commissioner announced the results that night, and Ayub was ushered to a microphone to give a victory speech drafted earlier by the Information Secretary. Gauhar reveals how a shaken Ayub, having won a narrow victory, that is, only 49,591 of the 80,000 electors, could barely read his prepared statement. Ayub demonstrated significant weakness in East Pakistan as well as in Karachi, where the democracy argument pressed by Miss Jinnah registered its greatest impact. In the areas won by the President, notably in West Pakistan, the Kashmir issue loomed large. Indeed, the running controversy with India, and especially Bhutto's role in framing the confrontation between India and Pakistan, had captured the attention of the rural and town constituencies. Thus the administration's use of emotional issues outweighed COP accusations of corruption and maladministration. Moreover, the democracy-autocracy question registered less impact in the towns and villages of West Pakistan, where paternalism remained an entrenched institution.

But in the final analysis no one, let alone Ayub Khan, could ignore that the political opposition, despite its divisions, had demonstrated a significant capacity to challenge the quasi-military dictatorship. Ayub's initial instincts, therefore, were to reform the governmental apparatus, but his Conventionist colleagues were determined to enjoy the fruits of their victory. Ayub's best intentions—modifying his government's programme, broadening its base, reaching out to the politically alienated—were lost in the swirl of events unleashed by the election campaign. Bhutto's many public declarations, notably his pledge to resolve the Kashmir dilemma after the election, had not been forgotten. Moreover, having wooed senior members of the armed forces, Bhutto was under considerable pressure to live up to his promises. Although Ayub Khan would have preferred shifting attention away from the Kashmir dispute as he began his second term, given the ambition of his Foreign Minister, he too was forced to accept the cost of his electoral victory.

The 1965 War

Ayub had long been removed from the day-to-day command of the army. His political conversion had given him a new role, and the engineering of a new political system consumed his time and his energy. Ayub was too engrossed in governing Pakistan to also oversee the operations of the armed forces. But the election campaign had rearranged the pieces on the chessboard. Bhutto was not only far more influential, he had also cultivated the highest-ranking officers in the Pakistan Army. As Foreign Minister, Bhutto was in regular contact with the army high command. Together they examined the relative strengths of the Pakistan and Indian armies, and given the latter's humiliation in the 1962 border war with China, there appeared to be ample evidence that Pakistan held definite advantages. Moreover, the March-April 1965 clash of Indian and Pakistan arms in the Rann of Kutch—a swampy, uninhabited borderland region on the Arabian Sea—only added to their confidence. Pakistani field commanders were ecstatic over the success of their forces in the Rann skirmish, and although nothing decisive had been demonstrated, they judged the Pakistan Army ready for a major campaign against their Indian adversary.

Ayub had been on a visit to the Soviet Union when hostilities erupted in the Rann, and it was only on 10 April 1965 that he was briefed on the situation there. Informed that the Indian Army had fled the battlefield, and that Pakistan might well exploit the situation, Ayub used all his leverage to contain his more enthusiastic colleagues. Nevertheless, not oblivious to Bhutto's pledge to liberate Kashmir, the Field Marshal found himself trapped between a hawkish Foreign Office and an overly self-confident army command structure. In addition, the events of recent years, capped by Nehru's death, had unleashed extremely jingoistic, anti-Indian calls to arms.

This sabre-rattling was mirrored on the Indian side, and even the otherwise mild Prime Minister Shastri had elevated his rhetoric to reflect Indian sentiment and bellicosity, both in and outside the Lok Sabha. From the beginning of the army takeover, Ayub had set a course calling for negotiations and, where possible, co-operation with India. The President knew the difficulties in such efforts, but he also cautiously measured Pakistan's defence capabilities, and he was hardly convinced that his army was ready for a showdown with its larger neighbour. Ayub, therefore, injected himself into the direct management of the Rann conflict, not with a view to countering the moves of his Foreign Minister, but in the belief that only he could rein in his field officers who seemed so eager to demonstrate their superiority. Ayub's intervention embarrassed General Mohammad Musa, but the officers under his command were even more distressed by the President's call to refrain from deepening the crisis. And when Ayub rejected a plan aimed at cutting off and destroying the Indian forces deployed in the Rann, he exposed himself to criticism throughout the ranks.

Ayub appeared to yield to international pressure when he agreed to a ceasefire rather than press what seemed to be an advantage. But given the probability of a protracted, more intense conflict, he was more worried about India opening a front elsewhere, no doubt in a region where the logistics favoured his adversary. Concerned with the defence of East Pakistan, Ayub could not ignore Indian statements that framed an assault on the distant province. Ayub therefore reached an agreement with his Indian counterpart in which both sides agreed to accept the *status quo ante*, that is, to enter into direct negotiations and, if unsuccessful, to transfer the Rann of Kutch dispute to international arbitration.

Ayub not only believed his actions avoided unforeseen consequences, he also thought his patient, more businesslike approach would stand as a model for the smouldering Kashmir problem. Diplomatic confidence-building centred on understandings between Pakistani and Indian leaders. A diplomatic solution in the Rann of Kutch might well reopen diplomatic channels on Kashmir. Moreover, Kashmir was a problem of international proportions and Ayub could not envisage a resolution without assistance from external parties. His preference for diplomacy in the Rann was, therefore, at least in part aimed at demonstrating Pakistan's peaceful intentions to the larger world. Furthermore, Shastri was hardly Nehru's clone, and Ayub anticipated a more positive relationship with New Delhi. He certainly did not want the Rann of Kutch controversy to define his relations with India, nor did he believe there were advantages in trying to weaken the new Shastri administration.

Ayub had paid a high price when he prevented his eager forces from moving into Indian-occupied Kashmir during the 1962 Sino-Indian border war. Now again he emphasized caution, displayed a preference for diplomacy, and avoided taking aggressive action against what his countrymen believed was a weak enemy. Ayub's Information Secretary cites the President's gamble and makes the point that Ayub exhausted his political capital, especially among those units of government upon which his administration rested: 'In senior Army circles and the Foreign Office, Ayub came under criticism for letting the Indians off the hook' (Gauhar, 1994, p.312).

Ayub could short-circuit army plans to punish India in the Rann of Kutch, but he could not dispel the feeling shared by his military high command and key members of the Pakistan government that Indian troops were no match for the Pakistani soldier. 'One Pakistani was as good as seven Indian soldiers' was a common theme heard in Lahore and Karachi in the spring of 1965. The Rann of Kutch skirmish was incorrectly but deliberately described as a major military encounter that had tested the two armies. Moreover, Pakistan had emerged the overwhelming victor. The re-arrest of Sheikh Abdullah in May, and stern military action against Kashmiri demonstrators, also redirected public attention to Kashmir. Moreover, the unrest in the mountain state coincided with the elections of the second generation of Basic Democrats, and the Kashmir dilemma again was central to the political discourse.

Violent demonstrations also erupted in West Pakistani cities and towns, with protestors demanding a military response against Indian forces in Kashmir. Anti-Americanism was also a feature of the gathering storm. US military assistance to India following the Sino-Indian conflict was seen as bolstering the Indian Armed Forces, and there was little doubt in official and unofficial circles that American arms were being used to subdue defenceless Kashmiris. It was not lost on Ayub Khan that the demonstrations, whether spontaneous or organized, were directed against his policies and that his support base, in spite of his electoral success, was slipping beneath him.

In the late spring and early summer of 1965 public opinion was riveted on the Kashmiri insurrectionists, and it was widely believed that Pakistan should assist those fighting for their liberation. Bhutto's Foreign Office contributed to the intensification of a war psychosis. The armed forces intelligence units followed a similar path, 'leaking' what they alleged were inside accounts of conditions in the Valley. No corroboration of evidence was demanded and none was supplied. Flights between Pakistan and India, and from New Delhi to Srinagar, however, were continued on their regular schedules. Visitors to Kashmir from Pakistan in mid-July 1965 found a quiet, tranquil vale. Tourists lived out their sleepy sojourn in houseboats on Lake Dal, while trips to the distant and nearby glaciers were commonplace. To passing observers, the only indication of tensions in the state were the stationary Indian army encampments arranged in scattered locations (author's personal observations). Eyewitness accounts during the period, therefore, did not reflect the reports in the Pakistan Press, nor could the statements made by Pakistani officials be reconciled with the realities on the ground. Nevertheless, given conditions within Pakistan, Ayub Khan found himself under increasing pressure to take some form of military action in Kashmir.

Pakistani manoeuvres were not ignored by the Shastri government, and the Indian Prime Minister also found it good domestic politics to elevate the rhetoric. He warned Ayub that India was reluctant to fight Pakistan, but that if war came, it would be at a time and in a place determined by Indian strategists, not a mere reaction to Pakistani initiatives. Ayub understood the significance of this 'war of words'. He also knew how thoughtless statements could precipitate actions that neither side was eager to take. He struggled with the matter of uncontrolled propaganda and how emotional parties on both sides of the border responded to calls to battle. Neutralizing such activity before popular dynamics overwhelmed rational decision-making was a monumental task, especially when Ayub had been upstaged by his Foreign Minister.

Bhutto chaired a key cabinet meeting in late July, informing the attending officials that a 'popular revolt' had broken out in Kashmir and that the situation in the Vale was desperate. Bhutto reported the movement of 'freedom fighters' from the NWFP into Kashmir. At his oratorical best, he declared history would not forgive 'us' if 'we' did not assist the liberators. Bhutto explained that the matter was so confidential that he was not in a position to respond to questions. Gauhar reports that Bhutto then left the room, leaving even General Musa and his aides in stony silence (Gauhar, 1994, p.316).

On 8 August the Pakistan army launched 'Operation Gibraltar', planned as a clandestine action against Indian forces in the Kashmir Valley. It fizzled out when four Pakistani soldiers were captured and, upon interrogation, revealed the purpose and plan of the attack. The failure of the operation exposed the activities of the Inter-Services Intelligence Directorate (ISI) whose agents were now ordered to break contact and retreat. Thus the plan that Bhutto said he could not discuss with the high command in the Ayub cabinet was aired by All India Radio with the entire world its audience. The Ayub government was left with no other alternative but to deny the Indian report. It was all enemy propaganda, Pakistanis were told.

Aziz Ahmad, the Foreign Secretary, worked in tandem with Bhutto in shaping the course of events. Both men had convinced themselves that the time was ripe for the introduction of Pakistani arms into the Kashmir dispute. Aziz Ahmad chaired a Kashmir Publicity Committee, and it was from that role that he influenced both the army high command on the one side, and Ayub Khan on the other. Often acting on his own, but always in consultation with Bhutto, it was the Foreign Secretary who had everyone believing that the Kashmiri people would rise up against their Indian tormentors once the first Pakistani troops entered the region. Bhutto and Aziz both tried to convince Ayub that India would be so paralysed by fear of another Chinese invasion that New Delhi would never deploy its forces in an all-out war against Pakistan. In effect, driving the Indians from Kashmir would be no more difficult than driving them from the Rann of Kutch.

The plan for the Kashmir operation had been developed prior to the Rann skirmish, and allegedly had been given to Ayub as a position paper during the December 1964 presidential campaign. Ayub, it is said, did not study the plan, but passed it on to his information officer and personal secretary who were asked to review it. Caught up in the election campaign, they did not examine it until after the presidential elections. Ayub's first serious reading of the plan occurred during a cabinet meeting and Gauhar, who was present, reports an angry response from the Field Marshal. Ayub verbalized his distress, questioning how an *ad hoc* committee of lay subordinates could draw up a plan that involved the use of Pakistani troops against dug-in Indian forces. Ayub's negative reaction was believed to have killed the project, but as subsequent events were to reveal, such was not the case.

Ayub's international commitments required his frequent absence from the country, and shortly after rejecting the Aziz Ahmad plan he travelled to China where, it is reported, he did not discuss anything even remotely linked to Pakistan's sending forces into Kashmir. Had he been preparing for such a campaign, he might have been expected to co-ordinate his operations with the Chinese, that is, if China was supposed to prevent India from using its main force against Pakistan. There being no evidence to suggest an understanding between Ayub and Mao Zedong or Zhou Enlai on this question, it appears reasonable to conclude that Ayub did not discuss with the Chinese contingency plans in the event of a war in Kashmir.

It will be recalled that Ayub's 1959 offer of joint defence, which he posed to Nehru, was intended to block Chinese attempts to penetrate the region on behalf of a Greater Nepal movement. Nehru's outright rejection of the Ayub proposal ended that effort at co-operation, but it did not change Ayub's view that the Chinese were not wanted in the subcontinent. Hardly six years later, it is doubtful that Ayub had altered his thinking. Nevertheless, there can be no mistaking the intrusion of new factors in the China equation, and most important, Bhutto approached the subject from a different perspective. Therefore, if the President did not call for Chinese assistance during his 1965 visit to Beijing, it can only be conjectured to what extent he was involved in the decision to move forces into Kashmir in the late summer of 1965.

But whatever the answer to this riddle, Ayub was responsible for the actions of his government. He alone had the authority to reappoint Bhutto to head the Foreign Ministry following the presidential election, nor did he caution his young Minister to subdue his rhetoric. Bhutto continued to insist that the time was right for a Pakistani thrust into Kashmir. To wait, he argued, only provided India with the needed time to access substantial stores of sophisticated weapons, which the Soviet Union was only too willing to supply. Combined with the military stores provided by the United States, India was destined to enhance its capability. Thus, if Pakistan was to realize its objectives in Kashmir, the time to resolve the Kashmir issue would never be more opportune. Never again would the two countries be so equal in military prowess, noted Bhutto. Moreover, the new government in New Delhi was still in the process of consolidating its power and hence was unprepared for war.

According to Bhutto, Pakistan's success in Kashmir would ensure a favourable balance of power between the two countries and also help to solidify Ayub's domestic reform programme. Bhutto also voiced the opinion that Pakistan would be better served in close association with China. Arguing that the American alliance was too distant, too strained, and had committed Pakistan to arrangements too far from its national interests, he urged a re-evaluation of all of the country's major foreign policy initiatives. Ayub knew Bhutto's thinking on foreign policy matters, and certainly he had chosen him to be his Foreign Minister because he demonstrated a deep understanding of international political issues, but Ayub never believed he had given Bhutto, or any of his other civilian colleagues, the authority to launch a military campaign against India or any other country.

Bhutto, however, had already established himself as the senior member of the cabinet. Ambitious and self-confident, Bhutto dreamed of a Pakistan in the forefront of the Islamic nations. Indeed, the Kashmir question was inextricably tied to this objective. Moreover, India would be in a poor position to threaten a Pakistan that was intimately associated with the world of Muslim states as well as China. Thus, Bhutto was prepared to burden Ayub with the 'hour of decision', but more significantly, he had ample opportunity to lecture and brief the army officers under General Musa's command. Bhutto had no difficulty in mesmerizing the more technically trained military officers. The Foreign Minister's presentations were cogently argued and the army commanders were easily won over. Gauhar speaks of General Musa complaining to Ayub that Bhutto had brainwashed his commanders (Gauhar, 1994, p.323). Musa was outflanked by the Foreign Minister, who now replaced Aziz Ahmad as Chairman of the *ad hoc* Kashmir Committee. With so many of his army commanders in agreement with the Foreign Minister, Ayub, too, succumbed to the often-repeated assumption that one Pakistani soldier was as good as seven Indians. In spite of his inclination to sustain a dialogue with New Delhi, Ayub allowed himself to be swept away by the Bhutto argument.

The initial infiltration of Indian-held Kashmir took place on 28 July by small groups of commandos who were ill-equipped for the task, and they either perished *en route* or were forced to retreat when Indian forces mounted their counterattack. Tipped off by this failed 'Gibraltar' mission, Indian contingents were quickly reinforced, but no less significantly, Kashmiri leaders who had been expected to rally local resistance were arrested or detained. Pakistan was not only denied the element of surprise, it could no longer expect assistance from the local population. By 16 August Indian troops had neutralized virtually all the Pakistani infiltrators and had assumed the offensive, swiftly moving into striking range of Muzaffarabad, the capital of Azad Kashmir. Operation Gibraltar having failed, General Musa was now compelled to save his remaining forces in the region. 'Operation Grand Slam', a more extensive strategy, had been held in abeyance because its execution would certainly mean formal war between India and Pakistan. Indeed, 'Grand Slam', required crossing a portion of Indian territory that was not part of the disputed state of Kashmir.

The decision-making process is clouded at this juncture. Ayub had retreated to the mountain state of Swat following the decision to pursue 'Operation Gibraltar.' It is argued that he did not know of the debacle that consumed the operation when he was asked to consider escalating the fighting. Ayub's response to a request to proceed with the larger operation was at best ambiguous, but Bhutto, who assumed responsibility for directing the forces, claimed that Ayub had approved the action. Launched on 30 August 1965, 'Operation Grand Slam' met stiff Indian resistance, and three days later it virtually collapsed. Ayub returned to Rawalpindi with the mounting of Grand Slam and only then learned that the news being fed the public, and indeed himself, about Pakistani successes was nothing more than fiction. An especially distressed Ayub is said to have called Bhutto and Musa to his private office where he demanded the unembellished truth. It was only then, according to Gauhar (p.332) that Musa revealed the collapse of Gibraltar and the stalemated situation in Grand Slam.

Ayub tried to salvage what he could from the situation and called for a termination of hostilities at the earliest possible moment. General Mohammad Yahya Khan was given the odious task of ending the campaign, but on 6 September, before the orders to stand down could be given, Indian troops opened an attack all along the West Pakistan frontier, the main force focused on Lahore, hardly a dozen miles from the Indian border.

Ayub had attempted to save his forces in Kashmir; more importantly, he wanted to avoid a general war. But the war he sought to avoid had come to Pakistan, and the nation had to be rallied to efforts not envisaged in the plans to capture Kashmir. The vast majority of Pakistanis knew virtually nothing about the course of the hostilities. All they knew came from Radio Pakistan, and in the name of national morale, the public was informed over and again of the successes on the battlefield, or at the very least, the heroism of units and individual members of the armed forces who had fallen in combat (author's experience). The fact that Pakistan itself had been targeted by Indian forces, that air raids had ranged to Peshawar on the one side and Dhaka in East Pakistan on the other, did not shake the Pakistani public's belief that the war was going well and that India was paying a heavy price for its audacious assault on Pakistani territory. Only when the war was suddenly halted by Ayub Khan did the general population begin to understand that their forces had not done as well as they had been led to believe. But even then, public opinion had been so influenced by the official media that it refused to accept the termination of hostilities as anything less than a sell-out by Ayub Khan. Long after the end of the war, Bhutto and others more responsible for the debacle would point the finger of blame at Ayub who, it was said, had lost his nerve and had caved in to international pressure (Brines, 1968).

A risky but minor operation in Kashmir had, in fact, escalated out of Pakistani control. Ayub had avoided involving himself in the operation because he did not wish to signal India that Pakistan contemplated a showdown with New Delhi. Ayub, however, had no reason to express surprise with the turn of events. The Shastri government may have been new but it was still the Congress government, and its roots lay at the core of the Indian experience. Moreover, after the Rann of Kutch incident, the Shastri administration had something to prove to itself, to its armed forces, and to the Indian nation. Its preparations for a larger campaign against Pakistan were made long before the Rann incident, but the character of that conflict and the vibrations emanating from Pakistan following the encounter were sufficient to activate Indian plans. Pakistani intelligence proved a total failure. Both political and military reporting was deficient: it was neither professional nor in any way related to the realities on the ground. Neither Bhutto nor Aziz Ahmad had read domestic conditions within India, and both operated on whims and personal perceptions. Their limited data was largely comprised of public events, transmitted by a news media not necessarily known for its reliability. Moreover, they read far too much into the Rann of Kutch incident and, in the end, that incident proved to be a dramatic instance of self-deception. If the highest level of Pakistan government really wanted a general war with India, their minimal preparation and the secretive character of the planning demonstrated their total unfitness for the roles they played.

Nor can Ayub be absolved from his responsibility in allowing the 1965 war to unfold. His was the greater failure. Ayub desperately and longingly searched for a formula that would bring peace and co-operation to the subcontinent, but he did not demonstrate the strength of his convictions at a crucial moment in his administration. Having been re-elected to the nation's highest office, irrespective of the questionable arrangements or the character of the exercise, he had nothing more too prove. He was responsible for the political transition to civilian government and had himself assumed political features and mannerisms. The times now called upon him to assume the role of statesman. Moreover, conditions in India beckoned him to take the initiatives needed to instil reality in the India-Pakistan relationship. Ayub failed this test. The troubled Hamlet, he could not be what he was not. His otherwise outgoing nature was transformed into a brooding personality, and the more he retreated within himself, the more he allowed his subordinates to shape the future.

Ayub did not fully understand the role played by Zulfikar Ali Bhutto, or how the higher officers in the Foreign Ministry adopted their Minister's thinking. Ayub had the opportunity to terminate Bhutto's services immediately following the election, but in spite of the private advice he received to sever his relationship with the overly ambitious young man, he nevertheless retained his services. Ayub's fragility during and immediately following the election led him to conclude that he needed Bhutto, that if not for his popularity among the nation's youth, his structural reforms would be impaired. But more than that, Bhutto was far brighter than Ayub, and like others who interacted with him, the President was no less impressed with his acumen, his analytical mind, and his thorough grasp of a wide range of issues. Bhutto was at once Ayub's life-jacket and his albatross, and little did the President understand that both elements could strangle him.

The War and its Aftermath

Pakistani authority followed its own mindset. One Pakistani was the equivalent of seven Indians, hence no matter what the reading on Indian preparations for general war, New Delhi would never attack Pakistan. The diminutive Shastri was not taken seriously, nor were his public statements given serious consideration in the top echelons of the Pakistan government. A message from the Pakistan ambassador in New Delhi similarly went unheeded. Again, personal attitudes, not hard facts, determined the course of Pakistani action. The Foreign Office had little respect for its ambassador, Mian Arshad Hussain, thus his communication was shrugged off as the work of a nervous, inexperienced commentator.

But with the Indian Army advancing along a broad front, Ayub rallied the nation in two radio addresses, one in English, the other in Urdu. Calling for sacrifices from all quarters, the President assured his countrymen that the nation would not only survive the ordeal, but as a consequence of its concerted action, it would attain new heights. The Pakistani Army was motivated to meet the aggressors head on and it penetrated Indian lines in several sectors. But despite some Pakistani successes, which included occupation of Indian borderlands, the momentum of war remained with New Delhi.

The United Nations Security Council was pressed into service in an effort to arrange a ceasefire, and the UN Secretary General, U Thant, flew to Pakistan to see if it was possible to broker a stand-down of forces. On the United States side, Ambassador Walter McConaughy was authorized by President Lyndon Johnson to inform the Pakistan government that American military assistance was being suspended. Johnson ordered an embargo on the transfer of arms to both sides, but the impact of the order fell heaviest on Pakistan. Almost totally dependent on American military assistance, Pakistan could not replenish its weapons needs and its stores were rapidly disappearing. India, on the other hand, had never been a major recipient of American weapons. New Delhi's flirtation with Moscow had given it significant access to Soviet arms, and the Politburo had taken an entirely different approach to the conflict in South Asia. India also possessed an arms industry which provided its armed forces with a steady flow of basic weapons and ammunition, something Pakistan could not expect to match with its very minor ordnance facilities. Thus, the US decision to deny weapons to the belligerents left the Pakistan Army with a three-front war, i.e., in Kashmir, along the length of the West Pakistan frontier, and in defence of an exposed East Pakistan, but without the needed reserves to protract the conflict.

No Muslim country came to Pakistan's defence. Even Iran and Turkey were foreclosed from shipping arms to their alliance partner. Indonesia made a faint gesture but it added nothing to the equation. Pakistan accused the United States of having pressurized its Muslim neighbours. Incensed by the American embargo, Bhutto would never again conceal the bitterness he felt toward Washington. For its part, the Johnson administration did not believe Bhutto's argument that India had initiated the conflict, had aggressively attacked Pakistan without provocation, or was bent on destroying the Muslim state. Bhutto's public posturing, however, notably his declaration that the Americans were in complicity with New Delhi, deflected attention away from his personal miscalculations. Moreover, Ayub had the responsibility for rallying the nation and he, not the Foreign Minister, was judged the supreme architect of the conflict as well as the state's defence.

A major propaganda campaign was initiated to convince the public that India had launched a surprise attack but that Pakistani arms were more than sufficient to beat back and punish the enemy. Nothing was said about the nation's limited capacity to fight a protracted war, and thus there was no need to explain why the armed forces were not better supplied, or why it was only after the Indian assault on West Pakistan that special efforts were made to obtain new weapons supplies from France, China, and other countries.

China was the only card Pakistan could play. The Chinese had consistently supported Pakistan's claim to Kashmir, and Beijing's running feud with New Delhi only hardened its ties to the Muslim country. Chinese officials spoke of Pakistan's 'just' cause and condemned what it described as India's 'chauvinist' policies (Brines, 1968). The 1962 border war had intensified recriminations on both sides, and Beijing continued to condemn New Delhi's aggressive actions in areas the Chinese deemed to be within its sovereignty or sphere of influence. This sustained controversy spilled over into the Indo-Pakistan War when, on 8 September, China warned India that a continuation of territorial violations would produce serious consequences. Four days later, China gave India an ultimatum that called upon the Shashtri government to dismantle military installations which it claimed were on sovereign Chinese territory.

The Shastri government assumed collusion between China and Pakistan, and indeed the Pakistani Press reinforced the popular belief that China had agreed to both assist Pakistan in liberating Kashmir and help thwart the Indian drive against West Pakistan. The Americans and British, as well as the Soviets, were likewise convinced that Pakistan and China had joined forces against India. Believing that conditions had reached a critical stage, they each contemplated some form of intervention. Moreover, the US had pledged to support India against renewed Chinese aggression and it had not, in spite of its several alliances with Pakistan, agreed to assist

Islamabad in fighting a war against a non-communist country, and certainly not against India. Here again, intelligence was faulty on all sides. There was no formal agreement between China and Pakistan in their different contests with India, nor were the Soviets or the Americans fully apprised of conditions on the ground. Washington's Cold War strategy involved containing Communist aggression, and with the Americans deeply committed to war in Indo-China, a war in which they perceived China as a major participant, all attention was given to the stabilization of the Indo-Pakistan conflict before Beijing complicated matters beyond repair.

With Chinese troops reported moving closer to the Indian border, Ayub publicly declared there could be no cease-fire without an agreement that would resolve the Kashmir dilemma. But the President's statement could not conceal his forebodings. Ayub was grateful for the Chinese action in deflecting the Indians, but any serious involvement of Beijing's forces would ruin Pakistan's associations with the United States, and the President, unlike his Foreign Minister, could not bring himself to believe that that would redound to the long-term benefit of Pakistan. Moreover, by 15 September, Ayub's generals were reporting the almost total exhaustion of military supplies and the virtual emptying of petroleum reserves. The troops would soon be left without ammunition, the aircraft without spare parts and fuel, and the armour without the necessities for battle. The war had been fought to a virtual stalemate, and although the Pakistani propaganda machine continued to indicate the imminence of a decisive victory, Pakistan's war-making capability had evaporated.

Ayub put out feelers to Washington that called upon President Johnson to intervene, to lend his good offices, and to make it possible for both sides to stand down without either being humiliated. Bhutto, however, was angered by Ayub's appeal to the Americans who, he believed, had conspired with New Delhi to humble Pakistan. Bhutto was inclined to accept Chinese assistance and, moreover, to encourage the Chinese to open another front along the Himalayan frontier that would cause New Delhi to redeploy its forces away from West Pakistan. The difference in postures between the two principals was never more distinct.

Ayub was wedded to the Western alliances, and through them to Turkey and Iran, who had also demonstrated that their American connections were more important than their ties to Pakistan, at least where India was concerned. Ayub sensed that his foreign policy would never be made coherent, nor Pakistan made secure, without some *rapprochement* with New Delhi. Bhutto, on the other hand, posited a different strategy. India had made its peace with Moscow, and Pakistan needed to become even more intimate with China. The escalation of the war in Indo-China threatened a wider conflict from which China would emerge a more formidable actor. Indeed, the Asian scene was undergoing a transformation that would alter international relationships, and for Bhutto, the 1965 war provided Pakistan with the opportunity to shed its colonial legacy and chart a course that would be more in harmony with its political culture and destiny.

Despite their differences, Ayub and Bhutto flew secretly to Beijing, where they met with Zhou Enlai and the Chinese Defence Minister on 20 September, but according to Gauhar, all that they got from the Chinese was encouragement to sustain the hostilities long enough to transform them into a people's war. Pakistani forces, the Chinese argued, should yield its border cities, retreat into the countryside, and allow the people of Pakistan to swallow the Indian advance. According to Beijing, while Pakistan endured its losses, China was prepared to sustain its pressure on the Indian frontier, but Beijing made no commitment on opening another front. Ayub rejected the Chinese plan, citing the destruction of his armed forces, and the problematic character of a successful guerrilla war in the Punjab plain. Moreover, a population untrained in the use of firearms or guerrilla tactics was not likely to turn the tide against a well-armed and sizeable military formation. The Pakistanis were not Chinese, and this was not a contest between two forces from the same nation. Ayub concluded that the trip to China was useful, but only because it reinforced a conclusion arrived at earlier, that the moment had arrived to end the hostilities.

Returning to Pakistan, Ayub instructed Bhutto to brief the senior officials on all that had transpired in Beijing, and to review with other members of the government the status of the fighting and the conditions under which a cease-fire could be arranged. A desolate Bhutto talked of resignation and exile, but he and others in the Foreign Ministry could not bring themselves to accept a cease-fire that would be interpreted as a defeat. It was at this moment that the message came from the Soviet Prime Minister, Aleksei Kosygin, that the Politburo was prepared to host a meeting of Indian and Pakistani leaders. Ayub's initial reaction was to reject the Soviet overture, but on reflection, and given the need to avoid even the hint of capitulation, he acknowledged that using Moscow, rather than Washington, to sort out differences with India would receive more popular support from an emotional, but unwary, public. Thus, with his commanding generals insisting on acceptance of the UN ceasefire resolution, and with international pressure also building in favour of such an action, Ayub cast aside the arguments made by his inner circle of civilian leaders that no cease-fire should be entertained without New Delhi's agreement to resolve the Kashmir dispute.

In accepting the cease-fire proposal on 22 September, just seventeen days into the war, Ayub declared he was not calling an end to the conflict but merely calling upon Pakistani forces to withhold their fire. Although the country at large had not been prepared for the President's announcement, and some elements decided to riot in expressing their sentiments, the general public, especially in East Pakistan, was relieved that the fighting had stopped. Ayub declared he would journey to Tashkent to meet with the Indian Prime Minister and that he would be hosted by the highest Soviet officials. He thus deflected attention away from a drumbeat of complaints in political circles, as well as in some of the print media, that he had again succumbed to American pressure. Nevertheless, anti-Americanism was even more pronounced after the acceptance of the cease-fire. Large throngs of demonstrators attacked official American installations in the country, notably in Karachi, where the American Information Library was sacked and razed, and where assaults were made on the American Consulate, the embassy having earlier shifted to Islamabad (author's eyewitness account). In the latter instance, however, the police beat back the demonstrators before they could do significant damage.

The anger directed against the Americans was contrasted with the gratitude Pakistanis registered towards the Chinese, and now too, the Soviets. Moreover, in the view of the public, it was Ayub who was held responsible for Pakistan's failure to liberate Kashmir, and Ayub's intimacy with the United States was judged a key factor. On the other hand, Bhutto was heralded as a great leader. His more abiding association with Chinese and Soviet leaders was credited with whatever Pakistani successes had been achieved, and in spite of the disastrous role he had played in helping to mount the conflict, he emerged more popular than ever. Always considering his options, the man who in a moment of deep depression had declared the end of his political career, overnight was transformed into a resolute leader. There is no mistaking that it was at this moment that Bhutto envisaged himself not only as Ayub's successor, but as the man to restore civil government to Pakistan. Ayub was still President of Pakistan, but the resentment against his rule was so deep and so widespread that there could be little doubt that his time was fast running out.

Ayub and Bhutto went to Tashkent after the Foreign Minister's preliminary meetings in Moscow in late November. Bhutto had agreed, although he would deny it later, to accept the Soviet terms that the discussions between Ayub and Shastri should be open and should not specify Kashmir as central to the deliberations. The Pakistani public continued to believe that the Tashkent talks would focus on Kashmir, and that the Indians were under considerable pressure to reach an agreement with Islamabad. The reality of the situation was far different. The Soviet Union, always closely aligned with New Delhi, provided details of the agreed agenda to the Shastri government and kept it informed on what it could expect from the Kremlin during the negotiations. In the meantime, the Indians were encouraged to flaunt their military power by reinforcing their positions in occupied territory as well as along the vital West Pakistan frontier.

For his part, Ayub had decided to first travel to Washington, to discuss the details of his plans for the Tashkent conference with President Johnson. *En route*, he stopped in London to engage in discussions with the British Prime Minister and his immediate associates. But Ayub came away with nothing from the London meetings, the British making it clear that they would not participate in mediating the Kashmir dispute, and that they absolutely refused to choose sides in South Asia.

The British talks were a harbinger of what Ayub could expect in Washington, where there was considerable distress over the rampant anti-Americanism in Pakistan. Following an opening address to the United Nations General Assembly in which he again called for Kashmiri self-determination, Ayub flew to Washington, where he went into private conversations with President Johnson. Later, in the more general session, Johnson rambled on about a number of world trouble spots, reserving major comments for Indo-China and the difficulties encountered in attempting to force the North Vietnamese to cease their onslaught against the South. Johnson did not speak directly of the Indo-Pakistan war or the Kashmir dispute, leaving that subject to Ayub. Nevertheless, it was apparent from their exchange that although Ayub was not prepared to alter his association with the United States, Washington would not assist Pakistan in the matter of Kashmir. Clearly, the Americans were preoccupied with the escalation of the fighting in Indo-China and fearful that Chinese meddling in South Asia hinted at more dangerous prospects. It was American opinion that the Soviet Union's offer of good offices was the better of the difficult scenarios. Ayub was, therefore, encouraged to make the trip to Tashkent.

Ayub returned to Pakistan empty-handed, and without the necessary international support to use in his encounter with Lal Bahadur Shastri. The Field Marshal was uncomfortable with the trip in so far as no agenda had been agreed upon, and he would have a difficult time in coping with the external pressures. On the one side, both the Soviet Union and the United States wanted an agreement between the parties that would terminate their conflict, while on the other, Pakistani society anticipated a breakdown in the deliberations and, egged on by China, a resumption of hostilities. After all, had not India suffered heavy losses, and had not the Pakistani Army demonstrated that, in spite of the enemy's greater numbers, they were by far the superior force? Ayub had avoided speaking directly to the Pakistani nation, and he never corrected their misperceptions of the conflict. Nor did he explain his decision to accept a cease-fire, or his reasons for going to the Soviet Union. He did not rein in the propaganda machine, nor did he silence his Foreign Minister or other cabinet members. Fearing that full disclosure would ruin his negotiating position in Tashkent, and also aware that any admission of failure would excite demands for his resignation, Ayub allowed events to take their own course.

Ayub flew to Tashkent after a two-day stop in Kabul, arriving at the conference site on 3 January 1966. Foreign Minister Bhutto accompanied the President, although it was obvious that the relationship between the two men had been severely strained by the events of the past several months. Indeed, the strain was so significant that the Foreign Office had not prepared an opening statement for Ayub, and no Pakistani agenda had been set for the meetings. Although it remained a secret at the time, Ayub was preparing to clean house in the Foreign Ministry following the Tashkent Conference, and he had every intention of holding to a tight schedule while improvising his way through the talks with the Indian delegation. Whereas Kashmir was the principal item for the Pakistanis, Ayub's personal agenda gave priority to the disengagement of the forces. The President envisaged sustained negotiations in India and Pakistan among the high-placed military commanders.

In the course of a long career, Ayub had seldom questioned the correctness of his actions. His self-confidence had carried him from one pinnacle to another, but the 1965 war had drained him of his pride, raised inner doubts, and caused deep psychological wounds. He blamed himself for the actions of his subordinates, and he was forced to acknowledge his gross miscalculation in delegating authority. Moreover, he understood that the ill-conceived plans of his government had done great damage to his beloved army. All the energy and time devoted to the building of a professional and contemporary armed force had been jeopardized by the chaotic decision-making of recent months. Ayub needed time to sort out the details of the debacle in order to begin major repairs, but he also knew that an expectant and puzzled nation awaited an explanation and, more important, direction. Ayub's strength had always depended upon the loyalty of the army, and that base was now shifting beneath him. No longer assured of his supremacy, Ayub wanted to keep the Tashkent deliberations brief. Indeed, the President was eager to return to Pakistan as soon as possible.

The Tashkent meetings, however, dragged on for several days, mainly because the Soviet leaders were insistent on an agreement that they could herald to the international community. Ayub and Shastri, however, did not agree on anything that involved concessions from the other. Sensing a breakdown of the talks, the Soviets prepared their own version of an agreement which they gave to the two delegations. The Pakistani contingent examined the document but rejected it because it could be interpreted as a capitulation. After all the Pakistani propaganda that nothing less than Indian concessions on Kashmir could prevent the renewal of hostilities, no one in Ayub's delegation was prepared to sanction an agreement that said nothing about the mountain state. Given this impasse, the talks broke off and the Pakistan delegation prepared for its return to Pakistan. Undaunted, Kosygin attempted to bridge the gap between Ayub and Shastri and, by his personal diplomacy, he was able to redirect the attention of the Pakistani delegation to the Soviet draft agreement. Again the Pakistanis baulked at the wording of the document, and Ayub asked that something be included to specify a future settlement of the Kashmir dispute. At this point, Kosygin reminded Ayub that Bhutto had agreed in the preliminary November meetings in Moscow that his government would not insist on the inclusion of the Kashmir issue in the negotiations.

The Soviet leader also said he would not permit the meetings to self-destruct. Thus the Pakistan delegation was pressurized to again review the draft, to modify some of the language, but to hold to the original intent of the document. Under extreme pressure, and apparently unable to resist the demands of his Soviet hosts, on 10 January, Ayub joined

Shastri, and both leaders signed a slightly modified Soviet-designed Tashkent Agreement. Ayub cited his dissatisfaction that the Kashmir problem had not been addressed and that a great opportunity had been missed to bridge the differences between the two nations. No one in the Pakistan delegation had reason to celebrate the agreement. The protracted nature of the talks, the lack of goodwill demonstrated by the parties, the rigidity demonstrated on both sides, and the less than neutral role played by the Kremlin did not suggest a successful conclusion. But Ayub none the less obtained an agreement on disengagement, and there was little likelihood of a resumption of hostilities. His major problem now was facing an expectant but ill-informed nation, and he knew that he would not be successful.

During the night, and prior to his departure for Pakistan, Ayub was informed that Lal Bahadur Shastri had suffered a massive heart attack and had died almost instantly. In the morning, Ayub was a pallbearer as Shastri's body was carried into the aircraft that was to fly the Prime Minister's remains back to New Delhi. Ayub said nothing to the nation on arriving in Islamabad, but the news that he had caved in at Tashkent had already rumbled through the country. Hardly a soul in Pakistan mourned Shastri's death. Ayub had been reluctant to sign the Tashkent Agreement, but having done so, he at least anticipated working with the Indian leader whose signature was also affixed to the document. That was not to be, and his disappointment mingled with a curious feeling of grief. Frustrated by his associates, abandoned by his allies, and now cut adrift by fate, Ayub had reason to ponder the uncertain future. Ayub's final exchange with King Zahir Shah on leaving Kabul for Tashkent is reported by Altaf Gauhar. 'General,' said the King, 'you have to be strong.' To which Ayub is reported to have replied: 'Yes, in the end you have to fight your own battle' (Gauhar, 1993, p.379).

The Last Years of the Ayub Era

Bhutto knew that Ayub would, eventually, dispense with his services. But too young to retire from his political career, ever confident of retaining a solid support base, and still burning with ambition, Bhutto plotted to strengthen his position by leading the opposition against the man he had intimately served for almost eight years. After returning from Tashkent, Bhutto virtually abandoned his role in the Foreign Office. He ignored the President's request for an official statement justifying the Tashkent Agreement, and more than that, first clandestinely and then openly, he voiced his personal criticism. Bhutto wanted all of Pakistan to believe that he had advised against accepting the Soviet draft but that Ayub had overruled him. By distancing himself from the agreement, by suggesting there were still other more secret understandings, Bhutto anticipated building upon his already strong political following. The fact that he exposed his President to even wider public condemnation also served his strategy. The Pakistan Army had suffered significant wounds in the 1965 war and its faith in Ayub Khan had been seriously shaken. Thus, if Ayub was forced to yield his authority, it was more than likely that the army would not interfere and would allow a civilian to assume the presidency. And of course, Bhutto anticipated being that civilian.

The cutting edge of Bhutto's following had always been the students. And it was not surprising that the students were the ones to spark the negative public reaction to the Tashkent Agreement. Student-inspired riots erupted almost from the first moment the agreement was announced, necessitating the closure of the colleges and universities. But the emptying of the universities only forced the demonstrators into the streets, and almost all the major cities in the northern half of West Pakistan were paralysed by their sustained actions. Curfews were imposed and ordinances were issued denying the right of mass assembly, but the more the government imposed limitations on the protestors, the more their numbers grew. Nor could the rioters be controlled without the loss of life. Bhutto allowed himself to become identified with the student agitators, which forced Ayub to publicly declare that the Foreign Minister had been a party in the Tashkent decision-making process, and that the Agreement could not be attributed to the President acting alone. Bhutto's manoeuvring, however, continued, and less than a month following their return from Tashkent, Ayub informed the Foreign Minister that he was being dropped from the cabinet. After taking this action however, Ayub hesitated and retained Bhutto, who he hoped would help quiet the demonstrators. But such indecision only allowed the Foreign Minister to explore his options with those politicians who had been energized by the government's failure at Tashkent. Chaudhri Mohammad Ali, who now led the Nizam-i-Islam, and Shaukat Hayat Khan, head of the Council Muslim League, condemned every feature of the Agreement. Maulana Maudoodi's Jamaat-i-Islami added its voice to the chorus of dissenters. But it was not so much the Tashkent Agreement as Ayub Khan himself who was the target of their abuse. Sensing a weakened President, the opposition believed the time was right to topple the Ayub government. In East Pakistan, Mujibur Rahman and Maulana Bhashani were less concerned with the Tashkent issue and more intent on pressing for a change in government structure and process. Not to be ignored, the National Awami Party in the eastern province muted their complaint on Tashkent in deference to the Soviet Union, but they were just as adamant in pressurizing Ayub to step aside. Mujib's Awami League displayed only marginal interest in the Kashmir issue, but they too believed that the time was ripe for a change in government that would bring benefits to the Bengalis.

The Ayub administration resisted all demands that it surrender its power and, in fact, managed to overcome the immediate reaction to Tashkent. Ayub pressed his reform programme, and long-postponed elections for the chairmen of Basic Democracies Union Councils in West Pakistan were conducted without interruption. During this period, Lieutenant-General Bakhtiar Rana, a hero of the 1965 war, signed an agreement with his Indian counterpart that officially disengaged the forces and returned territory lost to the opposed sides during the hostilities. The disengagement arrangements allowed the army to regain its equilibrium, to rearrange its personnel, and to develop procedures and tactics drawn from the war. The revitalization of the armed forces strengthened Ayub's hand and, in some measure, restored his confidence. Indeed, Ayub's resiliency surprised his detractors, and they now decided that only their capacity to speak with a single voice would bring appreciable change in the government and the country.

The West Pakistani political leaders announced the convening of a National Conference for 5-6 February 1966, but as much as this was a call for national unity, they nevertheless stressed that the central purpose of their sessions would be an examination of the Tashkent Agreement. The meeting received little positive response in East Pakistan, however, and only Mujibur Rahman announced his intention to attend the Lahore conference. 700 delegates were in attendance when the meetings were inaugurated, but only twenty-one of them were representatives of East Pakistan, where more than half of the nation's population resided. Moreover, the NAP decided to boycott the meeting *en masse*, and the Punjab and Bahawalpur NAP condemned the meeting as furthering the interests of the imperialists. The conference revealed more about the divisions within the opposition than their capacity for unity. Even a resolution calling for the revocation of the Tashkent Agreement failed to receive the required consensus, and the conferees had to settle for one of condemnation. Mujib came to the meeting for the purpose of presenting his Six Point Programme calling for East Pakistan's autonomy, but this too failed to pass and Mujib angrily marched his small delegation out of the hall and returned to the eastern province before the termination of the proceedings.

Following the Lahore conference, the government spread a broad net, arresting a number of political luminaries under Rule 32 of the Defence of Pakistan Rules (1965) for 'persistently indulging in activities which were highly prejudicial to the maintenance of public order'. Upon hearing of the arrests, virtually all the opposition parties issued their own condemnations of the government action, arguing that the right of free discussion had been guaranteed under the 1962 Constitution. The arrests were judged even more arbitrary in view of the citizens' sacrifices during the recent hostilities. But even this situation did not bridge the differences between the parties. Politicians spoke of political suffocation, but their own antics hardly relieved the condition. The incarceration of the opposition politicians, and their detention without trial, suspended the operations of their respective parties, and during this period of imposed calm the Tashkent issue was allowed to recede into the background. It was not until almost a year had passed that the detained West Pakistani politicians were set free.

In March 1966 Bhutto had the opportunity to bask in the attention given to the visiting Chinese leaders Liu Shao Chi and Chen Yi. Chairman Liu affirmed China's support for Pakistan and received a tumultuous welcome in Lahore from a population that credited China with helping to save their city during the recent war. Ayub decided not to accompany the two men on their parade through the Punjabi capital, and it was Bhutto who got to ride with them as they were enthusiastically and, in many instances, ecstatically greeted by throngs of humanity. Gauhar notes that this was the moment when Bhutto's political star reached its zenith, and it was almost 'as if Ayub himself launched Bhutto on his political career' (Gauhar, 1994, p.405).

It was during this sequence of events that rumours again circulated that Ayub was ready to dump his Foreign Minister. Ayub tried to deflect such thinking with his own caustic statements about 'fertile brains' and 'rumour manufacturing', but in June 1966, with Tashkent no longer considered a serious problem for his regime, Ayub asked Bhutto to submit his resignation, and he was immediately replaced as Foreign Minister by the Attorney-General of Pakistan, Syed Sharifuddin Pirzada. The Khan of Kalabagh, Malik Amir Mohammad Khan, the long-time Governor of West Pakistan, also tendered his resignation in September, following differences with Ayub, and General Mohammad Musa, who had been retired from command of the Pakistan Army, succeeded him. General Mohammad Yahya Khan was hand-picked by Ayub to become the new army Commander-in-Chief. Ayub transferred his control of the Defence portfolio to Vice-Admiral A.R. Khan, who also became Minister for Home Affairs. The long-envisaged changes in the Ayub government had finally materialized, but these changes left Ayub without intimate partners, save Altaf Gauhar, to buffer assaults on himself as well as his administration.

Bhutto, following his resignation, was quick to surface, this time with a vengeance, as he openly attacked Ayub's policies. In November 1966 he travelled to East Pakistan to show his support for Mujibur Rahman's Six Point Programme. As Foreign Minister he had condemned the autonomy scheme as anti-national; now, however, he favoured the proposal, and called upon other opposition leaders to follow his lead. Bhutto's initial thinking appeared to tie him to a 'Forward Bloc' notion in which he anticipated gaining control of the Conventionist Muslim League. He also toyed with becoming a member of the Council Muslim League and reuniting the two parties. But after a period of exploration and introspection, the former Foreign Minister was influenced to form a new political organization, one which better represented his personal philosophy and which carried none of the baggage of past events and personalities.

Feeble in attempting to neutralize Bhutto's political ambitions, the Ayub government allowed the release of documents which purported to show that Bhutto considered himself a citizen of India prior to 1958. The charge was based upon property owned by the Bhutto family in India which it had tried to recover, or receive compensation for, through the office of the Custodian of Evacuee Property. When he submitted that petition, Bhutto had declared he was an Indian citizen, a claim it is said he yielded only after his appointment by Iskandar Mirza to Ayub's first cabinet. Bhutto denied the allegations but admitted travelling to the United States in 1947 on an Indian passport. He argued that a Pakistan passport was not issued to him until July 1949. Bhutto hardly suffered from the publicity, however, and in October 1967 he announced the formation of his Pakistan People's Party (Rizvi, 1973). Bhutto's action came as no surprise. Nor was his career as a politician energized from a cold start. Bhutto was, without doubt, the most popular, most recognized political figure in the country at the time of the formation of the PPP, and he was destined to be the key player in the demise of Ayub Khan.

Ayub's attention, however, was diverted from Bhutto to Mujibur Rahman in East Pakistan. In January 1968 the government arrested more than a score of persons for allegedly hatching a plot to bring about the secession of East Pakistan. East Pakistan officials and politicians were accused of conspiring with Indian agents, notably the First Secretary of the Indian High Commission. The alleged betrayal was supposedly hatched at the border town of Agartala, and hence it was thereafter described as the 'Agartala Conspiracy'. Ayub was extremely sensitive to attacks on One Unit, and Mujib's Six Points and the NAP's Twelve Point Programme both seemed to address the question of breakup and separation. The Agartala affair was supposedly linked to both programmes. It was Ayub's judgment that to yield to demands for autonomy in the eastern province would inevitably lead to similar provincial demands in West Pakistan. For Ayub, therefore, any yielding to such expressions invited the dissolution of Pakistan itself. Ayub would have none of it, and he ordered that Mujib be arrested and tried with the others. It was just at this moment that Ayub fell ill. His ailment was initially diagnosed as viral pneumonia though little was said about his condition, and the government pressed its case against the accused conspirators in East Pakistan.

During Ayub's illness, and indeed there was a period during which it was believed he might succumb to the affliction, General Yahya Khan had assumed control of the country. Nothing in the constitution prepared the nation for Ayub's total incapacitation, and Yahya's assumption of power was considered a *coup d'état* by some of the President's closest observers. It was only two weeks into his illness that the nation was informed that the President had pneumonia complicated by a pulmonary embolism. But Ayub's recovery was no less dramatic than his illness. After a month of rumours about the President's health and the chances of his survival, Ayub returned to his office, but it was obvious to even the uninformed that he was a different, less dominating figure. Some concluded that Ayub appeared to have lost interest in the job.

While he was bedridden, the cabinet, under the chairmanship of Khwaja Shahabuddin, its most experienced member, had proceeded with plans developed earlier to celebrate the Decade of Development. Sensing that the public required a programme which detailed the many reforms undertaken by the administration, the cabinet allowed the celebrations to go forward without Ayub's participation, but they had the reverse effect of what was intended. Considered an expensive propaganda campaign by the opposition, the programme was criticized and ridiculed as wasteful and unwarranted. Indeed, the Decade of Development provided Ayub's enemies with one more opportunity to condemn the President and his government. Other issues had also provoked popular disfavour. Ayub's Muslim Family Laws were assaulted by members of the religious fraternity, and the head of the Islamic Research Institute was challenged on several propositions, not the least of which was his position on the use of birth control devices to slow population growth. The Director, Dr Fazlur Rahman, was hounded and his life threatened, and he was finally forced to seek asylum and accept political exile. Ayub, however, could not flee, and he was left to take the brunt of the public's criticism.

Bhutto's PPP drew strength from the repeated and more intense attacks on Ayub. On the one side, Bhutto appealed to the masses, calling for 'bread, clothing, and shelter' (roti, kapra, aur makan), while on the other, he continued to make deep inroads in the army high command. Given Washington's declared policy to sustain the arms embargo imposed on Pakistan in 1965, Bhutto was able to exploit his friendship with China, and thereby attract supporters in and outside the armed forces. Bhutto also drew upon Mahbub-ul-Huq's study that identified twenty-two Pakistan families who, he said, controlled the nation's economic resources. All were said to be in alliance with Ayub Khan, and Ayub's family members were also said to have acquired vast holdings during his tenure. Bhutto posed as the champion of the deprived millions, as a crusader against corruption, as the spokesman of democratic reform, and as a saviour of the Islamic heritage. Considering the energy that Bhutto brought to the political scene, even after his recovery Ayub could not successfully neutralize his former subordinate.

More withdrawn and introspective after his illness, Ayub was no longer the visionary of years past. Weakened from within, he was fair game for those who sought to capitalize on his loss of authority. Faced with dissension in the army and betrayal in his immediate political circle, besieged by the opposition and an enraged public, Ayub was hardly a

Solon or Lycurgus, the 'Great Legislator' that Samuel Huntington describes in a book published in 1968. There was nothing that Ayub could possibly do in the latter months of 1968 to reverse the momentum that would cause him to vacate his office. Ayub lingered on through January and February of 1969, but by this time turmoil had overtaken the country as well as the Field Marshal. An attempt on his life had failed in November 1968, but the incident left Ayub shaken and melancholy. Bhutto and Wali Khan, the son of Ghaffar Khan, had been arrested, Mujib was also in police custody, but even in the absence of these leaders, their followers were able to sustain their demonstrations and paralyse the country. Ayub became more dependent on the army and its commander, General Yahya Khan. The quelling of public unrest, i.e., preventing the destruction of life and property, was given major priority, but so too was the preservation and the discipline of the army. Given the adverse reaction to the Decade of Development, Ayub believed that the instability was prompted by economic factors (Feldman, 1972). Yahya, however, saw the national dilemma in political, not economic, terms. Only fundamental change in the political condition, he argued, could stabilize the situation. Economic remedies were meaningless without sacrificing much of the political changes introduced over the past many years. Ayub was told that all that he had contributed to the political evolution of Pakistan would have to be scrapped. Yahya listed the One Unit, the Basic Democracies, indeed the Ayubian Constitution—all would have to go in order to reclaim the high ground from an array of politicians with different, but less than national, objectives. In fact, in the whole panoply of political leaders, only Bhutto could claim something resembling a national following, but even he tended to encourage parochial expression.

Before Ayub accepted Yahya's radical proposition and agreed to step aside, he decided to make one more try at placating the opposition. A Democratic Action Committee had been formed representing a variety of political parties, particularly in East Pakistan, and Ayub, through the good offices of Khwaja Shahabuddin, tried to meet with its leaders. Ayub indicated a willingness to make concessions, notably to yield to their demand for direct elections that would be based upon universal franchise, to lift the state of emergency imposed during the 1965 war, as well as to release the detained politicians. But when the opposition leaders baulked at Ayub's offer, the President raised the ante, promising a full attack on corrupt practices and permission to alter those sections of the constitution that were deemed offensive. But even this did not satisfy the dissidents, who recognized that Ayub was now too weak to make concessions.

Ayub ordered Bhutto released from custody in anticipation that he would participate in serious discussions, but the PPP leader was especially reluctant to meet with the President, arguing that this would only strengthen Ayub's hand and protract his rule. At this juncture, even Manzur Qadir called upon Ayub to step aside and allow a caretaker government to run the nation. But Ayub still refused to yield his office. In the meantime, the riots that had started in the towns and villages of West Pakistan had inundated the major cities and had swept to East Pakistan, where the demands for self-government and autonomy had taken an ominous turn.

In a futile attempt to appeal to reason, Ayub declared he would not be a candidate for re-election. The announcement, however, only whetted the appetites of those who were now even more determined to drive him from office. Moreover, Ayub's statement had exposed other members of his government who had postured sternness in their dealings with the opposition, and who therefore, avoided deeper commitments and began to distance themselves from the President. Shahabuddin, who had attempted to broker an arrangement between the politicians and the President, was made a special target of their bitterness, but even this intra-cabinet dispute did not deflect criticism away from Ayub Khan. Problems continued to multiply and intensify, and Ayub acknowledged that only the most drastic action could save Pakistan. In conversations with Yahya, Ayub began to question the use of violence against the nation's citizens. Saving his government was no longer a primary option. Thus, on 10 March 1969, Ayub met with some of the country's top political leaders, but not with Bhutto, who preferred separating himself from the pack. Ayub informed the assembled politicians that he would soon step down, but that before doing so, he wanted assurances from all sides that they would respect the country's integrity, and that they would assist the police and armed forces in ending the nationwide disturbances.

Ayub was especially concerned with the deterioration of political conditions in East Pakistan. He therefore terminated the Agartala conspiracy trial, released the accused, and summoned Mujib to meet with him in Islamabad. In fact, under the influence of Manzur Qadir, Ayub even entertained ideas of reintroducing the parliamentary system and naming Mujibur Rahman the country's Prime Minister. Ayub was deflected from taking this route by General Yahya Khan, in whom he confided. Yayha told Ayub that such an action would embarrass the army, and he reminded the President that Mujib had been charged with anti-state activities, that it was tactically necessary to release him, but that neither he nor his brother officers could imagine taking orders from a Mujib who had never shown any affection for the men in uniform. Even the thought that Ayub could raise such a possibility was anathema to Yayha, who was now convinced that Ayub should vacate his office with all haste.

Yahya had developed his own persona in the years following the 1965 war, and he had also developed greater intimacy with the prevailing political process. Yahya knew whom he trusted among the politicians, and with the exception of Bhutto, he did not approve of a single one. Hence Ayub's meetings with the opposition, and the concessions he offered them in return for their support, did not sit well with the General. At best, politicians were to be tolerated, but if they expected to return to the game, they would have to do so under a different set of rules from those offered by a fatigued and beaten Ayub Khan.

Always concerned that the army would be seriously harmed if concessions were made to politicians espousing regional and provincial agendas, Yahya reacted negatively to the President's actions, and he not only forced him to reconsider his options, he demanded Ayub's formal resignation. A once all-powerful Ayub was compelled to accept the realities of a very changed situation that he no longer controlled. Thus, on

25 March 1969, Ayub Khan announced his decision to leave public life and to pass authority and the power of the presidency to General Agha Mohammad Yahya Khan.

Yahya, with the power vested in him by martial law, abrogated the 1962 Constitution and banned all the political parties. All members of Ayub's cabinet, as well as the provincial Governors, were sacked, and the country's new leader declared his intention to restore law and order and return the society to 'sanity'. In a public statement, Ayub said it was impossible for him to preside over the destruction of the country and that, except for the armed forces, there was no other way to save Pakistan. In a letter to Yahya, Ayub expressed the belief that he had exhausted all possible civil and constitutional means in trying to resolve the nationwide crisis. The politicians, he argued, had been given ample opportunity to accept and manage a political experience that would have given them an important role. While some of them had agreed to co-operate, others preferred to sustain their attacks on the public order. According to Ayub, the objective of the politicians was nothing less than the destruction of the national design, and he was left with no other option than to call upon General Yahya Khan to re-establish law and order (Ziring, 1971; Gauhar, 1993).

CHAPTER 8

THE DISMEMBERMENT OF PAKISTAN

Yahya Khan had anticipated the moment of his ascendancy for more than a year. Believing that he had demonstrated loyalty to his supreme commander, Ayub's failings, his widespread unpopularity, and especially his poor health, had convinced Yahya that power would be passed, and that given the political turmoil in the country, more than likely another army general would succeed to the presidency. Yahya acknowledged that he could be that general. Yahya was therefore forced to ponder his options during that period when it appeared that Ayub might not recover his health and he would have to address the question of reconstituting Pakistan's political experience. It did not require a savant to conclude that the Ayubian experiment had failed, and that patching the nationally-rejected system would only pour more fuel on an already roaring fire. Moreover, Yahya had his fellow officers to contend with, and his most immediate colleagues had not only lost respect for the President during and immediately following the 1965 war, they were convinced that Ayub had caused serious harm to the army.

The failure to liberate Kashmir was not to be blamed on the men in arms or those directing the campaign, but on the policies, and, indeed, the philosophical musings, of Ayub Khan. Ayub was made the scapegoat for ill-conceived plans and actions perpetrated by the very men who now absolved themselves of any responsibility. Ayub's mistake lay in placing far too much trust on faulty intelligence, and in not being able to recognize the ulterior motives of some of his most intimate civilian and military colleagues. Ayub was betrayed by virtually all those in his immediate circle, and it was only after he sensed their disloyalty that he summoned Yahya Khan, first to phase out the Kashmir débâcle, and then to take charge of the army itself.

Yahya was not only in line to succeed Ayub, he had also been groomed for Ayub's position by those of his brother officers who were determined to obliterate the Ayub record, using him as the instrument of their scheming. Yahya, therefore, was not allowed to tip his hand until he had Ayub's formal resignation, transferring power to his charge. To have acted prematurely, to have even hinted that he opposed virtually everything Ayub had done in his more than ten years in power, might well have resulted in Ayub clinging to office, in alliance with those members of the political opposition whom Yahya, along with his fellow officers, most detested. Manzur Qadir's advice to Ayub to restore the parliamentary system and to call upon Mujibur Rahman to form a government was unthinkable. Ayub's meeting with Mujib following the termination of the Agartala trial humiliated the armed forces, and was ample evidence for the cabalists that Ayub was tilting toward a political formula they could not tolerate.

Yahya allowed himself to become the instrument of several key officers in the command structure, namely: General Abdul Hamid Khan, the Punjabi Chief of Staff; Lieutenant-General S.M.G. Peerzada, a Bombay-born Principal Staff Officer and virtually the military Prime Minister after Ayub's departure; Lieutenant-General Gul Hassan Khan, the Chief of the General Staff, from the NWFP; Major-General Mohammad Akbar Khan, Head of Military Intelligence, a Punjabi; Major-General Ghulam Omar, Secretary of the Pakistan National Security Council, who had opted for Pakistan from the East Punjab; Air Marshal Nur Khan, who was made Martial Law Administrator of West Pakistan; and finally, Abubakr Osman Mitha, the Quartermaster-General, who hailed from a high-born Bombay family, and who directed the special commando force known as the Special Service Group. Also providing input in junta deliberations were Lieutenant-General Tikka Khan and Major-General Rao Farman Ali Khan, who were soon to be despatched to East Pakistan as the eyes and ears of the central command. To say that the principals were also rivals is to point to the obvious. But it is even more important to point out that they were some of the very officers whom Bhutto had cultivated during his years in the Ayub administration. Far more than Yahya, it was this small group of army commanders who appeared to relish the political struggle and who, in concert with Bhutto, sought the dismantling of the entire Ayubian system.

Initially, there was little hint of division within the junta as it began to issue ordinances and edicts that were aimed at returning the country to near normalcy, but it was also apparent that they could not expect to dominate the country's political life indefinitely. Moreover, the army was in the process of being reformed, and their attention, of necessity, had to be divided between their professional duties and what they judged to be the political necessities brought on by the collapse of the Ayub administration.

Perhaps no less important to the higher military officers, the US arms embargo that had been imposed on Pakistan in 1965 was now in its fourth year, and a number of the generals agreed with Bhutto that the country's foreign and national security policy had to be redirected away from its Ayub-developed ties with Washington, and toward the People's Republic of China, which Bhutto was credited with championing, but which had also demonstrated its strategic value to Pakistan during the 1965 war. Of all the ruling officers, Yahya was among the more reluctant to sever ties with the United States, believing that the US connection remained important and should be nurtured, in spite of Washington's ambivalent policy in South Asia.

Yahya is credited with having been a solid field commander and staff officer, but he was a novice at political intrigue. Moreover, his tenure as Commander-in-Chief of the Pakistan Army had been marked not only by broad delegations of authority, but also by long periods of professional indifference. Nor was Yahya's reputation as an alcoholic to be discounted; but whatever his failings, Yahya allowed his ambitious colleagues to play a major role in political as well as strategic planning. Yahya's *coup* during the period of Ayub's illness was, in fact, orchestrated by the officers around him, and he never fully measured the extent of the powers he shared with his colleagues. Clearly, Yahya was given the spokesman's role for a junta that he was destined to follow as much as lead. Yahya was the chairman of a board of directors which, when his problems began to mount, constantly frustrated his initiatives. As Mascarenhas (1972) has noted, the members of the inner circle constituted a powerful panel of advisors who, while acknowledging the chain of command, nevertheless influenced the course of policy. G.W. Choudhury (1974), a Bengali and former Political Science professor at Dhaka University, who became Yahya's chief advisor on constitutional affairs, also notes the heavy influence on Yahya by members of the junta.

Choudhury cites the alacrity with which Ayub relinquished control of the army after becoming President, and the little time lost in assembling a civilian cabinet. Yahya did none of this. He retained his role as Commander-in-Chief, and filled his cabinet with generals. Thus, Yahya assumed the portfolios of Defence and Foreign Affairs, General Hamid was made Home Minister, Air Marshal Nur Khan controlled the ministries of Education, Health, and Social Welfare, and the Navy chief, Vice-Admiral S.M. Ahsan, took responsibility for Finance, Planning, Industry, and Commerce. General Peerzada oversaw all government operations, and led the charge against the higher bureaucracy which resulted in the sacking of 303 of the key civilian officials serving during the Ayub era, notably Altaf Gauhar, N.A. Faruque, and Fida Hasan. Together with Nur Khan, Hamid, and Ahsan, Peerzada presided over a Council of Administration within the junta, which was served by two brigadiers whom Peerzada had elevated to Major-General status, namely, Generals Rahim, a Punjabi, and Karim, a Bengali. Two senior civil administrators, however, also served the junta: M.M. Ahmad, the President's Economics Advisor, and N.A. Razvi, the Director of the Civil Intelligence Bureau.

Choudhury's selection had been arranged by Peerzada for the purpose of assisting the junta in framing a new constitutional order. He recounts how Yahya's power was strengthened by his conflict with Nur Khan, who antagonized other high-ranking members of the junta by his radical positions on policy matters. Yahya eventually removed Nur Khan from the cabinet and made him Governor of West Pakistan. Admiral Ahsan, who also did not see eye to eye with the more conservative army representatives, was likewise sent to East Pakistan to assume the office of Governor. The subsequent formation of a civilian cabinet came at Yahya's urging, and in order to provide cover for the junta, which needed to resolve its internal differences away from public scrutiny. But the military junta, now essentially an army operation, continued to dominate the decision-making process. In the confusion between military and civilian decision-making, the need to restructure the government, and the urgency in coping with rising discontent in East Pakistan, Yahya lost control of daily, indeed, the everyday details of, governance. He therefore tried to confine his activities to the larger questions of constitution-making, but given his decision to defer to his colleagues, here too he confronted serious problems. More and more, therefore, Yahya came to depend upon G.W. Choudhury, and it was through him that he maintained an understanding of the major issues.

Yahya's speech to the nation following the transfer of power did not contain any of the arrangements agreed to in his conversations with Ayub. Ayub expected Yahya to operate under the terms of the 1962 Constitution, to accept all the necessary legal obligations, and to yield authority to civilian leaders as soon as law and order had been restored. But the imposition of martial law was the junta's, not Ayub's, decision. The abrogation of the constitution was a repudiation of the promise Yahya had made to his former President. When General Peerzada became Yahya's Principal Staff Officer, it became his job to empty the cabinet of Ayub holdovers.

As a professional soldier, Yahya was wedded to the principle of loyalty, but it is questionable how loyal he was in his later relations with Ayub, and he had to ponder the degree of loyalty his colleagues would show him. Yahya possessed little of the political acumen of his predecessor, nor did he wield the political power associated with military dictators. He could not manage without his closest associates, nor could he dispense with the expertise of the higher administration. Yahya shared the decision-making process with his intimate confidants, and given his obvious distaste for the job, they assumed significant leverage in the making and implementation of policy. Yahya therefore avoided interfering with general administration and, unlike Ayub, who in his early years reviewed the most mundane files, Yahya found the daily chores of government tedious and monotonous. Thus, daily decision-making was left to key administrators in the central secretariat. Yahya was the curious combination of introvert in matters of professional note and extrovert in social circumstances. He deferred to his subordinates on issues of state, while allowing himself maximum opportunities for personal engagements. It was not apparent at the time of Ayub's departure, but it became obvious later; Yahya failed to assume the posture of a 'great leader' in a political culture renowned for such posturing.

The Life and Times of Yahya Khan

Agha Mohammad Yahya Khan was born in Peshawar on 4 February 1917. A descendent of the Persian conqueror Nadir Khan, Yahya hailed from the Qizilbash tribe, and military tradition ran deep in his immediate family. After graduating from Punjab University he became a King's Cadet in the Indian Military Academy at Dehra Dun, and came first in his class. Commissioned in 1938, he was attached first to the 2nd Battalion of the Worcester Regiment and later to the 3rd Battalion of the Baloch Regiment, where he received his first command. During World War II, Yahya served in Egypt, Sudan, Libya, Cyprus, Iraq, and Italy. He opted for Pakistan after partition, was promoted to Colonel, and played a major role in the development of the Pakistan Army Staff College at Quetta. Made a Brigadier at the age of thirty-four, Yahya assumed command of an infantry brigade, and was later transferred to army headquarters, where he worked closely with Ayub Khan in the modernization of the Pakistan Army. The youngest officer to be promoted to the rank of Major-General, Ayub named him his Chief of Staff in 1957.

The sequence of events following the dissolution of the parliamentary system and the imposition of martial law are cloudy, but Iskandar Mirza had intended arresting Yahya at the same time that he sought the removal of Ayub Khan. Ayub's success in isolating Mirza, and ultimately in forcing him to leave the country, was in part due to the co-operation he received from Yahya, and the latter remained at Ayub's side in army headquarters throughout the forty-four months of martial law. Following the promulgation of the Ayub Constitution in 1962, Yahya was sent to East Pakistan as General Officer Commanding (GOC). But prior to that assignment, it was Yahya who assisted in the reorganization of the Pakistan Army, in the introduction of new weapons systems, and in the development of new tactical concepts. Yahya worked in close harmony with American military advisers and developed collegial relations with US officers, which strengthened Ayub's hand in Washington. He was also a key player in the work of the Federal Capital Commission that recommended moving the capital from Karachi to the Potwar Plateau near Rawalpindi. Yahya became the first Chairman of the Capital Development Authority and presided over the initial planning for the building of Islamabad.

Called to combat duty during the 1965 war, Yahya distinguished himself by retrieving a failed strategy, received his country's highest honour, was promoted to Lieutenant-General, and was made Deputy Commander-in-Chief of the Pakistan Army. He took full command of the army following General Musa's appointment as Governor of West Pakistan in 1966, and his years after the war were spent rebuilding the pride of the army and restoring its combat readiness in the absence of American support. The two goals were intertwined, and Yahya was forced to lean upon the services of a relatively young officer corps that had suffered significant psychological as well as physical damage in the 1965 war.

From the vantage point of the younger officers, Ayub's decision to terminate the 1965 war, and his acceptance of the Tashkent Agreement, had demonstrated his weaknesses and caused considerable dissension in the ranks. Defections, however, were kept in check by Yahya's diplomatic manoeuvring, but not without cost. Yahya was compelled to share authority with his immediate colleagues, and compromise, as well as collective decision-making, were made imperative. Thus, when riots spread from one end of the country to the other in 1968, Yahya could not take the necessary action without the approval of his comrades. Moreover, few in the higher ranks believed that the killing of unhappy citizens could be justified simply to keep Ayub Khan in office. Furthermore, most of the senior officers had already concluded that the anarchic situation was caused by the Field Marshal's reluctance to step aside. Having determined that it was time for Ayub to go, Yahya was urged to take the necessary action.

To the end, Ayub believed that his exit would be orderly and that Yahya would quickly stabilize the country, using the existing political system as the framework for his actions. Ayub, however, was not aware of the extent to which Yahya was controlled by his brother officers, or how they guided his public role. As Morris Janowitz (1964) has noted, Ayub never developed a personal military dictatorship, but during Yahya's administration, the military came to resemble a form of cabinet government without an electorate. In the beginning, however, Yahya played the collegial game to perfection and thus was able to neutralize efforts aimed at having Ayub tried for what were allegedly serious improprieties. It also enabled him to fend off those officers who sought closer ties with Communist China and who were demanding a sharp break with the United States.

Nixon's election to the American presidency in 1969 was judged a positive development in Pakistan-United States relations. Henry Kissinger, Nixon's National Security Adviser, had already signalled Yahya of Nixon's interest in improving relations with the People's Republic of China, and Yahya was encouraged to use his China connection in opening the way for a Washington-Beijing dialogue. Although this plan was held in the highest confidence, Yahya used the American entreaty to offset the pressure of those members of the junta who wanted a formal break with the United States. Yahya correctly read the changes in the Cold War, i.e., the American desire to extricate itself from south-east Asia, and the substitution of a policy of détente for that of confrontation with the communist states. Yahya therefore made it possible for Kissinger to meet with the Chinese leaders, and he had reason to anticipate a lifting of the arms embargo in return for his good offices. The American connection engineered by Ayub was in this way sustained, and the more radical members of Yahya's entourage were, for the time being at least, neutralized.

But while these matters were still in a state of gestation, Yahya's most immediate concern upon assuming power was the future of Pakistan's political experience. With Bhutto in the wings and a significant influence on the ruling junta, party political activity was rapidly reinstated on 1 January 1970, and in spite of the prevailing martial law, the politicians were emboldened to clamour for reforms and the restoration of civilian government. Yahya was imposed upon to permit political debate, and immediately the question turned toward the need for a new constitution. But before a new document could be drafted, a decision needed to be taken on the form of political system that it would describe. Attacks on presidential government appeared to guarantee that only a new parliamentary system would be acceptable, and it was with this objective in mind that Yahya announced that general elections would be conducted on 5 October 1970 for a new National Assembly. Declaring that the voting would be open to all adult males and females, the elections represented the nation's first experience with direct, mass voting since the country achieved its independence, twenty-three years earlier.

The Yahya Reforms

Yahya's preference for the parliamentary system was supported, but not without resistance, by the ruling junta, all believing that distance had to be established between the new military administration and that of Ayub Khan. Yahya therefore also agreed with his colleagues that the One Unit scheme should be scrapped and the former provinces of West Pakistan reconstituted. Thus a Legal Framework Order (LFO) was proclaimed on 30 March 1970, describing the distribution of seats to be contested from each of the provinces. The LFO also called for Provincial Assembly elections and, in effect, the clock was turned back to 1955, that is, prior to the drafting of the 1956 Constitution, and some three years before the 1958 declaration of martial law. The LFO described a National Assembly of 313 members, with thirteen of the seats reserved for women. The distribution of seats was as follows:

National Assembly of Pakistan

	General	Women
East Pakistan	162	7
Punjab	82	3
Sindh	27	1
Balochistan	4	1
North-West Frontier Province	18	1
Tribal Areas	7	

The military junta thus established the framework for the new political order. They uninhibitedly declared that much of the constitutional work had been completed years before (although the reinstatement of the 1956 Constitution was rejected), and that once the new Assembly was in place, it should quickly produce the new constitution. Yahya declared that 120 days was the time allotted to the politicians to complete their work, and if they failed to make good on their opportunity, the Assembly would be dissolved and another round of elections held for still another body. Thus, little attention could be given to the momentous decisions already made, that is, the breakup of West Pakistan and the distribution of seats to the reconstituted provinces. The LFO did not follow the parity formula between East and West; instead, East Pakistan had been awarded more seats than all the other provinces, including the tribal areas, combined. Although this was arguably a more appropriate arrangement than the one worked out in 1955, and in fact it more accurately reflected the distribution of the population, it nevertheless raised significant issues of public policy. West Pakistani politicians, notably from the Punjab, had objected to East Pakistan having a preponderance of votes in the National Assembly, and now the decision had been taken to elevate the Bengali component, and that change could only come at the expense of the less populous nationalities in the western portion of the country.

The generals, however, were not alone in drawing up the Legal Framework Order. Input had come from a variety of political circles, including those in West Pakistan. In addition to Bhutto, there were the leaders of the Frontier parties who had long demanded the breakup of One Unit. The more provincially-inclined politicians from West Pakistan saw an opportunity to thwart Punjabi power, and they had good reason to believe that the new arrangement would enable them to work in tandem with the representatives from East Pakistan who, they claimed, they had less cause to fear. And although G.W. Choudhury (1974) reveals his important role in the drafting of the LFO, it was Zulfikar Ali Bhutto who stood to profit from the breakup of One Unit. Bhutto's party had cut deep inroads in the Punjab, but his Sindh-based organization needed assurances that it could control western Pakistan's most important province. Bhutto envisaged a scenario in which he would neutralize both the traditional Punjabi Muslim Leaguers as well as the NAP, and, given an anticipated split in East Pakistan between Bhashani's NAP, the Jamaat-i-Islami, the rump Muslim League organizations, and Mujibur Rahman's Awami League, he had reason to believe he would be the person that the junta would call upon to form the new civilian government. Clearly, the junta's thinking tracked very close to that of Bhutto's.

Nevertheless, it was apparently Choudhury who convinced Yahya that 'one man, one vote' arrangements would save the Pakistan design by mollifying provincial interests, especially in East Bengal. Of the members of the inner military cabinet, only Generals Hamid, Tikka, and Omar were strongly opposed to yielding so much representation to the Bengalis. General Peerzada, although less than supportive, decided to maintain his neutrality but, along with the dissenters, he began the necessary planning in case the tactic failed. Thus the LFO was announced to the surprise of the nation, its success resting on the good faith of the principal politicians, whose task it would be to resolve their differences in assembling a new political order in the nation. The LFO distribution of seats in the National Assembly was supposed to placate the political leaders in East Pakistan. Bhashani, however, publicly renewed his call for secession, and more importantly, Mujib, swept along by the passionate demands of his constituents, secretly sought ways to extract further concessions from the military rulers. When it became known in Islamabad that Mujib was plotting a course that deviated from the intent of the LFO, not only did junta lines harden, but the situation allowed Bhutto to assume the role of statesman and saviour.

There had been nothing like a debate prior to the issuance of the LFO and the breakup of One Unit. Caught up in the fast moving events, few seriously pondered the consequences of the restoration of the original provinces in West Pakistan. Ayub had laboured for One Unit and had sustained it because he believed it was in Pakistan's strategic interests. He had looked for a way to transcend the ethnic competition that so often had deteriorated into displays of internecine violence. He had not entertained the breakup of the provinces into smaller and numerous administrative units because decentralization, in his thinking, merely played into the hands of traditional *biradris* and tribal leaders. Nor did he believe that a decentralized administrative system could long effect its rule in alien surroundings. One Unit and Ayub's Basic Democracies was the arrangement chosen because it linked the nation's many distinct units with a central core of decision-making and to Ayub this option, though admittedly imperfect, offered what was for him the best hope of transcending conventional patterns of rule.

The termination of Basic Democracies, coupled with the damage inflicted on the central bureaucracy, and indeed the repudiation of the centralized presidential system, was supposed to calm an aroused people, but returning to the early years of the republic meant revisiting the problems that brought the country to an impasse in 1958. The major difference this time was not only in the cast of characters, but the very legacy of the Ayub era. Yahya had, by this time, delegated much of his responsibilities as Chief Martial Law Administrator to his colleagues, and they in turn had begun to work more intimately with some of the political leaders, but none more so than Zulfikar Ali Bhutto.

The National Elections of 1970

When the elections were conducted in October 1970, twenty-five parties campaigned for positions in the National Assembly. There were 1,570 candidates for the 300 electable seats, and the activities and electioneering of the participants were nothing like anything yet experienced in the history of Pakistan. Considering the number of participating parties, the junta was assured of a divided vote that would necessitate the formation of a coalition government. Indeed, it was obvious long before the actual balloting that the Awami League and NAP, along with the Muslim League and lesser parties, would share the vote in East Pakistan. No single party was projected the dominant winner. West Pakistan, however, was another matter. There the PPP was envisaged carrying Sindh and the Punjab. Moreover, Bhutto anticipated substantial successes in the NWFP and Balochistan, thus giving his party a majority of West Pakistani votes. Overall, the PPP was expected to win the largest number of seats, and hence Bhutto had reason to anticipate a call to form the first civilian government in twelve years.

Moreover, some of the more important junta members much preferred working with Bhutto. And at least on one matter they were certainly in unanimous agreement: the junta vehemently opposed the Awami League Six Point Programme that would transform Pakistan into a confederation, allow for completely autonomous governments in East and West Pakistan, and leave the centre with vague responsibilities over defence and foreign policy. Mujib had also called for two separate but freely convertible currencies, and only the federated units would have the power to tax their citizens. The central government, it was said, would be granted funds necessary only for the conduct of its explicit business. Adding to their demands, the Bengalis called for separate accounts from foreign exchange earnings, and the right of the federating units to open trade links with foreign countries. Finally, the Six Points stated that East Pakistan would be allowed to raise a separate militia and generally manage its own internal security. From the vantage point of the junta, therefore, the Awami League demanded nothing less than the breakup of Pakistan.

The military leaders shared their concerns with Bhutto, who often met with them to exchange ideas and to ponder future prospects and possible courses of action. General Akbar Khan, the intelligence chief, had questioned the early revival of political party activity, and had argued against transferring power to any of the civilians. Akbar, his Punjabi credentials amply demonstrated, questioned the distribution of seats in the National Assembly under the LFO. He also read Bhutto's double game in both accepting the LFO and apposing the Awami League Six Points. Of all the members of the junta, only Akbar did not anticipate fractured results in East Pakistan. In spite of the numerous parties contesting the election, his intelligence revealed that the Awami League was guaranteed overwhelming popular support, and that the West Pakistan-based organizations would get no more than a handful of votes in the eastern province. Moreover, Bhutto had only months earlier visited East Pakistan to express his support for Mujib's Six Point formula. Akbar, unlike the other generals, did not trust Bhutto, nor did he believe the Punjab was well served by either the breakup of the One Unit or the rapid holding of elections. Outvoted by other junta members, however, especially Peerzada and Gul Hassan, the decision was taken to press ahead with the restructuring as well as the elections.

Flooding in East Pakistan had caused the postponement of the elections from their original date in October to another in December. But plans were well under way to hold the first ever national balloting when suddenly, and without warning, on 12 November 1970, a tidal wave more than thirty feet high, lashed by cyclonic winds of 120 miles per hour, blasted five of East Pakistan's coastal districts. The destruction wrought by the storm was inestimable, but it was said to be the worst natural catastrophe in modern history. The death toll was placed well above a million and property damage in the affected area was said to be total. In the chaos caused by the storm, the need for assistance was writ large, and East Pakistanis looked to West Pakistan, and especially to the military junta, for relief assistance. Yahya was returning from a state visit to China at the time of the disaster, and although he made a stop in Dhaka, he was not informed of the magnitude of the calamity, and he proceeded on to Islamabad.

With millions needing assistance, the government was ill-equipped to adequately deal with the situation. Rumours, therefore, quickly circulated throughout Bengal that the junta was indifferent to the plight of its own citizens. Thus, by the time Yahya returned to East Pakistan to tour the devastated region, he faced an angry reception but could still offer little to relieve the plight of the victims. When the Pakistan government finally acted, its assistance was only a fraction of that provided by international agencies, and this juxtaposition of concerns and needs only added to the sense of Bengali isolation. The central government was condemned for its inaction, but most of all for what was deemed its callous lack of sympathy.

Mujib articulated the sentiments of the Bengalis as the election campaign continued. Citing the obvious importance of his Six Point Programme and the absolute need to provide the province with maximum autonomy, his speechmaking fell on very receptive Bengali ears. Maulana Bhashani was equally outspoken, but he directed his anger not only at the martial law government, but at the people of West Pakistan as well. Bhashani declared it was painful to consider himself a Pakistani, and he announced that his NAP party had decided not to contest the elections. Holding to his promise, Bhashani left the field pretty much to Mujibur Rahman and his Awami League. Moreover, if Bhutto's PPP or any of the other West Pakistan-based organizations expected to win seats from East Pakistan constituencies, the developments in the period following the tidal wave did not augur success for their cause.

The military junta, as well as Bhutto and all the other principals, understood that if the elections were held in December, so soon after this tragic event, and if the NAP truly boycotted the elections, the Awami League would emerge the overwhelming victor. A decision, therefore, had to be taken on whether to postpone the elections again, or to proceed with the voting and accept the consequences.

The junta discussed the matter among themselves, and although there were serious questions about proceeding with the schedule, and indeed, Yahya considered still another postponement, at least until the situation in East Pakistan had stabilized, he was overruled and the elections were allowed to go forward. In holding to the election schedule, the military leaders put their faith in Bhutto winning a smashing victory in the provinces of West Pakistan, and thus bringing into question Mujib's success in East Pakistan, especially as the Awami League's principal competition in the eastern province had decided to sit out the exercise. In other words, the junta leaders convinced themselves that Mujib's victory would be tainted when compared with Bhutto's. Moreover, Mujib would not be allowed to form an exclusively Awami League government even if his party did win more seats than any other party. No matter what the final results, Bhutto and the PPP would have to be given due consideration. But still another scenario projected no political winners, with the fragmented vote making it all the more imperative that the junta remain in place. But whatever the outcome of the elections, expectations were heightened in both wings of the country.

In late November and early December Yahya had secret meetings with Mujib. No other politicians were consulted during these visits. Mujib told Yahya of the high tension in the province, and that any thought of postponing the elections would produce a violent uprising. Mujib assured the President that the Awami League would not jeopardize Pakistan's integrity, and that Yahya need not fear the election results. Moreover, Mujib tried to convince Yahya that his Six Point Programme and the five points described in the LFO were completely compatible and that both sets of principles would help in framing a new constitution. Yahya appeared to accept Mujib at his word, and returned to Islamabad believing that 'Pakistan had been saved' (Choudhury,1974, p.102).

The Election Aftermath

Pakistanis participated in their first national elections during the second week of December and, as expected, with the NAP out of the picture, the Awami League of Shaikh Mujibur Rahman swept the polls. Of the 169 seats allotted to East Pakistan, the Awami League eventually walked away with 167, making it the clear majority party in the country. The only other party receiving a respectable number of seats was

Bhutto's PPP, garnering 81 seats, or less than half of those acquired by Mujib's organization. Moreover, Bhutto's seats came exclusively from Sindh and the Punjab (except one in the NWFP), what with Balochistan and the NWFP opting for Jamiat-ul-Ulema (JUI) and the Frontier National Awami Party organizations. Neither the East Pakistan Awami League or Bhutto's PPP, however, won a single seat in the other wing of the country. What had been forecast by General Akbar, therefore, had in fact occurred. Under the parliamentary rules, Mujib had enough seats to establish the government without forming a coalition.

Relishing his victory, Mujib said that he would take into account the success of the PPP in the west, and a future cabinet would not ignore representatives from the other provinces. The Punjabis, however, were unreconciled, and they bitterly condemned the junta for allowing the elections to go forward in such a divisive environment. The *New York Times* of 13 December 1970 ran a banner headline that read 'Vote Jolts Punjabis'. The article went on to quote Punjabis as restive and angry. One comment summed up the sentiment in the Punjab: 'The Punjab is finished...We will be ruled by Sindh and Bengal. Our country has gone to the dogs.' But while Punjabis were crestfallen and demoralized, the Bengalis were jubilant and expectant. Having proceeded with the elections, having received an international stamp of approval that the elections were generally without incident and fair, the junta could not backtrack. To reverse field now would be to incite an explosion at home as well as invite opprobrium from abroad. Moreover, in addition to the Bengalis, the NAP and JUI had their provincial political expectations raised to new levels, and the junta had to consider the repercussions in Balochistan as well as the NWFP if any action were taken to nullify the returns. The junta's decision, therefore, centred on the validation of the election results, and allowing Bhutto and Mujib the opportunity to discuss their individual differences and to decide upon an appropriate course of action.

Bhutto, however, knowing the sentiments of the majority members of the military junta, now backed away from his earlier support of the Awami League Six Point Programme; in fact, he denounced it as anti-Pakistan, and insisted that any meeting with Mujib must focus on the withdrawal of the

Six Points from the negotiating table. Mujib, however, was flushed with victory and his old antagonism toward Bhutto could not be concealed. Mujib did not want Bhutto tampering with the election results. Sensing a Bhutto-junta cabal, Mujib was even more adamant in demanding a constitution that reflected the sentiments of the Bengalis. Nor could Mujib ignore his volatile constituents. The Six Points were non-negotiable. There was no longer any question as to the Bengali position; there would be no retreat from the minimum demand—that East Pakistan be granted full autonomy.

With demands in East Pakistan escalating into calls for independence, Bhutto's position was equally unyielding. Bhutto now claimed to speak for Punjabis as well as his brethren in Sindh, indeed for all West Pakistanis. Bhutto reiterated his declaration that there would be no meetings and no resolution of the impasse if Mujib did not relent on the Six Points. Facing a tidal wave of human dimensions, Yahya called upon Bhutto to put aside his rhetoric and meet with Mujib in Dhaka. The Awami League leader had, in fact, declined Yahya's invitation to come to Islamabad, and Bhutto was forced to make the trip to Dhaka. On arriving, Bhutto went into discussions with Peerzada, who was already in Dhaka. Choudhury refers to Peerzada as the 'Rasputin' in the Yahya regime, and there is little doubt that he briefed Bhutto on what the army was contemplating doing if Mujib did not reduce his demands (Choudhury, 1974, p.103). Close associates since the 1965 war, Bhutto and Peerzada shared political ideas, and together they agreed that a meeting with Mujib could be useful. Bhutto also learned that he had the support of General Hamid, Lieutenant-General Gul Hassan and Major-General Omar, none of whom was prepared to accept any of Mujib's points. Thus, whatever political settlement Yahya still contemplated was undermined by members of his own entourage, and before the first serious negotiations had even begun. Yahya had earlier told Mujib that he was prepared to make concessions, and perhaps his efforts· would have enjoyed some success if the Awami League leaders, by their intransigence, had not played into the hands of Yahya's detractors in the junta.

Yahya had called for the opening of the National Assembly on 3 March 1971, in Dhaka, and had insisted that its deliberations should proceed with or without the major participants. He had met Mujib in Dhaka shortly after the Awami Leaguer's electoral victory, and had returned to Islamabad with the declaration that Mujib would become Pakistan's new Prime Minister. But that statement proved premature. Neither General Peerzada nor a majority of his colleagues were prepared to accept a Mujib government. Yayha was forced to delay the proceedings and the Bengalis, sensing yet another betrayal, read his behaviour as stalling for time. As a consequence, the Mujib-Bhutto meeting was considered still another act of West Pakistani trickery.

By this time, the lines had hardened on both sides. Both Mujib and Bhutto were explosive orators in highly volatile circumstances. Each mustered passionate followings that numbered in the hundreds of thousands, and each rode a wave of history he could not control. Both were predetermined to contest the validity of the other's argument and bona fides. Mujib controlled a majority of the seats in the National Assembly but his representation was confined to East Pakistan. Bhutto held an impressive majority in West Pakistan, but the One Unit had been dissolved, and his political leverage was more a consequence of his success in winning the Punjab than his ability to lead a united West Pakistan constituency.

Mujib's electoral success was imperilled not only because the Awami League leader used his national status to press provincial objectives, but because he was expected to function as a parliamentary leader before a constitutional framework had legitimized his role. The abrogation of the 1962 Constitution, like the earlier decision to discard the 1956 Constitution, was not without its cost. Had a constitution been in place when the 1970 elections were held, the results would have been manageable. Moreover, the Awami League Six Points could not then have been used as a take it or leave it ultimatum. But as it was, the Bengali demands burdened the political process and cast a dark cloud over constitution-making. Ironically, the absence of a constitutional structure, and the attempt to create one from the election results, merely provided both Mujib and Bhutto with opportunities to press their separate, highly ambitious, political programmes.

The first-ever national election, tragically, was neither conducted under established legal guidelines, nor with the prior understanding of the competing political organizations. It needs to be remembered that the election was held during martial law, that it had been decreed by a military junta in the void created by the abrogation of the 1962 Constitution, and that it was aimed more at confirming the dismantling of the Ayubian political order than in erecting a new one.

Bhutto's response to Yahya's initiatives, therefore, was to further ingratiate himself with the army generals. Bhutto claimed the role of saviour of the Punjab, of the Pakistan of the Quaid-i-Azam, and, beyond that, of Islam in South Asia. Bhutto's appeal was broad and deep in the metropolitan areas, as well as in the Punjab and Sindh hinterland. Even if he had not cultivated the junta, the ruling generals would have had to notice the weight of his personality among the broadest sections of the West Pakistani public. Thus, as Mujib was given to exaggerations about 'revolution' and 'secession', Bhutto was no less capable of arousing the deeper sentiments of his audiences when he declared his willingness to martyr himself in a holy cause. Bhutto's exaggerated rhetoric matched Mujib's, and his audiences were just as delirious as those addressed by the Bengali leader. The problem in all this bombast, however, was the dearth of logic and national purpose. Each politician tried to out-perform the other, and little attention was given to their political bankruptcy, or the yawning vacuum that would suck the last vestiges of meaning from the original Pakistan design.

The Bhutto Factor

Bhutto was no more a national leader than Mujib. Both were provincialists to the core, and each represented constituencies that, almost from the moment of the transfer of power, had demonstrated their discomfort with the Pakistan of Mohammad Ali Jinnah. To that extent, both Mujib and Bhutto were representatives of what Pakistan had become in the years following independence. Only the army sustained the Muslim League vision of a united Pakistan that was, nevertheless, divided geographically in to two parts and separated by one thousand miles of hostile Indian territory. That is why Ayub Khan was so much more in the tradition of the Quaid-i-Azam and the Muslim League. This is also an explanation for Ayub's insistence on perpetuating the One Unit, on centralizing power through the presidential system. It also explains why he sought to depoliticize the national ethos. Ayub tried to focus the country away from politics and toward physical development. This also explains why he drew the United States into intimate embrace, believing, as did the Americans, that economic modernization would usher in an era of modified, but none the less assured, democratic development.

Ayub proved to be a bundle of contradictions. He was at once both a product of an older mindset, but also too far ahead of his time to successfully translate his vision into a people's reality. Ayub's programme of reconstruction was concerned with adapting the original Pakistan idea to contemporary conditions, but not only was he grossly misunderstood, his endeavour was complicated by the divisiveness of the Cold War, and especially the Cold War's impact on the generation of Pakistanis who attained their manhood when Pakistan became independent. And of course, in the forefront of all these complications was the conflict in the relationship with India, a relationship that was confounded by the intractable nature of the Kashmir question. The hostility generated by the Kashmir dispute made it impossible to bridge the divide between India and Pakistan, and also between East and West Pakistan. Not only did it deepen Indo-Pakistani antagonism, it guaranteed that West Pakistanis would see in the performance of their East Pakistani brethren only threat, conspiracy, and treason.

Claiming to know the most private and hidden motives of the Field Marshal, Bhutto's attack on Ayub Khan was vitriolic and relentless, and his popularity was a direct outcome of his demolition of his closest mentor and virtual shepherd. Although himself a wealthy member of the landed Sindhi aristocracy, Bhutto pilloried Ayub for his alleged support of the nation's twenty-two families, i.e., the industrial capitalists who had allegedly drained the nation's resources for their

PAKISTAN: A POLITICAL HISTORY

own private and personal purposes. Indeed, Ayub was not only linked with the exploiters, Bhutto also described the former President as being one of them. Bhutto wanted Pakistanis to know that Ayub Khan was a despicable character, totally self-serving, and without an iota of patriotism. By contrast, he projected himself as 'Simon pure', the people's friend and guide, and indeed, it would not be long before he would be addressed as the Quaid-i-Awam, the People's Leader.

It is important to note that Bhutto could not have come to the attention of the nation if Ayub Khan had not given him a platform upon which to play his part. Challenged by other Sindhi leaders, notably Ayub Khuhro, Bhutto would have remained a minor provincial figure (despite the notoriety of his father). But destiny ruled otherwise, and his supersonic rise to the highest level of Pakistani consciousness was a direct outcome of his association with Field Marshal Mohammad Ayub Khan. Bhutto achieved status during the Ayub era, and he embellished that status after Ayub's demise by continuing to hound the Field Marshal as well as ridicule his memory. Bhutto's popularity as a national leader was rooted in negativisms. The Shiva analogy would not be an exaggeration: Bhutto's elevation to the highest level of political power was a function of his destructive capacities; Bhutto destroyed people as well as ideas, institutions, and conventions. Claiming to be the vanguard of a great revolution, Bhutto fancied himself another Mao Zedong, in dress, in bearing, and as a social engineer. He also surrounded himself with persons whose convictions and aspirations dovetailed with his own.

In the beginning, Bhutto's objective was to assemble a coalition of followers representing a variety of persuasions. In time, Bhutto would demand their blind obedience and sycophancy, not their expertise or advice. But at this moment in history, he was content to consolidate his gains, to ensure his support in the army, and to press ahead with plans that would propel him into the highest office in the country.

By the time the election returns had been tallied, it was already too late to change course. Bhutto could never accept Mujib because the Bengali leader would never kowtow to the

PPP leader. More significantly, Mujib had won the election and rightfully anticipated forming the government. Bhutto's temperament, however, could never adjust to an Awami League-directed central government. It is important to note that of the two men, it was Mujib more than Bhutto who identified with the original Pakistan design. Yahya realized this, and certainly G.W. Choudhury and Governor Admiral Ahsan had drawn the same conclusion. The problem, however, was not their understanding of the two principals, it was the refusal of the army junta to entertain such a distinction. Thus, Mujib would never be permitted to demonstrate what he could do as Prime Minister, and his stubborn stand on the Six Point Programme simply provided his detractors with the justification needed to deny him his turn at the helm of Pakistani affairs.

Bhutto, on the other hand, although a representative of one of Pakistan's lesser provinces, did not conceal his national ambitions. And indeed, the junta showed no qualms in believing he could govern East as well as West Pakistan. Bhutto's condemnation of Mujib's Six Points as a declaration of secession hardly masked his real purpose. Bhutto cited his majority in West Pakistan and contrasted it with Mujib's majority in the eastern province. 'If you are going to talk about a Bangla Desh, we too, in view of our majority, can talk about Sindh Desh or Punjab Desh..in that case...where has Pakistan gone?' (Wolpert, 1993, p.150) Bhutto's question was not calculated to draw an answer, but rather to excite an emotional response. Wolpert (1993) describes how Bhutto, carried away by his own oratory, set himself apart from other Pakistani personalities, past and present. Notes Wolpert: 'he alone had the strength to stand against both superpowers and India...he was braver than the brave, bigger and tougher than any soldier or general. How could it be said that he would join with anyone or anything to destroy Pakistan?'

Not simply Mujib, but Abdul Wali Khan, the son of Abdul Ghaffar Khan, and the leader of the NWFP NAP, took umbrage at Bhutto's phrasings. Declaring that Bhutto had no standing in the Frontier province, he described the PPP leader's statements as audacious and unacceptable. So too, the retired Air Marshal, and now political leader, Asghar Khan, and

340   PAKISTAN: A POLITICAL HISTORY

Mian Mumtaz Daultana, leader of the Council Muslim League, denounced Bhutto's negativist statements. But interestingly, Bhutto did not take their criticism as an attack on his performance. All the political leaders, he argued, held the common view that Mujib should not be allowed to dismember Pakistan.

From the Bengali side of the divide, it appeared that no one in West Pakistan was prepared to acknowledge their electoral victory. The overriding popular impression in East Bengal was that of an illegitimate Pakistani government, dominated by West Pakistani soldiers, and supported by all shades of West Pakistani political opinion. Their central concern, it was said in East Bengal, was sustaining East Pakistan's servile status. Few Bengalis had reason to expect fair treatment from their countrymen in West Pakistan. Even before the elections, Bhutto had told Peerzada that Mujib's goal was 'nothing less than separation' (Choudhury, 1974, p.123). Bhutto further poisoned the relationship between Yahya and his colleagues when he told his friends in the junta that Yahya was too tolerant of Mujib, too naive, too trusting, and too likely to accept a compromise formula on the Six Points.

Thus, for one audience Bhutto could wax eloquent on the travails of the Bengalis how they had been exploited by capitalist forces, while to another he would cite Bengali failure to represent the Pakistan dream, to promote Islamic solidarity, or safeguard the nation's territorial integrity. Bhutto preached slogans that spoke of 'Islam is our Faith', 'Democracy is our Policy', and 'Socialism is our Economy', but the significance of these calls to action were lost on the Bengalis, whose major concerns had little to do with such matters. Bhutto had absolutely no appeal for the people of East Pakistan, nor could he match the speeches of Maulana Bhashani or Shaikh Mujibur Rahman. His message may have resonated among the people of the Punjab and Sindh, but it was hardly more than a whisper in East Bengal.

Nevertheless, Bhutto awakened a substantial constituency in West Pakistan. He articulated West Pakistani sentiments and reflected their complaints and aspirations. His call to liberate Kashmir was well received in the Punjab, and his connection with the youth of much of West Pakistan was undeniable. But neither his message nor the PPP strategy meant anything to the people of East Pakistan. Bhutto had certainly analysed the political conditions in the eastern province, and he knew he could never win the loyalty of the people there. This was a major dilemma for the man who wanted to rule Pakistan. Whereas he still believed it possible to overcome resistance in Balochistan and the NWFP, he understood he would never be judged a leader in Bengal.

Bhutto's frustrations with East Pakistan drove him to identify with the hardline army officers who, on the one side were not prepared to part with East Pakistan, but on the other, were not inclined to accept the loose confederation that Mujib and the Awami League were demanding. Junta ambivalence on the question, 'whither East Pakistan?' somewhat explains the failure of the martial law government to mount an all-out relief effort following the devastating cyclone. It also explains why, after the elections, plans were activated to reinforce the army garrison in the eastern province. Bhutto was generally of two minds in this matter. He needed the support of the Pakistan Army, but he was less than convinced that East Pakistan was worth saving. Nor did he believe that Pakistan could be governed from Dhaka.

The rejection of the Ayub system exaggerated the political credentials of Mujib and Bhutto. Representatives of a younger generation, each projected a radical approach to the Pakistan dilemma; each in fact postulated that there would be two Pakistan, not one, and only the colonial legacy, as represented by the armed forces, prevented them from realizing their similar but nevertheless conflicting objectives. To argue that Mujib's Six Points were incompatible with the LFO, which otherwise sustained a united Pakistan, is utter nonsense. The breakup of Pakistan could not occur without the antithesis of the Bhutto programme. It was the dialectical positioning of the two principals and their programmes that forecast the dismemberment of Pakistan, not simply the unaddressed grievances of the Awami League. The two forces represented by Mujib and Bhutto were in symbiotic relationship, the one reinforcing the other. It was this relationship that signalled the civil war that would rend the country and make it impossible, even without Indian intervention, to assure a unified future for the Pakistan state. Indeed, the army had suffered humiliation at Tashkent and because they saw the hand of New Delhi in Mujib's performance, they vowed that they would not again allow the Indians the opportunity to exploit Pakistani weaknesses.

Therefore, instead of facing the reality of two independent Pakistans, two predominantly Muslim countries within the Asian subcontinent, pride and the pursuit of personal power prevented the maturation of a civil society and led inexorably to a tragic convulsion. How much better it would have been for the Muslims of South Asia to be represented by two complementary, and moreover, co-operative Muslim states, than to allow differences over historic perceptions to override rational decision-making, and in so doing, play into the hands of their mutual nemesis. The peaceful and accommodative separation of the two wings was made impossible by men of limited vision and distorted egos. Too much history had already passed over the participants for them to choose the more meaningful options.

Yahya, with all his faults, saw the problem and he suffered personal abuse because he was prepared to take the courageous steps that the conditions demanded. So too Admiral Ahsan and General Yaqub, the last Governors of East Pakistan, counselled moderation and reconciliation prior to the storm. Both officers were conversant with the Bengali scene, and although they could never respect Mujib, they were realistic enough to understand the power of the Awami Leaguer's message and its impact on his fellow Bengalis. Yahya, Ahsan, and Yaqub were all prepared to make the necessary concessions, which meant controlling their pride, and more, facing the contemptuous assaults of their colleagues. But destiny and the junta, and Bhutto's ministrations, cancelled out their efforts. The consequence of the junta's override was the great tragedy that followed.

Prelude to Civil War

The situation was further complicated by the skyjacking of an Indian passenger plane in flight from Srinagar to New

Delhi. Landing in Lahore, the highjackers were first greeted as heroes and given their freedom, as well as a tumultuous reception. But this was not before the plane was blown up and India demanded compensation, which Pakistan refused to acknowledge. Moreover, New Delhi then took matters into its own hands and cancelled PIA overflights of its territory, thus lengthening the flight between Karachi and Dhaka by a multiple of three. Made to trace a route around India, over Sri Lanka and into East Pakistan, the restriction imposed a considerable burden on the Islamabad government's capacity to service its forces in East Pakistan. Moreover, when the decision was taken to reinforce the troops deployed in East Pakistan, it became necessary to commandeer all PIA flights, so for the foreseeable future, the only passengers moving from West to East Pakistan would be soldiers, albeit in civilian clothes, a requirement laid down by the Sri Lankan government. But more than the inconvenience and the burden this placed upon communications between the two wings of Pakistan, the situation elevated tensions between the two major subcontinental countries, and it more than fed the rumour mills of West Pakistan that New Delhi was in League with Mujib in his move to separate East Pakistan from its association with the West. Still another twist was given to the skyjacking episode when it was later argued that India had, in fact, orchestrated the incident, thus enjoying the necessary justification for its subsequent ban on Pakistani overflights of its territory. It was also during this crisis that Bhutto went to East Pakistan to meet with Mujib.

Bolstered by his election victory, and swept along by the frenzy of his followers, Mujib's public speeches had become even more demagogic, strident, and militant. Mujib's uncompromising outbursts made Yahya's task of making concessions all the more difficult, and the humiliating treatment meted out to members of the armed forces in East Pakistan, as well as Yahya's own embarrassment in trying to deal with the Awami League leader, contributed to an environment that was more confrontational than conciliatory. Moreover, Yahya did not operate alone. His colleagues were incensed by the proceedings, and Yahya was constrained from making the overtures he otherwise found necessary to preserve the integrity of Pakistan and above all, avoid the shedding of Pakistani blood.

Bhutto's performance only made a complex situation more impossible. His oratory was no less bombastic than Mujib's: stumping West Pakistan, Bhutto posed as the saviour of the Punjab, calling it the bastion of power in the country, and began hinting at there being two majority parties in the nation, and that the country needed two Prime Ministers. Yet, intensifying his intimacy with Generals Peerzada, Gul Hassan, and Omar, who he knew would never sanction two separate and distinct governments, Bhutto shifted his themes to Islam and democracy, stating that the elections should not be a prelude to the disintegration of the Muslim state. Bhutto's ever-shifting story line was more than the Generals could follow, but it nevertheless enhanced his power base for that time when he would have to shift attention from the junta to civilian authority. Bhutto sought to win over a variety of constituencies, and his nurturing of Punjabi army recruitment areas was no idle strategy. Moreover, his appeal to different sectors of the public and government, as Choudhury has said, placed him 'in position to challenge Yahya' if, in his judgment, the General 'betrayed' the national interest by promising too much to Mujib.

For his part, Mujib played a game no different from that orchestrated by Bhutto in destroying Ayub Khan. Bhutto did not give Ayub the opening he needed to press his reformation plans, and now Mujib did nothing to ease the path taken by Yahya. Bhutto was determined to bring Ayub down, and Mujib saw little lost if he facilitated the decline of Yahya Khan (Siddiqui, 1972). Neither politician, consumed by his own rhetoric and moved by the pressures of his constituency, was truly cognizant of his societal responsibilities. So blinded were both in their play for political power that neither paused to consider the needs of the country, or how his actions could be directed at reconciliation and healing.

Both Mujib and Bhutto were gifted men, the one more earthy, the other more erudite; but they were also men with enormous egos, and neither was able to transcend the limitations of his personality. Both had come to accept the idea of a larger role in a smaller circumstance; Mujib, in spite of his public declarations to the contrary, could only find contentment in an independent Bangladesh; and Bhutto, for all his national posturing, by February 1971 had resigned himself to governing a Pakistan free of the liabilities of the eastern wing.

Thus everything from this point on was mere charade. Bhutto flew to Dhaka in late January to discuss his differences with Mujib, and all that came of their meetings was the confirmation that there would be no agreement, no compromise formula, no way out of the impasse. Yahya had tried to negotiate an arrangement with Mujib a few weeks earlier but had been rebuffed. Although he had returned to Islamabad with the promise that Mujib would be Pakistan's next Prime Minister, the General was truly crestfallen and bitter. Yahya's response to Mujib's antics was to declare that he did not understand the mind of the politician. From this point forward, Yahya no longer really believed that a solution could be found to the impasse, and he deferred more and more to his brother officers and Bhutto. Yahya brought his tale of woe to Larkana, where he met privately with Bhutto, and for the PPP leader, this was his opportunity to reap advantages from Yahya's depressed state.

In his own words, Bhutto speaks of his support for the views of Generals Hamid and Peerzada, who were also present for the discussions in Larkana with Yahya. Bhutto cites their misgivings about the Six Points, but he also assured Yahya 'that we were determined to make every effort for a viable compromise' (Bhutto, 1971, p.20). In fact, with the exception of Yahya, who was heavily criticized for his efforts, there was no desire for compromise by any of the principals. Yahya was trapped by the intransigence of both Bhutto and Mujib, who although individually prepared to display flexibility in their talks with Yahya, were totally uncompromising in their relations with one another. Yahya was not in a position to cut the Gordian knot, to yield to the minimum of Mujib's demands, i.e., that the National Assembly meeting slated for 3 March be opened on schedule. Bhutto, with the support of key junta members, insisted that the convening of the Assembly be made dependent on the attendance of the two major parties, and he had ordered his PPP delegates not to participate.

With Yahya somewhat on the sidelines but compliant, the junta now accelerated and expanded the reinforcement of the army garrison in East Pakistan. 'Yahya's hold over the junta, which had never been absolute, was declining because of his failure to modify Mujib's policy. Both Ahsan and Yahya were discredited' (Choudhury, 1974, p.155). Ahsan was relieved of his command in East Pakistan and Lieutenant-General Tikka Khan was named his replacement. The civilian Shadow Cabinet also was dissolved, depriving Yahya of his token legitimacy. His attempt to retain some of the former cabinet officials as advisors met with little success. Only able to retain the services of Choudhury and former Chief Justice Cornelius, Yahya was essentially isolated from the decision-making process while the inner cabinet, that is, the army junta, now took full control of decision-making. During this period, it appeared that General Hamid might replace the beleaguered CMLA, but on reflection, the junta realized it would be the height of folly to expose the operations of the inner cabinet, especially when hard decisions needed to be made and there was already mounting criticism both at home and abroad. In other words, Yahya remained at the helm, at least in name, and it was he who was held accountable for the actions of his Byzantine administration.

The junta therefore ruled, and it was Yahya who declared that the scheduled 3 March meeting of the National Assembly would be postponed to give more time to the major political leaders to work through a formula of understanding. Bhutto's threat not to attend the session was enough to torpedo the plans that virtually all the other politicians had found acceptable. In fact, the members of the new National Assembly, including representatives from the PPP, were already arriving in Dhaka in considerable numbers. The news of the postponement, barely two days before proceedings were to commence, shocked all the delegates, but it struck the Bengalis with the force of an atomic bomb (Mascarenhas, 1972, p.91). Yahya's explanation was ambiguous and defensive but the message was clear. East Pakistan again was treated as a stepchild, almost a non-entity; its aspirations, and above all its rights, had been trampled upon by a distant authority that had lost all element of respect for function and due process. A tense and troubled province, long rocked by violence, now seethed with undisguised hatred for the masters in Islamabad. Moreover, the reaction was not confined to Dhaka. Wherever Bengalis congregated, the expression was the same; only the degree of demonstration separated one form of protest from another. The people of East Pakistan had become national, and the call went forward to metamorphose cultural identity into political experience (Jahan, 1972). The demand now was for an independent Bangladesh, with the focal point of popular anger directed against the 'treachery of the Yahya-Bhutto clique' (Mascarenhas, 1972, p.92).

If there was a formal declaration of civil war, it was Yahya's address on 1 March 1971; the first shots were verbal in nature but they were to prove just as deadly as those heard some three weeks later. The burning of the Pakistan flag and the flying of the Bangladesh standard symbolized the breakup of Quaid-i-Azam's Pakistan. The army was unprepared for the magnitude of the countrywide demonstrations and indeed, separated as they were from their reinforcements, not one thousand miles away but three thousand miles distant, the men in arms panicked. Curfews were imposed by the martial law authority, but they were ignored by the rampaging throngs that coursed through the cities, towns, and villages of the province. Nor could the army be everywhere to check the mayhem. Reports that Bengalis had assaulted non-Bengalis, that brutal displays of wanton killing and destruction were fomented by Awami League shock brigades, went unanswered as the army sought the safety of the cantonments. Mujib was perceived as orchestrating the disturbances, especially after his call to shut down the government and close all government offices was complied with. A nationwide strike brought all activity to a halt, and East Pakistan appeared perched at the very edge of total anarchy.

Lieutenant-General Tikka Khan was rushed to the troubled province to assume his assignment as Governor and CMLA; he immediately rallied his troops, instructing them that reinforcements would be arriving around the clock, but that in the meantime they should prepare themselves to meet the challenge, which he insisted emanated from New Delhi.

During the days that followed, Bengali units of the East Pakistan garrison were transferred to West Pakistan, and new units of Pathans, Punjabis, and Baloch arrived. The troops were instructed to defend themselves and they were prepared for the moment when they would assume an offensive aimed at rooting out conspiratorial elements whose purpose, they were told, was the dismemberment of Pakistan. Informed of the significant Hindu population in the province, the newly arrived *jawans*, never having visited East Pakistan before this moment, were encouraged to see the minority community as enemies of the nation and of their Islamic faith.

But such preparation for assault on the Bengali population at large was not well received among the members of the East Pakistan Rifles, where signs of disaffection began to emerge. Tikka called upon Yahya for still more troops, bragging he could tranquillize the province within twenty-four hours, once the required forces were on the ground. Yahya thereupon again spoke to the nation, declaring that his government would quell the disorder and that the National Assembly would be convened on 25 March. Yahya's message was not the palliative that might have been expected from the President of the country, but it caught Mujib at a difficult moment, and he hesitated in moving his army of common people against military headquarters where, it has been argued, they could have overwhelmed the relatively small garrison stationed there. Instead, Mujib allowed himself to enter into still another round of negotiations with Yahya, who was now very much in the grip of the junta he supposedly led. The role G.W. Choudhury had played in advising Yahya had now been surreptitiously assumed by Zulfikar Ali Bhutto, who also functioned as General Peerzada's closest political confidant.

Believing he held a winning political hand, and still believing it possible to avoid a violent showdown with the Pakistan Army, Mujib only seemed to back away from his unilateral declaration of independence when he added four more points to the six that had been the original bone of contention. They were: 1) the immediate lifting of martial law; 2) the army's return to the barracks; 3) the launching of a judicial inquiry into the army action that had resulted in heavy civilian casualties; and 4) an immediate transfer of power to the representatives elected to the National Assembly, with or without its convention, and before the framing of a constitution. These added points, however, made Yahya's task of reconciliation impossible. Time had run out, and there would be no reconciling the diametrically opposed positions. In fact, at this juncture, none of the principals truly believed that a compromise formula was possible.

Although Mujib was deadly serious in extending his latest ultimatum, he had totally misread the flow of events. Yahya had knowingly purchased what the junta believed was the necessary time to expand the East Pakistan garrison. Yahya, in effect, worked at cross-purposes with himself. Moreover, he played the role designed for him by the junta when he again flew to East Pakistan on 15 March, ostensibly to make one final attempt to hold Pakistan together.

Mujib was already addressing East Pakistan as Bangladesh when Yahya arrived. Indeed, he referred to the President of Pakistan as the 'guest of Bangladesh' (Choudhury,1974, p.161). Mujib had literally taken control of East Pakistan. All government offices answered to his directives, and those officials still loyal to the government in Islamabad found themselves under extreme pressure, or forced to seek refuge for themselves and their families. Observing the situation from West Pakistan, Bhutto publicly declared Mujib's action a violation of all understandings, and said that in the circumstances, the rule of the majority no longer obtained. Bhutto seemed to be leaning toward the recognition of two governments, but his public posturing insisted on the maintenance of Pakistan's territorial integrity.

Initially declining but then yielding to Yahya's urging, Bhutto went to Dhaka to join the President in one last effort at convincing Mujib to temper his demands and join in a government of common resolution. Yahya knew Tikka was planning a major strike against the Awami League. He also understood he was being used by the junta to distract Mujib and his followers, but he continued to hold out the possibility that a last-minute understanding could avert disaster. Moreover, he thought that if he could get Bhutto and Mujib together under his aegis, both men could be appealed to as patriotic Pakistanis, and that they would not miss this last opportunity to avoid the unthinkable. But when Bhutto flew to Dhaka on 21 March, he was confronted by angry and bitter Bengali demonstrators. All government operations had broken down, the city was in the grip of a total strike, and only hostile and vile epithets were encountered by the PPP leader and his entourage. Before meeting with Mujib, therefore, Bhutto met with Yahya so that the President could set the guidelines for the meeting.

Yahya informed Bhutto that Mujib had insisted on the immediate lifting of martial law, the convening of the National Assembly, the creation of two constitutional committees, one for East and the other for West Pakistan, the adoption of the Six Point Programme affirming East Pakistan's autonomy, and another autonomy manifesto that would be developed to serve the interests of the several provinces of West Pakistan. He also revealed that Mujib was agreeable to Yahya remaining President during the interim constitution-making period.

Bhutto knew Yahya had been sent to East Pakistan to help mask the junta's offensive strategy, and he was somewhat caught offguard by the President's apparent acceptance of Mujib's latest proposals. Bhutto saw himself being drawn into a situation wherein he could be accused by his associates in the junta of exposing or short-circuiting their plans. Bhutto, therefore, was most reluctant to sign the agreement that Yahya believed would save Pakistan and, no less important, avoid the agony of a violent confrontation. Bhutto, it is alleged, was prepared to accuse Yayha of violating a trust, but more than that, of betraying the army as well as his country. Bhutto concealed his true feelings, however, and requested time to study the agreement.

In the meantime, the PPP leader was closeted with Peerzada, Hamid, Gul Hassan, and Omar, who were all present in Dhaka. The discussions between these principals will be forever unknown, but from the course of events, it is possible to conclude that they focused attention on Yahya as much as they did on Mujib. After all, with the army assault on Awami League installations scheduled for the night of 25 March, with the troops already instructed where and who they were to strike, it was a matter of either proceeding with the operation or cancelling it in total. If the latter, then the junta would have to acknowledge Yahya's successful gambit and remove itself from the contest. Bhutto was certainly not prepared to accept that because it would expose his complicity in the matter. Instead, he argued in favour of holding to the assault schedule, and he promised his army colleagues that he would thoroughly embarrass Yahya by breaking off his talks with Mujib.

When finally Bhutto met with Mujib and Yahya on 22 March, Pakistan's fate had already been decided. Bhutto rejected the Bengali proposals, arguing that their acceptance would mean the formal and legal dismemberment of Pakistan. Yahya, according to Wolpert (1993), was playing a double game, having already agreed to use the army against the Awami League, its leaders and followers. Other accounts, however, dispute this conclusion. Yahya, it is argued, was sincere in trying to bridge the differences between the two wings (Williams, 1972). Moreover, Yahya wanted to honour the election results, which were conducted in an open and equitable manner, under the terms described in the Legal Framework Order.

East Pakistan was long the exploited fragment of the Pakistan nation. It had suffered numerous disadvantages as a consequence of independence and its economy which in the country's early stages had provided the foundation for the nation's development, did not see its burden lightened. West Pakistani and refugee entrepreneurs dominated East Bengal's commercial life, and investments were directed elsewhere, further impoverishing the province. On the political side, any move on the part of the Bengalis to represent their peculiar interests was judged treasonous in West Pakistan, and the Bengalis did not need to be reminded that their provincial election results of 1954 were rescinded, and Governor's Rule had been imposed on the province by a government representative of West-wing interests. In effect, the East Pakistanis had ample justification to demand autonomy. East Pakistan was the aggrieved party, and Bhutto might shout to the world his desire to save Pakistan from chaos, but the record reveals he did nothing during his long service in the

Ayub government to address the grievances of the people of East Bengal.

But more important, Generals Hamid, Peerzada, Omar, and Akbar Khan had all gone to East Pakistan to observe how Lieutenant-General Tikka Khan handled the situation. Tikka, after all, was expected to do what Admiral S.M. Ahsan, the former military secretary to the Quaid-i-Azam, could not do, and what Major-General Sahabzada Yaqub Khan had refused to do. Indeed, the junta had decided before Yahya's visit to Dhaka that even if Mujib yielded his Six Points, the army would still intervene. Bhutto knew the outline of the manoeuvre, and it was for that reason that he was told to remain on in Dhaka after the collapse of his talks with Mujib. Yahya had gambled that Bhutto and Mujib would find an eleventh-hour compromise, and he had lost. Now there was nothing left for him to do but to return to Islamabad and await the results of the army action.

The last minute Mujib-Bhutto-Yahya talks were programmed to fail. Before leaving Dhaka, Yahya knew the army was about to strike. Bhutto, also, was fully apprised of the situation, but remained in Dhaka so as not to give the appearance of colluding with the junta. Thus, the PPP leader was there when the assault on the university and Awami League installations was launched. Wolpert states that Bhutto tried to contact Yahya the next morning, but was surprised to learn he was already on a flight back to Islamabad. Bhutto's biographer infers that Zulfi (as he knew him) was left to witness the fires burning in Dhaka city while 'Yahya was sipping scotch and soda, at 40,000 feet over Ceylon'. The comment is gratuitous and, apparently, was drawn from a literary picture drawn by Mascarenhas earlier. The fact remains that Bhutto could well have prevented the slaughter that commenced on the night of 25 March, but chose not to do so. Indeed he truly could have been Pakistan's saviour had he not been caught up in his own fantasies and his lust for power.

Conveniently returning to West Pakistan on 26 March, Bhutto arrived at the airport in Karachi and, after disembarking from his aircraft, he uttered that fateful statement which placed him at the heart of the tragedy. 'By the grace of God Pakistan has at last been saved,' he declared.

Although there are those, like Wolpert, who would argue that Bhutto's words were misconstrued, and Bhutto himself was to argue that point, the record reveals that the PPP leader was apprised of the more intimate details of Operation Searchlight and, indeed, was himself a party to the action. J.A. Rahim, the PPP Secretary-General, and the single most important individual behind the formation of the PPP, accompanied Bhutto to Dhaka and returned with him on that fateful trip. Rahim later said that the separate PPP negotiating team which he led had gone to Dhaka with a compromise formula in hand. Unlike Bhutto, they knew nothing of the army plan to violently strike at the heart of the Awami League. He asserted that he and other members of his delegation had met with members of the Awami League, and that together they had come to an agreement on the matter of forming a government and drafting a new constitution for Pakistan (interview with the author). In fact, the negotiators had agreed on the need to draft three separate constitutions, i.e., one for East Pakistan, one for the provinces of West Pakistan, and another that would follow the federal principle and sustain Pakistan's territorial integrity. To put the plan into operation, the conferees insisted on the termination of martial law, an end to junta rule, and the establishment of a caretaker civilian government. Only Bhutto's approval was required, Mujib having given his assent. But when approached by Rahim, Bhutto vetoed their efforts. The PPP leader was on the one hand too committed to the junta, while on the other, he believed that his political future would be enhanced by the elimination of the Awami League.

For the junta, the humiliation of Agartala remained a live issue. Moreover, India was viewed as being at the heart of the East Pakistan disturbances, and the central figure in the East Pakistan resistance, namely Sheikh Mujibur Rahman, was assumed to be an Indian agent. Bhutto knew, before he returned to Karachi, that the army would arrest Mujib. Moreover, he took comfort in the thought that the army would make short work of the protestors, and with the apprehending of their leader, the way would soon be open for him to rally

the East Pakistanis opposed to the Awami League, especially
the Muslim Leaguers and members of the Jamaat-i-Islami.

Yahya did not oppose the violent action unleashed in East
Pakistan, but unlike his more hawkish and over-confident
brother officers, he would have preferred a political
settlement. Bhutto's intransigence, however, his total refusal
to accept Mujib as Pakistan's Prime Minister, his complicity
with the junta, made it impossible for Yahya to retrieve the
situation. Yahya had been warned by Ayub to watch out for
Bhutto. But after the 1970 election, Bhutto loomed large as
the most vital of the West Pakistani politicians, and that
position, as well as Bhutto's long cultivation of key members
of the junta, foreclosed any alternative arrangement Yahya
might have contemplated. Yahya did not want his troops
slaughtering unarmed Pakistani citizens, but he nevertheless
did nothing to stop it, and therefore bears major responsibility
for what followed. Yahya's radio address charging Mujib with
treason and putting full blame for the disorder on the Awami
League, while exonerating his troops from aggressive
intentions, placed the Chief Martial Law Administrator in the
middle of the calamity. The civil war in East Pakistan became
Yahya's war, just as the 1965 war had been Ayub's.

The Civil War

There were no saints in the civil war that consumed
Pakistan in 1971. Responsibility for the tragedy can be
found on all sides, within the political arena, among the
armed forces, in the bureaucracy, and throughout Pakistani
society. No war is ever simple, but civil war is the most
complex of human encounters, the most egregious, and
the most costly. In striking at the Awami League, the
Pakistan Army did more than assault a major antagonist; it
also struck at the heart of Bengali national consciousness.
This was no mere campaign against an aggressive
opponent; it was a direct attack on everything Bengali.
The West Pakistanis may have found solace in the belief
that the neutralization of Awami League influence was a
blow directed against India, but nothing could explain or
justify the brutalizing of the Bengali people. L.F.R. Williams
represents a minority opinion when he asserts that the

army was only doing its duty, that Awami League hooligans had committed 'frightful atrocities' upon innocent non-Bengalis residing in the province (Williams,1972, p.74). The Bengali units such as the East Bengal Regiment and the East Pakistan Rifles, according to Williams, were mutineers who threw in their lot with the Awami League, but not before killing off their non-Bengali commanding officers.

> It was the campaign of genocide perpetrated by the Awami League mobs, and not as the time-table of events shows, the action of the Army, which set in motion the flood of refugees seeking food, safety and shelter across the Indian border.

Following this comment, the author insists,

> a highly disciplined force like the Pakistan Army rarely gets out of hand, even when confronted by evidence of murder, rape and mutilation perpetrated on innocent civilians. Such occasional acts of personal vengeance as occurred were, I am informed by the competent authorities, dealt with by the full severity of military law (Williams,1972, pp.74-5).

Such argument need not be refuted. Mascarenhas, however, offers a totally different version of army culpability in citing the round-the-clock arrival of C-130 military transports from West Pakistan, the heavy equipment being stockpiled, and the clash between Pakistan Army units and contingents of East Pakistan Rifles on 19 March, almost a week before the launching of the major assault. In late February Mujib had warned the Bengali people that 'an artificial crisis is being fabricated to sabotage the making of the constitution' and that an army attack was imminent (Mascarenhas, 1972, p.109). The postponement of the 3 March meeting of the National Assembly was an ominous sign, and Mujib again had noted that the planes that were ferrying troops to the province might, instead, have brought the elected representatives. Mujib intimates that he was merely playing at politics; the army high command however, confirmed in their thinking by Bhutto's actions, believed that war had been declared against them and hence, against Pakistan itself. Not understanding the political game, their chosen playground could only be the battlefield.

Led by Mujib, who was in many respects a very naive individual, the Awami League leaders had sustained their negotiations with Yahya, and although they laid down certain conditions,e.g., the lifting of martial law, they also demonstrated that they could accept a compromise formula. Mujib wanted assurances and actions which showed that all the parties had accepted the election results and were prepared to acknowledge East Pakistan's many grievances. But in the absence of such actions, and in an atmosphere of rising tension, Mujib had to show his followers that he was in charge. His call for the assembling of *Sangram Parishads,* or revolutionary committees, was aimed at gaining control of the many people's organizations that had sprung up during the crisis. Given the breakdown of all government authority and services, individual groups arose to meet the needs of the population, but the Awami League was the only political organization capable of rallying these disparate elements (Ayoob and Subrahmanyan, 1972). Moreover, the raising of the Bangladesh flag on the Paltan Maidan on 23 March was the work of the Shadin Bangla Kendriya Chattra Parishad (Independent Bangladesh Central Student's Union), and it was they, not the Awami League, who declared the occasion 'Resistance Day'. It was the Awami League's task to try to bring these otherwise anarchic displays of disaffection under some form of central control, but the junta failed to see such Awami League involvement as anything more than a direct assault on the integrity of Pakistan.

From the perspective of the Pakistani junta, the flag incident was one more act of Awami League defiance and clear evidence of Mujib's complicity in a secessionist plot. The army, therefore, was even more justified in moving against those they believed were engineering a conspiracy. With hindsight, however, it is evident that the Awami League had little control over events, had made little preparation to withstand the onslaught of the Pakistan Army, and, in spite of all its highly charged public statements about its willingness to sacrifice Bengali lives, was not really ready to challenge the power of the Pakistan government, let alone a formidable armed force.

The Pakistan Army anticipated a brief campaign. On the one side, it expected to eliminate the principal bastions of Awami League power, arresting or killing its leaders, as it did with Lieutenant-Commander Muazzam Hussain, an Awami League leader and ex-naval officer who had been accused with Mujib in the Agartala Conspiracy in 1968. On the other, it expected to cow the population into submission while using East Pakistani politicians like Nurul Amin to regain control of the province. Mujib's arrest by General Mitha's Special Service Group, and the flight of other Awami League officials across the border to India, however, did not terminate the struggle. Nor did the destruction of Awami League newspaper offices, or the seizure of key rail, air, and telecommunications installations, restore the *status quo ante*. And although the army claimed it was only interested in the restoration of law and order, the murderous assaults in the middle of the night on Iqbal and Jagannath Halls, the living quarters of Dhaka University students, was an unconscionable act. So too was the rounding-up of university professors, doctors, lawyers, and writers, their removal from Dhaka, and their mass execution. The Bengalis were galvanized, not cowed, by these horrendous incidents. Confronted with what Mascarenhas has described as the beginning of a systematic and massive 'cleansing process' (Mascarenhas, 1972, p.115), the Bengalis were prepared for protracted conflict with or without the Awami League or their leaders. Indeed, the physical destruction of the Awami League was proof that the Bengali uprising was essentially spontaneous, and not the result of careful and co-ordinated planning (Chopra et al.,1971).

Moreover, even General Tikka was to acknowledge that the Awami League was but one of many actors in the unfolding scenario. Nevertheless, seeking justification for his use of brute force, the General expressed the view that the Awami League was linked to a Hindu-inspired conspiracy controlled by New Delhi. Totally neglected was the reality of the Awami League victory at the polls, an election played by junta rules and won fairly and convincingly. That the electoral winners were now to be judged traitors was too Kafkaesque to warrant further examination. Only the viciousness of the army action perpetrated against a relatively defenceless population can be noted. For Bhutto in later statements to talk of his quest for democracy was not simply hypocritical, it was nothing less than shameful and ludicrous.

So the army was launched upon a great campaign, a virtual holy war against the Hindu enemy inside East Pakistan, the Indian surrogate in the Pakistani midst. Special efforts, therefore, were made to destroy Hindu neighbourhoods, as well as to kill and intimidate the Hindu members of the larger Bengali community. 'The Hindus were marked out because the regime considered them to be Indian agents who had subverted the Muslims of East Pakistan' (Mascarenhas, 1972, p.117). But the army not only had its specific targets, it also unleashed indiscriminate assaults on the broad base of the province's minority population. For the leaders of the Pakistan Army, if the Hindus took flight and sought resettlement in India, so much the better for the long-term prospects of the East Pakistani population. Gone completely was Jinnah's articulated desire to see Muslims and Hindus live as nationals of one unified polity. The generals negated, indeed obliterated, such notions in their relentless and punishing attack. Nor were the urban-domiciled Hindus the most important target. But attempts by the army to move beyond the cantonment areas were met with stiff resistance in the countryside. And while the military establishment was able to gain control of the urban areas, the hinterland belonged to the Mukti Bahini, the Bengali Liberation Force. Moreover, given the constraints imposed on an army largely cut off from effective resupply, the vast jungle areas and riverain character of East Bengal made fighting the enemy a tedious and costly venture. While whole villages were destroyed as the Pakistan Army sought to neutralize members of the resistance, more of them remained the untouched havens of guerrilla fighters who prepared themselves for protracted conflict.

In this way, and again without Awami League mentoring, a Mukti Fauj sprang up, soon, however, to be transformed into the Mukti Bahini. Ostensibly controlled by the Awami League, and led by Colonel M.A.G. Osmani (elevated to General by the Bangladesh government in exile), the highest ranking Bengali officer remaining in East Pakistan. General

Osmani was the first to declare the independence of Bangladesh, although some would prefer to believe that Mujib did so before his arrest. Osmani found his task a virtual nightmare as he tried to organize and co-ordinate the many bands of Mukti Bahini guerrilla fighters. But even as this task proved impossible, the ill-defined structure of the Mukti Bahini made it more difficult for the Pakistan Army to target the 'miscreants', and although it was able to restore a semblance of calm in the major cities by April-May 1971, small-unit warfare raged on in the countryside (Loshak, 1971). Moreover, the establishment of a Bangladesh government-in-exile in India, and New Delhi's unconcealed sympathy and support for the Mukti Bahini and the Awami League, meant that the war would be protracted.

The Pakistani generals had opted for the use of violent force against their own citizens when all they had to do was nullify the elections and dissolve the National Assembly. New efforts at a political solution might have been attempted later (Mahmood, 1976, p.196), but army intelligence failed time and again to correctly assess the situation, and the demeanour of the generals was hardly conducive to rational decision-making. Seeking the victory that had eluded them in 1965, the army high command now saw the enemy in their own people, and they proceeded to conduct a military campaign that was unwinnable in any circumstance. As it was, the bloodletting drove millions from their homes and the bulk of the refugee community sought refuge in India.

New Delhi made it clear that they could not contend with such an influx of needy people, and they called for policies from the Pakistan government that would allow the displaced population to return to their homes. The difficulty with that demand, however, was the absence of homes to return to. The Pakistan government had also called upon the refugees to return home, but having personally witnessed the most unspeakable atrocities, the vast majority was not inclined to accept the invitation. India was, therefore, stuck with a monumental refugee problem that strained its capacity to provide even the most basic assistance. The Pakistan junta, however, ignored or brushed aside all Indian complaints. The Pakistani generals had concluded that New Delhi would adjust to the refugee situation, and that, despite India's perceived role in support of Mujib's demands, New Delhi would not dare intervene in what was deemed a civil insurrection (Ayoob et al., 1971).

With the passage of time, and in the erroneous belief that the army had successfully quelled a rebellion, Yahya did not seriously pursue a political resolution. Moreover, China's Zhou Enlai had indicated support for Pakistan should India launch an aggressive attack, and Nixon and Kissinger's China gambit in the summer of 1971 had also reactivated Yahya's diplomacy. Indeed, Yahya took pride in the forging of a link between China and the United States and, in gaining the American President's gratitude, he believed he had weathered the criticism levelled against his regime in the US Congress. With staunch allies in Beijing and Washington (although the US arms embargo was still in force), Yahya was even more firm in his belief that India would never interfere in his country's domestic affairs. Once again Yahya guessed wrong, and his intelligence proved no better, than before.

Imagining a Pakistan-United States-China Axis, New Delhi entered into a Treaty of Friendship and Co-operation with the Soviet Union, and proceeded to warn Islamabad that the conflict in East Pakistan could not be judged a local matter, given the flood of refugees that overwhelmed its aid-dispensing facilities. India provided sanctuary to the Mukti Bahini, and it also offered training and arms to Bengali guerrilla fighters. And after the declaration of an independent Bangladesh, it allowed a government-in-exile and a radio station to operate freely within its borders. India's assistance went far beyond the calls of humanitarianism, and as such, it stood in clear violation of the UN Charter and the rules of international law. But clearly the Indian assistance breathed life into a resistance movement which, although hard-pressed, continued to terrorize units of the Pakistan Army. India claimed it wanted a quick end to the hostilities, but its actions revealed it was very much interested in feeding the conflict. New Delhi was convinced that in a protracted encounter, with Pakistan's supply lines stretched and feeble, its garrison in East Pakistan could not fight a long campaign. Time, according to the Indian strategists, was on the side of the Bangladeshis so long as India was prepared to keep them supplied and in the field.

The indeterminate character of the civil war, indeed the cost of sustaining the war effort, was not made known to the people of West Pakistan. Foreign correspondents were ordered out of the war zone, and only censored, often fabricated, news was printed in Pakistani newspapers. All reporting blamed the Indians for the trouble in East Pakistan, and the West Pakistani public was led to believe that the people of East Pakistan opposed the Awami League and the guerrillas. All were described as either 'miscreants' or 'traitors', and Pakistan's cause was dramatized as serving national interests as well as those of the Islamic community. Moreover, in the name of saving country and religion, Tikka ordered General A.A.K. Niazi, who was in charge of operations in the province, to use all means at his disposal to eliminate the resistance, even if this meant burning the villages and slaughtering the inhabitants, who might be harbouring elements of the Mukti Bahini.

The actual figures of the lives lost in East Pakistan as a consequence of these actions will never be known, but estimates run from the hundreds of thousands to several million. Whichever the number, however, the bloodbath was of indescribable proportions, but none of this was conveyed to the people of West Pakistan. The Pakistan White Paper published in August 1971 was more a whitewash than a true account of the situation in East Pakistan. The government wanted everyone to believe that the fighting had subsided when, in fact, a campaign of ethnic cleansing had intensified. The outside world could not be shut out, however, and news of sustained atrocities filtered out of East Bengal in spite of all the government's efforts to manage the flow of information.

From his retreat in London, G.W. Choudhury writes about a letter he sent to Yahya pleading for an end to the killing. Yahya, he writes, replied pathetically, dilating on the insincerity of Zulfikar Ali Bhutto but lacking the will to reverse course (Choudhury, 1974, p.189). By the end of September, Yahya appeared to have abdicated all responsibility. On the other hand, Bhutto had risen in stature and, claiming to be the only true political representative of the Pakistani people, he demanded a share of the decision-making process. Peerzada, Gul Hassan, and Omar were mindful of the need to have civilian cover for their actions and they, unlike Yahya, drew Bhutto into their most intimate decision-making sessions.

In East Pakistan, the army was faced with the monsoons which made their operations virtually impossible, but the wet season was no obstacle for the Mukti Bahini. Thus the war continued, but it was obvious that it was reaching a point of stalemate. Neither side had demonstrated the capacity to subdue the other. In the meantime, the refugee population had swelled to several million, and New Delhi realized that nothing could be resolved by waiting for Pakistan to make peace with its own people. With the problems of East Bengal spilling over into a volatile West Bengal, New Delhi was compelled to act in its own interests. Believing that the pact with Moscow neutralized the Chinese threat, and with the United States government divided on support to Pakistan, the Indian Prime Minister, Indira Gandhi, decided to take forceful action.

Yahya attempted at the eleventh hour to placate India. Leaning heavily on President Richard Nixon's diplomacy, and defying his own junta, he had agreed to concessions which included the release of Mujibur Rahman, the return of the refugees under UN protection, and a pledge to address Bengali grievances. Indira, however, rejected the entreaty with the argument that the people had already spoken in the 1970 elections, and that the matter had come down to independence for Bangladesh. Convinced, that the Indians had fomented the disorder that had plunged the Bengalis into the maelstrom of war, Yahya anticipated still another Indo-Pakistan War, only this time, Pakistan would be at a gross disadvantage. Moreover, as much as Yahya looked to Washington for support, it was the American Press which featured the atrocities in East Pakistan, and American public opinion rejected any restoration of direct military aid. President Nixon had long put his faith in the Pakistani generals, but even his continuing words of encouragement could not dispel the anger registered in American circles when reports of Pakistani Army assaults on defenceless people were spread by the news media. Americans, in fact, were conditioned to look to India for relief, especially when only New Delhi was judged able to end Bengali suffering.

The attentive world was little interested in the manoeuvring of the subcontinental states, or in which of the major rivals would emerge triumphant, or how the success of one side or the other would influence the regional balance of power. Even the awareness that Moscow was supporting New Delhi failed to register Cold War points, notably because the United States was suddenly observed aligning itself with Communist China. All that really seemed to matter was the relaying of one horrific account after another, that a destitute and beleaguered people had been exposed to a terrible fate, and that the terror unleashed on 25 March by the Pakistan Army had to stop.

The fact that India was now openly calling for international recognition of Bangladesh's independence was of little consequence to those who had always perceived India as the predominant regional power. As early as 31 March 1971, the Indian parliament, at Prime Minister Gandhi's urging, had passed a resolution pledging full support to the Bangladesh freedom fighters. India made no pretences of supporting the breakup of Pakistan, nor did it, at any time, play the role of peacemaker. Efforts by the UN Secretary-General aimed at gaining Indian assistance in mediating the dispute went unanswered. On 23 November Yahya urgently appealed to the UN Secretary-General to address the matter of Indian forces that had crossed into Pakistan, but nothing materialized from that communication. Pakistan was left to fend for itself, to suffer the consequences of its own decisions, and to face the reality of yet another defeat at Indian hands.

The Indo-Pakistan War of 1971

India was virtually at war with Pakistan in the early weeks of November when Indian Army units struck across the East Pakistan frontier, inflicted casualties on Pakistani contingents, and quickly returned to base. By 21 November, however, Indian forces had eliminated Pakistan's forward emplacements, and they proceeded to dig in and await further orders. Within four days Indian Army divisions had moved all along the border with East Pakistan and, with armour and air support, they proceeded to wipe out Pakistani military units that had shelled Mukti Bahini sanctuaries in India (Zaheer, 1994). Using the Mukti Bahini, the Indians established operations inside East Pakistan and quickly neutralized the Pakistani defenders. The Pakistani generals in Dhaka knew they could not long resist a concerted drive by combined Indian forces, and urgent messages were despatched to Islamabad seeking additional assistance. The junta, however, still could not bring itself to believe that the Indian action was the beginning of a major offensive, and they concluded that the fighting would be confined to the border areas and involve no more than small unit skirmishes. The reply from headquarters, therefore, was to hold and defend, while more serious action was taken on the diplomatic front.

The Indians, however, had finalized their plan of attack, and it was to be a broadscale, major offensive with overwhelming force. The date for the frontal attack was set for 6 December, and it would not be terminated until Dhaka had fallen and the Pakistan Army had totally capitulated. The Indians set a course to end the Pakistani presence in East Bengal, and to ensure the independence of the new republic of Bangladesh. The Indian strategy was politically enhanced when, on 3 December, Pakistan air units attacked Indian military installations inside Indian territory, and New Delhi could claim that it was Pakistan that had, in fact, initiated the war. Thus when the Indian offensive began in earnest on 5 December, New Delhi could claim that it had been assaulted and had therefore taken the necessary action as a matter of self-defence.

It was, literally, no contest. India had superiority in everything, especially in logistics. The Pakistan Army, although a relatively sizeable force, was spread thin, bogged down in domestic police and counter-guerrilla operations, and hardly equipped or organized to take on the Indian forces. Moreover, resupply from West Pakistan was made impossible as Indian naval units took up blockade positions in the Bay of Bengal. Pakistani air capability was quickly eliminated, and Indian armour, despite the riverain terrain, moved virtually unopposed. Irrespective of how one defines resistance (Sisson and Rose, 1990, p.215), Indian forces passed quickly through the soft and undefended openings on East Pakistan's western border.

Nor was India content to confine its operations to East Pakistan. Although the creation of Bangladesh was a primary goal, New Delhi saw the war as an opportunity to destroy Pakistan's war-making capability. India anticipated striking in Pakistani-held Kashmir, and along the West Pakistan frontier as well. Pakistani military and communi- cations installations, as well as oil and industrial sites, were attacked by Indian air and naval units, especially in the Karachi and greater Sindh, areas. Indian forces punched their way into Sindh, and occupied land in Kashmir that would define a new line of control. The Pakistan Navy was overwhelmed in the action and a good portion of its fleet was sunk or put out of action. Oil storage depots in and around Karachi were bombed and consumed by flames, and the Pakistan Air Force, already deficient in spare parts, was effectively neutralized.

The swiftness and well-co-ordinated character of the campaign pointed to another short war; indeed, Indian strategists had projected a conflict not longer than two weeks in duration. The outside world was caught generally unprepared for the magnitude of the Indian assault, and it was certainly surprised when the civil war in East Pakistan escalated into a general war that seemed to threaten Pakistan's survival as a sovereign state. China's support for Pakistan proved to be no more than public verbalizing. Beijing avoided threatening India, and it did nothing to deflect New Delhi from its intended course. The United States also did relatively nothing. The despatch of the nuclear aircraft carrier *Enterprise* and its support ships to the Bay of Bengal was described by President Nixon as a safeguard in case Americans working and residing in East Pakistan needed to be evacuated. If the US naval presence was meant to intimidate the Indians, it certainly did not succeed. Nor did Pakistan's Muslim brethren come to the rescue. Lacking in capability as well as desire, the Muslim nations could hardly display concern for Muslim causes when the Pakistan government had itself launched an attack on Bengali Muslims. Moreover, Bangladesh had become still another Muslim state. Muslim-Hindu enmity remained an abstraction to Muslims outside the subcontinent, and also important was that India had long championed Muslim objectives as a leader of Third World causes.

The major battleground for Pakistan, therefore, was confined to the diplomatic arena, and notably to the deliberations of the UN Security Council, which had been called to address the hostilities in South Asia. And no one was better suited to lead the Pakistan delegation to the United Nations than Zulfikar Ali Bhutto. Yahya had appointed Bhutto Deputy Prime Minister just prior to the major Indian assault, and in fact it was at Bhutto's urging that the Pakistani Air Force attacked Indian bases on 3 December. Bhutto, much as he had done during the 1965 war, now again pressurized the generals to make 'total war' on India (Wolpert, 1993, p.165). By this time, Bhutto's rhetoric was known more for its fancy than its reality, but his passionate orations, and notably his sustained public appeal, swayed Pakistan's military leaders, and they launched their desperate strikes without consideration of the consequences. Pakistan was no match for India under any circumstances, and it was certainly far from making total war on any enemy, let alone the Indian behemoth. Logic, however, had long fled the scene, and the junta engaged in actions which could only be summed up in the term 'Yahya's war' (Jackson, 1975).

With Indian forces pressing their offensive toward Dhaka, and with Pakistan generally in a state of paralysis, Bhutto led a delegation to New York on 8 December. On leaving Karachi, the word-master spun a few more memorable quotations when he stated that there would be no rest until his mission had been crowned with success, and that even if it took 'a thousand years', Indian aggression against Pakistan would not be allowed to stand. Meeting with Kissinger before addressing the Security Council, Bhutto was informed that the United States had examined the options and had found Pakistan ill-equipped to meet the challenge of a full-scale Indian assault. Kissinger noted that saving Pakistan meant saving a portion of the country, that East Pakistan had been lost and could not be retrieved. Most important, Kissinger warned Bhutto that rhetoric alone would not save the situation. Conditions on the ground and in the war zone were moving to a climactic end, and what was needed was a formula that would ensure the stability and future of what remained of Pakistan when the shooting stopped.

This was not what Bhutto wanted to hear. He expected something more aggressively pointed at New Delhi and indeed, General Niazi had been ordered to put up the strongest defence in order to buy the necessary time for the Americans to make their move. Bhutto now knew the Americans were not about to move, that the *Enterprise* was stationed in the Bay of Bengal for symbolic purposes and would not assume offensive operations. Moreover, India had already demonstrated that it would not end its campaign until the Pakistani garrison in East Pakistan surrendered *en masse*. Bhutto flushed at what he considered another American betrayal. Kissinger never even hinted at lifting the arms embargo imposed on Islamabad during the 1965 War. Bhutto was angry and bitter, but the consummate Pakistani politician rose to speak to the Security Council knowing he was addressing his followers and countrymen at home, not the world's major nations.

Recognizing that defeat was staring him in the face, but confident that all the blame would be placed at the feet of Yahya and his army colleagues, the master orator made his emotional presentation. Wolpert describes Bhutto's speech as one of the longest and most sanctimonious of his political life' (Wolpert,1993, p.166). Describing the history of the subcontinent, Bhutto called the creation of Pakistan the realization of an ideal that would last 'even if it is physically destroyed'. Even the 'decimation' of 120 million people would not prevent Pakistan from re-emerging. Remembering Kissinger's admonition, and also mindful that he would return to Pakistan as the one and only person to whom virtually every Pakistani would look for future guidance, Bhutto appeared to extend his hand to India when he called for an end to their long years of bitterness. At the same time, he condemned India for creating Bangladesh, asserting that the people of East Pakistan had not been heard from, and that their deepest sentiments needed to be factored into any future equation of political forces.

Bhutto would have it every way if he could, but most of all he was preparing himself to succeed to the helm of a dismembered and demoralized country. He would, therefore, extend the olive branch to India while at the same time rallying his countrymen to a new and different experience that only he could be expected to engineer. Bhutto's presentation before the Security Council was not the organized piece expected of a political statesman. Its randomness, its contradictory character, made it difficult to follow, but one thing did not need clarification—it was Bhutto at his emotional best. Speaking again the following day, Bhutto wrote off Dhaka and with it, East Pakistan. Describing Pakistan as India's 'guinea pig', he said that India was using Pakistan to demonstrate its role as a regional power, Bhutto questioned the inability of the world body to take action against it. Then, moving from guinea pigs to rats, Bhutto declared

> I am not a rat. I have never ratted in my life. I have faced assassination attempts. I have faced imprisonments. I have always confronted crises. Today I am not ratting, but I am leaving your Security Council. I find it disgraceful to my person and my country to remain here a moment longer.

Stating that he would not legalize aggression, Bhutto, in a last burst of passion and high drama, declared he had lost all patience. 'We will fight; we will go back and fight. My country beckons me.' Tearing the papers lying on his desk and in his hands, and tossing them in the air, he strode defiantly from the chamber, declaring, 'you can take your Security Council!' (Wolpert, 1993, p.169)

Bhutto's performance meant nothing on the battlefield, where General Niazi, after first publicly stating that his troops would fight to the bitter end, quickly reversed course and indicated to his Indian counterpart that he was prepared to surrender his entire East Pakistan garrison unconditionally. The third and most costly Indo-Pakistan War was over, Bangladesh was a reality, Pakistan had been dismembered, and its junta-dominated government humiliated. Only Zulfikar Ali Bhutto emerged from the disaster intact, and in fact, stronger than ever. Bhutto returned to Pakistan in time for Yahya to announce his resignation, and for the young man from Sindh to succeed him as President of the demoralized country. Bhutto's charge was to pick up the pieces of a defeated nation whose physical state had been significantly altered, but more so, whose psychological condition needed immediate therapy.

Death and Transfiguration

The old Pakistan had died years before, but its burial was marked on 16 December 1971, when General Niazi formally surrendered his 93,000 man army to General Jagjit Singh Arora. It was a day of ignominy for Pakistan, a moment of high celebration for India. The number of Pakistani soldiers dead in the conflict was not revealed, but reports described acres of dead soldiers along the path of the Indian invasion. Pakistani forces had not surrendered without a fight and many paid the supreme price, never really knowing why they had been committed to such a hopelessly unequal struggle. Niazi spoke of the courage of his forces, but admitted the trap they had been led into by their superiors in Islamabad. Indeed, many of the dead would have been alive had it not been for Yahya's reassurances that aid, foreign aid, was on its way. Yahya, in fact, had reason to believe that Nixon would not let him down, but the American President, yielding to Kissinger's counsel, decided this was not the time nor the place for American arms to be demonstrated. The war in Vietnam was a major consideration, and the uncertainties of the subcontinent, and the meanness of the Pakistani assault on its own people, were not ignored. Thus, if Yahya gambled on the United States coming to his assistance, it was just one more of many bad calculations by the General and his inept colleagues.

Bhutto left the Security Council in a rush, but he did not return immediately to Pakistan. Flying to Florida to meet with Nixon on the yacht of his wealthy friend, he was to learn that the United States would assist him, following the transfer of power from Yahya to himself. It was only then that he returned to Pakistan, but not before meeting with the

Shah of Iran in Tehran. On his arrival at Islamabad, his supporters shouted his name, calling for long life for the PPP leader and demanding death for Yahya. The sentiments were no different in the general public, among the intelligentsia, and within the services. The junior officers were most disturbed, believing they had been betrayed and their comrades sent to either humiliating death or ignoble incarceration in Indian prisoner-of-war camps. Demanding the resignation and arrest of General Yahya Khan, they also called for the removal of the key generals in the army junta.

On arriving at army headquarters, Bhutto was met by broken men. Peerzada and Hamid had lost their swagger and acknowledged the termination of their careers. They would be satisfied to visit all the blame for the national tragedy on Yahya, if they could only quietly opt for retirement. Finally, at this late hour, almost two years after the 1970 national election and not before the country had been ripped asunder, the generals were ready to pass the mantle of governance to elected civilian officials. In the absence of East Pakistan, the representatives of the four West Pakistan provinces would comprise the National Assembly, and after Yahya announced his resignation, Zulfikar Ali Bhutto, leader of the Pakistan People's Party and the only unchallenged leader of a 'national' political organization in all of Pakistan, took the oath of office as Pakistan's first civilian President in almost fourteen years. It was 20 December 1971, and the Bhutto years had begun.

CHAPTER 9

THE BHUTTO LEGACY

Pakistan was thrust into history by a panoply of forces that left little time, if any, for a 'citizenry' to acclimatize itself to new circumstances and situations. Wayne Wilcox has argued that the refugee community which bore major responsibility for the creation of Pakistan 'pushed' their way in while others, indigenous to the territories that became Pakistan, were 'pulled' into a new socio-political and economic structure (Wilcox, 1977, p.27-8) But no matter how the formative period is viewed, it is clear that no war of national liberation galvanized the Indian Muslims. Few of them were aware of the magnitude of the 'Freedom Movement', and even fewer were concerned with the difficulties in constructing a new sovereign state in South Asia. The enthusiasm for an independent Pakistan came not from the people residing in the regions 'assigned' to the Muslim state, but from Muslims living in the upper Ganges Valley. Pakistan crystallized around the notion of an ill-defined Islamic state, which aimed at bridging the Muslims of the Gangetic Plain with those residing in the Indus Valley and along the mountainous, north-western limits of the subcontinent. The mobile Muslims, those who left their homes in an India dominated by Hindus, became the bridge-builders of a curious two-part federation, linking otherwise disparate regions that shared only their Muslim faith, a few common leaders, some similar views about the threat posed by an India devoid of British tutelage, and an imported language, namely English, that articulated their Great Leader's aspirations and intentions.

Pakistan's major architects were either dead or isolated within five years of the state's formation. However, it was not their vision, but the realities of communal tragedy, that influenced the direction of those who assumed their roles. No over-arching vision fueled their spirit or motivated their behaviour. No blueprint guided their actions or made them conversant with national experience. Even in the absence of a liberation war, the creation of Pakistan had cost an estimated one to three million lives, and caused the flight of millions on both sides of the partition line. In addition to the social dislocations, independence fractured the economies of the Punjab and Bengal, precious possessions and property were lost throughout the northern half of the subcontinent, and deep-seated enmities were formed that made permanent foes of the new neighbouring states.

The British left India with the sound of bagpipes in their ears, with their honour intact, and with their memories of a job well done. But the violence that Indians visited upon one another, as the last Union Jack was being lowered and ceremonially folded, deprived the recipients of independence with the needed opportunity to glorify their achievement, to consecrate their union, and to acclaim their national identity. The British returned to Old Albion as celebrated heroes of a 'civilizing mission', but there was little that was civil in the slaughter of the innocent and most helpless inhabitants of the subcontinent.

Pakistan was a dream that in subsequent years was transformed into a nightmare by men of personal ambition and petty pursuits. The refugees who flooded into the country left behind the legacies of their fathers, more than likely their kith and kin, and their more familiar lifestyles. They had reason to expect a new, even if difficult, beginning to their lives. The refugee encounter with those long domiciled in what was now Pakistan, however, was not the idealistic musings of poetic nationalists, but the realities of a human condition that viewed the sudden rush of newcomers as a disruptive intrusion. The melding of the settled and mobile communities did not occur, nor was it possible to integrate peoples of varying traditions and habits. Muslims did not blend with Hindus in a design of national making any better than one of imperial prescription. Nor could bridges be built between the Muslim population of the lush Ganges Delta and those in the semi-barren lands of the Indus Valley. Islam provided Pakistan with its ethos, but it could not promote the metamorphosis of a national culture. 'Islam in Danger' was aimed more at the British rulers of India than the people who were transformed into Pakistanis. The Muslim League convinced the Europeans to accept the painful division of their crown jewel, but it offered little in the formation of a coherent polity or civil society.

The resentment between and within the subcontinental regions that became Pakistan was manifested by those already there against those newly-arrived, and by those representing one sectoral experience against those expressing another. Essentially agrarian, the people of Pakistan who possessed or worked the land were ever fearful of losing their rights to interlopers whose claims they refused to understand. Power structures long in place were threatened by new arrangements and procedures that were too often arbitrarily dictated, or so ambiguous that they could not be coherently executed. Pakistan emerged in the years after the transfer of power not as a national community focused on compromise and consensus-building, but as a house divided against itself, a society wherein local and parochial expressions poisoned the wellsprings of national unity and perpetuated social divisiveness.

Even rivalry with India was less than a shared experience. Although it motivated a military response, popular understanding of the contest escaped most Pakistanis. Arguing the state's weakness *vis-à-vis* its larger neighbour, fear of Indian aggression was solidified in the dispute over the final dispensation in Kashmir. The early confrontation and protracted failure to close the Kashmir issue energized the hostility between the two states, denied the possibility of an equitable and rational settlement, and guaranteed the expansion of military establishments at great cost to the economic and political well-being of India, as well as Pakistan.

The Pakistan Army's intrusive role in the politics of the country was programmed by questions unresolved by partition, and the unfolding drama merely exaggerated the importance of the men in uniform. That the Pakistan Army prompted the nation's darkest hour, that a military junta bore primary responsibility for the country's humiliating dismemberment, that the army high command presided over the destruction of a unique socio-political experiment, can be traced to the gross amplification of the Kashmir question. Kashmir was sentimentalism writ large, and the Pakistani ethos paid a high price for the failure of its leaders to articulate, and hence communicate, the realities of independence to an unwary population.

Instead of centring attention on building coherence into their extraordinary nation, rather than celebrating the variety and complexity of psycho-social differences, Pakistan's leaders metamorphosed an ethos that in 1947 was supposed to be a rhapsody of diverse cultural and geographic experience, into an orgy of mindless conflict and bloodletting some twenty-five years later. As a consequence of the civil war in East Pakistan, no doubt internationalized and carefully sculpted by neighbouring India, the Pakistan that was to be, ceased to be. In the end, Pakistan survived the loss of its eastern wing, but it was a different Pakistan from that envisaged by its founding fathers. Moreover, the loss of East Pakistan ended the role played by the nation's first generation of political leaders. Those who survived to see the breakup of the nation were left with two options, either to fade into obscurity, or to accept oblivion. But it really made no difference. Their time in history had passed and their stunted record, illustrated by the duration of the military intervention, merely dramatized their ineptitude.

Pakistan's survival demanded a new generation of political leaders, but it would be a generation influenced more by the failures than by the successes of the one that preceded it. Represented by the looming presence of Zulfikar Ali Bhutto, this new generation of necessity set a different course for the Pakistan that was to be. They abandoned the original Pakistan design, and Bhutto's emergence as the Quaid-i-Awam punctuated the new beginning, even as it echoed a lost past. After more than a decade of military dominance, Bhutto's posture seemed to infer a shift from state-building to nation-building, but his idea of a People's Leader called for strength and vigour, not humility and deference. Bhutto did not come upon the scene unannounced. His ascent to the highest political office came at a time of profound crisis, but with supreme confidence in his capacity for leadership, he was absolutely certain that Pakistan could be born again. Bhutto's blueprint for Pakistan was more cerebral than intellectual, but he relished the thought of recreating the national entity. History, for Bhutto, meant that the Pakistan of the future would be the Pakistan of Zulfikar Ali Bhutto.

Bhutto and the PPP

If ever there was a leader who drew strength from the disgrace and demoralization of a nation, it was Zulfikar Ali Bhutto. Martial law remained in force after Bhutto's swearing-in ceremony as the new President of Pakistan, and given the humbling of the Pakistan Army and the disarray in its high command, he also became Chief Martial Law Administrator, the first civilian to hold such a position among the new nations. The duality and inter-relationship of the two roles illustrated the total power acquired by the PPP politician. The centralization of authority in his person, the rapt attention of those around him, and the animated popular support for his presidency, proved to be the most exhilarating experience of the young man's life.

Bhutto was born into aristocracy and nurtured to rule. He was hardly one to shrink from political opportunity. Moreover, he had had ample time to ponder the scenario which had now become reality. All his earlier actions had been predicated on the assumption that he would one day assume the leadership of Pakistan. His rejection of Ayub Khan, his decision to help in the formation of the Pakistan People's Party (PPP), his actions following the 1970 elections, and finally the civil war, taken together, had produced the moment he had always anticipated. Thus, while the nation despaired of its future, Bhutto could play the role for which he had prepared himself from the day he entered the Ayub cabinet. Almost by default, Bhutto had become the undisputed and total leader of the new Pakistan.

The PPP that Bhutto led was not a democratically organized or managed political party. Assembled in the home of Mubashir Hasan on 30 November and 1 December 1967, the PPP was the brainchild of a group of lesser-known leftist intellectuals, notably Mubashir and J.A. Rahim. Bhutto's initial impulse on leaving the Ayub government was to form a 'Forward Bloc' within the Convention Muslim League. He was dissuaded from such an action not only by the poor reception he received from high-placed Conventionists, but by Rahim, who was old enough to be Bhutto's father, and who counselled the young man to use his widespread popularity and unique oratorical gifts to lead a new party with fresh ideas and with none of the baggage of the older, more established organizations. Bhutto was never more open to advice than during this period. Rahim not only played to Bhutto's vanity, he also convinced the aristocrat that his major task was the mobilization of the masses, beginning with the politically-active youth of West Pakistan who had already identified him as their chosen leader.

Bhutto soon realized that if he could gather support from the dynamic elements in the general population, the more entrenched political interests would soon see the necessity of doing business with him. Bhutto, therefore, found the PPP a useful vehicle in the mobilization of his already considerable following. Bhutto's success at the polls in the Punjab and Sindh confirmed the thinking of his political advisers; it also brought key officers of the army under his spell. Basking in popular acclaim following the 1970 elections, Bhutto refused to acknowledge the even greater success of the Awami League. Instead of consolidating his gains in West Pakistan and sanctioning Mujib's right to form Pakistan's first civilian government since 1958, Bhutto, working in tandem with the country's military dictators, sustained martial law As a consequence, Mujib was never tested, albeit he was not given the opportunity to fail.

Had Bhutto demonstrated a degree of humility and some measure of self-control, he would have realized that Mujib would have prepared the ground for his inevitable succession. Moreover, if the procedural aspects of the succession had been followed, Mujib would have assumed responsibility for the government, but given the vagaries of the Pakistani political process, in time he would have fallen, and indeed,

Bhutto would have succeeded him. If Bhutto had been ready to show a little patience, his political legitimacy would have been assured, and the country would have avoided both a terrible civil war and the national humiliation that came with dismemberment. But the man from Sindh was too blinded by personal ambition, and far too impatient to allow matters to take their course. Bhutto's veto of Mujib's right to form the government was not what his PPP mentors advised, but by this time Bhutto was no longer in need of advice, and he virtually ignored the counsel offered by his PPP colleagues. Long wedded to a military strategy, Bhutto chose the intimacies of the army over those of his party (Syed, 1982).

Bhutto was intoxicated with power following his succession to the presidency. His meteoric rise in the country's military-political power structure had set him apart from others in the PPP. No Pakistani leader since Jinnah had attracted so wide an array of followers. And even more than Jinnah, Bhutto, acting as Chief Martial Law Administrator, dominated the permanent services. The civil bureaucracy was placed at his beck and call, and the leaders of the armed forces served strictly at his pleasure. In such circumstances, the PPP organization was little more than an afterthought. If ever a Pakistani ruler wielded absolute power, it was Zulfikar Ali Bhutto immediately following the 1971 war with India.

How Bhutto might have used his awesome powers to recreate the Pakistan experience remained to be determined, but an outline is found in the PPP's Foundation Documents. Authored by J.A. Rahim and Mubashir Hasan, the documents address Pakistan's attempt to merge Islam with socialist ideas and liberal democratic values. Moreover, the drafters of the documents believed that Bhutto was wedded to the form and substance of the PPP manifesto, and that his first concern would be their translation into workable policy. Primarily concerned with the nation's unbalanced economic development, the PPP set a course that claimed to serve the interests of the masses, not the 'captains of industry' who, it was said, had pillaged the country and left the people more destitute than during the period of colonialism. As Anwar Syed has noted, the 'wholesale plundering of the nation could not be called progress' (Syed, 1977, p.77). The Foundation

Documents were, therefore, radical in tone and content, reflecting the leftist orientation of the drafters, and although Bhutto seemed to echo their significance, his alliance with the army raised serious questions about his real intentions and inclinations.

Bhutto adapted socialist expressions, exploited his intimacy with China, and postured as a great reformer in the tradition of the charismatic Mao Zedong. But the Chinese experience with social renewal in no way paralleled the liberal democracy that was central to the philosophy of the PPP. Moreover, while Bhutto gave lip service to the rights of free expression and assembly, he was more comfortable dictating programmes that influenced a form of political behaviour which encouraged subservience. Bhutto demanded total obedience from his subordinates and, given his supreme position, he rejected any sharing of responsibilities among would-be equals. Even the notion of being first among equals did not suit him. Bhutto anticipated and demanded fawning loyalty and unquestioning respect from those immediately around him, as well as virtual homage from the masses. Bhutto sensed the power of his person, and even when martial law was lifted he could not shed the role of the determined autocrat.

Combining Islamic tradition and values with secular socialist thought was more the work of the PPP inner circle than that of Zulfikar Ali Bhutto. 'Islamic Socialism', however, was made synonymous with Bhutto's notionalizing about jihad, or holy war (Bhutto, 1973). Jihad was interpreted as applying to everyday human struggle the dedication needed if great goals were to be brought within reach. According to PPP doctrine:

> Jihad means eternal struggle for the expansion of man's creative capabilities and the safeguarding of decent values. It means abolishing artificial distinctions and making righteousness the criterion of honour among men, and establishing a democratic and egalitarian social order (*Foundation Documents of the Pakistan People's Party*, November 1967, p.7).

The envisioned jihad called upon the masses to respond affirmatively to the leadership of the PPP, with the promise that their support would usher in a new age for Pakistan and its otherwise forgotten and neglected people.

PPP appeal, therefore, was both abstract and pragmatic. The party's purpose was said to be social change, not a socialist revolution, but following the loss of East Pakistan and the collapse of the ruling junta, Bhutto cast all such ideas to the wind and proceeded to follow a course that he believed strengthened the redesigned Pakistan state. That course was more personal than institutional. Bhutto's landlord credentials, in fact his *wadera* circumstances, influenced the style of his rule. Always the patron, Bhutto was well-suited for Pakistan's viceregal tradition, and he instinctively ruled Pakistan as he did his Sindhi Larkana estate. Bhutto avoided the 'saint's role' in subcontinent parlance, and was more comfortable in guiding the people as a shepherd would tend to his flock, or a squire would succour his peasants.

Bhutto's temperament prevented him from becoming one with the people, meeting them at their level, or forming intimacies that were personal and sentimental. Bhutto insisted on all the trappings of the Great Leader, i.e., the mystique as well as the imperial mantle; indeed, he convinced himself that he was both the popular sage and the people's light. His Islamic Socialism sought to harmonize the mundane world with that of the profane, and the more successful he became at doing so, the more he distanced himself from both PPP doctrine as well as his colleagues. Thus, Bhutto would not hesitate to nationalize the economy, and his assault on the urbane *nouveau riche* was dramatic and decisive. According to PPP directives, the right to private property would always be subordinate to the interests of the community, and Bhutto used this idea to threaten or reduce the power of his real and imagined adversaries in the more sophisticated metropolitan centres. The new President, however, carefully separated communism from his emphasis on socialism. His socialist regime, it was said, would never threaten Islamic tradition, and it was often repeated that no law would be enacted that was repugnant to Islam.

Bhutto's overall purpose was the construction of a permanent majority that would ensure the longevity of his administration. Competitive politics were a means to an end, not central to his concerns. In his view, Pakistan required stable, effective, and enlightened leadership, not the give-

and-take of rival political parties. Conversant with the political conditions that had produced Ayub Khan, he was reluctant to open the political process to those for whom he had little respect, even if their political bona fides were no less sound than his own. Moreover, believing that the army posed no threat to his political ambitions, and that only the country's resurrected politicians challenged his authority or questioned his actions, Bhutto was forced to contend with those politicians who, like him, had organized followings. With the 1970 election results framing the revived political activity, Bhutto had to acknowledge that the frontier provinces had chosen other guides to lead them. How to wean the people of the NWFP and Balochistan from their local heroes and toward himself was not something he had fully contemplated. Bhutto's nemesis in the NWFP, Wali Khan, had vociferously opposed the PPP leader, and he was too towering a figure in his own right to lay himself at the feet of Zulfikar Ali Bhutto. So too, the *Sardars* of Balochistan, the tribal leaders whose paternalistic influence over their people was ever so much the measure of Bhutto's charm in Sindh or the Punjab.

Unable to win the periphery, Bhutto concentrated on the core of his power, and the core was in large part comprised of men with independent mindsets (Husain, 1972). Bhutto's vision verged on something resembling the *wali faqih,* or law-giver, but it was not mirrored in the behaviour of the men who built the Pakistan People's Party. Soon after the 1970 elections, cracks appeared in the PPP ranks. Ahmad Raza Kasuri, a noted jurist and man of letters, opposed Bhutto's decision to ignore Yahya's 3 March call for the formation of the National Assembly, and thus exposed himself to Bhutto's wrath. He eventually quit the party to join the opposition. Mukhtar Rana, another independently-minded political figure with a reputation for socialist militancy, targeted what he described as the 'fascist character' of the PPP, whereupon Bhutto, as Chief Martial Law Administrator, wasted no time in having him arrested and sentenced to five years rigorous imprisonment. Still another PPP stalwart, Meraj Mohammad Khan, a political activist and labour leader, likewise publicly accused Bhutto of converting the PPP into a fascist organization and the country into a dictatorship. He, too, was arrested and confined to a jail cell.

Arguing that party indiscipline, not his own behaviour, called for stern action, Bhutto ordered more than thirty PPP members of the National Assembly to tender their resignations. When they resisted the order and were joined by some twenty other MNAs, the clash between Bhutto and his party colleagues could not be mediated. Many bolted from the party and were hounded by Bhutto's Federal Security Force (FSF), an offshoot of the Special Police Establishment. The ranks of the FSF were filled by generally repulsive former members of the police and military communities, and more sensitive PPP members were appalled that Bhutto would countenance the formation of such a force. Moreover, because he saw fit to mobilize the FSF and turn it against friend and foe alike, Bhutto lost the services of a number of high-placed members of the PPP, one of whom was his Law Minister, Mahmud Ali Qasuri.

PPP weakness seemed to provoke and intensify political violence elsewhere in the country. Political murders and assassinations became routine. Labour leaders were killed in their offices or in their homes. The Speaker of the Balochistan Assembly and a member of the opposition were shot dead. The venerable leader of the NAP in Balochistan, A.S. Achakzai, was assassinated. Attempts were made on the lives of Wali Khan, the NWFP leader, and Asghar Khan, the mentor of the Tehrik-i-Istiqlal. Members of the Jamaat-i-Islami were also targeted, and some Jamaat officials were murdered while others barely survived the beatings inflicted upon them by unnamed thugs who were assumed to be members of the FSF. The elevation of political violence was observed in quantum terms, and much of it was attributed to the lawlessness unleashed by the Bhutto administration.

The attacks on lawyers, journalists, and virtually anyone engaged in public life, aroused the editor of Outlook, I.H. Burney, to jump-start his magazine. He had earlier taken on the Ayub government and been banned for his outspoken views. Now Burney took the field again, just as the Bhutto administration was assailing its critics. In his initial editorial, Burney cites the government's closing of three periodicals that had been critical of its actions. Later, noting the malevolent character of the PPP, he laments that Pakistan seems 'fated' to coexist with authoritarianism. Unafraid to

challenge the perpetrators of official wrongdoing, Burney
drew the anger of the party, and notably its Chairman, but he
nevertheless continued to write about the disarray in the
government party, as well as its corrupt and violent practices.
Arguing that the PPP was incapable of leading the nation in
troubled times, he urged his readers to rise to the occasion
and sweep the 'rascals' from power. But in the end it was
Burney who was swept away. His voice was silenced much
as it had been during the Ayub era, but this time his weekly
magazine would never resurface.

Burney's pleas, however, found support even in PPP
ranks: the disillusioned President of the Punjab PPP, Malik
Meraj Khalid, declared that his party had been discredited
in the eyes of the public, and that if it did not correct its
course, the country's suffering was destined to increase.
Meraj Khalid recalled the high expectations of the general
population following Bhutto's assumption of power, and
lamented that the organization's lofty goals had been
prostituted by some of the most corrupt political operatives
ever to walk upon Pakistan's political stage. Still believing
his Chairman could light the way out of the deepening
morass, he called upon Bhutto to restore the organization's
faith in itself.

PPP secretariat files which were scrutinized by Anwar
Syed (1977) reveal that Bhutto had cautioned his colleagues
against ambitious displays of power. The papers describe the
PPP Chairman as a concerned leader who anticipated nothing
but honest performance from his subordinates. Nevertheless,
the same records reveal that Bhutto was apprised of the
many malpractices but did virtually nothing to correct them.

Noting the conditions during the period of Bhutto's
administration, Burney wrote:

> In a society where corruption prevails at every level and there is
> little legitimate redress of grievances, the PPP's gradual
> transformation from an 'awami' party to a party of 'People's
> Guards' is not condonable by any standards.

And the author continues:

> The past eighteen months have seen such a disproportionate increase
> in cases of persecution and harassment that even to contemplate it is
> harrowing. Hardly a day passes without some political arrest or

victimization while crime rages comparatively unchecked on the streets (Burney, 1996, p.378).

Bhutto was hardly oblivious to the hooliganism that had overwhelmed Pakistani society. Syed reports examining a note that Bhutto sent his cousin Mumtaz Ali Bhutto which appears to show concern about the reign of terror visited upon the inhabitants of Sindh province, and the patronizing attitude of PPP officials to the utterly lawless. Bhutto sent a similar memo to the Punjab's Governor Khar that deplored the use of firearms against malcontents and members of the opposition. 'For the most trivial of things pistols are drawn and flashed,' he wrote (Syed, 1977, p.111). But instead of outright denunciation of these conditions, Bhutto acknowledged that in some circumstances it might well be necessary to use intimidation or even violence. Clearly, violence was justified when all other means had been exhausted. Syed notes:

> like many politicians, he (Bhutto) probably believed that in his craft an excess even of virtue is to be avoided, and that a certain amount of factionalism, graft, and arm-twisting are not only unavoidable but useful (Syed, 1977, p.112).

The issue, however, was not 'arm-twisting', but rather the widespread and official use of terror and violence.

Bhutto was not committed to the PPP. The organization was merely the vehicle of his success and the source of his legitimacy. Needless to stress, Bhutto considered himself above party politics, and although he was prepared to exploit its role in the post-civil war Pakistan, he allowed the party to wash aimlessly against the different shores of its composition.

International Dimensions

Soon after the transfer of power from Yahya, Bhutto released Mujib from captivity and allowed him to make his return journey to Bangladesh. Not yet prepared to acknowledge Bangladesh's independence, Bhutto had Mujib flown to London, from where Mujib made his way back to Dhaka. Having made this gesture of reconciliation, Bhutto turned his attention to domestic matters and ordered the nationalization of ten categories of major industries, including iron and steel, basic metals, heavy engineering, heavy electrical, motor vehicles, tractors, basic chemicals, petrochemicals, cement, and public utilities. These industries came under state control and a Board of Industrial Management, chaired by Mubashir Hassan, was created to oversee the implementation of the order. The unexpected action pleased members of the PPP constituency, but it also caused a precipitous drop in Pakistan's international credit, as well as a flight of capital.

Citing the adverse reaction to his policies abroad, Bhutto criticized western financial markets, and appeared to please some of his followers when he explained that Pakistan would begin to look more favourably on China and North Korea on the one side, and the Persian Gulf states and North Africa on the other. Arguing that he was dedicated to building a people's economy, Bhutto declared that the country would prosper once freed from the manipulative features of western financial interests. Bhutto's appeal to Pakistani workers and peasants was designed not only to promote economic reform, but to counter the criticism that the loss of East Pakistan was his responsibility. Thus, simultaneous with his nationalization decree was his condemnation of Yahya Khan, whom he now freely described as 'a liar, a drunkard, and a fraud' (Wolpert, 1993, p.177). Bhutto wanted everyone to understand that the loss of East Pakistan, indeed the civil war, was the responsibility of one man, namely, Yahya Khan.

Bhutto's personal and most public attack on Yahya was juxtaposed with his promotion of General Gul Hassan, who became the army's new Commander-in-Chief. Tikka Khan, though senior to Gul Hassan, was made Army Chief of Staff, and General Akbar became Minister of State for Internal Security. The President's actions were aimed at protecting not only himself, but also those within the junta who, even more than Yahya, had made the fateful decisions in the months leading up to the civil war. Yahya offered the necessary cover for a regime that was determined to deflect criticism from itself, and making a scapegoat of the much maligned former CMLA also enabled Bhutto to neutralize potential opposition within the armed forces. Dissension and resentment within the army was deep and widespread following Niazi's surrender in Dhaka, and a divided military establishment had given Bhutto the opportunity to form his Federal Security Force. It was only later that the professional soldiers realized that the FSF had been organized as a paramilitary force, and that its operations threatened the status of the conventional services.

All of Bhutto's actions, however, were couched in terms likely to receive popular approval. The times called for drastic procedures and daring acts of statesmanship. Bhutto epitomized the indomitable leader who alone could restore Pakistani morale and purpose. Thus he found considerable support for his wooing of the world's more radical nations (Bhutto, 1969). Pakistan's association with Muammar Qaddafi and Kim Il-Sung rankled in western circles, but validated Bhutto's popular credentials at home. Bhutto severed Pakistan's ties with the British Commonwealth of Nations and the South East Asia Treaty Organization (SEATO), but he clung to membership in the Central Treaty Organization (CENTO) so as not to disturb his relations with Iran and Turkey. Mindful that the United States arms embargo imposed on Pakistan during the 1965 remained in place, Bhutto found military suppliers outside the western orbit. He also saw advantages for Pakistan among the non-aligned countries, once the nation had distanced itself from western pacts and treaty commitments.

Admission to the Non-Aligned Movement (NAM) was a major objective of the Bhutto administration; it not only projected an independent foreign policy for the country, it also provided Bhutto with a platform from which to champion Third World interests. With a degree of deftness that earned him high marks in most diplomatic circles Bhutto made a number of adventurous moves without jeopardizing Pakistan's continuing dependence on the World Bank and the International Monetary Fund.

Bhutto believed that international status would also bring domestic security and guarantee his longevity. He therefore devoted himself to the externalities of performance, while doing little to repair the damage inflicted on the national experience by his flawed administration at home. Bhutto's rule, however, coincided with the new assertiveness of the

Organization of Petroleum Exporting Countries (OPEC). The Muslim component of the oil cartel dominated the world's oil supply, and Bhutto's cultivation of Iran, Saudi Arabia, and the Arab Gulf states, as well as Libya, was predicated on drawing support from those nations in return for Pakistan's assistance in championing issues of direct concern to them. Bhutto, therefore, placed great store in the Organization of the Islamic Conference (OIC) and he was quickly recognized as one of its more articulate spokesmen.

Within a year of taking office, Bhutto opened communications with his counterpart in New Delhi. Having released Mujib from custody, and by distancing himself from the United States, he anticipated a positive reaction from Indira Gandhi. Eager to gain the repatriation of the 93,000 Pakistanis held as prisoners of war, and fearing that war crimes show trials would only reopen unhealed wounds, Bhutto impressed upon Indira the need to sort out their differences. Having already briefed his army commanders on the subject of a negotiated settlement, Bhutto believed he had the backing for the concessions he would have to make in order to obtain the return of the Pakistani soldiers. He also believed he had the support of the Pakistani masses. Bhutto had lifted martial law in April 1972, and an interim constitution had been promulgated shortly thereafter. Both actions received a positive response from the Pakistani public.

Building up his strength at home, Bhutto was confident that his discussions with the Indian leaders would also have positive results. But then an article appeared in the local journals in which Indira was quoted speaking critically of the Pakistani President. Describing Bhutto as an 'unbalanced' personality, the Indian Prime Minister seemed to question the utility of doing business with the Pakistani leader. Bhutto thereupon invited the same European journalist to Pakistan, and in a calculated manoeuvre he attacked his counterpart, calling Indira a woman of 'mediocre intelligence' and a 'diligent drudge...devoid of imagination' (Wolpert, 1993, pp.189-90). Having said this, Bhutto also revealed that he was eager to meet with the Indian Prime Minister at a place of her choosing, and to no one's surprise, in June 1972, Bhutto got his wish. Whether the entire sequence had been planned was never disclosed, but the two leaders had their celebrated meeting in the mountain resort of Simla, and hardly a critical voice emanated from the Pakistani public .

Following several days of negotiations and ceremony, the two leaders announced they had reached an understanding on the main issues before them. India agreed to withdraw from the West Pakistan territory it had occupied during the war, and Pakistan accepted a new line of control in Kashmir. For New Delhi, the latter was a definable and legal border; it also acknowledged Pakistan's continuing presence in Azad Kashmir. The much-pursued plebiscite in Kashmir was never mentioned in the Simla agreement and it was assumed, at least in India, that Pakistan had accepted the permanence of the division that left the Vale of Kashmir in India (Burke and Ziring, 1990, pp.419-20). Of more immediate importance, however, there was no mention in the Simla agreement of the 93,000 Pakistani prisoners of war, and, given the appearance of sellout, Bhutto suddenly found himself the target of mounting criticism at home.

Defending his diplomatic efforts, Bhutto cited the need for realism, denied there had been secret agreements, and insisted he continued to support self-determination for the Kashmiri Muslims (Moody, 1973). According to Wolpert, Bhutto believed he had kept faith with his people and had not abandoned Kashmir, but rather had purchased the time necessary to restore Pakistan to full strength and that, at some future date, the issue of Kashmir would be raised anew and with even greater forcefulness (Wolpert,1993, p.192). In fact, Bhutto was able to deflect the criticism of his more determined detractors. Arguing that he had little choice if he was to avoid falling under the sway of Indian power, and indeed, if he was to avoid renewing hostilities with his neighbour, Bhutto convinced enough of his supporters that the appropriate course had been followed, and given his still popular mandate, his 'opposition melted before the fire of his (oratorical) eloquence' (Wolpert,1993, p.195).

The release of the 93,000 prisoners of war, and the cancellation of plans to have the Bangladeshis try Pakistani soldiers and civilians as war criminals, were not effected until February 1974, although some prisoners were released earlier. Bhutto celebrated his two years at the helm by hosting an Islamic Summit in Lahore. For the moment at least, Bhutto could bask in the praise of the Muslim rulers and governors who journeyed to Pakistan for the historic meeting. Joined by King Faisal, Anwar el-Sadat, Hafiz al-Assad, Muammar Qaddafi, Yasser Arafat, and leaders of most of the world's Muslims countries, the glaring exception being the Shah of Iran, Bhutto used the occasion to officially recognize Bangladesh and, in so doing, to invite Mujib to join those already in attendance. Bhutto avoided mentioning Kashmir by name during the conference, confirming what many believed to be his earlier decision to accept the *status quo*. He nevertheless satisfied his eminent visitors by lashing out at Israel and by offering Pakistan's unyielding support to the Palestinians.

Bhutto called upon the Muslim nations to unite their efforts and to overcome their intra-organizational rivalries, much as he had done in welcoming Mujibur Rahman to the conference. Bhutto had crafted the perfect setting in which to demonstrate his diplomatic skills, and in the euphoria of the Summit, he convinced Mujib that he should release the remaining 93,000 Pakistani prisoners of war and cancel plans to try the 195 Pakistani military and civilian officials who had been classified as war criminals.

Bhutto was at the top of his game, but neither his speech-making, nor the ceremony, nor the lavish hospitality, could conceal Bhutto's domestic difficulties. Pakistan remained a house divided and it was Bhutto's actions, not his words, that were most revealing.

The Domestic Front

Riots had overwhelmed the metropolitan areas of Sindh. The disturbances involved the indigenous Sindhi population and the *mohajir* community. Sindhis now openly accused the *mohajirs* of monopolizing the wealth of the province. Bhutto's Sindhi credentials as well as his statements had, at least in part, sparked the Sindhi campaign against the community. Karachi had become a *mohajir*-dominant city. It was also Pakistan's commercial and banking capital. The PPP had cast the *mohajirs* as 'capitalists' and 'exploiters', and along with their growing political influence, they had all but eliminated the native Sindhi as an active player. Bhutto had used the anti-*mohajir* argument to attract Sindhi followers. He had also promised those who followed his leadership that the uneven relationship between Sindhis and *mohajirs* would be corrected. Bhutto's divide and rule policy was successful in attracting Sindhi support for the PPP, but it also made life in mixed Sindhi-*Mohajirs* neighbourhoods more unstable.

Bhutto was the first Sindhi to attain high station, and his policy of reinvigorating the Sindhi lifestyle also enlivened G.M. Syed's provincial movement for a Sindh for the Sindhis. Moreover, an inspired Sindhu Desh Movement elevated tensions in the province and precipitated violent clashes that caught the *mohajirs* unprepared. When the embattled community looked to government for assistance, they found the authorities somewhat less than sympathetic. Nor were *mohajir* commercial establishments the only targets. A campaign was launched to reject *mohajir* culture, and notably, the Urdu language. This was interpreted as an assault not only on Pakistan's official language, but on the Pakistan Movement itself. Pakistan's identity crisis was made even more complicated by these developments.

The *mohajirs* had left their families and possessions in India, preferring to make their lives in a Muslim state. They were the cutting edge of the Muslim League Movement and they took considerable pride from the formation of Pakistan. But Bhutto's emergence as Pakistan's pre-eminent leader did not augur well for the community. Indeed, Bhutto was perceived as flouting their sacrifice and positive contribution. At the Islamic Summit, Bhutto addressed the need for Islamic unity, but his failure to promote unity at home distressed the refugee community, some of whom had only recently fled the inferno of Dhaka. Moreover, many more *mohajirs* awaited repatriation to Pakistan from Bangladesh, but the Bhutto government appeared reluctant to smooth the way for their passage. Believing Bhutto and the PPP were determined to reduce their number and exaggerate ethnic differences, the *mohajirs* began to form their own self-defence force and political organization.

Bhutto's energetic support of Sindhi as an official provincial language meant there would be no peace in the province. The *mohajirs* accused Bhutto of being a Sindhi, not a Pakistani, President. Described as the 'Raja of Larkana', his divide and rule behaviour was said to be more blatant than anything practised by the British. Bhutto nevertheless remained defiant, and he personally shepherded a Sindhi language bill through the provincial legislature. The elevation of the Sindhi language was not aimed at ending ethnic conflict, however, and the killing, looting, and burning spread from Karachi to the towns and villages of the province. Bhutto held the provincial government responsible for the law and order situation, but federal forces were no more successful in getting the aroused demonstrators to make peace with their neighbours.

Bhutto insisted he had inherited a terrible legacy, and that he needed time to set matters right. Arguing that he was a fighter who would never quit, that if necessary he would sacrifice his life for Pakistan, he pleaded for understanding and patience, and promised a new and better beginning for the Muslims of the subcontinent. Long on words, Bhutto's emotional speeches continued to captivate his constituents, but his adversaries preferred to mull over Indira's description of the 'unbalanced' personality who had come to preside over the Pakistani nation. Bhutto's public record revealed a man consumed by power, so driven by personal insecurity that he could not measure the impact of his own policies. Bhutto had come upon the scene at a desperate hour for Pakistan and, although he was the popular choice to lead the country into a new era, his behaviour resembled more that of a frightened usurper, indeed a figure who had achieved his place with ill-gotten gains.

Bhutto's Sindhi strategy was replicated in the frontier regions (Amin, 1988). Initially willing to enter into a tripartite agreement with Wali Khan's National Awami Party (NAP) and Mufti Mahmood's Jamiatul-Ulema-i-Islam (JUI), the dominant forces in the NWFP and Balochistan, Bhutto betrayed them by giving their Frontier adversaries key positions in his central cabinet. Abdul Qaiyum Khan, Wali Khan's number one nemesis, was made the Home Minister and, true to form, he poisoned an earlier understanding between Bhutto and his political rival. Wali Khan had every reason to believe that the attempt on his life had been planned by Qaiyum with Bhutto's approval. Although unproven, Wali Khan warned Bhutto that he was prepared to trade bullet for bullet. After this exchange, Bhutto's visits to the NWFP could only be managed under a cloak of PPP People's Guards and FSF shock troops.

But conditions in the NWFP were tame compared to those found in Balochistan. Balochistan was never comfortable with Bhutto's rule, and within a year of the PPP takeover, the provincial government challenged Islamabad's authority to intervene in local matters. Balochistan was a region where tribalism reigned supreme, and where regional *sardars* commanded constituencies in accordance with tribal practices. Historically, the writ of the *sardars* transcended central government law, and the PPP was determined to break the back of *sardar* power once and for all. Bhutto's policies were aimed at destabilizing traditional authority, but the tribals resisted the intrusion, forcing the PPP government to escalate the effort. Islamabad described the resistance as an insurgency, and what began as a minor display of force was transformed into a major military campaign.

By January 1973 Bhutto had ordered regular army units into Balochistan, their special focus being Lasbela, where, it was said, hordes of miscreants operated. The use of the term 'miscreant' to describe the resistance to Islamabad's rule reminded observers of East Pakistan, where the identical term was used to justify the use of extreme force against Bengali nationalists.

Bhutto's order calling on the troops to again fire on their own citizens, only two years after the civil war in East Pakistan, shocked the nation. On 16 June 1973 Burney raised the fundamental question in an article in *Outlook*. 'Have we learnt no lessons from the loss of East Pakistan? Dubbing political opponents secessionists has already cost us dear.' Explaining that Islamabad 'continues to find it difficult to reconcile the aspirations of the people whose tribal loyalty and allegiance are committed to their respective *sardars*', the author notes that the hour is late, but it nevertheless calls for 'tolerance and a non-partisan approach in the greater interest of Pakistan'. But neither Burney's pleadings nor any of those asking for rational decision-making could prevent the intensification of the fighting.

Bhutto assumed the posture of an embattled national leader struggling to preserve the integrity of the nation against nefarious forces. Information given to Bhutto spoke of the formation of a Baloch Liberation Front. He was also told that the Provincial Governor, Mir Ghaus Bakhsh Khan Bizenjo, was plotting secession. Contributing to Bhutto's fears was Abdul Ghaffar Khan, Wali Khan's legendary father, who, after almost a decade in self-imposed exile, had returned to Peshawar and was greeted with a hero's welcome. His negative views on all matters Pakistani were well known, and if he had found Jinnah distasteful, he was even more outspoken in his condemnation of Zulfikar Ali Bhutto.

Believing the Baloch and Pathan nations were planning an alliance, and fearing Indian and Afghan complicity—and indeed, there were signs that the Soviet Union was also involved—Bhutto ordered the application of even more aggressive tactics.

Bhutto removed Bizenjo as Governor of Balochistan and appointed a rival, Nawab Akbar Bugti, to succeed him. He also issued an edict dissolving the Balochistan government of Sardar Ataullah Mengal. He used the occasion to sack the Governors in the NWFP and Sindh as well, thus stirring up more controversy and, more importantly, destroying the PPP accord with the NAP-JUI that had been entered into earlier. Determined to tighten his control of the frontier provinces, Bhutto swept aside the elected governments and imposed PPP rule on the region. He also ordered General Tikka Khan to lead Pakistan Army units against the tribal resistance in Balochistan. The reputed 'Butcher of Bengal' was now given another moniker, namely, the 'Butcher of Balochistan'.

Bhutto also revealed that he had made Tikka the new head of the Pakistan Army after Gul Hassan, the erstwhile chief, was accused of 'Bonapartist' activities. Clearly, Gul Hassan had objected to the use of Pakistani soldiers in Balochistan, and had paid the price for his disloyalty. Through it all, Bhutto held to his refrain of building democracy in Pakistan, blaming evil elements, not himself, for the delay. Always defiant, Bhutto declared he would use all the force necessary to deny those who would threaten Pakistan's territorial integrity. After learning of Bhutto's statement, Wali Khan's response was simple and to the point. Describing the PPP leader as 'Adolph Bhutto', he said Bhutto's real objective was Pakistan's conversion to a fascist state.

The war in Balochistan demonstrated that Pakistanis were not yet a national people, that no lessons had been learned in East Pakistan, and that the Pakistan design remained a flawed vision. The nationalities dilemma was but one major element in the scenario. The problems posed by Sindhis and *mohajirs* revealed that the problem of national integration was more than an assertion of regionalism. Moreover Islam, although spiritually bracing across a broad spectrum of humanity, was nevertheless of lesser consequence in the formation of national consciousness. Pakistan suffered from conceptual deformities, as well as a paucity of national leaders. It should have been recognized much earlier that Pakistan was not a traditional nation-state. Regional loyalties were historically rooted in the experience of the subcontinent, and the formation of Pakistan had not altered relationships between local leaders and their followers. References to democracy no doubt captured the attention of urban populations, but they had little impact on rural people, who clung to the intimacies of their inter-personal relationships.

The formation of the United Democratic Front (UDF) that linked Wali Khan's NAP with the Sindhi Pir of Pagaro's Muslim League and Maulana Maudoodi's Jamaat-i-Islami was provoked by the war in Balochistan and, although facing great odds, the coalition worked to end the bloodletting. Bhutto, however, saw the UDF as a threat to his office and he ordered the Federal Security Force to stifle it. Indeed, throughout his tenure, Bhutto was more inclined to use coercive rather than persuasive powers.

In addition to the ubiquitous FSF, Bhutto frequently used the army to douse the fires he or his followers had either fanned or set. The Chairman's hand was obvious in the Sindh language riots and the Karachi labour disturbances in 1972, in Balochistan from 1972 onward, in the NWFP in 1976, and in the movement that became his ultimate undoing in 1977. Moreover, the Ahmedi controversy was needlessly intensified when the Pakistan National Assembly, at Bhutto's urging, declared the Ahmedi to be non-Muslims. The renewal of anti-Ahmedi rioting in June 1974 was a direct consequence of this legislative action (Ziring, 1980).

The New Constitutional Order

A new constitution was presented to Bhutto on 12 April 1973, by the Speaker of the National Assembly, Fazal Elahi Chaudry, the mild-mannered man whom Bhutto had personally chosen to be the country's new head of state. Bhutto had pressed for the creation of a presidential political system, but the PPP leaders were more inclined to revive the parliamentary experiment terminated by martial law in 1958. Bhutto yielded to his colleagues when he was assured that all significant powers would be centred in the office of the Prime Minister, and that the President would only be given ceremonial functions.

The constitution was not without controversy, but given the heavy PPP majority, opposition input was minimal. In fact, the opposition was left to debate the degree to which Pakistan should be described as an Islamic state, but it had few opportunities to question the empowerment of the Prime Minister. Thus, it was left to the more conservative orders to demand the application of Islamic penalties for criminal acts, or to call for limitations on the activities of women. The inclusion in the constitution of the statement that: 'all existing laws shall be brought into conformity with the injunctions of Islam as laid down in the Holy Qur'an and Sunnah...and no law shall be enacted which is repugnant to injunctions of Islam' (Article 227) was a consequence of these labours.

The incorporation of an Islamic Council in the document was also the work of the fundamentalist orders. The Council mirrored the one established by the Ayub Constitution, but its powers were strictly advisory and it was not empowered to interfere with secular performance. In fact, neither the National Assembly nor the provincial legislatures were obligated to accept the advice of the Islamic Council, and nothing prevented the legislative bodies from taking actions with or without its sanction. The 1973 Constitution also specified that only a Muslim could become President, and other sections in the Constitution referred to Islamic principles and policy. Bhutto was comfortable with all these provisions, especially with Article 40, which included a provision that the state 'shall endeavour to preserve and strengthen fraternal relations among the Muslim countries based on Islamic unity'.

Article 1 of the 1973 Constitution, therefore, described Pakistan as an Islamic Republic. Article 2 declared Islam to be the state religion of Pakistan, and Bhutto had no difficulty with any of these provisions. Moreover, none of the references to Islam infringed on his powers. The 1973 document, like the Ayub Constitution of 1962, reflected the interests of the maximum ruler, and from Bhutto's point of view, it was challenge-proof. Thus, the parliamentary system was crafted to buttress Bhutto's executive powers, and the Assembly was literally prevented from questioning the Prime Minister's behaviour or actions. The assignment of virtually absolute power to the head of government, however, caused the resignation of the Law Minister and provoked an opposition boycott of the closing proceedings.

Bhutto justified his extraordinary powers by citing the country's instability in the wake of war and dismemberment. Promising that the nation would one day develop full-blown democratic institutions, he pleaded for time and the opportunity to set a proper course. Parliamentary systems were exemplary in circumstances of extended tranquillity, he said, but Pakistan was a turbulent nation, and free expression was more likely to do harm than good. Although Bhutto avoided terms like 'basic democracy', he said it was necessary to limit attacks on his policies if the needed reforms were be implemented. Denied a presidential system, Bhutto had, in fact, argued for a submissive legislature, and his PPP followers had granted his wishes. The new parliament, therefore, was an institution in form and name, but it lacked substance, and it possessed none of the powers associated with such institutions. Wali Khan, speaking for the opposition, noted that Bhutto had been placed above reproach or scrutiny, and he said the matter would have to be taken into the streets, where the people could voice their opposition to what he described as an imperial Prime Minister. In a May 1974 article, Burney commented on Bhutto's intention to rule Pakistan 'for a minimum of eleven years'. The constitution had given him 'a straight run of six years', and he visualized a second term in a country 'where democratic institutions stand discredited and where they are further denigrated as a matter of policy'.

Bhutto wanted a constitution, but more than that, he wanted a political system that acknowledged his paramountcy. Operating on the basis of viceregalism, supposedly protected by the trappings of constitutional legitimacy, politically unchallenged at the national level, and surrounded by layers of security, Bhutto anticipated governing Pakistan almost indefinitely. But that expectation was threatened by the strife in the frontier provinces, and especially the raging conflict in Balochistan. Marri and Mengal Balochis continued to resist the central government intrusion, and sympathetic Punjabis and Pathans also volunteered their services. Bhutto's tactics were to divide the Baloch by siding with Governor Bugti against Sardar Mengal and Nawab Khair Bakhsh Marri, but his actions only intensified the struggle. In the unfolding circumstances, Bugti found governing the province an impossible chore, and scores were settled on the battlefield, not in the provincial legislature.

Moreover, the *coup* in Afghanistan that was perpetrated by Sardar Daud against his cousin, King Zahir Shah, in July 1973, was cause for more concern in Pakistan. Daud, more than any other high-ranking Afghan, had promoted the idea of an independent 'Pakhtunistan'. With the insurgency in Balochistan at an intense level, the seizure of the Kabul government by an old nemesis of Pakistan was viewed with alarm. Bhutto quickly recognized the new government and called upon Daud to assist in the pacification of their mutual frontier. Daud's positive response was a boost to Bhutto's morale, and on 14 August 1973 Bhutto yielded the Presidency and assumed his new the role as Pakistan's Prime Minister under the terms of the 1973 Constitution. Addressing the nation on that occasion, the Chairman of the PPP called for peace and co-operation, for national solidarity, and the development of democratic practices. But he had also just signed an order that directed the Balochistan Governor to arrest the leaders of the provincial opposition.

The PPP: A Crumbling Edifice

The men who created the PPP and the one man who could lead it to victory were never truly compatible. 'The enemy of my enemy is my friend', perhaps defines their relations; at best the leadership of the PPP was a marriage of convenience, a marriage that fell apart even before it was consummated. The central issue revolved around those members of the party who saw the opportunity to recast Pakistan as a country deeply committed to social issues, and a party Chairman whose major objective was the creation of a personality cult. The interaction between the organizers and the leader of the PPP was the powerlessness of the former and the almost absolute power of the latter. Rahim, Mubashir, Kasuri, Mairaj, and Rana pressed for the drafting of a parliamentary constitution, believing it would elevate their social objectives and at the same time restrict the otherwise freewheeling powers of Zulfikar Ali Bhutto. Bhutto yielded to their wishes, but not until he was assured of his mastery of the political process. Moreover, not all the PPP officials were prepared to accept the distribution of power that Bhutto demanded, and Mukhtar Rana and Mairaj Mohammad Khan, two of the more outspoken members of the party, were arrested and incarcerated without formal charges being brought against them. It was not that Bhutto was simply vindictive. He truly believed he was possessed of extraordinary abilities, that he was born to lead, and he demanded blind obedience, not alternative and hence obstructive viewpoints. In fact, Bhutto displayed little patience with those claiming to have insights that he had not himself contemplated. Therefore, Bhutto's initial opposition developed from within his own entourage, and some time before the official opposition could question his policies or direction.

The PPP was without a genuine opposition in the first three years of its taking power, but Bhutto had been thrown together with a group of men representing backgrounds and experience to which he could not readily adjust. The depth of his mistrust, his inability to overcome the fear of being used and, in time discarded, hardened his attitude; it also drove a deep wedge between himself and those members of the party faithful who were responsible for the organization's programme. The formation of the FSF was meant to protect the Chairman from his colleagues, as well as the political opposition. Moreover, the FSF was most obliging in containing, intimidating, or repressing Bhutto's real or imaginary enemies, no matter who they were.

The FSF was assembled largely from among the discredited members of the armed forces and police. Too often they were men of base reputation or persons who had, in one way or another, compromised their callings. Made responsible for securing the life of the Chairman of the PPP, they took their mission seriously, and quickly gained a reputation for excessive behaviour. The escalation in political murders was traced to the operations of the FSF. It was also held responsible for the arbitrary seizure of property, the surveillance of the regime's enemies, the bugging of telephone lines, and the intimidation of journalists. The original founders of the PPP had not envisaged the creation of a police state, but Bhutto's personal insecurity had shifted the emphasis away from a socialist society.

Moreover, the PPP's composition was changed when Bhutto insisted on the inclusion of landlords and industrialists in the organization. The action alienated the party's charter members and literally drove the more left-thinking radicals from the party. In July 1974 Bhutto broke with Rahim, declaring himself to be the People's Party and all its members his 'creatures' (*Outlook*, 13 July 1974, pp.7-8). Bhutto angered Rahim when he made Aziz Ahmad, a senator, a PPP member, and his Minister for Defence and Foreign Affairs. Rahim, a former civil servant, knew Aziz Ahmad personally and the two men never considered the other a friend. Rahim, therefore, accused Bhutto of destroying party ideology and morale, and he lashed out at Bhutto during a cabinet meeting. Enraged by Rahim's personal attack, Bhutto reminded the older man who was in charge, and ordered him to leave the room. (Wolpert's account differs in scene and character, not in outcome. The account described here came directly from Rahim in a personal interview at his residence in 1975).

Later, members of the FSF made a late-night visit to the

Rahim residence, ostensibly to inform him that he had been dismissed from the cabinet and had jeopardized his post as PPP Secretary-General. During the confrontation, a scuffle developed in which Rahim was severely beaten. Bhutto subsequently appointed Mubashir to succeed Rahim as Secretary-General, but the posting was done for public consumption, not the serious reorganization of the PPP.

The Pakistan People's Party was never the same following the Rahim affair. In January 1975 feeble efforts were made at redefining the party's socialist programme, but the ability to challenge the Chairman was markedly reduced by the departure of key members of the organization. Mustafa Khar, Hanif Ramay, Mubashir Hassan, Khurshid Hassan Meer, all had either been arrested, exiled, or put up to public ridicule. Even Bhutto's cousin, Mumtaz Ali Bhutto, had been forced to retreat from the political arena. Of his older and close associates, only Abdul Hafiz Pirzada, a childhood friend and Sindhi neighbour, remained at Bhutto's side. PPP confusion and disorganization was a direct and immediate consequence of Bhutto's monopolization of power. Many country-shaking events had occurred in the years following the organization of the PPP in 1967. The drawing together of students, factory workers, sharecroppers, and members of the professional and intellectual fraternity had produced the coalition that brought down the Ayub Khan regime. But the later inclusion of feudal aristocrats and industrialists strained the character of the PPP, even though Bhutto claimed that the 'capitalists and feudal lords who have joined my party have already taken an oath before me to abide by all the conditions laid down in the PPP Manifesto' (*Dawn*, 26 January 1975). Bhutto assured his party sceptics that if he could live with the new members, they too could do so.

Bhutto demanded blind faith from his followers, and given the spreading divisiveness in the country as well as within his party, signs of weakness began to emerge. Despite the heavy intimidation, Bhutto was resisted by some of his more steadfast foes. His alliance with the feudal class also revived the argument of his *wadera* lineage and upbringing—once a *wadera* always a *wadera*. The more radical elements in the PPP broke with the PPP Chairman, who was increasingly

pressurized to go to the people for a vote of confidence. It
had been five years since the 1970 election and the PPP had
never tested its popularity at the polls. Given the disarray
within the PPP, an election, it was argued, would galvanize
the organization, revitalize its ideology, and refocus its
programme. Moreover, given the fragmentation at the top of
the organization and the disaffection from below, some party
members believed an election was needed to demonstrate
that the PPP still commanded the support of the general
public.

Bhutto, however, was reluctant to put the party to an
electoral test. The party had broken into several factions,
each with its own leader, who in turn was surrounded by a
personal security force. Mustafa Khar was a prominent
example of a Punjabi PPP leader with a substantial following
and a private constabulary. His dismissal as Punjab's Chief
Minister left the province more unstable than ever, and his
successor, Hanif Ramay, could not repair the damage. Bhutto
was reluctant to inject himself into what was judged an
exclusive Punjabi contest, but he nevertheless ordered the
redrafting of the PPP manifesto so that it better reflected his
philosophy and constitutional prerogatives.

Bhutto was aware that he was losing his political base.
Moreover, a fractured PPP provided the political opposition
the opportunity to win more significant public support. Wali
Khan assumed the role of Leader of the Opposition in the
National Assembly, and he used the forum, as well as the
streets of West Pakistani cities and towns, to appeal to the
people in the most personal terms. He launched blistering
attacks on the PPP Chairman in his public meetings, many of
which were viciously interrupted by units of the FSF and
police. Wali Khan refused to be silenced, however, and his
courage motivated others, notably Asghar Khan, founder of
the Tehrik-i-Istiqlal, to add their voices to the chorus of those
deploring the use of police-state tactics. With the political
opposition intensifying its campaign, and with intimidation
of limited utility, Bhutto was more and more compelled to
seek a vote of confidence. But the venue for a test of his
popularity was not the National Assembly, where the debate
would be more deliberate and pointed, but rather in a national

election, where he could reach out to the people and, by his oratory, win their continued favour. The abstract character of an electoral campaign, although not without risks, began to appear the better of the available choices. Moreover, in winning a popular election, Bhutto envisaged a mandate that would allow him to root out those opposing his government. But the time was not yet right for such activity.

Bhutto toured Pakistan decrying the tactics of his opposition, criticizing their inflammatory speeches and blaming them for the resulting violence. Wali Khan led the opposition in refuting the Chairman's argument, holding Bhutto responsible for the country's persistent state of crisis. Bhutto struck 'fear' and 'terror' into the hearts of his countrymen, all in the name of saving the nation (Wolpert, 1993, p.241). This theme was repeated in the parliament and at every public gathering. The opposition shouted their defiance of one-man rule, and learned to embarrass Bhutto by walking out of the Assembly when he rose to speak. Wali Khan, therefore, became the PPP leader's principal nemesis. Exaggerations came easy to Bhutto, and now he chose to attribute all the country's ills to his Frontier antagonist, and even accused him of consorting with Kabul and New Delhi. Wali Khan's response was to chide Bhutto by citing the increasing public clamour for national elections and the Prime Minister's seeming reluctance to hold them.

Nor had the violence that gripped the country abated. In November 1974 his former ally, now a bitter foe, Ahmad Raza Kasuri, was returning to his home when his vehicle was hit by automatic gunfire. Kasuri survived the attack but his father was killed. Kasuri accused Bhutto of arranging his assassination. Displaying in the Assembly, his father's bloody garments, Kasuri identified Bhutto as the source of the 'hit' order. Again Bhutto fended off the attacks on his person while looking for ways to neutralize the opposition's assault. Then, on 8 February 1975, plastic explosives were ignited under the lectern of a PPP Frontier leader who was about to deliver a speech at Peshawar University. The blast killed Bhutto's closest aide in the province, Hayat Mohammad Khan Sherpao. Bhutto, who was abroad at the time of the incident, immediately cut short his itinerary and returned to Islamabad.

The Chairman claimed to know the perpetrators of the crime, and he ordered Wali Khan's arrest as well as the dissolution of his National Awami Party. The seizure of NAP assets and the imprisonment of the party's officers deprived the National Assembly of its Opposition Leader. It also led members of the United Democratic Front to boycott the proceedings of the parliament.

Needing to strengthen his hand, Bhutto reconciled with Mustafa Khar and reappointed him Governor of the Punjab, but his old comrade refused to rejoin the PPP. In reappointing Khar, Bhutto gambled that the Punjab at least would be secure, and that he would be free to shore up his constituencies in Sindh. Bhutto had toiled to win over the frontier provinces, but the continuing insurrection in Balochistan and the disaffection of the Pathans of the NWFP made that an impossible objective. Bhutto was, in fact, experiencing trouble even in his home province. Sustained inter-community violence, personal rivalries, and inept provincial governments had soured Bhutto's Sindhi supporters. The Chairman could still draw tens and even hundreds of thousands to his public meetings, but his political fortunes had dramatically changed following the promulgation of the 1973 Constitution.

Confronting mounting domestic problems, in 1974 Bhutto received an assist from India when New Delhi announced it had detonated a nuclear device. Bhutto rose to the occasion, and in one of his patented moments of oratory, declared that his country would match the Indian exercise; moreover, Pakistan would build an 'Islamic bomb' (G.S.Bhargava, 1983, pp.134-6). This very public declaration resonated to the Prime Minister's benefit in Pakistan, but it disturbed the western capitals. The world's Muslim countries were generally silent, however. Bhutto at once realized that the quest for a Pakistani nuclear device was a popular issue on both sides of the political divide, and he exploited it to the maximum in warding off the threat posed by his adversaries.

But even the 'Islamic bomb' issue was not enough to repair the damage done to both the PPP and the body politic. Bhutto had constructed a political system that did not allow for the normal range of competitive practices. For Bhutto, politics was a zero-sum game. He either had to monopolize power, control it absolutely, or he had to yield his high office. There was nothing in between his absolute command of the country's political institutions and his unconditional surrender. Bhutto acknowledged that there could be no retreat, and it was at this juncture that he truly acknowledged his mortality and publicly contemplated his early death.

Shaikh Mujibur Rahman's murder at the hands of Bangladesh army officers in August 1975 only added to Bhutto's increasingly morbid thinking (Ziring,1992, pp.102-3). Certainly a fatalist, Bhutto seemed prepared to cast caution to the wind as he more seriously contemplated calling national elections. Moreover, a glance at conditions in India, where Indira Gandhi had suspended constitutional procedures and imposed arbitrary rule, seemed to reinvigorate the PPP chairman. Sensing that he could gain advantage from the anarchy prevailing in Bangladesh and the dictatorship riding in India, Bhutto tried to craft a set of policies that gave Pakistan the image of a democratic polity.

The Chairman announced a new land reform which was to take effect almost immediately. The reform was drafted to help small landowners avoid the payment of customary land revenues. The move affected the vast majority of Pakistan's landholders in a positive way, but it also hurt some large landlords, who expected to see a doubling of their taxes. These reforms were judged an improvement over those made earlier, wherein landlords were limited to 150 irrigated and 300 unirrigated acres. Those reforms had applied only to individuals, not to families, and therefore the landed poor saw little if any change in their circumstances. The new reforms were different, however, and while they again did nothing for the landless and dependent cultivators, the declaration was generally well received, and Bhutto planned a wide range of others that he claimed would transform the economy and finally terminate the colonial legacy of dependency.

The year 1976, the centenary of the Quaid-i-Azam's birth, was to be used to bolster the sagging popularity of the Bhutto administration. Bhutto revived the PPP rallying cry of *Roti, Kapra, aur Makan* and rededicated himself to its central philosophy. The Prime Minister would again emphasize his interest in serving the common man, and the year-long celebrations of Jinnah's hundredth birthday also provided him with opportunities to popularize his theme of 'Islamic Socialism'.

1976 was also the year that General Tikka Khan's tenure as Army Chief expired, and the Balochistan conflict receded. Bhutto had found the General a helpful figure in so many ways, but none more important than in beating back his opposition within the armed forces. Moreover, Tikka had taken the sting out of army criticism over the formation and deployment of the FSF. So long as Tikka prevailed as Chief of Staff, the officers troubled by FSF operations were held in check. But now Bhutto had to find a replacement, and having done away with the office of Army Commander-in-Chief, he believed the next Chief of Staff would best be a subordinate officer who had no association with the Yahya junta, and who was professionally inclined to follow the orders of the Quaid-i-Awam.

Finding a 'junior' general, however, meant bypassing many senior officers, and Bhutto did not ingratiate himself with the army's upper echelon when he rejected Tikka's recommendation of Mohammad Akbar Khan. Nor did he select Tikka's second choice; instead he reached in among the aspiring generals to find Ziaul Haq, who had served in Jordan during the civil war. Zia had also escaped the humiliation of the surrender to India, and he did not appear to be familiar with the details of Bhutto's involvement in the East Pakistan tragedy.

In choosing Zia, it is said, Bhutto believed he had selected the perfect sycophant. Bhutto prided himself on reading the most mundane files, and he was not about to leave the dossiers of the candidates for the highest army post to others. In poring through the documents of the different candidates, he came upon Zia, who was described as a capable and reliable officer, professional to the core, true to his salt, and not one to interfere with political matters. Only recently a Major-General, his Lieutenant-General status was more a consequence of army retirements than of an outstanding record. Bhutto's judgment in selecting Zia has been questioned, but that was well after the fact of the General's appointment.

While it is true that the Chairman wanted an officer who was predictable and capable of taking orders from civilian authority, he also wanted someone who could hold the army in check, who would devote himself to the modernization of the force after the lifting of the US arms embargo, and who could oversee the development of a nuclear weapons programme. Bhutto did not want the army meddling in the country's internal affairs, and with an election campaign on the horizon, and most of the opposition politicians in prison or sidelined, Bhutto believed the expanded FSF was all he needed to maintain domestic stability. Bhutto, in effect, chose Zia carefully, not in an unguarded moment, as some argued later. Bhutto knew what he wanted in an Army Chief and in Zia he believed he had made the perfect choice, even if his personal knowledge of the man was virtually nil.

With the retirement of Tikka and the senior officers ranking above the new Army Chief of Staff, none of the old command structure remained. Bhutto, facing a crisis in his administration, with his party splintered and uncertain of its direction, presided over an army whose junior officers had suddenly become the institution's guiding force. Bhutto had not cultivated these men as he had those other serving officers. It was Bhutto's Ayub connection that had linked him with the army high command, and it was that same command structure that later cleared the way for Bhutto's succession to the presidency. By 1976, the Ayub generals had all retired and the new senior officers had an entirely different relationship with Zulfikar Ali Bhutto.

Having watched Bhutto rise to prominence when they were junior field officers, these were the men who had served the nation in the 1965 war and, to a lesser extent, in East Pakistan. In many respects better trained and more sophisticated than their predecessors, they were also more critical of the PPP Chairman. Few of this group appreciated Bhutto's methods, and most showed disdain for his mannerisms. Knowing that Bhutto had been a central actor in the destruction of both Ayub and Yahya, many held him responsible for the tragedy in East Bengal and the subsequent conflict in Balochistan. Uncomfortable with the power Bhutto delegated to the FSF, and forced to come to grips with the Pakistani version of a police state under the leadership of its new and untested commander, the army was no longer the collegial establishment that had brought Bhutto to power.

Everything negative that has been said of Zia was after the fact and from hindsight. At the time of his selection in 1976, Zia was a good choice, given the Prime Minister's state of mind. Zia proved to be a yeoman soldier, he followed orders, did his duty, and generally did not question the policies, programmes, or performance of the Quaid-i-Awam. If anything, Zia was too good a selection, because his perfect subordination to the PPP Chairman caused Bhutto to lower his guard. In fact, Bhutto followed Zia almost in the same way as the General followed the Chairman. With Zia in command of the army, and it was a command troubled by deep divisions and resentment, Bhutto believed the soldiers were less likely to pose a threat to his regime, and he could devote his energy to the election campaign which was now expected to follow the year-long celebrations of the Quaid-i-Azam's hundredth birthday.

The Elections of 1977 and the Aftermath

Bhutto revelled in the global spotlight as he hosted the International Seerat Congress, celebrating and memorializing the life of the Prophet (PBUH). Bhutto used the occasion to connect the Prophet's (PBUH) teachings with his foreign policy, and noted that he too concerned himself with the solidarity of the Muslim peoples. Bhutto also welcomed the Shah and his Empress to Pakistan, and spoke of the intertwined destinies of their two countries. He could not have known how intertwined their personal destinies were, nor indeed, how their fortunes would so tragically intersect three years later. But for the present, Bhutto could be euphoric. He had weathered so many conflicts, had seen so many stars fall; the fact that he was still a factor in the life of the nation and in the larger world was enough to generate the nostalgic reminiscences that buoyed his temperament and sustained his vitality. After all, the world had changed so dramatically in the few years he had been in power.

The war in Indo-China had finally ground to an end and the Americans, for the first time in their history, were required to accept something less than victory. Washington and Moscow concluded their first arms control agreement. The Egyptians had made a real show of it in breaking the Israeli Bar-Lev line, only to be forced to accept peace terms after their Third Army was cut off in the Sinai desert. Nevertheless, Egypt's Anwar el-Sadat indicated an interest in negotiating his differences with Israel and flew to Jerusalem, simply to demonstrate his resolve. Oil had become king. Saudi Arabia, although stunned by King Faisal's assassination, assumed superpower status by managing OPEC, while other Muslim oil-producing states reaped a harvest of profits unknown in modern history. Communist China had taken its seat in the UN Security Council, while an American President who had made his reputation in fighting communists had visited the People's Republic and had dinner with Mao Zedong. Closer to home, a two-hundred year monarchy had been terminated in Afghanistan, and Mujib, the light of the Bengalis, had been butchered in Bangladesh by members of his own army. India, too, was restless as popular forces struggled against an imposed 'state of emergency' and the dictatorship of the daughter of Jawaharlal Nehru. All these events, and so many more, had convinced Bhutto that the world was rapidly changing, and that Pakistan must adjust to the fast-moving events or be lost in the cruel dilemmas of dependency and second-rate status.

Deprived of oil, Bhutto envisaged Pakistan as a nuclear power and hence, a major actor in world affairs. Nuclear weapons capability was the balancer the country had sought in its conflict with India. Indeed, nuclear weapons capability was seen as providing Pakistan with the stature it needed to equalize its relations with New Delhi, as well as elevate Bhutto to a singular role as leader of the world's Muslim population. It was, therefore, with considerable discomfort that Bhutto sought to deflect American pressure to forego nuclear weapons development. Although the government insisted that the country's nuclear programme was solely concerned with the generation of nuclear energy, the Americans moved aggressively to prevent other countries from supplying Pakistan with the reactors and the technology otherwise contracted for. Ambassador Byroade's offer to provide the Pakistan Armed Forces with conventional weapons in return for a stand-down on the nuclear issue was not appreciated, but Bhutto hoped to calm American fears by appearing to accept the arrangement. Behind the scenes, however, Pakistan scoured the globe for the radioactive materials and the technology necessary to produce their Islamic bomb.

Bhutto also expanded his relationship with Sardar Daud, who prepared an elaborate greeting for the Pakistani Prime Minister. Bhutto waxed eloquent on the possibilities of a *rapprochement* with Kabul, and he invited Daud to Pakistan where, he said, a warm welcome awaited him. Enlisting the support of the Afghan leader was an important gambit in his tussle with Frontier dissidents, who anguished over the sustained incarceration of Wali Khan. The opposition was somewhat disoriented by the loss of Wali Khan and the banning of his National Awami Party, but they fell back on the old Sindhi Hur leader, the Pir of Pagaro, who led the Muslim League and whom Bhutto was most reluctant to antagonize.

In September 1976 Bhutto mapped out the programme for his election campaign, stressing the need to appeal to the country's youth, its women, factory labourers, and former servicemen. A book of Bhutto's quotations, much in the character of Mao's 'Red Book', was prepared in the several languages spoken in the country. Bhutto had already grown accustomed to wearing Mao's dress, including the Chinese leader's cap, and the book emulating the actions of his adopted mentor came as no surprise. Mao's death that year gave Bhutto's book of sayings even more attention.

Acting very much the people's leader, Bhutto extended his earlier nationalization programme when he ordered the government to take control of all cotton-ginning, paddy-husking, and flour milling. Justifying his action with the argument that the middlemen running such facilities were 'bloodsuckers', the Chairman wanted every Pakistani farmer to know that they could expect fair and honourable treatment from his government. No legislation was required to permit the seizure of private property, nor was it clear what, if any, compensation the government intended to pay for the takeovers. Bhutto's actions were pleasing to many farmers but were not so well received in the larger public or even among some of his former associates. These critics refused to credit Bhutto with trying to save the economy. On the contrary, much as Ayub was condemned for his 'Decade of Development', so too, Bhutto was accused of leading the country into deeper financial turmoil. Hanif Ramay's public criticism of the Prime Minister, who was then consumed in reinforcing his image as the country's economic saviour, landed him in jail with so many others. While applying the stick to politicians like Ramay, Bhutto offered barrels of carrots to others, especially junior army officers, who were granted bargain basement rates for the purchase of choice agricultural land.

Bhutto's economic tactics were all hitched to his political wagon. Everything he did was geared to propelling him to victory in the coming elections. It did not matter how many among the elite found fault with his manoeuvring; if the popular masses approved his actions, they more than offset the power of his detractors. Moreover, Bhutto was so convinced of his place in history that he truly believed that his was a greater destiny, and that no matter what the final outcome of his Pakistan experience, his vindication was assured. Bhutto genuinely thought of himself as a servant of the people. In a speech to the nation in December, he questioned why he was so misunderstood, so maligned by his enemies, especially when he had done so much to restore the people's faith and future. 'A nation that grudges honour to its leaders is a nation that thinks little of itself,' he said. Anticipating an outpouring of popular enthusiasm for his candidacy despite the barbs of his political foes, Bhutto was ready to announce the holding of the long-awaited national elections, indeed the first since the fateful polling of 1970.

Pakistan had had little practice with elections, and its only national experience had ended in the tragedy of civil war and dismemberment. Bhutto refused to anticipate anything resembling a replay of those events. The conflict in Balochistan had subsided, and the Chairman could cite the passage of enactments restricting the power of tribal *sardars*. Bhutto enjoyed the security that came from the imprisonment of some of his more potent rivals. The disarray in the ranks of the political opposition was especially gratifying given the conflict between younger and older politicians, as well as the philosophical and ideological differences that prevented the political organizations from finding common ground. Moreover, Pakistani politics was still more a matter of personality than group-think, and those political leaders who were able to avoid the FSF and remain active were most reluctant to pool their resources.

In the meantime, Bhutto continued to deal in patronage, to make promises, and to announce reforms. Reducing irrigated holdings to 100 acres, and 200 for unirrigated lands, he declared that the resumed lands would be distributed among the landless and tenant farmers. Resistance to this new ordinance, he warned, would be punished by long prison terms, and he would tolerate no delay in the transfer of excess landholdings to the government. Bhutto calculated that the urban vote was his, and that by appealing to the rural poor he could torpedo the landed interests, who remained key politicians in the countryside. Bhutto's frontal attack on the feudal system and rural power structure was a blow directed at the nation's long-term power-brokers, but he preferred to justify this latest decree as aimed at improving the output of the agrarian economy. A vast landholder himself, Bhutto prided himself in humbling the *zamindar*, much as he had cowed the country's corporate, financial, and bureaucratic elites. Indeed, it was Bhutto who had dissolved the elite Civil Service of Pakistan and integrated all the services.

In spite of all his difficulties, Bhutto had unquestionably changed Pakistan in ways that could never have been anticipated when he broke with Ayub Khan. With the possible exception of the armed forces, not one major institution was left untouched as Bhutto went about the business of systematically destroying all the traditional sources of power in the country. The steel frame had been replaced with one constructed of fear and intimidation, while the civil service had been thoroughly politicized.

The PPP was a political party in name only, its numerous factions tearing at the heart of the organization. Bhutto, however, transcended the organization, and having neutralized virtually all his major foes, he seemed prepared to face the nation's voters. If there was a domestic or foreign observer who believed Bhutto would not win an overwhelming electoral victory, he had not been heard from. Pakistan had undergone revolutionary changes, and no one was more responsible for the country's transformation than Zulfikar Ali Bhutto.

Convinced that victory would be his to enjoy, on 7 January 1977 Bhutto announced the holding of national elections within two months. Victory, however, was not enough to satisfy the Chairman. He not only wanted to defeat his adversaries, he was determined to destroy them forever. Bhutto's objective had little to do with boosting PPP morale or reviving the coalition that had produced such positive results in the previous election. Bhutto wanted nothing less than the total support of the Pakistani public, a veritable mandate, not only in Punjab and Sindh, but in the frontier provinces as well. Strengthened in his conviction that his next term would witness the submission of the entire nation, Bhutto plotted the strategy that ultimately was to be his undoing.

The quarrelsome and divided opposition acknowledged the few options in their quiver, and they soon realized that only by uniting their several programmes and forming a joint command would they have any chance of managing a meaningful campaign. Thus, just days after the call for elections, the opposition found the necessary common ground and agreed to establish an *ad hoc* body, which they named the Pakistan National Alliance (PNA). With the Press all but dominated by the government, it would not be a simple matter to get the message of the opposition before the public. Moreover, with so many politicians in prison, with a myriad of restrictions imposed on speech-making, and with transport to remote locations difficult to arrange, the government had all the advantages. Handicapped and outmanoeuvred, the PNA decided to centre all their efforts in a campaign slated to embarrass the Quaid-i-Awam.

The PNA was formed from the parties of the United Democratic Front, the Muslim fundamentalist organizations, as well as Asghar Khan's Tehrik-i-Istiqlal. In the absence of Wali Khan, Maulana Mufti Mahmood was elected its President. But right from the outset of the campaign the PNA found its path blocked. Required to file nomination papers for the different constituencies within barely ten days of their union, the PNA was hard-pressed to come up with a single slate of candidates. Not only was time a factor, when candidates finally appeared to register their intentions, they were often delayed or prevented from establishing their candidacy. Bhutto, for example, was determined to stand alone in his district of Larkana, and he was registered 'unopposed' when the election commission said that the opposition had failed to field a candidate. The same was true in districts dominated by other PPP notables, and though the PNA decried efforts at muzzling them, their complaints fell on deaf ears. So began the rigging of the 1977 elections.

Given Bhutto's absolute certainty of winning the election, it is curious that his administration would stoop to tactics that were so blatantly unfair, and in numerous instances, illegal. Nor is it possible to ignore Bhutto's complicity in arranging an election that guaranteed total victory. Bhutto did not adopt Mao Zedong's dress simply to make a point. Since the mid-1960s, Pakistanis who studied development theory thought they saw something in the Chinese experience that could be applied to Pakistan. To a large extent, it was their dissatisfaction with American teachings that drove both intellectuals and practitioners to consider China a more appropriate model.

Bhutto, too, was enamoured of Chinese achievements, and China's role in befriending Pakistan, especially during the 1965 War, had mobilized considerable popular support for Beijing's policies. China was also the balancer to Indian might, and in the competition for Third World leadership, Pakistan was keen to support China. Mao Zedong's passing, therefore, affected Bhutto in ways that are difficult to measure. Coming at a time when Bhutto was planning his election campaign, the Chairman sensed that he was not only standing for re-election in Pakistan, but was also establishing his mark in Third World circles. While India struggled with its two year 'state of emergency', this was the moment for Bhutto to reinforce his already substantial Third World credentials.

Thus, Bhutto would not be content with a simple victory at the polls. Nor were the elections aimed at assuring PPP control of the Pakistan government. Bhutto wanted stature and status, the kind of satisfaction that comes from knowing that in life you are the one indispensable leader, and even in death, the spirit that drives and shapes the future. Bhutto could not be content with a mere majority; his psyche, indeed his mystical temperament, demanded nothing less than the kingdom and all its subjects. On the more practical side, however, Bhutto needed a two-thirds majority in the National Assembly if he was to have any chance of revising the 1973 Constitution. Bhutto was most uncomfortable in the role of Prime Minister and his ambition would be satisfied with nothing less than the restoration of a highly centralized, presidential system.

All the more reason, therefore, that the PNA centred their campaign on Bhutto's rule, his personal habits, his family background, and his imperious and arrogant demeanour. The PNA concentrated their initial attack on Karachi, where the *mohajir* community was a dominant force and very much opposed to the policies of Zulfikar Ali Bhutto. More than the *mohajir* business community had reason to reject Bhutto. The internecine strife that had pitted Sindhis against *mohajirs* now had even greater political importance. Moreover, the more the PNA appealed to Karachi's vast refugee community, the more the PPP aroused the people of the Sindh hinterland. Thus the election campaign was also a stimulus for renewed, and in some cases more intense, ethnic conflict. Election districts had become war zones. The work of the politicians was impeded, and when the moment arrived for the people to cast their ballots, they found their avenues to the polls blocked. Bhutto had personally urged his administrators in the province to take aggressive action in getting the PPP voters to the polling places, and when the results were counted, it came as no surprise that the Chairman's party had swept 105 of the 115 seats, despite bruising losses in Karachi.

Approximately 17 million of the 31 million eligible voters cast their ballots on 7 March 1977, with the PPP managing some 60 per cent of the vote, but garnering 75 per cent of the National Assembly seats, far more than the two-thirds that Bhutto needed to change the constitution and the political system. And although the PNA had managed a respectable 35 per cent of the vote, it came out of the election with only 17 per cent of the seats. Moreover, the PPP monopolized all the seats set aside for women and minorities. In the course.of the campaign Bhutto had the use of a variety of intelligence-gathering organs, including Inter-Services Intelligence. Bhutto knew exactly which candidates he did not want in the Assembly and which PNA personalities were agreeable to him. Those likely to impede his programme were to be denied, those likely to be won over were to be allowed to win their elections, or at least this was the strategy developed for the occasion, and in no small measure these were the results of the election.

The opposition leaders knew they faced a formidable foe and they did not believe the contest would be fair, or that the managers of the election would be impartial overseers. In part, the conduct of the election could be attributed to inexperience, Pakistanis having had few polls in their history. But it was also apparent that the Bhutto administration influenced the conduct of the elections. The people charged with managing the ballots were either Bhutto zealots or so imposed upon, and so fearful of not delivering a PPP victory, that they did everything possible to guarantee the results that the Chairman had demanded. Bhutto would later deny knowledge of fraud and vote-rigging, but his message to subordinates was clear and unambiguous, and they were not alone in delivering what had been ordered.

The opposition was quick to denounce the elections as a travesty, totally flawed, and indeed, stolen by the government party, and particularly by its Chairman, Zulfikar Ali Bhutto. Arguing that they had lost all confidence in the Bhutto administration, the PNA leaders called for a countrywide strike that would shut down the nation at every level of public and private activity. Proprietors of establishments in all the country's major metropolitan areas closed their doors and boarded their windows, not only in support of the strike call, but fearing assaults on their property. And indeed, there were assaults by rival party groups that quickly degenerated into open rioting. The opposition focused attention on what they called the ballot-stuffing tactics of the government party, and they demanded the cancellation of the results and the immediate holding of new elections under more controlled conditions.

Bhutto's response was both defiant and conciliatory. On the one side he insisted that the election results were final and a 'settled matter', while on the other, he called for a dialogue between himself and the PNA leaders. The PNA stalwarts, however, saw no positive purpose in meeting with the Prime Minister, and Bhutto, who had himself rejected a critical meeting with Ayub Khan when he appeared conciliatory, found himself the target of the opposition's snub.

Bhutto did not have time to relish his electoral achievement. As with the other elections in Pakistan, this one, too, had a nightmarish aftermath. Bhutto had won a 'great' victory, but few of his countrymen were prepared to acknowledge the feat. Having failed to create the one-party state, he could not ignore the howls of foul play emanating from the many members of a disparate opposition (Burki, 1980). Moreover, even more so than during the campaign, the opposition zeroed in on the Chairman's un-Islamic habits and policies. The fundamentalist orders that had comprised the PNA, especially the Jamaat-i-Islami, the Jamaat-ul-Ulema-i-Islam, and the Jamiat-ul-Ulema-i-Pakistan, hammered at Bhutto's personal lifestyle as well as his overtly secular and socialist policies. Bhutto believed that the fundamentalists had also infiltrated the armed forces, and that the Jamaat-i-Islami had cultivated large segments of the army and had won over some of its key commanders. But conspiracies were hardly confined to fundamentalist machinations. On the one hand, there had been a long history of religious opposition to Bhutto. It had been a key feature in the 1970 campaign, when a *fatwa* was issued condemning his irreligious behaviour. Such assaults on Bhutto's lifestyle were not new, and it remains to be seen how questions of piety influenced members of the armed forces. On the other hand, and no doubt this was a more critical element in the rising tide of resentment over the election results, the country was facing an economic calamity, with uncontrolled inflation, crop failures due generally to the vagaries of nature, and PPP mismanagement of the nationalized industries, which were hardly functioning. Coupled with the attacks on the corporate and industrial community, government was hardly in a position to stem the flight of capital from the country. As a consequence, new investments were almost non-existent. Moreover, unemployment and underemployment gripped the public, and ethnic and sectarian strife paralysed serious economic performance. Finally, heavy government expenditures, especially those allocated for government security, were a constant drain on available funds.

The election campaign had framed these issues, but the results of the election, particularly the official tampering with the election process, energized and fueled the PNA reaction. In effect, the campaign against the PPP, and most important, against Chairman Bhutto, was galvanized after, not prior, to the election. All the issues surrounding the contest merged in the days and weeks following the election, and given the country's lack of tradition in conducting elections or honouring their results, the real politics were manifested only after the ballots had been cast. Elections in Pakistan were not developed to produce a government but rather to tear one down. Elections were not the beginning and source of political legitimacy, but confirmation that civilian authority is unworthy of wielding power. Bhutto's dream of a centralized, one-party state, with himself the President for life, ran head-on into a national legacy that associated 'real' power with the army.

Neither the leaders of the PNA nor the persons demonstrating their disaffection in the streets anticipated that their tactics would gain them control of the government. In escalating the riots, they knew both intellectually and emotionally that only the army could restore a semblance of balance to the country. The rioters risked placing the army in the camp with Bhutto; alternatively they risked the re-imposition of martial law and the military's return to politics. There were no other options, and General Zia's memo to his commanders warning them not to become embroiled in politics left little doubt he would ever contemplate substituting an Asghar Khan for a Zulfikar Ali Bhutto.

Bhutto desperately tried to stem the unrest without calling for army intervention. Believing he could manage the disturbances with the Federal Security Force, he was distressed to find the FSF failing in its responsibilities. Wolpert believes the FSF did not do their duty because Bhutto had squandered the Pakistan treasury and there was hardly the money to pay for their services, let alone honour his pledge to raise their pay by fifty per cent. He cites a call to the Shah of Iran in which Bhutto pleads for a $300 million loan that was not honoured, implying that that money would have been used to pay off the members of the FSF (Wolpert,1993, p.284). But whatever the reasons for FSF failure to manage the riots, and it is more likely that the ranks of the FSF had been infiltrated by Army Special Forces, FSF agents were induced to abandon their stations and save themselves. In effect, the FSF was in the process of self-destruction, leaving only its key officers to face the wrath of an angry public.

Distraught over the failure of his central security system, Bhutto tried again to talk his way out of a difficult situation. He asked his election commissioner to examine the complaints of rigging and ballot-stuffing, and special tribunals were assembled to try those accused of malpractices. But even these actions could not satisfy the demonstrators, who now turned to the results of the election in India, where Indira Gandhi had lost to her rival Morarji Desai. The fact that the Indian leader had lifted the two-year state of emergency to hold the elections, had lost the contest, and had quietly retreated from the central arena, contrasted with Bhutto's insistence on clinging to power. Bhutto's problem of only listening to his own inner voice prevented him from accepting the advice of a loyal colleague who advised him to call new elections. Too stubborn, too proud, too defiant, Bhutto refused to yield to people he had long since grown to despise. True to form, when his opposition refused to meet with him, Bhutto ordered their arrest. Addressing his newly-elected members of the National Assembly just three days later, the Chairman reiterated his willingness to meet with members of the PNA, but he also warned his detractors that they had to cease their 'politics of vandalism'. The street demonstrators never got the message, however, and the rioting continued into April.

The deaths of many protestors, and the arrest of many more, did not end the altercations. And as the crowds jamming the streets and thoroughfares grew with each passing day, the police and FSF were even more hard put to protect themselves. Shoot to kill orders were more numerous and the escalation of deaths did nothing to buttress the Bhutto administration. The country was confronted with yet another version of civil war, and the people of Lahore and Karachi got a taste of what it was like in the days leading up to the army action in East Pakistan just six years earlier. Frantic, and not knowing how to restore a semblance of law and order, various ministers in the Bhutto government declared their intention to scrutinize the controversial policies of the PPP government, including the more recent takeover of the agricultural processing industries.

The PNA leaders, however, sensed the weakness of the regime, and they sustained their efforts with calls to the citizenry to stop payment of their taxes. They also called another general strike that inflicted even more damage on an already collapsed economy. Bhutto was condemned by a variety of public and private organizations, but none was more telling than the resolution passed by the Karachi Bar Association, deploring the killing of innocent citizens. Even General Gul Hassan and Air Marshal Rahim Khan, who had help engineer Bhutto's rise to power, now deserted him. Having resigned their ambassadorial posts in Greece and Spain, both men accused Bhutto of playing at democracy while building a personal dictatorship, saying that if he had any honour left he would vacate his position and allow the country to regain its lost equilibrium.

In spite of the incredible pressure calling upon him to resign, Bhutto, citing his inability to quit a public responsibility, clung to power. To placate the Islamic fundamentalists, he announced a prohibition on the use of alcoholic beverages, banned gambling, and closed bars, nightclubs, and movie theatres. Neither Maudoodi nor the other religious leaders were impressed with these actions, however, and the gambit was judged too late to save his administration. Believing he had made all the correct moves, but still faced by an aroused populace, Bhutto now came to hold as true what he had always believed, that the United States had conspired with the opposition in a plot to destroy him. Desperate for an answer to his dilemma, Bhutto believed he had no recourse other than to call upon General Zia to assist him in establishing martial law in Karachi, Hyderabad, and Lahore, the cities that had experienced the more violent demonstrations. Before committing the army, however, he tried to reason with corps commanders, explaining that the country was being assaulted by external forces and that they were duty-bound to preserve its integrity. Although indicating that his government was expendable, Bhutto nevertheless dilated on the intertwining of his personal mission and the nation's future.

There is reason to believe that the principal commanders were torn between remaining loyal to their civilian leader and breaking with him. All understood the deep and expanding resentment within the army, especially among the lesser ranks, but none of them indicated knowledge of a plot aimed at ousting the Bhutto regime. Pakistan's field and junior officers were not expected to act without the co-operation of their senior commanders, and not since the Rawalpindi Conspiracy had there been anything resembling a move by the lower ranks against those at the top. Nevertheless, tensions had intensified since the humiliating loss of East Pakistan. The bloodletting in Balochistan had further impaired army morale, and the spreading violence in the NWFP and in *mohajir*-dominant Karachi could not be contained without army intervention. The heavy hand of the FSF also disturbed the men in service, not only because their professional integrity was involved, but because the secret police had been allowed to arbitrarily rampage through society, where even service families could not avoid being victimized.

Bhutto's questionable behaviour, his arrogance, his lust for power, as well as the policies of his government, only added to feelings that now bordered on despair. Bhutto was accused of unleashing the most violent forces in Pakistani society, of dividing the nation for self-serving purposes, of making a shambles of the economy, and of alienating and forcing into exile the nation's best minds and most industrious people. If allowed to sustain his performance, the man who was called upon to bind up the nation's wounds after a terrible civil war could very well be the same who would destroy what remained of Pakistan.

These were not the idle thoughts of the military's higher echelon, but the sentiments of a solid portion of the army's unit and field officers. As early as December 1976, no longer able to endure Bhutto's behaviour, field and junior officers of the Pakistan Army plotted his overthrow. It would take the elections of March 1977 and the resulting aftermath to bring their planning to a point of execution. It would also take substantial pressure to convince General Zia to lead the *coup*. Zia was not the strategist in the overthrow of Zulfikar Ali Bhutto, but he was made its instrument. Zia was faced with a win-lose situation and, in order to preserve the unity of the army as well as his command, he yielded to those younger majors and colonels who had earlier concluded it was either them or Bhutto.

The workers of Pakistan International Airlines and the Pakistan Railway left their stations in late April, partly in a display of solidarity with the Pakistan National Alliance and partly in an effort to force Bhutto to step aside. The pressure on Bhutto to resign was extreme, but still he refused to yield. For their part, the demonstrators continued, in spite of the arrest of virtually all the major PNA leaders (with the exception of the Pir of Pagaro). The Pakistan scene was no different in May than it had been in April, and even the attempt to broker an understanding between the government and the opposition by the Saudi Arabian ambassador failed to bear fruit. In early June, however, following a meeting with General Zia and his key commanders, Bhutto ordered the release of the PNA leaders, and the opposition announced the suspension of their agitation. Still another high-powered meeting was arranged, this time with the principal members of the PNA. These latter negotiations, however, were disturbed by a decree of the Lahore High Court declaring 'unconstitutional' the imposition of martial law in Karachi, Lahore, and Hyderabad. In spite of the confusion this caused the government, the conversations were not broken off. In fact, the ruling convinced the PNA leaders that time was on their side.

The PNA now demanded the scrapping of the March election results and the holding of new elections within thirty days. The government, however, refused to yield on its earlier position that the elections were fair, and it steadfastly resisted the opposition's complaint. Given the impasse, it was the government which shifted direction. Suddenly, on 15 June, an agreement was announced that called for new elections, with the details to be worked out by subordinate members of the different negotiating teams. Bhutto was buoyed by this understanding, and he flew to Riyadh to personally thank King Khalid for his country's good offices in trying to mediate the dispute between his government and the PNA. He also went on to Libya, Iran, Abu Dhabi, and Kuwait in a futile effort at re-establishing his bona fides as a prominent Third World leader.

When he returned to Pakistan, however, Bhutto was apprised of the difficulties in developing the details of the earlier agreement. For their part, the PNA leaders sensed that they were being outfoxed by the PPP Chairman. Bhutto had once again enlisted his once closest confidants, notably Mustafa Khar, in shoring up his base in Punjab and Sindh. Convinced that Bhutto was planning an end run, the PNA team demanded the introduction of central power-sharing to supervise all the agencies and instruments of government. Equal representation was demanded for the PNA and PPP, with each party coalition chairing a Supreme Implementation Council. Bhutto thought he had weathered the post-election storm and he was incensed over this later PNA demand. The Prime Minister called this latest ultimatum 'insulting' and a brazen ploy made by a dying coalition. But rather than blow the opportunity for a *via media*, the Prime Minister authorized Hafiz Pirzada to make a counter-offer that called for a joint government-PNA committee, but solely to supervise the new elections. When the opposition rejected that suggestion, Bhutto's suspicions were aroused as never before. Always believing the United States had a hand in promoting the opposition, he concluded it was time to hold fast and not make any further concessions. And although he resisted PNA demands to dissolve the National Assembly and form a combined cabinet, given the persistence of his negotiators, Bhutto was forced to ponder reconsidering his 'no-further' position.

Time, however, had run out. The younger officers had 'convinced' their senior commanders that the moment for action had arrived. Bhutto would be denied the use of the instruments of official violence and would no longer be permitted to silence his opposition. The Prime Minister, they concluded, would sacrifice the country, much as he had sacrificed East Pakistan. Truly believing that 'heads would roll' if Bhutto was allowed to remain in power, the majors and colonels forced Zia's hand. The generals would either go along with the *coup* or they, too, would be victims in the unfolding drama. Zia's choice lay in preserving the integrity of the army or saving Bhutto. In the end, he chose the army.

In the early morning of 5 July 1977, Bhutto was informed by General Zia that the Pakistan Army was back in the political game and that he, the Quaid-i-Awam, was out.

CHAPTER 10

THE ZIAUL HAQ DECADE

Ziaul Haq was a relatively unknown army officer when he was chosen by Bhutto to command the Pakistan Army in 1976, and it is doubtful that he ever contemplated assuming Pakistan's highest political office. Destiny was again at work in the transition from Bhutto to Zia, and indeed it was a transition, not a revolution, that substituted the General for the PPP Chairman. The *coup* was a white-glove affair. There was no aggressive action against Bhutto or any of his colleagues on the day the soldiers again took up the country's political reins. Bhutto was treated gingerly and with respect, and led to believe that his ouster was more a suspension than a termination. Zia described his reimposition of martial law as necessary to restore national tranquillity, and he therefore neutralized not only Chairman Bhutto and his associates, but also the key members of the political opposition. Zia called their detention 'protective custody', a condition that he said would last until law and order had been re-established throughout the country. In the meantime, Zia said, he had authorized the dissolution of the National Assembly and relieved all provincial government leaders of their charges, as well as those holding political office in the federal establishment. Unlike Ayub, however, Zia was mindful of maintaining a semblance of continuity, and he did not abrogate the recently enacted constitution. Instead, he declared its suspension, and thus hinted at its restoration at a date deemed appropriate.

Justifying the army's action in terms that echoed the past, Zia cited the inability of any of the political coalitions to

manage the country's affairs. Confronted with the degeneration of the political process, and witness to still another
national election that ended in chaos, Zia cited the
responsibility of the armed forces in serving the nation during
difficult times. Reassuring the citizenry that the army would
return to its professional duties as soon as the nation's stability
was guaranteed, Zia spoke of a new round of national
elections within three months, and led everyone to believe
that all the acknowledged politicians, including Bhutto,
would again be able challenge one another at the polls. As
for himself, the General emphasized his lack of interest in
politics, his strong belief in democracy, and his intention to
retire from the political arena once a new civilian government
had been appropriately installed.

Zia said all the Chief Justices of the provincial high courts
had agreed to assume the duties of Governor in their
respective provinces. This gesture to the judiciary appeared
to emphasize the General's desire to legitimize the take-over
while assuring the public that the rule of law had not been
affected by the declaration of martial law or the suspension
of the constitution (Mahmood, 1992). Zia spoke of impartiality
in the conduct of martial law and in dealing with the on-
going political process. He showed no particular or personal
animus toward Bhutto when he met with his fallen leader in
the 'protective' cottage set aside for him in Murree. Zia then
informed the deposed leader that he would be allowed to go
free within a few days. Bhutto, however, was both pompous
and frightened in his hill station 'prison'. On the one side, he
continued to behave as the much heralded Quaid-i-Awam;
on the other, he sensed a plot to not only discredit him, but
to destroy him. Allowed to mingle with some of his closest
confidants in his VIP chalet, Bhutto castigated those who had
betrayed him and vowed revenge when conditions enabled
him to return to power.

Bhutto's intemperate behaviour shadowed him throughout
his years, and even in his present predicament, his in-born
instincts told him to strike out verbally at his perceived and
imagined enemies. A mystic to the core, he continued to
nurture an omniscient posture, if not an attitude of
omnipotence, always believing that his destiny demanded

that he assert his superiority, even in circumstances where the odds against him were manifestly against his rebirth. Given to apocalyptic oratory, he had consistently talked of martyrdom, of making the supreme sacrifice for an idea, a cause, and especially for Pakistan. Convinced he was a man of history, Bhutto demonstrated defiance at his incarceration and manipulation by the very men in uniform he believed he had created. In his deepest thoughts, Zia and the others were his creatures, and the fact that they had turned on him only reinforced his determination to suffer their stings, but never in silence.

Popular reaction to the *coup* was mixed but, nevertheless, quizzical. One school of thought believed that Zia and Bhutto were in league with one another and had developed the perfect scheme to isolate, and permanently eliminate, all the Chairman's political opponents, another saw the flowering of a fundamentalist plot, with Zia the instrument whereby the secular state would be replaced by one of strict Islamic character.

Zia had spoken of the need for an Islamic system of politics and government, a *Nizam-i-Mustafa*, as more suited to the genius of the Pakistani nation. Zia's devout observance of Islamic tradition reinforced this view, and it was difficult for observers to imagine Bhutto being part of a scheme to transform Pakistan into an 'ideal' Islamic state. Moreover, Zia was convinced that only Islam bound Pakistanis to one another, and only the religious tradition could prevent a further unravelling of the political and social fabric. Bhutto suspected ties between Zia and the Jamaat-i-Islami, a marriage that he believed was bankrolled by Washington. Bhutto had reason to assume the United States was uncomfortable with his wooing of China and North Korea, and, more recently, the Soviet Union. Moreover, his aspirations in Third World circles had been significantly energized by his sustained anti-Western criticism. Furthermore, the US government had demonstrated its preference for strong military leaders and, in addition, it had long judged Islam a barrier against communist penetration of the country. Bhutto did not need convincing that Washington was less than grieved with his ouster and that in Zia they not only had a dedicated soldier, but also an officer who was determined to insulate Pakistan against Bhutto's socialist policies and orientation. But whatever the explanation for recent events, neither Zia nor Bhutto was destined to resurrect the *status quo ante,* and the *coup* dramatically terminated their short but curious relationship.

Wolpert (1993) presses the argument that Zia was not to be taken at his word, or even by his actions, after unseating and 'detaining' Bhutto. Bhutto's biographer insists that the plot to remove the Chairman not only from office, but from the world, was hatched in Zia's brain. According to the author, Zia detested Bhutto and he demanded the opportunity to savage the man who, while promoting him to head the army, had also enjoyed publicly demeaning and abusing him. While Wolpert pursues this theme from the moment of Zia's introduction, and while the author's facts are not open to question, his interpretation can be.

Whatever his personal feelings toward the Chairman, Zia did not initiate the overthrow of Zulfikar Ali Bhutto. He signed on for the operation, in part because his choices were limited. Moreover, given the countrywide unrest, there was the inevitable spectre of East Pakistan and India's near presence. Zia shared nothing in common with Bhutto, but he was not one to take matters into his own hands. There was no Iskandar Mirza to clear his path, nor did he fit the pattern that brought Yahya to prominence. Zia was a tactician and a strategist, not a conspirator, and if he found justification in the actions of his subordinate officers, it was more a reflection of his soldier's calling than a display of personal vindictiveness.

It was Bhutto, not Ziaul Haq, who had transformed Pakistan. The Pakistan of the Quaid-i-Azam was never clearly defined, and the pain experienced in trying to realize the dream of a secular, independent Muslim state within the subcontinent is documented in the events that culminated with the bloodletting in East Pakistan. In the thirty years between independence and the *coup* of July 1977, no one in Pakistan had held the centre stage longer than Zulfikar Ali Bhutto. Bhutto was a major actor in the Pakistan drama from the moment he entered the Ayub cabinet in 1958, through the break with the Field Marshal, the formation of the Pakistan People's Party, his tryst with Yahya Khan, the events leading up to and during the civil war, the 1971 conflict with India, and finally, his assumption of power following the country's dismemberment.

Assuming national leadership at a time of utter national despair, Bhutto was given the opportunity to recreate Pakistan. But with one eye on the domestic scene and another on the international arena, Bhutto effected a style of governance rather than new policies (F. Zaman and A. Aman, 1973). Always drawn to the big picture, that is, to his place in global space, Bhutto envisaged himself as a leader who transcended the limited circumstances of his country, whose larger destiny was written in the evolving character of the post-colonial world.

Bhutto was not content with simple ascendancy. Nor was the development of his nation his immediate concern. Bhutto was affected by, and infected with power and he measured success not in the sycophancy of his courtiers or the sentiments of the Pakistani masses, but in the adulation that he received from the kings, presidents, and dictators with whom he mingled and shared experiences. Bhutto projected a personality that was bigger than Pakistan, and because he did so with verve and majesty, he was believable and hence, respected in other lands beyond even his most fervent dreams. Pakistan therefore, despite its plunge into the abyss, was perceived new-born and youthful, like the fabled phoenix, risen from the ashes of its own despair to live yet another cycle under the tutelage of Zulfikar Ali Bhutto.

Bhutto projected an immortality for himself that, in his mind, intertwined with the nation. Thus, even the Pakistani national ethos was to be re-examined and re-engineered, and ultimately made more pliable and suited for the future imagined by the supreme architect.

Bhutto realized it was only the ideal Pakistan that was lost in the crushing defeat of December 1971. The real Pakistan, with its traditional bastions of power, remained untouched by the tragedy. So too, the different historic aspirations and enmities remained intact. The reality of Pakistan was its lack of national consciousness, and the loss of East Pakistan changed nothing. Pakistan remained a distant goal, and Bhutto preserved and nourished the parochial character of a polyglot, divided society. To argue that he should have used his energy to instil a sense of wholeness because the east wing had been lost fails in an understanding of the character of the real Pakistan. Bhutto was the least likely personality to address the totality of the Pakistan design. If there was even the hint of the national statesman in his bearing, he would have seized the occasion to congratulate Mujib on his electoral success. The time to demonstrate national leadership was before, not after, the unleashing of the dogs of war!

Bhutto was incapable of binding the wounds of a demoralized nation, a nation that grieved not the loss of East Pakistan, but of its *amour propre*. It was not that East Pakistan was free, but of that India had inflicted a humiliating defeat. Pakistan's divisive features remained untouched. Punjabis, Sindhis, Pathans, Balochis, were no more Pakistanis after Bangladesh than before it, and Bhutto, who prevented Bengalis from becoming Pakistanis, was not about to become one himself.

Bhutto took advantage of a weakened steel frame to introduce a system of governance that was contrived to neutralize threats to his authority. Though constitutionally denied a presidential office, he operated for the most part outside the established legal order, resting his authority not on being the nation's head of government, but rather its super ego, its mentor, and master power-broker. Avoiding statutory constraints, Bhutto functioned through the political party that he dominated and the paramilitary forces that he raised to serve his domestic needs.

Bhutto anticipated reshaping the steel frame to suit his purposes. The once-vaunted bureaucracy was forced into a new mould, but the reforms centred more on politicizing the services than on instilling higher levels of efficiency. So too, the armed forces were to be refashioned, especially the army, to dispense with their penchant for political intrusions. Bhutto endeavoured to recreate an armed forces that was conversant with civilian control, and he selected commanders who he believed would realize that goal. He chose Zia because he believed the General would be so grateful for the opportunity to realize the highest station in his calling that he would never question the orders of the Quaid-i-Awam. He chose Zia for other reasons as well: for his distance from Pakistan during the civil war and the humiliating surrender to India, for his strict professionalism, and indeed, for his piety. Zia was, by all accounts, the unassuming, quiet, simple soldier who could always be counted upon to do his duty. Bhutto did not so much trust Zia to perform on call, but he had concluded that the army high command had had enough of politics, and that the discrediting of Ayub and Yahya Khan, as well as the failure to tame India, had sufficiently chastened the men in uniform. Bhutto promised a new military establishment, less dependent on the United States and better equipped than the one that had emerged with American assistance. Everything seemed to point to an army more concerned with reclaiming its integrity and polishing its skills than one concerned with the game of central politics.

But Bhutto never got the *carte blanche* he needed. Inheriting a political experience that defied even his ministrations, he was constantly buttressing his power base. Unable to manage a diverse coalition of personalities and groups, always suspicious of those who would be his colleagues, Bhutto's imperious attitude created moats, not bridges. The elections were only the last of the glaring examples of Bhutto's preference for conflict generation, not resolution. One national election had already resulted in civil war and dismemberment, now the second one had raised a storm that threatened to destroy what remained of the country. Bhutto had contested the first election as he had the second, and his experience in the former defined his decision-making in the latter. Bhutto and his party were destined to win the 1977 election by a considerable margin, but not content with that reality, the Chairman determined that only a landslide in every province would suffice. Bhutto insisted on his mandate, and his henchmen were called upon to deliver that prize. Their fraud, committed in the name of solemn democratic procedure, was too public to be ignored or forgiven.

Bhutto allowed the weakest of his opponents to spark the explosion that would blow him from his lofty perch. The

PNA was hardly a threat to Bhutto's authority, but the Chairman was by this time so blinded by his own machinations that he failed to understand the real threat to his government and, indeed, himself. Zia was not 'a much shrewder politician for Pakistan than Zulfi Bhutto' (Wolpert, 1993, p.306), nor was the General fixated on the idea of hanging the leader of the People's Party (ibid.,p. 307). Zia was first and foremost a professional soldier, a new and untested commander of an army suffering from deep-seated psychological as well as physical deficiencies. Not yet having placed his stamp on the corps in his first year in the job, he was forced to confront bitter and angry men who had attained manhood after independence, and who had been instilled with the idea that they were well the equal of their Indian counterparts. Believing that their superiors had betrayed them, and convinced that that betrayal had done great damage to the army as well as put the country on a deviant course, they were determined to correct the situation before a point of no return had been reached.

Bhutto was the grey eminence in the collapse of the Pakistan dream. He was also the most unorthodox of all the Pakistani politicians. Having experienced his style of governance, having been called upon repeatedly to bloody their own people, the soldiers had had enough of the Quaid-i-Awam, and Zia was sufficiently perspicacious to realize that he could not deflect a movement dedicated to unseating him. Given the disarray at all levels and in all sectors of society, Zia could not stand by and allow the chain of command to disintegrate.

Bhutto had called upon Zia to lead the Pakistan Army at a critical time in his administration. Aware that the General had faithfully discharged his duties in the service of the Jordanian king during that monarch's most trying hour, he no doubt assumed that Zia could be depended upon to serve the Quaid-i-Awam in revamping the Pakistan Army. But never himself having been a soldier, Bhutto had no way of understanding the make-up and psychology of the men in uniform. Moreover, Bhutto, always fearful of the army, insisted upon a pliant establishment geared for external, essentially defensive, deployment, but stripped of its domestic interventionist potential. In Zia, he gambled on selecting the one officer who would not only realize those objectives, but would also remain loyal to his salt. Although the researcher may continue to discover references, expressions, actions that might point to the General's prior and original desire to dispose of the Chairman, it was Bhutto's own behaviour that brought mortal judgment down upon him. That Zia had the capacity to hang Bhutto is amply demonstrated by subsequent events. But to argue that this was the result of a personal vendetta, that Zia calculated Bhutto's execution prior to deposing him, remains unproven.

What is known is that the army not only swept the politicians from office and closed down the political institutions, it also moved to dissolve the Federal Security Force. The FSF Director, Masood Mahmood, and other high-ranking members of the special police were arrested, as were their underlings. Called upon to give testimony for their behaviour, they were 'encouraged' to account for their actions and, at every instance, to cite who issued the orders to intimidate, detain, torture, and murder the regime's opponents. It should have come as no surprise to anyone that, in an effort to save themselves, they would implicate their fallen and now defenceless leader.

The army was determined to obliterate the FSF; indeed, if there was a military target in the *coup* it was the secret police establishment that Bhutto had raised to ensure his security. Not unlike the history of other paramilitary forces, the FSF had far exceeded its charge and had become synonymous with rampant villainy. Accounts of its brutal methods were known throughout the country. Pakistani citizens found little comfort in a special police operation that clearly had no national function. Along with the PPP's militia, the FSF existed for one purpose alone, and that was to assure the totality of the Quaid-i-Awam's power. Pakistanis had never experienced anything resembling the FSF, and its emergence in Pakistan was not a consequence of the nation's political culture. Judged to be an imported institution, its likes were to be found in more dictatorial societies where personal rule was a fact of political life. Why a 'People's Leader' believed it necessary to surround himself with some of the nation's most discredited individuals, to endow them with sweeping powers, and to make a shambles of civil society, remains something of an enigma. Only by penetrating the deepest recesses of the Bhutto mind will answers be found. Failing this, however, it can only be said that the man never trusted his own popularity. Related to this contention is a matter that can only be notionalized, that is, that Bhutto was determined to keep the ghosts of his political career from weakening his hand. No one knew better than he what it had taken, indeed, what it had cost the nation, for him to realize his personal political objectives.

In the wake of the FSF dissolution, its former leaders and rank and file officers were routinely interrogated and, as expected, they not only revealed the corps' more heinous acts, they eagerly implicated the Quaid-i-Awam in virtually every one of them. Testimony of Bhutto's aggressive and illegal, if not corrupt, behaviour was derived from other sources as well. All the Chairman's enemies, many of them his intimate colleagues for shorter or longer periods, now found it possible, and to some extent personally necessary, to describe Bhutto's style of governance in the most unseemly terms. Bhutto was accused of committing the most venal sins, and in circumstances where so many had strayed from the solemn path, confessions came quickly. Religious scruples were again significant, and the number of sinners who sought repentance opened a cornucopia of sordid tales, all of which were traced to the behaviour and orders of the PPP Chairman.

The Zia-orchestrated *coup* built upon a resurgence of Islamic fundamentalism that was amply demonstrated during the election campaign. The assault on Bhutto's allegedly anti-Islamic behaviour had begun many years before, and at the time of his overthrow it had reached exceptional intensity. Bhutto's declaration calling for the banning of alcoholic beverages, the closing of amusement establishments, and new expressions of piety, could not expiate his previous actions. Thus, following the *coup*, and given the call for an Islamic renaissance and the cleansing of the Augean stables, Bhutto became the focal point of a military-led national catharsis. It was during this sequence of events that Zia began to ponder a political future. Seeing himself in a position not only to restore Pakistan's stability, but to guarantee the restitution of the nation's 'true' genius, Zia's religious devotions now included and centred on the revitalization of the national entity that had suddenly become his responsibility to direct. Religious calling and political ambition fused with the role of the professional soldier, and it was no longer simply a matter of re-establishing law and order or promoting democracy, but the reclaiming of a battered and lost national ethos. Zia's austere lifestyle stood in vivid contrast with that of the deposed Quaid-i-Awam. Zia claimed to be indifferent in the matter of creature comforts, and he would remain billeted in his modest cantonment residence for the more than ten years of his rule, never ignoring his obligation to observe the rituals of the pious Muslim. By sheer example of service without material reward, Zia would hold the confidence of his soldiers and reach out to those in Pakistani society who had had all they could take of the Quaid-i-Awam's performance. Like the *khalifa* of Islamic tradition, Zia declared he would release the politicians, but he also admonished them from conducting political activities until the sacred period of Ramadan had been completed. On July 28, some three weeks after Bhutto's overthrow, Zia flew to Murree with General Faiz Ali Chishti, the officer who had carried out the original 'arrest' order, to inform the PPP Chairman that he was free to return to his home in Larkana. After a brief stay in his ancestral home, Bhutto went on to Karachi and his residence in Clifton. Wherever he went, the crowds that had sung his praises earlier were just as eager to welcome him back to his familiar surroundings. Bhutto clearly retained the support of a sizeable segment of the Pakistani public, and in some ways, his mystique as a unique historical figure had expanded with his overthrow. For an unknown portion of the Pakistani nation, Bhutto was still the preferred choice over a discredited army command, and particularly one led by an officer few had ever heard of. By contrast with the fallen Bhutto, and despite his Islamic bona fides, Zia could hardly arouse the attention given to Zulfikar Ali Bhutto. Bhutto may have been a feared and even hated ruler, but he had demonstrated a capacity for leadership over a twenty-year period, and he seemed to best articulate the country's independent character. Moreover, as a soldier, Zia had betrayed a trust when he turned on the very man who had given him his rank and status. Bhutto was Pakistan's scoundrel, but he was also the embodiment of his own propaganda. Zia would find that coping with the Bhutto enigma involved playing a zero-sum game, a high-stakes game in which only one of the two principals would be allowed to survive.

Zia's Decision to Rule

Zia had appointed an Election Commission comprised of five respected judges, and had authorized the holding of Pakistan's third national election on 18 October. The political parties rushed to field their candidates for the contest, but none of the organizations were as prepared for the challenge as the PPP. Moreover, the Quaid-i-Awam was ever more eagerly embraced by his followers and supporters, especially those Pakistanis who would accept any civilian leader, if only in order to avoid the grasp of the army. Bhutto's triumphal return to Lahore, following his sojourn in Karachi, was clear proof that he and his party would carry the populous provinces much as they had done in the 1970 elections, and perhaps even more so. Bhutto remained strong in bearing and his speeches were never more forceful. It was obvious that he remained a dominant presence, and that nothing the military had done in deposing him had diminished his stature in the eyes of his public. Among the masses, leaders were identified for their strength of character and resolute demeanour, and Bhutto epitomized the oriental potentate whose lavish living and sometime cruel expression were acknowledged extensions of his power and privilege (Burki,1980). That the more erudite and sophisticated might find such adulation disturbing did not factor into the equation, and it was left to the opposition politicians and their dedicated followers to compete with the PPP juggernaut.

The *coup*-makers, therefore, questioned the decision to release Bhutto from protective custody and to reopen the election process. Those who had energized the operation and had succeeded in bringing the high command into play were overtaken by something approaching bewilderment as well as deep concern. Zia, they believed, had moved with too great haste and, in so doing, had jeopardized the entire action. There had not been the necessary time to make the case against the Chairman, and although considerable evidence had been assembled that placed Bhutto in the midst of a variety of criminal acts, it was still too early to hold him accountable. Moreover, Zia's expectation that appeals to chaste Islamic behaviour would be enough to turn the people against the PPP leader was not realized. In an effort to retrieve a failing strategy, Zia again met with Bhutto at the end of August, but he only hinted that he was considering moving back the date for the elections. Bhutto sensed that something more sinister than the postponement of the elections was afoot, however, and not six days later he was arrested in his Karachi home by special units of the Pakistan Army.

Unlike the July 'arrest', this time Bhutto was treated as a common criminal after being informed that he was being charged with murder and other serious crimes. Scheduled to be arraigned before the Lahore High Court on 13 September, Bhutto was released from prison on that day, but not formally charged. Set free on bail, he returned to his Larkana home. Some time past midnight on 17 September, however, a unit of commandos stormed Bhutto's estate, ignored his court-directed bail order and, citing martial law, bundled him off to Karachi, from where he was despatched to a dark cell in Kot Lakhpat prison, not far from Lahore. The ebb and flow of Bhutto's fortunes dramatized the divisions within the army, with one group signaling leniency while another demanded direct action. It could be argued that Zia's hand was forced for the final time; that he too now realized that Bhutto must be denied the opportunity to return to public life. Moreover, Bhutto did not have a private life. A major political actor for almost two decades, Bhutto personified the total politician. His imprisonment, therefore, was aimed at ending forever his role in the politics of Pakistan (Schofield, 1979). It meant taking his mortal life as well.

On 1 October Zia announced that the elections scheduled for mid-month would have to be postponed. Claiming that a variety of irregularities had been uncovered implicating a wide array of politicians, not the least of whom was Zulfikar Ali Bhutto, Zia said that the time was inopportune for the conduct of new elections and that the country needed more time to repair the damage done by the previous regime. The high-stakes game had moved from the political to the legal realm. With the Pakistani nation on the sidelines, it was the jurists who would be called upon to determine who was right and who wrong, who had committed unacceptable acts and who was justified in using extraordinary powers.

A.K. Brohi, perhaps Pakistan's most celebrated barrister, argued the case for martial law by citing the massive rigging and fraudulent acts perpetrated by the PPP government in the March elections. The disturbances that followed in the wake of the elections were a direct consequence of these events, and it was too late for the deposed Prime Minister to hide behind a constitution which he himself had so blatantly violated. Confronted with the spectre of another civil war, the army did its duty in terminating the Bhutto government, and the declaration of martial law was essential for the restoration of peace and tranquillity in the country. Moreover the constitution had not been abrogated, merely suspended pending a return to normalcy, hence, the Bhutto complaint was without merit. The nine members of the Supreme Court, finding that the martial law regime was lawful, then proceeded to unanimously dismiss the petition brought before it by Begum Nusrat Bhutto on behalf of her husband. Bhutto's fate had been sealed. He would remain in prison while his trial for conspiring to murder Ahmad Raza Kasuri proceeded in Lahore's High Court.

Utilizing the testimony of the FSF officers, particularly Masood Mahmood, Bhutto was linked with the order to kill his opponent, a matter that was corroborated indirectly by another FSF operator, Saeed Ahmad Khan. Bhutto denied the accusation. He also argued in his own defence that the available evidence did not prove his culpability. But plead as he did, he was helpless to reverse a verdict reached before the trial commenced.

The case was decided in March 1978. Bhutto was declared guilty as charged and sentenced to death, precipitating a long and agonizing appeal process. In the meantime Zia, who had so frequently expressed his disinterest in politics, declared himself President of Pakistan in September of that year. Also, during the passing months the martial law government prepared and released a series of White Papers that cited the many crimes of Zulfikar Ali Bhutto and his administration. Zia could now publicly describe Bhutto as a murderer, stating that Kasuri had not been the only victim of the Quaid-i-Awam's decision-making apparatus. Nevertheless, the General never raised the question of trying Bhutto on other murder charges, nor did he release documents to substantiate his statements.

To the end, Bhutto pleaded his innocence. Removed to the dank, dark, vermin-infested prison cell in Rawalpindi where he awaited his execution, Bhutto wrote to Zia, poetically accounting for his total, all-consuming, completely public life. Calling politics the soul of life, he spoke of his genesis to political fame as 'written in the stars' (Wolpert,1993, p.327). Earlier he had noted, 'it (politics) is my eternal romance with the people. Only the people can break the eternal bond. To me politics and the people are synonymous' (Wolpert, p.324). Believing to the last that no one other than his abstract concept of 'people' could take the measure of his life, Bhutto questioned how a common, obscure soldier, one he alone had brought to notoriety, would dare to wreck this ethereal marriage of folk and leader (Bhutto, 1979, p.223). Eloquence was never distant from the Quaid-i-Awam, but neither was the executioner. Bhutto knew full well he was in the grip of an unshakable earthly eminence, and solace could only be found in the mystical expression of a transcending spirit. 'The last days come for every actor on the stage,' he wrote (Wolpert, p.327). In preparation for his physical death, Bhutto soliloquized on the symbolism in his dying at the hand of a 'usurper'. The Quaid-i-Awam could hardly be expected to feign immortality. Bhutto penned his note to Zia neither for himself nor for the addressee, but for posterity. His message was to the generations of Pakistanis unborn who, in recounting the tale of those trying days, would not only exonerate him, but draw from his martyrdom the strength to do for Pakistan what in life he had failed to do. Bhutto's mysticism provided insight into an afterlife. From the darkness of his cell, Bhutto stoically found the glow of a life fulfilled.

Chief Justice Anwarul Haq had consumed hundreds of pages in explaining the deciding vote that sealed Bhutto's fate. A divided court, less two of its members, voted four to three to convict and to order the punishment of death on the gallows. Bhutto's appeal was poignant but fruitless. Left to languish in his musty dungeon while awaiting the call to final judgment, denied all but a few visits, his physical and mental state was allowed to deteriorate. Noting that his jailers did not have the civility to ease his pain in the year following the death sentence, Bhutto questioned the heartless vindictiveness of his captors who denied him even a ray of sunshine or an 'embrace of fresh air' (Wolpert, 1993, p.327).

Capitals around the world beseeched Zia, some asking for clemency, while others stated a willingness to take Bhutto into permanent exile. But none of these international pressures could budge the General, who now alone controlled the decision of life or death for the Quaid-i-Awam. In the end, Zia cast aside all entreaties and refused to pardon the one man who could prevent him from placing his own mark upon Pakistan. Like Bhutto, Zia too had a mystical core. Incubated in different surroundings and nourished by different experience, the General-turned-President envisioned a new order for the nation, a different Pakistan from that imagined by Jinnah, Ayub, or Bhutto. Zia believed his predecessors were all desirous of setting a path for the nation, but he had concluded that all were misled, all were too enamoured of alien devices and expressions, and hence, all had failed themselves, and most important, had failed the people of Pakistan.

Bhutto in his final agony believed Zia to be a 'strange and mercurial person, a liar and a double-crosser' (Wolpert, 1993, p.327). That was the Bhutto perspective, notably, under the most deleterious of circumstances—his imminent death by hanging. But Zia had already dispensed with Bhutto, and to him the Chairman's last days were meaningless, given his decision to lead the nation into a new era. Bhutto's cry for life fell on deaf ears, as the man who assumed all responsibility for his death prepared the groundwork for a Pakistan after the Quaid-i-Awam. Jinnah had dreamed the impossible dream, and Ayub's pragmatism was dead on arrival. Bhutto had borrowed an amalgam of experiences from distant places that had little or no significance in 'the land of the pure'. More so than those who had preceded him, Zia believed he understood the nature and essence of Pakistan and, hoping to avoid the pitfalls of his predecessors, he charted a course which he believed followed the rhythm and history of the Muslims of the subcontinent.

An ardent admirer of I.H. Qureshi, Zia had read the works of the noted historian, had acknowledged Qureshi's plight during the reign of Zulfikar Ali Bhutto, and had resurrected the old scholar to help him translate his ideas into policy. Qureshi, whose political activism began with the Khilafat Movement, had been the major author of the Objectives Resolution, and had long given resonance to the Islamic ideal. Treated with respect by Pakistan's military rulers, he had suffered harassment and abuse from Bhutto's legions. A former dean of St. Stephens College, Delhi, like Zia he had opted for Pakistan at partition, and had served in the Pakistan central cabinet until 1954. Named Vice-Chancellor of Karachi University during the Ayub era, his last assignment, overseeing the work of the Council of Islamic Ideology, was conferred upon him by General Zia who, it should be noted, was also a pall-bearer at his funeral in 1981.

The association of scholars like Brohi and Qureshi with Zia is instructive. Neither man relished military rule, nor were they enamoured of the Chief Martial Law Administrator or inclined to curry favour. Neither could be accused of sycophancy. Their intimacy with Zia tells a different story. More a reflection of their despair during the reign of Zulfikar Ali Bhutto, they were eager to give their support to the man who ended the rule of the Quaid-i-Awam—although it is doubtful they sanctioned his being put to death. Moreover, when Zia enlisted their services (Brohi as Law Minister) in the refashioning of national order, they believed they were serving the greater interests of a nation they had had some responsibility in creating.

The Kafkaesque character of the Pakistani experience was never more clearly illustrated than in the early morning of 4 April 1979, when Zulfikar Ali Bhutto, having said goodbye to Begum Nusrat and Benazir hours earlier, was led from his prison cell to the gallows and hanged until dead. Away from the scene of the execution, plans were well in train for the re-ordering of the Pakistani political system and society. And for those engaged in the reconstruction of the nation, there was little time or inclination to reflect on the demise of the PPP leader.

Bhutto's body was flown within hours to his ancestral estate, where he was intered almost immediately. Neither his wife or daughter were allowed to attend the burial and Bhutto's sons, Murtaza and Shah Nawaz were also absent, being in London, where they had earlier taken refuge to avoid Zia's wrath. The two surviving Bhutto males were, in fact, already engaged in the organization of an underground resistance movement which they called Al-Zulfikar, after their now deceased father. Begum Nusrat Bhutto and Benazir remained in Pakistan and were held under house arrest, but it was they who none the less took up the cause of the martyred Chairman of the Pakistan People's Party and vowed to reclaim his glory.

Thus began the decade of Ziaul Haq, the least likely of the personalities to grace Pakistan's centre stage. History had again demonstrated its fickleness as well as its unpredictability. Zia had had almost two years to contemplate his future, and more in keeping with the expressions of Macbeth than Hamlet, he accepted the brevity of the hours allotted to him. As a soldier, he could acknowledge the shedding of blood in the struggle for national survival, and judged by the dimensions of the blood shed in bringing Bhutto to power, his emergence as Pakistan's fountainhead was deemed serene. Believing he had silenced his only significant foe, Zia, who was now totally committed to ruling Pakistan from his cantonment residence, began in earnest the process of reclaiming the country's national ethos.

The Early Years

When the Pakistan Army deposed the civilian government of Zulfikar Ali Bhutto in July 1977, Pakistan's newest Chief Martial Law Administrator declared his intention to redirect the course of Pakistani politics. Martial law had become a customary and not unexpected feature of Pakistani political life. The masses were generally indifferent to the coming and going of the military juntas, but those claiming to represent their interests were quick to acknowledge this manner of political succession.

No Pakistani civilian government had ever completed its full term (unless it is assumed that Bhutto enjoyed a full term prior to the 1977 elections) and no election process had been in place long enough to smoothly transfer authority from one administration to another. Such was the condition up to the coming of Ziaul Haq, and so it would be long after his passing. Only the attaining of a critical national mass, seldom a predictable condition, foretold the termination of one government and its replacement by another, and always it was the army that became the instrument of transition. And more often than not it was the army that assumed responsibility for managing the nation. Nor did Pakistan enjoy the luxury of sustained direction under a single leader. No Qadaffis, Assads, Saddams, or Mubaraks graced the Pakistan scene. No monarchies hinted at who would succeed whom when the moment arrived to move from one ruler to another. Bhutto was the first of the Pakistani political personalities who seriously anticipated entrenching a political system that guaranteed his office for life. And perhaps he succeeded, but not, certainly, as he had imagined. His little more than five years in power were so brief that even the matter of consolidating his rule escaped his grasp.

Zia could not have anticipated an indefinite tenure, given the experience of his predecessors, and he was certainly conversant with the Pakistani succession dilemma. Nevertheless, he went about the business of governing Pakistan with the goal of sustaining his authority as long as possible which, in the parlance of Pakistan politics, meant so long as he could control the Pakistani Army. Although in his initial years he was considered an intellectual lightweight, Zia was, perhaps, the most erudite of the Pakistani generals. Never one to claim scholarly achievements, he was reasonably well-read, and when tasked, well-versed in matters of the human spirit. He seemed to enjoy conversations with scholars and men of ideas, and he proved to be a good listener in his more quiet and private moments. Zia's less than dominating appearance masked a quick, intelligent, and decisive mental capacity that was often equated with deviousness. Nevertheless, in the years that followed he would demonstrate a prowess for leadership unmatched by his predecessors. And although his many detractors were fixed on his daily performance as the ultimate decision-maker, Zia reinvigorated the armed forces and, at the same time, addressed the needs of an unstable society. He sustained the ban on political parties and kept the legislatures sealed while other forms of representation were pondered and, in time, institutionalized. But because all his reforms were judged to be self-serving, seldom would he be credited with introducing a programme of societal significance.

Zia was not one to talk about 'basic democracy', nor was he eager to reinvent the parliamentary experience. He truly believed that political parties were anathema in the Pakistan milieu and that little of value was produced in the parliamentary setting. Pakistani politics had developed from the beginning as negative expression, and political activity was too often conducted in the streets, rather than in the halls of the legislatures. In Zia's opinion, Pakistani politics had become the art of disarming your opponent, not doing the people's business. The Pakistani masses were generally a materially poor people, limited in educational attainments, grossly illiterate, and prone to exaggerated behaviour. Easy prey for demagogic personalities who claimed leadership over them, their pervasive gullibility offset efforts at constructing social responsibility. Pakistan was a far cry from the civil society that was the goal of contemporary nation-states, and the manipulation of power by the few was perpetuated in an environment of benign neglect.

Zia was challenged by two very different Pakistans. One was expressed in the ethnically diverse multitudes living on the margins of the modern world. The other represented the informed, educated, and involved members of a sophisticated political and economic experience. The latter articulated the sentiments of becoming national, they also monopolized the critical stations in society and created the patterns of contemporary discourse. Melding the two Pakistans was the task assumed by the country's previous leaders. Each had designed a different blueprint to chart their policies, but none was successful in harmonizing theory with reality, let alone in merging the two Pakistans. In fact, the record shows that they were more likely to pit the one world against the other, to bring them into collision rather than ease them along separate but parallel paths. As a consequence, their failure was writ large in the sustained turmoil of the Pakistan experience, and Zia's attempt to transcend the dialectical character of the Pakistan design was both laudable and foolhardy.

Starting with the constitutional order that addressed the second of the two Pakistans, by declaration and edict, particularly with the issuance of the Provisional Constitution Order of March 1981, Zia revised the 1973 Constitution so that it could not challenge his authority. Constitutions were meant to limit the power of authority, to compel actions that were predictable and centred on due process and the rule of law. The general purpose of constitutions was the safeguarding of the citizenry against the arbitrary uses of power. Government was by its nature powerful, and the essential requirement was not the conferment or confirmation of more or greater powers, but the enhancement of the public's welfare and interests. Constitutions were developed to close the gap between the rulers and the ruled, not to exaggerate the distance. In truth, constitutions promise democratic safeguards and military systems are, by their nature, undemocratic. Martial law is a condition least likely to evoke liberal ideas or allow diverse expression. But it is forever bewildering that the plea for democratic procedure is best articulated when the military replaces a civilian-led government that has failed to live within a constitutional order of its own making.

The army junta that took control of Pakistan in July 1977 shared much in common with its earlier counterparts, but it was also a unique body in that it represented generational change. Gone were the officers of the World War II period, that is, the men who bridged the colonial with the post-colonial world. Zia and his colleagues displayed little inclination for grand designs. More pessimistic than their predecessors, chastened by defeat and humiliation, forced to acknowledge their weaknesses, they were hardened by adversity and more inclined to accept survival as their essential goal. Finding strength in their Islamic heritage, the soldiers looked for ways to relate the teachings of the Prophet (PBUH) with those of Mohammad Ali Jinnah. Jinnah's secular expressions were muted in an ambience which demanded more substantial displays of piety as faith assumed operational importance. The merger of spiritual and temporal worlds, the combining of the immutable and unknowable with the profane and the pedantic, was the task the generals made their number one priority.

Zia's views, and it can be assumed those of his brother officers, were contained in a speech delivered in December 1982 celebrating the birth anniversary of the Prophet (PBUH). Zia stressed the need to direct Pakistani life in accordance with the teachings of the Koran and Sunna and to propagate the faith and performance of their spiritual leader. Attending the ceremony were the key ministers and advisers of the government, as well as leaders of the religious community. President Zia declared that nothing less than jihad could promote Islamic values, and his government searched for guidance in holy scripture as it went about the work of creating the *Nizam-i-Mustafa* or Rule of the Prophet (PBUH) in Pakistan. Citing the adoption of Islamic laws, he reiterated the need to strengthen the country's moral fibre, and for this reason he was determined to advance his Islamization programme.

Zia believed the riddle of the two Pakistans had an answer, and he anticipated transforming Pakistan brick by brick from a congeries of conflicting mindsets and regional societies into the solidary community that he associated with an Islamic state. The bricks included *zakat* (alms) and *ushr* (the tax on agriculture) which were supposed to provide the state with the resources needed to assist the less fortunate members of society. Zia also cited the government's intention to impose the Islamic rules of *qisas* (the right of pre-emption) and *diyat* (the laws of evidence in Islam), to establish *Qazi* courts (headed by religious judges), and to introduce an Islamic judicial system, as well as to eliminate the use of interest in all commercial and financial undertakings. Such reforms, it was said, were fashioned to root out the corruption and exploitation of the many by the few. But they nevertheless disturbed the established and more secular legal fraternity, and also undermined the power of cosmopolitan elites, causing many among the entrepreneurial class to move their assets abroad and, in some cases, to leave the country. Zia may have found an answer to the riddle of the two Pakistans, but it received only a partial response.

Zia made repeated attempts to assure his more adroit citizens that his Islamization programme was genuine and was aimed at neither destroying his rivals, nor perpetuating his rule. With a view to the larger Muslim world, which he described as too weak to resist foreign incursions, Zia believed that Pakistan too suffered from moral decay. Humiliation, division, and defeat, he noted, would continue if the country did not return to the source of its faith. Pakistan, he opined, must set an example for the entire Islamic world. Calling for true demonstrations of piety, selflessness, and high ethical conduct, he envisaged Pakistan's newly-found unity in faith becoming a beaton for Muslim nations everywhere. Zia's programme for Islamic reform, therefore, went well beyond the confines of the Pakistan nation, but he was candid enough to acknowledge that the basic test was very much at home.

Zia's principal concern on the political front appeared to be the history of Pakistan's political parties. An Islamic country, he would assert, had no need for political parties. The different organizations, with their conflicting philosophies and petty competition, caused unnecessary divisions within society, and obviated efforts at building national unity. Parties, he contended, lacked national purpose, denigrated discipline, and encouraged outlandish and reprehensible behaviour. Pakistan, a divided country at birth, could never bridge its differences while wedded to a political party format. In effect, parties had promoted anarchy, prompted chaos, and weakened national resolve. It was Zia's judgment that irreconcilable competition among the political parties had provoked the civil war in East Pakistan, and why, he puzzled, should political parties stand higher than the country? Convinced that Yahya Khan had allowed himself to be overwhelmed by the parties and their central spokesmen, he vowed it would never happen again.

For Zia, therefore, political parties were little more than alien importations, hardly relevant to Pakistani political culture. He rationalized their permanent banning and urged their supporters to find other vehicles to express their political interests. Zia acknowledged the absolute nature of the prohibition on conventional politics, but he argued his impartiality in doing so. All groups, at every level of Pakistani society, had been treated in the same fashion. Mainline politicians, students, representatives of the Islamic organizations, all had been neutralized. Once vibrant urban communities were restrained by martial law edicts, and the rural masses were insulated against those claiming to speak on their behalf. Stating that the politicians had long practised the 'politics of destruction', Zia insisted they could never again be trusted with the nation's destiny.

Having demolished the traditional role of the political parties, on 18 December 1982 Zia spoke about the need for a constitutional provision that would give the armed forces a legitimate and continuing role in any future political system. Noting its inspirational unity, its discipline and dedication to public service, Zia believed that the army was best equipped to assemble the new government. According to Zia, the military had sworn allegiance to the nation, had committed their lives to its defence, and eschewed personal gain. He assured the public that neither he nor his commanders were enamoured of power. On the contrary, the country had been so steeped in political intrigue, had been so abused by political personalities, that no institution save the armed forces remained untainted and hence, capable of fulfilling national aspirations. And because there were those who questioned his motivations, Zia wanted the world, and especially his Pakistani brethren, to know that 'if anything happens to me, there are other generals in the army who will take over', that the views he expressed and the ideas he espoused emerged from a professional calling, not personal desire or ambition (Nyrop, 1984, p.186).

The External Dimension

Zia's thinking, as well as his style of governing, were influenced in major part by external conditions. Pakistan was not the only country in the region experiencing climactic events. When Zia seized power in 1977, Indira Gandhi and the Congress had been overtaken by the Janata Party of Morarji Desai. By 1980, however, the anti-Indira coalition had disintegrated and she was returned to office. Her re-election came at a tense moment, given the Soviet invasion of Afghanistan in December 1979. The first-ever Soviet assault on an independent Muslim nation since World War II was supposedly aimed at sustaining a communist regime in Kabul, but the danger that it posed to Pakistan could not be ignored. Moreover, Prime Minister Gandhi's reaction to the Soviet incursion verged on the supportive, thus intensifying rumours that Moscow and New Delhi were engaged in squeezing and eventually partitioning Pakistan between them. More immediately, the Soviet foray into Afghanistan precipitated the flight of tens of thousands, and then hundreds of thousands of Afghan refugees, most of whom crossed over into Pakistan. Islamabad did what it could to receive and care for the hordes of desperate, impoverished people, but its resources were stretched thin in doing so. And although token relief in the form of money and supplies came from other countries, Islamabad was generally left to its own devices in managing one of the largest mass migrations in contemporary history.

Pakistan's western neighbours were both crisis-driven. Sardar Daud, his family members, and close confidants were all murdered in a bloody Marxist *coup* in March 1978. At the time of the uprising, Daud had been actively pursuing a diplomatic understanding with Pakistan. First Bhutto, and later Zia, had met with the Afghan leader who, somewhat influenced by the Shah of Iran, had agreed to turn from his long-term enmity toward Pakistan and begin the process of normalizing their cross-border relations. Daud was succeeded by a communist cabal known as the People's Democratic Party of Afghanistan, or Khalq led by Noor Mohammad Taraki and Hafizullah Amin. The PDPA's Soviet affiliation and the belief that Moscow had engineered the *coup*, caused Zia to hold up recognition of the new government. And in fact, the new government was one in name only. Within a year the PDPA broke apart, Amin murdered Taraki, and the Red Army pushed its way into Afghanistan to prevent further internecine warfare. The Soviet invasion of Afghanistan in December 1979 eliminated Amin and installed Babrak Karmal, leader of the PDPA-Parcham, as the head of the Afghan government.

Afghans, who had already taken up arms against the original Marxists, now centred their campaign on the forces of Babrak Karmal. Moreover, the scattered, small-unit character of the Afghan resistance, known broadly as the mujahiddin, made it virtually impossible to subdue. Provided with sanctuary in Pakistan, the mujahiddin established their headquarters in and around Peshawar, and from there prosecuted their war against both the Kabul and Soviet forces. Zia described Pakistan as a frontline state, and the defence of the country, barring the direct use of Pakistani forces, lay in assisting the mujahiddin, who were funneled arms and supplies. Because of the Soviet invasion of Afghanistan, Pakistan was again accorded priority status by Washington. Moreover, the inauguration in 1981 of President Ronald Reagan could not have come at a more auspicious moment. Unlike his predecessor, Jimmy Carter, whose offer of arms to Pakistan was rejected by General Zia as too meagre, Reagan made Islamabad a major arms recipient. Thus the Pakistan armed forces began to make up for the lean years caused by the American embargo, and the Afghan mujahiddin were assured a sustained flow of weapons.

Although confronted with a major threat to his country's territorial integrity, Zia was a major beneficiary of the Soviet invasion of Afghanistan, but it was not the only external issue influencing his administration.

Pakistan's other Muslim neighbour, Iran, was also the setting for dramatic events in 1978-9. The Shah never enjoyed the popularity that might have legitimized his rule, and despite the prosperity that the 1970s oil boom brought to the nation, by January 1979 he was forced to flee his country. The Iranian monarchy was terminated, and the country took on its new character as an Islamic Republic, led by Ayatollah Ruhollah Khomeini, a celebrated and charismatic member of the country's Shiite clergy. The revolutionary nature of the transformation in Iran, its turn toward theocracy, contrasted with the very secular Saur Marxist revolution in Afghanistan.

When Zia spoke of Muslim nations under pressure, in retreat, or searching for their true destiny, Iran and Afghanistan were uppermost in his thoughts. The revolution in Iran and the Soviet intrusion into Afghanistan affected Pakistan in different ways, but Zia believed an Islamic theme connected both situations.

Temperamentally, but also strategically, Zia was convinced that only by emphasizing Islamic precepts and tradition, by practising the socio-political values of the Muslim faith, could he expect to weather both the internal and external storms that shook his country. Nor did Zia for a moment question his actions in holding close the reins of power. Reinforced in his attitude by the United States, which perceived Islam as a bulwark against ideological communism and so was eager to supply the military aid Zia requested, he also drew strength from the support received from his regional Muslim neighbours, notably Turkey, Saudi Arabia, the United Arab Emirates, and Egypt.

Zia was never shaken in his belief that Pakistan was his to mould, and that Islamization was the only path to success. It would be pointless to argue the insincerity of Zia's intention to Islamicize the Pakistan design. Zia's faults were many, and the dictatorial character of his administration is a matter of record. But Zia was also a man in the middle, trapped by unprecedented domestic confusion on the one side, and uncertain, epoch-making external changes on the other. During his rule, all the indices of violence intensified. Moreover, the war in Afghanistan not only flooded the country with several million refugees, the newcomers also caused gun-running to spread, and the trafficking in drugs to expand. Given Zia's other priorities, socio-economic development was brought to a virtual standstill, and the country's dependence on international donors deepened. Nevertheless, Pakistan survived the harsh vicissitudes of the period, and there can be little doubt that its dauntless General-President deserved some of the credit.

The Junta

The soldier-politicians who have dominated the Pakistan scene almost from the inception of the state cannot be brushed aside as minor actors or, indeed, temporary usurpers. Clearly, they have played the major roles in steering the Pakistan state, and they have had the more significant long-term effect in sustaining and/or forming national institutions. Yahya authorized the country's first national election and tried to resurrect the parliamentary system, but it was Ayub Khan who is remembered as Pakistan's most constructive ruler. His lasting monuments are found in the gleaming city of Islamabad and the growth and expansion of the nation's middle class. From Ayub's Basic Democracies, to Yahya's Legal Framework Order, to Zia's Islamization Programme, the martial law generals have proven more innovative and industrious than the conventional politicians. More so than the country's civilian leaders, the soldiers have consistently centred attention on territorial integrity, national unity, and socio-political enterprise.

Martial law was never conceived as a mechanism for nation-building, but Pakistan was born in crisis and crisis has stalked the country from independence to the present. From the outset, the parochial character of Pakistani political life negated efforts at stabilizing political institutions, let alone centralizing authority. Weak centres were always forced to yield to a demanding periphery, and governments were only briefly capable of managing federal-provincial relations. Juntas, therefore, became surrogates for representative government. But even the strong and forceful character of the military succeeded only momentarily in masking, not subduing, deep-rooted fissiparous tendencies. Moreover, the persistence of the Pakistani dilemma, the enormous difficulties encountered in engineering a solidary polity, caused junta leaders to extend their political tenure. Thus, what was initially acceptable, even popular, became menacing and combative. Moreover, once the cast of military characters assumed tangible form and were not observed returning to their professional duties, public reaction became especially negative. Pakistani society proved fickle as well as naive. On the one side, only military intervention seemed capable of ridding the country of unpopular civilian governments. On the other, the very methods employed in neutralizing political foes never suggested more positive, let alone more democratic, performance.

The imposition of martial law is a partisan phenomenon in that a representative organization is often denied expression at the urging of another. But martial law authorities, and notably juntas, are not by their nature tied to one group or the other. Nevertheless, the fact that competitive political arrangements in Pakistan have not produced the desired results, that is, have not allowed predictable and peaceful transfers of power, has made it possible for the military to repeatedly assert its right to change governments and hence influence outcomes. Juntas are not tailored to satisfy diverse publics in the long term, and interposition is programmed to result in broadscale popular disaffection, particularly when the action is portrayed as self-enriching, and not a matter of public service.

But there is still another dimension of the junta experience in Pakistan that requires comment. A new country, Pakistan could not have been expected to spring fullblown and developed at the moment of independence. The country took form only with a transfer of power that was made by the colonial authority to the Muslim League. It was the Muslim League, its leaders and followers, but especially Mohammad Ali Jinnah, who were sanctioned by the former rulers of the subcontinent to represent extensive, disparate geographic regions, and it was only the Muslim League which was endowed with the freedom to address independent political views and speak for the totality of a reconfigured community. In effect, the power enjoyed by other groups and individuals prior to August 1947 was undermined and circumscribed by the power granted to the Quaid-i-Azam and his associates. A relatively loose political arrangement that had permitted local rulers to sustain their authority during the imperial period had been substituted for another that was more rigid in form as well as in purpose. The colonial experience meant different things to the different actors. The more traditional ones, in fact, lost their largely independent status after the withdrawal of the British Raj, whereas more recently organized assemblies, represented by relatively more enlightened, better educated, and sophisticated representatives of a somewhat distant, urban-based society, grew in stature and power. The juxtaposition of these different power centres, the older more conversant with the nature and uses of power, and the younger more given to ideational expression, were predestined to clash, and the complications experienced in fabricating a working relationship produced the instabilities that the military institution could not ignore.

The army's intrusion into the political arena was less a bridging manoeuvre than a substitution of one authority for another. The different sets of politicians, therefore, were never given the time necessary to demonstrate if they could themselves reconcile their differences and, at the same time, promote national unity along with the country's physical development. Moreover, faced with an external threat from their once joined and now hostile neighbour, and given the unresolved geopolitical issues at the time of independence, the armed forces concluded that protracted internal conflict only whetted the appetite of their near nemesis. According to prevailing military doctrine, security made it essential that political stability and national integration precede exercises in constitutional democracy. Thus it was not that the different Pakistan constitutions were poorly constructed, or that the politicians were inexperienced in the administration of government, but that the competitive political process encouraged too much conflict and too little consensus. Pakistanis of varied political experience failed to demonstrate that they could tolerate the behaviour and antics of their opposition, their equal right to hold power, or their management of national affairs having once achieved their goal. Moreover, constitutional protections appeared to intensify controversy rather than promote accommodation, and the country's several constitutions were abandoned with little understanding or concern for the consequences.

The result, therefore, was the atrophy of Pakistani political life, the perpetuation of unresolved problems, and the constancy of the military intrusion. Bhutto came into prominence because in collaborating with the military establishment, he also challenged it. Bhutto sought the freedom from opposition enjoyed by the juntas. He not only concerned himself with the need to make the armed forces an extension of his will, he was also determined to prevent deliberate challenges to his authority from the political opposition. Bhutto wanted nothing less than the extraordinary power and trust granted the Quaid-i-Azam, and he knew that had Jinnah wanted a throne and sceptre, a majority of his countrymen would have supplied them. Having contemplated the history of Pakistan, it was Bhutto's contention that the country desperately needed an absolute ruler who could not only insulate the nation against the vagaries of human ambition, but also represent its highest aspirations.

Like the commanders of the Pakistan Army, Bhutto played at democracy, but never believed it suited Pakistan's political culture. But even more than the leaders of the juntas, Bhutto ignored the pleas of the urbane members of Pakistani society. And whereas the Ayubs, the Yahyas, and even the Zias, were forced to consider the demands of the cosmopolitan members of the community, Bhutto turned a deaf ear. Paradoxically, the Quaid-i-Awam gave himself all the trappings of a people's leader but failed to enlist the very people who could assist him in realizing that quest. In spite of all his eloquence about contemporary democracy, Bhutto's representation of a people's leader was very much that of a feudal lord surrounded by obedient serfs whose every action focused on his personal gratification. Bhutto, almost from the beginning of his rule, alienated the liberal members of his party and disenfranchised key members of the opposition. In the end, he only succeeded in forcing a coalition between the army high command and the urban-based intelligentsia. Bhutto fell into a trap of his own making, and prompted still another junta to re-invent Pakistan.

The Zia-led junta consisted of an inner core of the highest ranking military officers, surrounded by a circle of serving and retired officers who, in turn, were interwoven with a phalanx of civilian specialists. By contrast, Ayub Khan was never really perceived as governing by junta, nor did he employ the army command structure in direct governance. Ayub quickly civilianized martial law, gave himself Field Marshal rank, but generally left managing the service to his commanders. In governing the nation, Ayub Khan leaned heavily on the established bureaucracy, especially the elite Civil Service of Pakistan (CSP), a service Bhutto dissolved in 1973. He gave special significance to the civil-military relationship and downplayed sophisticated democratic development. Ayub's belief that Pakistan was not prepared for full-blown democratic experience was never popular among the country's more enlightened intelligentsia, but it was an honest statement made by a determined figure who had assumed primary responsibility in guiding the nation.

Ayub elevated the role of the administrative state in virtually every developmental scheme, but by the time he was forced to vacate his office, the entire edifice had been discredited. His successor, Yahya Khan, found it more appropriate, as well as necessary, to use the army high command in the day-to-day management of the country, but those plans were short-circuited by sharp differences within the junta. Moreover, these were the same divisions that Zulfikar Ali Bhutto exploited in his play for power. The end result was the tragedy in East Pakistan, the Indian intervention, the Pakistan Army surrender, and the breakup of the country. These catastrophic events prevented serious experimentation with military rule, but following the Bhutto interregnum the generals again monopolized power, and this time they were determined to run the country from command headquarters.

Zia assumed the presidency following the expiration of Chaudhry Fazal Elahi's term, declaring that his succession was temporary and that he would step aside as soon as a suitable replacement could be found. Remaining as Chief of the Army Staff, he also retained his position as Chief Martial Law Administrator. Later, citing his desire to avoid the civil strife that would result from an open competition for the presidency, he also pointed out that eligible candidates would have to undergo considerable scrutiny, and that the contest should not be allowed to further divide the nation. Few members of the attentive public accepted Zia's reasoning or his statements, however, and it was widely held that the same officers who had convinced him of the necessity of removing Bhutto had urged him to occupy the President's office. Although somewhat awestruck with his high station, Zia fitted himself into the assignment with little fanfare and even less difficulty—which left his detractors to conclude that he had planned the manoeuvre from the beginning.

Ziaul Haq was born in 1924, the son of an army clerical officer from the East Punjab (now in India). He joined the British Indian Army and earned his commission as World War II ended. As a member of the ranks during the war, Zia saw service in Burma, Malaya, and Indonesia. He opted for Pakistan at independence and immediately entered the officer corps of the Pakistan Army. Provided with advanced training in the United States, he had achieved the rank of Lieutenant-Colonel when the 1965 war with India erupted. Following that conflict, the Pakistan Army sent a number of its men, both officers and *jawans*, to select Muslim countries. Zia was directed to Jordan, where he was attached to the Jordanian Army and where, in 1970, he was called upon to assist the King, whose government was under attack from forces associated with the Palestine Liberation Organization. His service in that encounter earned him a decoration from King Hussein, and he returned to Pakistan in time to experience the humiliating defeat of the Pakistan Army. Then holding Brigadier rank, in 1972 Zia was advanced to Major-General following the reorganization of the Pakistan Army after Yahya's fall and Bhutto's ascent to power. Zia, then an innovative commander of an armoured division, was brought to Bhutto's attention by General Gul Hassan, and in 1975 he had him promoted to Lieutenant-General and made a corps commander. Despite his junior status among the senior generals, in 1976 Bhutto personally chose him to be his Chief of the Army Staff, the first *mohajir* to attain that post.

Bhutto sensed that Zia, not a product of the Pakistani Punjab nor born a Pathan, was the ideal officer to lead the Pakistan Army in a period of political transition. But eminent rank alone did not provide Zia with the *carte blanche* to run roughshod over the proud, indigenous officers who occupied key posts within the establishment. In spite of all his intimacies with the military institution, Bhutto was unfamiliar with army protocol. Zia's promotion to head the army had been made for political reasons, and no one knew this better than the new commander. Moreover, Bhutto had publicized his concern with 'Bonapartist tendencies' in the armed forces, and his selection of Zia caused the early retirement of numerous officers who had anticipated longer tenures. Aware that Bhutto was playing a cat and mouse game with their careers and future, the generals were not prepared to give Bhutto unbridled control of the armed forces, nor had they prepared themselves for a *mohajir* commander. It was soon apparent from Bhutto's statements and actions that he had selected Zia not because he was the country's most able officer, but because he believed the General would need him to fend off attacks from his brothers-in-arms. Bhutto's tactics were aimed at bringing the army high command to heel. In the end, however, he only energized the movement that would unseat and destroy him.

The retirement of key army generals had opened the ranks to heretofore field officers who now assumed staff positions. Among these officers were those who were already plotting the overthrow of the Bhutto government. Thus Bhutto had inadvertently raised into positions of significant power the very men who were determined to drive him from office. If Zia was reluctant to betray the trust of his 'subordinates', he also realized his co-operation with the *coup* instigators would be critical to his administration of the army. Aided by recently retired military commanders, Zia agreed to join the conspiracy and, as the front-man in the operation, he also assumed principal responsibility for what followed. Neither Ayub or Yahya had taken power in this fashion. Their emergence as dominant figures stemmed from the role played by Iskandar Mirza, who precipitated the action against the parliamentary system, not any particular political personality. Ayub, in short order, replaced Mirza as the leader of the *coup*, and in subsequent years, Ayub transferred his authority to Yahya. There was far less of the military junta in these episodes than in the one that brought Zia to prominence. Moreover, the army had not been a target, and neither Ayub nor Yahya had been called to take on a titan of the likes of Bhutto.

Zia could not have eliminated Bhutto without the concurrence of the junta, nor could he have sustained his authority without its continuing support. The inner core of the junta included General Mohammad Iqbal Khan, Chairman of the Joint Chiefs of Staff Committee; Lieutenant-General K.M.Arif, Chief of Staff to the President; General Sawar Khan, Vice-Chief of the army Staff; Lieutenant-General Mujibur Rahman, the Martial Law Government's Information Secretary; and Major-General (retired) Rao Farman Ali, Minister of Petroleum and Natural Resources and Director of the Fauji Foundation, the latter an arm of the powerful and influential Army Retirement Organization that has in excess of one million members. Zia headed a Military Council that included Generals Iqbal Khan, Sawar Khan, and Arif, as well as Vice-Admiral Tariq Kamal Khan, Chief of the Naval Staff, and Air Marshal Mohammad Anwar Shamim, Chief of the Air Staff. Occasionally, General Mohammad Afzal Khan, Deputy Martial law Administrator, also attended meetings of the Council. Rounding out the junta were the seven army corps commanders and the four provincial governors, who were all high-ranking officers. Each military governor (replacing the temporary governor-jurists) also performed as provincial Martial Law Administrators. They were Lieutenant-General Ghulam Jilani Khan in the Punjab, Lieutenant-General S.M. Abbasi in Sindh, Lieutenant-General Rahimuddin Khan in' Balochistan, and Lieutenant-General Fazle Haq in the North-West Frontier Province.

In the circle surrounding these officers was still another support group that included Lieutenant-General (retired) Sahabzada Yaqub Khan, who also became Minister of Foreign Affairs in 1982; Major-General (retired) Abdul Rahman Khan, who was appointed President of Azad Kashmir in 1983; Brigadier (retired) Mansoorul Haq Malik, Director of Telephone and Telegraph; Lieutenant-General (retired) Saeed Qadir, Minister of Production and National Logistics; Major-General Ghulam Safdar Butt, Chairman of the Water and Power Development Authority; Major-General M. Rahim Khan, Secretary-General of the Ministry of Defence and Chairman of Pakistan International Airlines (PIA), and Lieutenant-General Jamal Said Mian, Minister of Northern Areas and Kashmir Affairs.

In the extended perimeter of the junta were the civilian specialists in the federal ministries. These included Ghulam

Ishaq Khan, Minister of Finance and Economic Affairs; Raja Mohammad Zafarul Haq, Minister of Information and Broadcasting; Dr. Mohammad Afzal, Minister of Education; Syed Sharifuddin Pirzada, Minister of Law and Parliamentary Affairs; Ghulam Dastgir Khan, Minister of Labour, Manpower, and Overseas Pakistanis; Mahmood Ali Haroon, Minister of Interior; Mohiuddin Baluch, Minister of Communications; Mir Ali Ahmad Talpur, Minister of Defence; Mahbubul Haq, Minister of Planning and Economic Development; Mohammad Abbas Khan Abbasi, Minister of Religious and Minority Affairs; and Nawabzada Abdul Ghafoor Khan Hoti, Minister of Railways. In addition to these civilians, other prominent figures in the outer circle were A.W. Halipota, Director, Islamic Research Institute; Justice Mohammad Haleem, Chief Justice, Supreme Court, and Chairman, Pakistan Law Commission; Supreme Court Justice Shafiur Rahman, Chairman, Zakat Council; A.G.N. Kazi, Governor, State Bank of Pakistan; and Niaz Naik, Foreign Secretary.

Although periodic changes occurred within the civilian group, the core military leadership remained relatively stable through the first five years of Zia's rule. On 5 December 1982, however, the government announced the retirement of Major-General Mohammad Iqbal Choudhry, who had served as Director-General of the Ministry of Health, Social Welfare, and Population. Never an active player in the junta, it was rumoured that Chaudhry had been relieved of his command and dismissed from the government because he had persuaded Zia to release Bhutto's widow from house arrest and permit her to seek medical treatment abroad. Nusrat Bhutto proved to be in little need of medical care, however, and she was well enough to make numerous public appearances, where her denunciations of the Zia government attracted considerable overseas support and also rallied her forces at home.

All told, however, there were few rifts within the junta. Zia also consolidated his hold on power and, increasingly, was the focal point for both the credit accorded the administration as well as the blame. In fact, with the passing years, the largely collective leadership was transformed into a one-man experience. Zia combined several virtues that gained him the respect of both the serving and retired officers. He was an indefatigable figure, working long hours, following a strict regimen in diet and bearing, and always mindful of his religious obligations. Zia neither aggrandized himself during his tenure, nor did he drift from the austere lifestyle that was his mantra. In Zia, the junta not only had the buffer they all desired, they also had the tireless administrator who was prepared to give himself totally to the task of ruling the country while at the same time restoring the army's lost dignity. Therefore, in spite of their several internal contradictions, the junta projected a harmony of interest that contrasted dramatically with the turbulence experienced during the Bhutto years.

The junta was so successful in its operations that the principal opposition emanated from outside the country. Publications like the American-based *Pakistan Progressive* attempted to appeal to the radical members of the armed forces. Another, the *Delhi Patriot*, published in India, printed a text prepared by an allegedly clandestine cell within the Pakistan Army. Appearing in 1983, the document called upon the Pakistani nation to join them in a rising against the junta. Identified as the Muslim Fauji Biradiri (Muslim Army Brotherhood), the would-be conspirators described the ruling junta as:

> A despicable gang of corrupt generals, which...continues to commit monstrous crimes... The generals are more interested in lining their own pockets than in defending the nation. The corrupt generals...had betrayed the ideas of Pakistan's founder Mohammad Ali Jinnah, and were leading the country to ruin (Quoted in Ziring,1984, p.194).

Nothing resembling the Muslim Army Brotherhood materialized in the more than ten years that Zia remained at the helm of state affairs, and it would appear to have been the invention of fertile minds in the neighbouring state. Nevertheless, Zia and his colleagues expended considerable energy in the maintenance of service solidarity, and they did not fail in that endeavour.

Junta Politics

Following Zia's decision to postpone the October 1977 elections, nothing more was said about the election process until after Bhutto's execution. Apparently seeking public support for the junta's policies, Zia again announced his intention to conduct national polls and November 1979 was given as the target date. But the PPP, now led by General Tikka Khan, viciously attacked the ruling generals and brazenly refused to follow the registration requirements established by the martial law government. Tikka's assertion that the PPP would run candidates clandestinely under little-known organizations and still win a majority of the seats was not considered idle commentary. Moreover, his open defiance steeled the will of other politicians, and the cacophony of diatribe which they directed at the ruling junta convinced the officers that holding the elections before other controls were in place would be dangerous. Thus on 16 October 1979 Zia again announced the cancellation of the elections, but this time he declared they would be postponed indefinitely.

Pakistan entered a new phase with the indefinite postponement of the elections. The junta was no longer a temporary, stop-gap phenomenon, and Zia behaved like a man with a mission. The military leaders no longer pretended tolerance in their dealings with the politicians, and Zia used every opportunity to denounce the political parties as irresponsible and devoid of any moral scruples. According to Zia, Pakistani politics had become synonymous with violence, while character assassination and narrow opportunism were its basic products. Only the surfacing of virtuous leaders could encourage him to transfer authority to civilian politicians, and only persons guided by Islamic values were worthy of serving the public. Zia refused to loosen the controls imposed on the mainline politicians, and Benazir Bhutto remained under house arrest. Asghar Khan was also prevented from leaving his residence, and Khwaja Khairuddin, Secretary-General of the Movement for the Restoration of Democracy (MRD) was repeatedly arrested.

Despite the tight security, in February 1983 leaders of the MRD met in Lahore in blatant violation of martial law regulations and decided to observe a 'political prisoner's day'.

When their meeting was broken up by the police, a group of female MRD members demonstrated their disfavour at the mausoleum of the Quaid-i-Azam in Karachi. The authorities were no less severe with the women, but the breadth of these attacks on the junta demonstrated that whatever reforms the soldiers intended to execute would have to be forced upon the nation. Although the MRD was an *ad hoc* and amorphous congeries of political organizations, it was by far the most successful vehicle for registering dissatisfaction with the ruling junta. Stressing that Islamization did not require a new political system, the MRD, comprised of PPP, Tehrik-i-Istiqlal, Pakistan National Party, Jamiatul-Ulema-e-Islam, Jamiatul-Ulema-i-Pakistan, Pakistan Democratic Party, Khairuddin Muslim League, Pagaro Muslim League and, on occasion, Jamaat-i-Islami members, repeatedly demanded the reinstatement of the original 1973 Constitution. Believing that the future of political organizations hung in the balance, the MRD tried to counter Zia's assault on the parties by arguing that the country's democratic prospects were doomed if they were permanently outlawed.

MRD efforts, therefore, centred on the preservation of the 1973 Constitution. In May 1983 the coalition announced a 31-point programme which they argued would allow for greater provincial autonomy, assure an independent judiciary, and guarantee fundamental rights. High priority was given to the lifting of restrictions on the Press, the promotion of trade unions, and their right of collective bargaining. The MRD also demanded an end to discrimination against women and religious minorities, and the strict accountability of all civil and military personnel. The MRD called for a reduction in tax burdens on workers with fixed incomes, and insisted on a clear demarcation between private industry and public corporations. The Leninist phrase 'from each according to his ability, to each according to his work' was also adopted. The MRD urged the establishment of compulsory military training and reiterated its policy to make Pakistan a non-aligned state. The organization questioned the heavy transfer of American weapons to Pakistan, and urged the government to pursue good relations with all the country's neighbours, the Third World, and especially the Muslim states.

Declaring that they would carry their 31-point programme throughout the country, the MRD named 14 August 1983 as the day they would hold a major protest meeting. Indeed, the date had been selected because Zia had announced his intention to reveal a new political system on the occasion of the nation's independence holiday. The junta, however, refused to be sidetracked by the opposition and restrictions were imposed on travel, let alone the holding of public meetings. The MRD saw itself as the last bastion of support for a more conventional parliamentary system, but events in the preceding two years had already convinced their supporters that they were too late to reverse the tide of reform.

Islamization

On 24 December 1981 Zia declared the formation of the *Majlis-i-Shoora*, calling it an interim arrangement to promote 'effective contact' between the people and the government. Described as an all-nominated body, and selected by the President from lists assembled by his staff and the bureaucracy, the *Majlis* initially consisted of 287 members. In theory the institution was to perform the tasks of a formal legislature, but it was not endowed with the powers normally associated with a law-making body. As a temporary substitute for a constitutional parliament, its functions were sharply defined and circumscribed. Zia justified the organization of the *Majlis-i-Shoora* on the grounds that the government wished to bridge popular demands with government policy. He also justified the selection process as a technique allowing for the rapid assembling of the body, but especially one geared to avoiding partisan competition. According to the General, the time was still not right for the holding of elections, and rather than risk a struggle that would weaken the nation's domestic defences, with an eye to the desperate situation in Afghanistan, he had decided to have the members of the Assembly appointed.

The powers of the *Majlis-i-Shoora* were defined in the Presidential Order that created it. It was given the power to recommend the enactment of laws, and it could suggest amendments to existing laws. It also could discuss the annual budget, review the five-year development plan, and request information from any agency of government. Finally, it could assume additional responsibilities on direct assignment by the President—but the *Majlis-i-Shoora* was not a true legislature, nor a permanent fixture. Although given the powers to scrutinize the work of the administration, it could neither initiate laws nor demand that its recommendations be adopted. Lawmaking therefore remained a monopoly of the junta government, and martial law rules and regulations were unaffected by the creation of this 'representative' institution.

The junta government made a determined effort to provide the *Majlis-i-Shoora* with broad representation. Members were selected from different provinces and regions, and a range of occupational groups. Members of the *ulema, mashaikh* (students of Islam), farmers, industrial workers, lawyers, teachers, medical doctors, and engineers were all associated with the body. Women and minorities also had reserved positions, and the voicing of diverse opinions was supposedly welcome. The *Majlis* was led by a Speaker who was chosen by the President from among the membership. The President also selected four vice-chairmen to work with the Speaker, and all officers were required to take an oath of allegiance to the government in accordance with the Provisional Constitutional Order 1981, which had laid the foundation for Zia's rule.

But in spite of the diversity of representation, critics of the *Majlis-i-Shoora* were quick to cite the large concentration of landlords in the body. Former government officials, as well as politicians favourable to the junta, were also counted among the members. In fact, approximately one-third of the members were former central government or provincial ministers. Nor were the political parties denied a form of representation. Many political operators had joined the junta bandwagon, and almost one hundred members of the *Majlis* had, at one time, enjoyed affiliation with the PPP. Their inclusion only added to the ambience of bitterness, and the Assembly was condemned as little more than a tool of the military junta. The leaders of the Tehrik-i-Istiqlal, the National Democratic Party, the Pakistan Democratic Party, and the

Khairuddin Muslim League followed the lead of the PPP and refused to recognize the legitimacy of the *Majlis-i-Shoora*. On the other hand, not all the parties were equally incensed, and rifts opened in opposition ranks when the Jamaat-i-Islami, the Jamiatul-Ulema-i-Pakistan, and the Pagaro Muslim League indicated some interest in the new Assembly.

The formation of the *Majlis-i-Shoora* prompted the government to deal even more sternly with its stubborn opposition. Martial Law orders were tightened, preventing any form of political expression. Dozens of prominent politicians who were still at large were either arrested, constrained, or simply prevented from travelling from one province to another. In these circumstances, differences of opinion could gain expression only within the confines of the new Assembly. Thus the *Majlis* Speaker, Khwaja Mohammad Safdar, an old-line Muslim Leaguer, was quick to take issue with Zia's prohibition against transforming the *Majlis* into a full-scale parliamentary institution. The General, however, had learned to cope with a whole range of political pressures, and Zia was not one to yield to argument, no matter how eloquently delivered. The Assembly soon found it could air the complaints of its members, or even speak on behalf of the unreconciled opposition, but it could not affect decisions already taken by the military government.

The *Majlis-i-Shoora* met in two sessions in 1982 and three in 1983. Debate in the Assembly focused on the need to hold national elections, and it was rumoured that Zia might allow new polls in 1984. Nor did Zia reject that possibility, but he made it clear that a new political system would have to be in place before such an event could be organized. In fact, the new political system was scheduled to be launched in August 1983, and a seventeen-member Constitution Commission had been authorized to examine the reports of the Council of Islamic Ideology, the *Majlis-i-Shoora*, and the cabinet before making its recommendations to the President.

In the meantime, Zia reinforced the local councils he had constituted in 1979. Local council elections had been conducted without formal political party involvement. Like Ayub before him, Zia insisted that the councillors should be entirely focused on constituent needs and had no need for political party affiliation. Organized in tiers, with union councils at the base and *tehsil* and district councils above them, councillors served four-year terms. Each union council was authorized fifteen members, with the chairmen of the lower bodies forming and serving the *tehsil* units, and from there, the district organizations. Towns were given the same basic structure as the rural areas, but in the larger cities, municipal committees and corporations were substituted. Not quite the Basic Democracies System of Ayub Khan, the local councils nevertheless provided the general population with a form of self-government. Moreover, the *Majlis-i-Shoora* was subsequently linked to the local councils, thus raising grass roots concerns to a national level. Totalling 50,000, the local councillors were given responsibility for agricultural production, education, health, and sanitation. They were also encouraged to assist rural technical staff in improving water supplies and road systems. Cultural and social matters were also made the concern of the common folk, and everything from the registration of births to the issuing of funeral notices came within their purview. Finally, along with economic development, disaster relief was made a joint enterprise between local administration and the provincial governments.

As in the past, the local bodies could not avoid dependence on the official bureaucracy which retained the expertise, the technical know-how, and especially the necessary funds. This continuing dependency on the career administrators was a perennial target of the politicians, who now also complained that the local bodies were nothing more than the reincarnation of the discredited Basic Democracies System. Zia, however, was unmoved by the criticism, and he found more than enough members of the general public who were eager to accept and work the local bodies.

Zia also introduced the Shariat Courts in 1979. Although it was argued that the religious courts were meant to supplement, not replace, the conventional court system, their establishment nevertheless aroused even greater controversy than the local bodies. A Federal Shariat Court was established in Islamabad and given authority to determine whether existing law was counter to or in violation of Islamic precepts and principles. Zia called the Shariat Courts a high-priority item on his reform agenda, and he justified the action by insisting that Pakistan had been created for the purpose of providing Islamic justice. A Hudood Ordinance dovetailed with the one creating the Shariat Courts and placed emphasis on Islamic codes of behaviour. From here on, crimes against Islam, or *hadd*, were to include the imbibing of alcoholic beverages, attendance at bawdy clubs, and any form of gambling. Zia said his decree would deal drastically with those in violation of Islamic codes of conduct, and he called upon the nation to find their need for escape and recreation in prayer, family activities, and constructive social acts. But for those convicted of breaking the law, harsh penalties in conformity with Islamic practices were to be imposed. Public lashings were, in fact, carried out on numerous occasions following the implementation of the ordinance, but the cutting off of limbs for criminal actions, particularly those involving theft, was generally avoided (Mahmood, 1992). Murder, however, brought the penalty of capital punishment, and Zia had, in fact, justified Bhutto's execution on the grounds that in ordering the death of another he had forfeited his own life.

Zakat was still another Islamic institution that Zia wanted slavishly followed in Pakistan. *Zakat* is the Islamic requirement that Muslims share their wealth with the less fortunate members of the community. Pursuant to his *zakat* ordinance, monies derived by the government were to be divided into three parts: a local account, a provincial account, and a central account. Such funds were earmarked for community use and were intended to spark development schemes from the village upwards. A hierarchy of control boards was created to administer *zakat* collections, and Zia also appointed an Administrator-General to oversee the entire programme making him directly answerable to the President. Although here, too, the critics found fault with his Islamization scheme, the most negative reaction came from the country's Shiite community, which claimed that the *zakat* tax was a Sunni Muslim contrivance and that they had their own collection practices. The Shiites argued that their religious observances had been undermined by the ordinance, and that it exposed the community to the manipulative capabilities of the majority Sunnis. At the height of the controversy, a Shiite group had stormed the Federal Secretariat in Islamabad and had held it hostage for three days when the government refused to answer their complaints. Following that episode, and not wanting to further excite religious passions, Zia exempted the Shiites from the otherwise obligatory rule.

Zia's reversal, however, stirred up resentment among members of the Sunni community, who described his concession as an act of appeasement. Members of the junta were also disturbed by their commander's willingness to yield to the pressure of a sizeable, but still minority community. Believing his action invited others to challenge the military authority, the junta warned Zia that he risked problems in a broad range of martial law edicts. Under attack from all sides, both inside and outside the government, Zia backtracked from his earlier position, but in doing so, merely provoked more street demonstrations. The resulting riots in Karachi that pitted antagonistic Shiite and Sunni groups in senseless bloodletting was exactly what Zia had tried to avoid. This time, the sectarian strife was triggered by a dispute involving the possession of a mosque in a mixed Muslim neighbourhood, but the authorities traced the origin of the conflict to unreconciled differences on the *zakat* issue. Moreover, the junta acknowledged its inability to counter demagogic manipulation of controversial social issues, and time and again it was forced to endure the embarrassment that stemmed from the Islamization programme. Although on the face of it, Islamization was deemed to be a desirable objective in a country more than ninety-five per cent Muslim, it had nevertheless shown itself to be a tedious and dangerous task.

The inability of the martial law authority to instantly quell the Karachi riots raised the level of national scepticism further. Nor could the matter escape the members of the *Majlis-i-Shoora*, who now called for a full debate on the controversy, as well as the junta's overall management of law and order. Anticipating an attack upon its bona fides, the government moved aggressively to neutralize the perpetrators of the violence. All forms of assembly were outlawed, curfews were imposed, and hundreds of demonstrators were arrested.

Zia broadcast a warning to anyone found disturbing the public peace, declaring that there would be no leniency and that his government knew how to punish 'miscreants'. Defying even this threat, however, the rioters sustained their indiscriminate attacks, inflicted more pain on the innocent, and reduced wide areas of Karachi city to cinder and ash.

The government's difficulty in containing the disorder was rumoured to be due to the demonstrators' Iranian Shiite connection. There was sufficient evidence to implicate Iranian students who had come to Pakistan ostensibly to study in Pakistani universities, but who in fact were engaged in conspiratorial activities that were directed against the United States-supported Zia junta. The Islamabad government found it difficult to crack down on the students without disturbing relations with Tehran. With the situation in Afghanistan at a critical stage, Islamabad was disinclined to cause more strain between itself and Tehran's revolutionary government. Moreover, Khomeini's Iran was locked in mortal struggle with Saddam Hussein's Iraq, and Zia had tried to play a major role in mediating an end to their war through the good offices of the Islamic Summit and the Organization of Islamic States. Zia, therefore, believed his best approach to the problem would be to slow his Islamization process.

Assuming a lowered profile, Zia called upon Ghulam Ishaq to explain that the introduction of *Zakat*, *Hudood*, and *Ushr* Ordinances was only the beginning of a long process, that Islamization remained the goal of the government, and that in more tranquil times the Islamic state would flower in Pakistan and spread to other Muslim nations. In a speech to the *Majlis-i-Shoora*, Ishaq declared that *ushr* laid the foundation for an Islamic welfare state, and that the funds generated by *ushr* would be used to expand Pakistani industry, construct pukka roads, and build modern state-of-the-art hospitals. More immediately, he noted, the monies collected through the Islamization programme would help expand social services for all Muslims, Sunnis and Shiites alike. The Education Minister followed this statement with another describing government's efforts in removing anti-Islamic reading materials from libraries and schools. The Ministry of Information and Broadcasting followed a similar theme. Arguing that the Press and Publications Ordinance would remain in force to block publication of obscene materials, the Ministry declared the government's intention to screen out all films and books judged to be hedonistic, immoral, and contrary to Islamic precepts. Provincial governments were even given the authority to police sermons during Friday's community prayers. Still another ordinance was issued making it a violation to preach hatred against another faith or sect, or against the ruling junta, which now claimed spiritual legitimacy for all its actions.

Islamization, therefore, continued to demonstrate its declaratory, rather than its practical, aspect. The deliberate and slower pace of the programme was also attributed to personnel problems, and indeed the stated expansion of the Shariat Courts required far more scholars of *sharia* and *fiqah* law (legal theology) than were readily available. Zia said his government would reach into the *madrasahs* for the needed personnel, but even this intention was destined to leave the courts shorthanded. Moreover, the problem was compounded by the *Majlis-i-Shoora*, which approved the Establishment of Courts of *Qazis* Ordinance in its winter 1983 session. *Qazi* Courts were ordered to be housed in all the provincial tehsils and were supposed to be made an extension of the local councils system. But the *Qazi* Courts also suffered personnel shortages, and those that were established were often presided over by less than competent staff. The same problem gripped the district Shariat Courts, which were supposed to have at least two learned exponents of Islamic jurisprudence in each unit.

Finding truly competent Islamic scholars proved an impossible task, and barring the importation of judges from other Muslim countries, the objective could not be realized in the short term. Moreover, district courts were organized to function under the guidance of the Federal Shariat Court, and staffing that august body was no less a problem. In point of fact, Zia's vision had ranged far beyond the country's human capabilities, and Islamic jurisprudence required no less training and enlightenment than that needed in other, more profane, human endeavour. Zia, therefore, for so many reasons, but certainly not because of personal disposition, was forced to slacken the pace of Islamization. The nation's underdevelopment in a wide array of categories, not the least of which was a paucity of Islamic jurists, prevented the instant manifestation of the Islamic state. Zia's critics would centre their criticism on lack of personal resolve or even personal probity, but in point of fact, he had attempted too much too soon.

Finally, Zia went to great lengths to assure the members of the secular legal fraternity that Shariat and *Qazi* Courts were not intended to replace the established secular court system. On many occasions he laboured to explain that the purpose of Islamization was to touch the lives of the masses, especially in the nation's villages, where conventional legal remedies were either non-existent or inaccessible. The grassroots too, he would assert, needed a legal system that addressed the peculiar needs of the peasant population, and he had little doubt that the religious courts were the best, and often the only, vehicles for rendering appropriate remedies. The common folk, he would opine, could not be expected to bring their everyday grievances to courts dispensing Anglo-Saxon justice. The rural people, though ignorant of their rights in the Common Law, nevertheless had legitimate grievances that could only be addressed within the cultural context of their religious lives. Justice for all the country's citizens involved different approaches, and for Zia, the intertwining of the Islamic and secular legal systems appeared to promise at least minimal satisfaction for the largest number of Pakistanis.

The New Political Order

Mohammad Ziaul Haq was vilified more than praised. But while hardly above reproach, he nevertheless proved to be an inventive and contemplative leader of a diverse, conflicted, seldom unified, and inchoate nation. Even his Islamization scheme was as risky as it was imaginative. His critics belittled his programmes and policies, decried his arbitrary decision-making, and agonized over his accretion of vast powers. But he also demonstrated a capacity for governing that surprised a wide array of observers. More in the tradition of Ayub Khan than Yahya, Zia was audacious when it came to repairing the governing apparatus, even more so when it came to changing or adding to its institutions. For this he was criticized, condemned, abused, and never given credit for more than cynically strengthening his own hand. But how was his creation of a national ombudsman (*wafaqi mohtasib*) to be judged? Was it simply a matter of personal gain, or a play for cheap popularity? The official he chose to occupy the post was not a sycophant but an eminent former Chief Justice of the Lahore High Court, Sardar Mohammad Iqbal. Moreover, the national ombudsman was given responsibility for identifying, investigating, redressing, and rectifying injustices committed against a citizen by any government agency, the only exception being the courts, judicial tribunals, and commissions established by law. Clearly, the ombudsman's authority did not extend to foreign affairs or defence questions, but he was empowered to range over the entire domestic condition, and a secretariat with an adequate budget was placed at his disposal.

Sceptics were numerous, and few believed that the institution would be permitted to operate according to its charge. Too many people believed that the bureaucracy would do anything to protect itself rather than stand the test of public accountability. Furthermore, the national ombudsman could not begin to address the number of grievances likely to be brought to his attention, and moreover, the fear persisted that he could be co-opted by the military junta. Citing the frustrations registered by the Speaker of the *Majlis-i-Shoora*, who also represented an 'independent' force, considerable doubt was expressed that Justice Iqbal would be any more successful in bringing the government to task. Furthermore, the President reserved the right to dismiss the ombudsman if it was determined he had violated specific understandings. Moreover, how could an ombudsman charged with challenging the prerogatives of the government function effectively under conditions of martial law?

Answers to such questions are never absolute, but the institution of the ombudsman was an intrinsic part of the junta's new political system which Zia laid before the *Majlis-i-Shoora* on 12 August 1983. Originally having scheduled his presentation for the nation's Independence Day, Zia had been informed that street demonstrations were planned for that occasion and the call went out to the police to seize, neutralize, and arrest all political leaders still at large.

Given the nationwide crackdown on the political opposition, Zia's presentation to the *Majlis* was somewhat paradoxical, appealing as it did to the democratic sensibilities of the legislators. The General-President revealed his willingness, by 1985, to dissolve the *Majlis-i-Shoora* and re-create the central parliament and provincial legislatures. He left no doubt, however, that the country would continue to have an all-powerful chief executive. The office of the prime minister would be revived, but only as a subordinate office to the presidency. Zia did not obscure the fact that the prime minister would serve at the exclusive pleasure of the president, not the parliament. True to Pakistan's viceregal tradition, the president would retain the extraordinary powers enjoyed by the colonial viceroy; thus, although the legislators were to be directly elected, the president would not be. Avoiding Ayub's electoral college system, Zia's president would be elected by the combined vote of the National Assembly and provincial legislatures. Perhaps more important, however, the president would perform the duties of both head of state and head of government. Indeed, it was customary in parliamentary systems to allow the prime minister to head the government, but ever since the administration of Liaquat Ali Khan, Pakistan's experience consistently reflected the uneven distribution of power between the president and the prime minister. Zia's monopoly, therefore, was hardly out of character and largely corresponded with the role played by Mohammad Ali Jinnah after the transfer of power.

Zia's new political system, therefore, resembled much of Pakistan's past practices. Zia demonstrated both rigidity and flexibility, but ever mindful of the centrality of power, he never allowed control to slip from his hands. Zia's performance as leader of a relatively successful military *junta* was less yielding than that of Ayub Khan, who was caught between his dependence on the professional bureaucracy and the demands of politicians whose stature derived from their pre-independence experience. By contrast with that earlier generation of politicians, Zia had to work with persons of lesser ability and far more limited experience (in major part, a consequence of the extended periods of martial law). More familiar with the politics of agitation and confrontation, they lacked the positive characteristics associated with legislating the country's socio-economic needs. Pakistan's second generation of political operators was a pale shadow of its predecessor, and Zia's behaviour was a direct response to the country's stunted political process. Politics remained an art form, and even quasi-democratic politics required a commitment and sense of purpose that the contemporary politicians either lacked or had little opportunity to display. Politics had become such a negative experience that it was virtually impossible to imagine that the country's work could be done in structured political circumstances.

Hence Zia could act as though he were preserving the 1973 Constitution, but in reality he amended it to the point where it became an entirely different document. During Bhutto's brief reign, the presidency had been reduced to a totally ceremonial role. With Zia's intervention, the presidency was elevated to, and endowed with, supreme powers. By contrast, the prime minister served only at the discretion of the Chief Executive and retained none of the powers associated with the office. Ironically, this was the very kind of system that Bhutto had contemplated, but which had been denied him when the political opposition demanded the guarantee that their voice would continue to be heard. More than Bhutto, therefore, Zia was in a position to transform the president into the principal and paramount decision-maker. This modification of the 1973 Constitution altered it beyond recognition, and this tampering became the central focus of debate during Zia's tenure.

The 1973 Constitution, as amended by the Zia administration, thus projected presidential power, and only marginally was the parliament considered an active and important actor in the political process. With the changed constitution in hand, and assured of his continuing mastery of the situation, Zia announced that elections for the new National Assembly and provincial legislatures would be conducted in March 1985. He also announced that martial law, in force since the 1977 takeover, would finally be lifted, but that the armed forces would remain on station to oversee the transition. And while holding high the carrot, Zia continued to wield the stick. True to his earlier position, he declared that the 1985 elections would be held without the participation of political parties. Arguing again that Islamic principles were at variance with factional politics, and citing the politicians' penchant for controversy, Zia saw no justification for subjecting the country to opportunistic displays that divided the nation and made enemies of otherwise compatible groups. Citing the objective of Islamic brotherhood, Zia warned the politicians that he would deal harshly with them if they disturbed the peace during this period of significant transition.

Ziaul Haq's confidence in his political leadership had obviously increased in the years following his somewhat hesitant assumption of power. The decision to allow Bhutto's execution to go forward was, no doubt, a turning point. Seemingly, it was from that moment that he fully grasped the meaning of the country's viceregal tradition. Moreover, having weathered the aftermath of Bhutto's passing, in no small measure with assistance from the chaotic conditions in both Afghanistan and Iran, he was convinced that it was destiny, *qismat*, that called upon him to govern Pakistan. The martial law years, combined with the Bhutto interregnum, had left few if any leadership choices, and only the army claimed the requisite capacity to manage the nation in so difficult a period. Pakistan's porous north-western frontier could be secured only with direct army intervention, and that same army had been called upon to service the vast Afghan refugee influx, and at the same time maintain normal services for the general population. The divisive, fragmented, and largely provincialized political parties were hardly prepared for national responsibility, and Zia's decision to rule out political party participation in the 1985 elections, examined objectively, involved something more than his plan to become Pakistan's president for life.

Zia's constitution, therefore, had the president, not the parliament, choosing the prime minister. The president also reserved the power to dissolve the parliament and call new elections. Such presidential powers were not unique to Pakistan, but when coupled with Zia's direct command of the army and his overall command of the armed forces, there was the high degree of probability that this president would behave in an arbitrary rather than a constitutional manner. In fact, no significant restrictions had been imposed on a president who was also the head of the military establishment, and in Zia, Pakistan had come very close to experiencing absolute rule. Thus, the heralded new political system was hardly geared to meet the needs or demands of the country's political leaders or their followers. The 'system' represented the consolidation of junta rule, not the sharing of national responsibilities. A civil-military arrangement had grown in confidence and literally monopolized authoritative decision-making. This left the politicians with but a single recourse, and that was the very street demonstrations that the junta had cited in denying them a place in the formal political process. It was a celebrated case of self-fulfilling prophecy, with the Zia administration provoking the very response that it then used to justify its sustained rule. The junta was not deterred by MRD verbal assaults, nor did it hesitate to use its police power to crush or neutralize opposition activities. Moreover, given the climate of mutual vilification, the principals in this drama closed every channel to possible compromise.

Demonstrations, protest meetings, and sporadic acts of violence spread throughout the country in the period following the declaration of a new political order, but nowhere was the turbulence more severe than in Sindh and Balochistan. Nor did the arrest of provincial leaders stem the tide of negative expression. Asserting that the mayhem was instigated by leftists and radical elements who drew their sustenance from external sources, the government showed little patience with those they had labelled troublemakers, and so Zia's projected new political system appeared dead on arrival.

By January 1984 the unrest in Sindh had subsided, but not before hundreds of deaths had been registered. Moreover, scattered acts of looting, kidnapping, and murder persisted. The most violent protests, because of their Sindhi base, were believed to be linked with the PPP, which continued to draw a broad following despite the efforts by the junta to discredit it. Zia decided to release many of the incarcerated politicians, but he argued the need to hold in detention PPP stalwarts and also Rasul Bux Palejo, leader of the Sindhi Awami Tehrik. Both Palejo's party and the PPP were accused of masterminding the disorder, and the generals wanted the released politicians to know that they could expect significant freedom if they were prepared to follow a more tranquil strategy.

It was during this period of seeming political transition, that General Iqbal Khan and General Sawar Khan, key members of the ruling junta, retired from service. Iqbal was replaced as Chairman of the Joint Chiefs of Staff Committee by General Rahimuddin Khan, who had been serving as Governor of Balochistan. Sawar Khan's position as Vice-Chief of the Army Staff was assumed by General K.M. Arif, Zia's chief aide and confidant. Retired General Rao Farman Ali also resigned his ministerial post, and two new civilian officials, Zafarullah Khan Jamali and Sartaj Aziz, became Ministers of Local Government and Rural Development, and Food, Agriculture, and Co-operatives, respectively. The changes signalled a shift in junta tactics, so that in addition to maintaining a strong hand, the military leaders also delegated greater responsibilities to civilian, but not necessarily political, figures.

Zia acknowledged the necessity of easing the country toward more intensive civilian involvement, but he nevertheless displayed perplexity when he allowed the country to mull over his musings on the conduct of the forthcoming elections. Voicing concern that even a partyless election may not be the proper course, Zia raised the possibility of holding a referendum rather than a formal election. But such thinking in public only infuriated his detractors, and even lost him the support of his sometime supporters, notably within the Jamaat-i-Islami. Moreover, the students were agitated over the banning of their celebrated unions, and they found common ground with the Jamaat's student wing, the Jamiat-i-Tulaba, who in concert launched a major assault on the institutions of military government. In the ensuing disturbances, the authorities arrested more than one thousand students in cities stretching from Karachi to Lahore to Peshawar. Moreover, the government shut down all the country's universities, hence only adding to the number of students participating in the demonstrations.

It was at this point that the more conservative and fundamentalist Islamic parties formally broke with the Zia regime. Along with the Jamaat-i-Islami, the Jamiatul-Ulema-i-Pakistan, too, joined in a collective display of disaffection. The president of the JUP, Shah Ahmad Noorani, citing the failure of MRD, called for still another, but more effective, coalition, whose central and sole purpose would be to defeat and ultimately oust Ziaul Haq.

Zia's response, therefore, was even more draconian. He issued an ordinance forbidding the Press from publishing anything related to the political parties. Furthermore, having just ordered the release of many of the politicians, he now issued orders returning them to prison. In an effort at placating his fundamentalist erstwhile supporters, Zia also issued an order depriving the Ahmedi community, which during the Bhutto administration had been formally decertified as Muslims, from using any Islamic symbols or in any way leading people to believe that the community was connected with the Islamic faith (Ahmad, 1959). The more conservative members of the orthodox community had argued for even harsher penalties, insisting that the Ahmedis were heretics and hence, subject to the death penalty. Zia did not adopt that extreme view, but the government was immediately challenged by sectarian strife in which Shiites and Sunni Muslims clashed in their mixed neighbourhoods in Karachi. It was not until many had died and many more were wounded that the authorities could restore a semblance of law and order to Pakistan's major commercial centre.

If these problems were not enough to tax the military government, in late September 1984 Zia revealed that ranking army officers and some *jawans* were implicated in a plot to overthrow the government. Accused of being in league with both Indian and Libyan agents, their trial was in some ways linked with another that involved the two sons of Zulfikar Ali Bhutto who, it was said, were the brains behind the Al-Zulfikar terrorist organization. Because of the latter's domicile in Libya, the two brothers were to be tried *in absentia*. But irrespective of where or how these trials were conducted, they revealed both the strengths and weaknesses of the Zia regime. Moreover, in an open act of defiance, Benazir, who had been allowed to leave the country to join her mother in exile, had circulated a letter in Pakistan that called upon her PPP supporters to refrain from participating in any election sponsored by the Zia government.

Zia nevertheless went ahead with the scheduled polls. In fact, just days prior to the balloting the government arrested several hundred persons who, it alleged, planned to disrupt the electoral process. For its part, the political opposition described the elections a sham and a disgrace, and having been disallowed from participating, they called upon the public to boycott the proceedings. But when the polling was completed, neither side was especially pleased. The Zia government was distressed that less than the anticipated electors cast their ballots, and the political opposition was unhappy because more had voted than they had hoped would turn out. The opposition took heart from the fact that Zia's slate of candidates failed to achieve a ringing endorsement, and that only two of nine cabinet-level officials were successful. Moreover, voters drove from office some thirty members of the National Assembly who were closely identified with the administration. Nevertheless, the government was assured that Zia's fiat would be sustained.

Several months prior to these elections Zia had orchestrated a referendum on his Islamization programme which, he said, would also be a test of his popularity. The overwhelming support given the programme thus became the vehicle of 'legitimacy' whereby Zia would govern Pakistan for an additional five years. The 1985 elections had never been a factor in Zia's remaining in power. Assured of his continuation in office prior to the polls, the results of the election did nothing to weaken his hand or threaten his demise. On the contrary, the continuation of the Zia presidency for an additional five years provided the General with sufficient time to repair whatever damage may have been done to his rule by the losses in the National Assembly. Moreover, so long as Zia remained at the helm, and so long as the President's power remained unchallenged, the National Assembly, no matter its composition, was his to mould and influence.

Zia had had the constitution amended so that the legislature was reduced to an advisory body, and the President alone determined the extent of his powers. Indeed, the courts were not permitted to question the extraordinary powers Zia had now amassed. Finally, in establishing his new political system, Zia made it certain that all the ordinances enacted during martial law would carry over and hence endow him with the necessary legal authority to overrule any future effort by the legislature to assert its authority. Having completed his fail-safe system, Zia imposed heavy restrictions on the further amending of the constitution, and thus guaranteed that the laws in force which legalized his powers would not be tampered with.

The lifting of martial law seemed to matter little in the circumstances, but military rule nevertheless remained in force. Zia had promised to lift it, but he was also determined to seek ways to civilianize, and hence indefinitely perpetuate, the condition but without describing it as martial law. To help him build the bridge between martial law and the new political system, Zia chose a Prime Minister with whom he believed he could be comfortable, and who could assist him in releasing the country from the junta's, but not his own, iron grip. Zia called upon Muhammad Khan Junejo, a quiet-spoken Sindhi who had been brought into the Zia Cabinet in 1978 as Minister of Railways. A subdued critic of protracted martial law, Junejo had left the cabinet after only one year, and in the 1985 election he won an unopposed seat in the National Assembly. In choosing Junejo to be his Prime Minister, Zia sought to neutralize his more vocal opposition in the troubled Sindh province. He also had expectations of drawing PPP defectors to the Junejo fold. Junejo, therefore, became the instrument whereby martial law would be lifted.

Soon after his appointment, the new Prime Minister assembled a nine-person committee to study the gradual lifting of martial law. Building on the effort, his political colleagues urged Junejo to help in lifting the ban on political parties as well, but here the new premier displayed his reluctance, arguing that the elimination of martial law should be the immediate and unencumbered goal of his administration. When the politicians defied martial law restrictions and took their followers into the streets, Junejo pleaded with Zia to remove martial law as soon as possible in order to demonstrate his genuine desire to restore the government to civilian control. Zia responded by ordering still more arrests while Junejo, in apparent disagreement with Zia, informed the nation that martial law would be withdrawn by the end of the year. Zia was forced by his own actions to accept the Prime Minister's timetable. In fact, Zia went a step further, declaring that political parties, after all he had said to the contrary, would be permitted to function as soon as the National Assembly had completed legislation guaranteeing that they would function under rules prescribed by the administration.

Realizing that the country was rapidly moving from junta rule to a form of representative government, the administration submitted an 'indemnity bill' to the National Assembly which, when passed, would pardon all acts of the military government since its seizure of power in 1977. The bill also aimed at constitutionalizing martial law edicts, and prevented any future civilian government from questioning the acts of the martial law regime. The indemnity bill was not well received, however, and while the Zia-Junejo administration struggled to beat back the attack from an angry political public, word reached Pakistan that Shahnawaz Bhutto had been found dead in an apartment in Cannes, France. In Pakistan, the news of the young man's death only added to the assault mounting against the administration. Believing that Zia had ordered the death of still another Bhutto, there was little comfort and less belief in reports that he had been poisoned by his estranged wife. In an effort to relieve the tensions caused by these multiple and tragic events, Zia granted Benazir Bhutto's plea to have her brother's body returned to Pakistan, where it could be buried next to her father.

Benazir's return from her London exile was a singular event which added considerably to the emotional occasion of Shahnawaz's funeral. Hailed as the great leader of the PPP, the successor to her father, and hence the most noteworthy politician in Pakistan, Benazir led a procession of tens of thousands of mourners and followers to the family gravesite in Larkana. Following the burial ceremony she met with leaders of the PPP, and together they planned the revitalization of the party, which had split into a couple of major and several minor factions during her absence from the country. In an effort to bridge party differences, Benazir declared her intention to lead the political struggle against President Zia. She joined, and indeed now led the chorus of those demanding the immediate lifting of martial law and the reinstatement of full political party activity.

The Zia government's response was not unexpected. In fact, it was Benazir's strategy to incite the administration, to force it to deal harshly with her and her compatriots. In the absence of a formal political forum, courting arrest and forced detention had long been a tried and tested technique of political activism. The sacrifices made by those challenging authority, and that same authority's furtive behaviour in trying to silence its critics, was the stuff of which leadership was made. Zia could argue as much and as long as he wished that Benazir had betrayed a trust, had abused his act of compassion, but the daughter of Zulfikar knew that the man who was known as her father's 'hangman' would scarcely receive the support that he hoped to solicit. Zia had to face the reality of the situation, that Benazir had manipulated her brother's death to mobilize the nation's political forces that were even then on the eve of re-emerging. Aware that he could only add to her leadership credentials, Zia was saddled with a Hobson's choice, neither of which was likely to redound to his benefit. Benazir was therefore rearrested for violating martial law edicts, the order ostensibly coming from Prime Minister Junejo's office.

The Zia-Junejo Administration

Benazir was held under house arrest for less than three months. Faced with continuing demonstrations in her behalf, in November 1985, the government decided to put her on a plane destined for Europe, knowing that she would not be silenced. Indeed the young woman arrived in London to an exuberant reception and immediately launched her campaign to return to Pakistan to 'test the political waters' which had shown signs of surging during her brief visit. Moreover, Zia was on record as being apparently convinced, that the political parties had to be accommodated. Zia had purchased a bit more time, but cumulative events now were forcing his hand, and on 30 December 1985 he formally declared the end of a martial law period that had lasted approximately eight years, the longest in the country's history. The National Assembly had earlier passed the constitutional amendment pardoning the military government for all acts committed during martial law. It had also stabilized and made secure all the reforms, notably the Islamization reforms, that the junta had authorized. Moreover, the amending process added credence to the December 1984 referendum that not only approved Islamization programmes, but also confirmed Zia's presidential tenure into 1990.

In January 1986 the government made it compulsory for all political parties to register with the Election Commission. It also stated that their right to participate in political activity would be determined on the basis of a test that measured their acceptance of the country's 'ideology' and to what extent they worked toward the goal of national unity: But while the way was being prepared for the return of the parties, Zia continued to press his theme that an Islamic state had no need for such organizations. Zia obviously could not have it both ways. Having agreed to revive the parliamentary process, he could not prevent Prime Minister Junejo from linking forces with Pir Pagaro's Muslim League, and he quickly rallied some two-thirds of the National Assembly members to join that organization. Succeeding in this endeavour, the government followed with a directive that prevented any other parties from bearing the Muslim League name.

The Pagaro Muslim League, therefore, assumed the role of the party that had been given the responsibility for creating Pakistan. By association, therefore, it was declared the heir to the legacy of Mohammad Ali Jinnah and Liaquat Ali Khan, and hence, the only organization capable of projecting the Pakistan idea into the 1990s and beyond. The other Muslim

League factions were appalled by the government action and, along with the other opposition parties, they accused Zia and Junejo of mendacious and deceptive behaviour. They also refused to comply with the order. Sensing that Zia was preparing the nation for one-party dominance, the politicians cited the devious nature of the government's action, but they could not prevent Junejo from becoming president of the new Muslim League, or from arranging a cabinet drawn from compliant members of the political fraternity.

Working in tandem with his Prime Minister, Zia removed the serving generals who doubled as governors in the different provinces and replaced them with civilians, two of whom were retired generals, thus providing more grist for the opposition mills. The politicians hurled epithets at the president, charging him with duplicity and self-serving tactics, as well as with sustaining a dominant military presence. Zia's reluctance to pass his control of the army to another senior officer was likewise attacked as disingenuous and still another sign that martial law had not been totally abandoned. But these opposition complaints were less than effective given the unbridgeable divisions within the MRD. The coalition that had set as its goal the destruction of General Zia and the restoration of the pre-*coup* constitutional system continued to pillory the General-President, but they no longer agreed that the re-invigoration of the Bhutto Constitution was in all their interests.

With the opposition in disarray, the Zia-Junejo government received National Assembly approval for the amendments to the constitution that conferred virtually unlimited power on the president. The MRD response was weak and indecisive, given the decisions of its component parties to follow different tracks. The Tehrik-i-Istiqlal, for example, agreed to accept the terms laid down by the government for its participation, while PPP leaders refused to comply with the order to register their organization. Attempts to hold reconciliation meetings between and among the different organizations also proved unsuccessful, and Zia, believing he had outwitted his detractors, and because Junejo had convinced him that Benazir was more a threat to the MRD than to the government, even allowed the chief Bhutto heir to return to the country, only this time to freely engage in the unfolding political process.

Zia's, let alone Junejo's, optimistic reading, however, was short-lived. The PPP called upon all the parties to join forces behind Benazir's leadership in what they described as an Awami (People's) Movement. This call was answered affirmatively by most of the leaders, and when Benazir arrived in Karachi on 10 April, she was met by what some observers called the largest throngs ever to greet a Pakistan politician since the days of Mohammad Ali Jinnah. Benazir, it was asserted, had surpassed the popularity of her father, whose martyrdom and legacy had propelled her into this moment. Exhilarated by the outpouring of affection, Benazir moved quickly to the task of organizing the popular sentiment that had been mounting against the Zia-Junejo administration. Aided by the discipline of the crowds that came to hear her speak, Benazir raised all the salient issues without giving the government the opportunity to curtail her campaign. She even took pains to complement Junejo and to bestow praise upon the armed forces. With a strategy aimed solely at isolating Zia, Benazir managed to draw together many of the remnants of the PPP, and her reorganization plans proved successful in enlisting the support of the heretofore recalcitrant politicians.

Both Zia and some of the more radical elements among the opposition struggled to find strategies to offset Benazir's gambits. At the end of May the National Assembly took the drastic step of removing its Speaker, Fakhr Imam, who it was said, had become too much of a Zia critic. Among the opposition leaders, it was Wali Khan who distanced himself from Benazir by organizing several leftist parties from the frontier region into a new organization called the Awami National Party. Fearful that the ANP could undermine opposition efforts, the PPP declared its intention to release 150,000 political workers, labelled 'doves of peace', to spearhead a nation-wide protest that would force businesses to close, pressurize labour to strike, and generally paralyse the country. Describing it as a peaceful campaign, PPP strategists hoped that the army would not move against unarmed civilians, and that some of the very tactics that had, in fact, driven Zulfikar Ali Bhutto from office could now force Zia to step aside.

Zia and Junejo, however, continued to pool their efforts and, bolstered by a somewhat successful economy, in part assisted by American aid programmes, they managed to deflect the central opposition assault. Pakistan had become the third largest recipient of American assistance during this period, and with the expiration of a $3.01 billion arrangement, another $4.02 billion had been made available by the Reagan administration. Coupled with the World Bank transfer of $850 million in 1986, a sum seventy per cent higher than in 1985, Pakistan was able to demonstrate growth in both its private and public sectors. Moreover, the Asian Development Bank had granted Pakistan more than $2 billion for a host of projects, and the government seemed able not only to withstand the challenges posed by Soviet actions in Afghanistan, but also to ward off threats posed by trans-national terrorist organizations. Therefore, with one eye on the Afghan, front which had now moved across the border into Pakistan proper, the National Assembly approved still another amendment to the constitution which made Islam the supreme law of the land and officially established the religious courts. The amendment was also supposed to bring all fiscal and tax laws into conformity with the injunctions of Islam.

Forced to struggle on multiple fronts against determined foes, the government did what it could to withstand the Afghan-related bombings in Peshawar and Karachi. It also had to contend with civil strife that pitted fundamentalists against radical secularists, students against police, Muslims against members of the minute Hindu community, and, toward the end of 1986, Pathans against *mohajirs* residing in Karachi and Hyderabad. The resources needed to quell the many disturbances and to repair the damage to the social fabric sapped the energy of the Zia-Junejo Government, but the President and the Prime Minister nevertheless emphasized their intention to press ahead with economic development as well as to declare 'a jihad against corruption, bribery and injustice'. The government cited statistics showing significant increases in the gross domestic product, and a twenty-one per cent growth in exports, especially rice and cotton, between 1984 and 1986. Thus, in spite of the multidimensional dilemmas confronting the nation, the administration wanted it known that the country was in firm hands and that the business of the people was not lost in the management of anti-state and subversive political forces.

The MRD must have realized that it was in a poor position to attack the government's handling of the economy or its policies toward Afghanistan. Moreover, having failed to hold the coalition together, the MRD leaders decided to confront Zia head-on. Zia was abroad when the MRD planned its demonstration, and the Junejo government was quick to ban all public assemblies. When the decision was made to defy the government ban order, Junejo ordered the police and the army to intervene, and in the ensuing mayhem Benazir and numerous other high-placed politicians were again detained. Junejo's insistence on law and order, coupled with the army presence, isolated the MRD leaders and discouraged their rank and file political activists. More to the point, the general population seemed to have lost patience with the politicians and, already overburdened by multiple threats, it appeared to have abandoned the struggle. After gaining her release, Benazir acknowledged that it was futile to try to salvage the MRD, and she devoted herself to the restoration of her PPP.

While the politicians plotted new strategies against the Zia-Junejo government, the war in Afghanistan spilled over into Pakistan with greater intensity. The bombing of public places in and around Peshawar included the destruction of the central bus station, and suspicion increased over the operations of Afghan agents and saboteurs who were hidden among the hundreds of thousands of refugees housed in frontier camps. Gun-running and trafficking in drugs were also linked to such operatives, who, it was said, were under orders from Kabul and Moscow to destabilize the Zia government by escalating the violence within the country.

On the diplomatic front, United Nations mediation efforts had resulted in long drawn-out proximity talks between Pakistani and Afghan government officials, but they never met each other face to face, and it was only the tireless efforts of the Secretary-General's representative, Diego de

Cordovez, that brought the talks to a point of resolution. By stepping up the pressure inside Pakistan, the Moscow-Kabul axis believed they could force Islamabad to yield some of its major negotiating positions and accept the reality of a Marxist regime in the Afghan capital. Through the several years of the talks, however, Zia refused to budge on his principles and, backed by the United States, and to some extent Saudi Arabia and Egypt, he continued to supply the mujahiddin and to insist on the withdrawal of all Soviet troops from the country, as well as the return of the refugees to their former homes. Moreover, he steadfastly clung to his policy of non-recognition of the Babrak Karmal regime.

Zia, clearly, had more than one front to defend against his determined foes. Internally, the Sindh problem continued to vex the administration, but the conflict between *mohajirs* and Pathans in Karachi also spread and deepened. The neighbourhood of Sohrab Goth was a case in point. The authorities had launched an extensive campaign that was intended to disrupt the smuggling of arms and narcotics in Karachi. But when the police raided the neighbourhood of Sohrab Goth, they precipitated communal rioting that was described as the worst since the tragic events of partition. Pathans accused *mohajirs* of instigating the police raid on their stronghold, and the battle escalated when Afghan refugees joined the Pathans and attacked innocent members of the *mohajir* community. Before the authorities could restore calm to the region, more than 200 lives had been lost and several neighbourhoods had been torched. Given the intensity of the conflict, the Government took pains to separate the refugee Afghans from the Pathan community, and tent cities were erected to house them in monitored locations.

The Sohrab Goth incident, however, caused the entire Junejo cabinet to resign, and a new one was not fully assembled for several months. Zia was criticized for allowing the Afghans to settle in different sectors of the country and for not providing the necessary security for its citizens. In his defence, the General argued that the riots were planned and executed by foreign governments which were determined to embarrass him, but more importantly, to force him to agree to terms that favoured the Marxist-installed regime in Kabul.

Zia also offered the opinion that the riots were aimed at provoking another round of martial law, at destroying his Islamization programme, and ultimately, at inciting a new civil war that might well be the undoing of Pakistan. But even as Zia attempted to define his position, fighting erupted in Karachi again, this time sparked by *mohajir* factory workers and their Pathan bus drivers. Again the strife focused attention on the seeming incompatibility of *mohajirs* and Pathans, and given the ferocity of the ethnic warfare, the police were unable to   control it. In fact, they too were targeted by the rioters. Only the army had the capacity to restore order to the region, and Zia was compelled to use his troops to quell the disturbances.

The Junejo government, denied the experience of so many of its key cabinet officials, was virtually paralysed by these events. Moreover, uncomfortable with his role as Zia's puppet, Junejo began to plot alliances with the politicians, who had begun to display a new vitality. Local and provincial political leaders had laboured to improve the status of their several organizations, and they renewed their appeal at levels that guaranteed substantial grassroots support. In the meantime Benazir, who was also engaged in reorganizing her party, suspended her activities long enough to marry a wealthy Karachi businessman, Asif Zardari. Having been betrothed to her new husband only five days after their initial meeting, Benazir declared that her marriage would permit her to increase her political activities, not limit them. While rumours circulated that her marriage to Zardari would provide her with the resources needed to fight her political battles, Benazir insisted that her decision to marry was a personal matter and made from 'religious obligations and family duty'. But despite this disclaimer, it was obvious that Zardari had married the PPP as well as the daughter of Zulfikar Ali Bhutto.

Zia celebrated the tenth anniversary of his seizure of power on 5 July 1987. In the decade of his rule, the General-President had never received the acclaim of the nation, and on the very day marking his ascendancy, the political opposition commemorated the occasion with a 'black day'. The bombing of the Lahore central train and bus stations on that day, though not traced to 'black day', nevertheless illustrated the prevailing insecurity in all the major urban centres. A week later, explosions again occurred in Lahore, this time in a crowded bazaar. And almost simultaneous with that event, bombs were exploded in Karachi, notably at the central bus station. The dead and injured from these several blasts ran into the hundreds, and the fact that such public places had been targeted demonstrated over and again the capacity of terrorists to strike anywhere and at any time with virtual impunity. These terrorists seemed bent on destroying what little confidence the defenceless and innocent folk of Pakistan had in their leaders. The psychological damage they wreaked was considerable. Nor was the political opposition above taking advantage of the situation to increase their pressure on the Zia-Junejo regime.

Zia, while noticeably distressed that the opposition would make capital from such tragic circumstances, continued to believe that the attacks were ordered from Moscow and Kabul and that they were meant to force him to accept a permanent Marxist presence in Afghanistan. Soldier that he was, he said he would not yield to such tactics, and in standing his ground, he also sustained his negotiating posture while continuing to assist the embattled Afghan muhajiddin. Zia seemed to draw strength from the multiple challenges. Seldom did he leave an opening to his opposition or to those terrorizing the nation.

More than the bravado, however, what surprised observers was how an administration so burdened by terror from within as well as from without could nevertheless promote relatively successful economic development. The country continued to demonstrate progress in its output of wheat and cotton, and Pakistan also benefited from a fall in world petroleum prices. Remittances from Pakistanis working in the oil-rich Muslim states also increased during the period, and the government's budget for 1987-8 reflected more than the usual optimism (Burki et al., 1991). Dr Mahbubul Huq, the Planning Minister, however, pointed to future problems if inflation, the rising cost of consumer products, and the fall in real wages were not arrested. Mahbubul Huq also called upon Zia to come to grips with increasing official corruption which, he said, was a scourge on the nation and a serious threat to administration.

National Security

Before his overthrow, Zulfikar Ali Bhutto had re-established formal diplomatic relations with New Delhi. But the years following Bhutto's removal and death were not years of positive Pakistan-India activity. Always concerned about military rule in Islamabad, the Indians had long suspected that the Pakistani generals would attempt to recover some of their lost glory in a renewed contest with India. On the Pakistan side, however, the Red Army's invasion of Afghanistan, coupled with a Soviet-Indian Treaty of Friend- ship and Co-operation in 1971, had convinced the military strategists that New Delhi and Moscow planned a pincer movement against Pakistan, and that the two 'allies' had a long-range plan to divide Pakistan between them. Indeed, the Soviet thrust into Afghanistan was perceived more as an assault on Pakistan than an attempt to absorb the neighbouring mountain state (Burke and Ziring, 1990). More-over, the dismemberment of Pakistan as well as the sustained instability among the different Pakistani nationalities, espe- cially the insurgency in Balochistan and the civil unrest in Sindh, had signalled to Pakistan's adversaries that the country might be near to falling apart.

But Pakistan did not fall apart. The assassination of Indira Gandhi by her personal Sikh bodyguards in 1984, a follow-on to her orders to invade and shoot up the Golden Temple in Amritsar, demonstrated that India was, perhaps, only slightly less volatile than Pakistan. And in 1986 India and Pakistan again threatened one another when they massed forces across their mutual frontier. Zia, however, made a Sadat-like gesture by suddenly flying to New Delhi. Stating that his purpose was simply to attend a scheduled Pakistan-India cricket match, the Pakistani President was soon locked in conversations with Indira's successor, Rajiv Gandhi. In what was described in the media as 'cricket diplomacy', the two subcontinental leaders agreed to withdraw their forces and allow their subordinates to examine ways to avoid similar confrontations in the future. Zia's diplomacy was not greeted with much enthusiasm in Pakistan, but observers in the outside world judged it an impressive performance.

With the war continuing in Afghanistan, Islamabad wanted no part of a war with India. By the same token, Rajiv's willingness to pull back his forces was evidence that New Delhi was not conspiring with the Soviet Union to destroy Pakistan. On the other hand, there was reason to believe that the Kremlin was no longer interested in working with India against Pakistan. The new leaders in Moscow, led by Mikhail Gorbachev, appeared ready to break off their war in Afghanistan and normalize relations with Pakistan. Diego Cordovez had indicated that a breakthrough in the proximity talks was possible, but no one knew that better than Zia, whose negotiating team had already informed him that the Soviets had overspent themselves in the mountain state.

The problem for Pakistan, therefore, remained India, not the Soviet Union, and to prove the point, in September 1987 Pakistani and Indian troops skirmished in Kashmir, on the remote Siachen Glacier. India was the first to publicize the hostilities, citing the clash of arms as the most serious between the two neighbours since the 1971 war. New Delhi claimed 150 Pakistani soldiers had been killed in the course of the conflict but Islamabad reported it as a minor incident. While admitting some loss of life, the Pakistan Foreign Office said the skirmish was by no measure as significant as the Indians portrayed. The Siachen Glacier appeared to be of little value to most lay observers, but Pakistani military strategists later noted that the region was vital to the security of Azad Kashmir. The skirmish, therefore, was a sign that Pakistan-India relations remained troubled and that the Kashmir issue was still the major point of contention.

The Indians also accused the Zia government of fomenting trouble in India's Punjab state, where Sikh separatists threatened to paralyse the region. Sikh militants had been responsible for a variety of attacks, ranging from the skyjacking of commercial aircraft, to the assassination of government officials, to assaults on innocent citizens utilizing the country's rail and road systems. Islamabad declared its innocence on all counts, but New Delhi was not dissuaded. Thus, while Islamabad wished to avoid a full-scale war with India, it was nevertheless viewed aiding guerrilla and terrorist campaigns in the neighbouring state. By the same token, Islamabad had long concluded that Indian agents were linked to the terror campaign inside Pakistan. In sum, the appearance of complicity on both sides of the border detracted from the efforts at reconciliation, and no one in high position in either country believed that an improvement in relations was in the offing.

And as illusive as peace with India appeared to be, tranquillity still seemed a distant goal in Afghanistan. Afghan warplanes and artillery bombed and shelled Pakistani towns along the troubled border in 1986 and again in 1987. A raid against the village of Tera Mengal was especially tragic, in that more than one hundred lives were lost. Pakistan brought down an Afghan transport aircraft which had been mistaken for a bomber, while Kabul gloated over the destruction of a Pakistani fighter plane. Afghan warplanes also carried out air raids on mujahiddin targets in the North-West Frontier Province. Islamabad protested against all these assaults on its sovereignty, but its pleas fell on deaf ears as each side endeavoured to force the other to make concessions pending a breakthrough in the Geneva-based proximity talks.

Pakistan's insecurity also prompted it to intensify its pursuit of nuclear weapons. Although hiding its weapons programme behind oft-repeated claims of a nuclear energy project, Zia authorized the army to take charge of the mission and to realize the goal (Ali, 1984). But while the administration devoted much of its scientific resources to the production of an atomic weapon, Pakistan also pressed the United Nations General Assembly to approve a resolution declaring the Indian Ocean and the region of South Asia a nuclear-free zone. Islamabad also stated its willingness to sign the Nuclear Non-Proliferation Treaty if New Delhi did so, but India decided not to opt out of the nuclear club and the Zia Government reacted by accelerating its weapons programme.

Rajiv, echoing his mother, criticized the United States for providing Islamabad with state-of-the-art fighter-bombers that could be fitted with nuclear weapons. Citing what he called the hypocrisy in the American quest for a nuclear weapons-free world, the Indian Prime Minister declared India's sovereign right to protect its territorial integrity, and in a cynical world he called for maximizing his nation's security. More than just a war of words, the undiminished bitterness between the two countries was cause for concern in other capitals.

Critics of US policy toward Pakistan in the US Congress cited statutes that barred doing business with a country that was shown to be developing nuclear arms. The Reagan administration, given the conflict in Afghanistan, had waived the law so that military transfers could be made to Pakistan. By 1987, however, with the war in Afghanistan winding down, members of the Congress questioned the continued transfer of military aid to Pakistan. Moreover, Pakistan had been featured in a number of high-profile cases in which it was alleged that its agents had stolen, or tried to obtain surreptitiously, nuclear technology. The much-publicized cases energized the American Congressmen to pressurize the Reagan administration to reconsider its Pakistan programme. And in September 1987 a number of Congressmen called upon the President to suspend aid to Islamabad. The period marked the end of the American-Pakistani honeymoon, and the sequence of events that dominated 1988 reversed a process that had begun with the Soviet invasion of Afghanistan.

The Final Chapter

1988 began much as 1987 had ended. Internally, Pakistan was torn by rival ethnic, regional, and political groups, each with its own agenda, and hardly one among them interested in the restoration of normalcy. Try as he did to balance and neutralize opposed forces, Zia was unsuccessful in rallying the critical coalition that might have brought domestic peace to the nation. Stubbornly avoiding intimacy with the different leaders of the political opposition, and seldom in a position to reconcile his world view with theirs, Zia was condemned to toil virtually alone, and the eleventh year of his rule was little different from the ten that preceded it. Zia had demonstrated that he could sustain his authority, but he never found the formula that might have enabled him to reconcile disparate elements.

Zia never really had the chance to move Pakistan forward. The legacy of the Ayub, and especially the Bhutto, years weighed heavily upon him. Nor could he fall back on more than his survivor instincts when faced by a hostile India and an aggressive Soviet Union on his frontiers. Even Zia's vision of an Islamic state was overshadowed by developments in Iran which brought the Ayatollah Khomeini to the attention of the world. The cataclysmic shift in neighbouring Iran from a progressive and secular ally to a reactionary theocracy made Zia's own experiment in appropriate Muslim behaviour less than believable. Moreover, the war that Iraq launched against Iran in 1980 dragged on through all the years of the Zia administration, and although the protracted war added credibility to the Iranian revolution, Zia could not prevent it from spilling over into Pakistan and negatively affecting his own Islamization scheme.

Zia had an overflowing plate of problems in the years he ruled Pakistan, and the fact that he was still able to engineer a political and social equilibrium, to demonstrate economic resiliency, and to fasten attention on Pakistan's multiple goals of Islamization and military preparedness, was no small achievement. Zia had kept Pakistan afloat through years of turmoil and division. Surrounded by violent experience as well as immersed in it, pressurized by one of the world's two superpowers on its fragile borders, and by the other demanding not only a steadfastness of character but also a modicum of democratic performance, the Pakistan of Ziaul Haq laboured to be all things to outsiders, but it was something else to its own citizens.

Clashes between rival student organizations, and between students and police, made a shambles of the nation's higher education experience, and the government was forced to extend the closure of most of the universities and colleges. On the one side, the educational institutions found it impossible to conduct their programmes; on the other, however, their closing meant that the nation's volatile and politically active youth would have still more opportunity to expand their ranks and sustain the unrest. In the early months of 1988, the bloodiest incidents involving the student population were experienced in Sindh's largest cities of Karachi and Hyderabad. Mobs of young people indiscriminately attacked bystanders and set fires that caused the deaths of scores of innocent residents. Nor were the students alone in their wild escapades. This latest uprising reignited enduring ethnic hatreds, and once more the different communities found nothing to celebrate in national unity.

Pathans and Afghan refugees again represented some of the principal combatants and, as with their earlier displays of lawlessness, they found their enemies in the people who shared their locales. Having been evicted from some of their shantytown habitations in 1986, many Afghans and Pathans returned to their old neighbourhoods to find the *mohajirs* in their once familiar surroundings. Already irreparably estranged, the one refugee community vented its anger on the other hapless community. And although the Zia government attempted to restore law and order and placed Karachi and Hyderabad under even tighter constraints, the perpetrators of violence could not be adequately contained. Their furious assaults on one another continued to take a heavy toll of people and property and virtually paralysed the country's economic life.

The government's demonstrated inability to guarantee the security of its citizens drove the relatively defenceless *mohajirs* to fall back upon an organization of young militants. The Mohajir Qaumi Movement (MQM) was formed in 1986 by Altaf Hussain, a young man who, along with his youthful followers, had decided to give the community a political voice and who, in the absence of established and identified leaders, articulated what they argued were the sentiments of the larger community. Thus the MQM was spawned in an atmosphere of hate and vilification, of fear and civil disorder. Although never truly welcome among the movers and shakers of Pakistani society, the MQM nevertheless filled a peculiar leadership vacuum. And it was Altaf Hussain who came to embody the ordinary *mohajir's* concern for the protection of life and physical property. Sensing their marginalization in a divided and provincialized Pakistan, these lower-middle-class descendants of the Pakistan Movement found comfort and purpose in the expressions of their charismatic leader, but not the peace and contentment that were their real objectives.

But the bitter conflict between opposed refugee groups was fuelled by still other historical, more indigenous economic and social factors. Having spread their influence from Karachi to Hyderabad, the Indian refugee community had come to monopolize the economic life of Sindh province. The Sindhi reaction to this 'alien' takeover was illustrated in their struggle to prevent the Muslim League from declaring Karachi the federal capital in the country's early years. Native Sindhis were generally less educated and more impoverished than the newcomers in their midst, and their expression was nurtured and shaped by the more articulate members of their ethnic group who represented a variety of experience, some urban, some rural, but nevertheless highly personalized. Sindhis, too, tended to deify their leaders, to endow them with powers they could not manifest in themselves. Such leaders had long dominated rural Sindh, where the *wadera* landlords enjoyed all the powers of life and death over their tenant-subjects. Inferior-superior relationships shaped Sindhi political consciousness and the different leaders, whether landlords or *pirs*, were all capable of galvanizing huge followings.

Sindhi nationalism was exploited at the national level by Zulfikar Ali Bhutto, whose central purpose was the neutralization of a perceived threat to his PPP, but who nevertheless did not hesitate to intensify the already deep divisions within society. The unrest that overwhelmed Sindh following the loss of East Pakistan was often attributed to the divide and rule policies of the Quaid-i-Awam, but even after Bhutto's passing, no individual or institution was able to bridge the differences between the indigenous Sindhis and those who had adopted the province. Sindhis were uncomfortable with the Pathans who first came to Karachi in quest of employment, they were distressed by the later inflow of Afghan refugees who trafficked in illicit trade, but they were even more disenchanted with the *mohajirs,* whose new militancy and concentrated numbers had given them not only economic and financial advantages, but also political control of the key urban centres.

During the Zia years, the unresolved Sindhi problem did substantial damage to the social fabric of both the province and the nation. The war in Afghanistan was also significant in that it further aggravated an already complex socio-psychological condition. Challenged by a congeries of peoples who only abstractly shared common Pakistani identity, no one in Pakistan, and certainly not the Zia-Junejo combination, was in a position to cope with the hardening of exclusive mindsets. The government of Ziaul Haq was pressured to find a formula that offered results beyond the use of physical coercion; but positive programmatic development could not be implemented in an atmosphere of fear and insecurity.

The dilemma of the Sindhi cities spread to the towns and villages, and neither provincial nor federal governments had the tools or the experience to address the central questions of the multi-ethnic state. The MQM, like the other Sindhi organizations, flourished in these circumstances and Zia, a *mohajir* without an ethnic constituency, offered no alternative to Altaf Hussain. It was the MQM which tried to dominate the life of Karachi and Hyderabad, and its candidates won control of the municipal governments. But the opposition to the MQM was unreconciled to these electoral victories, and what could not be successfully challenged at the polls was moved to the streets and neighbourhoods. Hence the protracted disorder, the provincial government's utter helplessness, and the federal government's deployment of the armed forces in a futile attempt to limit the destructiveness. Nor was Sindh the only ethnic trouble spot engaging the Zia administration as it entered its eleventh year of imposed rule. Sectarian conflict was evident even in the remote northern region of Gilgit. And perhaps linked to that unrest was the assassination of Allama Arif al-Hussaini, a leader of the Shiite community, who was gunned down in Peshawar only weeks after the Gilgit altercations. His death provoked still more disturbances and highlighted the depth of national, let alone regional, instability. Moreover, this most recent display of disaffection came just as Pakistan and Afghanistan were to announce the finalization of an agreement on the disposition of forces in the mountain state.

On 14 April 1988 Afghanistan and Pakistan entered into an agreement after six years of tedious, indirect negotiations mediated by the United Nations representative on behalf of the Secretary-General (Rais,1994). The United States and the Soviet Union were made guarantors of the accords, while Islamabad and Kabul promised not to interfere in each other's affairs. The accords provided for the return of the refugee population, the phased withdrawal of Soviet troops, and a Pakistani pledge to cease assisting the Afghan mujahiddin

Soviet assistance to the Kabul government was also to be terminated, and the Afghan people were to be given the opportunity to determine their own government and future.

Neither the Afghan mujahiddin nor the Soviets were participants in the negotiations, however, and although Moscow seemed relieved of a great burden, the Afghan resistance was far from satisfied. Too much blood had been spilled, too many sacrifices made, and too many divisions created for there to be general and overall acceptance of the accords by the mujahiddin. Moreover, Zia had favoured the Islamic fundamentalists, and they were unified on only one matter, namely, the removal of Soviet troops. They now struggled over the question of sustained Marxist rule in Kabul, and they were not prepared to put away their weapons until Babrak Karmal's successor, Najibullah, had been defeated.

Nevertheless, the Soviet troops began their withdrawal from Afghanistan on 15 May. Moscow expected Islamabad to police the Afghan resistance and, especially, to tame the guerrilla groups which its Inter-Services Intelligence organization had supported through the long conflict. When Zia could not satisfy that Soviet demand, Moscow warned the Pakistani President that he risked another form of warfare which would inevitably have an impact upon his own country. Moscow did not trust Zia. The Kremlin saw him playing for time, waiting until the last Soviet soldier had left Afghanistan before turning his fundamentalist organizations against the Kabul government. Indeed, Zia's well-publicized Islamic proclivities, his desire to see Pakistan and Afghanistan in common cause, were not lost on the Kremlin. Moscow reminded Islamabad that the agreement had been entered into, indirectly or not, between Pakistan and Afghanistan. The Soviet Union had agreed to honour its part of the arrangement; it was Zia's responsibility to see to it that the mujahiddin also complied with the Geneva understandings. The Kremlin made it clear that it had not abandoned the Marxist government in Kabul, and that the agreement rested on Pakistan's sincerity in reining in the Afghan resistance.

Despite Soviet complaints and threats, Zia held to his commitment to the fundamentalist orders, and with the Soviets locked in Najibullah's embrace, the only section of the April accords that could be implemented was the Soviet troop withdrawal. And with Gorbachev anxious to cut his losses in the region, there was little likelihood of a Kremlin reversal. The Afghans, however, were not prepared to lay down their arms and the war did not cease with the accords. Pakistan, therefore, was forced to accept the continued presence of the several million refugees who had wandered into the country in the eight years of war. Moreover, because the Afghans were now more than ever engaged in a civil war, the refugees continued to move in Pakistan's direction. Zia hoped to provide the resistance with enough support to win a quick victory over Najibullah's forces, but that strategy was only developing in the summer of 1988. Nor could it be determined at the time if the capture of Kabul would indeed end the hostilities and allow the Afghans to return home.

Even before the April agreement was announced, the cost of the war to Pakistan was inestimable. Generations of Pakistanis yet unborn would pay the price for the war in the neighbouring state. And a tragic, and more immediate, example of that cost was registered just as the accords were to be announced. On 10 April an arms dump located at Faizabad, a village between Islamabad and Rawalpindi, blew up, raining ordnance on the village and outer regions of the nearby cities. More than one hundred people were reported killed and in excess of one thousand injured by the exploding shells and falling buildings. These figures, however, did not account for the affected military personnel who were handling and guarding the arsenal, and estimates of their losses made the tragedy the single most costly event suffered by Pakistan in the course of the Afghan war. Moreover, there was ample reason to believe that sabotage was the cause of the explosion. Simultaneously with the Faizabad disaster came news of an explosion in a Lahore arms factory, and another in a busy Karachi neighbourhood. Although the Pakistani authorities, with a view to the Geneva accords, sought to play down the incidents, it was General Zia who publicly declared that the explosions were the work of foreign agents; indeed, he fingered members of Najibullah's clandestine service. Najibullah, according to Zia, had sent a message to Pakistan, and that message said it was Islamabad's responsibility to neutralize the mujahiddin.

The April accords, therefore, were not the panacea that the outside world imagined. Zia, in particular, was confronted with even greater challenges now that Soviet forces were in full retreat from Afghanistan. Not only was the war not over, Islamabad was about to lose the services of the retiring Reagan administration, and the American Congress was already inclined to reduce the military commitment the US administration had made to General Zia. Moreover, Zia was trapped by the character of the Islamization programme which he had pressed on the Afghans with even greater enthusiasm. The Geneva accords could not be reconciled with Islamization, but Zia was already too deeply committed to backtrack now.

Confronted with questions he could not answer, Zia struck a blow against his own inner circle when in May he announced the dismissal of Prime Minister Mohammad Khan Junejo. He also sacked his cabinet and dissolved the National Assembly and all the provincial legislatures. Zia justified his actions with the argument that Junejo and the other governments were weak, and therefore unable to stem the tide of social conflict that had swamped the country. Identifying ethnic, communal, and sectarian strife as mortal dangers, Zia said that only the sternest measures could restore the nation's equilibrium. Zia noted that the Soviet withdrawal from Afghanistan had done little to improve conditions within the country. He said that he feared sustained domestic unrest would again play into the hands of the nation's enemies, and that the armed forces must be alert to the new challenges.

Zia accused the Junejo government of failing to eradicate corruption. He also said that it had joined with the opposition in opposing his Islamization programme. In June Zia announced the formation of a new caretaker cabinet, but surprisingly, it was a facsimile of the one he had sacked, less Junejo and four other ministers. A few days later General Zia declared the implementation of an Islamic legal code that would be the supreme law of the land, and the superior courts were ordered to strike down laws that were in conflict with Islamic law. Some observers drew the conclusion that Zia had panicked, that the new equation in Afghanistan required symmetrical developments on both sides of their shared frontier. The Junejo ouster and the rush to implement the new Islamic reforms disturbed the more sophisticated members of Pakistani society, but the consequences of all these actions were still to be clarified.

Zia's Islamization scheme aroused suspicions, given the fading of the Soviet threat. It was no longer clear what Zia's intentions were, but there was general agreement that he planned a new assault on the country's legal system. A case in point was Zia's attack on the 1961 Muslim Family Laws, which he portrayed as protecting the female population against male preferences. Early in July a formidable body of Lahore women characterized the assault on the Family Laws as an assault on their dignity and self-worth. Identifying their cause with that of Benazir Bhutto, they carried the flag of the Pakistan People's Party and petitioned Zia to reconsider his actions.

Zia was not oblivious to the political climate that clouded his administration. Feeling more isolated, he announced the holding of new elections to the National Assembly for 16 November, and provincial assembly elections three days later. With Benazir Bhutto supposedly anticipating the birth of her first child in November, Zia's selection of the election date, appeared to be directed at reducing her presence on the political scene at a critical moment. Zia knew that Benazir led the most successful of the surviving political parties, perhaps the only national party in the country. Therefore, limiting Benazir's chances was a definite feature of Zia's overall electoral strategy. But the autumn elections were another matter. Zia also needed to tend to army business and, very much in need of state-of-the-art weapons for his soldiers, he was eager to observe the operations of a new United States armoured vehicle that was to be the Reagan administration's final gift to the Pakistan Armed forces.

On 17 August 1988 Zia boarded a United States-built C-130 military transport at Bahawalpur for the 300 mile flight back to Islamabad. The General had gone to Bahawalpur with almost all his highest-ranking army officers to observe a demonstration of the American M-1 tank. Having witnessed the exercise in the company of the American Ambassador to

Pakistan, Arnold Raphel, and the US Chief Military Attache, Brigadier-General Herbert Wassom, all the principals, including Raphel and Wassom, joined Zia and the senior Pakistani generals for the brief flight back to Islamabad. Within minutes of take-off, however, the plane exploded and crashed. All aboard perished, and the Zia reign ended amid the flaming debris that spread across a broad area of the Bahawalpur region.

CHAPTER 11

DEMOCRACY REVISITED

The death of General Ziaul Haq dramatized the extreme divisions in Pakistani society. His supporters grieved his passing and arranged that his remains be laid to rest in the compound of the soaring and majestic King Faisal mosque in Islamabad. His opponents, however, were uncontrollably gleeful, and virtually oblivious to the heavy loss of life on the ill-fated aircraft. They publicly and unashamedly celebrated the 'tyrant's demise'. '*Pakistan Zindabad!*' (Long Live Pakistan!) was meant to drown out the cries of the mourners. Thus Pakistan ushered in yet another era in its history, with one segment of the nation sombrely reading the prayers for the dead while another exuberantly welcomed the transfer of power and heralded a new democratic age. How to reconcile these two totally different expressions requires more wisdom than any serious participant or observer of the Pakistan scene is likely to possess. Nevertheless, it is instructive that, in spite of the relatively even split between the one group and the other, much more voice was given to Zia's adversaries than to his followers.

Pakistan was seized by great expectations following the passing of General Zia, and those expectations were articulated not only by the dead President's political opposition, but also by the country's literati and intellectual elite, which dominated the print media. The latter were unimpressed with a government report issued on 16 October 1988 describing the explosion aboard Zia's aircraft as 'a criminal act or sabotage'. It was an irrelevant disclosure to those who had put the matter behind them, and irrespective of how the General met his end, they believed that the principal obstacle to Pakistan's brighter future had been removed. Zia's dead spirit was therefore resurrected not so much by his colleagues as by his antagonists, who sought to demonstrate that all of the nation's problems had been caused by the evil machinations of one man. It was their argument that fate, if not good fortune, had willed an end to Zia's personalization of power, had allowed the country to rediscover its lost ethos and to begin again the business of building a great nation.

One paragraph says it all. According to Zulfikar Khalid Maluka, 'Zia exploited the deeply-held religious sentiments of various factions and set them against the minorities for the perpetuation of his hold on them.' The author continues:

> There is a consensus among political scientists that Zia employed the civil and military intelligence agencies to create and arm ethno-cultural and communal groups and entangle them in confrontation with other sections of society which were reluctant to yield to his ignominious rule. While deliberately generating the kalashnikov and heroin culture, Zia completely neglected socio-economic development and thoroughly corrupted all aspects of national politics (Maluka, 1995, p.276)

It is not apologetic to cite the strained aspects of this characterization. Zia was as much a prisoner of the Pakistan experience as he was its judge and jury and, in the matter of Zulfikar Ali Bhutto, its executioner. But Zia did not emerge from nowhere. A product of the conditions that had brought him to prominence, it was his destiny to preside over the nation at a critical period in its history. Zia was part of the Pakistan story, hardly its maker. Moreover, he was an extension of a deeper past that intertwined with the age of the Mughals and the reign of the British Raj. Zia was no less a Pakistani than those who preceded him or those who came after. Trained to accept responsibility and dedicated to service, he was nurtured in an environment that demanded discipline and required blind obedience. Moreover, Zia combined religious commitment with his soldiering, and there was little in his demeanour that allowed for liberal expression or democratic behaviour. Other Pakistanis, less encumbered by an autocratic life experience, also failed the test of democracy, and to cite Zia as the singular culprit, the one person who denied the nation its true destiny, is not only disingenuous, it is deliberate distortion.

Zia played the role of the viceregal ruler in his own way and in response to the conditions prevailing at the time. To accuse him of corrupting the nation's political life is to ignore the stages of Pakistan's history. Embellishing history is an art form; fabricating it becomes dangerous licence. Zia did not destroy the democratic experience in the Muslim nation, nor did those who followed him revive it. Democracy is more than rhetoric, more than good intentions, and certainly more than the natural order of things. Pakistanis have waxed eloquent on the subject of democracy but the record reveals it was seldom within their grasp. A divided nation at birth, democratic experience was made impossible by the inability to reconcile competing claims or relieve deep-seated fears. Zia's emphasis on Islamization was not divisive, it was society's many divisions that rejected his portrayal of Islamization. Moreover, Zia's determined foes would be the last to consecrate his power, let alone to acknowledge his desire to bind the nation's wounds. In their eyes, Zia was an usurper and an illegitimate presence, and hence combat, not co-operation, was their reaction to his entreaties. But in choosing confrontation and conflict, they too failed to bridge the differences that have stalked Pakistani society from its inception.

The Transition

Zia's immediate successor was Ghulam Ishaq Khan, then the Chairman, or presiding officer, of the Pakistan Senate. Ghulam Ishaq Khan was quickly sworn in as Acting President, and as soon as he took the centre stage, he too became the target of those demanding a more 'democratic' leader. Ghulam Ishaq Khan had distinguished himself as a civil administrator over a period that spanned the entire history of Pakistan. A Pathan, Ghulam Ishaq was born in 1915 and raised in the North-West Frontier Province, where he came under the influence of the colonial administration and where he set his goal on a career in public service. Already thirty-two years of age at independence, his preparation and prior experience as a maturing frontier administrator won him an appointment to the CSP, the elite Civil Service of Pakistan.

Ghulam Ishaq established his reputation as a formidable member of the Pakistan Government only after Ayub Khan asked him to manage the West Pakistan Water and Power Development Authority. He was later shifted to the post of Secretary in the Ministry of Finance, and then to the even more prestigious office of Governor of the State Bank of Pakistan. Subsequent to this role, he became Secretary-General in the Ministry of Defence, where he nurtured his intimacies with the highest serving officers in the Pakistan armed forces. Sharing the views of his colleagues in the higher bureaucracy that political stability was a *sine qua non* in the development of democratic institutions, and mindful of the country's difficulty in achieving national integration, Ghulam Ishaq justified the periods of martial law. He served Ayub Khan, Yahya Khan, and Ziaul Haq with classic bureaucratic dedication. More balanced than Ghulam Mohammad and less ambitious than Iskandar Mirza, Ghulam Ishaq nevertheless shared their contempt for the politicians, and it came as no surprise when, in 1985, some time after his retirement from the administrative service, General Zia arranged his 'election' to the Senate.

Ghulam Ishaq Khan had made a reputation for dedication and commitment to public service. Whereas his professionalism was never questioned, nor his administrator's neutrality to successive serving governments, he had reason to ponder the course of democratic experience. Ghulam Ishaq had little respect for politicians in general and they, in turn, were less than pleased with his administrator's demeanour, which they characterized as colonial and oppressively paternalistic. Firm in the opinion that Pakistan was not a democratic nation, Ghulam Ishaq was entirely focused on stable government. He ignored the posturing of self-proclaimed political leaders and temperamentally, as in practical matters, identified with the country's military establishment.

At an advanced age when he assumed the presidency, he was nevertheless a powerful figure. Endowed with all the powers conferred upon his predecessor save leadership of the army, Ghulam Ishaq was familiar with the country's viceregal tradition and experienced in authoritarian decision-making. Moreover, guided by the amended 1973 Constitution that had expanded the role of the President, Ghulam Ishaq Khan had the power to make and break governments, to dissolve the legislatures, and to virtually paralyse political activity. A personality to be reckoned with, Ghulam Ishaq was a pivotal actor in the Pakistan after Zia.

Not since the days of Ghulam Mohammad had a civil administrator assumed the prominence that Ghulam Ishaq enjoyed as President of Pakistan. The Eighth Amendment to the Constitution was deemed to be the source of his power and, although challenged in the courts, no tribunal had argued the impropriety of the statute. Nevertheless, the Eighth Amendment and the powers it conferred on the President were seen as a subversion of the political process. Ghulam Ishaq's instincts, experience, and training influenced his behaviour, however, and when faced with a chaotic moment in the destiny of the nation, he responded in the only way he knew: he was forceful, direct, and entirely focused on the nation's tenuous equilibrium. Accusing him of playing toady to the higher military, of misapplying constitutional provisions, his detractors were convinced that his actions were solely prompted by personal ambition and an insatiable quest for power.

The new President's declaration of a state of emergency was not well received, nor was his decision to delay appointing a caretaker Prime Minister and cabinet. His critics believed that the old civil servant had set his sights on monopolizing power, and none of his actions were deemed to be in the true interest of the nation. Moreover, Ghulam Ishaq allied himself with what remained of the army high command, and especially with the new Chief of the Army Staff (COAS), General Mirza Aslam Baig, who had been present at the Bahawalpur demonstration but had returned to Islamabad on another aircraft. Given the deaths of many of the senior generals accompanying Zia, Baig was selected to lead the Pakistan Army.

Linkages between Baig, General Hamid Gul, Chief of Inter-Services Intelligence, and Ghulam Ishaq Khan were given sinister meaning, the assumption being that the President and the surviving officers had conspired to deny the formal return of civilian government. Nevertheless, the elections authorized by President Zia remained on track, and Ghulam Ishaq demonstrated every intention of honouring his predecessor's promise. In the interim, however, the new President preferred governing the country through a special council of senior ministers and armed forces Chiefs that he had hastily formed. Declaring the emergency council necessary in the name of continuity and consistency, he said he was committed to the continuation of Zia's domestic and foreign policies. Moreover, he did not believe that the immediate aftermath of Zia's death was the appropriate time for a return to competitive politics.

In October, in response to a writ petition, the Punjab High Court declared Zia's earlier dissolution of the National Assembly illegal, while the Pakistan Supreme Court ruled in favour of the political parties and cleared the way for the normalization of political activity. Within days of these judicial rulings, no less than eighty-two parties announced they would run candidates in the November election. If Ghulam Ishaq had any intention of blocking their participation, there was no indication from his statements or behaviour. The time had passed when the parties could be denied their traditional role, and given the legal judgments, opposing their participation was no longer in question. Furthermore, while generally supportive of Zia's overall programme, the new President did not share the late General's Islamic emphasis. Closer to the thinking of Ghulam Mohammad and Iskandar Mirza, Ghulam Ishaq was uneasy with Islamization, and by boosting the return to conventional politics he also demonstrated his preference for secular politics.

Thus Ghulam Ishaq proved to be a balancer and an equalizer, and not the devious monopolizer of power the politicians made him out to be. He agreed to work with the politicians as they moved back into the mainstream of public life, but he was also ever mindful of their divisive tactics, and he refused to remain a distant and aloof bystander. The new President encouraged the many parties and factions to find common ground and he was generally relieved when a host of them decided to form their coalitions. Moreover, one of the coalitions came to represent the larger programme of the late Ziaul Haq, taking the name of the Islamic Democratic Alliance or Islami Jamhoori Itihad (IJI). The other major coalition was the resurrected Movement for the Restoration of Democracy, but its failure to enlist the services of Benazir Bhutto's PPP destroyed any chance it might have had to re-establish its bona fides. The PPP had decided that it did not need to throw in its lot with a coalition, that its popular strength was sufficient to give it a majority and hence, absolute control of the government. The electoral contest, therefore, was clearly between the IJI and the PPP and somewhat strangely, between the policies of the late President Zia and the programme and philosophy of yet another dead leader, namely, Zulfikar Ali Bhutto.

With little time to present their platforms to the electors, the PPP and the IJI prepared general manifestoes that broadly described their opposed views, but which were meant more to appeal to elector sentiments than to edify them on subjects of national policy. Under the leadership of Benazir Bhutto, the PPP virtually abandoned references to socialism and called upon the public to acknowledge its democratic credentials, notably when contrasted with the legacy of the IJI. The IJI was not constrained from running on the Zia programme, and it positioned itself to capture the vote of those who not only approved of the Islamization programme but who also desired a government with a mundane business outlook. Both the PPP and the IJI were expected to do well, but the competition they faced from the MRD and a host of lesser parties hinted at a divided electorate and an inconclusive result.

More candidates competed in the different constituencies than in any of the previous elections, and a divided polity left all the basic questions unanswered. Moreover, forecasting election results was made more difficult given the voter requirement of a National Identity Card. In fact, the election results were not known until 16 November, when the Election Commission announced that of the 215 contested seats in the the National Assembly, the PPP had garnered more than any other party, although only 92 of the total. By contrast, the IJI had received only 54. It was obvious that neither organization commanded a majority and thus could not straight away be called upon to form a new government.

The PPP complained that their plurality might well have been a majority had the identity cards been issued to all their supporters, but the IJI was not yet prepared to yield to Benazir Bhutto. The matter of who should form the government therefore fell to President Ghulam Ishaq Khan. He met with the leaders of both the PPP and the IJI. When the PPP declared it had entered into an alliance with the Mohajir Qaumi Movement (MQM), the PPP not only strengthened its hold on Sindh province, it also gained control of Karachi. With that leverage, it also won over the Awami National Party in the NWFP and spread its influence into the Punjab and Balochistan. The IJI's power remained in the Punjab, where it had already taken command of the provincial legislature, but its lower rating in the national polls made it a poor choice to form the central government. Thus, after a number of meetings between the major actors, Ghulam Ishaq called upon Benazir Bhutto to form the first post-Zia civilian government.

The First Benazir Government

Benazir's emergence as the President's choice to form the new government came as no surprise, given her status at the head of the country's most successful political organization. But in other respects it was surprising that a young, thirty-six-year old woman would be called upon to preside over the government of a Muslim country. She was, after all, the first woman in modern history to head a government of a Muslim nation, and references to other successful women politicians, e.g., Indira Gandhi or Golda Meir, were without significance. Benazir was cast in a unique role, and the lady was hardly one to shy away from the experience. Seeing her victory as both a vindication of her dead father and popular disaffection for the late Ziaul Haq, she was determined to reinvigorate the memory of Zulfikar Ali Bhutto as well as trample on the legacy of the deceased General-President. The personal vendetta that Benazir had carried on against General Zia did not end with his death, and the new Prime Minister's immediate comments on assuming her high station were less a response to national need than her own desperate and private longing for inner satisfaction.

Zia's death had cleared the way for Benazir's ascension, but his sudden and violent passing had also prevented her from confronting her father's hangman on an even playing field, where she very much expected to get the better of him. Benazir's internalization of what was a deeply psychological matter and her inability to put her feelings of irreparable loss to rest, were apparent the day the Prime Minister assumed her high office and stalked her throughout her brief tenure.

Pakistani society, however, was ready for a new age, and the young woman who now led Pakistan was expected to open a new chapter in the history of the nation. Democracy was in the air, as well as in the sentiments of the people, when Benazir entered the National Assembly accompanied by the President of Pakistan and assumed her new responsibilities. No longer simply the leader of a much denied and much maligned opposition political party, Benazir took the oath of office, pledging to serve the entire nation, to practise the positive arts of reform, and to deliver to the country what had been overlooked in decades past. In her first televised address to the nation, the celebrated orator from Oxford University thrilled her listening and watching audience with her appeals for sacrifice and hard work. Noting that the road ahead would be difficult, she also said it was lined with great promise. It was a fitting start to her administration, which had already been punctuated by a meeting with the IJI leader, Nawaz Sharif. Focused on co-operation and accommodation, Benazir said she was committed to a government of understanding and consensus-building, and thus anticipated a positive response from her rivals.

But that peacemaking side of the Benazir equation also concealed a combative soul. Her first formal press conference brought out the angry Benazir. She used the occasion to direct a fusillade of complaints against Nawaz Sharif, who had become the Chief Minister of the Punjab. Accusing Nawaz Sharif and his IJI of having stolen the provincial election, she condemned what she called his separatist tactics, 'branding him the G.M. Syed of the Punjab'

(Inayatullah, 1993, p.2). Having ordered her PPP associates in the Punjab provincial assembly to vacate the house as a protest against Nawaz Sharif's election as Chief Minister, Benazir turned aside the olive branch extended by the IJI and encouraged the appointment of her party's Secretary-General as Governor of the Punjab. Not only was Nawaz Sharif bypassed by this manoeuvre; the new Governor had failed even to carry his constituency in the recent election.

Benazir had made a personal, not a wise choice and by her actions she unnecessarily placed herself on a collision course with her principal rival in the country's pivotal province. Not content with having thrown down the gauntlet, the Prime Minister imposed a retinue of federal civil servants on the province, again without seeking the approval of the Punjab's Chief Minister. As her father before her had plotted the undermining of the frontier governments when they failed to vote for the PPP, so now Benazir also seemed to believe she could offset the results of the Punjab elections and somehow manage the province from Islamabad. If Benazir had read the lessons in her father's exploits, she might have adopted different tactics, but she was her father's daughter and she could not avoid a fight, even if her intellect told her it was a chancy manoeuvre.

By promoting conflict between the PPP and the IJI, Benazir prolonged Pakistan's long night of division and mistrust. If her real purpose was the creation of a democratic experience, it would be found in her actions, and her performance in the Punjab did not promise a successful outcome. Benazir was a split personality, one side projecting cosmopolitan and worldly experience, the other revealing narrowly-defined and restricted lifeways (Ziring, 1991). It was the latter personality that influenced her behaviour as Prime Minister. Never before an office-holder, still a very young and inexperienced leader, she remained the youthful firebrand, the young activist that had captured the attention of the Pakistani public. It would not be unfair to say that Benazir's inexperience in matters of state quickly turned the promise of her coming into a painful departure. Benazir was the epitome of a Pakistani opposition politician. But she had never served in the legislature or in the administration, and she had none of the practical experience that was expected of a head of government. It is, therefore, not surprising that Benazir chose to challenge Nawaz Sharif rather than work with him. Benazir was not unaware of the give-and-take of democratic politics, but believing in her heart of hearts that democracy was dysfunctional in her country, she set her sights on destroying her rival before, as she believed, he could destroy her.

If Benazir had been familiar with the history of her country, she might at least have been reminded of the controversy that engaged another Prime Minister and his Punjabi Chief Minister. Liaquat Ali Khan's struggle with Mian Mumtaz Daultana had terrible consequences, and needless to emphasize, neither emerged from the fight intact. The political vacuum created by their inability to reconcile damaged the democratic experiment and set in motion the forces that would ultimately overwhelm the country's initial attempt at building representative institutions.

Inayatullah (1993) has written of those first days and weeks of the Benazir administration. In January 1989, writing in the *Daily Nation*, the retired career civil servant commented on how 'lucky' Benazir was to have at her side a President like Ghulam Ishaq, whose 'highest qualities of head and heart and...vast experience of handling national affairs' should prove most helpful if she would but 'seek his advice and guidance'. Cautioning that Benazir was 'riding the wave of democracy', Inayatullah cited the need to keep one's balance while developing the requisite experience in governing a nation with a difficult and tragic past. Pleading for a rational and objective approach to the questions of governance, he wrote that the opportunity to realize the democratic promise must not be missed.

Benazir, however, was oblivious to the thoughts of men like Inayatullah. As a national leader, her inability to control the country's most vital province frustrated her efforts at expunging the Zia record and, as she saw the situation, left her weak and threatened. Believing she had the momentum to overcome the IJI majority in the Punjab, she challenged Nawaz Sharif and sought to drive him from office. Nawaz Sharif, however, was hardly prepared to cave in to the pressure and, left with no alternative, he met the Prime

Minister head-on. The intensification of this rivalry was not lost on anyone in the Punjab, and it certainly could not escape the attention of the President.

Ghulam Ishaq was not prepared to stand aside and allow the confrontation between the country's two strongest politicians to paralyse both the national and provincial governments. Acknowledging that both officials held positions as a consequence of their electoral achievements, he felt that it was not a question of supporting one against the other, but rather of finding the common ground for compromise. Others like Maluka (1995) might conclude that Ghulam Ishaq conspired with Nawaz Sharif to destroy the PPP government. Writing in *The Muslim* on 25 June 1993, Altaf Gauhar was likewise angered by the President's apparently conspiratorial behaviour on behalf of the Punjabi Chief Minister. But after acknowledging the appearance of collusion, how was the President to judge his responsibilities when the country's two leading political figures were determined to ignore each other's electoral victory?

Cases are made with great enthusiasm on both sides of the question, but the failure to accept the uncertainties of democratic government prompted the President to employ his extraordinary powers. Benazir knew that Ghulam Ishaq had the constitutional authority, no matter how controversial, as well as the will, to use the powers of his office if he believed the country was foundering. Had she wanted to forestall the President's use of those powers, Benazir would have had to accept the full consequences of the 1988 elections. But the Prime Minister's desire to control the Punjab was so obsessive that it had to trigger a Presidential response. In the circumstances, Ghulam Ishaq could not refrain from playing the role of the viceroy. Subsequent events, years later, would demonstrate that it was Benazir's behaviour that sparked the attack which eventually swept her from office. Moreover, that she would commit the same error on two separate occasions, with two different Presidents, demonstrates either a high degree of arrogance or gross miscalculation.

Benazir brought youth and vitality to a role traditionally played by members of the feudal oligarchy, and although a scion of a celebrated *wadera* family, she was also a prominent representative of Pakistan's urban, professional, and artistic intelligentsia. Her preparation for life experience included both the mentoring provided by her father and the formal education she received in the United States and Great Britain. Benazir, even more than her father, was the product of a new cosmopolitan age, and she was reasonably comfortable in both oriental and occidental tradition. In so many ways her youthful vigour, her obvious intelligence, and her oratorical gifts were a refreshing change from the austere, more circumscribed, and rigid demeanour of her predecessor. Moreover, Benazir enjoyed the support of the new army high command, and it was General Aslam Baig who sheltered her from the opposition and neutralized the impact of their attacks on her government. She was able to ward off criticism that her administration was responsible for soaring inflation and rising unemployment, and even the Voice of America ignored the country's plight in describing Benazir as a 'symbol of the new democratic Pakistan'.

With friends in high places, Benazir survived a debate on her budget in her first summer as Prime Minister, but defections within her coalition pointed to still greater obstacles ahead. Both the MQM and the ANP broke with the PPP, the former as a consequence of the army crackdown in Karachi which fell heavily on the refugee community. The turbulence in Sindh was undiminished following General Zia's death, and Benazir was no more successful in bringing the ethnic conflict to an end than her predecessor had been. In fact, in May 1989 Benazir described the situation in Sindh province as a 'mini-insurgency', and directed the army to quell those responsible for the violent conditions.

The targeting of the MQM by the army was believed to have been ordered by the Prime Minister, although she denied all such accusations. Instability in Sindh also prompted the Jiye Sindh leader, G.M. Syed, to renew his call for an independent or autonomous Sindhu Desh. His followers turned out in significant numbers to demonstrate their resolve, and in the ensuing riots, they temporarily seized Sukkur airport. The anger of the protestors was dramatized by the burning of the Pakistan flag, and only the army was able to restore law and order, but not before 3,000 followers of the Jiye Sindh movement had been arrested.

Benazir's difficulties in her native Sindh province and her dependence on the army did not augur well for her future. Moreover, one separatist movement begot another, and suddenly a Seraiki Qaumi Movement sprang up, demanding a new province from the merger of the Multan, Bahawalpur, Dera Ghazi Khan, Dera Ismail Khan, and Jhang divisions. Mumtaz Ali Bhutto, Benazir's uncle, had also broken with the PPP to form the Sindh-Baloch-Pushtoon Front. A strong supporter of a confederal Pakistan, this member of the Bhutto clan believed that the country could be saved only by honouring the wishes of the many regions for greater autonomy. Ever refining his ideas, in March 1989 Mumtaz announced the formation of still another organization, which he called the Sindh National Front. Presenting a fifteen-point formula that included the devolution of sovereignty to the several 'nations' comprising Pakistan, he amplified the call of G.M. Syed for a separate Sindh for the Sindhis. Mumtaz Bhutto called for the abandonment of all Pakistan army cantonments in Sindh province, and insisted that the different units of Pakistan be permitted to enter into agreements with other nations. Mumtaz declared that his objective was the preservation, not the dissolution of Pakistan, which in his opinion could survive only in a confederal form. Wali Khan was more restrained on this subject, given the unstable conditions in Afghanistan, but Balochistan's Akbar Bugti echoed similar ideas in calling for a 'Balochistan for the Baloch.'

The ANP drifted from the ranks of the PPP over differences with the government's Afghanistan policy. The last of the Soviet troops left Afghanistan in February 1989, but the struggle in the neighbouring state did not end. Rival factions fought for control of the provinces and the Marxist Najibullah government remained in place in Kabul. Pakistan's Inter-Services Intelligence (ISI), under the leadership of Lieutenant-General Hamid Gul, had sustained its assistance to the various Afghan fundamentalist orders that operated out of Peshawar, but they were prevented from taking strategic Jalalabad, which remained under Najibullah's control. Wali Khan, leader of the ANP, condemned the operations of the ISI, declaring that they had prolonged the war and inflicted even greater hardship on both the Afghans as well as the people of the frontier province. Benazir, however, did not move to replace General Hamid Gul until after the ANP broke with her administration.

General Baig's loyalty to the Prime Minister was seemingly assured, but Hamid Gul's largely secret operations had aroused concern that the President, who had serious differences with the COAS, was conspiring with the ISI to undermine his command. Rumours also were allowed to circulate that connected Hamid Gul with Nawaz Sharif, it being intimated that both had consorted with the President in a manoeuvre aimed at undermining the Benazir-Baig relationship. Gul had been appointed to his post by General Zia in 1987, and he had developed the ISI into a formidable institution that was relatively free of Baig's authority. Both Baig and Benazir, therefore, had reason to rid themselves of the General, and the Jalalabad fiasco proved to be the opportunity to restrict the operations of the ISI. It also opened the way for Benazir to have Hamid Gul dismissed and replaced by Lieutenant-General Shamsur Rahman Khan.

The opposition led by Nawaz Sharif refused, however, to let up their assaults on the Prime Minister. The combined opposition filed a motion of no-confidence in the PPP government and called for a vote on 1 November 1989. The essentially IJI motion carried the signatures of eighty-six members of the National Assembly, and only 119 were needed to bring down the government. When the vote was about to be taken, differences over the appointment of judges to the Supreme Court had opened deep rifts between Benazir and Ghulam Ishaq. Other matters, involving appointments and retirements of government and high-ranking members of the armed forces also dramatized the serious disagreements between the President and Prime Minister. In fact, so inflamed were relations between the head of government and the head of state that astute observers had concluded that Ghulam Ishaq had thrown his support behind the no-confidence motion. Moreover, when Nawaz Sharif sought an audience with General Baig, the latter declined to meet with him, leading the public to believe that Baig's 'neutrality' was, in actuality, support for Benazir.

With the lines apparently tightening, Nawaz Sharif moved between Lahore, Murree, and Islamabad in a desperate attempt to assemble the needed votes to unseat the Prime Minister. The MQM had joined with the IJI in September and its Members of the National Assembly (MNAs) announced their intention to vote with the opposition. It was said that never in the history of Pakistan had there been so much trading and purchasing of party loyalties. Millions of rupees were reported changing hands in the manoeuvre, and when government overtures sought to win back the defecting members, the more 'vulnerable' were placed in what were called safe houses, and police escorts were arranged to ferry MNAs between their place of refuge and the Assembly in Islamabad.

But despite all these efforts, as well as the heavy expenditure, the IJI strategy failed. The no-confidence motion fell twelve votes short of its goal and Benazir's precarious majority in the Assembly was sustained. When the Speaker, Meraj Khalid, announced the defeat of the move, the government benches were ecstatic. Benazir used the occasion of her victory to thank her supporters and to pledge a programme of national renewal. Her government, she noted, had received an important message, and she intended to pursue a vigorous programme of reform that would 'live up to the expectations and aspirations of the people of Pakistan' (Ziring, 1990). Calling upon the opposition to join ranks with her government, she acknowledged the healthy character of democratic debate, but said that opposition for opposition's sake alone was counterproductive and, if perpetuated, would ruin the experiment in self-government. 'I have no rancour or ill-will against those who have moved that no-trust motion against me,' Benazir declared, but she hoped 'saner elements' in the Assembly and throughout the nation would join hands with her to make democracy work in Pakistan. She concluded her remarks with the view that it was a time for 'taking stock' and that both the government and opposition parties needed to review their performances.

In a news conference later, Benazir cited the passionate debate in the Assembly but also opined that everything had been done within the rules and that, overall, it had been a very positive experience. Responding to the opposition's repeated demands for new elections, Benazir questioned the utility of such an exercise, noting that the country had just held one national election and it was premature to talk of another. Meraj Khalid appeared to agree with the Prime Minister. The Speaker also reminded the public that the no-confidence motion was the very first in the history of Pakistan and that it had been pressed with great enthusiasm, but also with great concern for democratic procedure. What both Benazir and Meraj Khalid wanted stressed was Pakistan's growing political maturity and, having made their point, the Prime Minister proceeded to rearrange her government so that she might be better prepared to ward off the next assault from her opposition.

How democratic the no-confidence proceeding actually was, however, is recorded in the verbal attacks that continued between the government and opposition benches. Whereas the government accused the IJI of subverting the neutrality of the armed forces and questioned the role of the President, the PPP had resorted to its own form of extraordinary tactics when it flew ninety MNAs to Peshawar and held them incommunicado, thus preventing the opposition from enticing them to join their ranks. Ghulam Mustafa Jatoi, who had broken with Benazir to join the opposition, cited the many manoeuvres that had negated the success of the opposition effort. He pointed to the absence from the Assembly of Wali Khan, whose ballot in support of the motion might have swayed the additional votes, but he too acknowledged the utility of the experience, and anticipated that the contest between the PPP government and the opposition would continue.

Both sides appeared to claim a measure of victory, but it was Benazir who demonstrated the most resonant voice. Noting that her term of office had only begun, she reiterated her intention to complete her five-year term and, not one to hide from the challenges, hinted that her difficulties were not so much with Nawaz Sharif or the IJI as with President

Ghulam Ishaq. In an even political contest, Benazir had little doubt she could outfox her opposition. But the President and the army were another matter, and serious collusion between them would not augur well for her administration. On 23 November, Benazir cited new efforts at unseating her government. Insisting that she could never be defeated in a fair election, that her removal could only be managed by surreptitious means, she listed numerous attempts at discrediting her government, which, she argued, included the attempt to destroy a Saudi Arabian airliner in Karachi.

Brushing aside Benazir's complaints as well as her accusations, Mustafa Jatoi called upon the Prime Minister to honour her pledge of co-operation. He repeated the opposition's claim that it was not plotting a behind-the-scenes action against the PPP government, nor was the IJI enlisting the services of the President or seeking to provoke the army to again intervene in the country's political life, and called upon Benazir to transcend her suspicions, to clean up her administration, to address the many charges of corruption that had been hurled at her government, and to acknowledge that she and her ministers had made 'some mistakes' that could not go unattended. Benazir, however, was not one to ponder opposition appeals, let alone pressures from a politician who had broken ranks. Guided by her own inner beliefs and deeply committed to the tragic memory of her idolized father, she could not deliver on her much proclaimed promises. Many continued to believe in her, in no small part because she represented a departure from the years of military rule, but her administration was not the democratic experience Pakistanis had hoped for.

Benazir's PPP was an autocratic arrangement that had never adopted democratic practices, and her government promised much but delivered very little. Inflation and unemployment bedeviled her administration, and even the minimal needs in health care and education went unattended. Moreover, the trafficking in drugs had attained national significance, and government attempts to manage the affliction were feeble at best. Benazir was also challenged by her gender: a young woman, she had enormous difficulty in winning the support of the country's fundamentalists. Her balanced approach to religious issues, most notably on the Salman Rushdie affair, was not calculated to please Muslim clerics or their devotees. Moreover, Benazir was perceived as a creature of the Americans, and although she was able to secure the transfer of already purchased US weapons, she had been heavily pressurized by Washington to curtail Pakistan's nuclear programme. Even the appearance of yielding to such pressures damaged her popularity. But perhaps nothing was more significant in shaping Benazir's destiny than her inability to control the provincial governments. Having tried unsuccessfully to force Nawaz Sharif from power in the Punjab, Benazir had stirred up a hornet's nest, and given the defection of her coalition partners in the MQM and ANP, she was left to fend off the opposition virtually alone.

Benazir's decision to make her mother, Nusrat, a senior minister without portfolio, and her father-in-law Chairman of the Parliamentary Public Accounts Committee, dramatized a paucity of trusted associates and an abiding dependence on family members. More than that, it demonstrated a level of nepotism that dishonoured her democratic claims. Benazir's husband, Asif Ali Zardari, was no less involved in the activities of her administration. Perceived as a notorious and corrupt businessman and politician, Zardari's practices sullied the Prime Minister's reputation as an honest public servant. Benazir retaliated by describing Nawaz Sharif as the handmaiden of the late Ziaul Haq, but the more she belaboured that theme, the more the excesses of her family members were magnified and the more she suffered from the constant exposure. Sensing that confrontation was the only possible response to the ploys and gambits of her opposition, Benazir ignored calls for conflict resolution, and the country was allowed to drift aimlessly from crisis to crisis. Not a single piece of meaningful legislation was passed by the National Assembly during her administration. All Benazir could show for her time in office were a few amendments to existing legislation. She blamed the Senate for the legislative gridlock, but in fact it was sustained political instability that had sapped the energy of the House.

Conflict and Resolution

An MQM-orchestrated strike in Karachi in February 1990 resulted in still more widespread disorder as well as in killing, burning, and looting. The major commercial city was again paralysed and, to restore calm to the community, the Prime Minister was once more compelled to call upon the army to tranquillize the vandals and repair the damage. Moreover, Benazir had delivered a second child in January 1990, and even while she was recuperating in Lady Dufferin Hospital, sixteen opposition parties, apparently mobilized by the MQM, massed in a demonstration in the streets outside. Cries of corruption and incompetence were shouted in the direction of her hospital room, and the crowd renewed the call for her resignation. To add to the fury of the assault, portraits of the late President Zia were unveiled, and thousands of women, many carrying their own babies, hurled unpleasantries that were meant to disturb the Prime Minister's convalescence.

After returning to her responsibilities, Benazir was confronted by renewed fighting in Kashmir between Indian paramilitary forces and mujahiddin. With New Delhi continuing to accuse Islamabad of fomenting the disorder, India reinforced its units in the mountain state, and Pakistan responded by massing its forces on the ceasefire line. Pakistani officials declared it their intention to avoid another war with their neighbour, but they also declared they would not be cowed into submission. Again calling on New Delhi to honour the long-postponed plebiscite in Kashmir, the Pakistan National Assembly was summoned for a special session to debate whether it was necessary to declare a 'nationwide state of emergency' after reports were received that India's clandestine intelligence agency, RAW, had infiltrated Azad Kashmir. On the Indian side, General V.N. Sharma, India's Army Commander, declared relations between the two countries had not been more tense since the 1971 war.

Burdened by issues and events she could not control, the riots that rocked Karachi in February 1990 further weakened Benazir's administration. The frequent use of the army to quell domestic disturbances drew precious resources from the nation's defences without strengthening the country's

social fabric. Hundreds of demonstrators were arrested, but
the movements that they represented continued to press their
demands, while terrorist bombings and the deaths of innocent
bus travellers in Karachi caused Benazir to cancel a trip to
the Middle East. Holding fast to her diminishing authority,
differences over tactics as well as strategy emerged between
the Prime Minister and her Army Commander. Baig wanted
a free hand in Sindh. He also wanted the opportunity to
strike at PPP militants who, along with their counterparts in
the MQM, prevented the restoration of law and order. Benazir
refused to grant Baig his request, however, and their once
solid relationship began to fall apart when the General was
forced to acknowledge the uneasiness among his senior
officers. Faced with problems from within and without, the
visit to Pakistan of Deputy US National Security Advisor Robert
Gates in May presented still another dilemma.

Gates had been sent to Pakistan by President George Bush
with the express purpose of ascertaining the severity of the
confrontation between Pakistan and India. Fearing a nuclear
confrontation, Gates called upon Benazir to smother the
invective which her government had directed at New Delhi.
An emissary from the Kremlin had carried the same concern
and the identical message to New Delhi. The respective visits
of superpower officials lightened the atmosphere, and in July
India's Foreign Secretary travelled to Islamabad for direct
negotiations between the two governments. Benazir had
promised Gates that she would work to reduce tension, and
in her conversations with the Indian official she called for an
Indian pull-back from the border regions. But while this series
of talks was described as productive, it left the Kashmir
problem unresolved, and the Kashmiri resistance showed no
inclination of ceasing its operations.

Following these events, Benazir left for her postponed tour
of the Middle East, and visited Iraq, Kuwait, Morocco, Algeria,
and Bahrein. Apparently assured of Saddam Hussein's
support in her struggle with India, she went to Kuwait for a
ceremonial meeting with the royal family. Benazir had the
dubious distinction of being the last head of government from
a non-Arab Muslim state to visit the region. Shortly after her
return to Islamabad, Saddam sent his forces into Kuwait, and
within twenty-four hours had conquered the kingdom,

declared an end to the Sabah monarchy, and announced Kuwait's new status as Iraq's nineteenth province. Benazir had not been apprised of the pending conflict and was caught flat-footed by the Iraqi blitzkrieg. Nor did she have time to respond adequately to an event that traumatized the Islamic world.

Four days after the Iraqi Army marched into Kuwait, Ghulam Ishaq declared an end to Benazir's government. The President used the powers granted him under the Eighth Amendment and Article 58 (clause b) of the Constitution to dissolve the National Assembly and the provincial administrations, and to dismiss the first woman ever to head a Pakistan government. Ghulam Ishaq declared that Benazir Bhutto had lost the capacity to govern, had demonstrated an inability to stem domestic violence, and had also nurtured nepotism as well as corrupt practices by both family members and associates. The President called for calm and announced that he had asked Ghulam Mụstafa Jatoi, a heretofore dominant PPP force in Sindh, indeed the last of Zulfikar Ali Bhutto's Sindhi Chief Ministers, to form a caretaker government.

Jatoi had broken with Benazir shortly after he had arranged her triumphal return to Pakistan in 1986. Differences with Benazir in matters related to Zardari had driven him to form his own PPP splinter group, the National People's Party; furthermore, Benazir had embarrassed Jatoi when she had forced him to yield the chair of the Sindh PPP. A confirmed progressive and a principal exponent of the Islamic welfare state, Jatoi preferred to cite his philosophical differences with Benazir, but it was obvious their estrangement was far deeper and personal.

Benazir was not one to accept her fate without a struggle. She lashed out at the President, describing his actions as arbitrary and unconstitutional, and unbefitting a democratic country. Her cries, however, had a hollow ring, and they had little impact. Nor could anyone reverse Ghulam Ishaq's decision. Moreover, the President ordered the arrest of PPP leaders and the immediate investigation of their activities. On 1 September, the government announced it was also likely to arrest Benazir on grounds of improper behaviour. And later, a special court ordered the former Prime Minister to stand trial on charges of corruption and misconduct. Benazir continued to profess her innocence of the charges filed against her, and commented that the government's objective was her permanent removal from the political scene.

Ghulam Ishaq, nevertheless, pressed the government's case against the former Prime Minister, declaring that Benazir had violated a public trust. Promulgating the Special Courts and Speedy Trial Ordinance, 1990, the President also activated the Holders of Representative Offices (Prevention of Misconduct) Act, originally enacted during the administration of Zulfikar Ali Bhutto. The caretaker government charged numerous PPP officials with corruption and threatened to prevent them from seeking public office. Benazir was charged with having allotted hundreds of costly residential plots in Islamabad to PPP stalwarts at 'throwaway prices'. She also was accused of using gifts and bribes to win the support of members of the provincial assemblies. On 10 October, however, a heavier blow was levelled against Benazir's husband, Asif Ali Zardari, who was arrested for allegedly kidnapping a Pakistani-born British citizen from whom he was said to have extorted a large sum of money. Zardari was, in fact, the target of a number of investigations, it being argued that he had used his wife's position to increase his personal wealth. While judicial proceedings paralysed PPP activity, the Election Commission was busy printing ballot papers for the upcoming election. At the same time, the IJI announced that it had coalesced with other organizations to form a broad-based electoral alliance and that it would field a single, united slate of candidates. The central core of the IJI was formed from the Muslim League led by Nawaz Sharif. Former Prime Minister Mohammad Khan Junejo and Eijaz-ul-Haq, the son of the late General Zia, also lent their services. Between them they captured a solid portion of Sindhi landowners, fundamentalists, the urban middle class, and the entrepreneurial elite. Mohammad Afzal Khan was elected President of the IJI, and two senators, Qazi Abdul Latif and Asif Fasihuddin Vardag, jointly exercised responsibility as alliance Secretary-General. Wali Khan's Awami National Party and Altaf Hussain's MQM rounded out the coalition, thus guaranteeing an IJI victory. On 13 October, the IJI issued an electoral manifesto that described its central objective as the supremacy of the Koran and Sunnah 'in every sphere of Pakistani life' (Ziring, 1991).

The IJI turned the election into a referendum on the Benazir administration, and the PPP was unable to get its message out. Benazir filed a complaint against the Pakistan Television Corporation (PTV) but these efforts, too, were frustrated. The situation was only slightly different in the print media, where a muted Benazir faced a government-controlled Press that continued to vilify her. Moreover, with her electoral campaign in tatters, Benazir was called before the Lahore High Court to show cause why she should not be found guilty of misconduct in matters pertaining to the implementation of the Liquified Petroleum Gas (Production and Distribution) Rules, 1971. Accused of providing members of her government, as well as personal acquaintances, with illegal marketing rights in liquified petroleum, she again denied all the charges but could not muster sufficient support to mount a serious campaign (Mahmood,1992).

It was in this environment of unrelenting charges that Jatoi, the caretaker Prime Minister, called upon the voters to cast their ballots for the IJI coalition. The IJI, he argued, was a democratic organization representing a broad range of interests, whereas the PPP represented only the wishes of a single family. Jatoi prophesied the total defeat of the PPP and the repudiation of its leadership. Benazir, he exclaimed, would more than likely abandon the country and seek domicile abroad. Syeda Abida Hussain, the caretaker government's Information Minister, echoed the Prime Minister's statements, and voiced the opinion that Benazir would be more comfortable in foreign lands. Questioning Benazir's patriotism, she asked why the former Prime Minister had hired the services of an American public relations expert (Ziring, 1991). Attacking a practice which had become common elsewhere in the world, Abida accused Benazir of paying the American publicist 'almost half a million dollars' in public funds in a futile endeavour to improve her image. This assault on her personal behaviour complicated Benazir's attempt to clear her name (Manheim, 1994).

Operating at a gross disadvantage, Benazir's only recourse was to go directly to the people. At every opportunity, she described the wide array of forces that opposed her, and, taking strength from her previous successes as well as the sustained adulation of her followers, she insisted she would redeem her honour as well as that of her family and party. Benazir, however, suffered another setback when the Bush administration decided to terminate its aid programme to Pakistan. Arguing that he could no longer certify to the Congress that Pakistan was not developing nuclear weapons, on 1 October 1990 President George Bush ordered the curtailment of all assistance to Pakistan. Benazir's enemies, citing her intimacies with Washington, asserted that she had influenced the American decision. Moreover, Washington had considered Benazir a brake on the Pakistan military, and her ouster had been judged a blow against the restoration of democracy in the country. With the IJI the dominant political force in the country, the Americans also worried over the spread of Islamic fundamentalism. Always concerned with the popular appeal of reactionary forces in the Muslim world, and confronting Iraqi aggression in Kuwait, the United States may have acted in its own interests, but if the decision to cut off aid was supposed to assist Benazir, it had quite the opposite consequences.

Clearly, the American action drove more Pakistanis to support the IJI. Benazir, already confronting a no-win situation, suffered another blow when the Lahore High Court ruled that the President had the constitutional power to dissolve the National Assembly and call new elections. Declaring that the Benazir Bhutto government had failed to perform its legislative responsibilities, had also failed to bring peace to Sindh province, and had refused to call a meeting of the Council of Common Interests, the Court ruled that the country had become more polarized and confrontational. It said that it therefore had no other option but to rule in the President's favour, and under Article 48(2) of the Constitution, it legitimized Ghulam Ishaq's action in calling upon Jatoi to head the caretaker government. Thus Pakistanis went to the polls, for the second time in two years, on 24 October. And there were no surprises in the results. The IJI coalition soundly defeated the PPP in all the provinces, taking 105 seats in the new National Assembly. Parties aligned with the IJI won an additional 50 seats, while the PPP People's Democratic Alliance managed only 45. The PPP lost ground in every province, with its greatest defeat coming in the Punjab. Benazir, running in several constituencies, lost her election in Peshawar but won in her home constituency at Larkana. Nusrat Bhutto also won her election, but Asif Zardari lost in his native constituency of Nawabshah. Zardari, however, won a seat in Lyari, a pro-Benazir haven.

The IJI success propelled Nawaz Sharif from his commanding position in the Punjab to the central government in Islamabad and Ghulam Ishaq called upon and him to form the new government. Benazir's reaction was hardly conciliatory. Declaring that the election had been rigged against the PPP, that ballot boxes had been stuffed, and that the count was fraudulent, she promised to fight the results in the courts. Observers were left to weigh and compare Benazir's actions out of power against her performance while she held the reins of government. Her democratic propensities were always more apparent in the opposition than in service of the nation. Her apparent inability to understand the significance of this contradiction, let alone to correct it, would hound her in the years yet to unfold.

Enter Nawaz Sharif

Nawaz Sharif was born in Lahore in 1949, two years after the independence of Pakistan. Like Benazir, he was a product of the Pakistan experience, but unlike her upbringing in the Sindhi feudal tradition, Nawaz was exposed to the cosmopolitan lifestyle of the new industrial elite. More at home in the upper middle class capitalist environment, he devotedly practised Islamic rituals while at the same time developing a taste for liberal politics. Home grown, he went to school in Pakistan, receiving his undergraduate education at Government College, Lahore, and a law degree from Punjab University. Long at odds with the Bhutto family, he found himself in opposition to the policies of Zulfikar Ali Bhutto when the late Prime Minister seized and nationalized his family's industries. A fierce believer in free enterprise, Nawaz

Sharif championed the cause of free property, and found Bhutto's contrived socialist policies a threat to the democratic experience as well as to traditional Islamic principles and practices. Eager for a role in politics from the time he left college, Nawaz became a Finance Minister in the Punjab during the Zia years and later was named the province's Chief Minister. Acknowledging Pakistan's dependence on a form of welfare, Nawaz blended his capitalist and legal training with an abiding Muslim commitment. More than Benazir, Nawaz represented a new generation of Pakistani leadership, and in a country still dominated by feudal lords, his rise to the highest position in the government was no small achievement.

Nawaz Sharif rode a wave of anti-PPP expression all the way to Islamabad. Moreover, his success had again placed the Punjab at the centre of Pakistani political life. But he could not have claimed victory without the support of the anti-PPP politicians. Jatoi, for one, continued his assault on Benazir Bhutto following the election, citing her lack of sportsmanship and her futile efforts at smearing the IJI's success. Benazir, however, continued to express her dissatisfaction with developments and was not prepared to acknowledge her party's repudiation at the polls.

Sensing that the public had developed a more sophisticated interest in politics, Nawaz Sharif signalled a desire to fulfil his campaign promises, and his more urbane approach to government contrasted with the conventional feudal expression that had dominated the political stage from the first moments after independence. Indeed, the IJI was a different kind of coalition from those experienced earlier. Representing urban constituencies, it gave voice to an industrial-commercial class that had long remained in the shadow of the country's agrarian elite. The merger of the business and commercial class with fundamentalist and ethnic orders proved a formidable combination.

Thus, the elections for the provincial assemblies produced similar results. The IJI won an overwhelming 208 of 234 seats in the Punjab, and sufficient seats in the NWFP and Balochistan to form coalition governments. The PPP was again denied in the frontier provinces, but its greatest disappointment came in Benazir's home province of Sindh, where the PPP could not pull a simple majority and had to stand by as the IJI coalesced with the MQM and other parties to form the provincial government.

The newly-elected National Assembly convened on 3 November 1990, but the PPP and Pakistan Democratic Alliance members refused to attend until the government agreed to release Benazir's husband from prison. That ploy apparently worked, because Zardari was released the next day and entered the Assembly to be sworn in with other members of his party. Nawaz Sharif declared his government would be one of reconciliation, not revenge, and he opened the way for the Awami National Party, the Jamaat-i-Islami, and the MQM to join with him in a government of mutual support and national awareness. On 6 November, Mian Nawaz Sharif took the oath as Prime Minister of Pakistan after receiving 153 votes to only 39 for his rival, Mohammad Afzal Khan. Pledging an administration that would rise above confrontation, Nawaz Sharif declared it was his intention to work with all the political orders, including the PPP, on issues of both domestic and international concern. 'All the major issues,' he intoned, 'would be confronted on the basis of co-operation' (Ziring, 1991). Even Benazir's statement about standing with the government when it stood by the people seemed to herald a more positive beginning.

The state of emergency was lifted the next day, following which Nawaz Sharif promised a government totally committed to serving the nation. 'Education, health, employment, shelter, peace, and protection are the basic rights of all citizens,' he declared. Citing women's rights, the expansion of the industrial sector, improved working conditions for factory labour, and a new focus on the needs of rural cultivators as most significant, the new Prime Minister pledged to serve all the people without rancour and certainly without favouritism. One additional item was given special place. Nawaz Sharif reiterated his government's policy to develop the peaceful uses of nuclear energy, but he insisted that there was no intention to produce nuclear weapons.

On 9 November, Nawaz Sharif announced his new cabinet, which retained Sahabzada Yaqub Khan as Foreign

Minister and Sartaj Aziz as Minister of Finance and Economic Affairs. In commenting on his appointments, Nawaz Sharif declared it his objective to transform Pakistan into a 'real welfare state', but he also set about the business of privatizing the public sector. After fifteen years of nationalization programmes, the country was set on a path of economic renewal in which the private sector was to be allowed greater responsibility. Deregulation of the economy received high priority and an immediate impact was felt in industry, banking, and insurance.

Off to a rousing start, the IJI government was embraced by MQM leader Altaf Hussain, who offered full co-operation to Nawaz Sharif and the Chief Minister of Sindh, Jam Sadiq Ali. The MQM, Altaf noted, was excited by the prospect of working in harmony with Sindhis, Punjabis, and Pathans. Moreover, the violence that had paralysed the province since the Zulfikar Ali Bhutto years appeared to subside with the inauguration of an era of good feelings. In the euphoria of the transition, Nawaz Sharif assumed the appearance of a miracle worker. Moreover, with the total cut-off of American assistance for the first time since the mid-1950s, Pakistan was ready to go it alone. Self-reliance was tied to tax reform, to export promotion, to deregulation and disinvestment, and to an aggressive industrial policy. Nawaz Sharif called for new understandings with Washington, but he was emphatic on the matter of the country's independent policy. Noting that Pakistan had for too long allowed its dependency on the distant superpower to influence its behaviour, the Prime Minister received popular approval for his decision to accelerate the nuclear energy programme. 'Pakistan need not depend on any aid from any country,' he said.

Challenged by the crisis in the Gulf region, Nawaz Sharif went to Saudi Arabia on 19 November and there met with members of the royal family as well as with the Emir of Kuwait, who had taken refuge in the neighbouring kingdom. Using the occasion to condemn the aggression against Kuwait, the Prime Minister announced he would despatch 3,000 men to Saudi Arabia to join the 2,000 already in the country. Given the international effort in shoring up Saudi Arabia's defences, Pakistan's increased commitment was welcomed as a gesture of brotherly support at a defining moment in the Muslim world. Within a week of that tour, Nawaz Sharif was in the Maldives for a meeting of the South Asian Association for Regional Co-operation (SAARC), where he met with his Indian counterpart, Prime Minister Chandra Shekhar, who had assumed his office in the wake of Rajiv Gandhi's assassination. The two new leaders addressed the old question of Kashmir, but came away from their meeting with little to show for their conversation other than their capacity for face-to-face exchange. Nawaz Sharif, like all his predecessors, insisted on the holding of a plebiscite in Kashmir, and Shekhar argued in support of the irreversible decision that made the disputed territory a state within the Indian union. Indications that the latter talks had only confirmed the crisis nature of the dispute came with General Baig's statement that the Indian troop build-up was a threat to Pakistan's security and that vigilance could not be relaxed.

Nawaz Sharif had inherited a most difficult legacy, and although there were small signs of domestic peace, there was little indication of peace in Kashmir, Afghanistan, or along the eastern border with India. Moreover, the greater region was especially turbulent given the behaviour of revolutionary Iran and, of course, the Gulf, where an almost million-strong force had been assembled under United Nations auspices, led by the United States, whose more than half a million combat-ready army, air, and naval personnel were poised to liberate Kuwait from its Iraqi occupiers. The Iraqi conquest of Kuwait and the violent American response had divided Pakistani public opinion which, at both official and lay levels, was uncomfortable with the heavy American response, as well as the presence of non-Muslim troop concentrations in the vicinity of the Islamic holy places. Given the cessation of American aid to Pakistan, anti-Americanism was already apparent, and this demonstration of American arms against another Muslim state, irrespective of the circumstances, tended to intensify dissatisfaction with Washington policy. Nawaz Sharif had entered the Prime Minister's office with the expectation that he could be all things to all his countrymen, but events external to the nation had already demonstrated the impossibility of playing that role to its fullest.

The IJI Administration

Nawaz Sharif's first cabinet was considerably smaller than that of Benazir Bhutto. Tightly drawn, the cabinet reflected the different regions of the country, but drew the heaviest representation from the Prime Minister's own province. Nawaz had come to his responsibilities surrounded by international trouble spots, and the sudden demise of the Soviet Union did more to confuse the situation than clarify his government's options. It was Nawaz Sharif's judgment that, rather than become too embroiled in foreign policy issues, it would be better for his administration to address domestic questions. Indeed, the country required stabilization in a period of worldwide uncertainty, and Nawaz Sharif believed he had the formula for internal change. Moreover, the success of his programmes would also determine the degree to which Pakistan could position itself in a transitional world. The Prime Minister, therefore, centred his policies on economic stability and growth. In addition to self-reliance initiatives, he moved swiftly to eliminate the strait-jacket that Zulfikar Ali Bhutto had imposed on the nation in the 1970s, returning confiscated properties to their original owners and generally providing encouragement to the private sector.

A series of reforms was forecast in taxation, foreign exchange arrangements, and administrative law. The government sensed the need to balance industrialization programmes with agricultural reforms that enhanced the lives of the nation's largely impoverished peasants and tillers of the soil. His central answer to the country's multiple problems, however, reflected his background in the industrial world. Rural areas were to be made more adaptable to agro-based industries, and a variety of incentives was offered to the country's entrepreneurial class to invest in both capital industrial projects as well as agrarian schemes that promised high returns in productivity and profits. Overall, the Prime Minister expressed a commitment to the private sector and its free enterprise economy, hence he stressed the need to deregulate the many spheres of human endeavour, to attract back to the nation capital secreted abroad, and to unleash the forces of capitalism in the name of national renewal and reconstruction.

Ambitious as this scheme was, it nevertheless opened the way for profit-seeking money managers to exploit new opportunities and to reap advantages that seldom trickled down to the average citizen in the city or the village. Nawaz Sharif had conceived a plan that was destined to result in huge gains for the more affluent, aggressive members of the economic community, while the anticipated expansion of the job market simply did not occur. In time, Nawaz Sharif proved unable to satisfy the expectations of the larger public, and the criticism levelled against his administration produced some of the same unstable conditions that had brought down the Junejo and Benazir governments. Pakistani elections, no matter how frequent, were no panacea for the country's ills, and successive elected governments found the task of governing the divided nation a dismal experience. Moreover, given the powers conferred on the President by the Eighth Amendment, no government was capable of sustaining its popular mandate. Indeed, elected Pakistani governments had difficulty in completing their full terms, and the Nawaz Sharif administration had reason to believe that its fate would be no different from those that had preceded it.

Nevertheless, Pakistan appeared to be on the verge of creating a two-party political system. The IJI's central core was the redesigned Muslim League, and although it was a far cry from the party that founded the nation, it all the same drew its strength and its bona fides from that original organization. On the other side was the PPP, which, although having metamorphosed since the days of J.A. Rahim and Mubashir Hassan, continued to pay homage to the memory of its martyred leader. The juxtaposition of the revived Muslim League and the modified Pakistan People's Party resurrected the spirit of the two Quaids, Jinnah and Bhutto, as well as their different, but nevertheless intertwined, missions. Nawaz Sharif found his roots in the political experience of Mohammad Ali Jinnah, but he could not help being provoked by the spectre of Zulfikar Ali Bhutto.

Some observers saw the spirit of Ziaul Haq in the 1991 Shariat Bill that Nawaz Sharif pressed through the National Assembly. But the references to the Koran and Sunnah were prompted by forces long in place in the country. Reflecting more the purpose of the Muslim League's original Objectives Resolution, Nawaz Sharif had found a way to placate, but at the same time to limit, the influence of Islamic orthodoxy. Both the Muslim League of Mohammad Ali Jinnah and the revived organization led by Nawaz Sharif reflected secular as well as religious concerns. Prepared to accept the criticism of the conservative orders, even to risk their defection, Nawaz Sharif was hardly the dogmatic leader that the PPP described. The Muslim League that he led proved relatively free of ideological expression, and its social pragmatism offered the country a range of choices, not the least of which was the opportunity for Pakistanis to observe their religious traditions.

The Shariat legislation appeared to call for a more stringent Islamic legal system, a religiously ordered educational set-up, enforced prayer schedules, as well as limitations on the print and electronic media. It also addressed the need to alter the banking system so that it, too, conformed to the tenets of Islam. Moreover, the Federal Shariat Court's ruling in November 1991 that a score of federal and provincial laws were repugnant to Islam and therefore null and void, seemed to underline the administration's ultra-conservative objectives. But while Nawaz was prepared to acknowledge and honour the more devout members of the religious community, he was also determined to satisfy the requests of his more cosmopolitan followers. Himself a representative of the latter group, the Prime Minister's economic programme was dependent on the support and commitment of Pakistanis functioning in the profane world of commerce and banking. Melding these different constituencies, however, was a herculean undertaking.

Debates over the question of interest in financial and commercial transactions could not be avoided, nor could the criticism which first one group, and then another, directed at the IJI administration. The fundamentalist orders complained of foot-dragging and lack of commitment to Islamic principles, whereas the secularists denounced what they believed was a programme to convert Pakistan into a theocratic state. Women's organizations and minorities were most vocal in the latter instance, and it was they who forced Nawaz Sharif, to publicly declare that he was not a fundamentalist. But whereas the Prime Minister's declaration may have satisfied one group, it antagonized others. Clearly, Nawaz Sharif could not satisfy the vast assortment of constituencies that demanded his attention, and in the attempt to manage a middle course between the different and many expressions, he ended up damaging only himself. He had inherited the cumulative problems of all the previous administrations. Pakistan's inchoate nature, its failure to become national after more than forty years of independence, left the IJI government with the task of building the Pakistan of the future. Indeed, each major actor in the Pakistan experience had turned his hand to this purpose, and none had succeeded. The belief that Nawaz Sharif would achieve what his more illustrious predecessors could not do weighed heavily on the young Prime Minister. In fact, his task was far more difficult than that of the earlier leaders. So many contradictions had been allowed to invade the polity that just managing the day-to-day life of the nation was as tedious a chore as any experienced in the earlier years.

Governments are composed of people, and the personnel representing the Nawaz Government started from the lowest grade police officer or administrative scribe, all the way to the highest-ranking army commander and most senior politician. Individual behaviours had been nurtured in a climate of instability verging on anarchy, and the corruption that permeated government at all levels also involved members of the broader society. Moreover, discontented regional and ethnic groups, as well as conflicting religious orders, had long plagued efforts at Pakistani unity, and although a moment of calm followed the IJI victory at the polls, it was not long before the bombings, the kidnappings, and the assassinations were again on the ascendant. A term was coined to describe the violence that inundated the nation. The 'Kalashnikov culture' meant no one felt really secure anywhere in the nation, neither in their homes or on the public thoroughfares. Hooliganism, robberies, and terrorist assaults on public transport, in the workplace, or the schools, had become common. The use of narcotics increased dramatically during the Benazir and Nawaz administrations, and the addiction sapped the vitality of, and did serious injury to, a growing number of Pakistani citizens. Government attempts to deal with these multiple problems were not insignificant, but their widespread effect, coupled with endemic civil disobedience and complicated by the multitude of Afghan refugees, meant all solutions would be temporary at best.

Following acts of lawlessness in the Punjab in the summer of 1991, the government enacted the Twelfth Amendment to the Constitution that provided it with the power to impose summary justice, but the violence did not end. The police could not cope with the disorder, and even the army failed to guarantee more than a brief respite from the spreading civil strife. Differences over tactics caused problems within the IJI coalition and whetted the appetite of the opposition, which condemned the government's use of extraordinary and often arbitrary powers.

Defections by Jatoi's National People's Party, Qazi Ahmad's Jamaat-i-Islami, and Altaf Hussain's MQM were not unexpected, but they exposed the Nawaz government to direct assaults by the PPP. Describing Nawaz Sharif's economic development programme, notably his privatization scheme, as 'loot and plunder', Benazir regained the spotlight, and more the support of the disenchanted. Blaming government for the ills of society was an established Pakistani tradition. Economic scandals were inevitable in the shift from the public to the private sector, in the unleashing of entrepreneurial forces—especially in programmes allowing the commercial world to involve itself in the generation of electricity—in the construction of roads, in the development of telecommunications, and in the management of the shipping and airlines industries. The rising cost of basic commodities, the inflationary spiral caused by careless planning, and the seeming indifference to the plight of the poor and lower middle classes could be attributed to the social and economic costs of modernization, but they nevertheless adversely affected a desperate population.

Thus, when the Bank of Credit and Commerce International (BCCI) was cited for its worldwide abuses, and especially its greedy and corrupt banking practices, the embarrassment suffered by the Nawaz Government was extreme. But perhaps more detrimental to the administration was the failure of the Co-operative Societies in the Punjab, where some two million

people lost most of their life's savings and Nawaz Sharif lost
his credibility as an honest leader. Left with a diminished
coalition represented by his Muslim League and the Awami
National Party of Wali Khan, Nawaz Sharif ceased to be
effective.

Seeing a new opportunity to revive her political fortunes,
Benazir accused the Nawaz Sharif Government of stealing
the 1990 election as well as the people's personal bank
accounts. Benazir championed a variety of popular causes,
notably those calling for economic and financial probity.
Defying government restrictions on public demonstrations, in
1992 Benazir organized a civil disobedience movement and
immediately faced a government order aimed at silencing
her. Undaunted, Benazir condemned the government's
repressive, police-state tactics. Appealing as it did to
deepening popular disfavour with the Nawaz government,
the PPP could be neither isolated nor silenced by law
enforcement. It was Nawaz Sharif's turn to be pilloried, and
by 1993 his administration had lost a considerable portion of
its popular support.

Seeing the weaknesses in the ruling coalition, Benazir
continued to hammer away at its undemocratic practices
and let it be known that she would not object to a military
take-over. General Mirza Aslam Baig's retirement in August
1991, however, gave command of the Pakistan Army to
General Asif Nawaz, who immediately declared his neutrality
in the political tug-of-war.

With pledges of support from his new Army Chief, Nawaz
Sharif tried to buttress his position by citing the resolution of
two long-standing issues, i.e., the allocation of the Indus
waters and the distribution of revenue between the provinces
and the central government. But the glow that came with
these achievements faded rapidly. More intractable problems
refused to yield a solution, and the Prime Minister was forced
to backtrack on a variety of issues. Moreover, under pressure
to offer more and more patronage in return for pledges of
continued support, his original cabinet, which began with a
talented few, soon became an unwieldy body of almost fifty
members. Similar problems had an impact on the provincial
governments, where a large portion of the legislators cajoled

their way into lucrative but otherwise vacuous ministerial roles. Nawaz Sharif's once seemingly strong position crumbled under the weight of the country's multiple legacies, and his retreat on the home front was replicated in his foreign policy.

The American-led military offensive against Saddam Hussain had unpredictable consequences in Pakistan. Pakistan became an outspoken critic of the American-directed campaign, and although Islamabad sent several thousand soldiers to Saudi Arabia, they were not deployed in the liberation of Kuwait. More important, General Baig questioned the aggressiveness of the operation against Iraq, and found considerable fault with the Arabian monarchs. The General's retirement, therefore, was not unwelcome in the Gulf states, but Nawaz Sharif was nevertheless embarrassed by the episode, and relations with important neighbours had been unduly strained.

Nawaz Sharif tempered his personal assaults on American foreign policy following the Baig incident, but Washington did not acknowledge his peace overture and American aid was not resumed. On the other hand, New Delhi began to develop new intimacies with Washington. India also used the opportunity to pour fresh troops into Kashmir and, with the outer world ignoring the on-going conflict in the Himalayan state, the Indians intensified their operations against the resistance. These developments, as well as a failed peace initiative in Afghanistan, added to Nawaz Sharif's burden. Moreover, while Najibullah was finally forced to yield to the mujahiddin, the different factions that occupied Kabul displayed considerable difficulty in forming a new Afghan government. Unable to agree on a collective formula, they proceeded to attack one another, and Pakistani mediation efforts were also unsuccessful. Akram Zaki, Secretary-General for Foreign Affairs in the Foreign Ministry, spoke for all the higher officials when he noted that 'Pakistan's foreign policy used to be walking on a tightrope; now it is walking a minefield and it does not have a map' (The News, 21 August 1992).

Constitutional Crisis

It was not Benazir or the PPP that threatened Nawaz Sharif and the IJI government, but rather the country's traditional power source, the higher military and bureaucratic institutions. The incident that sparked the final confrontation between the Prime Minister and the President was the appointment of a new COAS, following the sudden death of General Asif Nawaz on 8 January 1993. Observing the multiple problems burdening the nation at home and abroad, Ghulam Ishaq apparently decided not to consult Nawaz Sharif before announcing Asif Nawaz's replacement. The President chose Lieutenant-General Abdul Waheed Kakar, but the manner of his decision angered the Prime Minister, and he reacted by calling for the repeal of the President's Eighth Amendment powers. A desperate move, the manoeuvre was orchestrated to draw the broadest popular support, but it also destroyed Nawaz Sharif's ability to work with Ghulam Ishaq. Nawaz Sharif said that his objective was a constitutional system that empowered the Parliament and limited the role of the President, and the proposition had considerable support among the general public. The civil-military establishment, however, did not find the assault on the prerogatives of the President salutary. The Prime Minister's actions were reminiscent of a 1954 attempt to limit the powers of Ghulam Mohammad. That strategy was sabotaged by the permanent services, and although Ghulam Ishaq was no Ghulam Mohammad, and Nawaz Sharif was no Mohammad Ali Bogra, the outcome was not different.

Nawaz argued for the same powers enjoyed by the British Prime Minister, but Ghulam Ishaq stressed his responsibility in protecting the established system. Each man accused the other of tampering with the democratic process for personal gain. Observers were surprised that Nawaz Sharif would take on the President at a time of parliamentary weakness, when he had serious differences with the PPP, and Benazir had made gestures that strengthened Ghulam Ishaq's hand (Amin, 1994). Benazir had sustained the drumbeat of dissatisfaction with the elections that had produced the Nawaz Sharif victory in 1990, and only the use of the President's extraordinary powers promised to reverse the course of events. Although critical of the President's use of the Eighth Amendment in forcing her from office, Benazir now urged him to use those same powers against her Punjabi nemesis.

The plot thickened when the widow of the late General Asif Nawaz claimed he had been poisoned, and appeared to accuse Nawaz Sharif of the deed. Forced to respond to the accusation, the Prime Minister convened a three-man judicial commission which was mandated to examine the charges and to receive expert testimony as to the cause of the General's death. But before the special committee could bring forward its findings, Benazir manoeuvred herself into a more advantageous position. Ingratiating herself with the President, Benazir called upon Ghulam Ishaq to dissolve the IJI government and call midterm elections. Citing the defections in the Pakistan Muslim League, the resignation of key cabinet officials, and the virtual breakdown of government, Benazir promised to support Ghulam Ishaq in his quest for another term as President if he removed her rival.

Nawaz Sharif, somewhat belatedly, recognized the folly of his campaign against Ghulam Ishaq, and tried to outmanoeuvre Benazir by announcing his party's support for the President's candidacy. Nawaz Sharif's incredible performance, however, was too little and too late. Faced with imminent dismissal, the beleaguered Prime Minister made a final broadcast to the nation citing the President as the 'root cause' of the country's woes. In a moment of empty bravado he declared that he would not resign, nor would he submit to dictation.

Nawaz Sharif had crossed his Rubicon and had left himself trapped on the wrong side of the power struggle. Outfoxed by both Ghulam Ishaq and Benazir Bhutto, his behaviour and statements had only increased their desire for revenge. The President described the Prime Minister's statement condemning him an 'act of subversion'. Charging the Nawaz administration with rampant corruption, with arbitrary assaults on the political opposition, with secret deals and payoffs in the name of privatization, and finally with the political assassination of General Asif Nawaz, on 18 April 1993, Ghulam Ishaq again used his powers under the Eighth Amendment to dismiss the Prime Minister and his government as well as to dissolve the National Assembly. As he had in forcing Benazir Bhutto from power, so here too he said his purpose was the preservation of the constitutional process and the public peace. Asserting that his actions were in no way personal, the President called for fresh elections on 14 July, but in the interim, asked Mir Balkh Sher Mazari to organize a caretaker government in which the PPP would play the principal role.

Nawaz Sharif declared the President's action illegal and unconstitutional, and he immediately appealed to the Pakistan Supreme Court to cancel the directive and to reinstate his government. Confronted with the same argument on other occasions by other ousted officials, the last being Benazir Bhutto, the Court was again expected to rule in favour of the Chief Executive. This time, however, the jurists decided to challenge the very viceregal tradition that their predecessors were, in major part, responsible for nurturing and institutionalizing. The Supreme Court responded to Nawaz Sharif's writ petition with steadfastness as well as surprising alacrity. Six weeks after the President's action, they ruled that he had acted illegally and unconstitutionally, and thus insisted that the government be restored and that Nawaz Sharif resume his prerogatives as the country's head of government.

The courage demonstrated by the Court was unprecedented in the history of Pakistan, but the judges had apparently been dumbstruck by General Aslam Baig's disclosure, just weeks before Ghulam Ishaq's action, that he, as COAS, had sent a confidential message to the Supreme Court in 1988 arguing that it should not reinstate the Junejo government. The public airing of the behind-the-scenes power struggle, but particularly the collusion between high-placed officials in the political, military, and judicial arenas, had forced the Supreme Court to take a different position in the case before it. Moreover, attempts at refuting Baig's assertion had failed, and Chief Justice Afzal Zullah was compelled to step aside and allow Justice Nasim Hasan Shah to assume the leadership of the Supreme Court.

The Supreme Court's ruling against the President was aimed at salvaging the judiciary, which had been severely damaged by Baig's public confession. The action had not only compounded the confusion, but had demonstrated the nation's institutional shallowness after more than forty-five years of independent government. Sorting out the details of this constitutional disaster would not be simple in a country strong on personal rule and weak in due process. Moreover, none of the principals were prepared to go quietly into the night and simply disappear. Certainly not Ghulam Ishaq, whose legitimacy had been blown away by the unfolding of events. The old civil servant insisted on holding his position, irrespective of the consequences. For a man who had all his life claimed to place public service above personal privilege, it was strange to see Ghulam Ishaq so passionately committed to the political struggle. His blocking of a Lahore High Court order reinstating the Punjab provincial government was aimed solely at denying Nawaz Sharif the leverage he needed to reform his government. Chaos was everywhere and in everything, given the virtual breakdown of the political system in all its parts. The dissolution of the NWFP Assembly and the attempt to destroy the Sindh government also bore the hand of the President, who by this time had transformed himself into a Shiva-like god who seemed ready to take everything down with him in one great fit of personal rage.

What was especially difficult to understand in the unfolding scenario was the army's apparent decision to support the President's destructive escapade. The Zia-amended Constitution had so linked the President with the armed forces that even in the critical circumstances of the day, the army high command had great difficulty in acknowledging the almost paranoid actions of the President. Ghulam Mohammad's mental condition in 1954 was of significant note to those around him, especially to Iskandar Mirza and General Ayub Khan. Although Ghulam Ishaq did not suffer the disability of his early predecessor, his behaviour none the less raised great concern among those responsible for the nation's welfare. It was, therefore, with considerable reluctance that General Waheed Kakar agreed to intervene, and to referee an arrangement agreed upon by both Ghulam Ishaq and Nawaz Sharif. Appeals were made to both men to do no further damage to the nation, and to make the necessary personal sacrifices that the time demanded. Both were 'requested' to submit their resignations and allow still another caretaker government to be formed. Hesitatingly, and mindful of the fallout that might affect them if they agreed to yield their positions, both men were assured that their personal interests would be protected and that their actions would receive the plaudits of the nation.

Following a round of intense negotiations, on 18 July 1993 both Ghulam Ishaq Khan and Mian Nawaz Sharif simultaneously resigned their respective positions and allowed a caretaker government to be formed by the Senate Chairman, Wasim Sajjad. Sajjad assumed the office of the President, while Moeen Qureshi, a former Vice-President of the International Bank for Reconstruction and Development (World Bank), and now a private businessman residing permanently in the United States, was urged to return to his strife-torn country and take up the unenviable responsibility as Pakistan's interim Prime Minister.

The Interim Government

Moeen Qureshi was to serve as the nation's Prime Minister for a period of three months. Engaged at the time of his appointment on a consultancy in Singapore, he was not tinged by any of the events of the preceding years. And although his appointment came as a surprise to the nation, he proved to be a good choice in that he assumed his tasks unencumbered by the political controversies that had incapacitated virtually all the country's political principals and derailed the once vaunted legal system. Chosen by the officials of the higher military-bureaucracy because he carried apolitical credentials, and also because he had assembled a record of accomplishment as an international civil servant, Qureshi had the integrity as well as the expertise to command the attention of the nation's powerbrokers. Operating over the heads of the politicians, he had no patronage to bestow, no personal ambitions to conceal, and given the country's demoralized state, he seemed to be the one man who could restore confidence in the governmental system. Moreover, and not of small consequence, Qureshi had strong and intimate ties to the international community, and especially to the United States.

The interim Prime Minister, by his own wishes, had little time to remedy the ills afflicting Pakistani society. Provided with the special and almost *carte blanche* powers needed to grapple with the more prominent and well-publicized ailments, Qureshi did not delay in introducing a series of reform measures that he anticipated, or at least hoped, would be perpetuated by his elected successor. Concentrating his reforms on the drifting economy, he took the drastic step of devaluing the inflated rupee. Playing the role of the white knight, he exposed years of deceit and corruption when he issued a public list identifying 5,000 loan defaulters. He also condemned policies that had allotted expensive tracts of land to politicians and their supporters, and he did not hesitate to cite the failure of the well-to-do to pay their utility bills. His government let it be known that stiff penalties would be imposed on anyone found negligent in meeting their tax obligations.

The Acting Prime Minister called for belt-tightening measures, and his austerity programme was a refreshing contrast to the profligacy of his immediate predecessors. In a money-saving move, but also with a view to their inefficiency, he ordered the closure of fifteen ministries and ten embassies, and dramatically ordered a reduction in the size of the government. He even struck a blow against the landed gentry by imposing a temporary levy on agriculture, a matter avoided by successive Pakistani governments. Qureshi let it be known he had no intention of harming the small cultivator, but he was earnest in his desire to uncover hidden sources of landed wealth. The sum of money resumed by all these measures was hardly enough to return solvency to the treasury, but the campaign centred popular attention on the need for individual as well as societal purification and probity.

Qureshi went after the druglords, and called for police reforms that improved discipline and at the same time elevated the stature of the agent of law and order. By requiring the politicians to pay their outstanding loans or face a ban on their election expectations, he was able to retrieve a considerable sum of money, but he also embarrassed both Nawaz Sharif and Benazir Bhutto, whose brother and husband respectively, were forced to meet their neglected obligations. Given the sincerity of Qureshi's effort, law enforcement, and particularly the army, gave him their total commitment. As a consequence, a number of politicians were banned from participating in politics, and some of the highest-placed drug dealers took the option of leaving the country.

The Acting Prime Minister lived up to his reputation as an effective, efficient, no-nonsense, and dedicated administrator. Indeed, more the civil servant-cum-politician than a true politician, his talented, technocratic abilities were amply demonstrated in the limited period of his tenure. Qureshi's administration was a welcome respite from the business-as-usual politics that had ravaged the Pakistani scene, but it was not without its costs. The devaluation of the rupee and the restrictions imposed on the country's commercial life took its toll in a rise in the price of essential commodities. Gasoline, electric power, natural gas, wheat flour, cooking oil, and a host of everyday items became more costly and made life for the average Pakistani more difficult, and in the case of the poor, more bitter. Qureshi did not escape criticism, and with the Jamaat-i-Islami leading the way, the Acting Prime Minister's actions were condemned as excessive and in the worst interests of the common folk. Such critics were quick to cite Qureshi's extraterritorial credentials, his close and intimate association with the United States, and the temporary nature of his residence in Pakistan. Arguing that he had been foisted on the nation by the Americans, the World Bank, and the International Monetary Fund, they enthusiastically called for his early retirement and the holding of new elections.

Qureshi would have preferred a more receptive public, but he argued his policies had a negative impact on all the people of Pakistan, not just those who had greedily advantaged themselves. Qureshi, however, was a man in a hurry. Called to render a service of the highest magnitude in the briefest time, to restore the national equilibrium, and to give the government the breathing space needed to repair the damage done the highest governmental institutions, he had acted as he saw fit and without concern for the consequences. Moreover, only Moeen Qureshi had the courage, some would say the audacity, to announce the capping of the country's nuclear programme, but he did so, ever mindful of the popular enthusiasm for the project and also aware that the Pakistan Army was its most interested party. Thus, when the time arrived for Moeen Qureshi to yield his powers, to pack his belongings, and return to the United States, many Pakistanis were eager to urge him on his way. At the same time, many others acknowledged his presence and cited the unique character of his administration, the industry with which he approached the country's multiple problems, and the essential success of his mission.

Chapter 12

The End and the Beginning

The people of Pakistan cast their ballots yet again for another National Assembly on 6-7 October 1993. In the ambience created by the outgoing caretaker government, the elections were largely without incident and judged to be fair by both national and international observers. Although some rigging was later uncovered, and a number of disqualifications resulted from the disclosures, the PPP was returned to power by the narrowest of margins. Indeed, if the country had been in the process of developing a two-party system, the 1993 election bore out the extent to which that goal had been achieved. The PPP won 86 seats to 72 for the Pakistan Muslim League. Neither party, however, achieved a majority of the 207 seats in the National Assembly and coalition government was once more assured. Nawaz Sharif's party had actually drawn more of the popular vote, 39.7 per cent, to the PPP's 38.1 per cent. Yet another important aspect of the final counting was the relative success of the smaller parties, but the dismal failure of the vocal and ever-active religious organizations. Compared with the secular minority parties which had demonstrated their not inconsiderable popularity, the Islam-*pasand* organizations managed only nine parliamentary seats among them. The Awami National Party, as well as the ethno-based parties of Sindh and Balochistan, did poorly in the national elections. The MQM, on the other hand, had decided to sit out the elections as a show of defiance and in the belief that its non-participation would discredit the polling. In a way the tactic seemed to work, because far fewer than fifty per cent of Pakistan's eligible voters actually exercised their franchise. In the final analysis, however, the stay-at-homes and the boycotts merely played into the hands of the PPP and the Muslim League, who again dominated the political arena.

The PML was, unsurprisingly, the most successful party in the Punjab with 106 seats, but the PPP was not far behind with 94. Nawaz Sharif's control of the Punjab was affected by a renegade Muslim League splinter group which joined the PPP and helped to give the latter a controlling interest in the province. The PPP was triumphant in Sindh, taking 56 seats to the MQM's 27, and the PML's 8. Another interesting sidelight to the Sindh provincial elections was the victory of Murtaza Bhutto, Benazir's brother, who won a seat in the Assembly for his Shaheed Bhutto Committee. The PPP was also successful in the NWFP, where it took 22 seats to 21 for the ANP, and 15 for the PML. Only in Balochistan did the PPP secure less seats (3) than the PML (6).

The combination of voter support and coalition building had allowed the PPP to form the government and Benazir Bhutto, after three years in the opposition, was again made Prime Minister of Pakistan. Taking the oath of office on 19 October, Benazir pledged to revitalize Pakistan, to heal the wounds opened in the recent political wars, and to begin the process of reconciliation. Moreover, the PPP, with the help of the Junejo PML organization, also took control of the Punjab, as well as Sindh province. Therefore, more so than in her first administration, Benazir could claim solid representation in the different regions. If she was inclined toward proving that democracy was alive and well in Pakistan, her opportunity had now come. Given a second chance to minister to the needs of an expectant but no longer naive public, it was Benazir's responsibility to demonstrate that her years in opposition had not been wasted. Although Nawaz Sharif's party was able to coalesce with organizations in the NWFP and Balochistan to form the provincial governments there, the IJI was a matter of history, and the PML was now cast in the role of the loyal opposition. How loyal, of course, would be determined by subsequent events.

Benazir's fortunes were further heightened on 13 November, with the announcement that the PPP candidate for President, Farooq Leghari, had defeated his PML rival, Wasim Sajjad. Given the problems Benazir had had with Ghulam Ishaq Khan, Leghari's victory heralded a new era in Pakistani politics wherein the head of government and the head of state were expected to work in concert with one another. Moreover, although Leghari was endowed with all the trappings of power, including the Eighth Amendment, Benazir was perceived as having little to fear from the President. In fact, one of Leghari's campaign objectives was the rescinding of the Eighth Amendment, and expectations ran high that the new President would cease interfering in the work of the government, and certainly would not do anything to undermine the administration of his own Prime Minister.

It was not surprising, therefore, that observers drew the conclusion that Pakistan was entering a new era, that for virtually the first time an elected government could be expected to complete its full term, and most important, that the country's viceregal tradition, born in the crucible of colonialism, had at long last been laid to rest (Ziring, 1993). Furthermore, the Pakistani citizen had matured; the several elections had been a genuine educational experience, and despite the low turnout of eligible voters, the nation had demonstrated its clear preference for rational, secular government. Moreover, the two-party system that had been much heralded, finally appeared to crystallize. Although there were still those who found the caretaker government of Moeen Qureshi a less than satisfying experience, even his more harsh critics had to acknowledge that it was by his efforts that a constitutional crisis had been successfully weathered. For the first time in memory, Pakistan seemed to be on a relatively smooth track toward its much-proclaimed democratic objective.

While the people of Pakistan were hardly euphoric, a positive attitude framed their political world. The country ended a very critical year and entered another with greater hope. Nevertheless, there were those who cautioned a more conservative view (Amin, 1994). Noting that the country was far from economically or socially stable, that the creation of a civil society continued to elude the nation, that the socio-political balance was still maintained by a steel frame of civil-military administration, that the parties were not yet disciplined expressions of societal aspirations, and that the externalities of the Pakistan experience remained a negative factor in the development equation, there was every reason to suspend judgment until Benazir could demonstrate that her second administration would be far different from her first.

Benazir inherited an economy that had suffered considerable losses in the agricultural sector due to catastrophic floods that had done serious damage to the cotton, rice, and sugar-cane crops. And what the floods had not taken, a leaf virus did, virtually ruining the nation's cotton production. The manufacturing sector presented a mixed but on the whole gloomy picture, and what successes were achieved in small business operations could not make up the failure registered in larger firms. Only in transport was there a remarkable surge, but this was mostly due to Nawaz Sharif's pet project of jamming the thoroughfares and byways of Pakistan's urban centres with fleets of small taxis. Indeed, the expansion of the transport sector was paid for in the loss of foreign exchange that was needed to pay for the vehicle imports.

Gross investment had declined dramatically during the tenure of Nawaz Sharif, and even the austerity measures introduced by the later caretaker regime could not reverse the condition. The nation's fiscal management was in substantial disarray, with a budget deficit on the ascendant and repayment schedules on the national debt an ever increasing burden. Moreover, Pakistan continued to allocate heavy resources for defence and hence had little, if anything, left for socio-economic improvements.

Moeen Qureshi only had time to point up the disastrous consequences of careless spending and the arbitrary allocation of resources. Alarmed by the magnitude of foreign reserve depletion and rampant inflation, Qureshi called for drastic belt-tightening and, in addition to the collection of monies due in taxes and loan repayments, he called for an end to hare-brained schemes that continued their drain on the meagre treasury.

Moeen Qureshi departed from Pakistan, leaving it with problems that the new Benazir administration was called upon to address. But unlike the caretaker government, which had functioned under administrative fiat, Benazir would have to operate within the context of a society deeply divided along political as well as regional and social lines. The PPP government confronted a political opposition that was more inclined to sustain its rivalry with Benazir Bhutto than address the nation's socio-economic needs. Benazir had little time to savour her electoral victory and return to power. Confronted with a challenge to her authority from the moment she resumed her role as head of government, she reverted to the more familiar Benazir of her initial tenure.

In many ways it was the more familiar Benazir that was needed on the foreign policy front. Relations with the United States had reached a new low during the Nawaz Sharif administration and improvement had only sparked with the Qureshi interregnum. Washington was increasingly wary of Pakistani intentions in the nuclear area and, ever fearful that the country's nuclear weapons capability would only intensify Pakistan-India rivalry, it pressurized Benazir to freeze the country's nuclear programme. Some United States officials implicated Pakistan in the sustained *intifada* in Kashmir as well as the Sikh insurrection in India's Punjab state. Moreover, former Afghan freedom fighters had surfaced in some celebrated terrorist incidents in Europe and the United States. In January 1994, therefore, Pakistan was placed on the 'watch list' of potential terrorist states, and the Benazir government was hard put to it in making its case that the country should not be so labelled.

It came as a shock to cosmopolitan and largely pro-American Pakistanis that their country, in a few brief years, should be moved from its classification as the third largest recipient of United States assistance to something of a rogue or pariah state that threatened the peace of the subcontinent, and by inference, the extended world. Most Pakistanis viewed themselves as doing no more than other sovereign states in managing their security, and the American reaction was judged insensitive as well as uninformed. Under pressure from her constituents, Benazir declared that she was duty-bound to maintain the country's nuclear programme, nor had she assumed power to satisfy distant friends, let alone sacrifice the country's national security.

Benazir, however, had to marshal all her diplomatic resources to convince Washington of her country's peaceful pursuits. Competing with the Indian foreign office, which was only too eager to apply the terrorist label to Pakistan, Benazir entered into co-operative arrangements with the United States that involved a heavy commitment of Pakistani Army personnel to United Nations peacekeeping operations. Moreover, Benazir's return coincided with the change in American government that had brought Bill Clinton into the Presidency in January 1993. Although the new Washington administration would not lift the Bush-imposed embargo on assistance to Pakistan until 1995, the new President's foreign security advisors had stressed the need to sustain previous defence arrangements between the two countries. Thus, joint exercises between Pakistani and American forces continued, albeit at lower levels, and the Clinton administration hinted at the possibility of releasing the F-16 fighter aircraft for which Islamabad had paid $658 million.

What Benazir was able to do was accomplished by dint of her positive credentials in Washington circles. Thus, it was Benazir who persuaded the Clinton administration to reconsider Pakistan's argument that either the aircraft purchase contract be honoured or the country be refunded its money. She also caused the US Department of State to re-examine its position on Kashmir, and won a small victory when an American official publicly announced the government's interest in reopening the plebiscite question in the disputed territory. As a consequence of her successful lobbying, Benazir also convinced the State Department to refrain from pursuing the terrorist designation.

Benazir had more difficulty, however, in convincing the Americans that the government's purchase of missile systems from China was not a violation of treaty commitments entered into with the United States. Islamabad also justified its acceptance of Chinese assistance in the development of its Chashma nuclear facility. Arguing its right as a sovereign nation, Benazir was constrained to emphasize that Pakistan was an independent country, and that her government was responsible for the nation's defence as well as its modernization. Pakistan, she declared, wanted good relations with the United States, but not at the cost of the country's security or dignity. To demonstrate its commitment to international peace, Pakistan had posted 5,000 soldiers in Somalia as part of a UN peacekeeping mission that had been initially prompted by the United States. Contingents of Pakistani forces also served in UN missions in trouble spots stretching from Asia to Africa to the Carribean in the western hemisphere, but although these services were generally acknowledged, they did little to move the international community on the matter of Kashmir. Nor did Pakistan's display of international co-operation give it the advantage in its contest with India.

Benazir inherited still another tense situation in Pakistan's relations with its adversarial neighbour when the Babri Mosque, an old Mughal structure, was demolished by a frenzied mob of Indian Hindu zealots. That event had provoked retaliatory assaults on Hindu installations in Pakistan and Muslim-dominant Bangladesh. The incident also precipitated a rash of bombings and communal assaults in both India and Pakistan. New Delhi accused Pakistan's Inter-Services Intelligence (ISI) for the bomb blasts in Bombay, whereas Islamabad pointed the finger of blame at New Delhi's clandestine service, RAW, accusing it of committing a number of terrorist attacks in Sindh, the Punjab, as well as in Islamabad. The fire that burned a portion of Pakistan's Assembly building on 9 November 1994 was also attributed to RAW agents. The expulsion of diplomatic representatives by each country only heightened tensions, and the massing of troops on their mutual frontier, as well as the recurring skirmishes on the ceasefire line in Kashmir, were not aimed at improving the atmosphere between the two neighbours. In sum, it was not an auspicious beginning for Benazir's second coming.

The Second Benazir Administration

Benazir did not have the proverbial honeymoon that new governments sometimes enjoy upon taking up their responsibilities. There was no respite from the political wars or the multiple socio-economic problems that burdened the nation. Civility had eluded the Pakistani political scene early in the nation's history, and it would have been naive to assume that the bitter rivalry between Benazir and her major competitor, Nawaz Sharif, would be suspended long enough to give the new government the opportunity to assemble its operative organization and chart its course. Moreover, as if Benazir did not have enough difficulty in countering the assaults from her official and principal opposition, she was also confronted with another, more personal challenge, from within her own family. Her only surviving brother, Murtaza Bhutto, had won a seat in the Sindh Assembly on a ticket representing his personal views, but also on a platform that was highly critical of his sister and the PPP. Having passed sixteen years in self-imposed exile, and wanted in Pakistan on terrorist charges, Murtaza timed his return to Pakistan to coincide with Benazir's re-acquisition of power. He believed himself to be the genuine heir to his father's legacy and was warmly greeted by his mother, who implored Benazir to give her brother a prominent position within the PPP. Indeed, Begum Bhutto insisted that she remained the true leader of the PPP and that her daughter, though she was the country's Prime Minister, was still beholden to her.

Benazir could not prevent a gross public display of family feuding, nor could the print media ignore the drama of the confrontation, or what the sustained controversy did to Benazir's mystique and the country's image abroad. If it were not so serious a matter, it would have been laughable, but few people in Pakistan saw the humour in the family contest of wills. Benazir accused her mother of engineering Murtaza's election as well as his return, and more important, she declared that it had all been done to embarrass and discredit her. Nusrat Bhutto was already a feeble woman at the time of the confrontation, but she had sufficient energy and enough presence of mind to recognize the devious behaviour of Benazir's husband, Asif Zardari. It was Zardari who insisted on representing the Bhutto clan, and he had manoeuvred Benazir into a position where her only option appeared to be the repudiation of her brother. Moreover, Murtaza was a

wanted man and had been implicated in the death of a
Pakistani diplomat through his leadership of the Damascus
and Tripoli-based Al-Zulfikar terrorist organization. Nusrat,
however, was determined to protect her only living son, and
she feared that Zardari's machinations would be the ultimate
death of the Bhutto family.

Benazir was cast in a no-win role. When her mother tried
to block PPP followers and officials from visiting Bhutto's
grave-site, and arranged with Murtaza to set up a defence
perimeter around the burial ground, Benazir ordered the
breaking of the cordon and, in the resulting conflict, the
family feud took its first blood. The deaths caused Nusrat to
condemn her daughter and, in a moment of high emotion,
she accused Benazir's government of being worse than that
of Ziaul Haq. Murtaza's incarceration on long-standing
terrorist charges did not ease the relationship between mother
and daughter, or between Benazir and Murtaza, who now
committed himself to his sister's destruction. Benazir had no
option but to relieve her mother of her titular PPP
responsibilities and to reaffirm her leadership of the party by
leaning more heavily on her husband.

The bitterness of the Bhutto family conflict was replicated
in the behaviour of the political opposition represented by
Nawaz Sharif. More determined than ever to avenge himself
for what he believed were PPP tactics in denying him a
political voice commensurate with his party's popular status,
Nawaz opened a vicious campaign of vilification against
Benazir and her organization. And the more heavily the
opposition pressed against the crumbling edifice of the PPP,
the more Benazir resorted to extra-legal actions in shoring up
her beleaguered Government.

The country's economic and social plight was ignored in
the struggle to retain power, and a classic example of
intrigue, influence peddling, and outright bribery ripped apart
the relative tranquillity in the NWFP, where a PML-ANP
coalition had formed the government. PPP operators, armed
with huge sums of money, enticed and ultimately won over
enough borderline members of the ruling coalition to weaken,
and thus bring down, the provincial government. In the chaos
that followed, Governor's Rule was imposed on the province

but it was soon lifted to allow the PPP to form the government. Demonstrations and riots followed on the heels of the PPP award, with Nawaz Sharif insisting that the actions in the frontier province were unconstitutional and a travesty of democracy. Boycotting the National Assembly session, the opposition took their anger into the streets of Islamabad, Lahore, and Peshawar, where the Benazir government was exposed to a fusillade of charges that could not be effectively countered.

Nothing was sacrosanct as the Nawaz forces opened heretofore unrevealed files on Benazir's personal excesses, as well as her government's failures in domestic and foreign policy. Benazir's public pronouncements on a number of issues were dissected in ways that revealed her duplicitous actions, and in her foreign policy, like her father before her, she was denounced for befriending India and, it was alleged, even encouraging New Delhi to advantage itself at Pakistan's expense.

Benazir also found herself trapped in a banking scandal which had even greater public impact than the co-operatives and BCCI scandals of the Nawaz Sharif administration. The arrest of Younus Habib, President of the Mehran Bank, on grounds that he had diverted huge sums of money to political leaders as well as former high-ranking army officers, ultimately led investigators to the President's House, where President Farooq Leghari was alleged to have personally benefited from the bank's sale of a piece of worthless property. Leghari was forced to admit the transaction and the lucrative return, but he insisted that it had all been done within the strict tenets of the law. To dramatize the episode, Nawaz Sharif escorted a group of journalists to the desolate region of Dera Ghazi Khan, where the land in question was located, and where the observers affirmed that it was indeed virtual wasteland. And although the President resisted this assault on his integrity, there was no mistaking the harm that the disclosure had done to Leghari and the Presidency. The opposition, however, had demonstrated its capacity to marshal evidence that dramatized the questionable behaviour of the highest members of the Benazir government and, indeed, the Prime Minister could only hope to deflect the charges that were levelled against her personal activities, as well as those of her husband.

Encouraged by her husband, who was also her principal adviser and confidant, Benazir sought to divert attention from herself and her administration by ordering the arrest of Brigadier Imtiaz, the Intelligence Chief during the Nawaz Sharif administration. Imitiaz was accused of plotting the overthrow of Benazir's first administration, and the Prime Minister sought to demonstrate to her current detractors that she would not hesitate to act against them if they persisted in their tactics to undermine her rule.

With increasing frequency and vengeance, Benazir ordered investigations of the Nawaz Sharif family fortune and, as was to be expected, the government uncovered cases of tax evasion, significant defaults on loans, and general tampering with the governmental process. Benazir ordered the arrest of Nawaz Sharif's father, Mian Mohammad Sharif, on grounds of illicit commercial transactions, despite the aged industrialist's poor health. She also found sufficient evidence to imprison some of Nawaz Sharif's closest associates, who were also articulate leaders of the opposition. Asif Zardari took on the character of the 'grey eminence', Benazir's 'Rasputin', as the government sought to silence its critics by ferrying them off to distant jails. Members of the National Assembly representing the PML were likewise apprehended by the authorities, and the appeals made to gain their release by the Speaker of the Parliament and the Senate Chairman went unanswered. The isolation of the opposition paralysed the work of the Assembly, which had now become the scene of raucous displays as members castigated and physically abused one another in and outside the forum. Through it all, Asif Zardari was reported to be especially pleased with the imprisonment of so many of his enemies, so many individuals whom he held personally responsible for the more than two years that he had languished in the jails of the Nawaz Sharif administration.

Zardari did not function without Benazir's acquiescence, and in the final analysis, it was the Prime Minister who aggressively sought the prosecution of the more vocal members of her opposition. In an attempt to assure the success of her campaign against her political foes, Benazir forced the early retirement of judges in the Supreme Court as well as in the provincial high courts, replacing them with persons deemed to be loyal to the PPP administration. Democracy proved to be another empty concept as the government's draconian measures sought to neutralize the voices of dissent. Nor could the arbitrariness of the government's actions be justified on anything but personal grounds; the Bhuttos were engaged in a vendetta and the whole country was witness to the unleashing of nightmarish forces.

Demonstrating that he too could successfully play the opposition game, Nawaz Sharif attempted to rally support from among the general population. Boarding a train in Karachi, Nawaz Sharif moved through Pakistan's towns and villages until he arrived at Peshawar, all along the way citing the Benazir government's tyrannical actions and calling for public outcry. The crowds that lined his route forgot the inadequacies of his previous administration and enthusiastically welcomed his arrival. Comparing his governance to that of the Bhutto clan, Nawaz Sharif called upon the Pakistani nation to join with him in a work stoppage that would dramatize the extent of their popular dissatisfaction with the Benazir regime. And indeed, on 11 October 1994, a solid portion of the nation answered his call and semi-paralysed the country. But if the demonstration was launched to force the resignation of the government, it did not even come close to realizing that objective.

Nor did the government yield to the civil disturbances that continued to rock the nation. Still another PPP-MQM coalition arrangement broke down when the *mohajir* organization split into factions and the one made open war on the other. By 1994 the situation in Karachi had become so embattled that it had become more a magnet for the violence-prone than the peacemakers. No one truly appeared interested in a brokered solution to the complaints of the different communities, and both government and non-governmental organizations took advantage of an authority vacuum to wreak more havoc on the metropolitan scene. Extremist elements representing both Sunni and Shia practices, and, there is little doubt, aided and encouraged from outside the country, joined in the mayhem. India, Iran, Saudi Arabia, were all implicated.

Pakistani intelligence organizations as well as Indian security agencies were all geared to intervene in the troubles of Sindh province. Moreover, neither the Pakistan Army, nor the provincial or federal government appeared capable of returning the region to sanity. The strategy of the Pakistan intelligence units called for dividing the MQM movement, neutralizing the factions, and eventually destroying them. But the execution of that programme had only intensified the struggle, and neither the random killings nor the damage done to private and public property could be reversed.

Members of the *mohajir* community had reason to question the basis of their loyalty to Pakistan: why in fact their forebears had left India for Pakistan, and had given so much of themselves in the formation of the Muslim state. Contrasting their plight with that of the Kashmiri Muslims, they wondered aloud how the Pakistan Army could target them and yet claim to honour its commitment to the Muslims of the northern territory (author's interviews, 1995). The question that they constantly posed to themselves was how a government that had pledged itself to safeguard the Muslims of Kashmir could unleash such ferocity on the Muslim *mohajirs* of Sindh province. The Pakistan army, in the eyes of the *mohajir* community, had ceased to be their army, and in fact, had no more integrity than the Indian Army, which had launched still another brutal campaign against the Kashmiri people.

The MQM leader, Altaf Hussain, had been tried *in absentia* for high crimes against the nation, and had been sentenced to twenty-seven years in prison. No one expected him to return from his London exile, and the judicial procedure did more to dramatize his cause than to temper the chaotic situation. Moreover, revealing the depth of their despair, some members of the MQM demanded nothing less than separation from Sindh province. The creation of a *Mohajir* Desh raised the spectre of the Bengali demands of the 1950s and 1960s, and caused many to draw the parallel between events precipitating the civil war in East Pakistan and those building in Sindh's principal cities. Perhaps in a gesture aimed at relieving the tension in Karachi, in December 1994 the army decided to withdraw some of its troops, but the assassinations and the bombings did not end. Prominent members of the country's literati were singled out for elimination, as were two American Consulate employees who were gunned down in broad daylight on a busy Karachi intersection. The bombing of the Egyptian Embassy in Islamabad caused another fifteen deaths and many more wounded, and it was not surprising to find those with travel options leaving the country for more secure locations. The government's response to all these problems was hardly directed at a solution. The closure of the Indian Consulate in Karachi was a futile answer, and was aimed more at deflecting public opinion than truly coming to grips with a deeply divided polity.

How deeply divided and socially regressive Pakistan had become was dramatized almost a thousand miles north of Karachi, in the tribal Malakand region, where in late 1994 a movement identified as the Tehreek-i-Nifaz-i-Shariat-i-Mohammadi (TNSM) sparked a rebellion against the Pakistan government. Malakand had been organized into a self-governing division in the later stages of the Ayub era, but a much pressurized Supreme Court had rejected it's unique status. The TNSM argued that the Benazir government sought to spread its influence in the region for the purpose of substituting its law for that of the Islamic Sharia. Demanding that they be permitted to govern themselves according to their own rules and principles, the demonstrators, who were also described as the 'Black Turbans', cut the roads into and out of the districts of Swat, Malakand, and Dir, occupied the airport at Saidu Sharif, and seized and murdered government officials. The seriousness of the situation, given the unrest elsewhere in the country, necessitated the despatch of army units, and the insurrection was not quelled until another year had passed and only after many more lives had been lost.

The only positive developments were the statistical reduction in the nation's trade deficit and a slight rise in foreign exchange reserves. Benazir's return had attracted external funds, and a sizeable investment in the country's energy sector was made by American, South Korean, and Hong Kong Chinese financiers and business interests. Pakistan also continued to receive loans and grant assistance from the World Bank, IMF, and the Asian Development Bank.

And in September 1995 the United States Senate voted to lift the economic as well as some of the military sanctions that had been imposed on the country in 1990. Hillary Rodham Clinton and her daughter also visited the country as guests of the Prime Minister, and there were ample signals from Washington that new understandings with Pakistan were desirable.

But these achievements could not conceal the deepening socio-political divisions within the country or the sustained failures in the country's agricultural and industrial sectors. Nor could the government ignore the increasing levels of unemployment, or the ever more inflated prices of everyday necessities. The administration sought to cast blame for these latter problems on the International Monetary Fund and its structural adjustment policies. But whether or not the international agency had contributed to the disastrous economic situation, large sections of the citizenry found greater difficulties in their day-to-day lives.

The Gathering Storm

In 1995 Benazir had almost three years remaining in her term, and with the army indicating a hands-off policy in the political arena, the administration was reasonably equipped to beat back the challenges of the political opposition. Given the climate of fear and intimidation, as well as its capacity to use extreme measures in the neutralization of rivals, the PPP government, in spite of the nation's socio-economic plight, appeared quite capable of holding its position. The army, therefore, held the key to both Benazir's survival as well as her demise. And it was with considerable interest that the public learned from the mouth of the Prime Minister that an 'Islamic plot to overthrow the Pakistani government' had been uncovered in the army. Benazir reported that a number of army officers, including a Major-General and several Brigadiers, had been implicated in a conspiracy aimed at derailing her government and installing a regime that would be more properly guided by the principles of Islam. The reported 'conspiracy' was the first indication that the army might again interfere with the management of the civilian government, but after the initial disclosure, strenuous efforts were made to belittle the episode and to suggest that everything was normal within the services.

Nevertheless, slippages in Benazir's support-base had become more significant. Not only was the Prime Minister called upon to placate key members of the armed forces, she also had to maintain the support of President Leghari who, since the Mehran Bank incident, had sought to place more distance between himself and the head of government. Sensing that his honour as well as his status was at stake, Leghari had grown uncomfortable with Zardari's influence in the party, and especially Benazir's tacit approval for the use of more violence-prone PPP elements. The President was already under pressure from civilian leaders and groups to assume a more direct role in the governing process. Benazir was not unaware of the jockeying for favours and influence and, believing that she could neither trust nor expect informed leadership from her political associates in and outside the cabinet, she had shifted her attention to the civil bureaucracy and to the key officials in the central administration. This dependence on the civil administrators caused the widening of the gap between Benazir and the PPP hierarchy, a gap that had become pronounced in December 1993, when Benazir formally took sole control of the party. Moreover, the consequences of this growing separation within the PPP hierarchy was observed in the decline of PPP influence in both Sindh and Punjab.

The most precipitous decline, however, occurred in the urban areas of Punjab, where Benazir had lost considerable ground to Nawaz Sharif (Wilder, 1995). Philosophically and ideologically, the PPP and the PML had come to represent and espouse many of the same interests. With the PPP more in the hands of Zardari, the commercial interests of the party attempted to rival those represented by Nawaz Sharif's PML. But it was the PPP which had come to public notice on a programme of social justice, and its deviation from that objective not only caused defections among its members, it also convinced those in the supporting public to abandon the organization.

Moreover, Murtaza Bhutto and his mother combined forces to form yet another PPP, which they claimed was true to the principles and purposes of Zulfikar Ali Bhutto. Addressing a crowd in Rawalpindi in late November 1995, Murtaza said he had returned to Pakistan not recognizing either the policies or the People's Party that had been founded in the name of 'farmers and the poor' (*The News*, 1 December 1995). Explaining that his father had made his mother Chairperson of the PPP for life, he demanded her reinstatement. But even more outspoken on the subject of his sister's crimes against the people, he called upon the Prime Minister 'to kick out the killers' of her father, hold new elections, and denounce her husband, Asif Zardari who, he asserted, had 'plundered the country's wealth'. Although Murtaza promised a more people-oriented government, unhappy PPP members and their supporters did not flock to his Shaheed Group. Its existence, however, was a constant reminder of the fragility of the Benazir-led government, and a source of intense bitterness between family members. Benazir's obvious weaknesses, let alone the machinations of Asif Zardari, and now the aggressive nature of Murtaza's sniping, were a disaster for PPP fortunes. Nor could the situation be ignored by President Leghari and the higher military.

Now wedded to unaccustomed privatization policies, the PPP had a difficult time in associating itself with the country's business interests, which had already demonstrated a preference for Nawaz's PML. Weaning the financiers and industrial leaders over to the PPP camp required overcoming the damage rendered to the community by Zulfikar Ali Bhutto's nationalization schemes of the 1970s, and the PPP government's arbitrary, and often vindictive, expropriation of private property. Memories were ever fresh. More important, the Zardari manipulation of the government's financial and commercial policies to satisfy special, and often personal, interests could not go unnoticed. Nor, for that matter, was the open intimidation of prominent business-sector supporters of Nawaz Sharif slated to win new converts from the business community. In addition, the government's use of the legal system to harass leading members of the economic community raised anew the spectre of Zulfikar Ali Bhutto and his anti-capitalist practices. Nawaz Sharif, too, was among the prominent businessmen who had their property seized, and he, along with others of his class, were also subjected to questionable arrests and court procedures.

Intimidation and arbitrary arrest had become commonplace by the beginning of the third year of the Benazir Bhutto administration. Among the more notable incidents was that which occurred in Punjab when Chief Minister Mian Manzoor Ahmad Wattoo was dismissed because, it was said, he had lost the confidence of the provincial legislature. Wattoo was a member of the Junejo PML which had coalesced with the PPP to form the government in Lahore. Before joining the PML of Junejo, Wattoo had been a member of Asghar Khan's Tehrik-i-Istiqlal, and like other leaders of the latter organization, he had defected to the Junejo group when the Tehrik's principal leader compromised his position.

Benazir's belief that opposition political party leaders might embrace Wattoo as an alternative to Nawaz Sharif meant that the Chief Minister had to go. In September, following the resignation of fifteen members of Wattoo's cabinet on the grounds that the Chief Minister had performed illegal acts, Wattoo was officially dismissed, and Governor's Rule imposed, that is, until a government favourable to Benazir could be assembled. In the meantime, Wattoo's closest associates were arrested on trumped-up charges, including Javed Zia, a personal friend and assistant, and Rana Gul Nasir, a political confidant. Warrants of arrest were also issued against Sardar Nasrullah Dreshak, a member of the Wattoo political committee, who managed to evade the authorities. This did not prevent the PPP Government from raiding his sugar mill office, however, or from indicting him on gun-running charges. But not content with these measures, Benazir, and now too Zardari, believed it necessary to totally destroy Wattoo lest he emerge again to haunt their political future. Thus Wattoo was accused of misappropriating discretionary funds and he too was arrested.

The political game in Pakistan had come to mean more than the pursuit of power and patronage. The contest had degenerated into a life and death struggle, with the violence in the streets paralleled by officially-organized, but nevertheless clandestine, assaults on, and even assassinations of political opponents. In Karachi alone in 1995, approximately 2,000 persons had been murdered, but only a few arrests were made, and even then it was difficult to conclude that the accused were, in fact, the perpetrators of the crimes. Notable political personalities were among the list of victims, with the MQM losing some of its leading figures, including the brother and nephew of Altaf Hussain. Indeed, Press reports describing the condition of their bodies indicated that they had been tortured before being executed.

From the vantage point of her adversaries, Benazir's PPP, in spite of the democratic rhetoric, had come to mean the pursuit of total power. For them, Pakistan was being transformed into a fascist state in which there would be no tolerance for dissenters, and no patience with those arguing a different method of governance. The last bastion of democratic procedure, the nation's judiciary, according to Benazir's critics, had been mutilated by the packing of the judiciary with her hand-picked political workers. Moreover, her personal selection of an *ad hoc* Chief Justice, as well as additional judges who were chosen to carry out her directives, underlined the direction in which the nation had been pointed. Zulfikar Ali Bhutto had laboured to bring all Pakistani institutions under his control. He succeeded in all departments save that of the army. Benazir set the same goal for her administration. Believing she had neutralized the Presidency, co-opted the bureaucracy, and sidelined and weakened the political opposition, her formula in tackling the army was somewhat different from that used by her father, but the prospects of her bringing the military to heel were, nevertheless, questionable.

The forty army officers who were arrested in October 1995 were accused of plotting the overthrow of the Bhutto government. It was alleged that the cabal had been hatched by retired Lieutenant-General Javed Nasir, a former ISI chief, and that he and his co-conspirators had targeted the army's nine Corps Commanders. Thus, what was first suggested to be a minor rumble within the ranks was quickly transformed into a major event, warranting a court martial of the accused. The manner in which this event split the army reached all the way to General Waheed Kakar who, it was reported, refused an extension of his service as COAS and was to be replaced by General Jahangir Karamat. The delay in confirming General Jahangir, however, hinted at difficulties between the army high command, President Leghari, and Prime Minister Benazir Bhutto. It also suggested that the different actors were in the process of seeking ways to reinforce their individual roles. But of all the contending parties, it was Benazir who stood to gain or lose the most from the selection, and the best chances for stabilizing her regime appeared to rest on the continuing disarray within the military establishment.

The Second Going

In a public display of exasperation mixed with disgust, Benazir aired much of her personal displeasure while inaugurating the First International Congress of Writers and Intellectuals in Islamabad on 30 November 1995. Citing what she described as the forces of tyranny, she pointed to the malevolence of the Zia administration and its offspring, the IJI, now the PML of Nawaz Sharif. Making what her supporters claimed was one of her 'finest speeches', the Prime Minister accused religious zealots and politicians of forming an 'unholy alliance' that was aimed at destroying the democratic principles of Mohammad Ali Jinnah. Deploring the continuing disruptive tactics of the 'stooges of Ziaul Haq', she declared that she would not cease in her labours until she had liquidated those whose lust for power was so abiding that they would trample the nation's constitution and destiny (*The News*, 1 December 1995).

Commenting on the disclosure of an abortive army *coup* attempt, she said that those who would have perpetrated the action would have killed the President, the Prime Minister, the Army Chief, and all the Corps Commanders in order to establish their sectarian state. Describing the *coup* leaders as a 'small group of power-hungry adventurers who would have plunged Pakistan into a civil war, destroyed the cream of the armed forces, and opened to attack our sensitive military institutions', she said that the government would act aggressively against them. Stating over and over again that Ziaul Haq had created these evil foes, had introduced the politics of corruption and violence, had unleashed the traffic in drugs and guns, and had spawned a 'new class of fortune-hunters' who made their wealth 'on the backs of political prisoners, the cries of the lashed, and the screams of the tortured', she vowed to defeat them. Declaring that the real American agents were 'those clerics toting their guns bought with CIA funds and running their organizations by CIA money given for the Afghan Jihad', she concluded by noting that the battle between the free world and communism might be over 'but the battle between democracy and dictatorship still rages' (*The News*, 1 December 1995).

President Farooq Ahmad Leghari, however, continued to distance himself from Benazir's views as well as her administration. Although her supporters continued to sing her praises and find fault with the 'conspirators' around her, she revealed even greater difficulties in managing the positive side of the political equation. Charged with the responsibility of governance, Benazir was only as successful as her colleagues. A case in point was Punjab where law and order problems had spread from Karachi to the northern Mughal city. Bus and market bombings had taken a toll of the innocent and had reduced confidence in government to its lowest point. Although reports sought to expose the corruption of the Wattoo administration, and especially how the deposed Chief Minister had stolen public funds for his personal use, the new Chief Minister, Arif Nakai, was compelled to increase his provincial cabinet to more than sixty members, a solid portion of the Legislative Assembly. The expansion of the governing structure centred on the doling out of patronage, not a serious assault on the province's problems. The public could see little difference in the accusations hurled at Wattoo and the behaviour of the serving officials who continued to drain the public treasury. Moreover, Wattoo's successor could not assure the safety of the average citizen who daily used public transport or shopped in the neighbourhood bazaar.

Fearing the collapse of legitimate government institutions, and aware that the public bureaucracy, the armed forces and the judiciary had been seriously compromised by the manoeuvring of all the major politicians, President Leghari tried to reassure the nation that its institutions could still function in a reasonable and constitutional manner. Prior to

General Waheed Kakar's formal retirement from his post as COAS, Leghari moved to end the speculation on his successor. Understanding that the army had been wounded by the disclosure of a cabal engineered by a retired general, the President placed tradition and convention above expediency and politics, and insisted on the appointment of the most senior member of the army as the new COAS. Centring his decision on the principles of seniority, professionalism, and merit, in the spring of 1996 Leghari officially appointed General Jahangir Karamat to be Pakistan's twelfth Chief of the Army Staff.

The action represented the first time in Pakistan's political history that a change in army command was announced well before the retirement of the COAS. Moreover, the decision and the method employed by the President in making the selection received the approval and support of Lieutenant-Generals Naseer Akhtar, Mohammad Tariq, and Javed Ashraf Qazi, those next in line for the COAS post. General Karamat's appointment not only allowed the other officers to remain in the service, it also acknowledged the dedication, expertise, and professionalism of a disciplined and loyal high command. Moreover, Karamat had distinguished himself in all key areas, i.e., in command, staff, and instruction. Most importantly for the army, his promotion ended the rumour-mongering that still another political appointment was imminent, while even more importantly, Karamat's promotion to the to post terminated speculation concerning unrest within the forces. It gave a morale boost when it was most needed and it demonstrated the strict separation of the army from politics. By his actions, President Leghari also signalled to the politicians that they would not again be permitted to tamper with the command structure, nor supersede senior officers, sow dissent in the ranks, or seek to manipulate the services.

From this point forward, it was President Leghari who emphasized the need for transparency in all government operations. Reportedly sickened by reports of malpractice and mismanagement at all levels of government and throughout the political and economic system, he stressed the need to change course while time still remained. It was in this same vein that the President attempted to clean up the judicial mess that the PPP government, as well as its predecessors, had created.

Operating on an injunction from the Supreme Court, and given his powers under Article 193 of the Constitution, Leghari appointed Justice Khalilur Rehman as the permanent Lahore High Court Chief Justice, Mamoon Qazi as permanent Sindh High Court Chief Justice, and Justice Nasir Aslam Zahid as Chief Justice of the Federal Shariat Court. Other appointments to the Supreme Court and the provincial high courts followed, and in total, the actions essentially terminated the lawyers' movement which had pressurized the government to restore the dignity of their profession. More than that, however, Leghari had begun a process of reconstruction, and his salvaging of the lost independence and prestige of the judiciary was a notable achievement. Now praised by his heretofore staunchest critics in the Bar Association of Pakistan, Leghari had not only instilled new confidence in the armed forces and reclaimed the integrity of the judicial system, he had also placed the presidency on a constitutional track. Leghari himself had been transformed. Emerging from behind the edifice of the PPP, he seemed to realize for the first time what it meant to be the President of all the people of Pakistan.

The collision course followed by the President and the Prime Minister was now obvious to almost everyone. Leghari, whose relationship with Benazir had ranged over a fifteen-year period, had been Benazir's choice for the President of Pakistan, and that marked a significant difference from her father's selection of Ziaul Haq to command the Pakistani Army. Bhutto did not personally know Zia when he made his appointment. Nevertheless, in making their selections, both father and daughter believed that they had selected persons who would serve them dutifully, ignoring all their foibles and manoeuvrings. Time would show that Zulfi underestimated Zia, and it was now ever more apparent that Benazir had misjudged Leghari. President Leghari rejected a ceremonial role from the moment of his election, nor was he inclined to insulate Benazir from her enemies. The President had grown uncomfortable with the constant intrigue, the plotting, and the mayhem, and observing the dismantling of the only institutions fashioned to perform the nation's business at home and abroad, a showdown between the two principals was made inevitable.

Indeed, the PPP had never been a disciplined organization and, in the hands of Asif Zardari, it had ceased to inspire even its most faithful members. And because of the intimacy of the Benazir-Zardari political alliance, Benazir was perceived as using all the instruments at her command merely to remain in power, and hence both the party and the constitutional system could be sacrificed if in so doing, Benazir's rule could be guaranteed. Observers believed that Benazir's choice of new cabinet ministers had angered the President, and again revealed the expedience of her actions. Others speculated that it was Benazir's intention to issue an ordinance legitimizing raffle-type funding for the country's Jubilee celebrations in 1997 that precipitated an irreparable break.

Disclosures that Zardari had purchased 'Rockwood', a mansion in Surrey, for a reported £ 2.7 million, touched off a storm of recriminations that Leghari could hardly ignore. When the story was first published in the London *Sunday Express*, the Prime Minister's office issued an official denial, and Benazir and Zardari threatened to take the newspaper into court. The tabloid, however, stuck to its story and declared that it was prepared to defend itself against the filing of any libel case brought by the Bhuttos. In fact, the newspaper later published a report that Zardari had purchased two luxury flats in London's prestigious and fashionable district of Belgravia that were paid for from a foreign bank account. It also was alleged that Zardari had a mortgage account in the Channel Island of Guernsey and that obligations were transferred to it from an account in Karachi. The paper reported that a huge monthly sum was transferred from the one account to the other to pay for the apartments. The newspaper also reported that Zardari's father, Hakim Ali, owned an apartment in the same area which he was prepared to sell for £ 200,000. Whether true or false, the stories exploded like bombshells when they were reported in the Pakistan Press, and Leghari had more reason to part company with the Prime Minister. In the opinion of the President, considering the desperate conditions within the country, Pakistan did not need the scandals associated with the Bhuttos.

On 12 September 1996 the International Monetary Fund informed the Pakistan government that its continued support would be made dependent on the administration imposing a tax on agricultural income, on a sizeable reduction in military expenditure, on the removal of regulatory import duties, on the slashing of tariffs, and the management of flexible exchange rates. Cited in the IMF's 1996 Annual Report, the demands explained the strain that had developed in Pakistan-IMF relations. The IMF had early on intruded itself in Pakistani governmental decisions, and now, even more forcefully, it called for a general sales tax and the phasing out of tax exemptions and concessions to select industries and business establishments. The Pakistan government was urged to control its expenditures, improve its efficiency, and pay more attention to development programmes. The IMF also cautioned the administration that it could not use privatization proceeds to finance unsustainable increases in government expenditures, and that it would have to follow the doctrine of transparency in its budget management. Only when the nation's fiscal account was strengthened would the IMF be prepared to conduct business as usual with the Pakistan government.

The IMF attack came only two days after the devaluation of the Pakistan rupee, which was aimed at easing the country's balance of payments problem. Gearing for an austerity programme, the State Bank had called for a sharp curtailment in imports, and had pleaded with Pakistanis working abroad to remit their earnings through the nation's banks. The devaluation, however, was difficult to accept in all sectors of society, including the trading and industrial communities, which anticipated that the scheme would cause a vicious devaluation-inflationary spiral that could only further destabilize the economy. If the level of imports remained the same, more output would have to be diverted to exports, and away from domestic consumption and investment, simply to maintain the *status quo*. Thus the devaluation could actually lead to a loss of real income without any benefit in the balance of payments. Moreover, the impact of devaluation would cause imports to rise in price, and would also provoke increases in wages and salary demands by domestic workers, who would have to find ways to preserve the real value of their purchasing power.

The devaluation also produced a demand for higher agricultural support prices, and with the higher wage demands, Pakistan's balance of payments was noticeably worsened. In effect, Pakistan's devaluation decision exacerbated the external balance of payment problem while generating runaway inflation. The Pakistani rupee moved from a value of 9.90 to the American dollar in 1982 to 36.97 in 1996, and before the year was out, to a point well above 40. The havoc these fiscal readjustments spread for the public, especially the country's middle and lower classes, was inestimable and, coupled with the pressure from the IMF and the World Bank, it was obvious that drastic action needed to be taken to strengthen the country's institutions. Pakistan was awash in a range of problems that the Benazir government seemed incapable of addressing, and sorting out the mess was impossible with an administration trapped by the personalization of power. The President was now left with no other option than to separate himself from Benazir and her administration.

The metamorphosis of Farooq Ahmad Khan Leghari was not lost on Benazir, her party, or the political opposition. The office of the President again loomed large over that of the Prime Minister, but this time the Chief Executive was not perceived by the public to be the intimidating, vindictive, and overbearing figure that for so long had plagued Pakistani political life. The maturing of Leghari was seen as the key to a resurgent Pakistan, and to a nation whose democratic rhetoric seldom measured up to its general practices, Leghari seemed to offer the best hope for a Pakistani future that a majority of citizens had despaired of ever realizing. Projected as an impartial leader who was solely concerned with the welfare of the nation, Leghari ceased being Benazir's other, lesser half in the PPP hierarchy. Moreover, Benazir had reason to fear the changing political climate, and she realized that, while the President had pledged himself to follow even-handed, constitutional precepts, given her bitter contest with

Nawaz Sharif and the still extraordinary powers of the presidency, she remained a vulnerable target. Thus, while Leghari received all the plaudits of the public, it was Benazir who anticipated the stings not only of the opposition, but of a people grown tired of her complaints as well as her antics.

Benazir's opposition had swelled, not diminished, as she attempted to beat back the assaults on her personal life as well as her government. Nawaz Sharif held to his role as chief opposition leader, but the lesser lights in the political constellation were no less troublesome. Murtaza continued to capture attention, and his tirades against his sister and her government increased in fury as he searched for a platform to launch a more successful bid for political attention.

Joining the political chorus in 1996 was the former cricket star, Imran Khan, who claimed a role as Pakistan's saviour. Domiciled in the United Kingdom and married to an exceptionally wealthy British woman, Imran Khan's political campaign was supposedly to be financed by his father-in-law. Organizing his Tehrik-e-Insaaf, the legendary cricketer stormed Pakistan with his speeches, pillorying the Benazir regime and insisting, that only he could bring social justice to the nation. While few Pakistanis gave him any chance of establishing himself as a main contender, his buffoonery illustrated the feeble character of Pakistani politics. Like Murtaza, Imran was a political neophyte, but he was furthermore totally without a real or solid constituency. In another time, his performances would have gone unnoticed. But given the desperate plight of Pakistani politics, and the general indifference of the public to political orations, Imran Khan offered a diversion, and even added a bit of humour to the humdrum tedium of everyday life.

During their separate but mutual assaults on the Benazir government, it was reported that Murtaza welcomed Imran Khan's entry into politics and had even suggested that they might co-operate with one another. Murtaza insisted that Imran Khan could assist him in exposing the deceit in the Benazir government. Citing the devaluation of the rupee as the action of a corrupt government and State Bank, he was convinced that Asif Zardari was the most corrupt of all the villains that had filled the history of Pakistan. Murtaza revealed that he had had but two brief meetings with his brother-in-law since his sister's marriage, and that he faulted Benazir for not having better sense than to allow herself to be victimized by such a personality. Murtaza proved to be an indefatigable campaigner, and though his play for power appeared futile to most Pakistanis, he was cited for his courageous efforts. Murtaza's base in strife-torn Karachi was reinforced by youthful supporters who seemed inspired by his fearless behaviour. Moreover, Murtaza was a towering presence and an indomitable politician. Dynamic as well as dashing, he attracted the adventurous to his side, and even the larger anti-Benazir public found something amusing as well as purposeful in his assaults on his sister and her husband.

Thus the news on 21 September 1996 that Murtaza Bhutto had been gunned down by police shocked the nation. The initial report described an encounter near Murtaza's Clifton residence where a police contingent, which claimed to be checking vehicles following a series of Karachi bomb blasts, said it was fired upon by Murtaza's bodyguards. In the return fire, Murtaza was fatally wounded and died *en route* to the hospital. Six members of his entourage also died in the reported exchange of fire. Murtaza had registered a complaint only the day before, accusing the government of blocking his political party activities. He had also reported the arrest of some seventy members of his breakaway PPP faction, and had charged the administration with harassment and with inhibiting his campaign. Murtaza had met with his sister some two months before, their first meeting since his return to the country almost three years earlier. Appearing to have arranged a truce, the two siblings of Zulfikar Ali Bhutto soon parted ways when it had become more than evident that Zardari had warned the Prime Minister not to have anything to do with her brother. In a later interview, Murtaza had revealed that his meeting with Benazir was disappointing and that nothing of positive substance had developed. 'We disagreed on virtually everything,' he was reported to have said. Moreover, it was after that meeting that, it is believed, Zardari personally instructed the Sindh government to obstruct Murtaza's politicking.

Benazir was reported grief-stricken at the news of her

brother's death, but she did not attend his funeral with the thousands of mourners that bore his body to the family cemetery at Garhi Khuda Baksh in Larkana. It was said that female members of the family are seldom present at burials, and that Benazir's non-attendance was more a sign of respect than one of sustained bitterness against her brother. Moreover, the Prime Minister was reported to have visited the hospital where Murtaza's body had been taken and to have wept profusely at his bedside. But even then the family feud continued. Begum Nusrat Bhutto was in London at the time of the shooting and had to be rushed back to Pakistan. But Murtaza's wife, Ghinwa Bhutto, was outspoken, accusing Benazir's government, and notably, Asif Zardari, of having arranged her husband's assassination. Indeed, the mystery of how Murtaza and his colleagues died when two police officers were only slightly injured, raised speculation and gave credibility to the belief that a high-level conspiracy had, in fact, been engineered. Persons on the scene described Murtaza leaving his car and walking toward the police when he was shot down. Furthermore, the police party knew that the brother of the Prime Minister had been seriously wounded, but they nevertheless hesitated nearly one hour before moving him to a hospital, and it was said that if he had received immediate and prompt attention, his life might have been saved.

Given the discrepancies in the stories and the public outcry for the facts in the case, Benazir had little option but to call for a special inquiry. But Murtaza's death had ended the forty-two-year old politician's career even before it had begun. Murtaza had no doubts that Benazir would lose her office and that in the maelstrom of Pakistani politics, he would yet rise to a position of particular prominence. But that ambition ended with the sudden closing of his life, and with him, too, went the last of the male line of Bhuttos. If, in fact, as Nusrat Bhutto had argued earlier, it was Asif Zardari's intention to destroy the Bhutto clan in order to inherit its legacy, Murtaza's death and the feebleness of his mother appeared to set the scene for Zardari's ascension. Moreover the PPP, which Zardari had come to dominate, was now more firmly in his grasp and he might well do with it what he pleased. The murder just six days later of Haq Nawaz Sial, the police officer credited with killing Murtaza, further heightened suspicions. And while the government portrayed the incident as a vendetta killing or a suicide, there were others who believed that Sial had been silenced by those who had authorized Murtaza's assassination.

President Leghari was now convinced that the Benazir administration was a menace to the nation and had to be replaced. Citing the chaotic law and order situation throughout the country, Leghari declared that if the brother of the Prime Minister could be killed in such mysterious circumstances; if another twenty-one innocent worshippers could be shot down while praying in a Multan mosque; indeed, if the Commissioner of Sargodha division could be killed in broad daylight; then all government law enforcement agencies were questionable and no Pakistani could feel secure anywhere. Repeating Benazir's assertion that Murtaza had been targeted, not simply the victim of a random shooting, the President called for increased vigilance by those Pakistanis who had already suffered enough rampant violence.

Benazir's questioning of the President's actions in appointing judges to the country's courts without consulting her had also given Leghari cause for rancour. The President put his powers to the test by asking his private lawyer, whom he trusted, and not the Attorney-General, whom he did not— an obvious affront to Benazir—to ask the Supreme Court to define those powers. President Leghari also agreed to a meeting with Nawaz Sharif, the first between the two principals since the President's election three years before. Prior to his scheduled conference, Nawaz met with Wali Khan and with an emissary of Altaf Hussain, who remained in exile in England. The President acknowledged the need to repair the damage in the political system, and his meeting with Nawaz Sharif was aimed, it was said, at opening a dialogue with all the competing factions. Leghari had also informed the National Assembly and Senate that he wanted to form a Commission of Inquiry to examine the charges of corruption levelled against individuals and groups throughout Pakistani society and government. Sensing a cabal, Benazir's Interior

Minister, General Naseerullah Babar, cited the need for
accountability in all walks of life, and recommended that the
inquiry also include retired government and military officials,
as well as industrialists, bankers, and commercial agents. In
a wry comment, the official declared that the President
should not be excused from those to be scrutinized. The
President, he argued, does not have immunity from inquiry
tribunals, and he prodded Leghari to state if the investigations
he intended to authorize would begin from the period of
independence in 1947, or during the rule of Ziaul Haq in
1985.

The meeting between President Leghari and Nawaz Sharif
was held on 26 September and their discussions ranged over
the critical conditions prevailing in the country. Leghari
informed the PML leader that he did not want to utilize his
special powers under Article 58(2)b of the Constitution but, if
the nation's social fabric further unravelled and the national
interest demanded his intervention, he would not hesitate to
dismiss the Benazir government and dissolve the Assemblies.
After their three-hour exchange, a press statement said:

> the President took note of the contention of the Leader of the
> opposition that the Government was not being run in accordance
> with the Constitution, and action should therefore, be taken under
> Article 58(2)b of the Constitution. The President stated that this
> was a matter that lay in his discretion. He said he would act in
> accordance with the constitutional provision if the supreme
> national interest so demanded.

Commenting on the meeting, Leghari noted that the issues
discussed were all vital to the interests of the country, and
that they should be debated and resolved in the National
Assembly. If the government and the opposition agreed to
hold new elections and the President was called upon to
perform his duties, he assured the members of the Press that
he would see to it that 'the elections were conducted honestly,
justly, fairly, and in accordance with the Constitution and
Law'.

Benazir's reaction to the Leghari-Nawaz conversations, as
well as the public statements following their get-together,
was not unexpected. Accusing 'people' of engineering
conspiracies against her government, she declared that they

were also conspiring against Pakistani democracy. Benazir said she had learned of a 'timetable' for her 'illegal dismissal'. Nevertheless, she declared her determination to remain at the head of the government and, in an aside, she questioned how such an attack could be made upon her when she was in the midst of grieving the death of her brother. Declaring that those who had plotted the deaths of her father and two brothers, now were also planning to kill her, she said she was not afraid and would not run away; indeed, she would fight tenaciously to retain her elected office. Noting that Nawaz Sharif was a 'product of martial law', she insisted that there would be no retreat from principle and that she would never compromise with those who had violated democratic practices. Seeking a respite from the struggle, Benazir left Pakistan for the United Kingdom, where she met with Prime Minister John Major, and later the United States, where she addressed the United Nations General Assembly in New York City. In her public address, Benazir said nothing about her situation at home, but she made an impassioned plea to the world body to assist the people of Kashmir who, for half a century, had struggled to free themselves from Indian domination.

But Benazir could not escape the commentary of her critics, no matter where she was. Writing in *Dawn* on 7 October, Ayaz Amir cited the discredited government of Benazir Bhutto, asserting that it was the 'brazenness' of the men and women 'running this latter-day Mughal court which passes for a Government of Pakistan that would have discredited a nunnery or a college of cardinals'. Amir advised Benazir to read the 'writing on the wall' and correct her behaviour before it was too late. He wrote:

> Ms. Bhutto's great contribution to the art of government, has been to focus her formidable energies relentlessly on the non-essential. In the process she has manufactured artificial crises which the government, to the exclusion of other business, is then required to resolve.

And he continued, 'Is Ms. Bhutto capable of curbing her instinct to tilt at windmills?' Accusing the Prime Minister of surrounding herself with incompetents, the writer asserted that there was not 'a sliver of independent thinking in all the glittering array of Ms. Bhutto's court'. And finally coming to the climax of his piece, Amir noted that the struggle had always focused on power, not the welfare of the people of Pakistan: Bhutto vs. Zia, Zia vs. Junejo, Ghulam Ishaq Khan vs. Benazir, Ghulam Ishaq Khan vs. Nawaz Sharif, and now Farooq Leghari vs. Benazir Bhutto, none of these 'mighty battles' had any relevance for the common Pakistani citizen. Nor did Ayaz Amir believe that the current National Assembly was capable of moving beyond the oratorical dimensions of the corruption issue, and he lamented Benazir's inability to reverse course, to admit her mistakes, to clean house, and to move forthrightly to tackle the nation's pressing business.

On 14 October Ayaz Amir penned still another *Dawn* piece, laying the major dilemmas confronting the nation at Benazir's feet.

> What other governments could not achieve in ten years, it has done...in three...Through its inadequacies and its almost surreal capacity to mismanage everything, the government is also presiding over a subtle but sure shift in the equilibrium of the Constitution, with power slowly moving in the direction of the Presidency...With her position weakened by quixotic adventures, the Prime Minister has left herself with no choice except to go along with a more assertive Presidency, a process that can only gather strength as the shadows lengthen over what arguably is the most grimly incompetent government in the nation's history...Pakistan has been left prematurely with a lame-duck administration, unable to govern effectively and helpless before the sharp winds that have begun to flow from the Presidency.

And in the last bit of sarcasm, Amir called the educated Benazir one who, since regaining her office in 1993, had demonstrated 'that she is incapable of learning anything'.

Shaheen Sehbai on 15 October, also in *Dawn* noted the utter failure of the Benazir government, describing the 'murky mess' created by the Prime Minister and her colleagues. Citing her and her husband, Asif Zardari, as the main culprits, the author noted that her three years in power had been productive, that is, 'productive in the sense that she and hubby Asif Zardari enjoyed unlimited powers and political, economic, and financial control,' over virtually everything. But the couple had overplayed their hand, he concluded, and the President was now his own man, the judiciary again independent, the army had been reclaimed, and even the bureaucracy was shifting its support. Meanwhile Nawaz Sharif had achieved heights of popularity never scaled before. Sehbai advised Benazir to retreat to the opposition benches, and once there, to ponder her future. Clinging to power would not serve her short term or future interests, especially with 'the odds now stacked against her'.

Benazir, however, refused to acknowledge the pungent advice of her articulate critics. Pugnaciously holding her position, on 20 October the Prime Minister announced she would present herself for a test of her accountability before any special prosecutor. Praising President Leghari and the generals who maintained the neutrality of the army, she applauded her completion of three years in office and called it a record that compared only with the term served by her father. She therefore rejected the demand for mid-term elections, and instead called upon the opposition to join with her in restoring the nation's equilibrium. That same day, Benazir's Minister of State for Law initiated legislation described as the Constitutional Fifteenth Amendment Bill. If approved, the Constitution would include a new Article 175(A) specifying that any holder of public office or any person involved in corrupt practices would be punished and disqualified from taking part in elections in accordance with the provisions specified in the Eighth Schedule. The Eighth Schedule laid down the procedures for trial and punishment for corrupt practices. The proposed bill envisaged setting up a special committee comprised of the Leader of the House, the Leader of the opposition in the National Assembly, the Chairman of the Senate, the Speaker of the National Assembly, and four members to be nominated by the Leader of the House and the Leader of the opposition from among the members of the Assembly. Similar committees were to be organized in the provinces. These committees would be made responsible for the selection of the special prosecutor who would examine allegations of corruption against all and any members of the government. If approved, the amendment would enable the legislative branch to invade the prerogatives of the judiciary, including the impeachment of members of the superior courts. In situations where members of the military were implicated, the special prosecutor would refer the cases to the Defence Ministry.

Addressing the National Assembly following the presentation of the bill, Benazir spoke of 'taking the wind out of the sails of the opposition,' and offered herself as the first case for accountability while allowing the Leader of the opposition to escape scrutiny. Claiming she had heard enough unsubstantiated stories about alleged corruption involving herself and her husband, she said she wanted the issue settled once and for all. Benazir's action in the face of mounting criticism demonstrated her determination to remain in office. Hoping to deflect attention away from herself and thereby to weaken her opposition, Benazir waxed eloquent about the national interest overriding personal ambition, and she again commended President Leghari for his personal rectitude as well as his genuine distaste for the powers conferred upon him by the Eighth Amendment. Benazir endeavoured to ingratiate herself with a President who she knew had developed strong differences with her administration. She also played to the vanity of the generals, who were embittered over the IMF's demand that military expenditure be dramatically reduced. Benazir noted that she had faced down the IMF, and said that her government had no intention of complying with the international organization's demands.

Also, in an effort to blunt the criticism levelled against her government by President Leghari for mismanaging the country's energy policy, indeed, for allowing the Oil and Gas Development Corporation to be victimized by international business interests, on 22 October Benazir described the entire planning and development policy as 'defective and faulty', and she ordered a review of all foreign-assisted projects. All the provinces were called upon to revise their development programmes and to co-ordinate their efforts with the Planning Commission. Presiding over a meeting of the Social Action Programme (SAP), she forcefully expressed her dissatisfaction with the Planning Commission, noting that the foreign-funded projects had done nothing more than increase the country's indebtedness. Condemning some of the key officials in her government, but reserving her sharpest comments for members of the bureaucracy who, she said, were only interested in 'lucrative jobs with power', she rejected all the recommendations of the SAP committee and demanded a total overhaul of the developmental process.

Commenting on the Prime Minister's insistence on finding fault everywhere but in herself, on 28 October Ayaz Amir, again writing in *Dawn,* described Benazir's performance as 'bizarre' and said that:

> Among the long line of failures and mediocrities who have flitted through the halls of government in Pakistan, her name and that of her husband's who has shared power with her, will perhaps shine the brightest...The dyarchy of Benazir Bhutto and Asif Ali Zardari will be remembered not so much for its slime and corruption as for its sublime heedlessness for doing things, questionable things most of the time, without caring for the consequences.

Noting that even the Ayub and Zia governments had some notion of the rules of the game, Amin charged the Benazir administration with the flouting of all established understandings, of riding 'roughshod' over all the conventions that had sustained Pakistani society through so many turbulent years.

The Jamaat-i-Islami put the words of critics like Ayaz Amir into practice when, on 27 October, the party led a procession to the Assembly building in Islamabad. The PML had also demonstrated their strength but they were deflected by a heavy concentration of special Ranger forces and police. The Jamaat group was also stymied by the show of arms, and rather than excite the troops, the decision was taken to peacefully protest their displeasure with the Benazir government. Declaring that the PPP government had created lawlessness in the country, the demonstrators questioned whether any of the country's institutions would be left intact if it were allowed to remain in power. But whereas the Jamaat followers were physically restrained, their speeches were not, and someone among the assembled police decided to break up the meeting. The police use of teargas precipitated a response from the crowd, and when stones were hurled at the police, a general mêlée ensued. In the disturbance that followed the police made numerous arrests, and casualties were recorded on both sides. Later, paramilitary forces were mobilized to prevent another display and to ensure that the sit-in which the Jamaat had declared as its goal would not occur. It took two days of scuffling for the Army and the police to quell the disturbances, but the use of force hardly served the interests of the administration.

Nawaz Sharif convened a meeting in Islamabad of all the major opposition parties on 29 October. The decision was taken to call upon all opposition members in the National Assembly to resign their positions, and to increase the pressure on the government by holding street rallies throughout the country, with the first one slated for Rawalpindi on 12 November. The timing for the resignations was set for 8 November, when Farooq Leghari was to address the Parliament. The theme pressed by the opposition was similar to that expressed in the recent Jamaat-i-Islami protest meeting, that is, the administration's destruction of all the institutions and the rampant corruption unleashed on the nation by the ruling party. Noting the government's over-reaction to the Jamaat demonstrators, and the possibility that they too could be assaulted by a panicky administration, the opposition leaders nevertheless committed their organizations to a united endeavour that would not yield until the PPP government had fallen.

At midnight on 5 November 1996 President Farooq Leghari issued a declaration stating that the National Assembly had been dissolved and the Prime Minister and her Federal Cabinet had been dismissed. The status of the four provincial assemblies, however, was not clarified. Leghari nevertheless sacked the Punjab Governor and detained both the Punjabi Chief Minister and Asif Zardari, who was also the Federal Minister of Investment and who, at the time of the decree, was reportedly in Lahore to deflect efforts at reinstating the Wattoo government. The army had been ordered to surround Governor's House in Lahore and no one was permitted to make contact with anyone inside the building. Also arrested in the middle of the night were the persons accused of murdering Murtaza Bhutto, namely, Masood Sharif and Wajid Durrani.

President Leghari appointed as caretaker Prime Minister Malik Meraj Khalid, an original founder of the PPP. Now an octogenarian, he had served as Speaker of the National Assembly. Never too far from the PPP, he had left the political wars to assume the rectorship of the Islamic University in Islamabad, and it was from that post that Leghari chose him to become the caretaker Prime Minister. Taking the oath as Pakistan's head of government at nine o'clock in the morning on 5 November Meraj Khalid's appointment not only marked the end of Benazir's second coming, it was also the termination of a Bhutto era that had spanned almost forty of Pakistan's first fifty years.

The Immediate Post-Bhutto Period

The President's reasons for dismissing the Benazir government and dissolving the National Assembly centred on the uncontrolled violence in the country, highlighted by the killing of Murtaza Bhutto, the manipulation of the judicial system, the political interference with administrative postings, the use of draconian measures in neutralizing the political opposition, the tampering with and corrupting of national institutions, rampant nepotism, and not the least, the disastrous state of the economy. The selection of Meraj Khalid to lead the caretaker government, however, was not meant to resolve these problems, but to keep the country on the rails during uncertain times. Thus the appointment of Sahibzada Yaqub Khan, a former Foreign Minister, and Begum Syeda Abida Hussain, a former Ambassador to the United States, was seen as maintaining continuity in Pakistan's external policies, while the appointment of Shahid Javed Burki as the country's chief economic advisor (a role he played in the Moeen Qureshi caretaker government), was aimed at restoring confidence in financial markets in Pakistan and abroad. The additional choices of Javed Jabbar, a former Information Minister, and Irshad Haqqani, a journalist, were supposed to assist the President and Meraj Khalid in the public relations department, while Omar Afridi (Interior), Shahid Hamid (Defence, Law), Sadiq Awan, Mohammad Zubair, and Shafqat Mahmood were called upon to administer to the needs of government and help ameliorate provincial and ethnic problems.

Acknowledging that the higher bureaucracy had been compromised by the former PPP government, President Leghari also ordered the removal and replacement of Federal Secretaries in the Defence, Cabinet, Interior, and Establishment positions. Similarly, the Chief Secretary of the Punjab was transferred and subjected to retirement proceedings. The latter posting had been necessitated by a decision of the Lahore High Court that called for the reinstatement of the Wattoo administration just hours before the President's action against the Bhutto government. Indeed it was because Wattoo, after a long court battle, was to be returned to his office as Punjab's Chief Minister that Asif Zardari had gone to Lahore to organize a no-confidence vote against him. Following the President's action, however, Wattoo, in the name of peace and stability in Punjab, decided of his own accord to resign his position and permit the President to assemble a new and less controversial government for the province. On 17 November the provincial Assembly and the cabinet were dissolved, and Mian Afzal Hayat was sworn in as the caretaker Chief Minister. Efforts at restoring the nation's equilibrium received high priority in all the provinces, hence the provincial governments were given time for the transition to the new circumstances, and new governments for the different provinces emerged under less dramatic circumstances than those affecting the central administration.

With the President leading the way, the caretaker government attempted to purge all those bureaucrats who had colluded with the PPP and thus were deemed to have compromised their professional offices. They included the Deputy Chairman of the Planning Commission, the Secretary of Culture, members of the Federal Anti-Corruption Committee, and the Secretary of the Women's Division. Also resigning their posts were the Attorney-General and the Managing Director of Pakistan Television. The new caretaker administration set a course whose objective was a thorough housecleaning of all Benazir Bhutto associates.

In the meantime, Benazir, who was initially placed under 'protective custody', was soon allowed to move freely, and she wasted no time in condemning the President's actions as undemocratic and unconstitutional. Claiming she had been illegally detained and her husband 'kidnapped', Benazir said she would fight Leghari's actions in the highest courts.

Benazir questioned why was it that a Punjabi like Nawaz Sharif could be reinstated by the judiciary, while Sindhi leaders, from Zulfikar Ali Bhutto to Junejo to herself, were never the recipients of similar justice. Revealing an abiding persecution complex, Benazir also took the opportunity afforded by her freedom to indirectly implicate President Leghari in the death of her brother. If not the perpetrator of a conspiracy, asked Benazir, then why did the President make a point of Murtaza's killing in his dismissal order, and why was the judiciary so determined to operate against her? Though her statements were made while in a state of high emotion, Benazir's questions were, nevertheless, aimed at undermining the credibility of Leghari, who only days before she had praised for his fairness and dedication to principle. Forced to the conclusion that she had been betrayed, Benazir still refused to acknowledge her own missteps and how they might have led to the prevailing condition.

Pakistan was essentially calm immediately following the removal of the Benazir Bhutto government. The extended population of Pakistan had grown indifferent to the actions and behaviour of the politicians, and they felt no personal loss with the departure of those in high places. The people's plight was too severe, and the politicians too wanting, for the majority of Pakistanis to take much notice of the high drama in Islamabad. If Benazir's charisma had worn thin among the general population, it had also been significantly tarnished abroad, where some of her most ardent supporters were located. The official US reaction to the ouster was illustrative of such outside opinion. On learning of the President's action, the State Department issued a statement that said very simply: 'It was an internal matter of Pakistan and President Leghari appeared to have acted within his constitutional authority.' If Benazir truly expected a reversal of the conditions that now confronted her, there was little interest in her complaint from outside the country, and her efforts internally were solely dependent on the judgment of the very judiciary she had herself so deeply undermined.

As Benazir sought to marshal her case and pleaded for support from among her countrymen, the caretaker government was busy at work trying to stabilize the nation and prepare the scene for the next round of National Assembly elections, which were slated for 3 February 1997. In the interim, however, the nation's economy was in need of major repair, and the principal burden in that realm fell to Shahid Javed Burki, the newly-appointed adviser to the Minister of Finance and Economic Affairs.

Burki called for an 8 to 10 per cent growth in the economy, but before positive actions could be taken, bank loans and back taxes had to be collected, and defaulters and tax evaders punished. He estimated that Rs. 120 billion remained to be recovered. Agreeing with the decision to slash the federal budget by twelve per cent (less defence and debt servicing), Burki also declared the need to abolish some long-operative institutions, including the Pakistan Banking Council and a host of industrial, agricultural, and investment organizations that allegedly had squandered the public's money and permitted the accumulation of unacceptable debts. Burki called for the privatization of all state-managed banks, but did not immediately reveal how shareholders and depositors were to be protected, or how thousands of employees were to be cared for. Moreover, Burki was inclined toward market reform and the privatization of the country's physical infrastructure, which included the nation's airports.

Commenting on the long-term character of these proposals, Burki's detractors questioned how programmes launched by the caretaker administration would be continued by the government that would be elected in February. Nor was Burki's response reassuring when he said that President Leghari would oversee the fulfillment of the reform objectives. Burki would have been a controversial figure under any circumstances, considering the nature of his role, but when it was later alleged that he had assured the IMF that there was no chance of the Benazir Bhutto administration being restored, he embarrassed the caretakers and the President and made his situation still more difficult.

In spite of the vagueness of the caretaker government's economic programme, President Leghari sustained his effort to purge the government of anyone judged to have compromised his position and damaged the national condition. On 18 November the President promulgated the Accountability Ordinance which created a Chief Ehtesab (accountability) Commissioner to scrutinize the activities of allegedly corrupt government officers and politicians, and to bring them to trial within two months of their indictment. The Law and Justice Minister said the ordinance would apply to all officers in Grade 20 and above, and include army officers serving in civil organizations. If found guilty under the law, a politician or public official could be imprisoned for seven years and be disqualified from future elected office for another five years; in the case of government career officers, conviction would mean dismissal from service.

Benazir immediately denounced the ordinance and claimed it did not apply to her, to which President Leghari replied that the lady was behaving like a historic French potentate. Leghari said that whatever he had done was in the best interests of the country, that the elections would be conducted on time, and that Benazir would be permitted to contest them. He added, 'if Mohtarma (Benazir) wins, she will be welcome to form the next government'. Rejecting Benazir's demand that he step down and allow an interim President to prepare for the February polls, Leghari declared he had done his constitutional duty and 'there is no reason for me to step down' (*Pakistan News Service*, 11, 1016, 21 November 1996). Benazir, however, was not ready to yield. Taking issue with the appointment of the caretaker governments in the provinces, she was especially critical of the appointment of her uncle, Mumtaz Ali Bhutto, who was named Chief Minister of Sindh province. Asserting that he was anti-Pakistan and the leader of a movement that aimed at breaking up the nation, she said:

> Nobody will accept results of elections by the caretakers, comprising elements who believe in a confederal system, secessionists, loan defaulters, and liars who have a vested interest in taking over the PPP and raising a king's party.

Unable to control her anger, Benazir added that 'the man I hand-picked to be the President, who called me sister, whom I considered as the third brother, stabbed me in the back' (*Dawn*, 26 November 1996).

Prime Minister Malik Meraj Khalid brushed aside Benazir's charges and countercharges, and pledged to ensure the accountability orders. Indeed, Mumtaz Ali Bhutto, along with the late G.M. Syed and the late Abdul Ghaffar Khan, had been acquitted of secessionist treason charges following Benazir's removal, and Meraj indicated that there were more genuine culprits who would be pursued by the caretaker government. Revealing that there were legions of politicians under scrutiny, and hence considerable pressure upon him to forego the proceedings, Meraj declared that the 'feudal lords' would not again be permitted to plunder the nation's wealth. 'We have marked hundreds of politicians and corrupt officials for investigation,' he said, adding that the process would be completed within sixty-five days and no one, no matter how powerful, would be spared (*Pakistan News Service*, 11, 1017, 3 December 1996). Following this announcement, on 30 December 1996 the caretaker government approved an amendment in the Representation of the People's Act 1976 giving special powers to eight election tribunals to debar loan defaulters and evaders of taxes and utility charges from contesting the general election. In addition, the government released a list identifying 1,538 declared candidates for public office or their relatives who fitted those categories. Meraj noted that after the amendment had become law through Presidential ordinance, the nomination papers of persons on the list would be rejected.

The ordinance, therefore, fell most heavily on the PPP and former members and officials of the Bhutto administration, and it was a reasonable prediction that Benazir's party would not fare well in the forthcoming polls. But more than simply sidelining the PPP, the caretakers, and notably President Leghari, set about reforming the government of Pakistan. The Defence, Establishment, and Law Minister, Shahid Hamid, announced in January 1997 that the government had categorically rejected suggestions that a 'state of emergency' be imposed in the country. Rather, the government had taken the initiative in creating the Council for Defence and National Security (CDNS) which included the President, the Prime Minister, the Defence Minister, the Interior Minister, the Chairman of the Joint Chiefs of Staff, the Chief of the Army Staff, Chief of the Naval Staff, and Chief of the Air Staff. The CDNS, it was said, represented a new and innovative approach to the Pakistan constitutional system which, it further explained, brought the nation abreast of current realities.

The Leghari argument discounting the continuing significance of the parliamentary constitution, and his call for recognition of the country's mixed executive-legislative realities, was dramatized in the formation of the CDNS. Although described as an advisory body, it was obvious the Council's creators wanted to think of it as a permanent institution. Indeed, President Leghari declared it to be his hope that the government elected in February would sustain the body and work closely with it in assuring the nation's future political stability and security.

Addressing the forthcoming elections, on 7 January 1997 Shahid Hamid, said that they would be conducted impartially, freely, and fairly, and that the CDNS would neither interfere with their conduct nor question the results. The purpose of the body, he said, was to guarantee democratic expression in the country, not to stifle it. Nevertheless, the reaction of the political parties to the formation of the Council was at best sceptical, and at worst, disapproving. The Central Committee of the Tehrik-i-Istiqlal decided it would not participate in the elections under the arrangements outlined by the caretaker government. Moreover, it complained that accountability tests had not separated the corrupt from the honest participants, and that in all likelihood, the same dishonest politicians would again win political office. The Jamaat-i-Islami also found the election procedures repugnant, and Jamaat leaders too agreed to sit out the election campaign. It was not immaterial that the Tehriq-i-Istiqlal did not expect to carry many votes, or that the Jamaat had repeatedly failed to attract the voters in successive elections. Their public reasons for not participating, therefore, were not nearly as significant as the understanding that another thrashing at the polls would do nothing positive for their organizations. Designed to make life miserable for sitting governments, both parties were content to confine their politics to street demonstrations and public orations.

The screening of election papers had nevertheless, proved to be a tedious procedure, and although many filing abuses had been uncovered, it was clear that not enough time remained to remove all the politicians with questionable records. Hakim Ali Zardari did not need disqualification. The father of Asif Zardari had been arrested earlier and then released, and his brief incarceration had drained all his prior enthusiasm for public office. On the other side of the divide, however, were the defaulters who had had their loans written off. These included the sitting Punjab Governor, Khwaja Tariq Rahim, and Sardar Jafar Leghari, the President's cousin, as well as several other members of the Leghari family. A number of Nawaz Sharif family members were similarly excused, as was the Speaker of the National Assembly, Syed Yousef Reza Gilani, former Speaker Gohar Ayub Khan, and a host of others. Observers could not be blamed if they detected double standards in the application of the disqualification and rejection orders.

While plans were moving forward for the holding of the elections, and the institutions safeguarding them were locked into place, Benazir was in court pleading for a reversal of the President's 5 November edict. Confronted with only a partial Supreme Court bench, the former Prime Minister questioned why, in all the history of Pakistan, she was the first to be denied bringing her complaint before the total body. When her request was rejected, she asserted that the Court had been enlisted in the plot to defame her. Moreover, the day before this proceeding, the Supreme Court had held that the Eighth Amendment was a valid part of the Constitution, and that Article 58(2)b, which conferred special powers on the President, was a proper and preferred deterrent to the imposition of martial law. Try as Benazir did, and her lawyers were aggressively committed to pressing the case against the President's powers, there would be no turning back the clock. Benazir and her supporters, therefore, had every reason to believe that Leghari had been won over by the higher military.

Reflecting on the formation of the Council for Defence and National Security, it was the opposition's belief that the President had so isolated himself that he could not escape dependence on the civil-military bureaucracy. The CDNS, in effect, reinforced and legitimized the extraordinary powers of the President. It also aimed at institutionalizing a permanent role for the armed forces in the political life of the nation. Ziaul Haq had sought a permanent place for the military in Pakistan's political life, and it was no doubt with some bewilderment that Leghari should be the one to realize that objective. Nevertheless, by bringing the President, Prime Minister, and other state functionaries into direct and continuing association with the country's formal and principal security and intelligence branches, technically all the forces of government would be prepared to deal with crisis situations before they festered and spread. Supporters argued that if the nation was ever to find the political stability needed for its growth and development, all the elements of government had to work in concert. Asserting that the neutrality of the armed forces would not be compromised by the operations of the CDNS, Minister Shahid Hamid nevertheless explained that twenty-six per cent of the country's budget went annually for the maintenance of the defence services, and he therefore questioned why the armed forces should not be an intrinsic part of the governance equation. The Defence Minister decried those who called the CDNS a supraconstitutional body, and noted that it had been formed under Article 90 and Article 99 of the Constitution, which empowered the President to establish the rules of business for the operation of the federation.

Critics of the Council persisted, however, and the politicians received some assistance from the Human Rights Commission of Pakistan (HRCP) when its Director, I.A. Rehman, criticized the formation of the body and demanded that it be dissolved. Rehman questioned the authority of the President to impose a non-elected institution on the constitutional system. Providing the CDNS with the power to impose tariffs on gasoline, petroleum products, and even electricity without the sanction of Parliament, he said, was totally unacceptable. Speaking for the Pakistani Non-Governmental Organizations (NGOs), Director Rehman cited their efforts at relieving the burden of the unspoken-for masses, and suggested that an institution like the CDNS should be concerned with similar matters, while leaving the issue of public policy to the country's elected officials. Subsequent to the HRCP's complaint, a division bench of the

Lahore High Court, chaired by the Chief Justice, issued notice to the caretaker government of a challenge to the formation of the Council for Defence and National Security. The petition, which had been filed by a Lahore advocate, called upon the High Court to declare the CDNS unconstitutional, and argued that the President's actions, if allowed to stand, 'destroyed the basic structure of the Constitution' (*Dawn* Wire Service, 16 January 1997).

Taking another approach to the question, two PPP Senators from Sindh appealed to Air Marshal Farooq Feroz Khan, Chairman of the Joint Chiefs of Staff Committee, and a member of the CDNS, to demand that President Leghari be compelled to submit himself to an accountability test. The Senators cited loans to the D.G. Khan Woollen Textile Mills, owned by President Leghari's cousin and son, which were written-off just two days after the sacking of the Benazir government. The appeal also cited the President's land deal with the Mehran Bank, the spending of huge sums of money from the contingency fund, and the assistance he provided to his brother-in-law, who was trying to sell a defunct BCCI Pakistan branch bank, in which he was a partner, to a Gulf group. The charges listed other questionable financial transactions involving Leghari, but their real purpose was to force his resignation. Stating that the President was behind a 'false and malicious' campaign to discredit the PPP, they questioned how the forthcoming elections could be conducted freely, fairly, and impartially if they were held under the auspices of a dishonest politician.

With charges and countercharges the order of the day, the judiciary had more than its share of responsibility in sustaining national decorum. Confronted with three separate petitions challenging the 5 November 1996 dissolution order, the Supreme Court decided to combine them so that a ruling could be produced before the scheduled elections on 3 February. Benazir, however, was not content with that arrangement, and she filed still another petition alleging that the caretaker Prime Minister and his adviser on finance had assured the IMF, a foreign body, that the Supreme Court would not rule in favour of the petitioners, and hence would not restore the dissolved National Assembly or return her government to power. Benazir's lawyers questioned how the finance adviser, Shahid Javed Burki, could offer such assurances without the Supreme Court itself being compromised. The proceedings appeared to hinge on the accuracy of the newspaper accounts reporting what Burki had said in a Karachi seminar. For his part, Burki insisted that he made no such statement, or at best, that his words were misconstrued. The Court, however, was called upon to sort out the allegations from the facts, and the knowledge that it, too, had been implicated did not make its task any easier.

Considering that an election campaign was under way, the country's essential focus appeared to be not on the choice of candidates, but on the drama surrounding the President and the caretaker government. Pakistanis were clearly inundated by events and issues that no rational citizen was capable of understanding or inclined to sort out. The sacking of the Benazir administration had failed to stir the nation, and the events following that dramatic event only added to the general sense of drift and confusion felt by the public. By this time, the average, reasonably attentive citizen had lost not only faith, but also interest, in the political scene. With accountability charges flying everywhere, and with no luminary, let alone lesser light, free from the taint of corruption, the public saw nothing in the candidates that distinguished one from the other. Moreover, the austerity measures introduced by the Meraj Khalid Government cut deep into the reserves of the nation's middle and lower classes, and their concerns for their general security, in what they concluded was a largely lawless society, were heightened by the economic pressures caused by out-of-control inflation and ever higher unemployment. Imran Khan did what he could to arouse a disconsolate electorate in a letter to the President which was published in the nation's Press on 27 January. The Tehrik-e-Insaaf leader demanded the immediate resignation of President Farooq Leghari, accusing him of being party to an 'unholy troika of corruption, nepotism, and opportunism' (*Dawn*, 28 January 1997). Reading like a campaign platform, the letter contributed something to the political debate, but it registered zero impact on the Pakistani voter.

Determined to ignore both the personal attacks of the anti-government politicians and the apathy of the public, the administration moved closer to the date set for the national election, and announced several amendments to the Representation of the People Act, 1976. The amendments empowered an election tribunal to hold in abeyance the results of an election where a candidate whose accountability had not yet been judged had been returned to the Assembly. Anticipating that loan defaulters and tax and utility fee evaders would have slipped through the disqualification screening process, the government indicated that it was determined to commence the new National Assembly with members who had all passed the test of accountability. In the meantime, the election campaign was reaching a crescendo, with a feeble and almost robot-like Nusrat Bhutto appearing on a platform in support of her daughter's and her own candidacy, and with the MQM and the renegade PPP faction of the late Murtaza Bhutto agreeing not to compete with one another in the same constituency.

The last obstacle to the holding of the elections was swept aside on 29 January, when the Supreme Court ruled against Benazir Bhutto's petition. The Court, ruling in favour of the President, cited the Chief Executive's constitutional powers to dissolve the National Assembly, and noted that the Justices were duty-bound to accept the judgement of the President as well as to defer to him. The President had cited the crisis situation in the country, and the use of his special powers in the interests of national security, and the Court found no reason to deny his judgement or action. This final ruling in favour of the President meant that the elections could proceed on schedule. Addressing the nation on the eve of the elections, the President voiced the hope that the new government would not only complete its full term, but would provide the nation with much-needed political stability and economic continuity. Noting that he had kept his promise to hold new elections within ninety days of the previous government's dissolution, President Leghari said:

If I had been a dictator intent upon furthering personal ambitions or settling scores, I might have sought ways to transform ninety days into two years or would have tried to extend the time-frame and used the state apparatus to knock on doors after midnight, put people into prison, and exploit state witnesses and approvers to convict political opponents. But I have done no such thing' (*Dawn*, 3 February 1997).

The 1997 Elections

Pre-election projections hinted at a low voter turn-out, and few were surprised when that forecast proved correct. Those casting ballots in 1997 were significantly fewer than in 1993, thus illustrating the lack of citizen interest in the contest. The percentage of eligible voters casting ballots was estimated at about thirty, with the overwhelming number showing a preference for Nawaz Sharif's Pakistan Muslim League. By contrast, the PPP was trounced, winning only seventeen seats in the National Assembly and two in the Punjab. Independent candidates, in a number of instances, made a better showing than the party of the Bhuttos, but Imran Khan's Tehrik-e-Insaaf failed to win a single constituency in either the National or Provincial Assemblies. In the Punjab, former Chief Ministers Wattoo and Nakai were defeated, as was Mohammad Haneef Ramay. In fact, all the former PPP and PML(Junejo) ministers, advisers, parliamentary secretaries, and chairmen of Punjab Assembly standing committees, were routed. But the PPP was wiped out in Lahore, Faisalabad, Rawalpindi, Multan, Sarghoda, Bahawalpur, Sahiwal, and Sheikhupura, as well as in the party's traditional rural strongholds in the southern and central regions of the province. By contrast, the PML of Nawaz Sharif won all the seats allotted to the metropolitan and urban areas of the Punjab. The PML was second best in the NWFP, winning a little more than half the seats obtained by the Awami National Party of Wali Khan. But the close association between Nawaz Sharif and the frontier leader pointed to their co-operation in forming a coalition government. Balochistan, however, was another matter. The Balochistan National Party and the Jamhoori Watan Party emerged as the two largest vote-getters in the province, and these parties demonstrated sufficient capacity to form the new government. The Nawaz group could muster only five successes, some three less than the PML achieved in the 1993 polls. By contrast, the PPP managed only one victory in Balochistan. Even in Sindh, the PPP had a difficult time maintaining a significant presence, and was unable to overcome the combination of an MQM and PML victory.

Nawaz Sharif's PML was credited with having amassed two-thirds of the total vote, not only enough to claim a mandate, but with a majority that virtually neutralized the official actions of the PPP. The election results were reminiscent of the provincial elections in East Bengal in 1954, when a formidable Muslim League was demolished by a United Front led by Fazlul Huq and H.S. Suhrawardy. That defeat marked the demise of the original Muslim League, not only in the province, but throughout the country. Although it was too early to count the PPP out of the political game, its voice in the legislatures had been significantly reduced, and it was doubtful that the party would be able to block the policies of the PML government.

The PPP rout was attributed to low voter turnout, a phenomenon linked more to voter disgust with the PPP than approval for the PML. According to observers, the elections were conducted fairly, and although there was confusion in some constituencies over proper female names, PPP assertions of wide-scale rigging were difficult to entertain. On the other hand, the massive mandate accorded the PML and its leader, Nawaz Sharif, raised interesting prospects about the course the new government would follow.

Benazir was surprisingly gracious, if not realistic, in the first rush following her humiliating defeat. Although she insisted that the balloting had been 'engineered' and her defeat pre-arranged, she noted it would be pointless to pursue the matter. Having been chastened by events, not the least of which were two ousters by two different Presidents, Benazir had finally decided it was time to make peace with her rival politicians and focus attention on the country's institutions which were so heavily tilted in favour of the country's Chief Executive. What purpose, she asked, would be served by agitating for justice and in the end only causing the dissolution of still another National Assembly? She acknowledged that the people of Pakistan had grown weary of the political game and had developed a special distaste for all the politicians. Sustained political infighting would only do more damage to the constitutional system, and no doubt, open the way for even deeper inroads by civil-military power brokers.

> For better or worse, Nawaz Sharif and the PML have been given charge of this country. They have been...given a blank cheque to re-write the Constitution. I wish Mian Nawaz Sharif good luck' (*Dawn*, 5 February 1997).

Asserting that it was time to break the 'vicious circle,' Benazir declared she would redefine her role and begin the process of building a loyal opposition.

Having analyzed the election results, Benazir had come to the conclusion that President Leghari and the Council for Defence and National Security had provided Nawaz Sharif with far more leverage than even they had intended. Already having discounted the parliamentary system, the President and higher civil-military complex anticipated sustaining their domination of the political process after the elections. Nawaz Sharif's two-thirds majority, however, had given the Prime Minister-elect a popular mandate that was aimed at reviving the parliamentary experience. Nawaz had already registered considerable discomfort with a super council that did not answer to the people. Nor were Farooq Leghari and Nawaz Sharif intimate associates. The President had been a pivotal actor in laying the groundwork for Nawaz Sharif's return to high office, but the two men had yet to prove they could work together, let alone collectively manage the nation's business.

Benazir's assertion, that Nawaz would have to tackle the problem posed by the Eighth Amendment, was not lost on the new Prime Minister. The country could not continue with two powerful figures, the one an acknowledged, popularly-elected leader, and the other an extension of the country's colonial experience. Moreover, the matter of who governs Pakistan would determine how the nation's many crises would be handled in the future.

Nawaz Sharif basked in the glow of an epoch-making return to political power. Always the determined politician, and now even more convinced of the rightness of his ideas, he was quick to establish his personal bona fides as Pakistan's major political personality. For the moment seemingly oblivious to the near presence of the President and the Council for Defence and National Security to which he had earlier agreed to give his full support, Nawaz Sharif spoke of his commitment to normalizing relations with India, as well as the need to review the policies that had contributed to the growth of the fundamentalist Taliban Movement that now dominated so much of Afghanistan.

Nawaz Sharif took note of the economic programme constructed by Shahid Javed Burki, and, while not prepared to display sharp differences with the caretaker government's financial adviser, he nevertheless believed that his government would do best by striking out on its own. Indeed, the Prime Minister-elect declared that he had his own views and plans for the revitalization of the economy. Echoing Burki, he acknowledged the need to honour international commitments and to continue those programmes that came within the national interest, but he was also eager to cite his own reform package, which stressed rationalizing the tax system, drastically cutting government expenditures, and stimulating the investment climate. Tax holidays and the removal of foreign exchange restrictions were some of the schemes needed to offer incentives to the business community, he said. Responding to a question about the future of the Council for Defence and National Security, Nawaz Sharif declared that the body had not been institutionalized, and that it would be necessary to examine its positive and negative aspects before concluding whether it should be retained or scrapped. By the same token, Nawaz Sharif believed that the Eighth Amendment power of the President was a matter for the new National Assembly to examine, and he intended to ask the legislature to determine its fate.

It was not only Benazir who cautioned Nawaz Sharif to beware of the President's extraordinary powers and his recently-assembled council of military associates. Although the United States government confined itself to diplomatic protocol, *The New York Times*, in a lead editorial, urged Nawaz Sharif to 'abolish' the newly created Council for Defence and National Security. Arguing that the new Prime Minister's principal challenge arose not from a chastened Benazir Bhutto, but from the military establishment that had long dominated Pakistani politics, the newspaper did not believe Pakistan would establish the necessary civilian institutions if the army and its allied intelligence services, as well as the clerics and wealthy feudal landlord families, continued to exert unusual influence in the making of public policy.

But such 'foreign intervention' only made Nawaz Sharif's. tasks more difficult. Pakistani politics were a function of the country's internal dynamics, and there was no simple method of reversing a course that was deeply rooted in the nation's history. On 6 February the Lahore High Court answered the complaint registered by those challenging the formation of the Council for Defence and National Security, and ruled that it was indeed constitutional. The court noted that:

> The federal government is well within the amplitude of its executive powers to set up an advisory council like the CDNS for obtaining advice on defence, security and incidental matters under Article 97 read with items 1, 58 and 59 of the Federal Legislative List' (*Dawn*, 7 February 1997).

The writ petitions were dismissed, but the High Court did not stop there. It ruled as unacceptable the government's claim that the Eighth Amendment had transformed Pakistan's government from a parliamentary into a mixture of presidential and parliamentary systems. 'The system remains parliamentary as consistently held by the Supreme Court because it provides for the supremacy of the Parliament.' Finally, the Court stated that matters of defence and security should be brought before the appropriate forum, namely the parliament and not the judiciary.

The Lahore High Court ruling clarified some matters but raised anew the fundamental questions of where political power actually rested. It would remain for the principals to sort out their respective interpretations as to who governs and who rules, who commands and who determines the nation's future. The elections of 1997 had set the scene for yet another confrontation between the forces of history and those seeking to rewrite it.

The New Administration

With the PPP leadership trying to make the most of a difficult situation, its charges of gross rigging of the elections were not unexpected. Moreover, the Election Commission did reverse the results of a few constituencies, providing the PPP with a small bit of solace. But the defeated party was forced to face the humiliation of its enormous loss and to acknowledge the reality that so many of its workers had abandoned the organization. Benazir stated her willingness to resign from the leadership of the party, but agreed to remain in place only after the pleadings of her chief associates. Moreover, try as she did to make alliance with the MQM in Sindh, she did not succeed, and Nawaz Sharif proudly revealed the formation of a coalition between the PML and the MQM. Most significant was Altaf Hussain's declaration of support for the Nawaz Sharif administration. In return for MQM assistance in the National Assembly and in Sindh province, however, Nawaz Sharif pledged his government to an investigation of the killings in Karachi that had taken so many *mohajir* lives. More immediately, the success of the PML in Punjab, the frontier provinces, as well as in Sindh, compelled Benazir to withdraw the names of her party's candidates for high positions in the National Assembly. On 16 February, therefore, Illahi Bakhsh Soomro was unanimously elected Speaker of the National Assembly, and his colleague Chaudhry Jaffer Iqbal was made Deputy Speaker. In a gracious moment, Nawaz Sharif, joined by Gohar Ayub Khan, walked to Begum Nusrat Bhutto's and Benazir Bhutto's seats in the House and officially expressed their appreciation for allowing the election to proceed without opposition.

The scene in the chamber was remarkable for its cordiality when Nawaz Sharif was sworn in as Pakistan's Prime Minister. All the major participants thereupon addressed the need for co-operation and pledged their adherence to the principles of parliamentary order and democracy. The outgoing Speaker cited the mandate given Nawaz Sharif and his PML by the people, and called for a government that must complete its full term. Addressing the needs of the people of Pakistan, the politicians were urged to put aside their partisan manoeuvring and work toward the common objective of national reconstruction. Special attention was focused on the need for accountability checks at all levels, and the cleansing of the body politic, it was intimated, must begin with the people's representatives. Even Benazir noted that Nawaz Sharif had received broader electoral support than any leader before him, and she called upon the new Prime Minister to aggressively pursue accountability investigations and to root out the 'wrongdoers' wherever they may be found. In her new role as opposition leader, Benazir again emphasized the need to save the parliamentary system, and she warned those who would listen to her words that 'anti-democracy' forces had damaged the parliament and that only the newly-elected officials could save it.

On 18 February, as required by Clause 3 of Article 91 of the Constitution, Nawaz Sharif sought and received a vote of confidence from the National Assembly, and on that same day declared that his government would not tolerate even a hint of corruption from among its members. Pledging himself to clean up the political system, from the lower courts and police stations to the highest positions in government, the Prime Minister gave himself no more than five months to reclaim the honour of the public services and of those whose responsibility it was to maintain law and order. Declaring that the elections were as fair as might be expected in a developing country, Prime Minister Nawaz Sharif attributed the PPP loss to its 'undemocratic policies', and said that he would not allow his party to commit the same error. For the first time, Nawaz Sharif admitted that his party's success in Sindh, Balochistan, and the NWFP, as well as his veritable landslide in Punjab, was a major surprise. Seemingly humbled by his popular mandate, he declared it his intention to keep faith with the people and to govern the nation with a lean, small, and accomplished federal cabinet. Nawaz Sharif appeared to imply that political patronage was a thing of the past. Even the Prime Minister's staunchest critics acknowledged that Mian Nawaz Sharif had matured since he last held the reins of government, but no one doubted that Pakistan was paused at a crossroads, and that the fateful next steps, those that would lead the nation into the twenty-first century, were yet to be taken.

CHAPTER 13

THE MEANING OF HISTORY

History is fickle. A human contrivance, it draws its importance from the mortal human beings who want so much to understand the nature of their existence, their purpose in a limited span of time, and their connections with a buried past and a never realized future. History is meaningless in the absence of human industry, but it is more a reflection of the human mind than the material world of life forms. Life, in all its aspects, would continue without history, but human life loses its substance without the signposts that mark the trail of human evolution and adaptation. The stages of history describe the increments of human experience on an ever shrinking earth, but it is the individual actors of historic legend that continue to fascinate and provoke interest long after they have passed from the world of the living. History, after all, is a summing up; it is the interpreted record of particular events, fashioned by observers who may or may not be intimate with their subject, who may or may not be participants in the life experience they describe, who may or may not be able to distance themselves from the story they choose to tell. That there can never be true history, that is, that no historian can ever reveal more than a glimpse into the past, explains why history is forever being written and rewritten. The volumes that address a particular moment, an event, a personality, address the human yearning for explanation long after the moment, the event, the personality, have passed from the scene. Ultimately, history is the cumulative record, a glance back to where we were before we arrived at where we are. And tomorrow, the glance back will be to today, and so it will be tomorrow, and in all tomorrows.

The Elements of the Pakistan Paradigm

By what standard does one judge the political history of Pakistan in the twentieth century? Fifty years is but a moment in the time of states—or is it? The Soviet Union was one of the two most prominent of the world's states when Pakistan achieved independence—but fifty years later it is hardly more than a memory, a virtual footnote to history. Read in such context, fifty years is not a flash of light or the blink of an eye. Fifty years of human events cannot be passed over so casually that we fail to grasp the meaning of the life experience and its manifestation in the contemporary nation-state. And perhaps that is one key to the conundrum that draws our attention.

The world of the twenty-first century will increasingly be ever more so the world of nation-states. By contrast, when the twentieth century began, nation-states were few in number and, except for the United States, the earth was blanketed by empires and their colonies. Empires had their roots in traditions and conventions that described defined status and purpose, and the systems they imposed were not very far from the lifeways of the colonial people they victimized. Alien rule was rule from a point beyond the reach of the colonized, but it was none the less, predictable and readily grasped by those long versed in superior-inferior relationships. Empires enjoyed exceptional staying power, in major part because the many who suffered the rule of the few acknowledged the uneven juxtaposition of the others' strength and their weakness. Moreover, time was measured differently in that now distant age. The lifetime of imperial states was read not in years and months and days, but in dynasties and epochs, and little if any significance was given to periods connecting generations to one another.

Nation-states are the inevitable result of collapsed empires. Nation-states were spawned in the popular revolutions that challenged and defeated aristocratic and alien rule. Nation-states are vehicles for the realization of mass politics. Self-government, the inherent right of a citizenry to choose its leaders, to demand their accountability, and to establish the limits of their prerogatives, lies at the heart of the process defined as constitutionalism. Limited powers, contractual responsibilities, and fundamental guarantees frame the relationship between the governors and the governed. Moreover, law under-girds the functions of the nation-state. No one is above the law, and ignorance of the law is no excuse for breaking it. But as law applies to all, and justice is deemed to be blind, the procedures whereby law is defined and imposed are given as much weight as the law itself. Due process is what ensures that the law will be fair and equitable, that it will not be used arbitrarily, and that the individual's rights are paramount.

The nation-state is all these things and more. It is the safeguarding of its weakest members, the sanctity of the pluralist community, and above all, it is the creation of a civil society. The world of empires has become the world of nation-states, but whereas the former were practical undertakings and relatively simple to comprehend, the latter are more abstract, theoretical, and burdened by complexity. Nation-states are idealized, not realized, political expressions, and few if any contemporary nation-states conform to the expectations of their proponents. Becoming a nation-state and being a nation-state are not similar occurrences. Moreover, the spread of the nation-state to every sector of the planet reveals more about its appeal than its fruition. Nation-states, therefore, remain goals that may never be reached. Like democracy itself, the nation-state is more a quest than a reality.

How then is one to think of Pakistan as a nation-state? Pakistan was removed from the womb of one of the most successful imperial systems in human experience, but it began its life in an ambience totally out of phase with its incubation. Born from an imperial mother, Pakistan was not genetically structured for the world of republics and federations that dominated the thinking of the post-World War II era. A clone of a yet untested species, its surrogate birth provided little if any nurturing, and virtually no guidance. Given existence as a nation-state, Pakistan was, from the beginning, the antithesis of such expression. The embryonic origins of the new entity were rooted in Islamic tradition, but no other sovereign Muslim-dominant state of that period, save perhaps the Republic of Turkey, centred its performance on nation-building. The other self-governing and quasi-self-governing Muslim states of the immediate post-World War II condition were replications of older monarchical models, and their performance offered nothing by way of advice or example to fledgling Pakistan. More significantly, however, Pakistan was the product of a multiple birth. Connected to its Indian sibling during the sequence of gestation, the separation of the two abstractions was manifested in a transfer of power that conferred individual identities, but failed to ensure the positive interaction of the two offspring.

Pakistan was the consequence of a colonial dispensation made possible by two world wars and by the resolute members of a Muslim League movement who, having failed to receive adequate assurance from the majority community that their commingling was a feasible option, insisted on the right to determine an individual future. The actual division of the subcontinent, however, was the work of the retreating imperial mentor, and its less than evenhanded treatment of the partition arrangements, instead of ameliorating the transition, exaggerated the fears and intensified the bitterness of those who would be forever unreconciled to the proceedings. Pakistan was as inchoate as it was complex. Formed from two territorial segments that were separated from each other by vast distances, the units were even more distant from one another in culture and history. Except for their shared religious experience, the two geographic regions that became Pakistan in August 1947 had few assets with which to bridge their great divide.

More demanding of attention at the time, however, was the issue of Kashmir. A natural extension of the northern areas of the new Pakistan, only the withdrawing British Raj can explain why the territory was left in such an ambiguous state. But Britain has long since disclaimed any responsibility for the Kashmir conflict that consumed Pakistani and Indian forces in the days immediately following their attainment of independence. Kashmir was not another colonial dispensation, but rather an imperial confirmation. The inclination of the colonial Raj to restore the powers extracted earlier from the Indian princes made greater sense than the exercise creating two dominions, albeit two nation-states. And although the former colonial authority would have been content with an independent kingdom in the mountain state, they also made certain the region would remain outside the Pakistan camp if the Hindu monarch was unable to perpetuate his rule.

But while India and Pakistan clashed over Kashmir, there were no conflicts between the two states when communal violence took its heavy toll in Pakistan and India proper. The slaughter of the innocent on both sides of the great divide set in train a mass exodus from both India and Pakistan. But the plight of the hapless millions from central India and Pakistan did not spark the same military reaction that occurred in Kashmir. The fact that Kashmir became a matter of cross-border interest, while the sufferings of millions of refugees were perceived as domestic problems, illustrates the state-centric character of the new political entities. Territorial, not human, questions drew the attention of the new governments. Thus, when limited strategic interests, not collective regional concerns, established the limits of co-operation and accommodation, the two nation-states were predestined to emphasize the negative features of their relationship.

These early developments influenced Pakistan's political behaviour, and the country never escaped the legacy of its colonial past. Had Pakistan chosen monarchy instead of the inclusive nation-state, it would have been a more appropriate choice. Had the predominantly Muslim nation chosen theocracy in fashioning its political system, that too would have been more in keeping with the nation's exclusive self-image. The Muslim League leaders, however, the persons most responsible for the creation of Pakistan, rejected the distant as well as the most recent past. Democracy, not autocracy, was the tenor of the post-World War II period, and nations justified their demand for self-determination in the firm belief that the opportunity for self-government demanded distinguishing between the power of the colonial few and the aspirations of the popular masses. By the same token, English-schooled Muslim Leaguers gave substance to the Muslim dream of a reconstituted political order within the subcontinent, but few among them entertained a system of government that measured up to fundamentalist demands.

Pakistan, therefore, was conceived and given substance as a secular state, guided by parliamentary practices, and conversant with the rule of man-made law. Mohammad Ali Jinnah articulated this choice of political experience, but the historic record reveals that even his closest associates, in spite of their intimacy and genuine commitment, never fully grasped his full intention. Jinnah created Pakistan, but he did not transform it into a nation-state.

The Pakistan idea and the Pakistan reality could never be reconciled. The idea was a dream sequence in which the Muslims of South Asia would find satisfaction and fulfilment in a secular, democratic experience. The reality was the full awareness that Pakistan would be carved out of regions that were then, and for centuries had been, Muslim-dominant and were, in some ways, already self-governing. The people who were transformed into Pakistanis in 1947 did not experience their liberation, but rather, their entrapment. While the more independent peoples of the north-western regions of the subcontinent were motivated to hasten the departure of the Europeans, Pakistan was the consequence of a legal act, not a battlefield victory. Moreover, legal authority was conferred upon those who were not, and had never been, rulers. Because they were made the recipients of the 'legitimate' symbols of power did not mean their legitimacy superseded that of long-established local authorities. Kinship, tribal, filial, and landed interests wove the fabric of traditional leadership and governance in the different regions of western Pakistan, and from their perspective, one alien intruder had replaced another. In the eastern territory, the conditions were different but the inevitable outcome was not dissimilar. In East Bengal, a small urban intelligentsia and Muslim commercial class assumed the principal leadership roles following the flight of the Hindu landlords to India. The Muslim League, which had its origin in Dhaka, became the vehicle of their expression and the mechanism of their authority, but here too, the monopolizers of power were forced to test their credentials against those who spoke for the vast majority that inhabited the province's rural hinterland.

Considering the dissatisfaction pervading the lands of western Pakistan in making the Muslim League the sole agent of the subcontinent's Muslim population, the war in Kashmir was transformed into a rallying cry for the party and its followers. And although Kashmir was never liberated, it nevertheless provided a justification for the consolidation of the nation. The Muslims of western Pakistan were galvanized by the Kashmir struggle. The mountain state was made synonymous with the Pakistan nation, and although Pakistan addressed its essential unity, it could never be whole in the absence of Kashmir. Pakistan, in effect, remained an ongoing quest.

Thus the meaning of Pakistan was altered at the moment of independence by the Kashmir dispute. With attention riveted on the northernmost region of the subcontinent, the secular conception of Pakistan was sacrificed for another representing its spiritual *raison d'être*. This reversal in fortunes and direction was unintended by Pakistan's founding fathers, and especially by Mohammad Ali Jinnah. Not only did Pakistan acquire a natural and permanent enemy in its rival sibling, but the confrontation between the two offspring elevated Muslim-Hindu differences and, given the stirring of high emotions, the way was opened for those opposed to the secular state to enter the political arena.

'Islam in danger' was the popular strategy motivating the Pakistan Movement, and the unresolved contest with India over Kashmir guaranteed the perpetuation of that fear. Pakistan's leaders emerged from the periphery to question the hegemonic role of those at the centre, and neither the periphery nor the centre could avoid the challenge made manifest by Hindu India's insistence on dominating Kashmir. In the psyche of the Muslim Pakistani was the strengthened belief that his tryst with destiny was somehow a contemporary version of the biblical story that pitted Cain against Abel.

Jinnah's death so soon after the transfer of power collapsed the Muslim League centre, and opened the floodgates to the many lesser actors on the fringe of the party, or totally outside it. Jinnah, not the Muslim League, represented Pakistan;

Jinnah, not the Muslim League, created Pakistan. In the absence of the Great Leader, Jinnah's disciples were either powerless or persuaded not to press the goals that he had envisaged for the new nation. The Muslim League sought to redefine itself in the years that followed, and indeed, the Objectives Resolution was supposed to frame the future Pakistan. But the difficulty encountered in attempting to do justice to the nation-state, while at the same time honouring the Pakistani citizen's commitment to his religious tradition, intensified the controversy between those more inclined to separate religion from politics, and those who believed the two were inextricably intertwined. The more sophisticated members of the Muslim League, therefore, were encouraged to entertain the views of their more tradition-oriented members, and the latter also opened the path for the country's religious leaders to enter the debate.

The strenuous efforts and the time consumed in the attempt to draft a suitable and proper constitution, describe the shift of power from the centre to the periphery, and the emergence of leaders with questionable political credentials. The more conservative and orthodox leaders, in spite of their limited constituencies, had accrued the leverage needed to influence the decision that denied a cardinal feature of the nation-state, i.e., that sovereignty must reside in the people. Instead, there was a reaffirmation of faith, that sovereignty belonged to God alone, and that mortal men merely held it as a trust. Clearly, this orthodox concept of sovereignty meant that Pakistan could not be a nation-state, nor would it be one that limited the powers of government. Indeed, this interpretation made it virtually impossible for Pakistanis to choose their leaders, let alone restrict their powers. The Muslim League definition of sovereignty in effect assured the perpetuation of the subcontinent's authoritarian experience. Sovereignty, that is, the supreme power over subjects and citizens, remained a monopoly of entrenched authority. Constitution-writing, therefore, became a surrealistic experience wherein the traditional sources of power and privilege endeavoured to produce a document that enhanced, rather than diminished, their prerogatives.

More significantly, viceregalism was sustained, and with it, personality politics took precedence over institution-building. In the absence of a viable political centre, the competition between the provinces was exaggerated, and although the Kashmir question continued to fuel Muslim sentiment, no leader emerged to remind the nation that Punjabis and Bengalis were also brothers. Instead, inter-provincial and west-east controversy was allowed to swirl around the matter of separate or joint electorates, a meaningless conflict in the aftermath of independence, but nevertheless a potent issue for those searching for the lost legitimacy of the Muslim League. The struggle between the centre and the periphery, and among the major provinces, made a mockery of Muslim League claims and actions. And no longer standing for anything, the party that had received the transfer of power was easily manoeuvred to the sidelines by the permanent services. Pakistan's failure in contemporary nation-building, tragically dramatized by the loss of East Pakistan, meant that the country's political experiment would remain suspended in time. Pakistan would be sustained in the condition of a classic administrative state.

Whither Pakistan?

Pakistanis deserve better. A people of significant accomplish-ment and promise, the Pakistani nation has passed from crisis to crisis and been subjected to horrors to which a proud and honourable people should never have been exposed. The problem for Pakistanis appears not to be in their stars, but in their ill-defined presence as a nation-state. The people of Pakistan cry out for honesty and integrity, but those cries have never been answered affirmatively, nor are they likely to be answered so long as the population remains divided between the educated few and the illiterate masses. The vast majority of Pakistanis are a gullible congeries of factions, clans, and tribes, and their manipulation by traditional, as well as contemporary, powerbrokers remains the central focus of the political experience. The pleas of the educated few for more balanced government, for a share of the decision-making process, do not go unnoticed, but they are no match for the machinations of entrenched elites.

Educated Pakistanis must confront the realities of their world. The country is not a nation-state, and it will be some decades yet before such a goal is brought within reach. Too much time has been lost, and too many resources squandered in the attempt to fashion a nation-state from the social milieu that makes up the country. Better it would be if the more sophisticated members of the Pakistan experience acknowledged that while Ayub Khan may not have got it right, his reaching out to the faceless masses was not an idle gesture. Government clearly is not the answer when it comes to bridging the great divide between the modern and traditional folk who populate this state. If Pakistan is to survive and flourish, and there is every indication of the resiliency of this country, it will be because the different worlds of Pakistan will draw closer together. Before Pakistan can achieve coherency, before it can assume the role of a nation-state, it will have to construct a civil society. The absence of such a condition, and it is a condition, not a structure, can only perpetuate the turmoil that government is unable to address.

Viceregalism can preserve Pakistan, but it will not sustain it. Government will remain intimidating, but it will also be a weak government, one that cannot address the fundamental needs of Pakistani society. Pakistanis must reach out to one another, interact with each other, and assist one another in meeting the demands of the modern world. The armed forces are not the answer to the Pakistan dilemma. Nuclear weapons may deter Pakistan's aggressive neighbour, but they cannot provide the nation with the guidance it requires in bridging complex social and psychological differences. Pakistanis will succeed in their quest to create a haven for the Muslims of South Asia only when they transcend their sectarian and regional distinctions and begin to see the merit in their Islamic diversity. Pakistan will survive only if the people who inhabit the region believe they are a community, that, in spite of their peculiar diversity, they are, after all, one people.

PUBLICATIONS CITED AND CONSULTED

Abbott, F. (1966), 'Pakistan and the Secular State', D.Smith, (ed.), *South Asian Politics and Religion* (pp.352-70), Princeton, NJ: Princeton University Press.

Abbott, F. (1968), *Islam, Critical Essays in Social Anthropology and Pakistan*, Ithaca, NY: Cornell University Press.

Adams, J. (1966), 'The Ideology of Mawlana Maududi', D. Smith. (ed.), *South Asian Politics and Religion* (pp.371-97), Princeton, NJ: Princeton University Press.

Afzal, M.(1976), *Political Parties in Pakistan, 1947-1958*, Islamabad: National Commission on Historical and Cultural Research.

Ahmad, A. (1964), *Islamic Modernism in India and Pakistan, 1857-1964*, New York, NY: Oxford University Press.

Ahmad, A. (1969), *An Intellectual History of Islam in India,* Chicago: Aldine.

Ahmad, A.S. (1976), *Millennium and Charisma among Pathans: A Critical Essay in Social Anthropology,* London: Routledge & Kegan Paul.

Ahmad, A.S. (1980), *Pakhtun Economy and Society: Traditional Structure and Economic Development in a Tribal Society*, London: Routledge & Kegan Paul.

Ahmad, A.S. (1986), *Pakistan Society: Islam, Ethnicity, and Leadership*, New York: Oxford.

Ahmad, J. (ed.), (1952), *Some Recent Speeches and Writings of Mr. Jinnah*, Lahore: Ashraf.

Ahmad, M. (1963), *Government and Politics in Pakistan*, New York, NY: Praeger.

Ahmad, M. (1964), *The Civil Servant in Pakistan*, Karachi: Oxford University Press.

Ahmad, M. (ed.), (1980), *Contemporary Pakistan: Politics, Economy, and Society*, Durham, North Carolina Academic Press.

Ahmad, M. (ed.), (1988), *The Politics of Islamic Revivalism*, Bloomington: Indiana University Press.

Ahmad, M.B.M. (1959), *Ahmadiyyat*, Rabwah: Tahrik-i-Jadid Ahmadiyya Pakistan.

Ahmad, M. (1960), *My Chief*, Lahore: Longmans, Green and Company.

Ahmad, M. (1985), *Pakistan at the Crossroads*, Karachi: Royal Book Company.

Ahmad, S.N. (1985), *From Martial Law to Martial Law: Politics in the Punjab, 1919-1958*, Boulder, Colo: Westview Press.

Akram, Muhammad (1977), *Martial Law Proclamation 1977 and Laws*, Lahore: Lahore Law Times Publications.

Al-Mujahid, S. (1981), *Quaid-i-Azam Jinnah: Studies in Interpretation*, Karachi: Quaid-i-Azam Academy.

Ali, A. (1984), *Pakistan's Nuclear Dilemma*, Karachi: Economist Research Unit.

Ali, C.M. (1973), *The Emergence of Pakistan*, Karachi: Pakistan Research Society.

Ali, I. (1988), *The Punjab Under Imperialism, 1885-1947*, Princeton, NJ: Princeton University Press.

Ali, S. (1992), 'City Under Siege', *Far Eastern Economic Review*, 3 December.

Ali, Tariq (1970), *Pakistan, Military Power or People's Power*, London: Jonathan Cape, 1970.

Ali, T. (1983), *Can Pakistan Survive?* New York, NY: Penguin.

Amin, Tahir (1988), *Ethno-National Movements of Pakistan*, Islamabad: Institute of Policy Studies.

Amin, T. (1994), 'Pakistan: Some Dramatic Changes', *Asian Survey*, 34, No. 2,pp. 191-99.

Amin, T. (1995), 'Pakistan in 1994: The Politics of Confrontation,' *Asian Survey* 35, No. 2 February, pp. 140-46.

Ansari, S.H. (1996), *Political Thought of Inayatullah Khan Mashriqi*, Ph.D. dissertation. Quaid-i-Azam University.

Asghar Khan, M. (1983), *Generals in Politics: Pakistan, 1958-1982*, New Delhi: Vikas.

Askari, H. (1964), 'Problems of Leadership', *Today*, December.

Awan, A.B. (1985), *Baluchistan: Historical and Political Processes*, London: New Century.

Ayoob, M. (1971), *Bangla Desh: A Struggle for Nationhood*, Delhi: Vikas.

Ayoob, M. and Subrahmaniyam, K. (1972), *The Liberation War*, New Delhi: S. Chand and Company Ltd.

Ayub Khan, M. (1967), *Friends Not Masters: A Political Autobiography*, New York, NY: Oxford University Press.

Azad, M.A.K. (1959), *India Wins Freedom*, London: Longmans, Green and Company.

Aziz, K.K. (1967), *The Making of Pakistan: A Study in Nationalism*, London: Chatto and Windus.

Aziz, K.K. (1976), *Party Politics in Pakistan, 1947-1958*, Islamabad: National Commission on Historical and Cultural Research.

Bahadur, L. (1954), *The Muslim Leaque*, Agra: Agra Book Store.

Bahadur, L. (1979), *The Muslim League: Its History, Activities, and Achievements*, Lahore: Book Traders.

Basham, A.L. (1954), *The Wonder That Was India*, New York, NY: Grove Press.

Baxter, C. (1984), *Bangladesh: A New Nation in an Old Setting*, Boulder, Colo.: Westview Press.

Baxter, C. (1985), *Zia's Pakistan: Politics and Stability in in Frontline State*, Boulder, Colo.: Westview Press.

Becker, M.L. (1957), *The All-India Muslim League: 1906-1947*, Cambridge: Radcliffe College.

Bhutto, B. (1983), *Pakistan: The Gathering Storm*, New Delhi: Vikas.

Bhutto, B. (1988), *Daughter of the East: An Autobiography*, London: Hamish Hamilton.

Bhutto, B. (1989), *Daughter of Destiny*, New York, NY: Simon and Schuster.

Bhutto, Z.A. (1964), *Foreign Policy of Pakistan*, Karachi: Pakistan Institute of International Affairs.

Bhutto, Z.A. (1969), *The Myth of Independence*, Karachi: Oxford University Press.

Bhutto, Z.A. (1971), *The Great Tragedy*, Karachi: Pakistan People's Party.

Bhutto, Z.A. (1973), *The Political Thinker*, Lahore: People's Publications.

Bhutto, Z.A. (1979), *If I Am Assassinated*, New Delhi: Vikas.

Binder, L. (1963), *Religion and Politics in Pakistan*, Berkeley, CA: University of California Press.

Binder, L. (1986), 'Islam, Ethnicity, and the State in Pakistan: An Overview', *in* A. Banuazizi & M. Weiner, (ed.), *The State, Religion, and Ethnic Politics: Afghanistan, Iran, and Pakistan,* Syracuse, NY: Syracuse University Press.

Birkhead, G. (ed.), (1966), *Administrative Problems in Pakistan*, Syracuse, NY: Syracuse University Press.

Bokhari, I.H. and Thornton, T.P. (1988), *The 1972 Simla Agreement: An Asymmetrical Negotiation*, Washington: Foreign Policy Institute, Johns Hopkins University.

Bolitho, H. (1954), *Jinnah, Creator of Pakistan*, London: John Murray.

Braibanti, R. (1963), 'Public Bureaucracy and Judiciary in Pakistan', *in* J. LaPalombara, (ed.), *Bureaucracy and Political Development*, Princeton, NJ: Princeton University Press.

Brines, R. (1968), *The Indo-Pakistani Conflict*, London: Pall Mall Press.

Burke, S.M. (1974), *Mainsprings of Indian and Pakistani Foreign Policies*, Minneapolis: University of Minnesota Press.

Burke, S.M. and Ziring, L. (1990), *Pakistan's Foreign Policy, An Historical Analysis*, Karachi: Oxford University Press.

Burki, S.J. (1986), *Pakistan: A Nation in the Making*, Boulder, Colo: Westview Press.

Burki, S.J. (1988), *Pakistan Under Bhutto, 1971-1977*, London: Macmillan.

Burki, S.J. (1989). 'Pakistan', *in* F. Robinson, (ed.), *The Cambridge Encyclopedia of India, Pakistan, Bangladesh, Sri Lanka, Nepal, Bhutan, and the Maldives*, Cambridge: Cambridge University Press.

Burki, S.J. (1991), *Pakistan: The Continuing Search for Nationhood*, Boulder, Colo: Westview Press.

Burki, S.J. and Baxter, C. (1991), *Pakistan Under the Military: Eleven Years of Ziaul Haq*, Boulder, Colo: Westview Press.

Burney, I.H. (1996), *No Illusions, Some Hopes, and No Fears*, Karachi: Oxford University Press.

Callard, K. (1957), *Pakistan: A Political Study*, London: Allen And Unwin.

Callard,K. (1959), *Pakistan's Foreign Policy: An Interpretation*, New York, NY: Institute of Pacific Relations.

Chishti, F.A. (1989), *Betrayals of Another Kind: Islam, Democracy and the Army in Pakistan*, Delhi: Tricolour Books.

Chopra, P. (1971), *The Challenge of Bangladesh*, Bombay: Popular Prakashan.

Chopra, P. (ed.), (1983), *Contemporary Pakistan: New Aims and Images*, New Delhi: Vikas.

Choudhury, G.W. (1963), *Democracy in Pakistan*, Dhaka: Green Book House.

Choudhury, G.W. (1967), *Documents and Speeches on the Constitution of Pakistan*, Dhaka: Green Book House.

Choudhury, G.W. (1969), *Constitutional Development in Pakistan*, (ed.), Vancouver: Publication Center, University of British Columbia.

Choudhury, G.W. (1975), *The Last Days of United Pakistan*, Bloomington: Indiana University Press.

Choudhury, G.W. (1988), *Pakistan: Transition From Military to Civilian Rule*, London: Scorpion.

Cohen, S.P. (1989), *The Pakistan Army*, Berkeley, CA: University of California Press.

Coupland, R. (1942), *The India Problem, 1833-1935*, London: Oxford University Press.

Coupland, R. (1944), *Indian Politics, 1936-1942*, London: Oxford University Press.

Coupland, R. (1944), *The Future of India*, London: Oxford University Press.

Faruki, K.A. (1974), *Islam, Today and Tomorrow*, Karachi: Pakistan Publishing House.

Faruki, K.A. (1987), 'Pakistan: Islamic Government and Society', *in* J.L. Esposito (ed.), *Islam in Asia*, New York, NY: Oxford University Press.

Feldman, H. (1955), *A Constitution for Pakistan*, Karachi: Oxford University Press.

Feldman, H. (1967), *Revolution in Pakistan: A Study of the Martial Law Administration*, Karachi: Oxford University Press.

Feldman, H. (1972), *From Crisis to Crisis: Pakistan, 1962-1969*, London: Oxford University Press.

Feldman, H. (1976), *The End and the Beginning: Pakistan, 1969-1972*, London: Oxford University Press.

Fox, R.G. (1985), *Lions of the Punjab: Culture in the Making*, Berkeley, CA: University of California Press.

Fraser, L. (1911), *India Under Lord Curzon and After*, London: Heinemann.

Gandhi, M.K. (1948), *Gandhi's Autobiography: The Story of My Experiments with Truth*, (Translated by Mahadev Desai), Washington, D.C.: Public Affairs Press.

Gankovsky, Y.V. and Moskalenko, V.N. (1978), *The Three Constitutions of Pakistan*, Lahore: People's Publishing House.

Gardezi, H. and Rashid, J. (eds.), (1983), *Pakistan: The Roots of Dictatorship*, London: Zed Press.

Gardezi, H.N. (1991), *Understanding Pakistan: The Colonial Factor in Societal Development*, Lahore: Maktaba Fikr Danish.

Gauhar, A. (1993), *Ayub Khan: Pakistan's First Military Ruler*, Lahore: Sang-e-Meel Publications.

Gilmartin, D. (1988), *Empire and Islam: Punjab and the Making of Pakistan*, Berkeley, CA: University of California Press.

Gledhill, A. (1957), *Pakistan: The Development of Its Law and Constitution*, London: Steven.

Goodnow, H.F. (1964), *The Civil Service of Pakistan*, New Haven: Yale University Press.

Government of East Bengal (1952), *Report of the Enquiry into the Firing by the Police at Dacca on the 21st February 1952, by the Honourable Mr. Justice Ellis of the High*

Court of Judicature at Dacca, Dacca: Government of East Bengal Press.

Government of Pakistan (1954), *West Pakistan as One Unit*, Karachi: Government Printing Office.

Government of Pakistan (1957), *Statements on Foreign Policy and Defence by H.S. Suhrawardy, Prime Minister of Pakistan*, Karachi.

Government of Pakistan (1979), *White Paper on the Performance of the Bhutto Regime (Volume One—Mr. Z.A. Bhutto, His Family and Associates; Volume Two—Treatment of Fundamental State Institutions; Volume Three—Misuse of the Instruments of State Power; Volume Four—The Economy*, Islamabad: Government of Pakistan Press.

Government of the Punjab (1954), *Report of the Court of Inquiry Constituted Under the Punjab Act II of 1954 to Enquire into the Punjab Disturbances of 1953*, Lahore: Government of Punjab Press.

Gupta, S. (1966), *Kashmir: A Study in India-Pakistan Relations*, Bombay: Asia Publishing.

Hamid, A. (1971), *Muslim Separation in India*, Karachi: Oxford University Press.

Hamid, S. (1986), *Disastrous Twilight: A Personal Record of the Partition of India*, London: Leo Cooper.

Haq, M.U. (1970), *Muslim Politics in Modern India*, Meerut: Meenakshi.

Hardy, P. (1971), *Partners in Freedom and True Muslims: The Political Thought of Some Muslim Scholars in British India,1912-1947*, Lund: Student-litteratur.

Hardy, P. (1972), *The Muslims of British India*, Cambridge: Cambridge University Press.

Harrison, S. (1981), *In Afghanistan's Shadow: Baluch Nationalism and Soviet Temptations*, New York, NY: Carnegie Endowment for International Peace.

Hasan, K. (1966), *The Transfer of Power*, Karachi: Pakistan Institute of International Affairs.

Hayat, S. (1991), *Aspects of the Pakistan Movement*, Lahore: Progressive Publishers.

Hayes, L.D. (1984), *Politics in Pakistan: The Struggle for Legitimacy*, Boulder, Colo.: Westview Press.

Hunter, W.W. (1872), *Our Indian Mussalmans*, London: Trubner and Company.

Hussain, A. (1972), *Parties and People's Representation in Pakistan*, Lahore: Ferozsons, Ltd.

Hussain, A. (1979), *Elite Politics in an Ideological State*, Folkestone: Dawson.

Hutchins, F.G. (1967), *The Illusion of Permanence: British Imperialism in India*, Princeton, NJ: Princeton University Press.

Hyman, A. (1990), *Pakistan: Toward a Modern Muslim State*, London: Research Institute for the Study of Conflict and Terrorism.

Ikram, S.M. and Spear, P. (eds.), (1955), *The Cultural Heritage of Pakistan*, Karachi: Oxford University Press.

Ikram, S.M. (1964), *Muslim Civilization in India*, New York, NY: Columbia Press.

Inayatullah (1993), *Pakistan's Politics: A Personal View*, Lahore: Ferozsons.

Jackson. R. (1975), *South Asian Crisis*, New York, NY: Praeger.

Jacobs, V.K. (1994), *The Woodpecker Story*, Cambridge: The Pentland Press.

Jahan, R. (1972), *Pakistan: Failure in National Integration*, New York, NY: Columbia University Press.

Jahan, R. (1974), 'India, Pakistan, and Bangladesh', in G. Henderson, R.N. Lebow, and J.G. Stoessinger (eds.), *Divided Nations in a Divided World*, New York, NY: Mckay.

Jalal, A. (1985), *The Sole Spokesman: Jinnah, the Muslim League and the Demand for Pakistan*, Cambridge: Cambridge University Press.

Jalal, A. (1991), *The State of Martial Rule: The Origins of Pakistan's Political Economy of Defence*, Lahore: Vanguard.

James, M. and Peter, L. (1993), *Pakistan Chronicle*, New York, NY: St. Martin's Press.

Janowitz, M. (1964), *The Military in the Political Development of New Nations*, Chicago: Chicago University Press.

Jennings, Sir I. (1957), *Constitutional Problems in Pakistan*, Cambridge: Cambridge University Press.

Jillani, A. (1991), 'Pakistan and CENTO: An Historical Analysis', *Journal of South Asian and Middle Eastern Studies*, 15, No.1, Fall, pp. 40-53.

Jillani, A. (1993), 'Judicial Activism and Islamization after Zia: Toward the Prohibition of Riba', C.H. Kennedy (ed.), *Pakistan: 1992*, Boulder, Colo.: Westview Press.

Kennedy, C.H. (1987), *Bureaucracy in Pakistan*, Karachi: Oxford University Press.

Kennedy, C.H. (ed.), (1993), *Pakistan: 1992*, Boulder, Colo.: Westview Press.

Khaliquzzaman, C. (1961), *Pathway of Pakistan*, Karachi: Longman.

Khan, F.M. (1963), *The Story of the Pakistan Army*, Karachi: Oxford University Press.

Khan, M.A. (ed.), (1985), *Islam, Politics and the State*, London: Zed Books.

Khan, M.H. (1981), *Underdevelopment and Agrarian Structure in Pakistan*, Boulder, Colo.: Westview Press.

Khan, R.A., Rais, R.B., and Waheed, K. (1989), *South Asia: Military Power and Regional Politics*, Islamabad: Islamabad Council of World Affairs.

Khan, R.A. (1992), 'Pakistan in 1991: Light and Shadows', *Asian Survey*, 32, No.2, February, pp. 197-206.

Khan, R.A. (1993), 'Pakistan in 1992: Waiting for Change', *Asian Survey*, 33, No.2, February, pp. 129-40.

Kochanek, S.A. (1983), *Interest Groups and Development*, New Delhi: Oxford University Press.

Korbel, J. (1966), *Danger in Kashmir*, Princeton, NJ: Princeton University Press.

Korson, J.H. (ed.),(1974), *Contemporary Problems of Pakistan*, Leiden: Brill.

Korson, J.H. (1993), *Contemporary Problems of Pakistan*, Boulder, Colo.: Westview.

Khuhro, H, (1978), *The Making of Modern Sind*, Karachi: Indus Publications.

Lamb, A. (1992), *Kashmir: A Disputed Legacy, 1846-1990*, Karachi: Oxford University Press.

Lamb, A. (1994), *Birth of a Tragedy, Kashmir 1947*, Herting Fordbury: Roxford Books.

Lambrick, H.T. (1964), *Sind: A General Introduction*, Hyderabad: Sindhi Adabi Board.

LaPorte, R., Jr. (1975), *Power and Privilege: Influence and Decision-Making in Pakistan*, Berkeley, CA: University of California Press.

LaPorte, R., Jr. (1996), 'Pakistan in 1995: The Continuing Crisis', *Asian Survey* 36, No. 2, February, pp. 179-89.

Lelyveld, D. (1978), *Aligarh's First Generation: Muslim Solidarity in British India*, Princeton, NJ: Princeton University Press.

Loshak, D. (1971), *Pakistan Crisis*, London: Heinemann.

Low, D.A. (ed.), (1977), *Congress and the Raj*, London: Arnold-Heinemann.

Low, D.A. (1991), *The Political Inheritance of Pakistan*, New York, NY: St. Martin's Press.

Lumby, E.W.R. (1954), *The Transfer of Power in India*, London: George Allen and Unwin.

Mahmood, A. (1964), *Basic Democracies*, Lahore: All Pakistan Legal Decisions.

Mahmood, D.D. (1992), *The Judiciary and Politics in Pakistan*, Lahore: Idara Mutalia-e-Tareekh.

Mahmood, S. (1976), *The Deliberate Debacle*, Lahore: Sh. Muhammad Ashraf.

Mahmood, S. (1990), *Constitutional Foundations of Pakistan*, (ed.), Lahore: Jang.

Mahmud, S.H. (1958), *A Nation Is Born*, Lahore: Feroz Printing Works.

Majumdar, R.C. (1953), *An Advanced History of India*, London: Macmillan.

Malik, H. (1963), *Muslim Nationalism in India and Pakistan*, Washington: Public Affairs Press.

Malik, H. (ed.), (1971), *Iqbal: Poet-philosopher of Pakistan*, New York, NY: Columbia University Press.

Maluka, Z.K. (1995), *The Myth of Constitutionalism*, London: Oxford University Press.

Manheim, J.B. (1994), *Strategic Public Diplomacy and American Foreign Policy*, London: Oxford University Press.

Mansergh, N. and Lumby, E.W.R. (eds.), (1970), *The Transfer of Power, 1942-47*, (5 vols.), London: Her Majesty's Stationery Office.

Marshall, C.B. (1959), 'Reflections on a Revolution in Pakistan', *Foreign Affairs*, 37, January, pp.247-56.

Mascarenhas, A. (1972), *The Rape of Bangla Desh*, Delhi: Vikas.

Mason, P. (1974), *A Matter of Honour: An Account of the Indian Army, its Officers and Men*, London: Cape.

Mayne, P. (1956), *Saints of Sind*, London: John Murray.

Mayo, K. (1927), *Mother India*, New York, NY: Harcourt, Brace and Company.

McCullough, D. (1992), *Truman*, New York, NY: Simon and Schuster.

Merriam, A. Hayes. (1980), *Gandhi vs Jinnah: The Debate Over the Partition of India*, Calcutta: Minerva.

Metcalf, T.R. (1964), *The Aftermath of Revolt: India, 1857-1870*, Princeton, NJ: Princeton University Press.

Minault, G. (1982), *The Khilafat Movement: Religious Symbolism and Political Mobilization in India*, New York, NY: Columbia University Press.

Mody, P. (1973), *Zulfi, My Friend*, Delhi: Thomason Press Ltd.

Moon, P. (1964), *Divide and Quit*, London: Chatto and Windus.

Moore, R.J. (1974), *The Crisis of Indian Unity, 1917-1940*, Oxford: Clarendon Press.

Mosley, L. (1961), *The Last Days of the British Raj*, New York, NY: Harcourt, Brace and World.

Mujeeb, M. (1967), *The Indian Muslims*, London: George Allen & Unwin.

Munir, M. (1980), *From Jinnah to Zia*, Lahore: Vanguard.

Muqeem Khan, F. (1973), *Pakistan's Crisis in Leadership*, Islamabad: National Book Foundation.

Nasr, R.V.R. (1992), 'Students, Islam and Politics: Islamic Jami'at-i-Tulaba in Pakistan', *Middle East Journal*, 46, No.1, Winter, pp.59-76.

Newman, Karl F. (1986), *Pakistan Under Ayub, Bhutto, and Ziaul Haq*, Munich: Weltforum Verlag.

Nyrop, R. (ed.), (1984), *Pakistan: A Country Study*, Washington, D.C.: US Government Printing Office.

Pakistan People's Party (1967), *Foundation Documents of the Pakistan People's Party*, Lahore.

Page, D. (1982), *Prelude to Partition: The Indian Muslims and The Imperial System of Control, 1920-1932*, Delhi: Oxford University Press.

Palmer, N.D. (1977), 'Pakistan: The Long Search for Foreign Policy', L. Ziring, R. Braibanti, and W.H. Wriggins, (eds.), *Pakistan: The Long View*, Durham, NC: Duke University Press.

Philips, C.M. and Wainwright, M.D. (eds.), (1970), *The Partition of India: Politics and Perspectives, 1935-1947*, London: Allen and Unwin.

Qureshi, I.H. (1956), *Pakistan: An Islamic Democracy*, Lahore: Institute of Islamic Culture.

Qureshi, I.H. (1957), *Islamic Elements in the Political Thought of Pakistan*, unpublished manuscript.

Qureshi, I.H. (1965), *The Struggle for Pakistan*, Karachi: University of Karachi Press.

Rahman, A. (1982), *Pakistan and America: Dependency Relations*, New Delhi: Young Asia Publishers.

Rais, R.B. (1994), *War Without Winners*, Karachi: Oxford University Press.

Rajput, A.B. (1948), *Muslim League: Yesterday and Today*, Lahore: Muhammad Ashraf.

Rajput, A.B. (1987), *Religion, Politics, and Society*, New York, NY: Oxford University Press.

Raza, S.H. (1982), *Mountbatten and Pakistan*, Karachi: Quaid-i-Azam Academy.

Richards, J.F. (1993), *The Mughal Empire*, New York, NY: Cambridge University Press.

Richards, W.L. (1993), 'The 1990 General Election in Pakistan', *in* H. Kennedy, (ed.), *Pakistan: 1992*, Boulder, Colo.: Westview Press.

Rizvi, H.A. (1973), *Pakistan People's Party: The First Phase 1967-1971*, Lahore: Progressive Publishers.

Rizvi, H.A. (1981), *Internal Strife and External Intervention: India's Role in the Civil War in East Pakistan (Bangladesh)*, Lahore: Progressive Publishers.

Rizvi, H.A. (Ed.), (1986), *The Military and Politics in Pakistan, 1947-1986*, Lahore: Progressive Publishers.

Rose, L. (1989), 'Pakistan and the World', *in* F. Robinson, (Ed.), *The Cambridge Encyclopedia of India, Pakistan, Bangladesh, Sri Lanka, Nepal, Bhutan, and the Maldives*, Cambridge: Cambridge University Press.

Saeed, M. (1989), *Lahore: A Memoir*, Lahore: Vanguard.

Salik, S. (1977), *Witness to Surrender*, Karachi: Oxford University Press.

Samad, Y. (1995), *A Nation in Turmoil*, New Delhi: Sage.

Sayeed, K.B. (1960), *Pakistan: The Formative Phase*, Karachi: Pakistan Publications.

Sayeed, K.B. (1967), *The Political System of Pakistan*, Boston, Mass: Houghton Mifflin.

Sayeed, K.B. (1977). 'Political Leadership and Institution-Building under Jinnah, Ayub, and Bhutto', *in* L. Ziring, R. Braibanti, and W.H. Wriggins, (eds.), *Pakistan: The Long View*, Durham, NC: Duke University Press.

Sayeed, K.B. (1980), *The Nature and Direction of Change*, New York, NY: Praeger.

Sayeed, K.B. (1982), 'The Historical Origins of Some of Pakistan's Persistent Political Problems', *in* A. Jayaratnam, and D.Dalton, (eds.), *The States of South Asia: Problems of National Integration*, New Delhi: Vikas.

Schofield, V. (1979), *Bhutto: Trial and Execution*, London: Cassell.

Sen. S. (1955), *Birth of Pakistan*, Calcutta: General Printers and Publishers Ltd.

Shafiq. M. (1987), *Islamic Concept of a Modern State: A Case Study of Pakistan*, Lahore: Islamic Book Foundation Distributors, Al-Maarif.

Shahi, A. (1988), *Pakistan's Security and Foreign Policy*, Lahore: Progressive Publishers.

Shaikh, F. (1989), *Community and Consensus in Islam: Representation in Colonial India, 1860-1947*, Cambridge: Cambridge University Press.

Shakir, M. (1970), *Khilafat to Partition*, New Delhi: Kalamkar Prakashan.

Sherwani, L.A. (1980), *Pakistan, China and America*, Karachi: Council for Pakistan Studies.

Siddiqui, K. (1972), *Conflict, Crisis and War in Pakistan*, New York, NY: Praeger.

Sisson, R. and Rose, L.E. (1990), *War and Secession: Pakistan, India, and the Creation of Bangladesh*, Berkeley: University of California Press.

Smith, W.C. (1946), *Modern Islam in India*, London: Gollancz.

Smith, W.C. (1951), *Pakistan as an Islamic State*, Lahore: Ashraf.

Smith, W.C. (1959), *Islam in Modern History*, New York, NY: Mentor Books.

Spear, P. (1951), *Twilight of the Mughals*, Cambridge: Cambridge University Press.

Spear, P. (1961), *India: A Modern History*, Ann Arbor: The University of Michigan Press.

Suleri, Z.A. (1962), *Pakistan's Lost Years*, Lahore: Progressive Papers Ltd.

Syed, A.H. (1977), 'The Pakistan People's Party: Phases One and Two', *in* L. Ziring, R. Braibanti and W.H. Wriggins, *Pakistan: The Long View*, Durham, NC: Duke University Press, pp. 70-116.

Syed, A.H. (1984), *Pakistan: Islam, Politics, and National Solidarity*, New York, NY: Praeger.

Syed, A.H. (1988), 'Political Parties and the Nationality Question in Pakistan', *in Journal of South Asian and Middle Eastern Studies*, 12, 1, Fall, pp.42-75.

Syed, A.H. (1992), *The Discourse and Politics of Zulfikar Ali Bhutto*, New York, NY: St. Martin's Press.

Symonds, R. (1951), *The Making of Pakistan*, London: Faber.

Tahir-Kheli, S. (1982), *The United States and Pakistan: The Evolution of an Influence Relationship*, New York, NY: Praeger.

Talbot, I. (1988), *Provincial Politics and the Pakistan Movement*, Karachi: Oxford University Press.

Taseer, S. (1979), *Bhutto: A Political Biography*, London: Ithaca Press.

Tinker, H. (1954), *The Foundations of Local Self-Government in India, Pakistan, and Burma*, London: Athlone Press.

Vertzberge, Y. (1983), *The Enduring Entente: Sino-Pakistan Relations, 1960-1980*, New York, NY: Praeger.

Vorys, K.V. (1965), *Political Development in Pakistan*, Princeton, NJ: Princeton University Press.

Waseem, M. (1987), *Pakistan under Martial Law, 1977-1985*, Lahore: Vanguard.

Waseem, M. (1992), 'Pakistan's Lingering Crisis of Dyarchy', *Asian Survey*, 32, No. 7, July, pp. 617-634.

Weinbaum, M. (1977), 'The March 1977 Elections: Where Everyone Lost', *Asian Survey*, 17, No. 7, July.

Wheeler, R.S. (1970), *The Politics of Pakistan: A Constitutional Quest*, Ithaca, New York, NY: Cornell University Press.

Wilcox, W.A. (1963), *Pakistan: The Consolidation of a Nation*, New York, NY: Columbia University Press.

Wilcox, W.A. (1977), 'The Wellsprings of Pakistan', in L. Ziring, R.Braibanti, and W.H. Wriggins, (eds). *Pakistan: The Long View*, Durham, NC: Duke University Press.

Wilder, Andrew (1995), 'Changing Patterns of Punjab Politics in Pakistan: National Assembly Election Results, 1988 and 1993', *Asian Survey*, 35,4, April, pp.377-93.

Williams, L.F.R. (1966), *The State of Pakistan*, London: Faber and Faber.

Williams, L.F.R. (1972), *The East Pakistan Tragedy*, London: Tom Stacey.

Wirsing, R. (1991), *Pakistan's Security Under Zia, 1977-1988: The Policy Imperatives of a Peripheral Asian State*, New York, NY: St. Martin's Press.

Wolpert, W. (1962), *Tilak and Gokhale: Revolution and Reform in the Making of Modern India*, Berkeley: University of California Press.

Wolpert, S. (1984), *Jinnah of Pakistan*, New York, NY: Oxford University Press.

Wolpert, S. (ed.), (1992), *A New History of India*, New York, NY: Oxford University Press.

Wolpert, S. (1993), *Zulfi Bhutto of Pakistan: His Life and Times*, New York, NY: Oxford University Press.

Wriggins, W.H. (ed.), (1975), *Pakistan in Transition*, Islamabad: University of Islamabad Press.

Wriggins, W.H. (1977), 'The Balancing Process in Pakistan's Foreign Policy', *in* L. Ziring, R. Braibanti, and W.H. Wriggins (eds.), *Pakistan: The Long View*, Durham, NC: Duke University Press.

Yusuf, H, (1980), *Pakistan in Search of Democracy, 1947-1977*, Lahore, Afroasia.

Zaheer, H. (1994), *The Separation of East Pakistan*, Karachi: Oxford University Press.

Zakaria, N. (1958), *Parliamentary Government in Pakistan*, Lahore: New Publishers.

Zaman, F. and Zaman, A. (1973), *Z.A. Bhutto: The Political Thinker*, Lahore: Cosmopolitan.

Ziring, L. (1966), 'The Administration of Basic Democracies', *in* G. Birkhead, (ed.), *Administrative Problems in Pakistan*, Syracuse, NY: Syracuse University Press.

Ziring, L. (1971), *The Ayub Khan Era: Politics in Pakistan, 1958-1969*, Syracuse, NY: Syracuse University Press.

PUBLICATIONS CITED AND CONSULTED

Ziring, L. (1975), 'Perennial Militarism: An Interpretation of Political Underdevelopment, Pakistan Under General Yahya Khan, 1969-1971', in W.H. Wriggins, (ed.), *Pakistan in Transition*, Islamabad: University of Islamabad Press.

Ziring, L., Braibanti, R., and Wriggins, W.H. (eds.) (1977), *Pakistan: The Long View*, Durham, NC: Duke University Press.

Ziring, L. (1980), *Pakistan: The Enigma of Political Development*, Boulder, Colo.: Westview Press.

Ziring, L. (1984), 'Government and Politics', Richard F. Nyrop in (ed.), *Pakistan: A Country Study*, Washinngton, D.C.: US Government Printing Office.

Ziring, L. (1990), 'Pakistan in 1989: The Politics of Stalemate', *Asian Survey*, 30, No. 2, February, pp. 126-35.

Ziring, L. (1991a), 'Pakistan in 1990: The Fall of Benazir Bhutto', *Asian Survey* 31, No. 2, February, pp.113-24.

Ziring, L. (1991b), 'Benazir Bhutto: A Political Portrait', *Asian Affairs* 18, No.3, Fall, pp.178-89.

Ziring, L. (1992), *Bangladesh, From Mujib to Ershad*, Karachi: Oxford University Press.

Ziring, L. (1993a), 'Dilemma and Challenge in Nawaz Sharif's Pakistan', *in* C.H. Kennedy (ed.), *Pakistan: 1992*, Boulder, Colo.: Westview Press.

Ziring, L. (1993b), 'The Second Stage in Pakistan Politics: The 1993 Elections', *Asian Survey*, 33, No.12, December, pp.1175-85.

Index